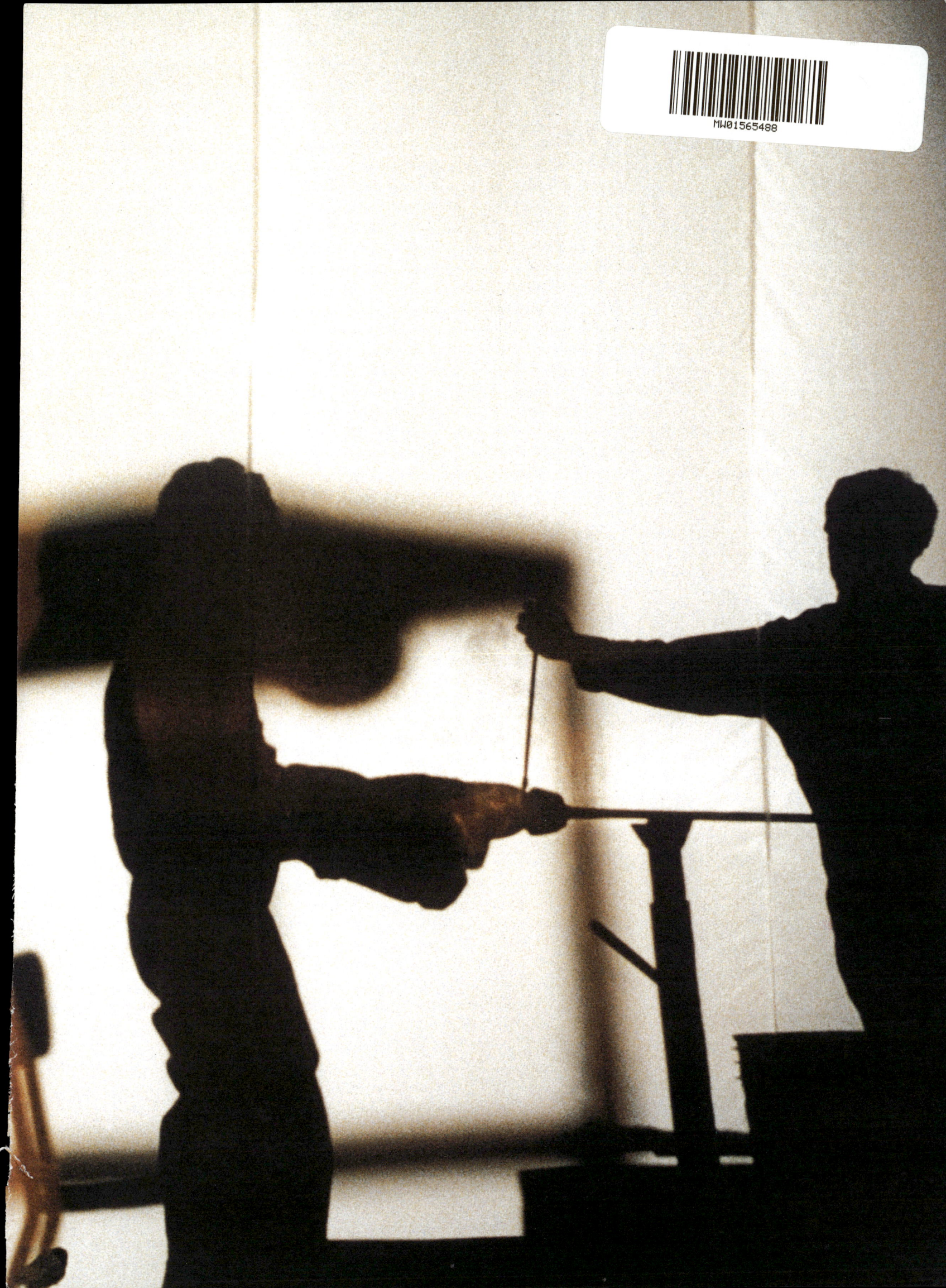

GLASS ART

RICHARD WILFRED YELLE

From UrbanGlass

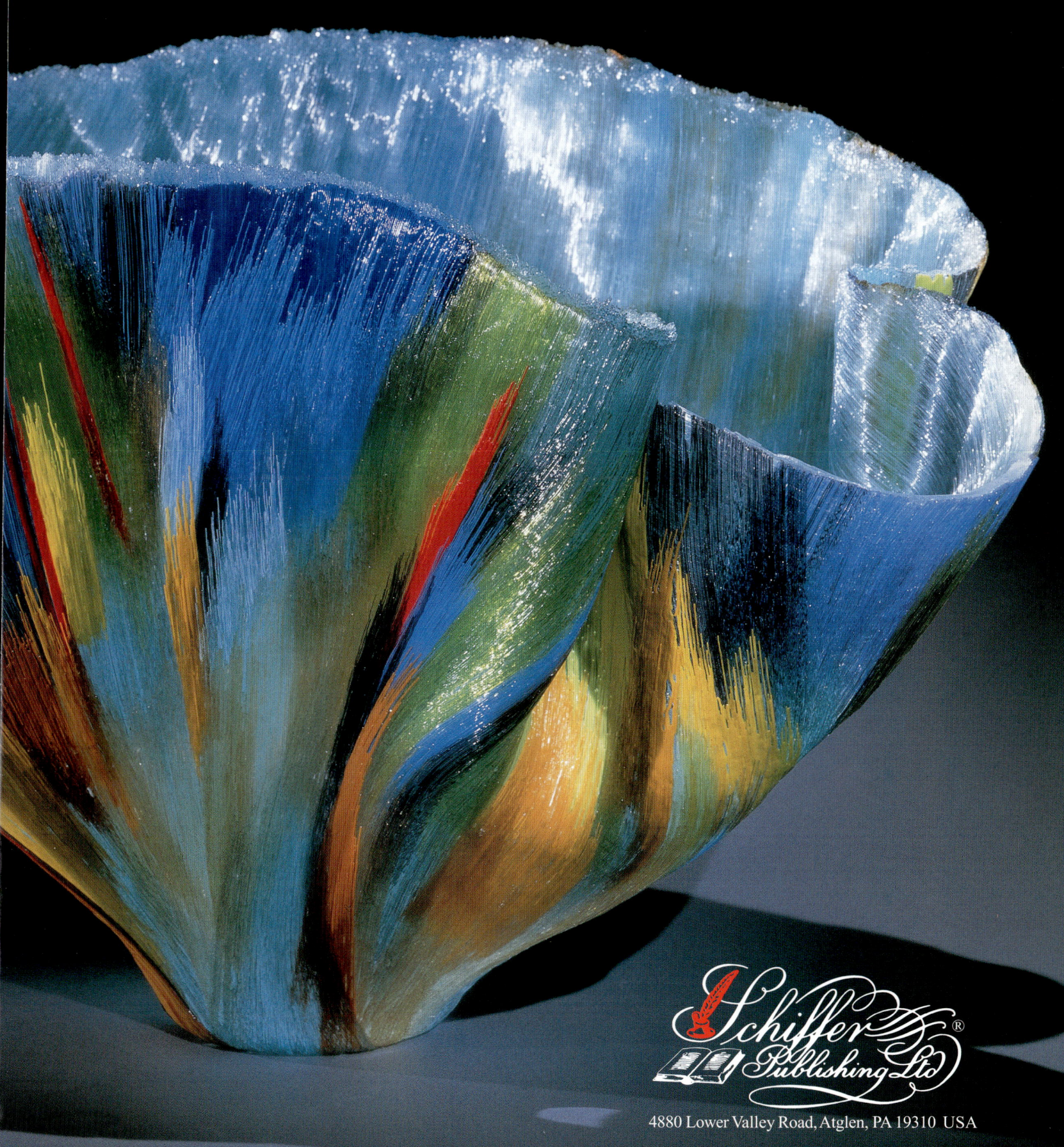

Schiffer Publishing Ltd
4880 Lower Valley Road, Atglen, PA 19310 USA

DEDICATION

Tina Yelle
UrbanGlass Executive Director, 1984-95.

My sister Tina's vision, optimism, and persistence made it possible to build UrbanGlass' spectacular diverse programming and state-of-the-art facilities in down-town Brooklyn, New York, and catapult *GLASS* magazine to the preeminent status it enjoys today. We all owe Tina our deepest thanks on a job well done!

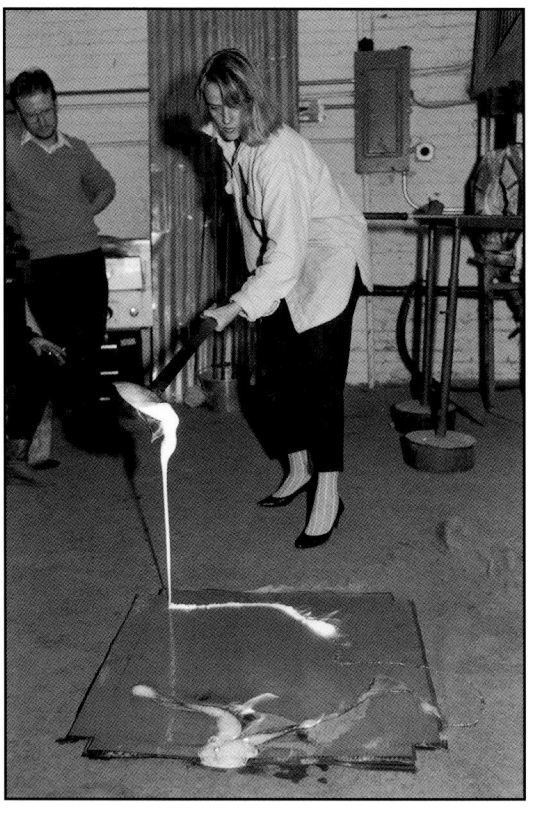

Tina Yelle creating a hot glass drawing, UrbanGlass, 1988. Photo: Helen Kitchen.

Library of Congress Cataloging-in-Publication Data

Contemporary art from UrbanGlass/ [compiled] by Richard Wilfred Yelle.
p. cm.
ISBN 0-7643-1116-6
1. UrbanGlass (Center) 2. Glass art--New York (State)--New York--History--20th century. I. Yelle, Richard Wilfred. II. UrbanGlass (Center)
NK5198.U73 C65 2000
748'.09747'1--dc21
00-008155

Copyright © 2000 by Richard Wilfred Yelle

All rights reserved. No part of this work may be reproduced or used in any form or by any means—graphic, electronic, or mechanical, including photocopying or information storage and retrieval systems—without written permission from the copyright holder.
"Schiffer," "Schiffer Publishing Ltd. & Design," and the "Design of pen and ink well" are registered trademarks of Schiffer Publishing Ltd.

Design by Blair Loughrey
Type set in Zurich

ISBN: 0-7643-1116-6
Printed in China

Published by Schiffer Publishing Ltd.
4880 Lower Valley Road
Atglen, PA 19310
Phone: (610) 593-1777; Fax: (610) 593-2002
E-mail: Schifferbk@aol.com
Please visit our web site catalog at
WWW.SCHIFFERBOOKS.COM
or write for a free catalog.

We are always looking for authors to write books on new and related subjects. If you have an idea for a book, please contact us at the above address.

This book may be purchased from the publisher. Please include $3.95 for shipping.

In Europe, Schiffer books are distributed by
Bushwood Books
6 Marksbury Ave.
Kew Gardens
Surrey TW9 4JF England
Phone: 44 (0)208 392-8585; Fax: 44 (0)208 392-9876
E-mail: Bushwd@aol.com
Free postage in the UK. Europe: Air mail at cost.
Please try your bookstore first.

Title page photo:
Toots Zynsky, **Night Street Chaos**, 1998. Fused and thermo-form glass threads, h. 7.15 x 13 x 7 inches. Tampa Museum of Art, Florida. Gift of Dale and Doug Anderson.

C·O·N·T·E·N·T·S

ACKNOWLEDGMENTS *5*
by Richard Wilfred Yelle

UrbanGlass: NEW YORK CENTER FOR CONTEMPORARY GLASS *6*
by David C. Burger, Chairman of the Board of Directors, UrbanGlass

GLASS! GLORIOUS GLASS! *7*
by Kenneth R. Trapp, Curator-in-Charge, Renwick Gallery of the Smithsonian American Art Museum

GLASS *9*

THE GLASS WORLD: *316*
Essays by Prominent Curators, Critics, and Writers

QUESTIONING GLASS *316*
by Karen S. Chambers, Freelance Curator and Critic-at-Large, New York, New York

THE CURRENT STATE OF CONTEMPORARY STUDIO GLASS *317*
by Elaine D. Gustafson, Curator of Contemporary Art
Tampa Museum of Art, Tampa, Florida

GLASS: A NEW ROLE IN A NEW CENTURY *318*
by Bruce W. Pepich, Director, Charles A. Wustum Museum of Fine Arts, Racine, Wisconsin

VALUING GLASS *319*
by William Warmus, Writer, Lansing, New York

WHAT WILL LAST: THE CHALLENGE OF GLASS *320*
by Neil Watson, Curator of Exhibitions and Contemporary Art, Norton Museum of Art, West Palm Beach, Florida

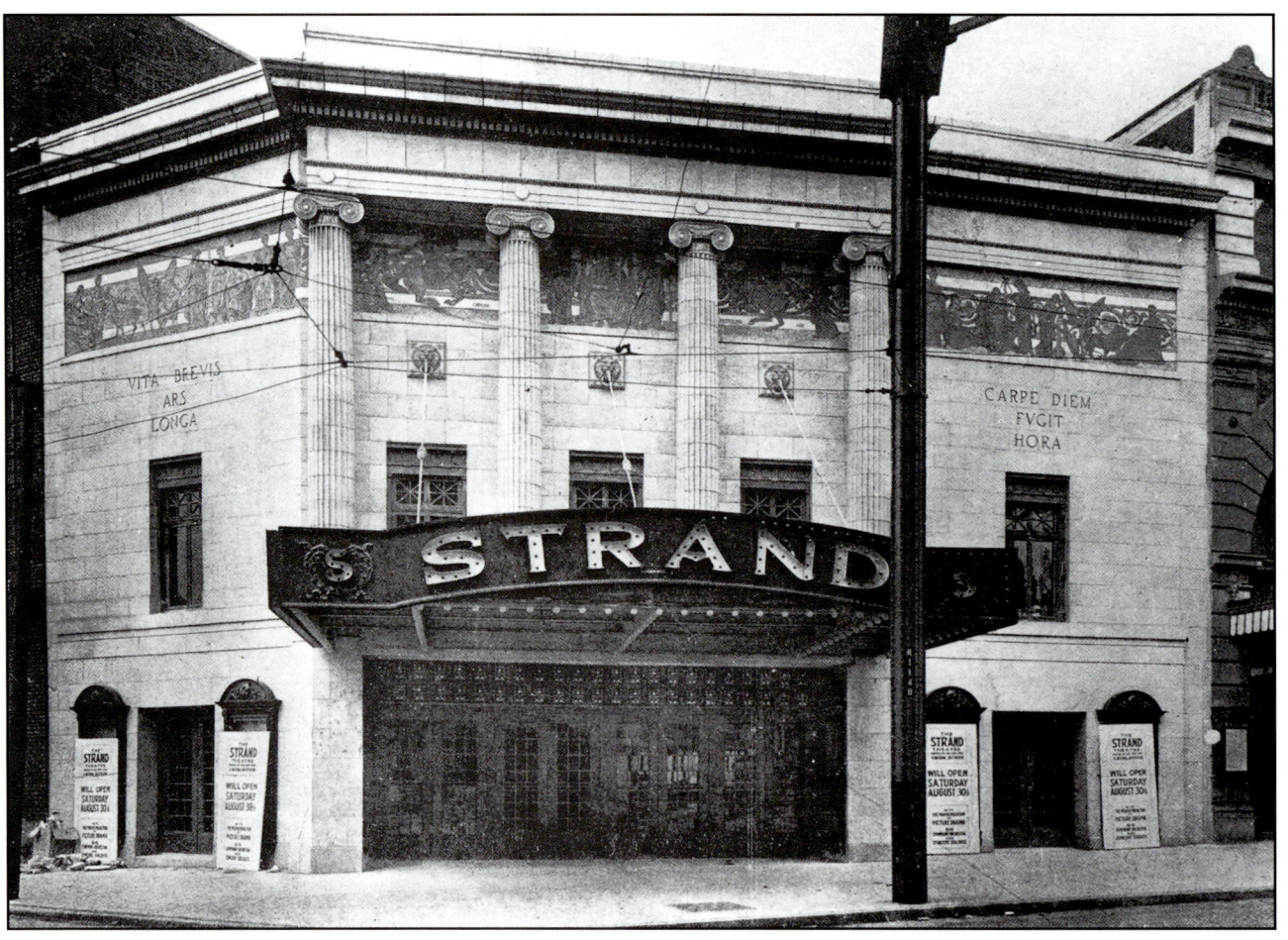

UrbanGlass, Brooklyn, New York
The Strand Theater was completed in 1919 as a music hall and moved quickly into Vaudeville theater. Later the Strand became the first talking-picture theater in Brooklyn. In the '50s it was converted into the largest bowling alley in the world before becoming vacant in the early 1970s. Abandoned in the '80s, the City of New York installed three floors in the Strand Theater shell, hoping to attract new tenants. UrbanGlass' architect, Jeffrey G. Beers, began plans to renovate the fifty-foot high top floor of the Strand in 1989, and completed construction of a state-of-the-art hot glass facility in 1991. Photo courtesy of the New York Historical Society.

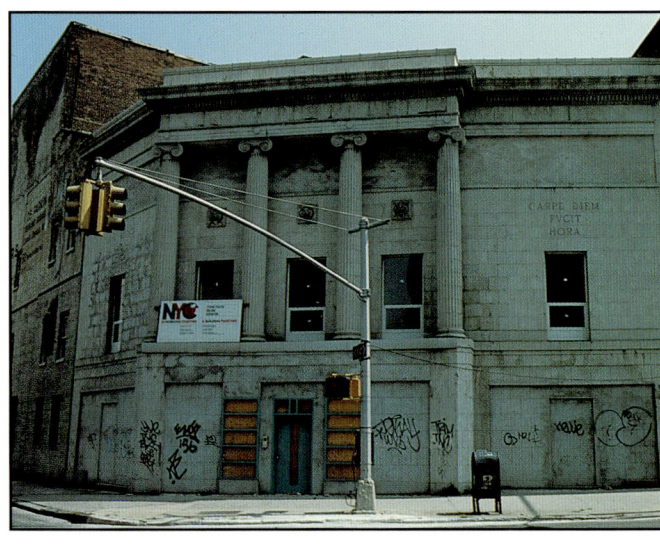

The Strand Theater today.

ACKNOWLEDGMENTS

When I learned that Parsons School of Design, a division of the New School University, had awarded me a sabbatical leave for the Fall 1999 semester to prepare for a retrospective exhibition of my work at the Robert Lehman Gallery in conjunction with UrbanGlass' 25th anniversary in 2002, I immediately realized this was also my opportunity to write the book on UrbanGlass I have always wanted to do. For over 20 years, an incredibly diverse group of artists and designers have been associated with UrbanGlass in many different ways. My goal has been to document the work of some of these artists and designers in pictures and to celebrate their achievements in art and design using glass as the material of choice.

I wish to thank Anthony Whitfield, Chair, Product Design Department; Randolph Swearer, Dean, Parsons School of Design; and Jonathan F. Fanton, President, New School University for this wonderful block of time, which allowed me to take a break from my teaching and administrative routine at the fast-paced and academically intense environment of Parsons.

My thirteen-year-old son Scott deserves special thanks. Although I have always maintained a painting studio in our home, which Scott has often used for his own artistic work, this was the first time he had to put up with an "office" in our home. Thanks big time, Scott! Of course, I talked about this book endlessly at the family home on Cape Cod this past summer. So, a warm thanks for putting up with me to my mother, Margaret Yelle; my brother, Jay Yelle; my sisters and their families: Pam and John Mannes and their children, Jason, David, and Tanya; Andrea Yelle and Mo Jahanbaksh, and their daughter Setareh; Mary and Gary Pforzheimer, and their children Adrian and Anya. Adrian, thanks for the loan of the Harry Potter book by J.K. Rowling and for our really fun talks about it.

Any endeavor of this scale requires help from talented people who know the field of contemporary glass. I was lucky to find a distinguished group of advisors— people who not only know the field inside and out, but were willing to put in endless hours of work to make this an accurate and important record of UrbanGlass' history.

My Advisory Group was made up of Dale Anderson, Doug Anderson, Amye Price Gumbinner, Paul S. Gumbinner, Geoffrey J. Isles, and Cynthia Manocherian. It is a pleasure to thank Dale for her sharp eye and special wit; Doug for his professionalism and energy; Amye for her enthusiasm and taste; Paul for his marketing savvy; Geoffrey for his encyclopedic knowledge of contemporary glass and UrbanGlass history; and Cynthia for her brilliant insights. You all helped make this book possible.

I simply have to thank Doug Anderson a second time. Doug's assistance extended far beyond the advisory capacity to almost daily nitty-gritty help with names, phone calls and numbers, and real down-and-dirty editorial help. David Burger, too, provided invaluable help, without which this book would not have been possible.

I also wish to mention John Perreault, Executive Director of UrbanGlass, and Brett Littman, Associate Director for providing UrbanGlass images, and the list of artists and designers from which the invitations were made for this book. Douglas Heller and Michael Heller of Heller Gallery, Terry Davidson of Leo Kaplan Modern, Kate Elliott of Elliott Brown Gallery, Bill Traver of William Traver Gallery, Dara Metz of Barry Friedman, Ltd., Lillian Zonars of Habitat Galleries, and Katya Garrow also provided important help.

It is an honor to now thank the writers who contributed to this book. Without the efforts of David Burger, Kenneth Trapp, Karen Chambers, Elaine D. Gustafson, Bruce Pepich, Bill Warmus, and Neil Watson there would have been no art and design context within which to view the wonderful glass art and design in this book. Your combined efforts have helped everyone to enjoy glass art and design in a richer and more understanding way. Thank you all!

Last, but not least, I wish to thank my editors, Tina Skinner and Molly Higgins, and Publisher Peter Schiffer, for their support and encouragement.

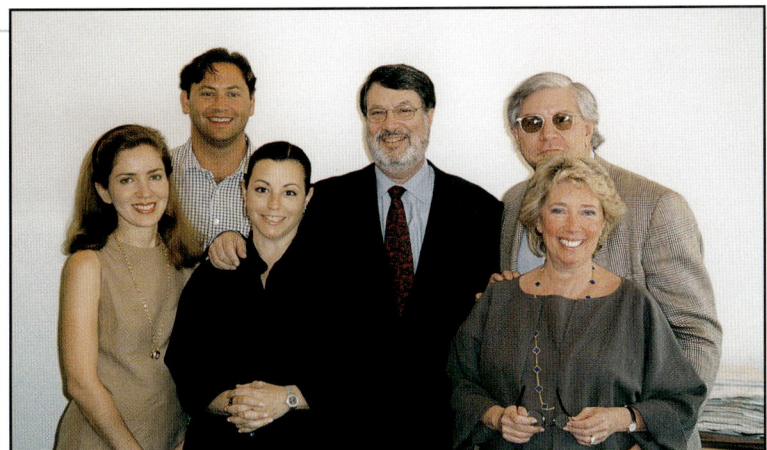

Advisors, (from left to right) Cynthia Manocherian, Geoffrey J. Isles, Amye Price Gumbinner, Paul S. Gumbinner, Dale Anderson, and Doug Anderson.

UrbanGlass has a profound, and unrivaled, role in supporting the use and appreciation of glass as an art and design medium. The depth and breadth of UrbanGlass' programs impart a unique influence on all aspects of contemporary glass. UrbanGlass, a not-for-profit organization, provides studio facilities for virtually every glass working technique, including glassblowing, casting, neon, lampworking, molding, slumping, fusing, cold working, stained glass, and mosaics. We offer training in those techniques to over 600 students each year in the form of group and individual classes, weekend workshops and other intensive classes. Our facilities are also utilized as the primary studio space of over 300 artists each year. In addition, residencies have been granted to many visiting artists.

UrbanGlass:

NEW YORK CENTER FOR CONTEMPORARY GLASS

UrbanGlass publishes *GLASS*, The Urban Glass Art Quarterly, the foremost English language periodical on contemporary glass. The annual UrbanGlass Awards honor outstanding achievements in, and contributions to, the field of contemporary glass. The Robert Lehman Gallery at UrbanGlass offers exhibitions of established and emerging glass artists, including many who have worked at UrbanGlass. The Store at UrbanGlass offers the retail sale of works by a select group of glass artists. The unique UrbanGlass Abroad program offers summer classes in various glassworking techniques at locations throughout Europe. Through the UrbanGlass Atelier program, we also work closely with sculptors, architects, and other design professionals in executing commissions. These programs have provided immeasurable benefit to many an aspiring artist.

Several of today's established glass artists recall the inspiring and yet somewhat ramshackle beginnings of UrbanGlass, then known as the New York Experimental Glass Workshop, on Great Jones and Mulberry streets in Manhattan. It is more than a little breathtaking for those of us who have been involved in this venture to recognize that, in just over twenty years and especially in just the last decade, we have built the largest glass school and open-access glass artists' studio in the world.

It is certainly fitting that Richard Yelle should be the one who conceived of, and edited, this volume celebrating many of the artists who are part of the UrbanGlass family. Richard was a founder of the New York Experimental Glass Workshop and *GLASS* magazine, served as the first president of its Board of Directors, and was a long-standing member of the Board and of the Editorial Committee for *GLASS*. In those roles, and in many other official and unofficial capacities, Richard has been a critical force in shaping this organization and its influence on the many artists and students that it serves.

David C. Burger
Chairman of the Board of Directors, UrbanGlass

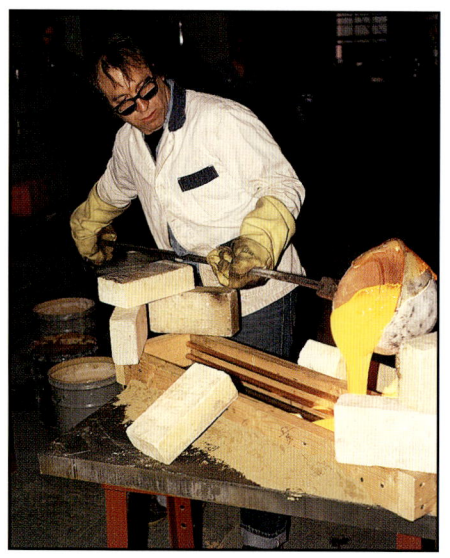

Howard Ben Tré doing a pour into a wood mold at an UrbanGlass seminar, 1983. Photo: © G. Rose

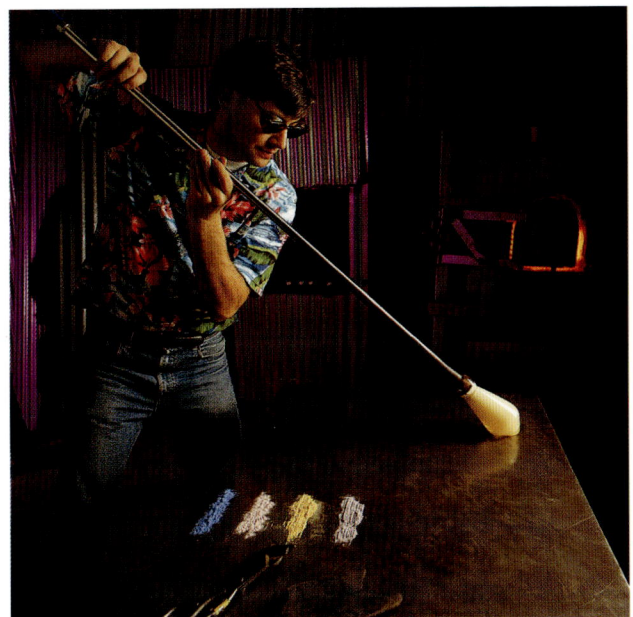

Geoffrey J. Isles blowing Glass In UrbanGlass' hot shop.

GLASS!
GLORIOUS GLASS!

What is Glass?

Glass is an ancient substance that dates back some 5,000 years. A vitreous glaze on stone and ceramic beads that originated around 3,500 to 3,000 B.C. in ancient Mesopotamia (now Iraq) is thought to be the precursor to glass. The earliest glass vessels, discovered as fragments near Nineveh in ancient Assyria of Mesopotamia, date from about 1525 to 1475 B.C. It has taken fifty centuries for glass to become the material we now know, and our knowledge of glass has progressed more in the past two hundred years than in all the previous centuries.

Composed of earthen materials transformed by fire, glass is a sister to pottery and metal. Excavations of ancient sites have revealed that glasslike substances or glass itself sometimes appear with evidence of pottery and metals. That glass did not evolve isolated from ceramics and metals is most evident in the appearance of the metal blowpipe—an extended hollow rod—which was necessary before free-form glassblowing could occur.

Believed to have been developed in the mid-first century B.C. in Syria as a glassworking technique, free-form glassblowing forever transformed glass production, and its influence is still felt today.

Several centuries ago, owning glass—a rare and precious commodity—was the privilege of wealth and royalty. Knowledge of how to make and work glass was a carefully guarded secret controlled by royalty and specialized trade guilds. Today, however, glass is so common that it is found in the remotest parts of the world and has become a solid waste problem in industrialized countries.

Although glass occurs in nature as volcanic obsidian, this book focuses on man-made glass. Reduced to its essential elements, artificial glass is composed of silica (quartz sand or pulverized pebbles or flint) and an alkali (potash or soda ash). Lime or lead oxide may be added to facilitate fusion when the batch is subjected to extreme heat. Glass may be transparent, translucent or opaque. Cold glass is hard, inorganic, amorphous, and noncrystalline. The artist Fritz Dreisbach describes the structure of glass: "As (molten) glass cools, it gets thicker and stiffer, but the process of stiffening is very slow compared to molten steel, molten silver, or molten rock. Those materials hold the temperature constant while the molecules within them line themselves in rows and columns like soldiers on the field. Once they are lined up, the material becomes crystalline and changes suddenly from a liquid to a solid. Glass never does that. It never crystallizes. The molecules never organize themselves into a pattern or structure. They are just as random in the hard, cold, rigid pieces as they were when they were molten in the furnace."

A versatile substance, glass can be worked in many ways. Molten glass can be free blown, poured into a mold, or pressed into a form. In a method called slumping, cold glass is heated slowly to a pliable state, then shaped to create new forms. Cold glass also can be pulverized, mixed with fluxing agents to facilitate melting, poured into a mold, and then heated slowly to fuse the powder into a cohesive mass. The French call this method *pâte de verre*, or glass paste. Common methods of working cold glass include sandblasting, acid etching, engraving, carving, cutting, enameling, polishing, painting, and assembling pre-existing pieces by using industrial adhesives.

While glass is often taken for granted, our ancestors held the medium in awe, for it was a difficult substance to master and forgave few mistakes. Nowhere is their awe more evident than in the poetic metaphors and images that enliven our language and folk tales. Because glass can transmit light and transform that energy into prismatic bursts, and because glass intensifies colors when penetrated by light, this wondrous material is commonly associated with the spiritual.

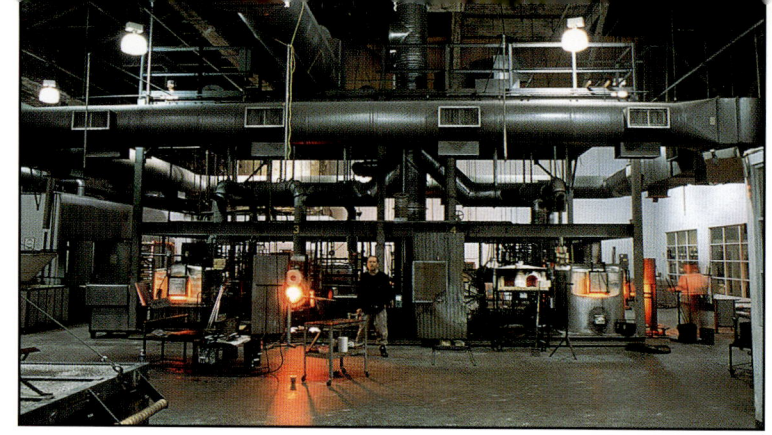

Executive Director John Perreault in the hot shop at UrbanGlass.

The Studio Glass Movement

The studio glass movement in the late twentieth century has stimulated a fresh look at this ancient substance. Though not yet four decades old, the movement has already gifted us with a stunning array of artistic creativity, allowing glass to transcend utilitarian function and mass production as "serviceable" goods. Its role as a medium for art, historically limited to the medieval tradition of stained glass in ecclesiastical art, is now firmly and fully established.

Studio glass is a recently coined term that refers to one-of-a-kind works created in a workshop in which usually one person conceives of or directs (with assistants) the production of the art. Studio glass is the antithesis of industrial glass, which is mass-produced according to rigidly controlled standards that maintain conformity.

The studio glass movement is just one in the broader international craft movement that has flourished in the industrialized world since the 1960s. The international craft movement embraces clay, fiber, glass, metal, and wood, each a material that formed a mechanized industry in the Industrial Revolution. The premise of the craft movement is simple: art is not defined by its materials but by its concept and content.

In 1962 the Toledo Museum of Art—renowned for its historical glass collection—hosted two glass workshops to explore glass as a medium for art separate from industrial uses and specific function. Dominick Labino and Harvey K. Littleton, two of the "fathers" of studio glass who were involved with the Toledo workshops, played seminal roles in establishing glass as a viable medium for art. These two landmark workshops heralded the studio glass movement in the United States. By the end of the 1960s, it was clear that glass is a dynamic medium for art, joining the craft materials of clay and fiber as media for creative expression.

Early in the movement, studio glass was defined as art that originated with one person: the artist develops the concept and then carries it through to the final work of art. But for an artist working with hot glass, such romanticized adherence to the ethos of the solitary craftsman, rooted in the Arts and Crafts movement of the turn of the century, was almost impossible. Because glass melting and glassblowing demand enormous amounts of energy, spacious facilities, specialized tools and equipment, and highly developed skills, it is a medium beyond the reach of most individual artists.

Not surprisingly, the evolution of the studio glass movement was fostered largely by studio art programs in major universities, art schools, and specialized workshops. Teaching institutions and art schools and programs were vital in developing studio glass as a legitimate art. Further legitimizing contemporary studio glass were the development of museum collections, the flourishing of important galleries and private and corporate collectors, the rise of such organizations as the Glass Art Society, the Art Alliance for Contemporary Glass, and the Creative Glass Center of America, as well as the publications devoted to the medium. The Pilchuck Glass School located in Stanwood, Washington, was founded in 1971, and UrbanGlass: New York Contemporary Glass Center, the publisher of *GLASS*, located first in Manhattan and now in Brooklyn, was founded in 1977. Both have been influential in promoting studio glass and shaping the character of the movement.

How to make glass and how to work it are not necessarily exclusive domains in the studio glass movement. An artist is often both a consummate glassmaker and a broadly skilled craftsman and technician. Some artists are innovators of glass technologies and have led glass engineers to new understandings of this endlessly challenging material.

While some artists immerse themselves in glass chemistry and create special varieties of the medium for their artistic ends, others use existing glass to achieve their art. Both approaches are at home within the studio glass movement. More than any other feature, exceptional richness and diversity characterize the studio glass movement.

Kenneth R. Trapp, Curator-in-Charge Renwick Gallery of the Smithsonian American Art Museum.
Excerpted from the *Glass! Glorious Glass!* Exhibition Brochure.

GLASS

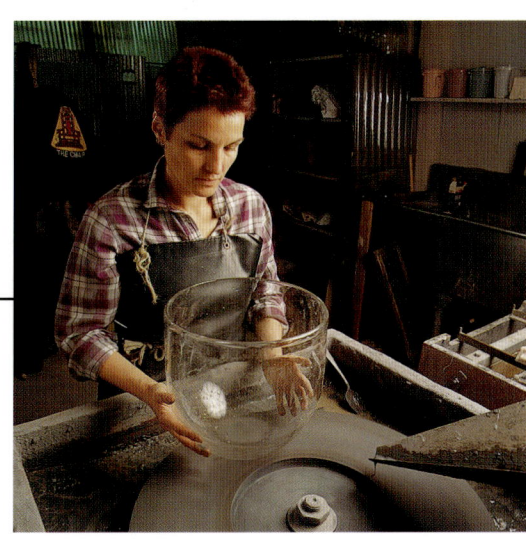

Jane Bruce grinding a vase in UrbanGlass' coldworking shop.

Michael Aschenbrenner
(b.1949)

UPLAND, CALIFORNIA

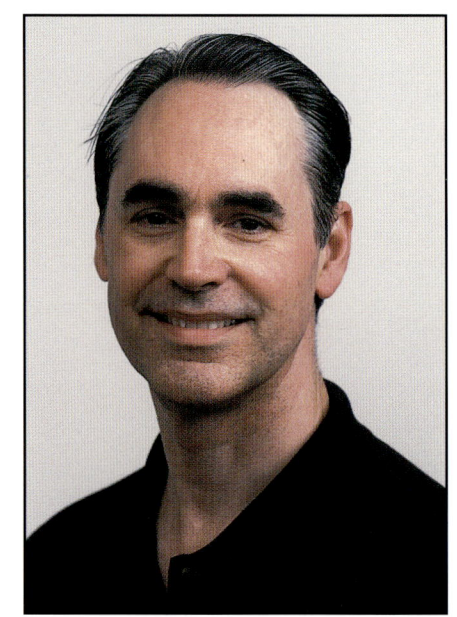

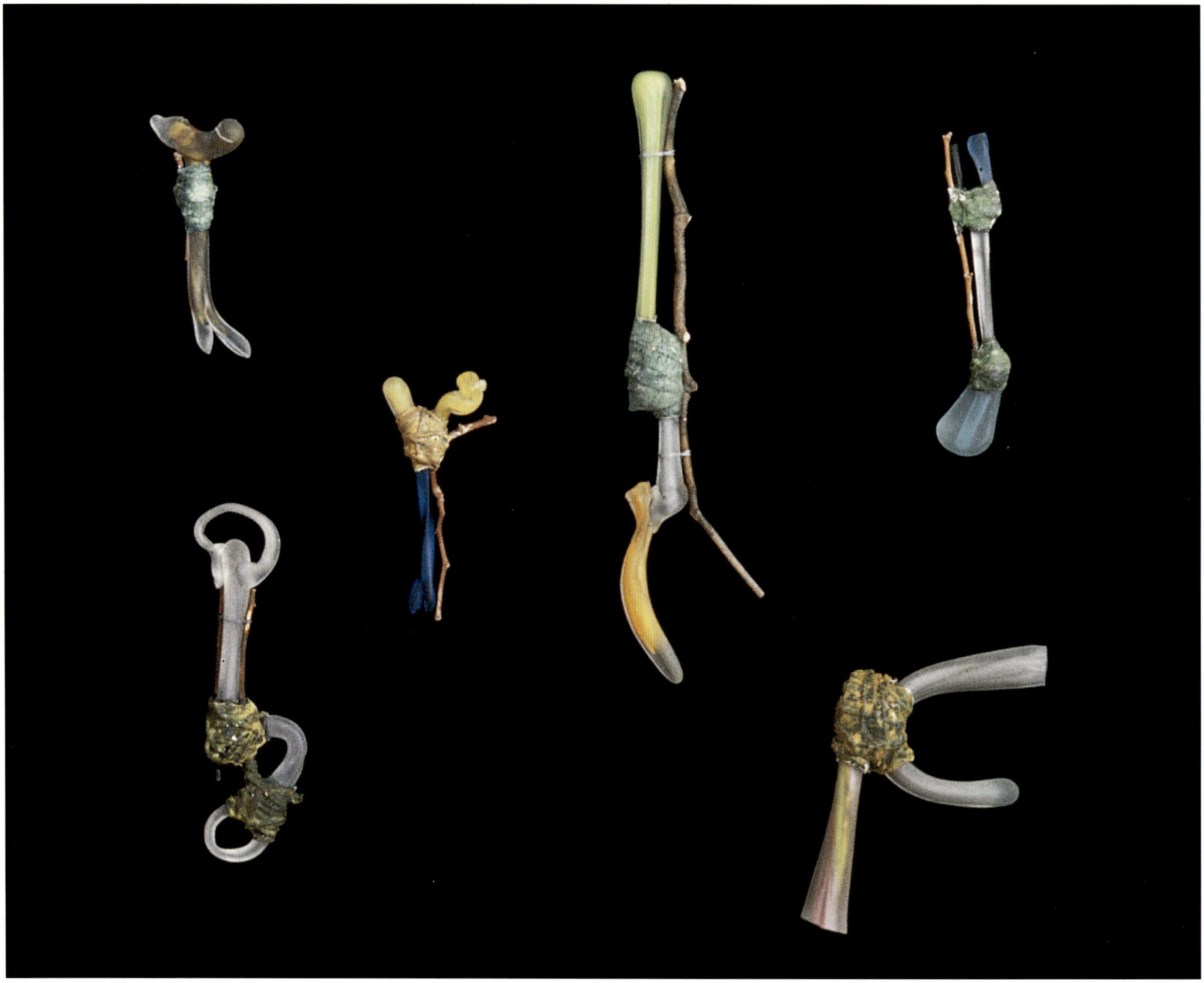

Composition of Ancient Tools; Implement Series, 1994.
Glass and mixed material. h. 60 x 50 x 6 inches

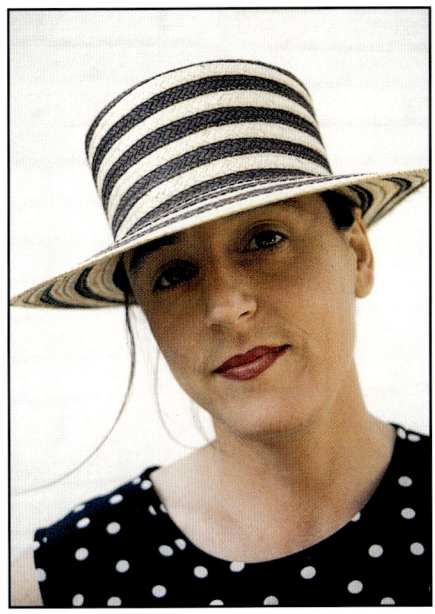

Photo: Greta Olafsdottir

BROOKLYN, NEW YORK

Tina Aufiero
(b.1959)

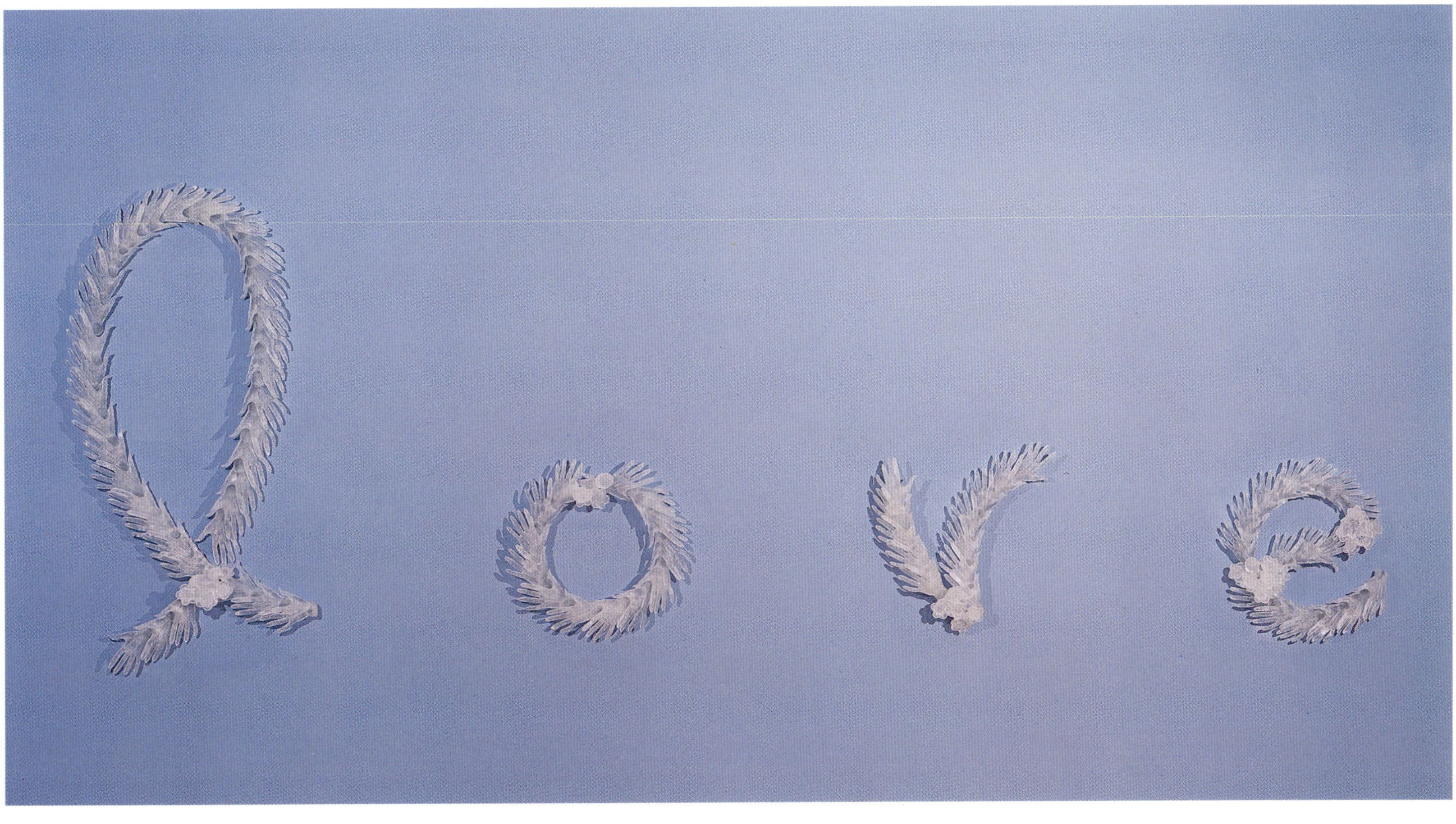

Love, 1995. Wall relief, cast glass, cast hands, flowers, dolls, fit and glued to steel armature, h. 66 x 22 x 4 inches.

Herb Babcock
(b.1946)

OXFORD, MICHIGAN

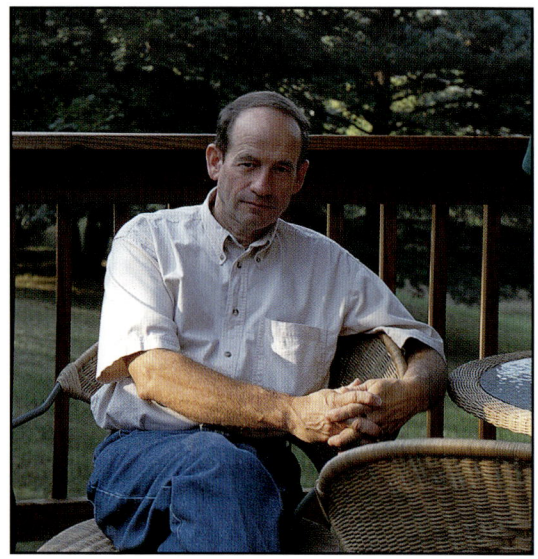

Young Bamboo in Wind, 1995. Cast glass, steel, stone, and fiber-optic light, h. 22.5 x 22 x 22 feet. Hsinchu Cultural Center; Hsinchu City, Taiwan.

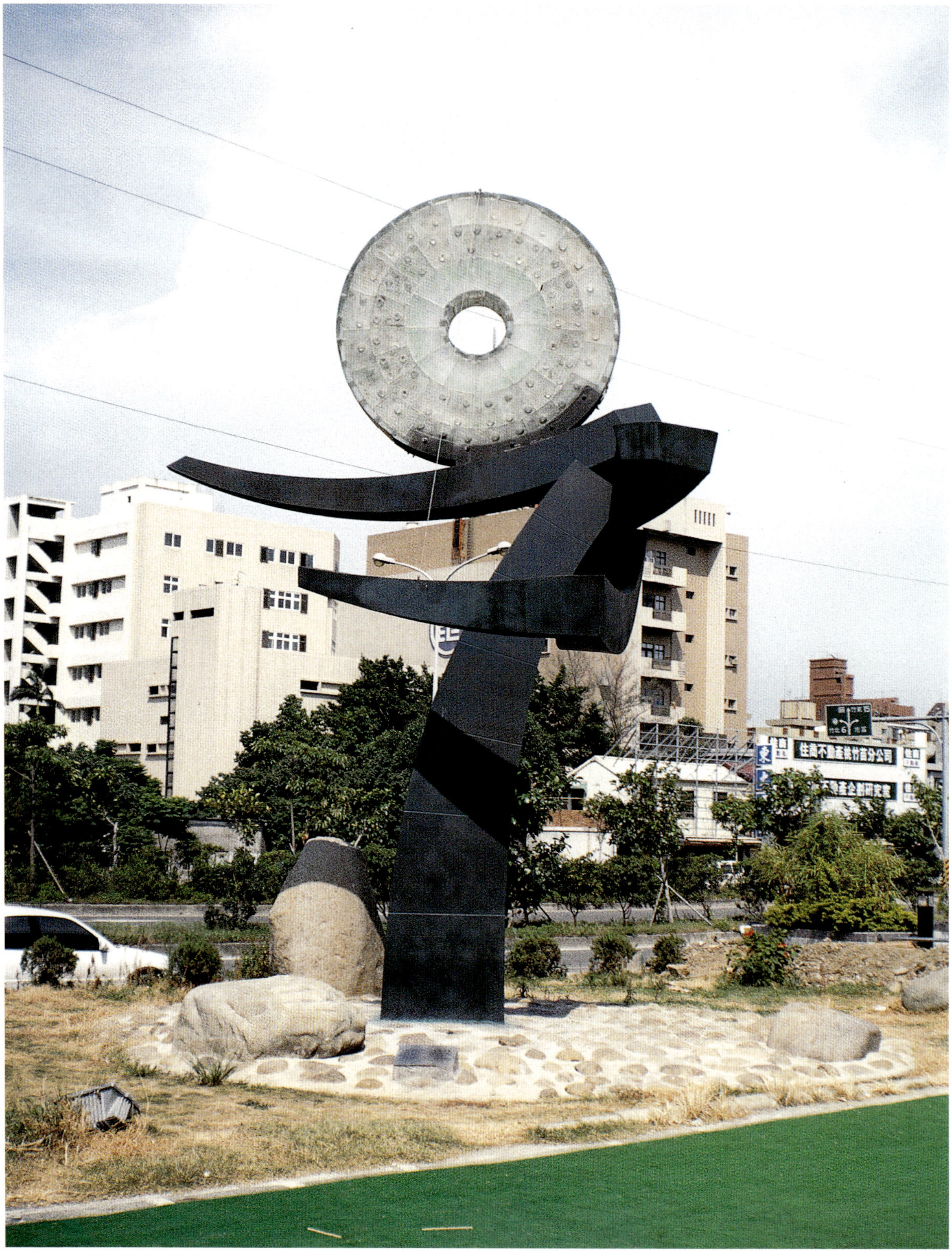

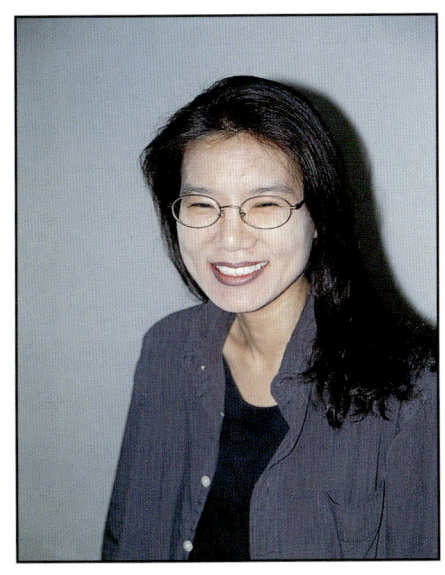

DAEGU, SOUTH KOREA

Kyoung Joo Bae
(b.1963)

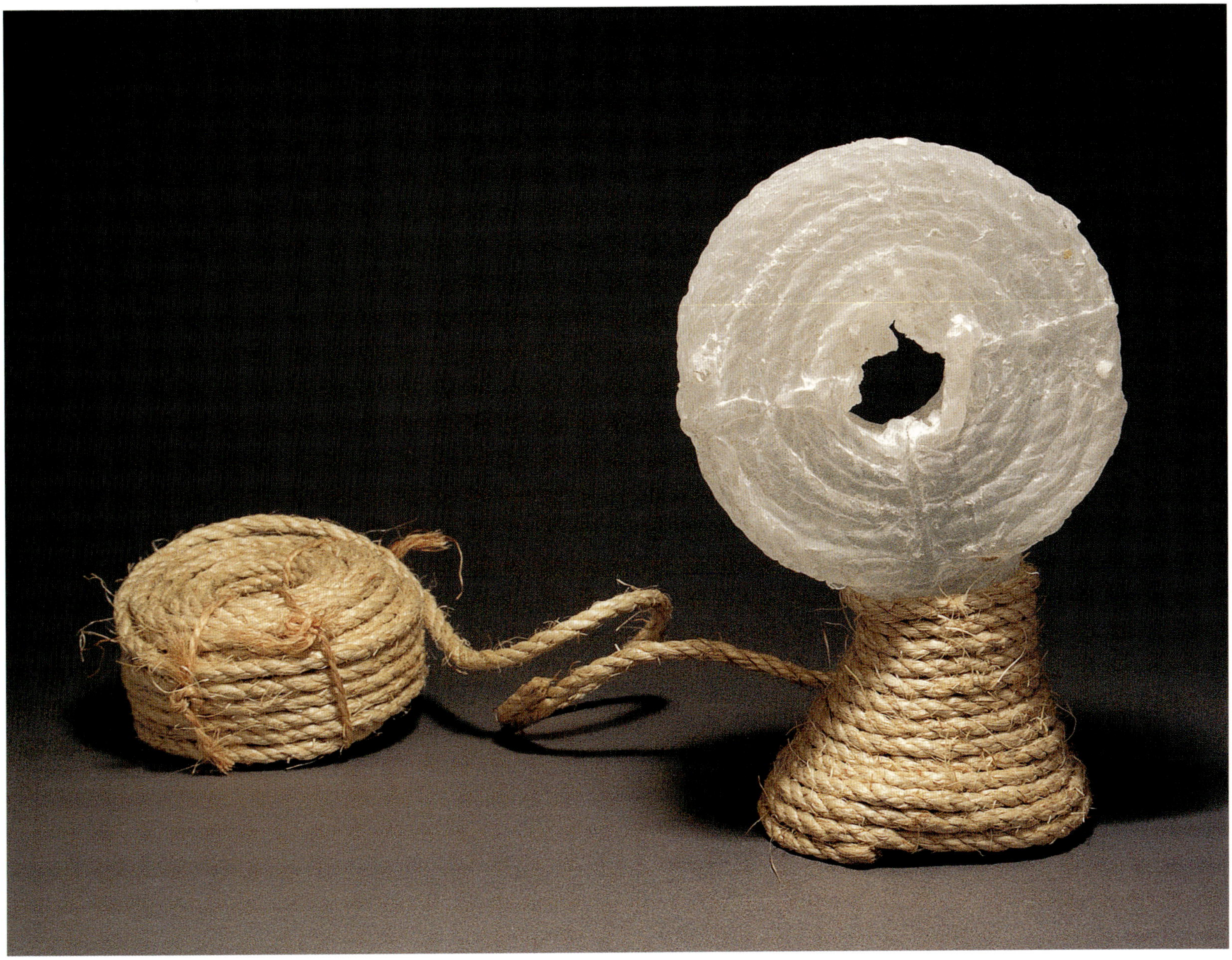

Untitled II, 1996. Lost wax, cast glass, and straw, h. 10.5 x 5.2 inches.

Christine Barney
(b. 1952)

JERSEY CITY, NEW JERSEY

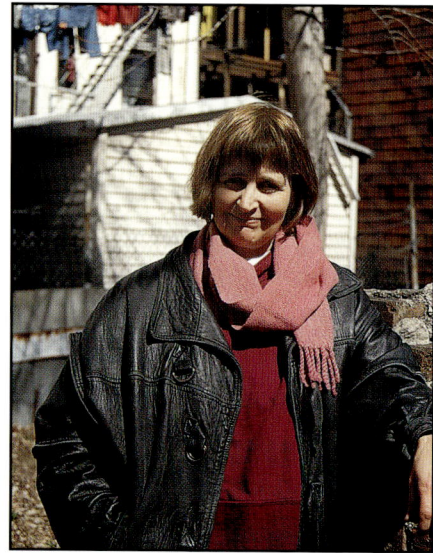

Ruby Fusion, 1998. Cast glass, h. 12 x 8 x 5.5 inches.

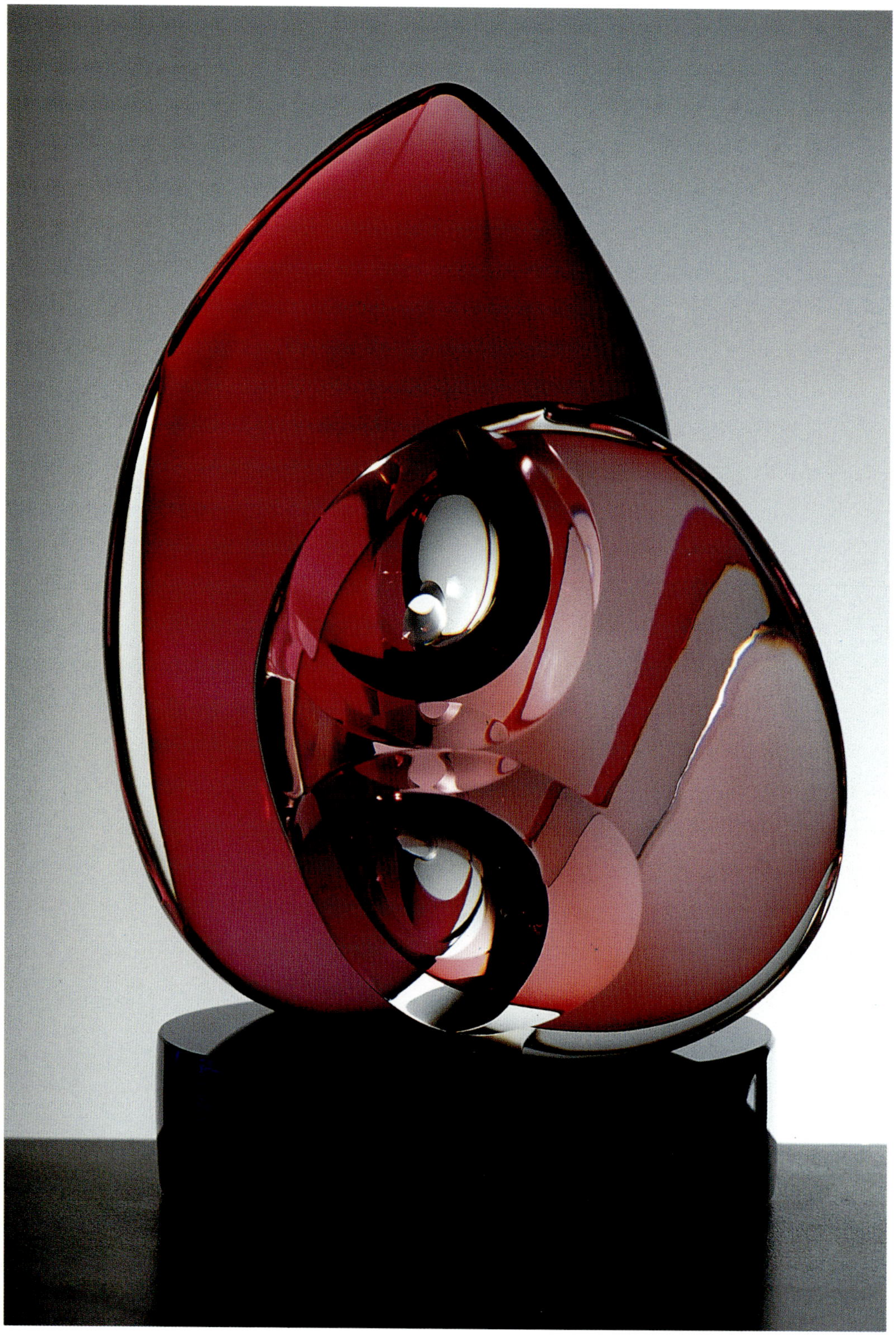

Paula Bartron
(b.1946)

STOCKHOLM, SWEDEN

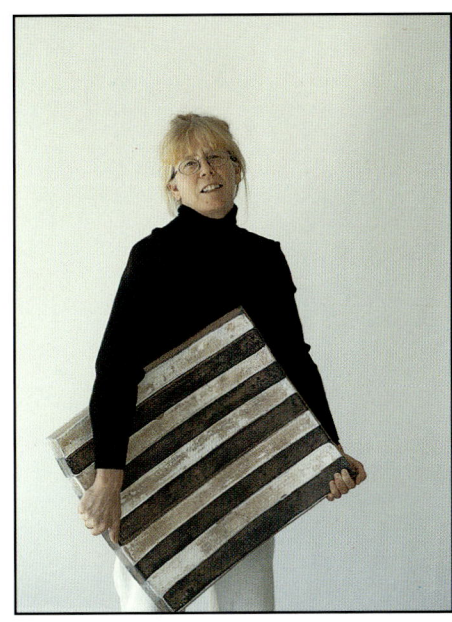

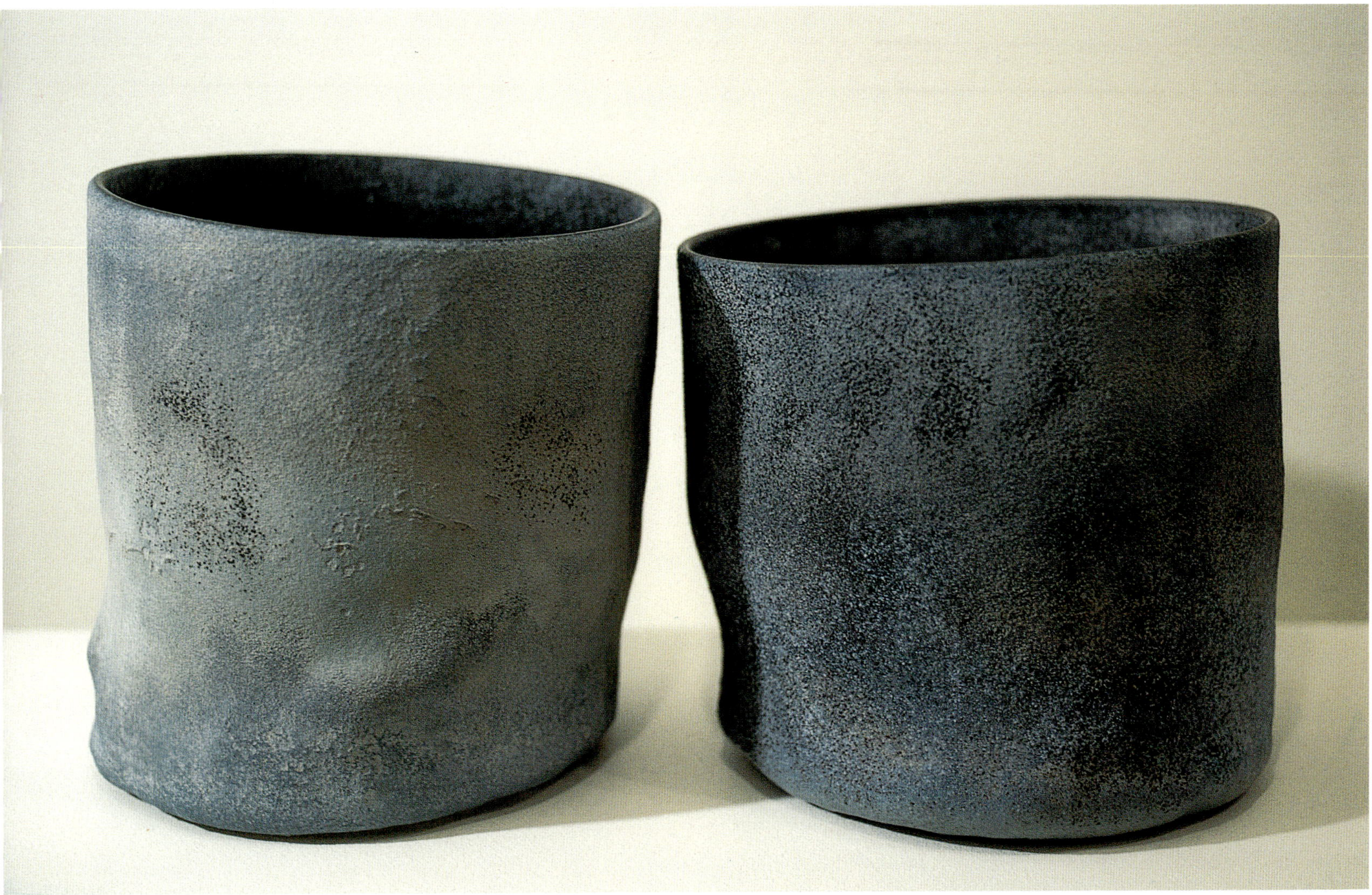

***Soft Cylinders**, 1999. Blown glass in sand mold, h. 8.5 x 9.2 & h. 9 x 8 inches.*

Lynda Benglis
(b.1941)

NEW YORK, NEW YORK

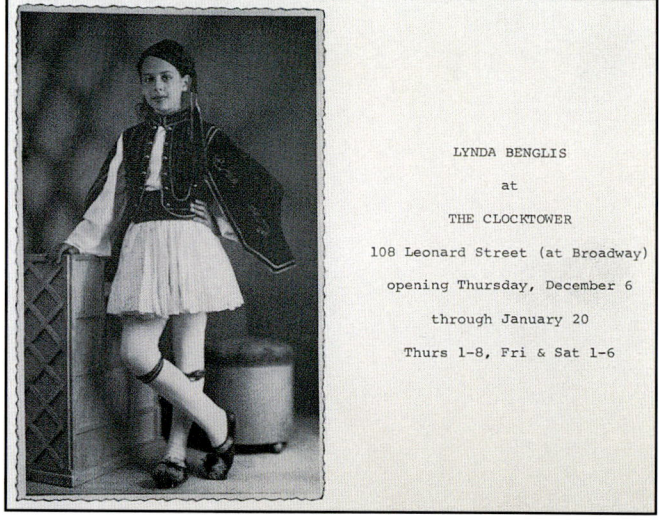

Exhibition Invitation, 1973-74,
The Clock Tower, New York City.

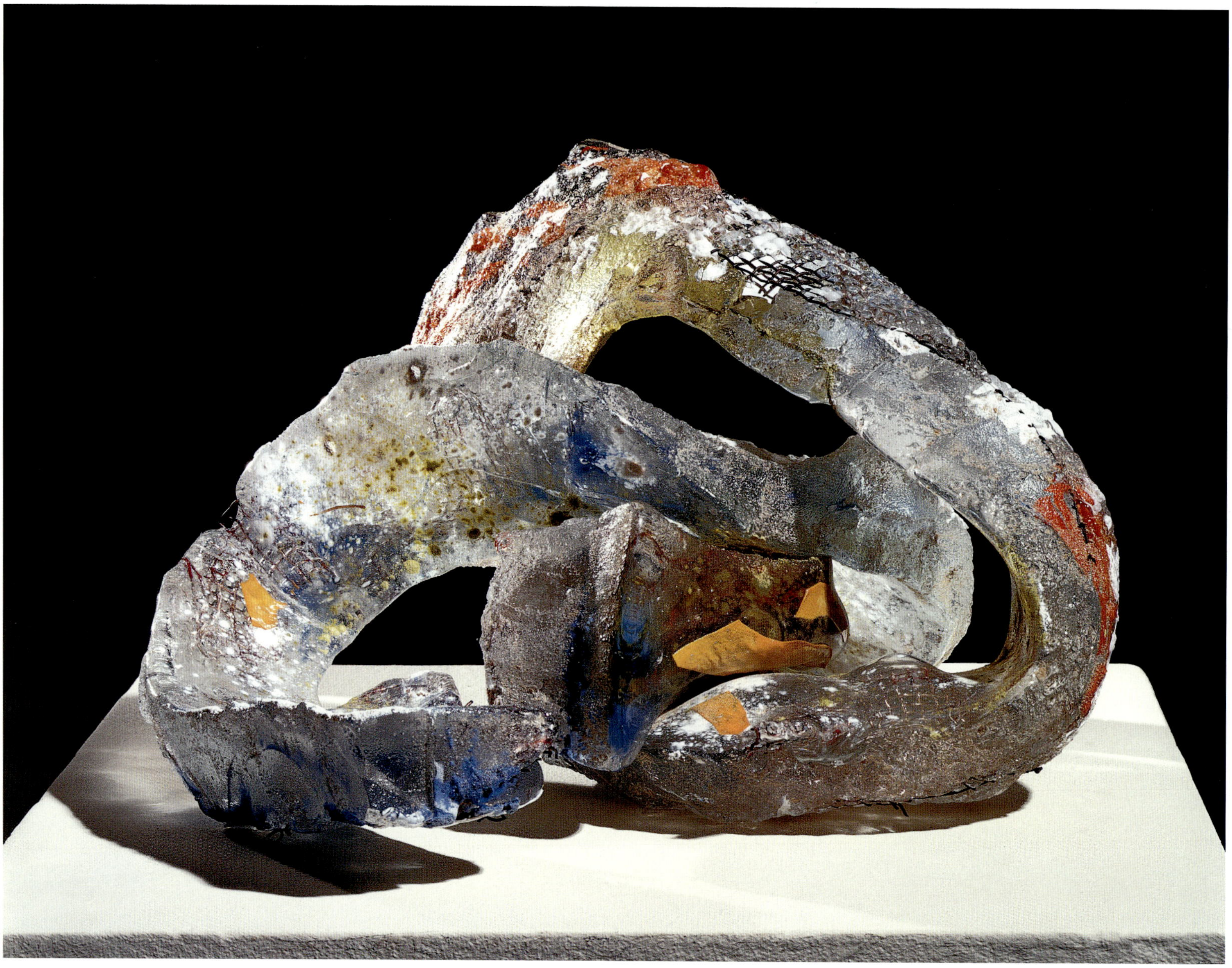

Bowfin, 1985. Sandcast glass,
h. 10.5 x 16 x 14.5 inches.

PROVIDENCE, RHODE ISLAND # Howard Ben Tré
(b. 1949)

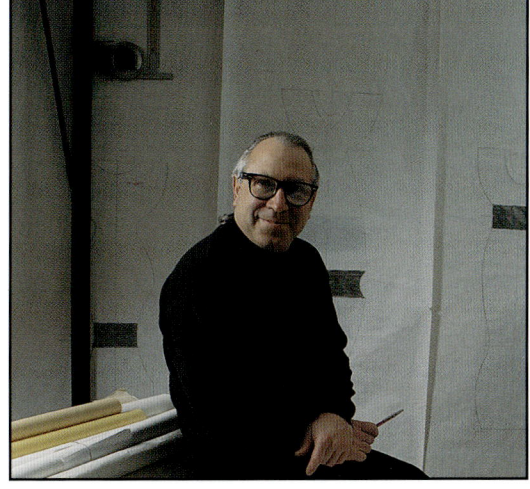

Photo: Ric Murray

Wrapped Form 16, 1999. Cast glass, and iron powder, h. 53.5 x 18.5 x 17.25 inches. Photo: Ric Murray.

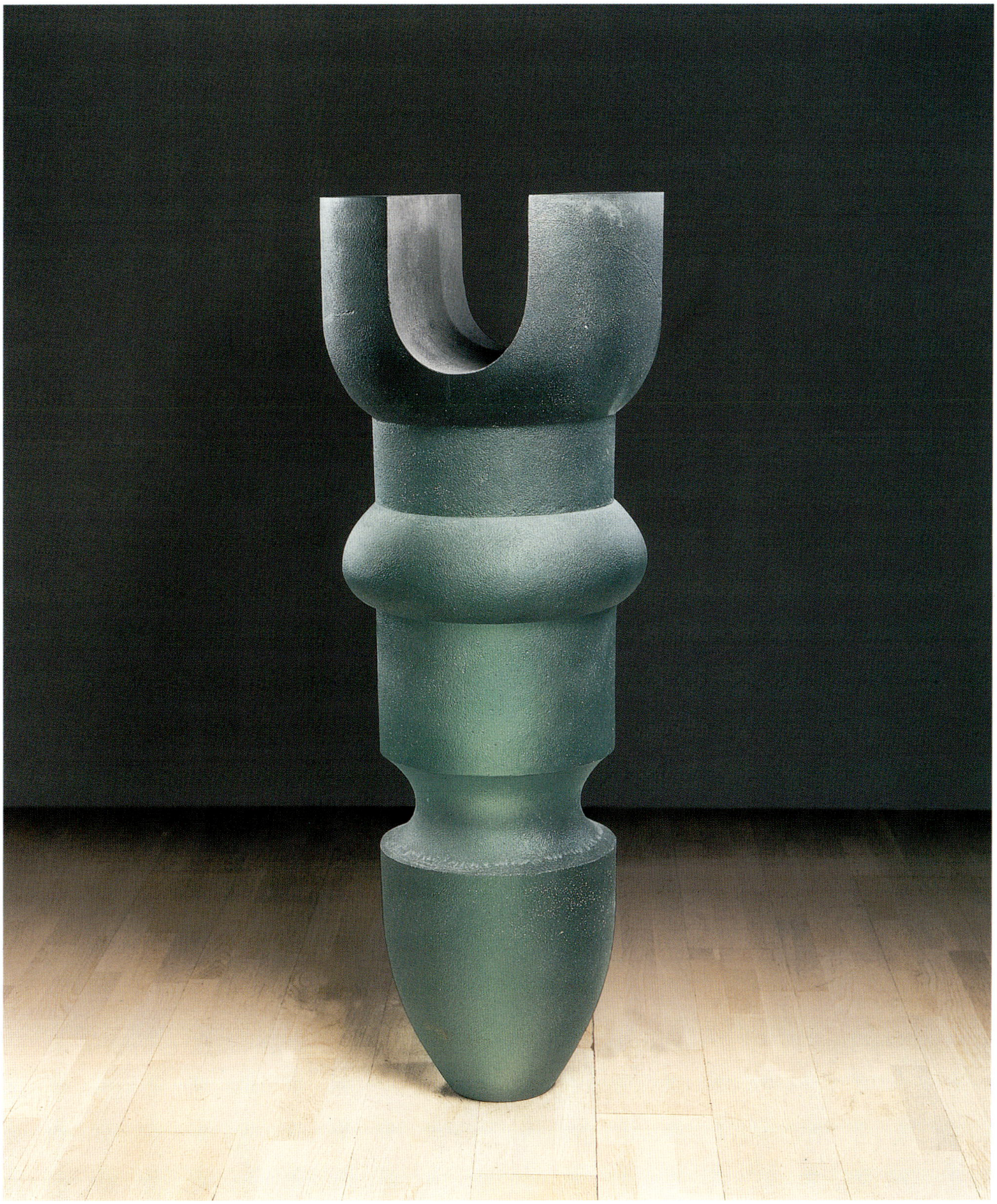

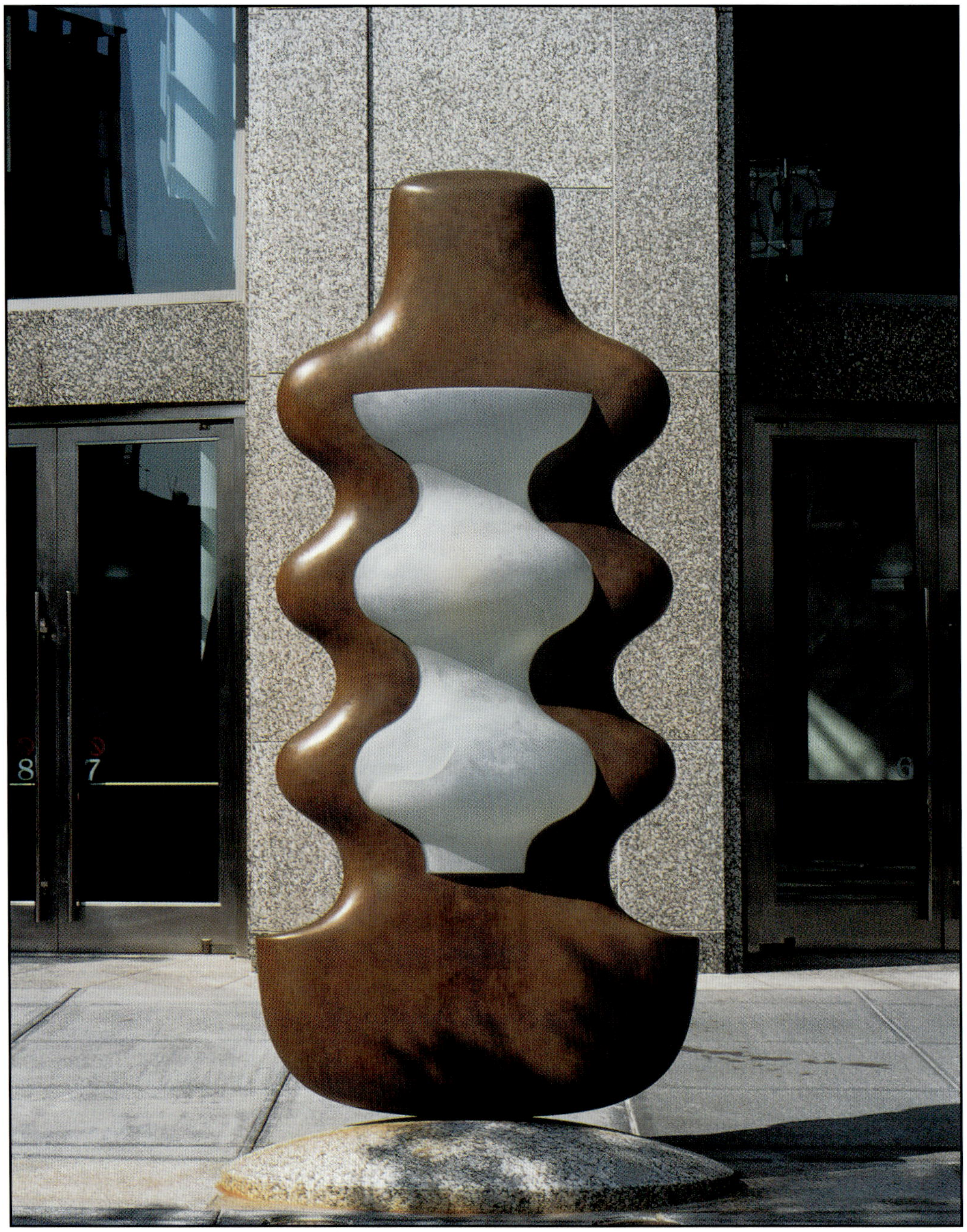

HOWARD BEN TRÉ

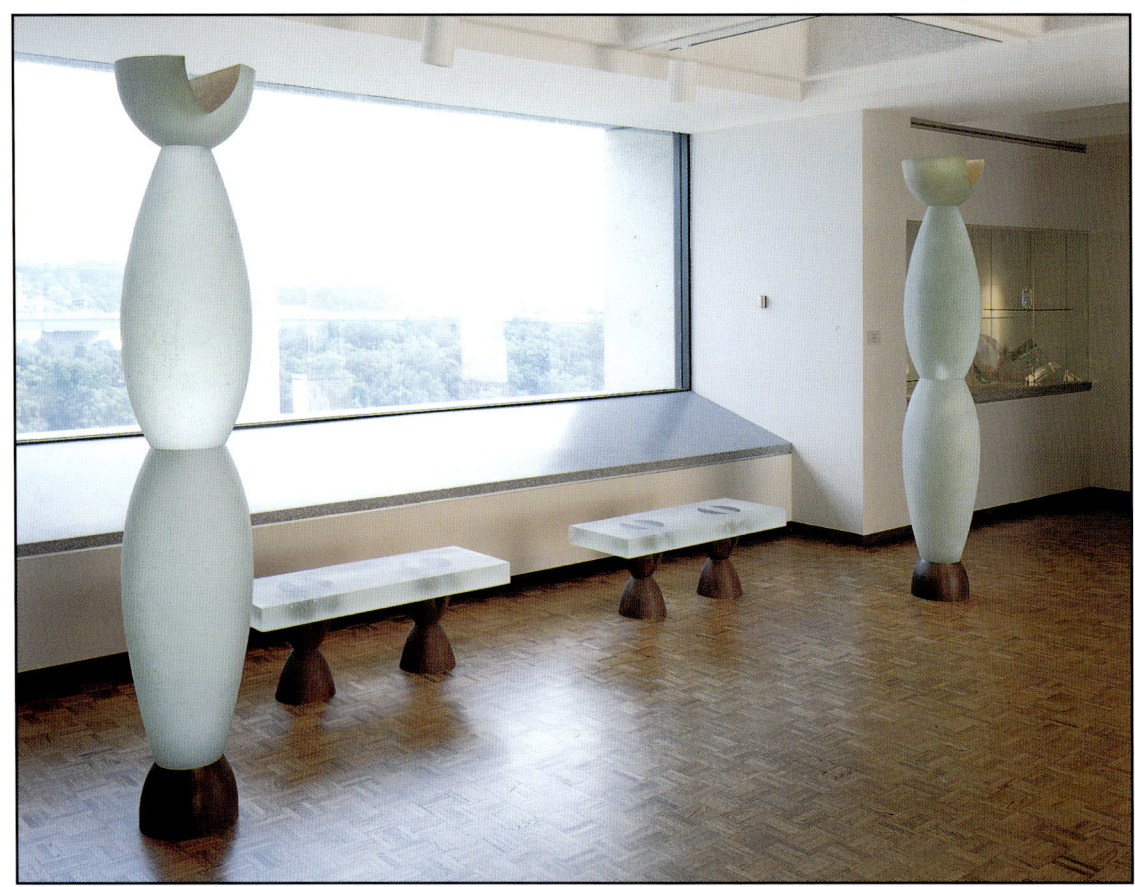

Top:
***Caryatid Columns with Benches**, 1998. Cast glass, bronze, gold leaf, and pigmented wax, (each column) h. 96 x 16 x 16 and (each bench) h. 18.25 x 48 x 17 inches. Permanent installation for the Hunter Museum of American Art, Chattanooga, Tennessee. Photo: James Maddon.*

Bottom:
***Bearing Figure**, 1996. Cast low expansion glass, bronze, gold leaf, patina, and granite base, h. 120 x 54 x 29 inches. Rhode Island Convention Center. Photo: Ric Murray*

Opposite:
***Bearing Figure with Amphora**, 1997. Cast low expansion glass, gold leaf, and granite, h. 84 x 36 x 18 inches. Photo: Tim Thayer.*

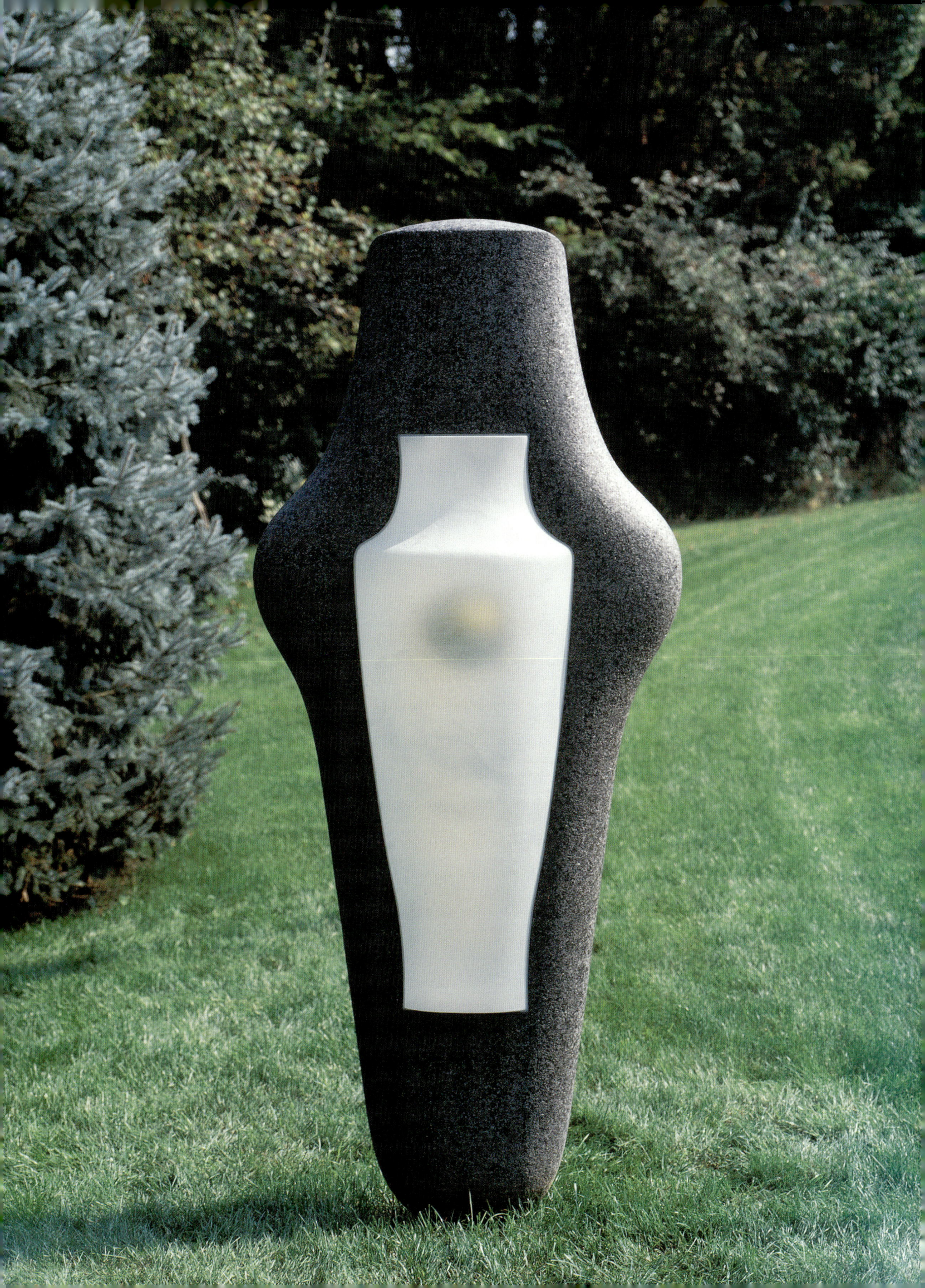

Giles Bettison
(b.1966)

MAYLANDS, AUSTRALIA

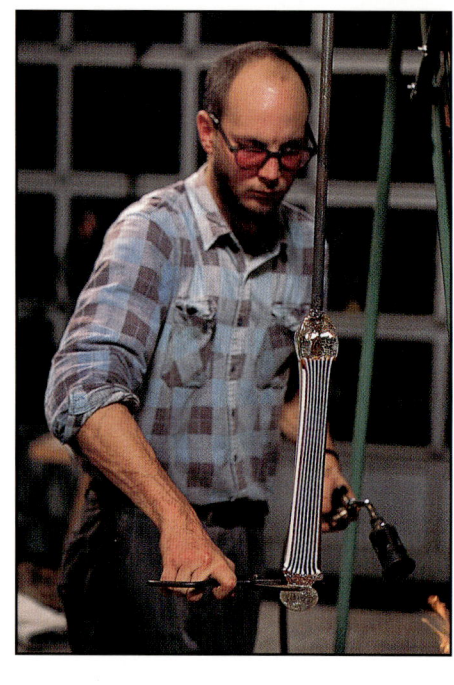

Right:
Cell #35, 1999. Blown glass, h. 16.9 x 5.3 inches. Photo: Andrew Dunbar

Opposite:
Cell #37, 1999. Blown glass, h. 17.9 x 5.7 inches. Photo: Andrew Dunbar

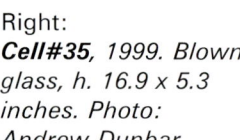

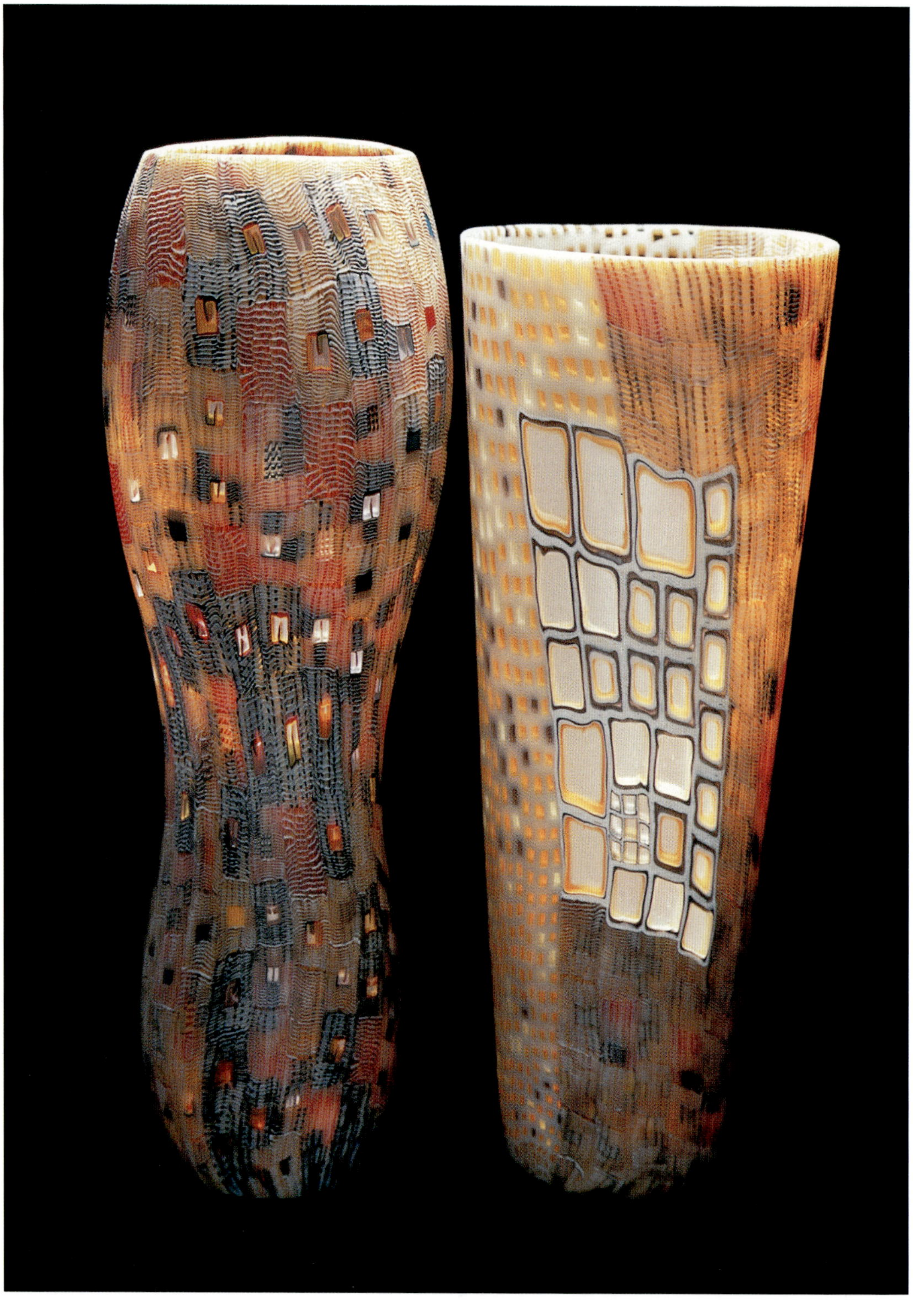

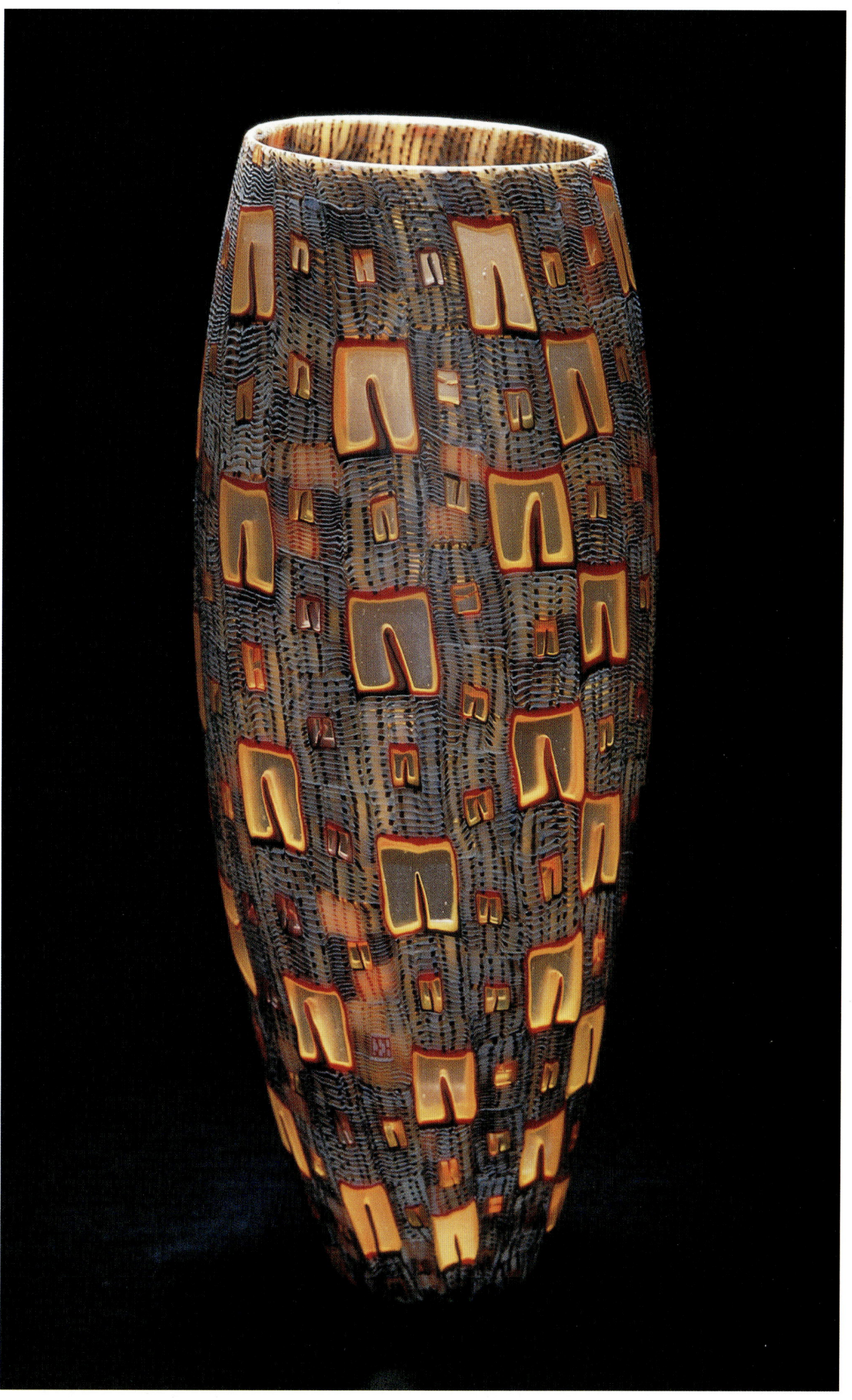

Reino Björk
(b.1952)

NEW YORK, NEW YORK

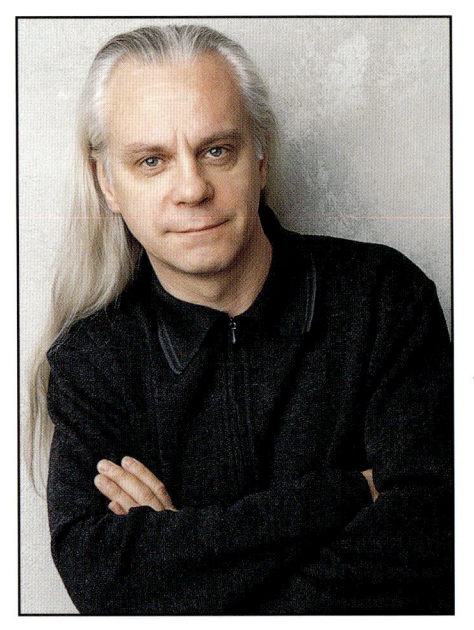

Photo: Timothy Greenfield-Sanders

Flat with Dots, 1999. Blown glass, murrine incalma, h. 22 x 20 inches.
Photo: Timothy Greenfield-Sanders

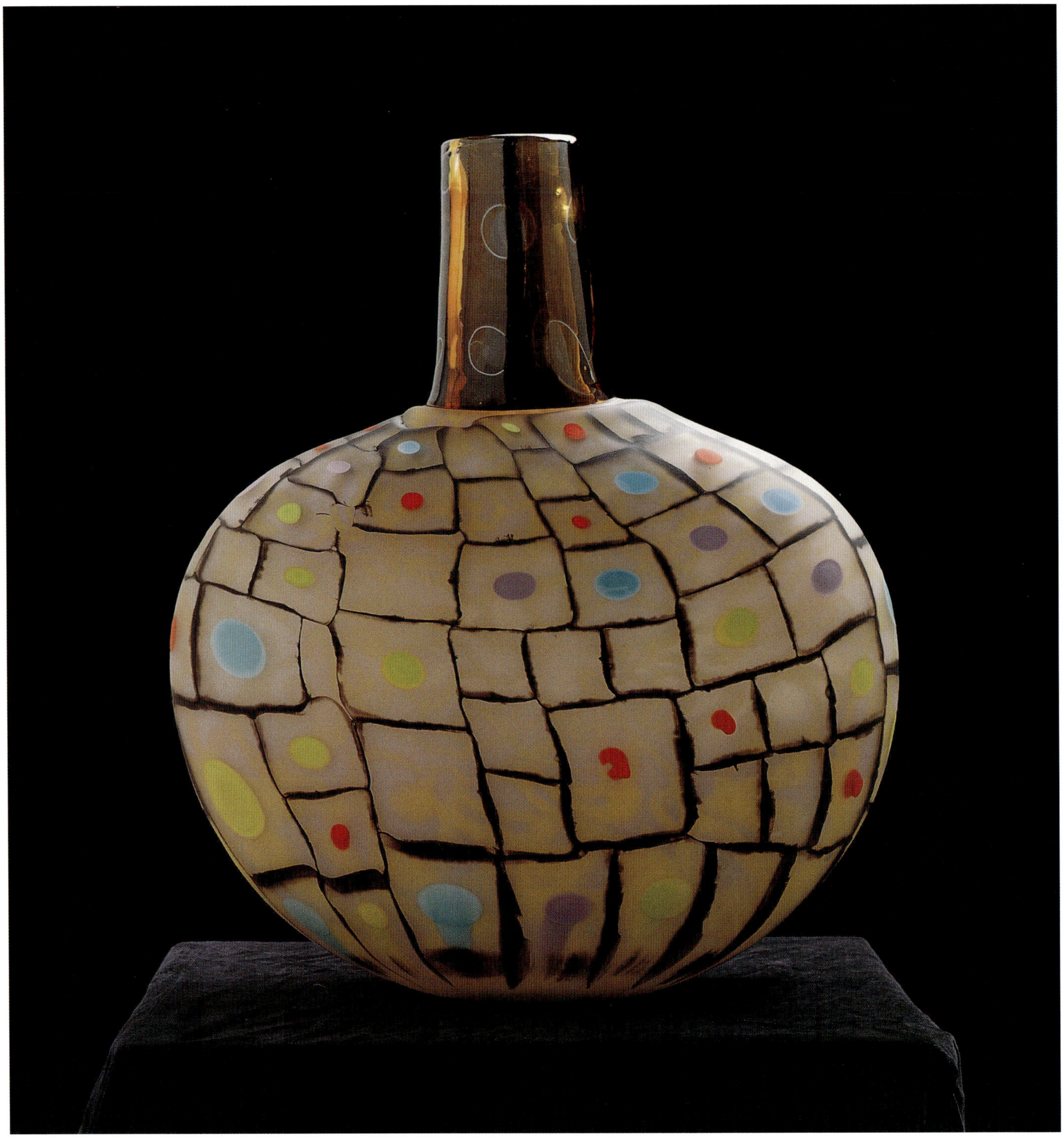

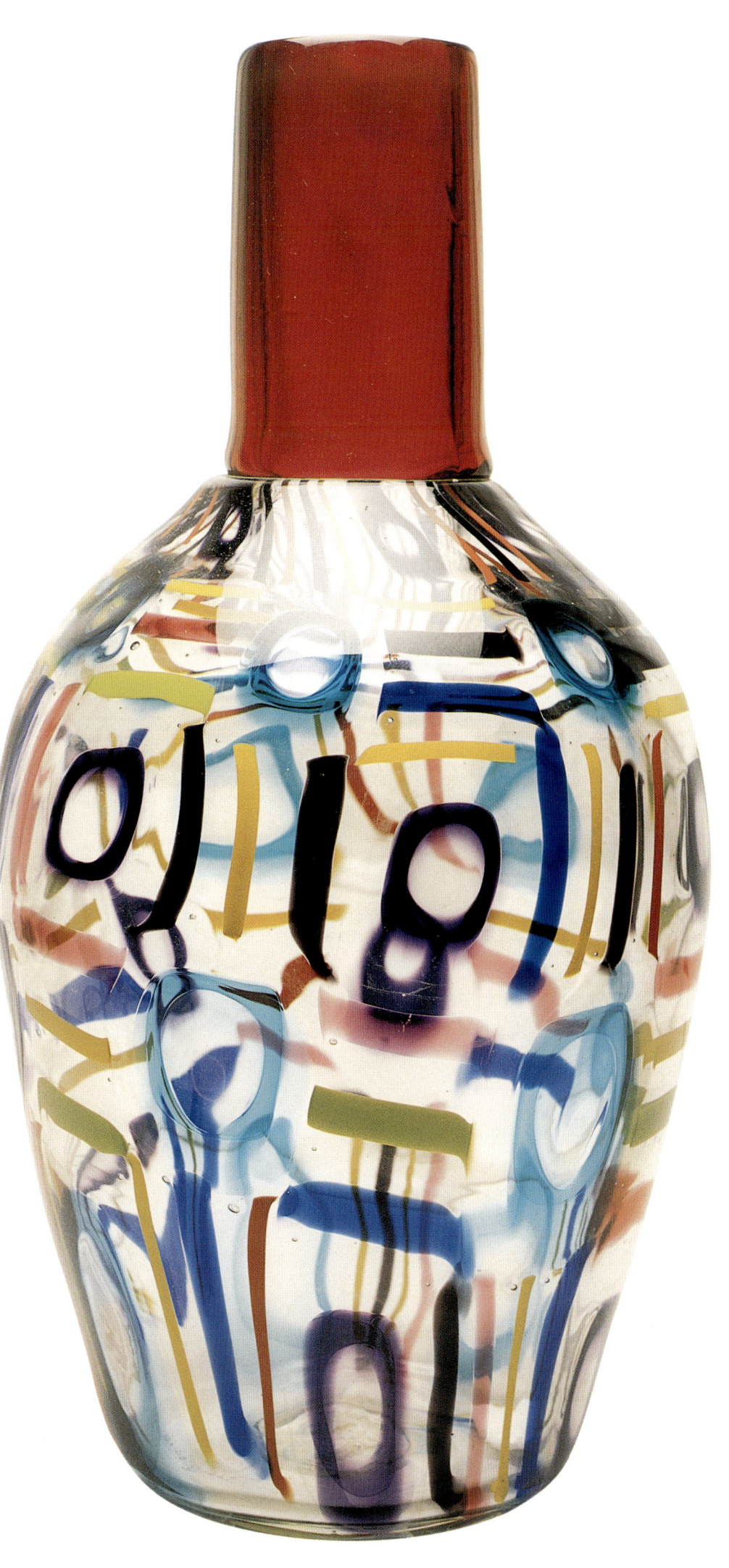

Red Neck, 1996. Blown glass, and murrine incalma, h. 22 x 11 inches. Collection of Cynthia and Jeffrey Manocherian

23

Sonja Blomdahl
(b.1952)

SEATTLE, WASHINGTON

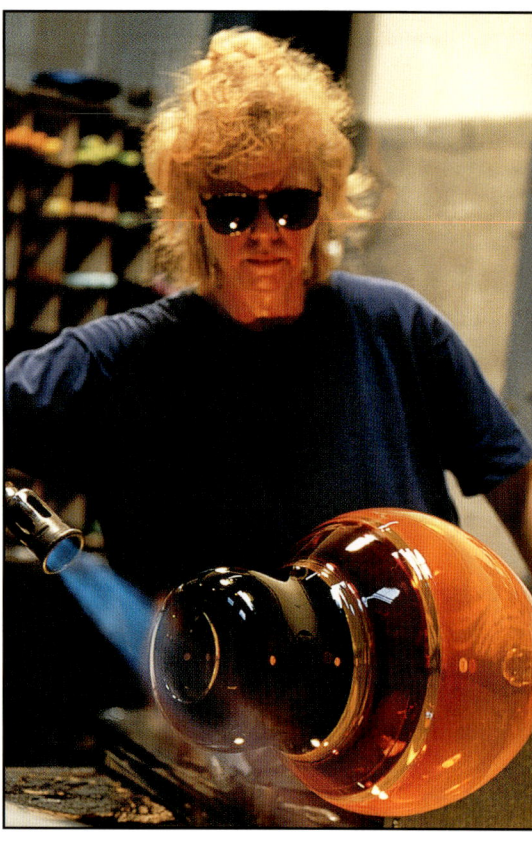

Photo: Russell Johnson

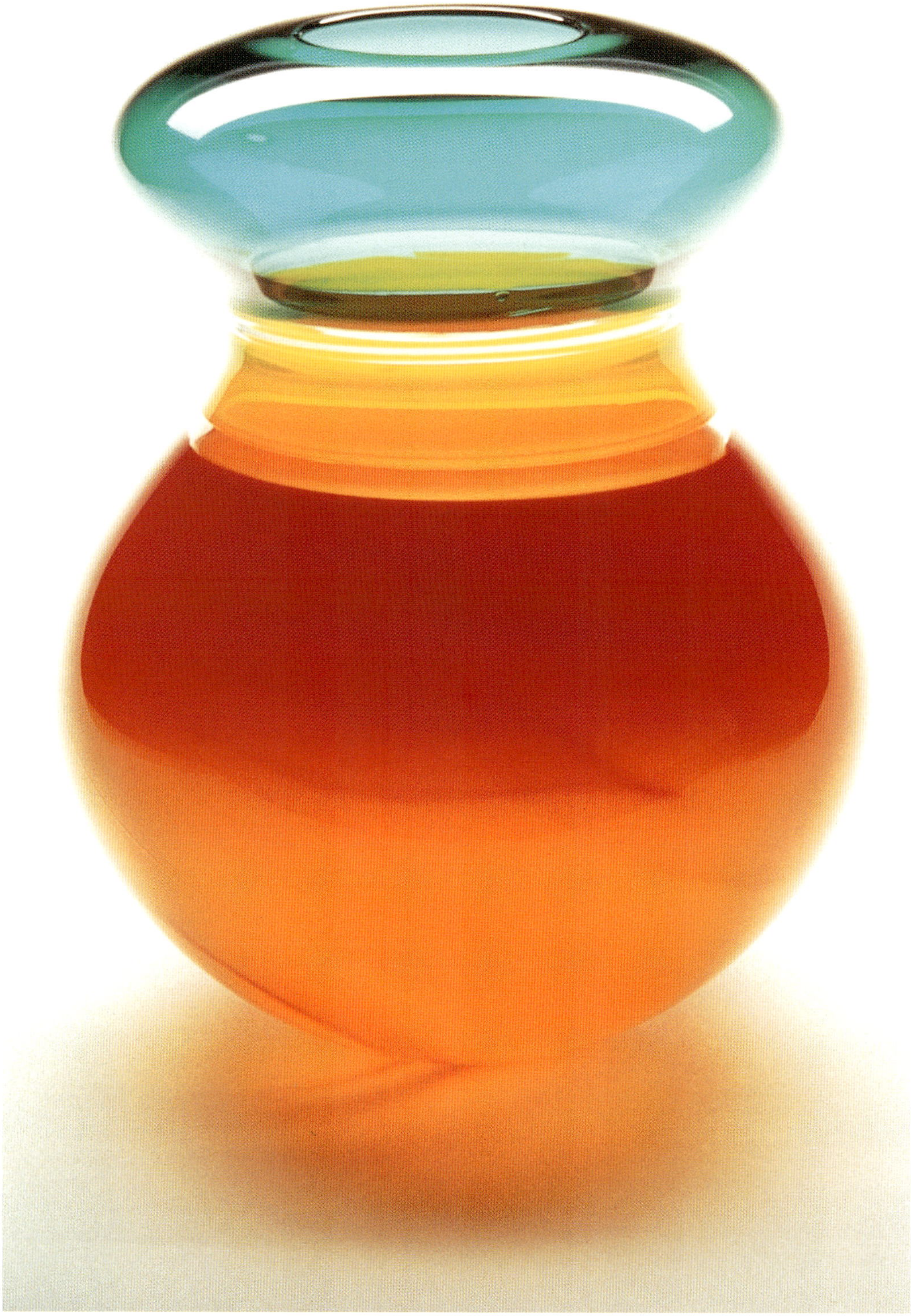

Red/Yellow/Green Vessel, 1992.
Blown glass, h. 15.5 x 12 inches.
Charles A. Wustum Museum of
Fine Arts, Racine, Wisconsin.
Gift of Dale and Doug Anderson.
Photo: Jon Bolton.

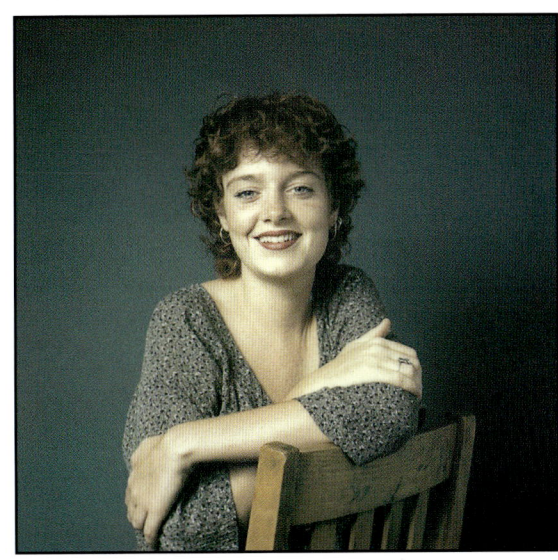

BROOKLYN, NEW YORK

Katie Bochicchio
(b.1974)

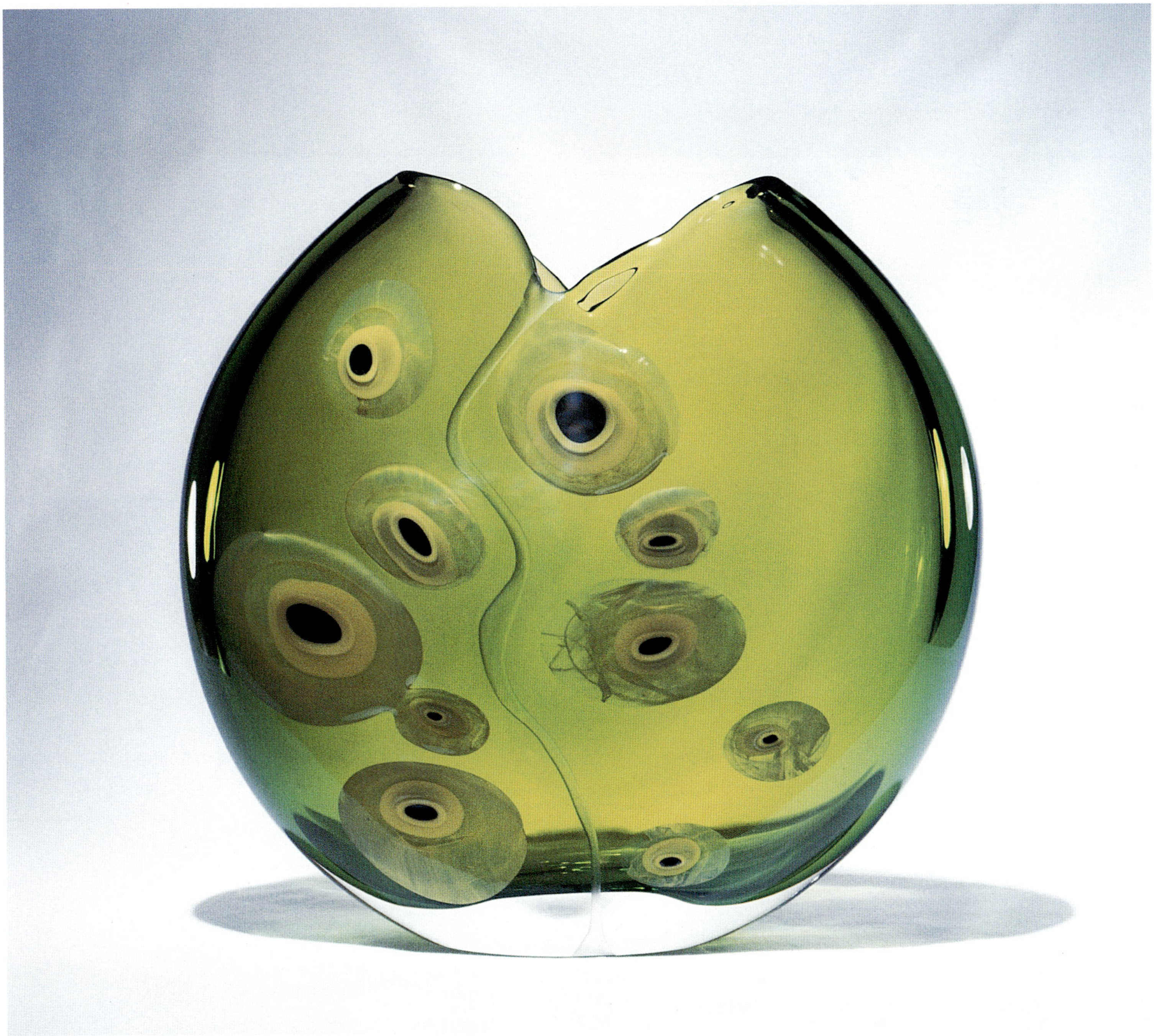

Lotus Vase, *1999. Blown glass,*
h. 7 x 3 x 12 inches.

Nancy Bowen
(b.1955)

NEW YORK, NEW YORK

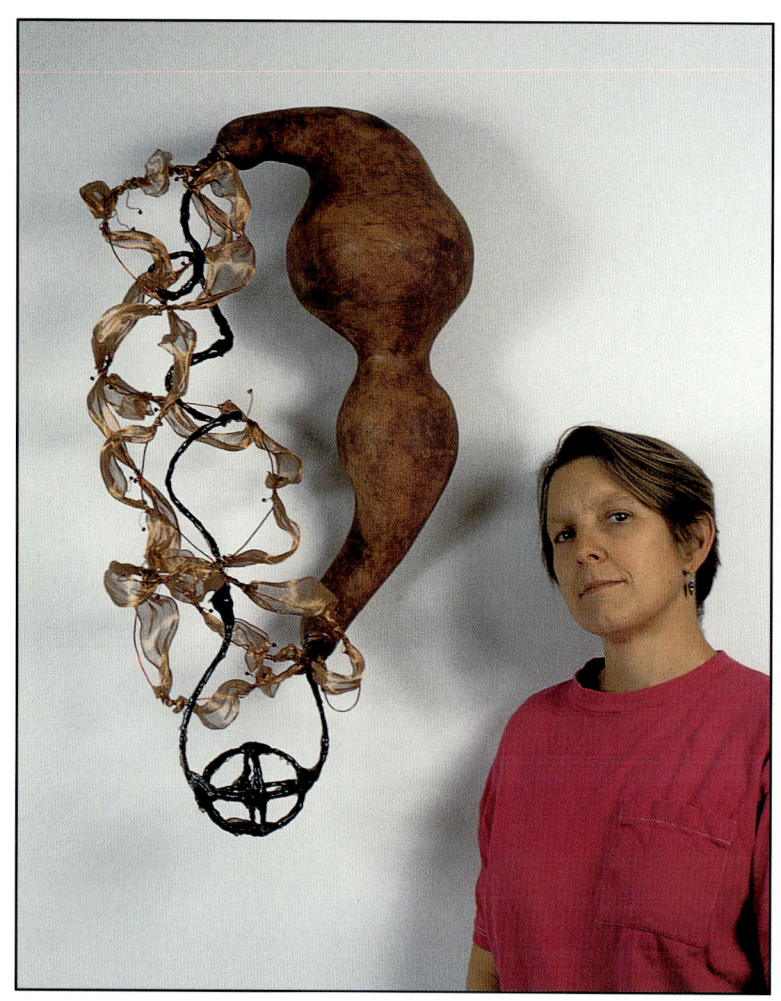

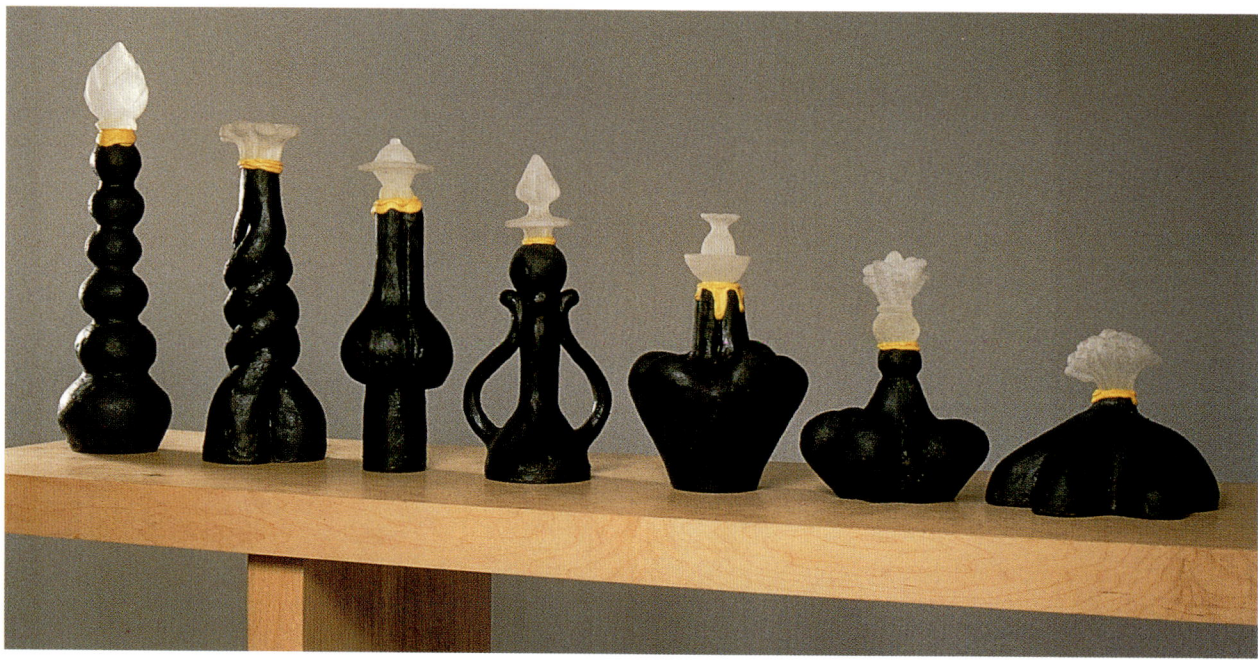

7 Aspects: Florets, 1994. Clay, glass, and modeling plaster, c. 23 x 80 x 24 inches.

BROOKLYN, NEW YORK

John Brekke
(b.1955)

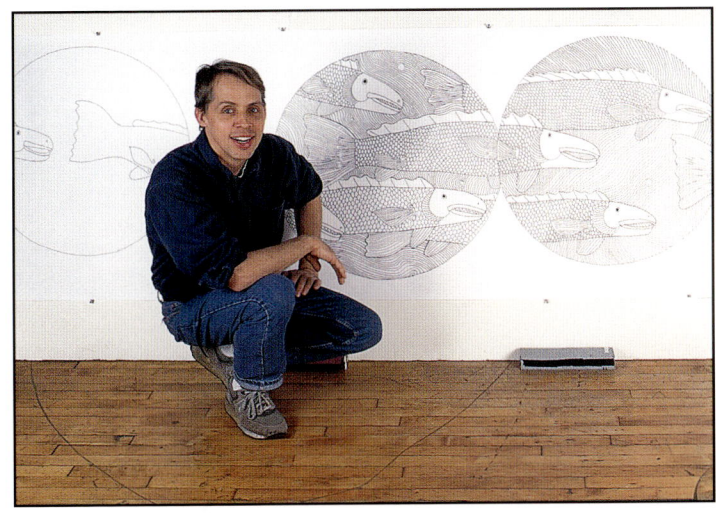

Photo: Dawn Marie Hale

***Squirrel**/Tattoo*, 1992. Blown glass, sandblasting and acid etched, h. 12.75 x 9 inches.

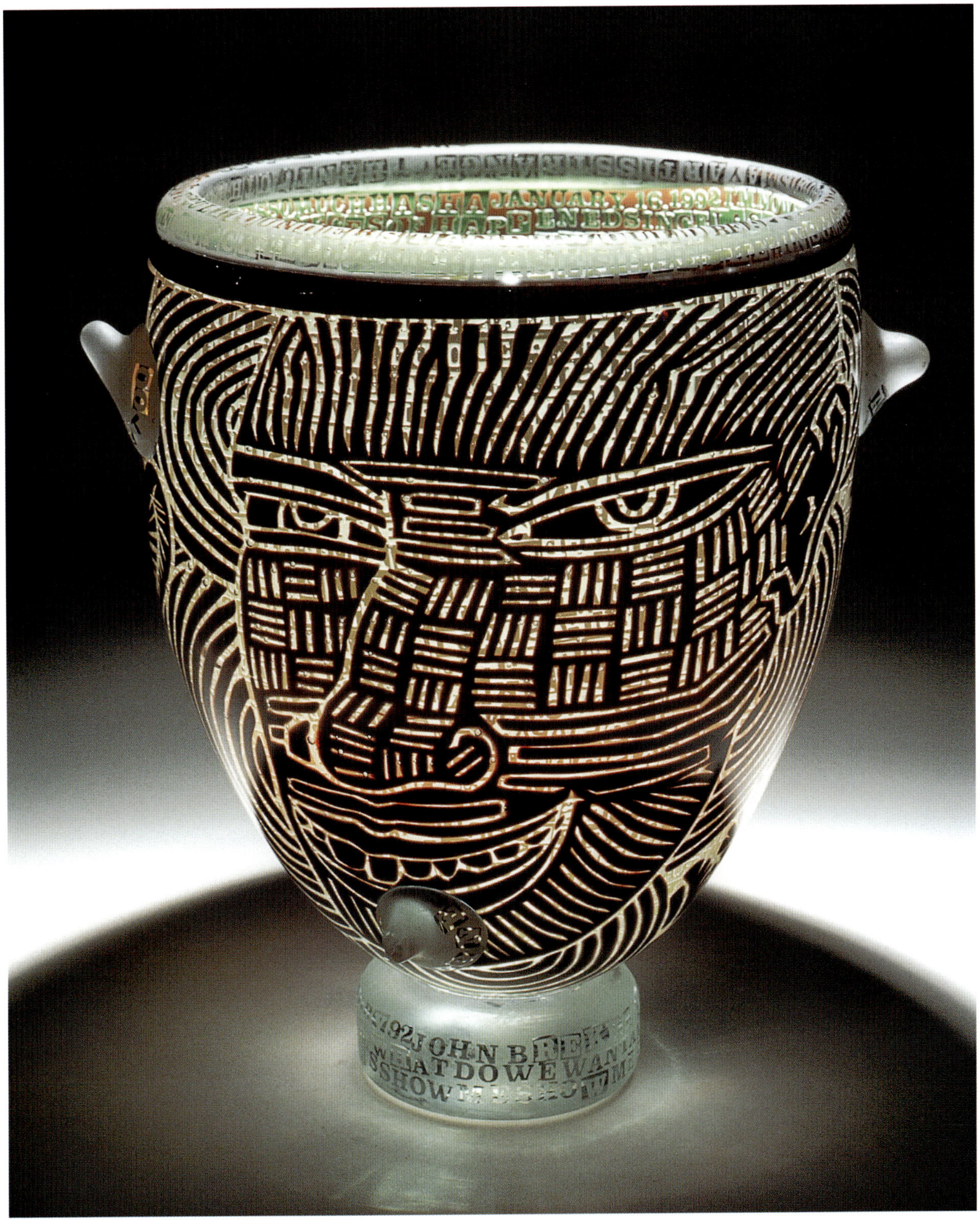

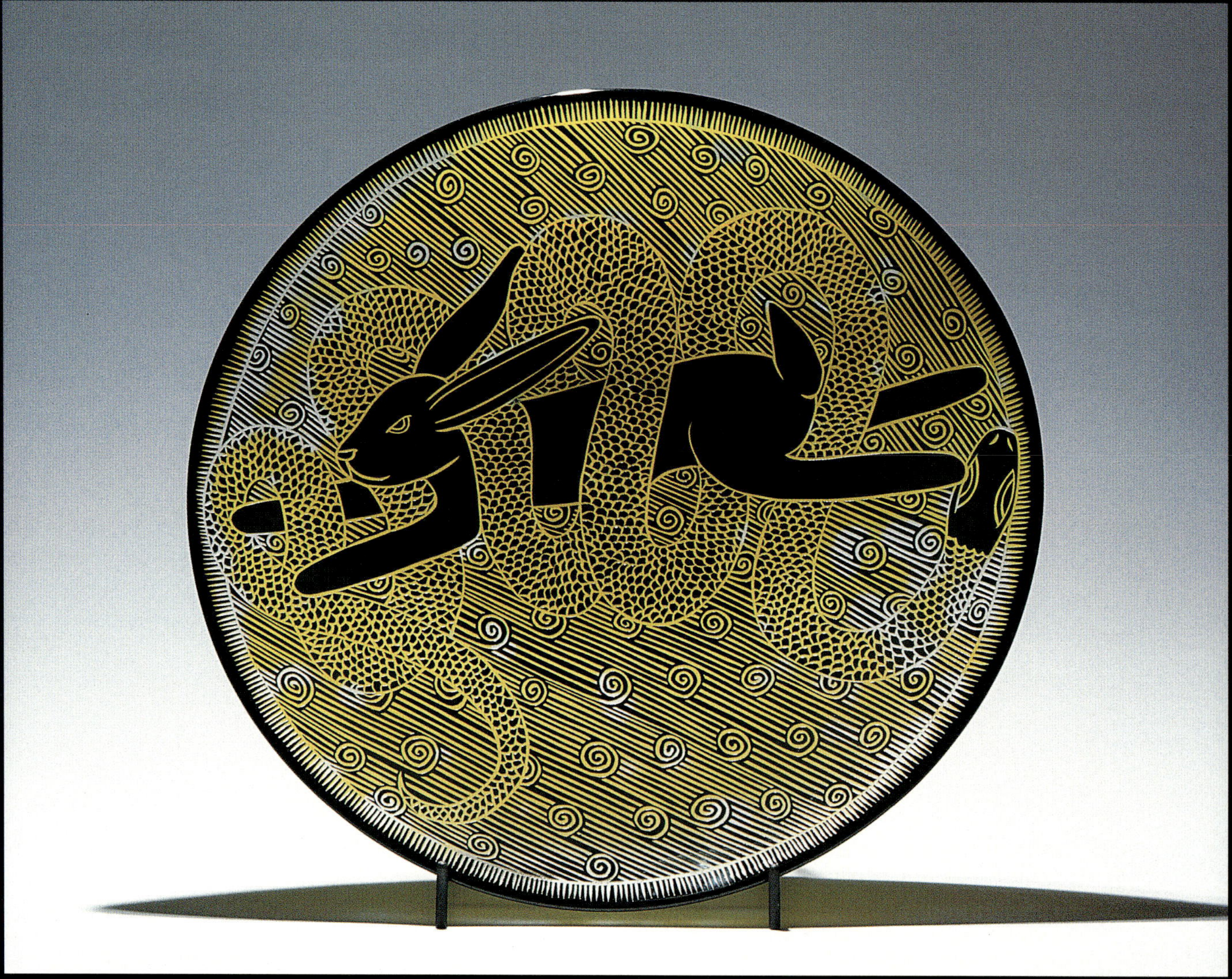

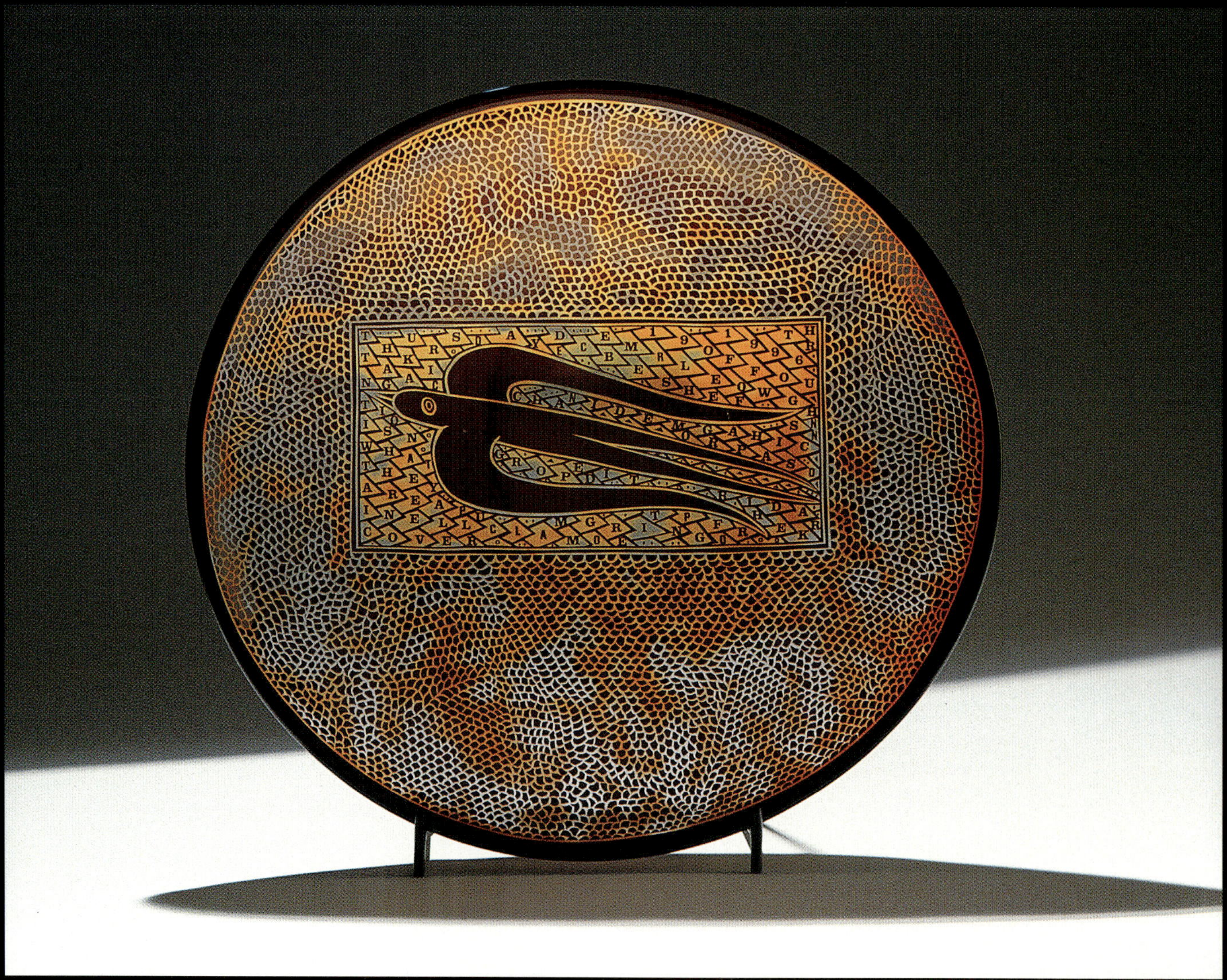

JOHN BREKKE

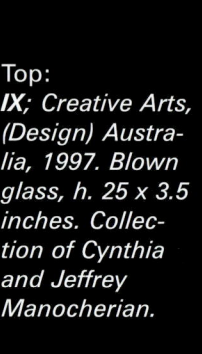

Top:
***IX**; Creative Arts, (Design) Australia, 1997. Blown glass, h. 25 x 3.5 inches. Collection of Cynthia and Jeffrey Manocherian.*

Bottom:
***VI**; Creative Arts, (Design) Australia, 1997. Blown glass, h. 22.5 x 4 inches.*

NEW YORK, NEW YORK

Jane Bruce
(b.1947)

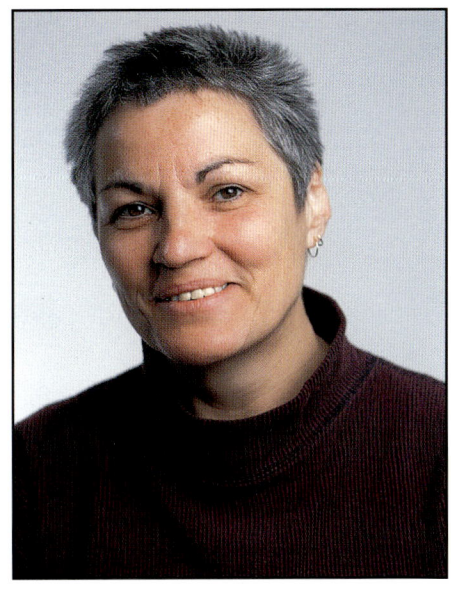

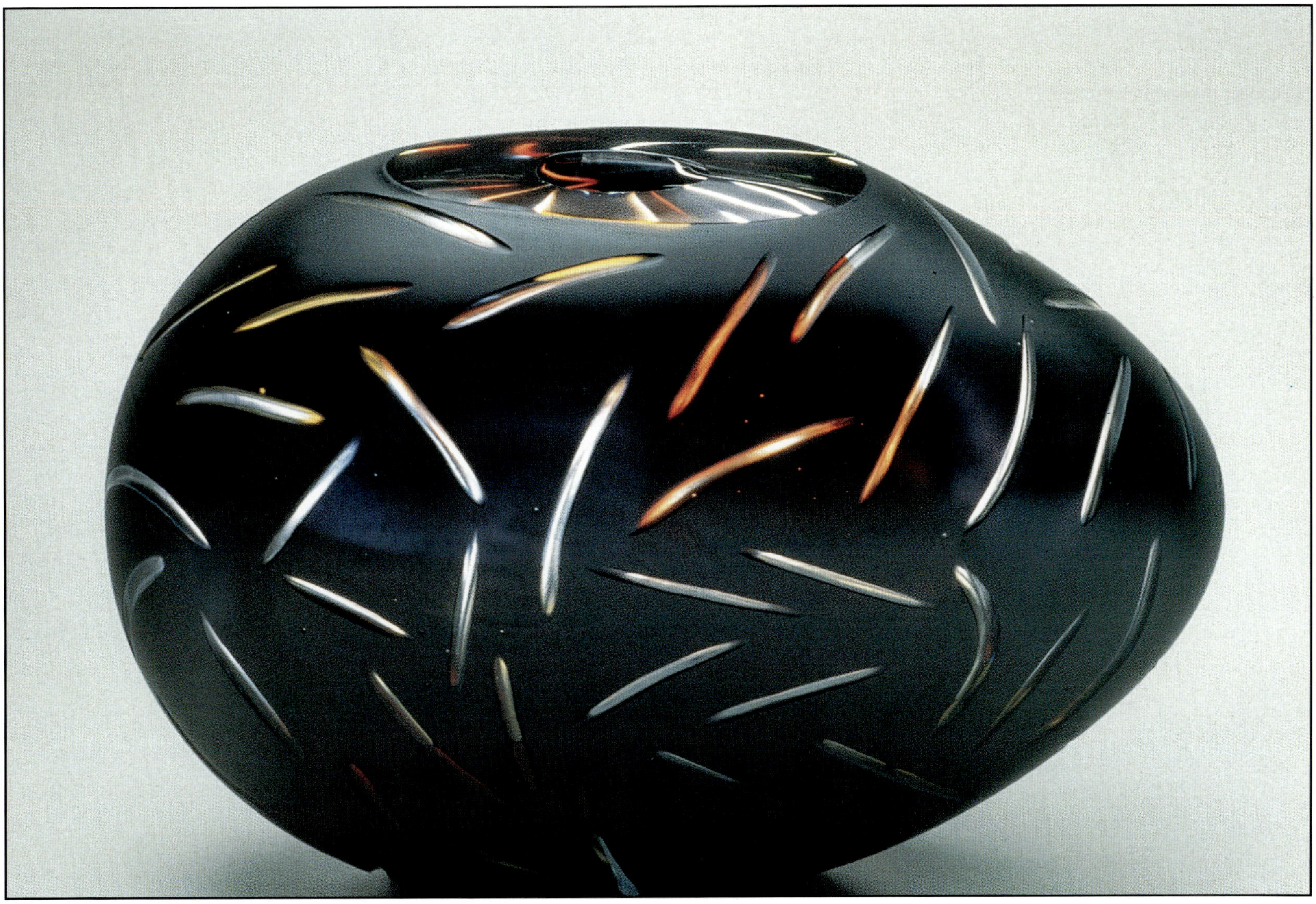

Large Object, 1998. Kiln-formed, blown Bullseye glass, wheel cut, and hand finished, h. 9.5 x 11 x 5.5 inches. Photo: David Paterson

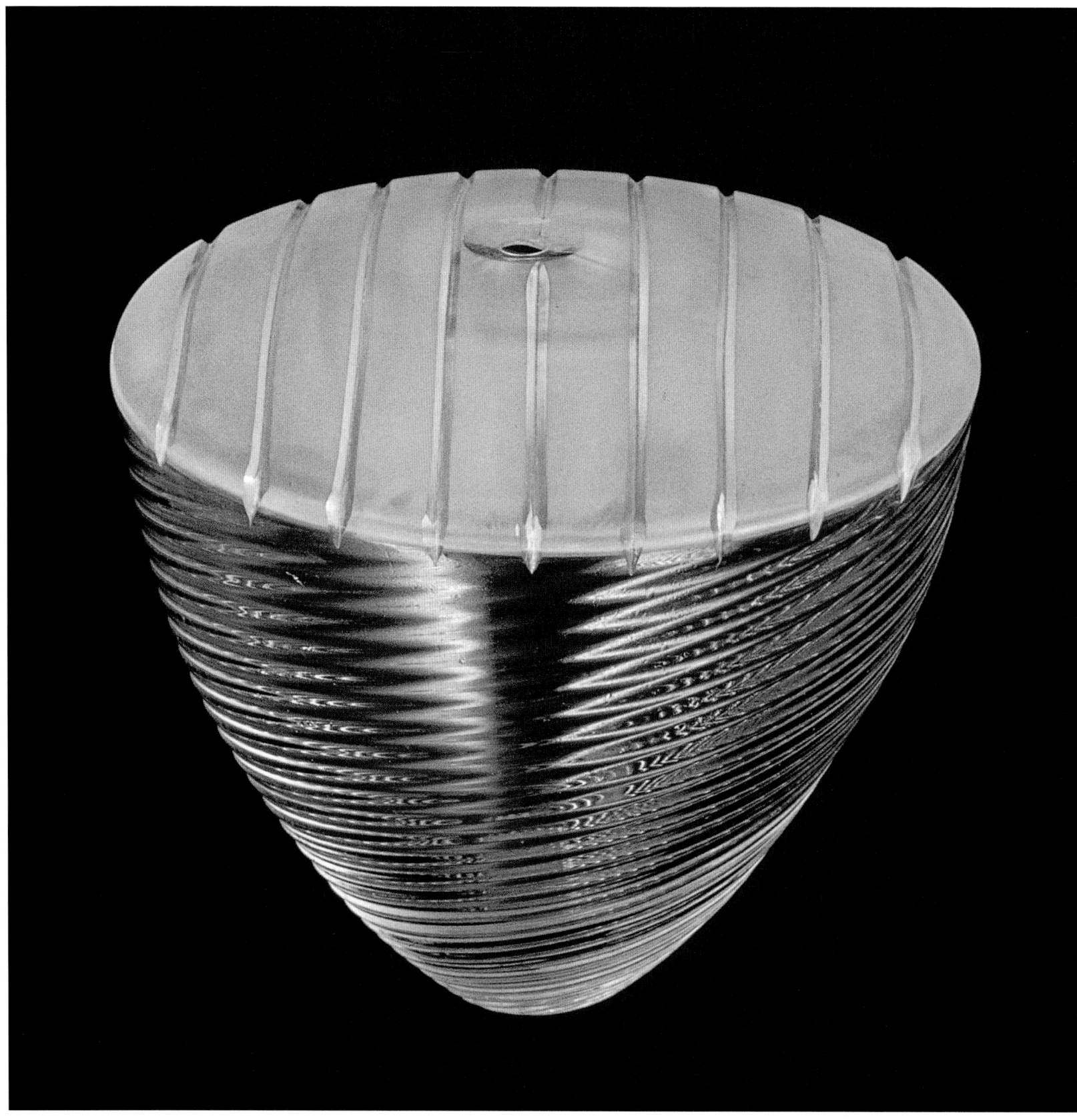

Clear Lidded Vessel, 1998. Blown glass, wheel cut, and hand finished, h. 8.25 x 8.75. Photo: David Paterson

B- Team

NEW YORK, NEW YORK

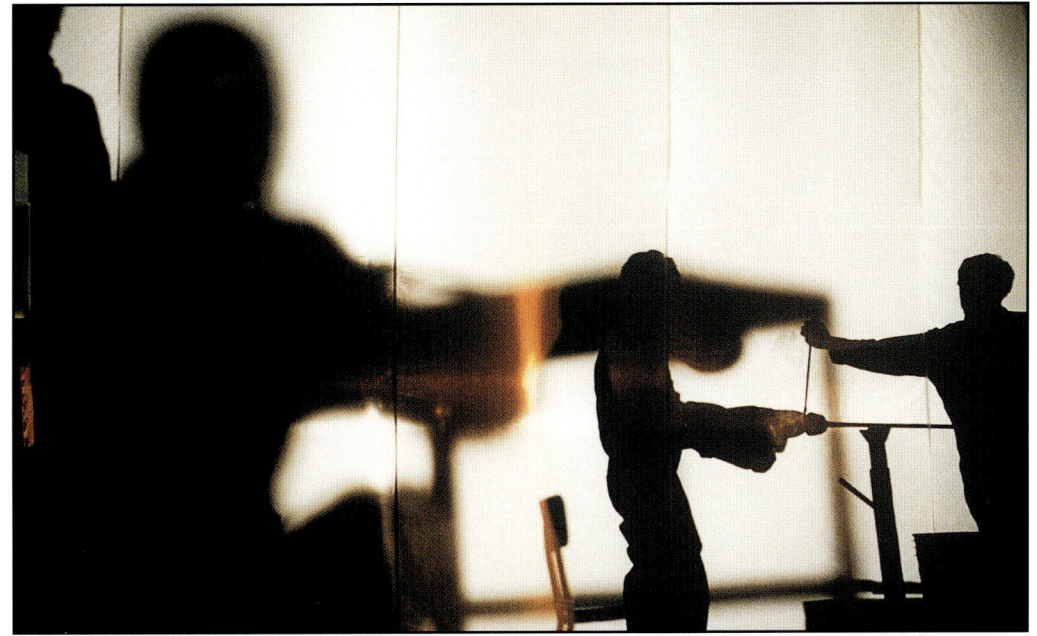

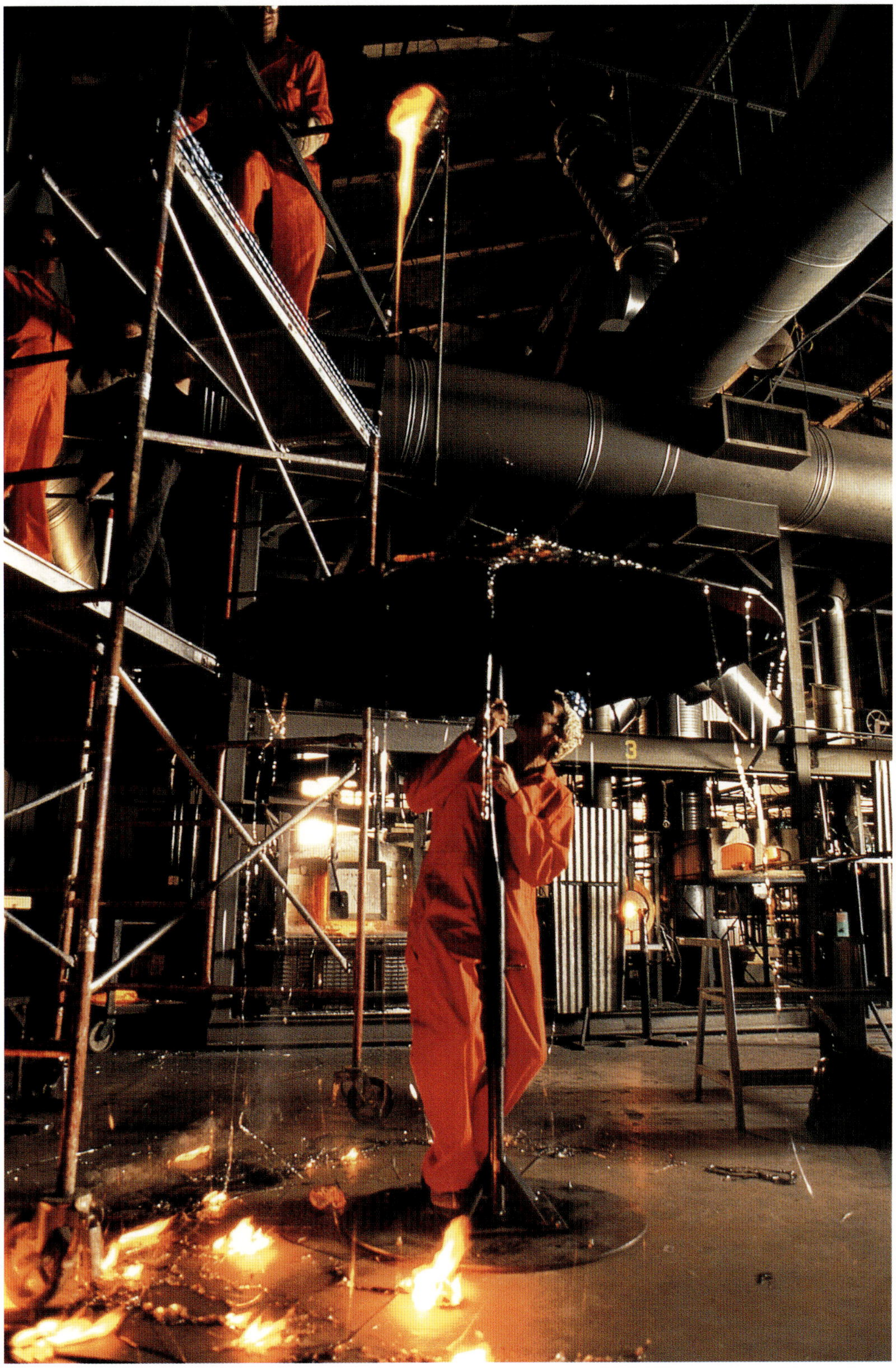

Top:
Performance Artists Zesty Meyers, Evan Snyderman and Jeff Zimmerman. Photo: Eva Heyd

Bottom:
***Spontaneous Combustion**; Hot Glass Rainstorm*, UrbanGlass, 1996. Photo: Eva Heyd

Mary Ellen & Kevin W. Buxton-Kutch
(b.1950) (b.1951)

BROOKLYN, NEW YORK

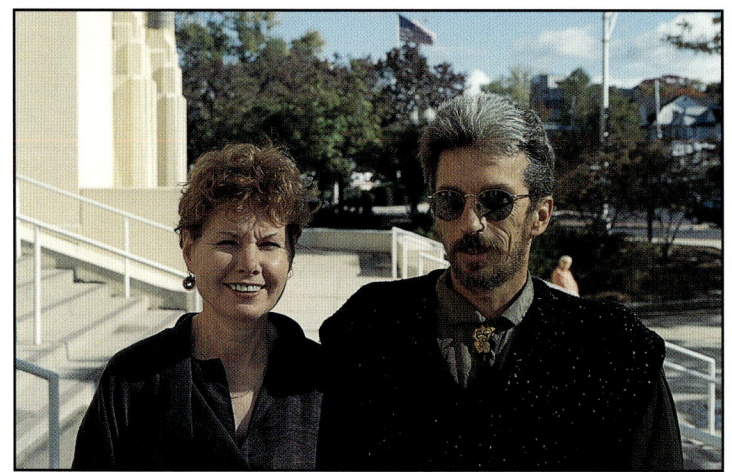

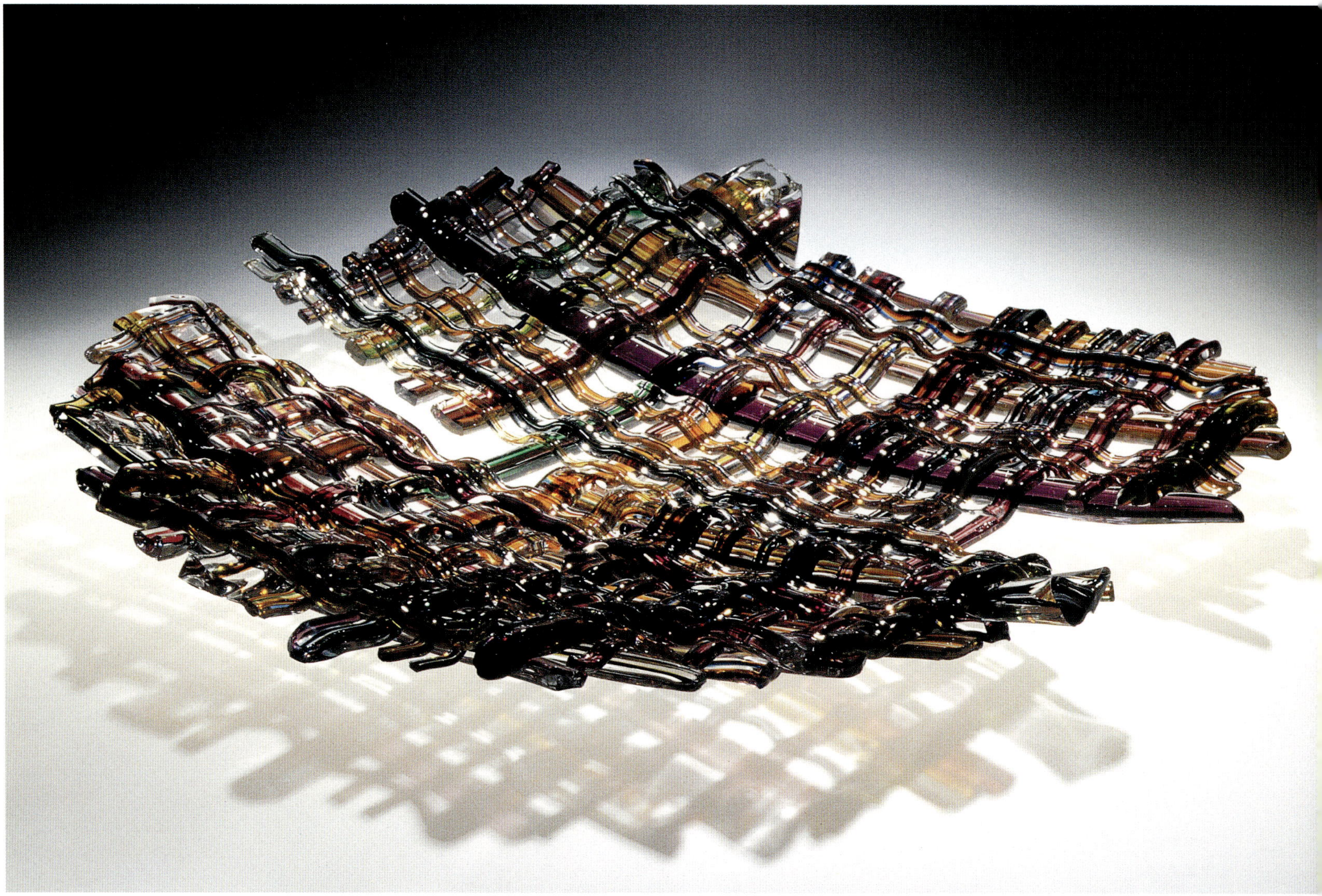

Woven Bowl, 1999. Slumped and fused cane, h. 30 inches.

NEW YORK, NEW YORK

James Carpenter Design Associates, Inc.
Richard Kress
Luke Lowings
James Carpenter
(b. 1949)

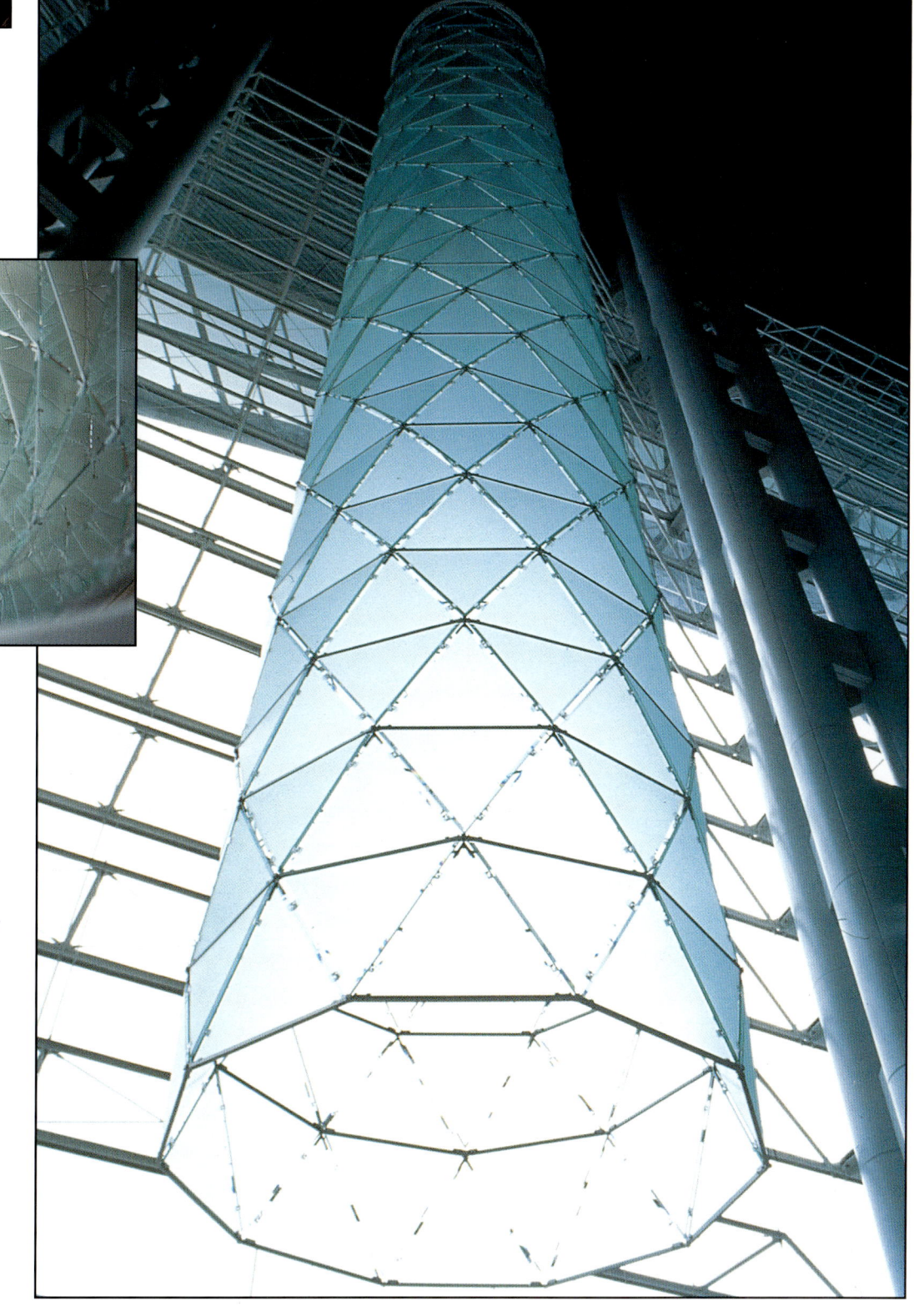

Right:
Suspended Glass Tower, 1997. Laminated glass panels with acid etched surfaces and prismatic edges, stainless steel rods, and machine aluminum components, h. 64.3 x 8.25 feet, suspended 11.5 feet off the ground. Hong Kong Convention & Exhibition Center. Client: Hong Kong Trade Development Council.

Above:
Suspended Glass Tower, 1997. Installation view showing how a helical pattern emerges from the stacking arrangement of glass ring enhancing the columnar effect.

JAMES CARPENTER DESIGN ASSOCIATES, INC.

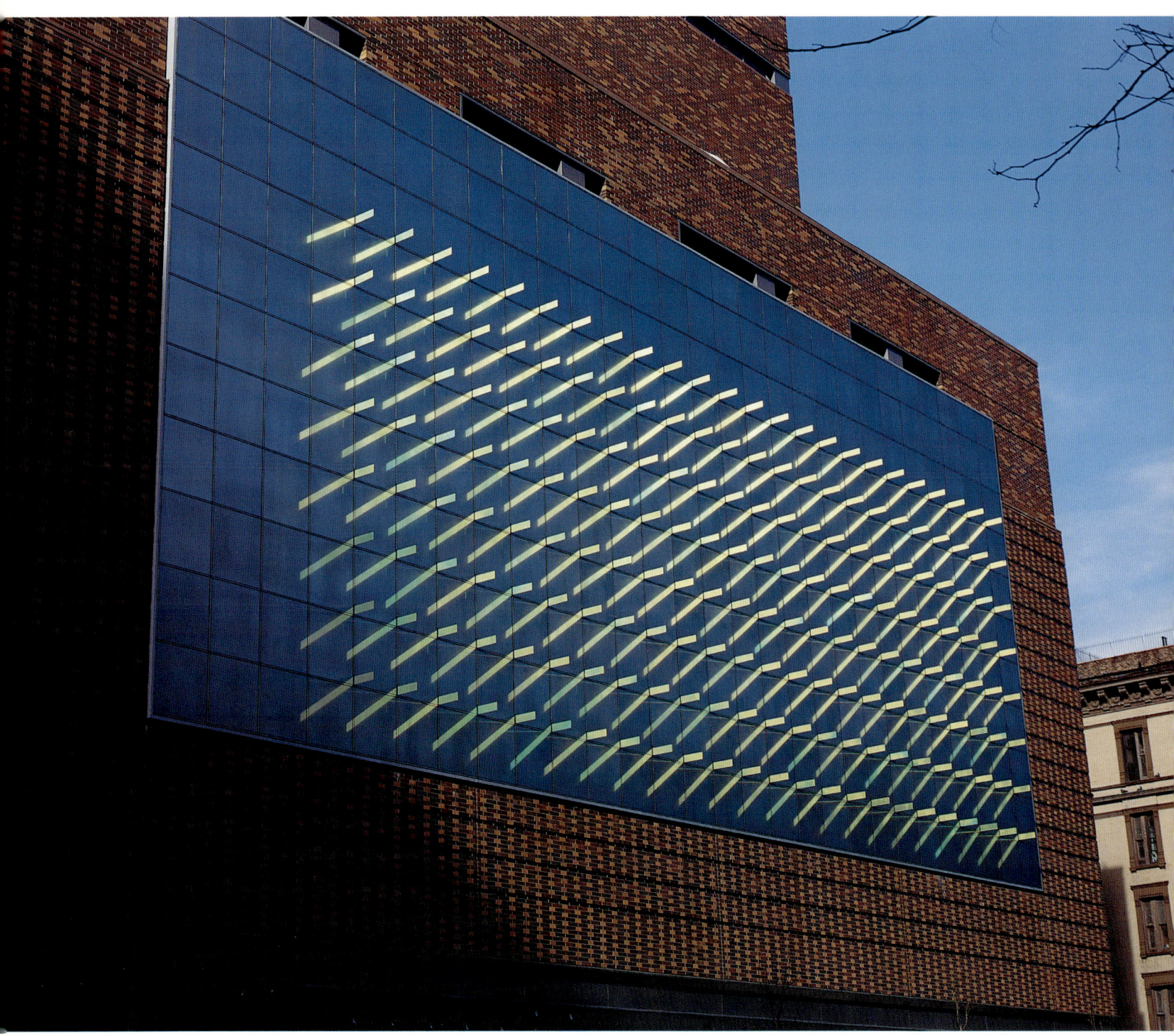

***Dichroic Light Field**, 1995. This project captures and heightens the public awareness of the movement of the sun and the passing seasons, within a dense urban context. Background panels: laminated glass, textured and semi-reflective, in anodized aluminum frames. Fins: laminated glass with dichroic coatings, h. 46 x 100 x 2 feet. Columbus Avenue at 68th Street, New York City. Client: Millennium Partnership. Photo: David Sundberg.*

MARLBORO, NEW YORK

Sidney Cash
(b. 1941)

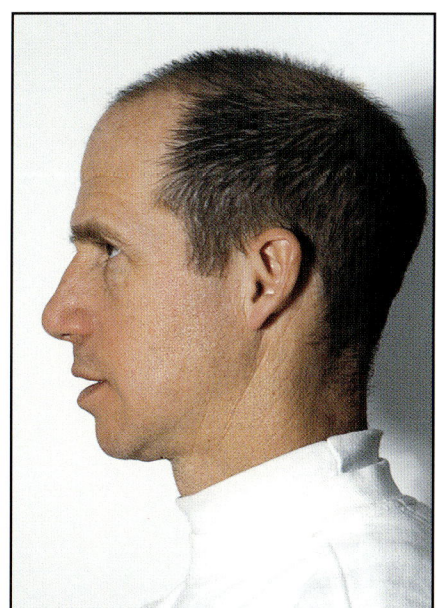

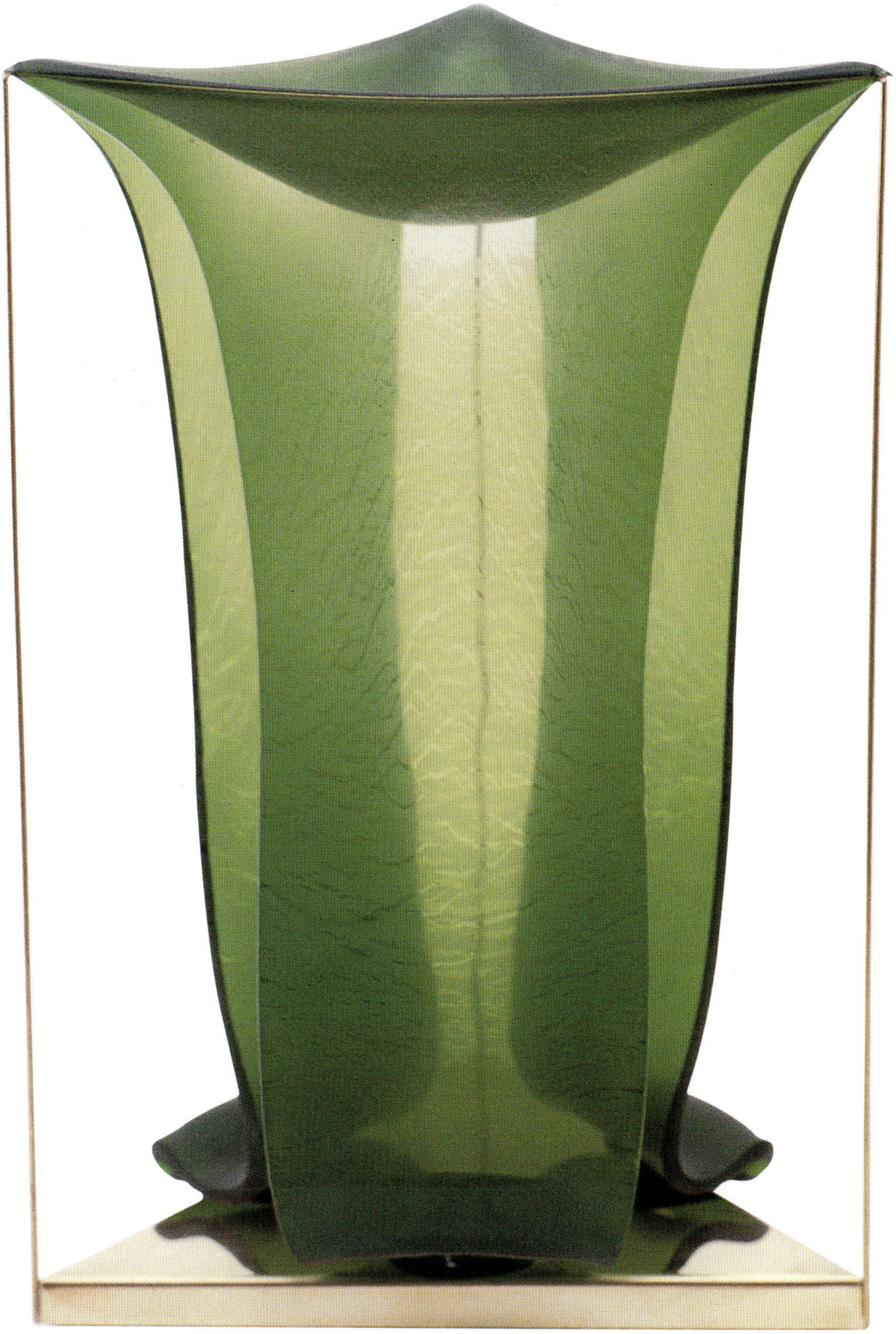

**Slumped Glass Form;
Large Tri-fold**, 1980.
Glass, wire and brass,
h. 10.5 x 7 x 6.5 inches.

Suzanne Aimee Charbonnet
(b.1967)

BROOKLYN, NEW YORK

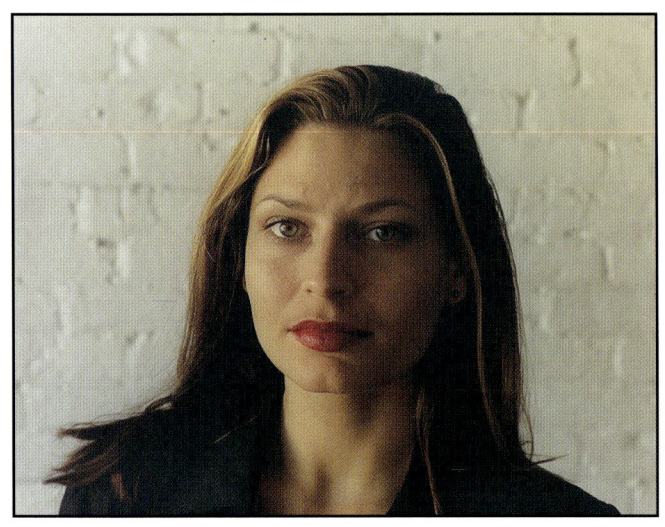

Submarine Vase, 1999. Blown glass with encolmo, h. 19 x 15 x 6.5 inches. Photo: Eva Heyd.

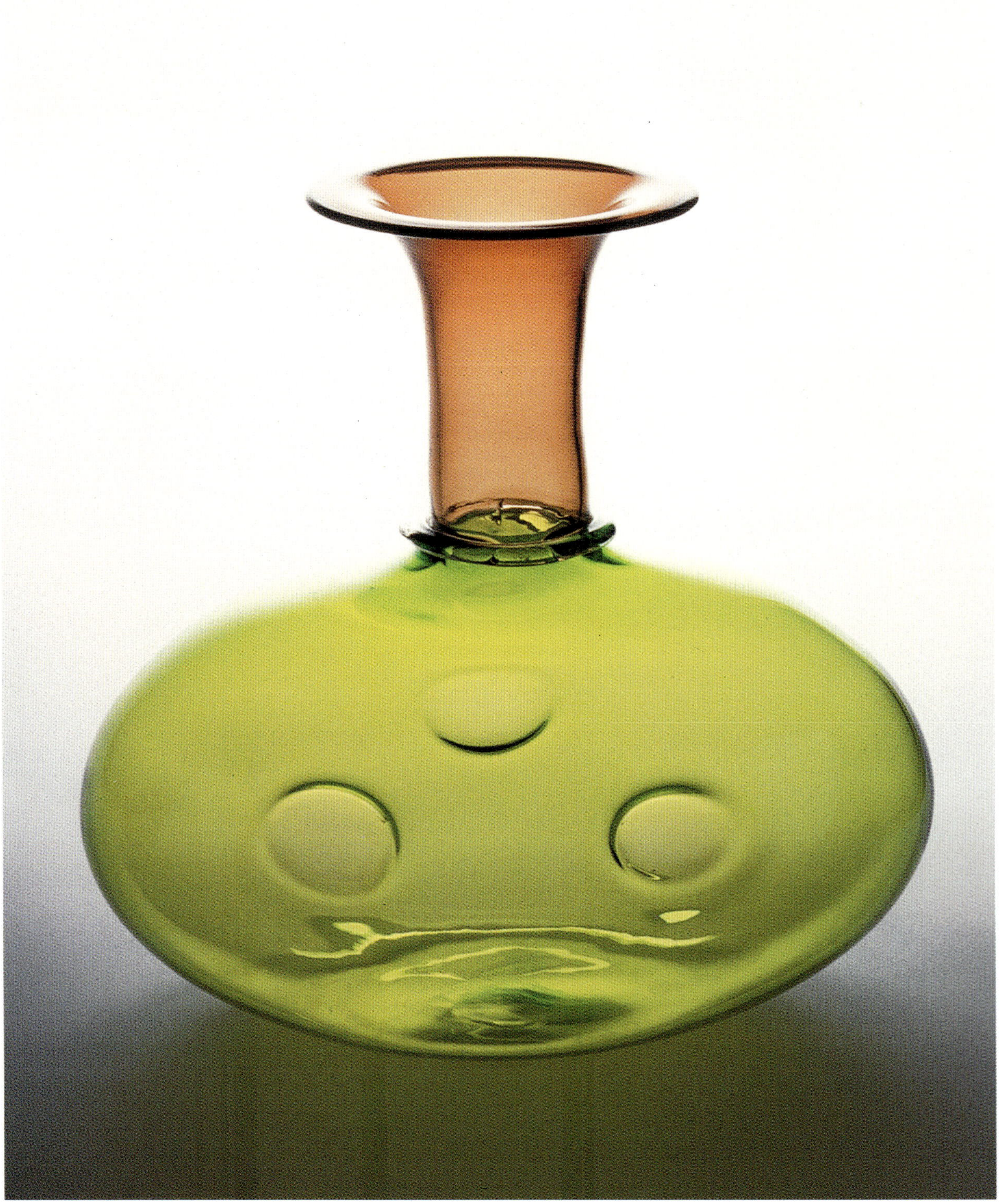

SEATTLE, WASHINGTON

Dale Chihuly
(b.1941)

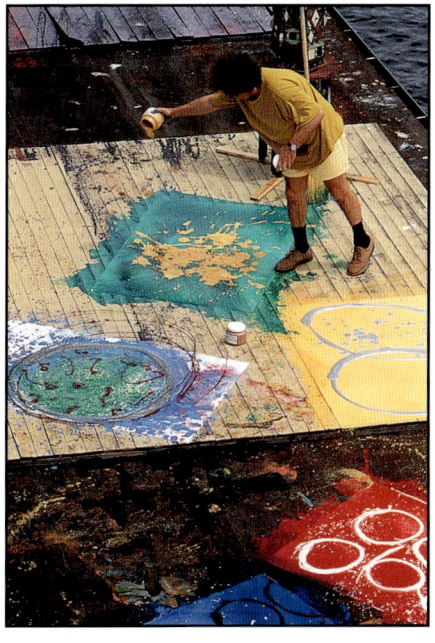

Photo: Russell Johnson

Icicle Creek Chandelier, 1996. Sleeping Lady Conference Retreat, Leavenworth, Washington. 1000 pieces of glass on steel armature, h. 12 feet. Photo: John Marshall.

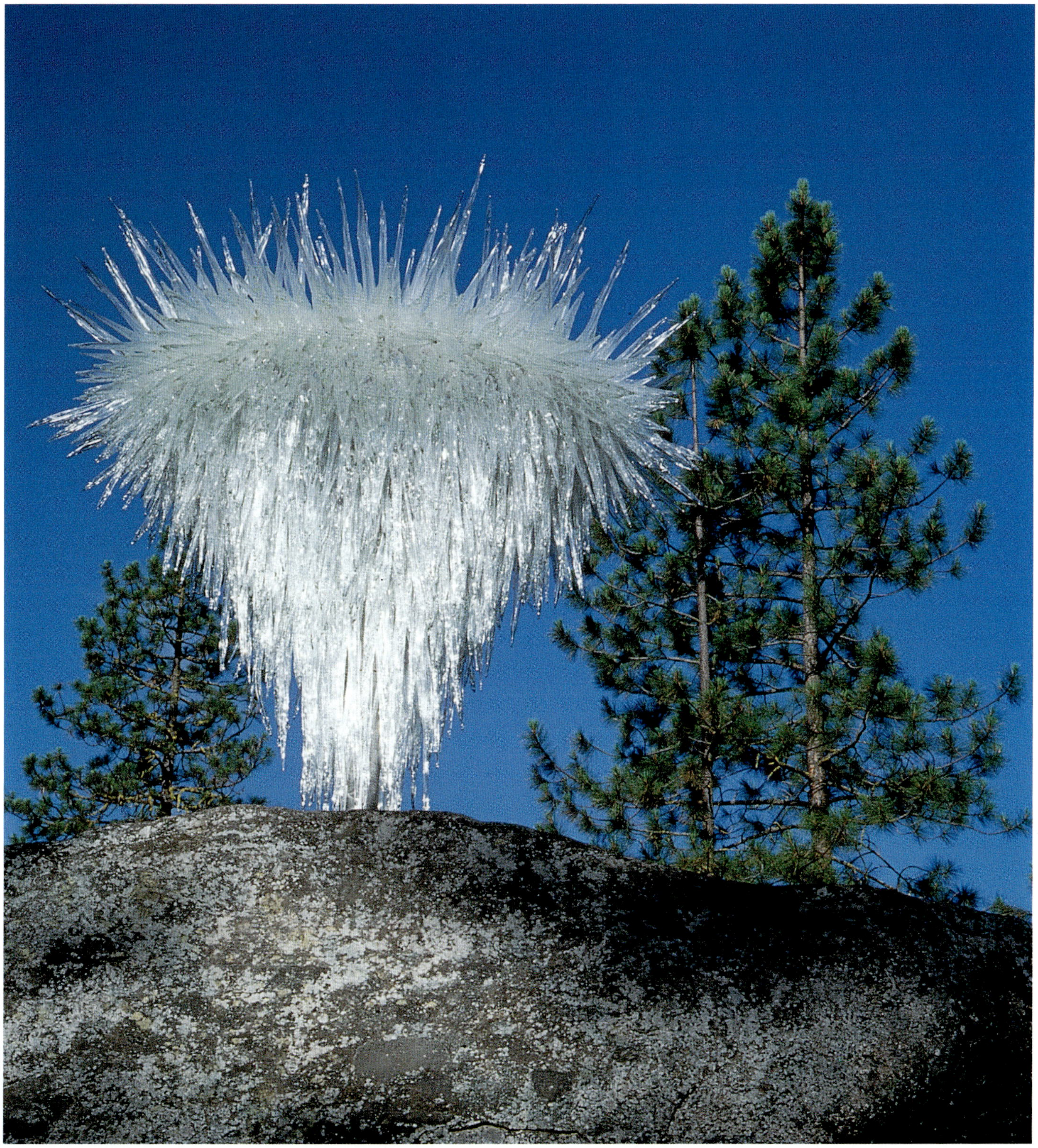

37

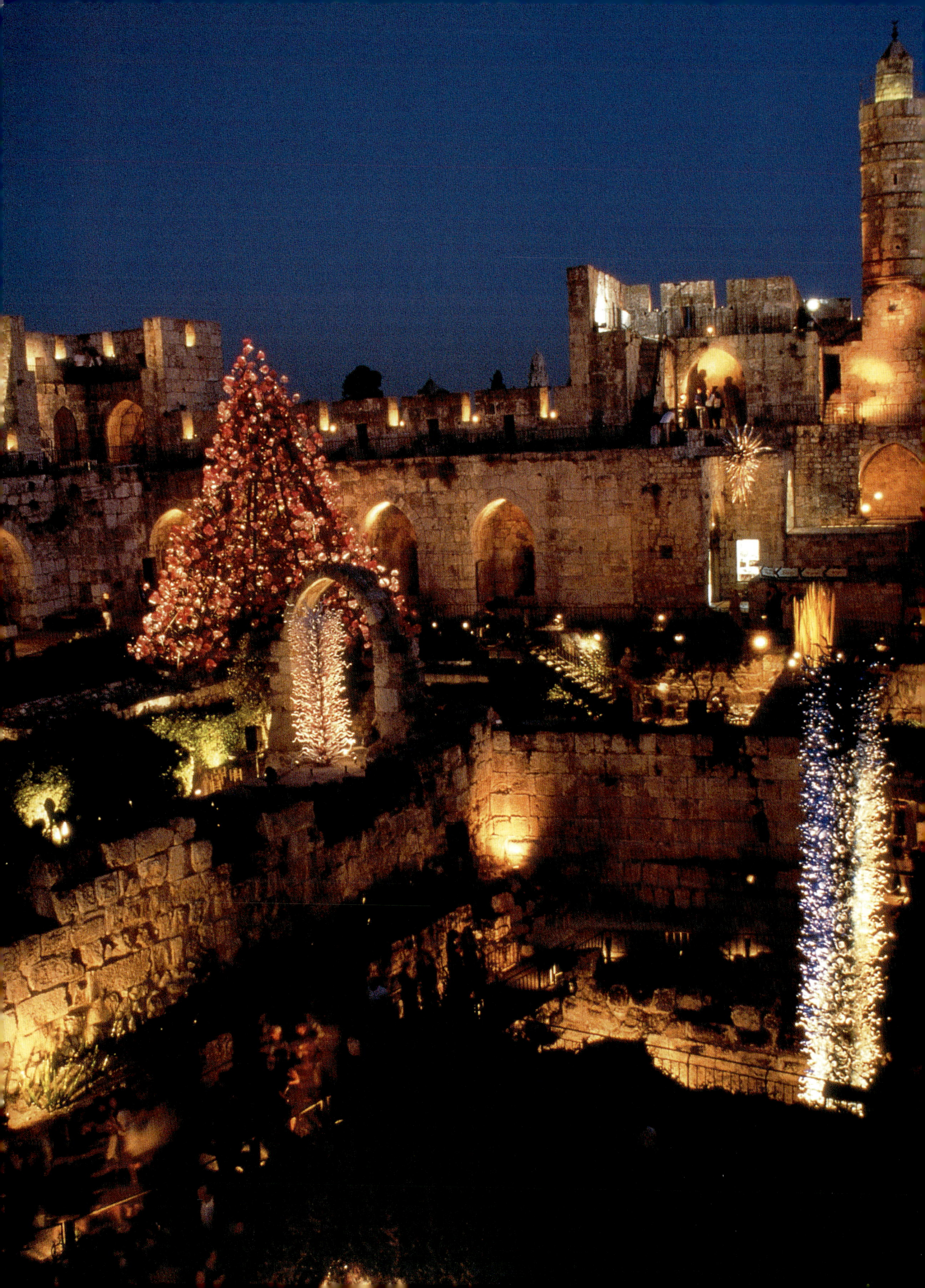

DALE CHIHULY

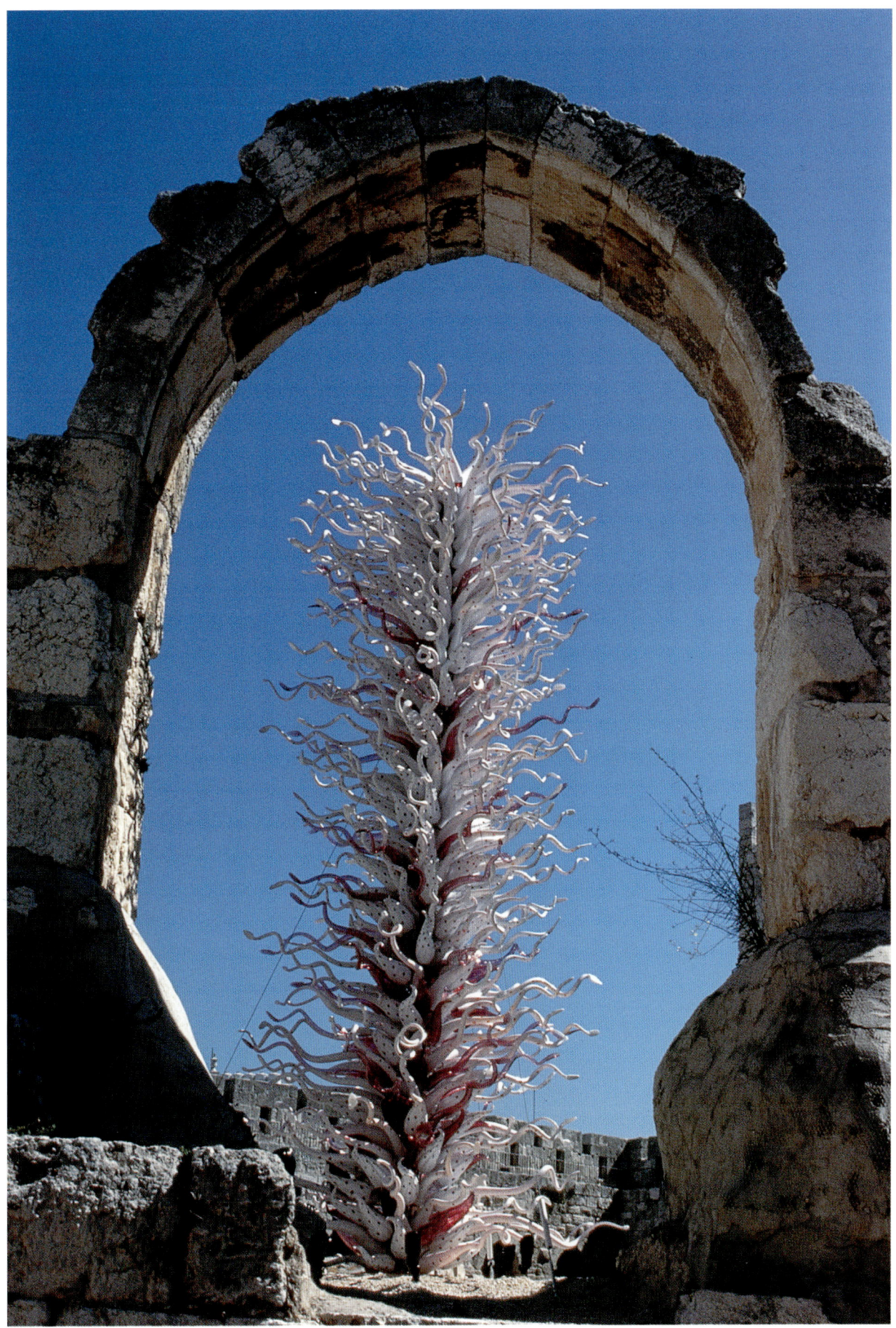

Opposite:
Chihuly In the Light of Jerusalem 2000; Installation, 1999. Tower of David Museum, Jerusalem. The exhibition, Dale Chihuly's homage to Jerusalem on the eve of the millennium, is made up of 17 large installations in the courtyard of the Tower of David. The glass, weighing over 42 tons, was shipped to Israel in 12 containers from factories in Seattle, Finland, France, the Czech Republic, and Japan. Photo: Terry Rishel

Above:
White Tower; Chihuly in the Light of Jerusalem 2000, 1999. Tower of David Museum. 2000 pieces of glass on metal frame, h. 15 x 6 feet. Photo: Terry Rishel

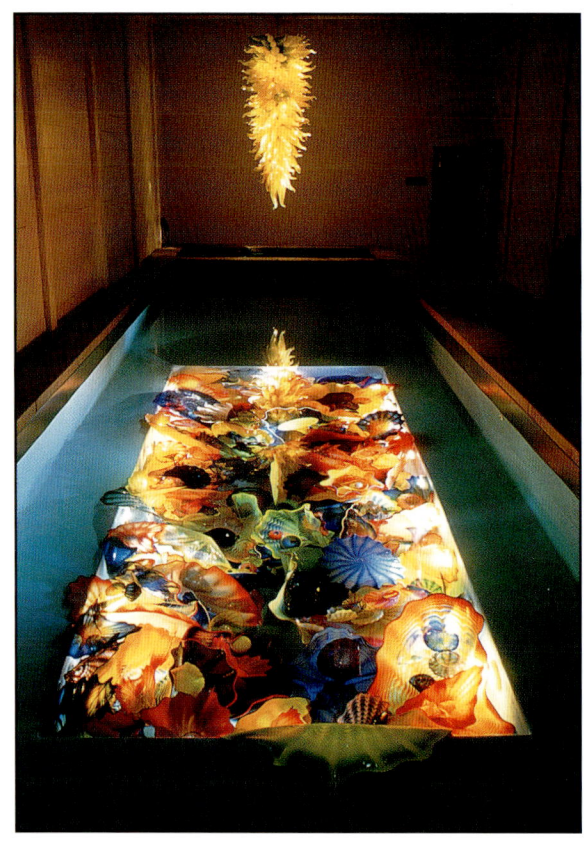

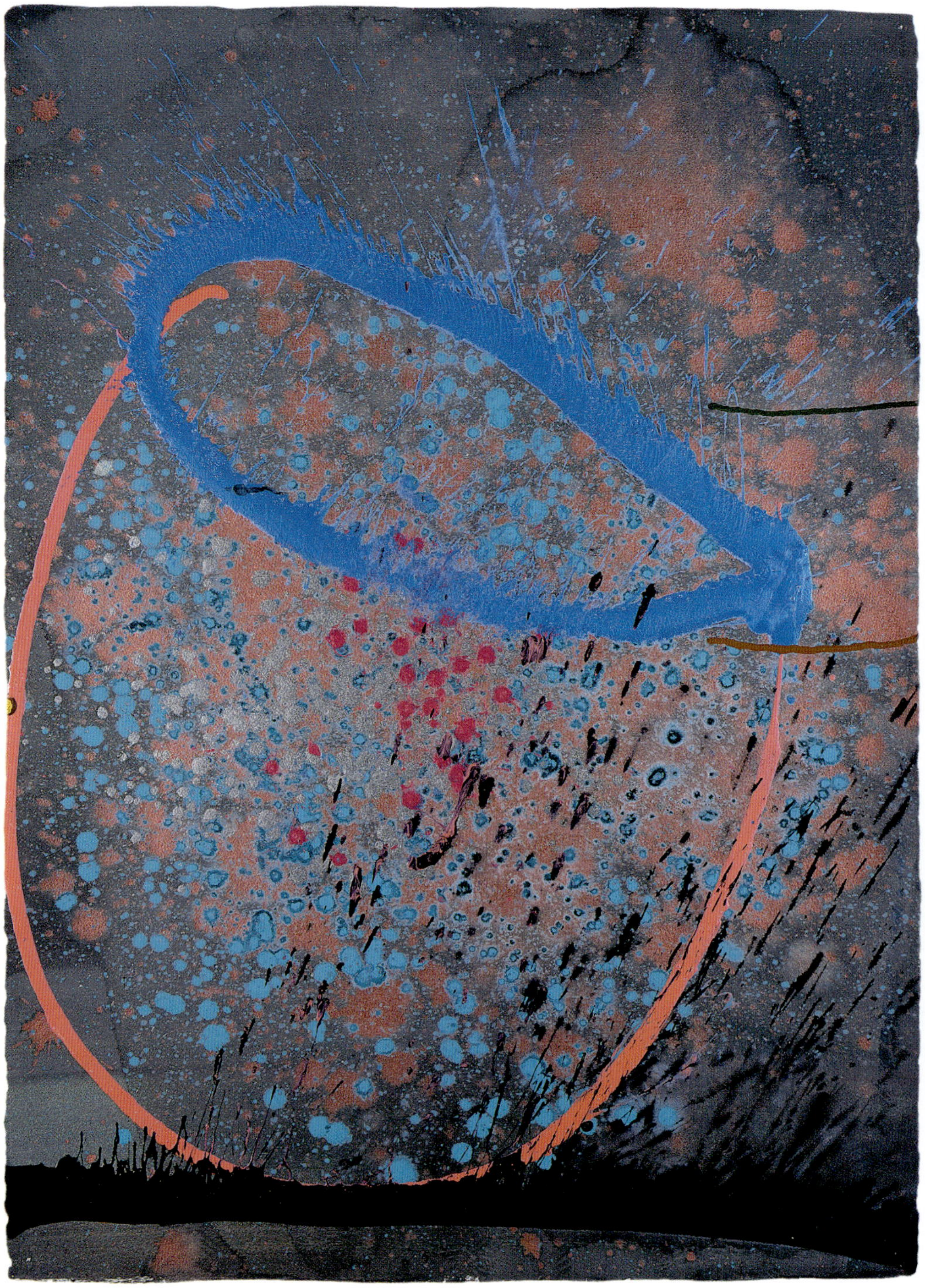

Left:
Seaform Lap Pool, 1994. The Boathouse, Seattle, Washington. 54 x 12 feet. Photo: Claire Garoutte

Right:
Drawing, 1998. Acrylic on paper, h. 30x18 inches. Norton Museum of Art, West Palm Beach, Florida. Gift of Dale and Doug Anderson

WESTON, VERMONT

John Chiles
(b.1962)

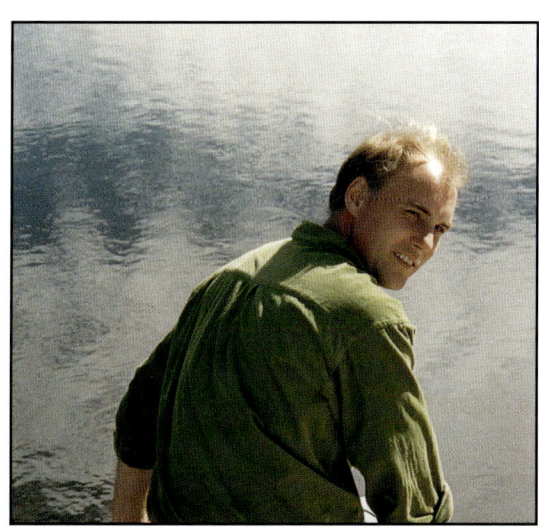

Grumpy, 1997. Blown glass assembled hot,
h. 21.6 x 6.8 inches. Photo: Charlie Parker

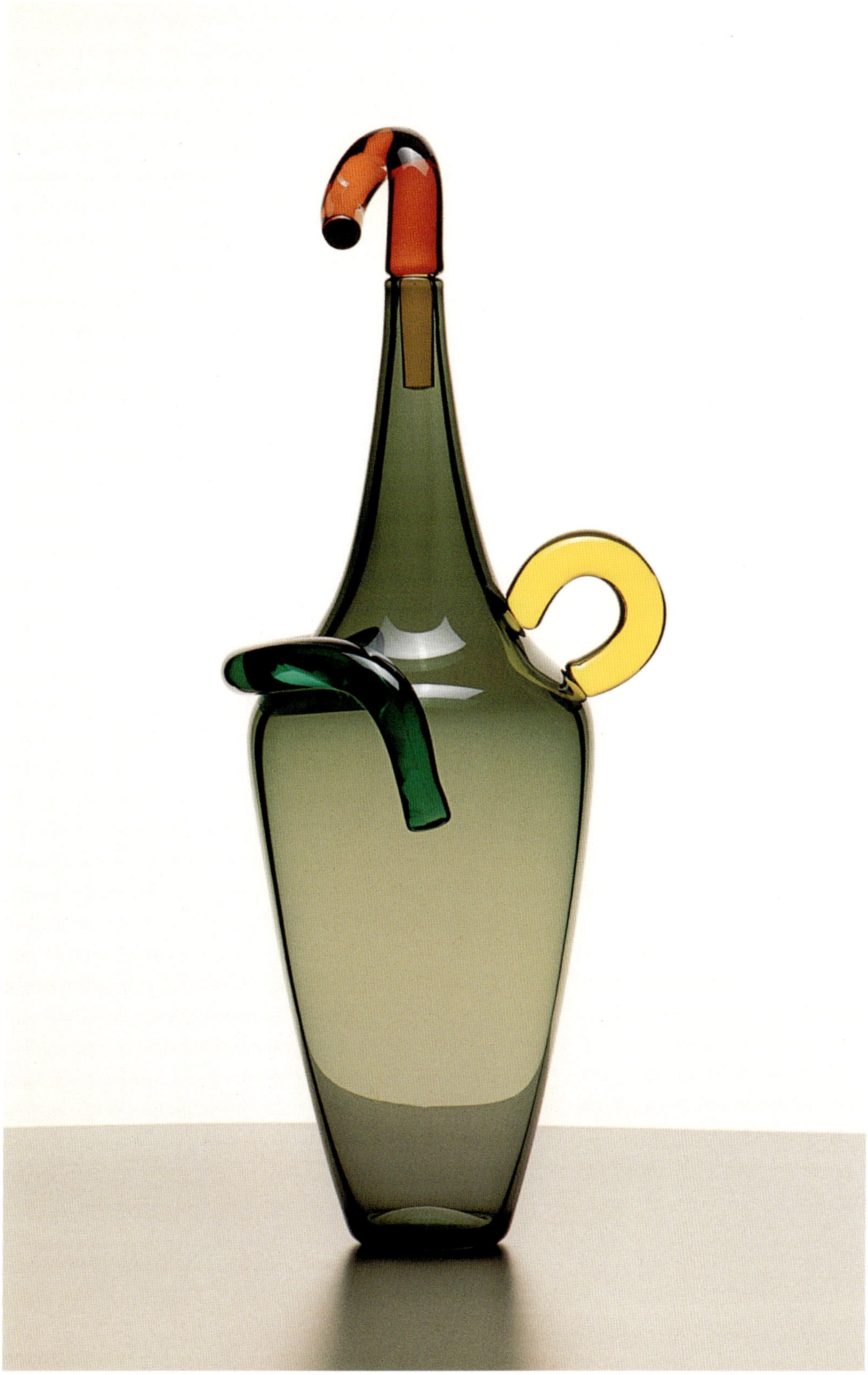

Jon Clark
(b.1947)

ELKINS PARK, PENNSYLVANIA

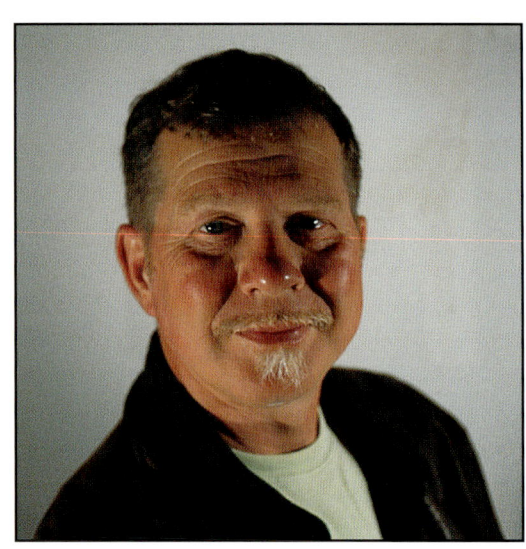

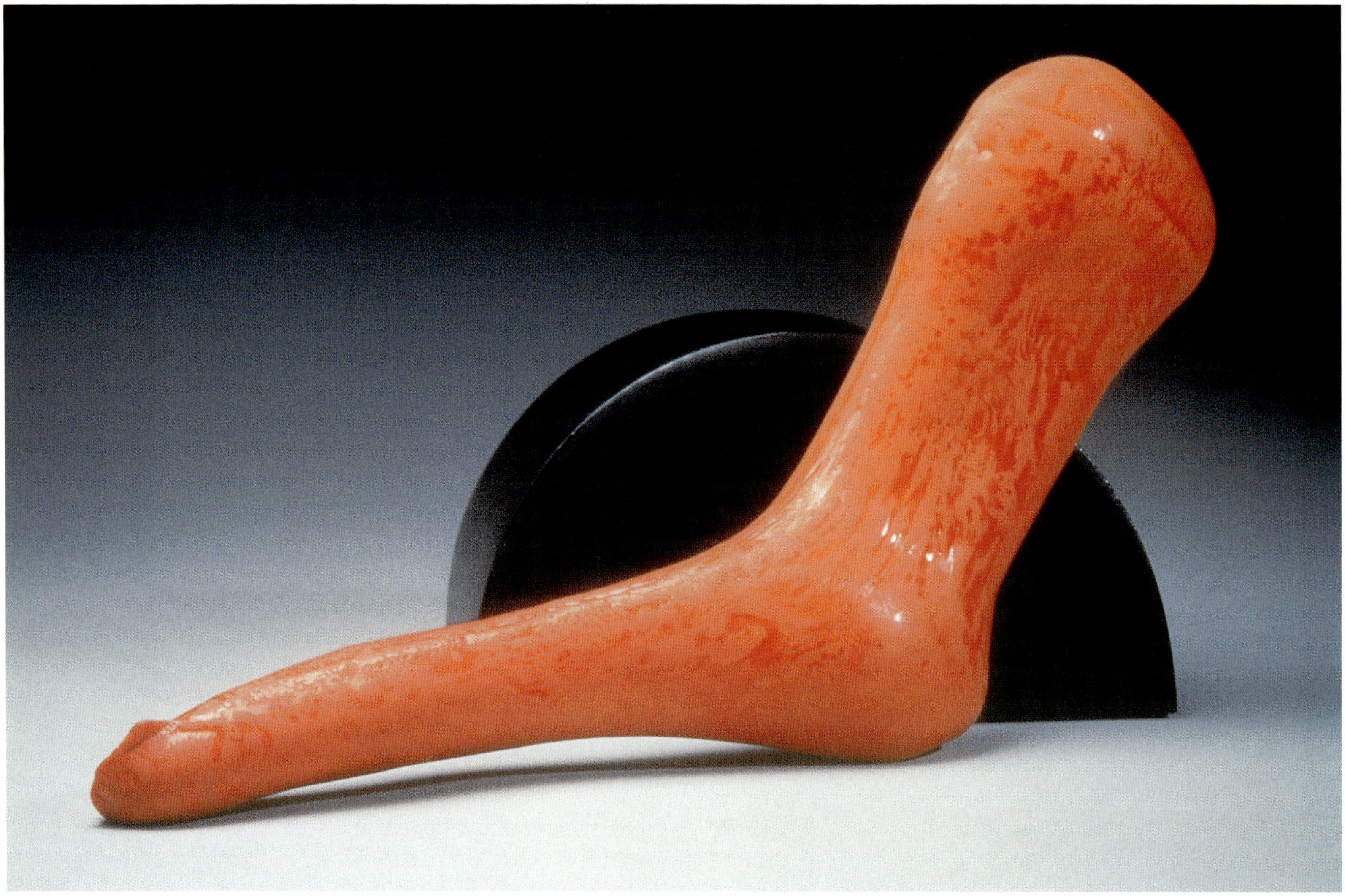

Orange Joint, 1999. Glass and painted wood, h. 8 x 13.75 x 9.25 inches.

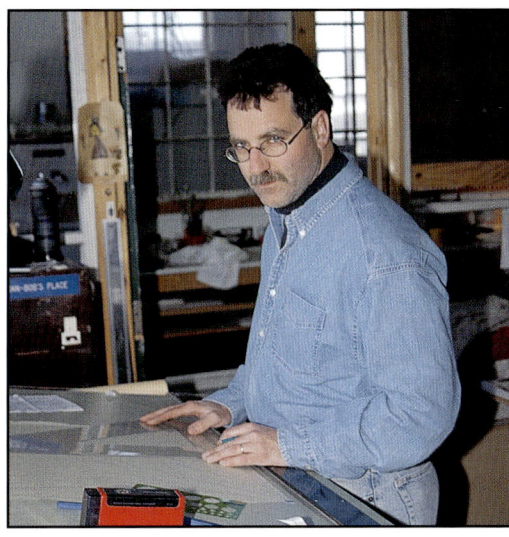

RUMFORD, RHODE ISLAND

Daniel G. Clayman
(b.1957)

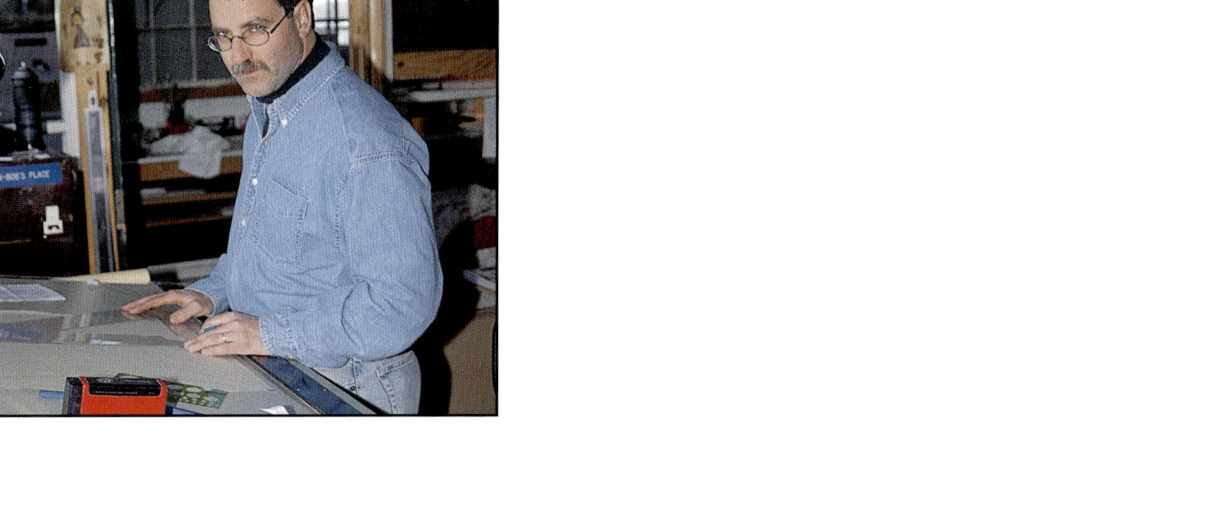

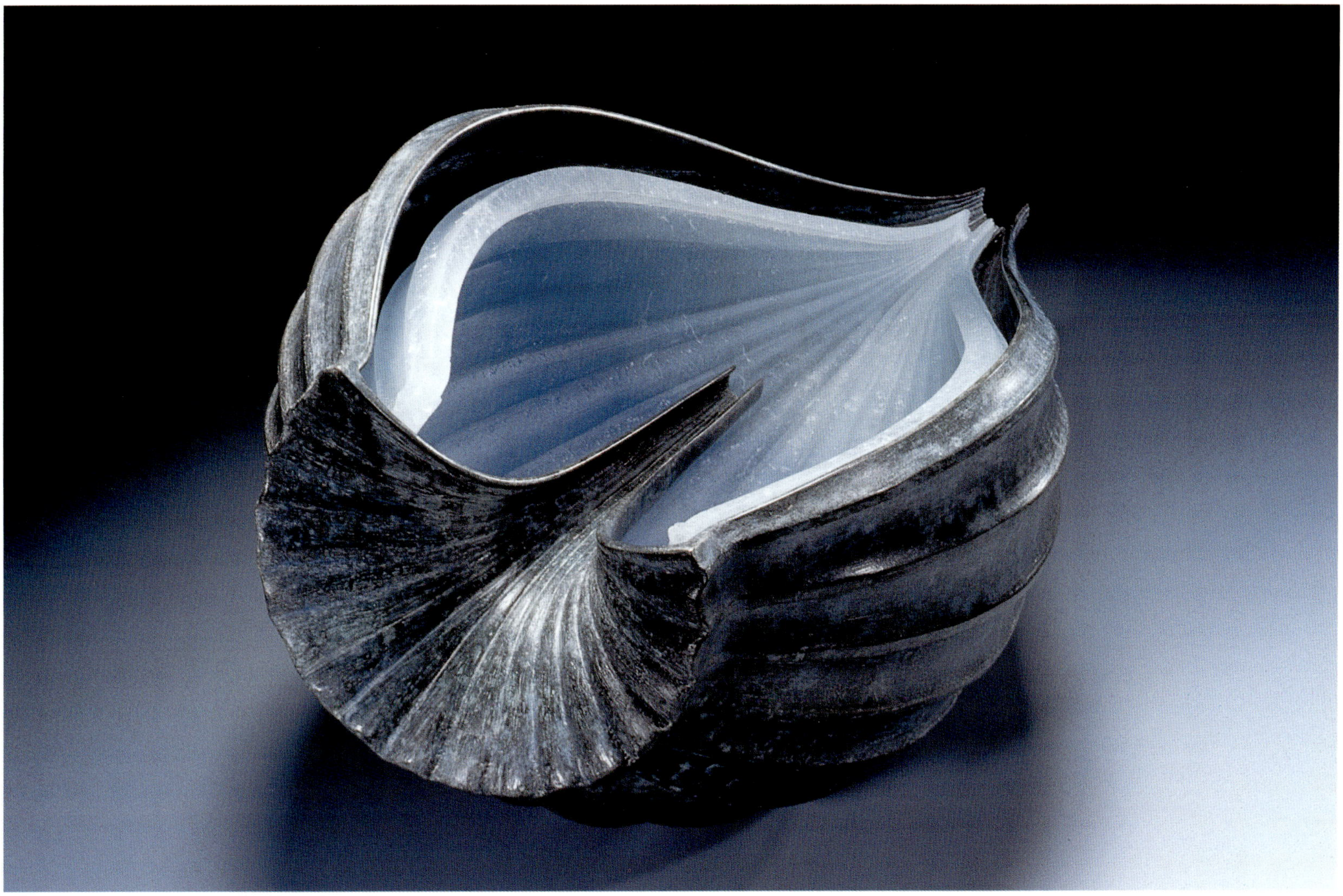

Umbra, 1999. Glass and bronze, h. 9 x 18 x 9.5 inches..
Photo: Jessica Marcotte.

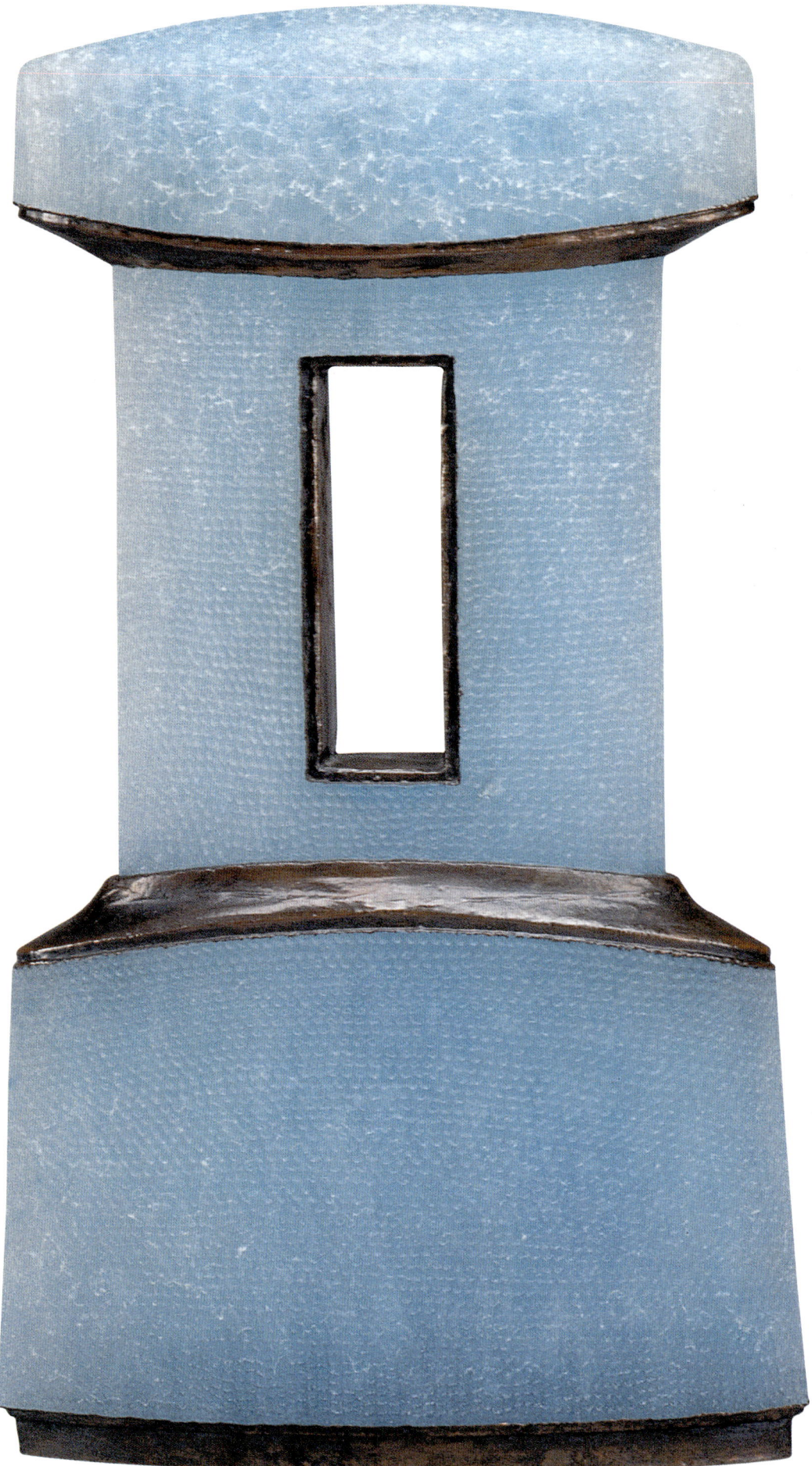

Dagoba, 1989. Cast glass, and electroformed copper, h. 11.75 x 6.5 x 1.25 inches. Charles A. Wustum Museum, Racine, Wisconsin. Gift of Dale and Doug Anderson. Photo: Jon Bolton.

SEATTLE, WASHINGTON

Jeff Crandall
(b.1964)

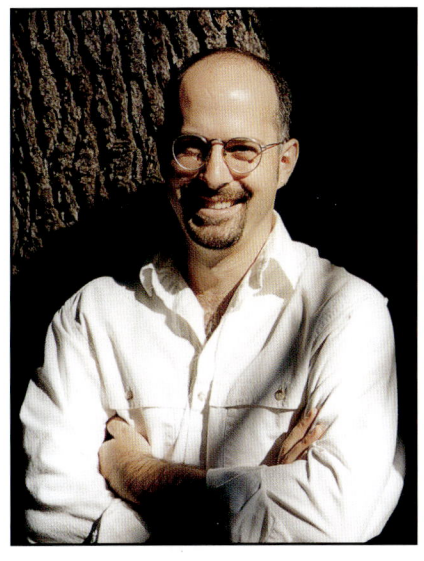

Poet's Bottles; Faith: Danger: Do not lose, Hope: Warning: Do not abandon, and Truth: Caution: Do not dilute, 1999. Sandblasted and acid etched glass. Photo: Rob Vinnedge

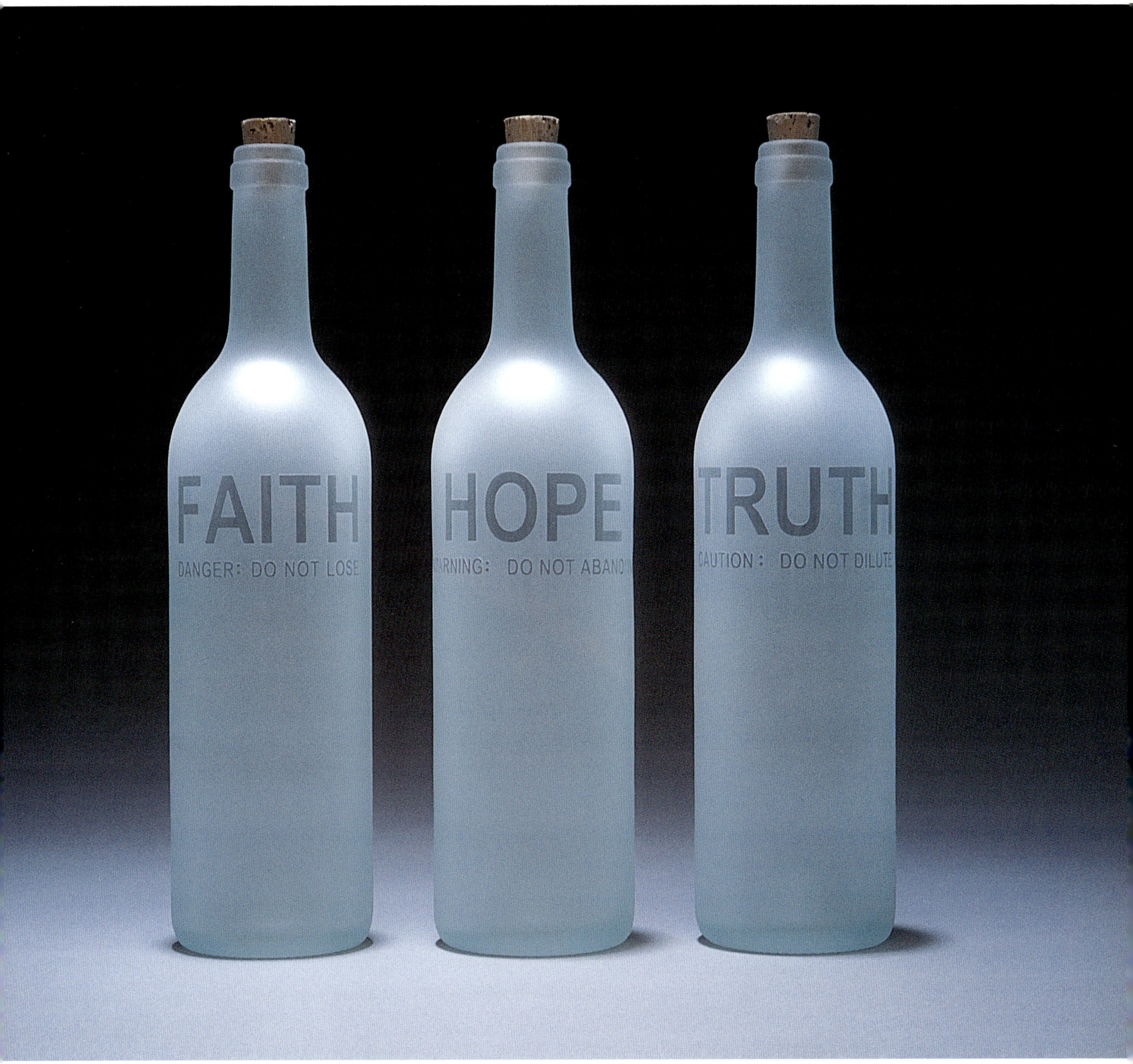

Rene Culler
(b.1960)

CLEVELAND, OHIO

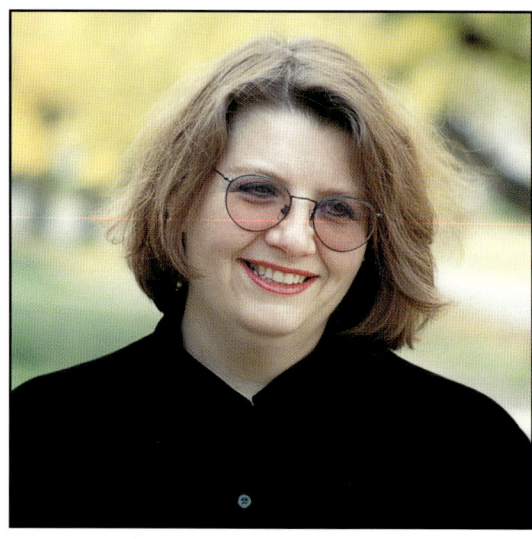

Jelly Bean Grail, 1996. Glass, paint and mixed media, h. 18 x 10 x 10 inches.

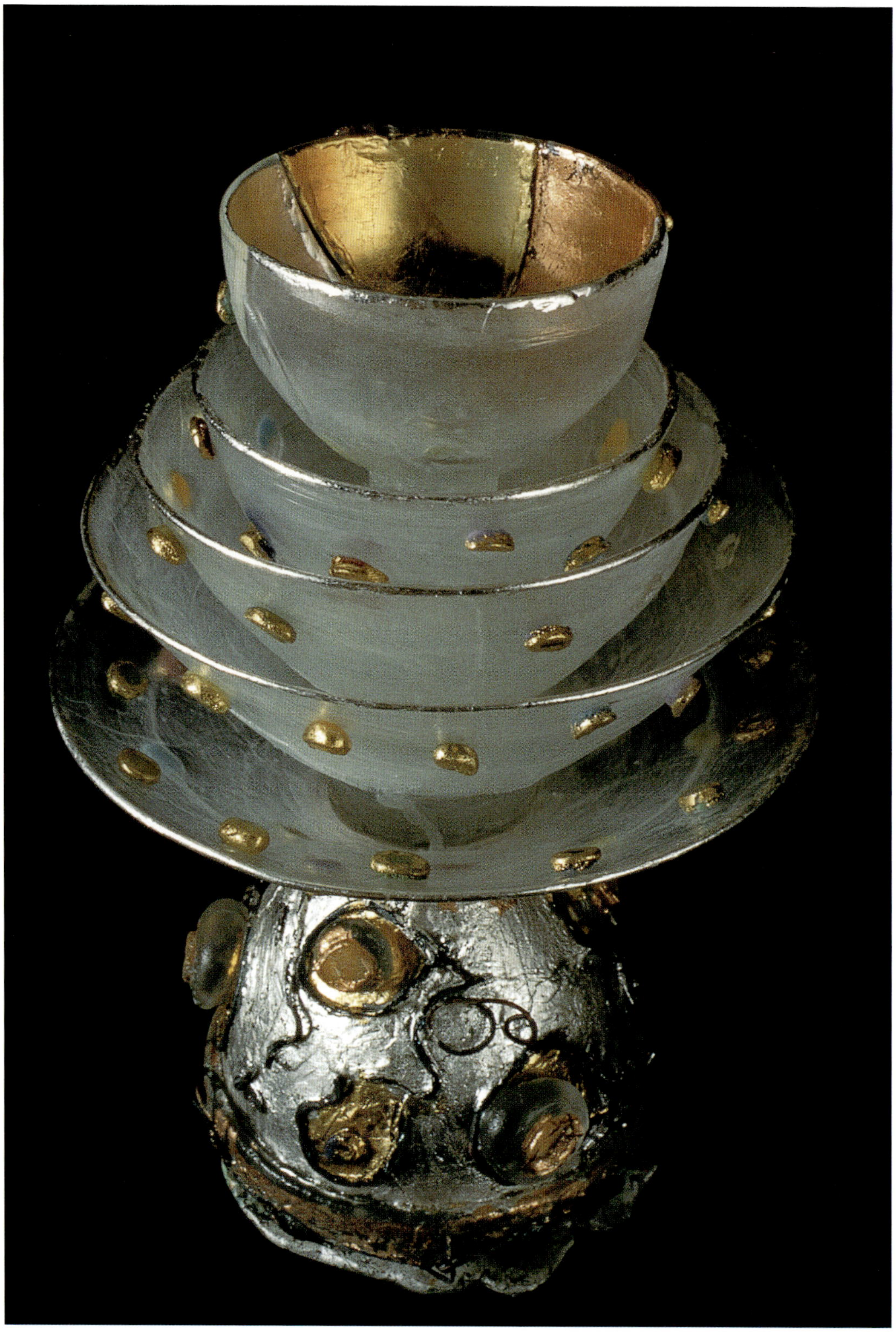

KENSINGTON, NEW HAMPSHIRE # Dan Dailey
(b.1947)

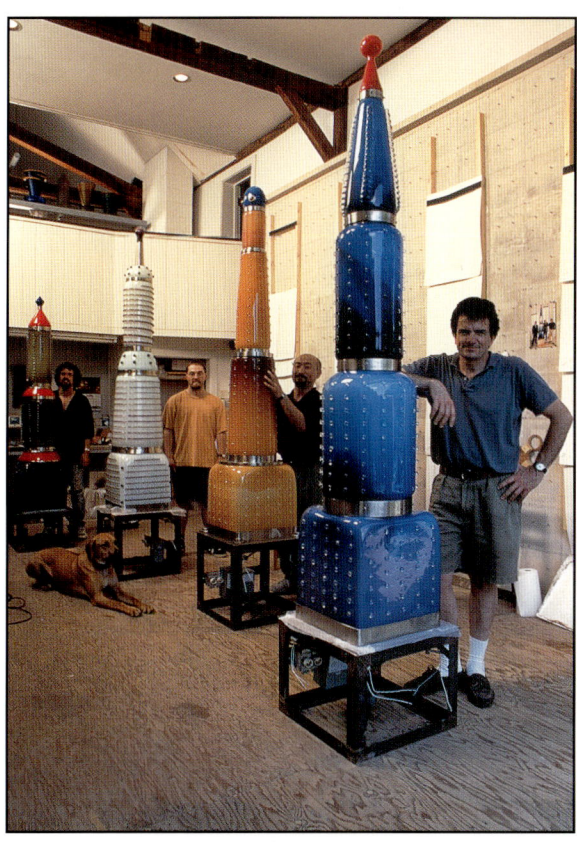

Left:
Four Skyscraper Structures, "Greatest Bar on Earth", Windows on the World restaurants, World Trade Center, New York City, June 1996. (Assembly of sculptures at studio, Kensington, NH.) Photo: Russell Johnson

Below:
Jungle Dancer; Console, 1997. Plate glass top, pâte de verre figure and leaves (Daum, France), cast bronze branches and base, fabricated and gold plated bronze detail elements, h. 36 x 38 x 12 inches. Collection of Mimi and Bob Rieder. Photo: Bill Truslow

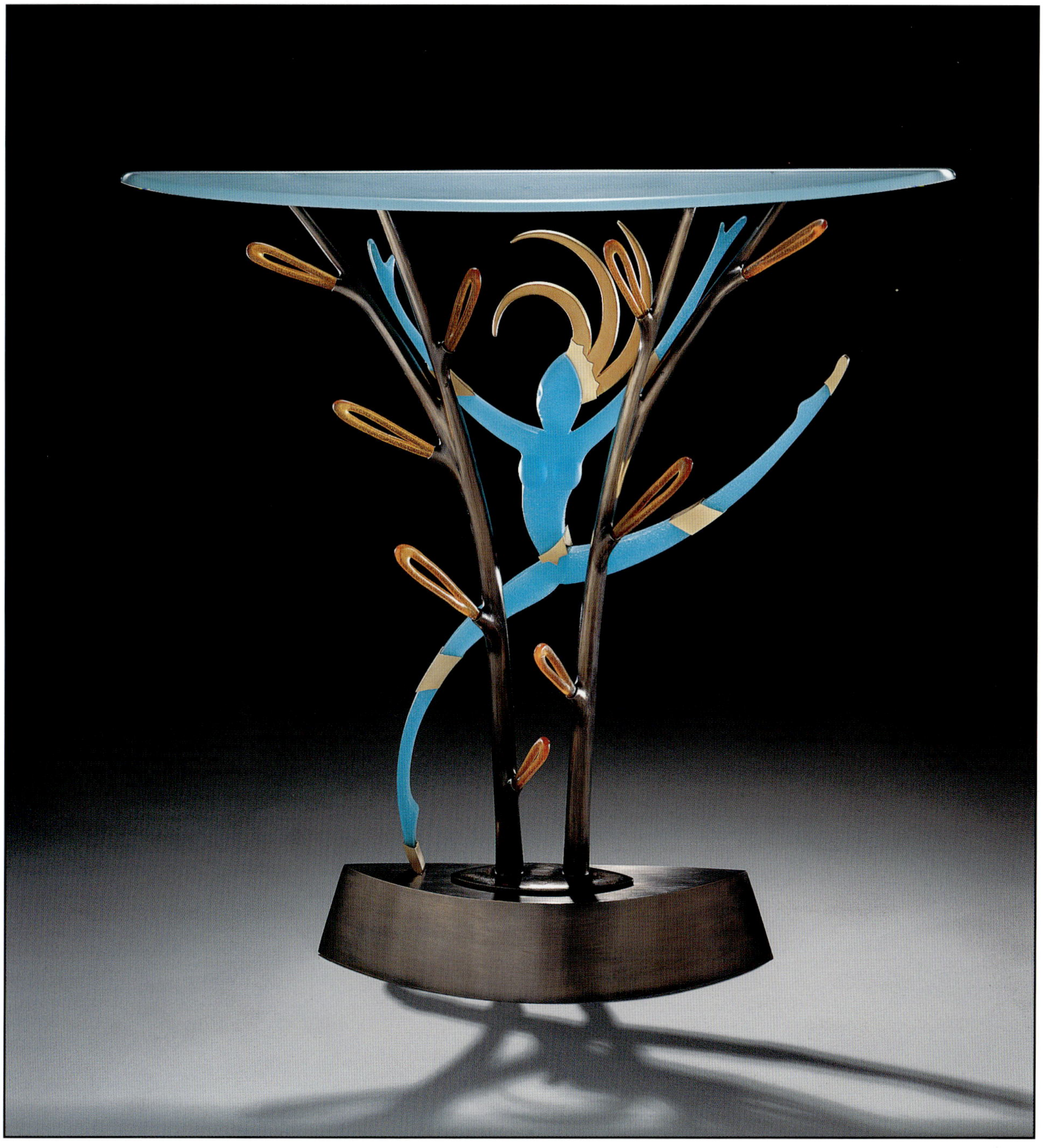

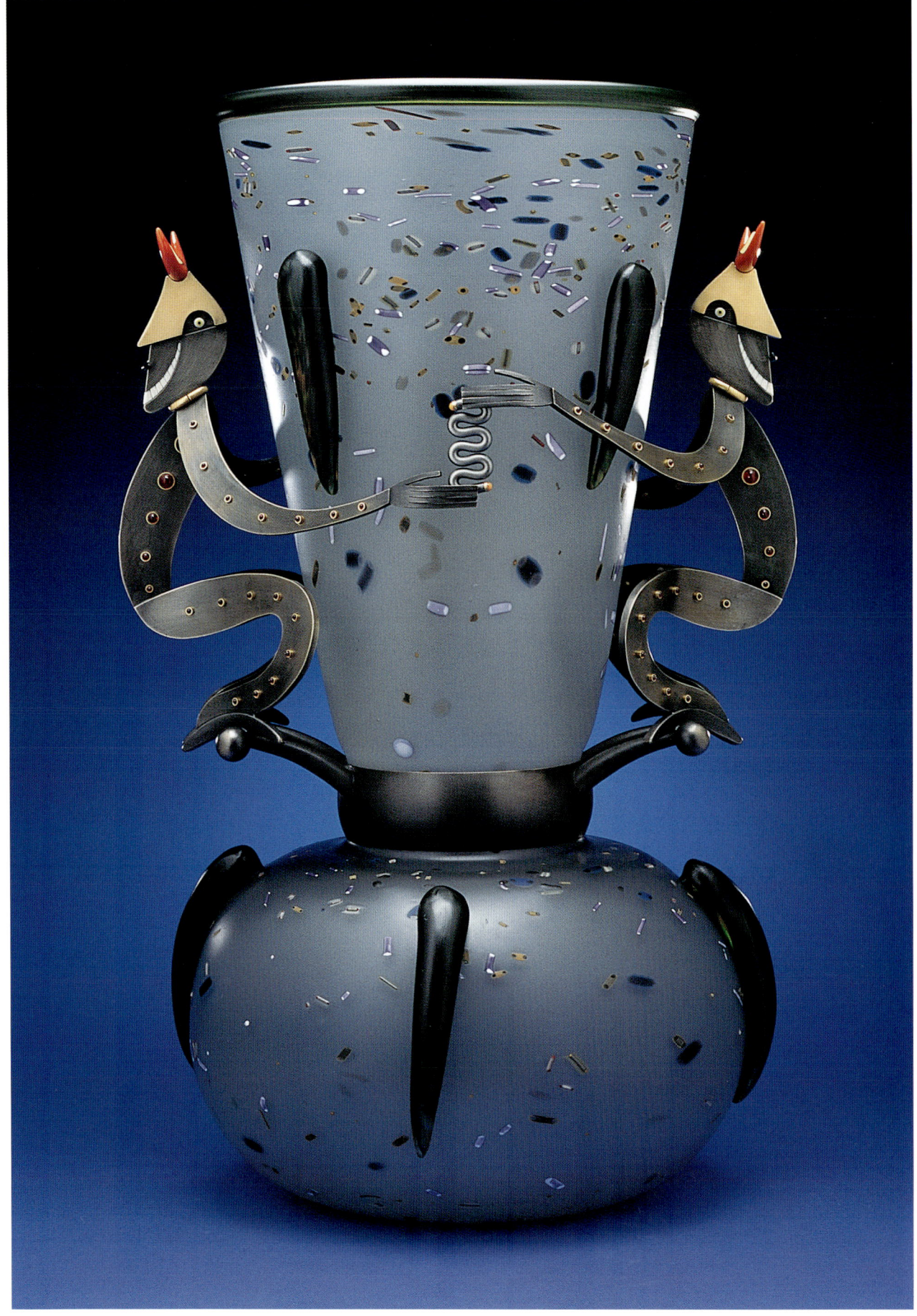

Above:
Zany Actors; Cirus Vase, 1999. Blown glass, fabricated patinated and gold plated bronze figures with glass details, h. 25 x 17 x 14 inches. Hunter Museum of American Art, Chattanooga, Tennessee. Photo: Bill Truslow

Opposite:
Masked Seducers; Cirus Vase, 1999. Blown glass, fabricated patinated and gold plated bronze figures with ivory, lapis, green, red, and yellow plate glass elements, h. 58 x 38 x 21 inches. Collection of Buddy and Debbie Menin. Photo: Bill Truslow.

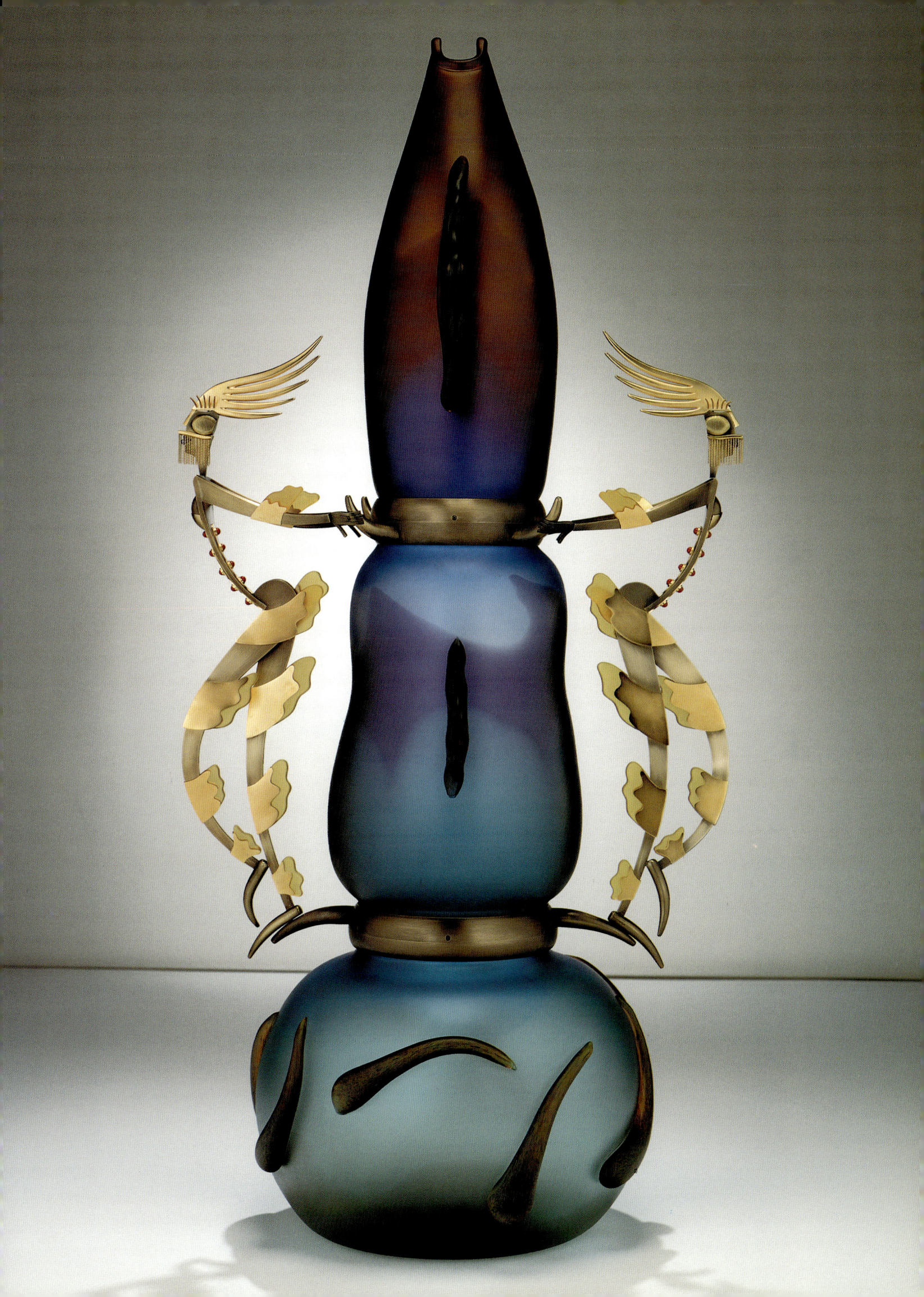

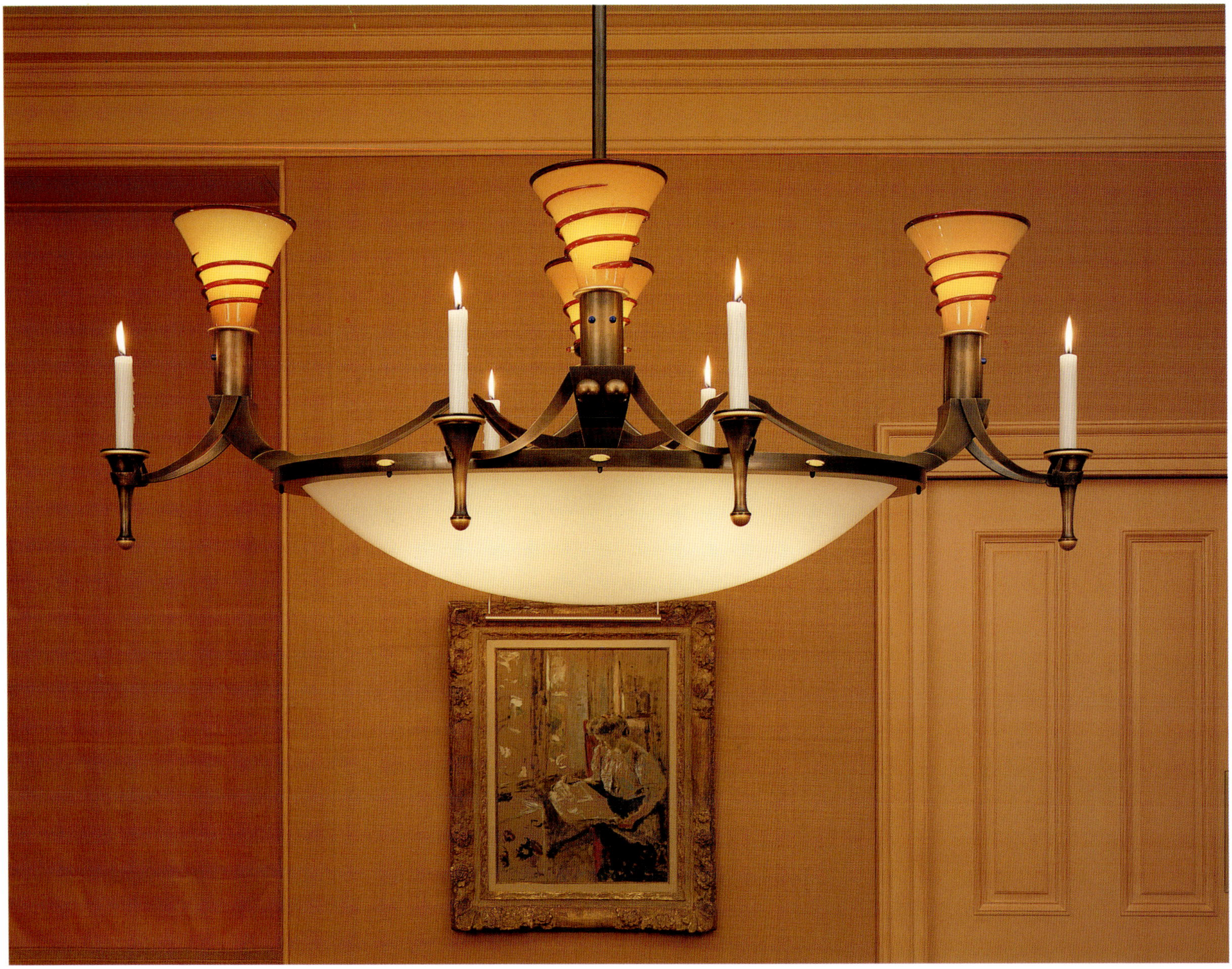

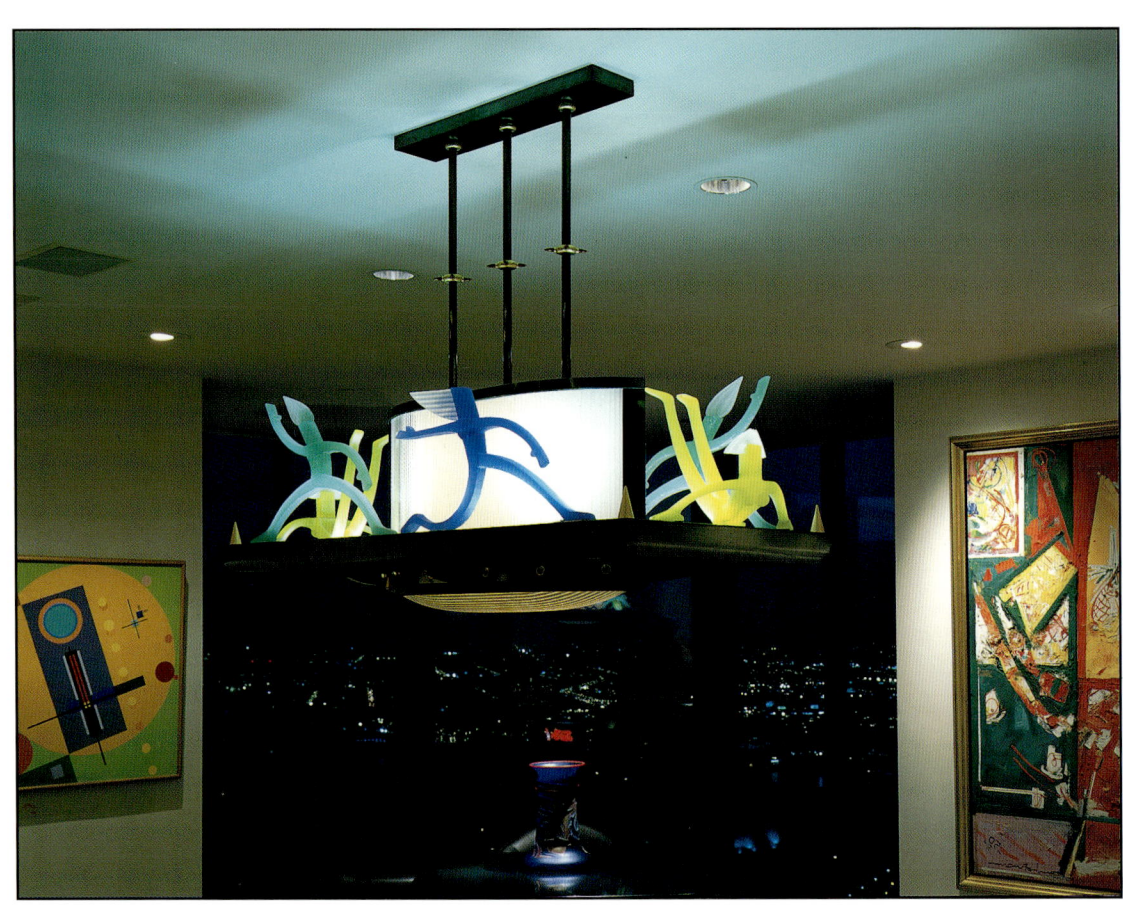

Above:
Four Balancing Women; Chandelier, 1996. Blown, slumped, ground, and polished glass elements, machined aluminum and bronze chassis, fabricated, patinated and gold-plated bronze figures, h. 22 x 52 inches. Private Collection. Photo: Bill Truslow.

Right:
Chandelier, 1999. Pâte de verre, plate glass, pulled glass rod, bronze, and aluminum, h. 36 x 42 x 20 inches. Collection of Simona and Jerry Chazen. Photo: Bruce Schwartz.

PROVIDENCE, RHODE ISLAND

Jill Henrietta Davis
(b.1969)

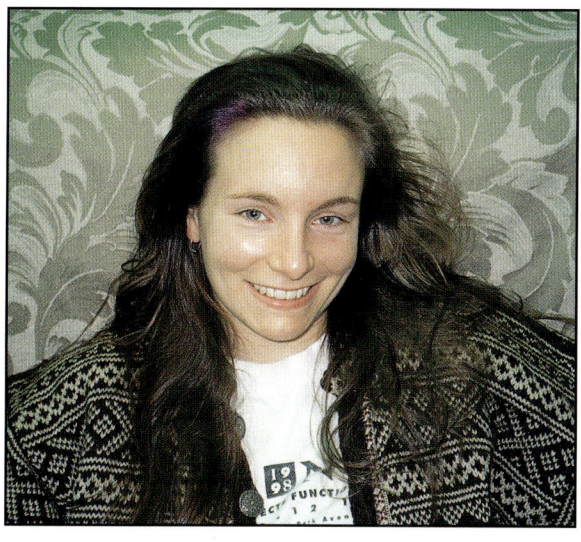

Brocade Push-Me Pull-Me. 1999. Blown and slumped glass and copper leaf, h. 14 x 17 x 12 inches. Photo: M. Scott

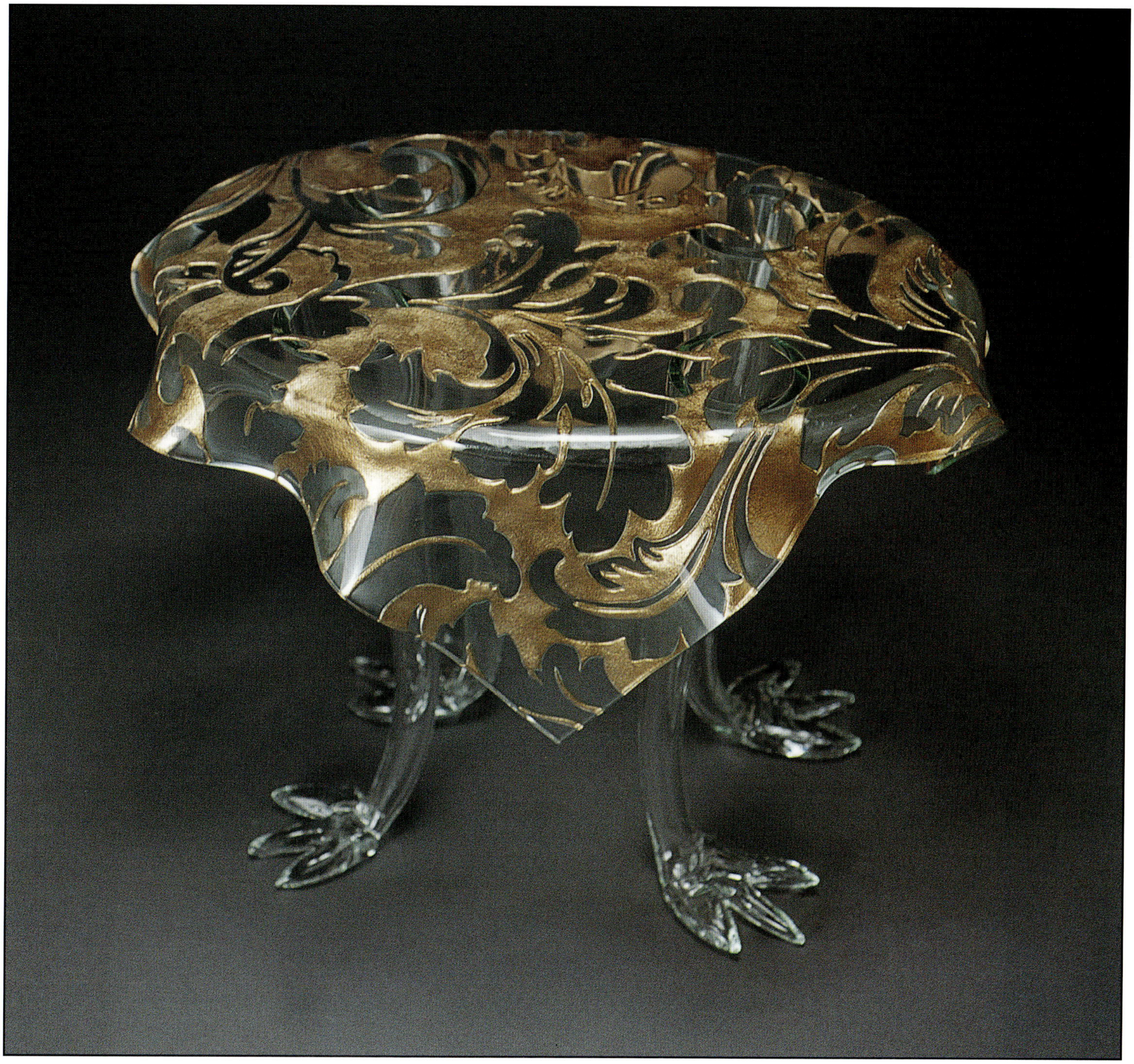

Michael Davis
(b.1953)

NEW YORK, NEW YORK

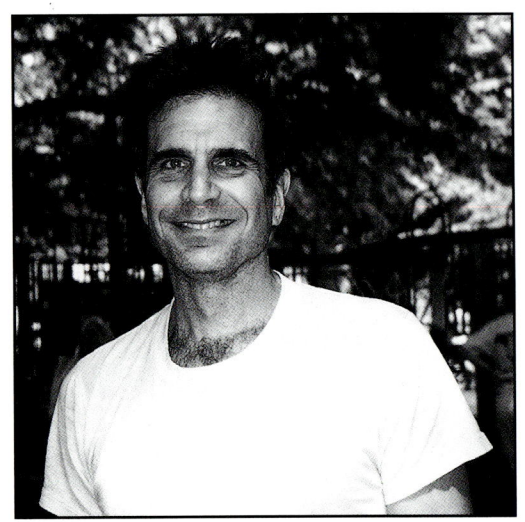

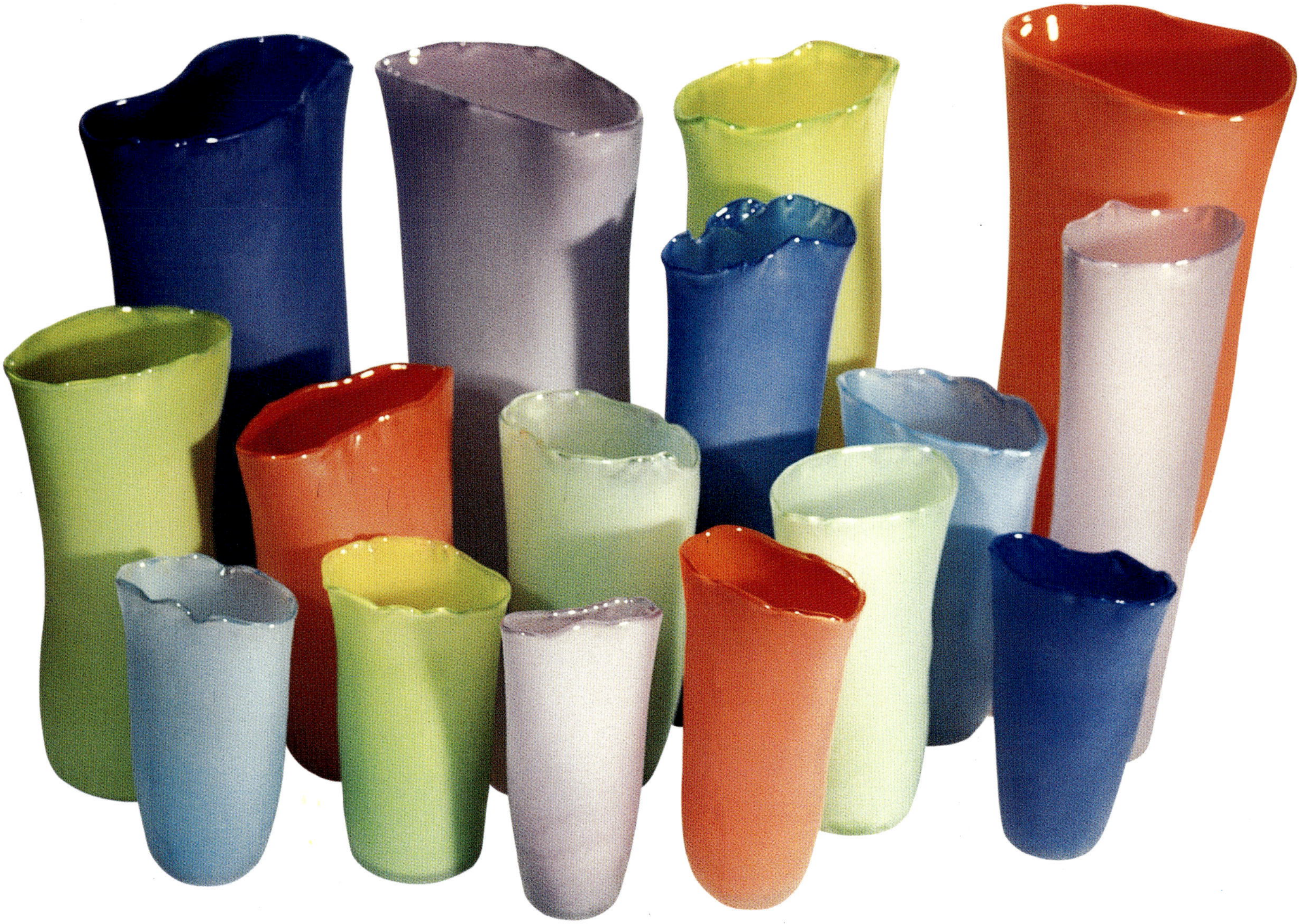

Ameoba Vases. 1999. Blown glass, h. 6-8 inches.

Einar & Jamex de la Torre
(b.1963) (b.1960)

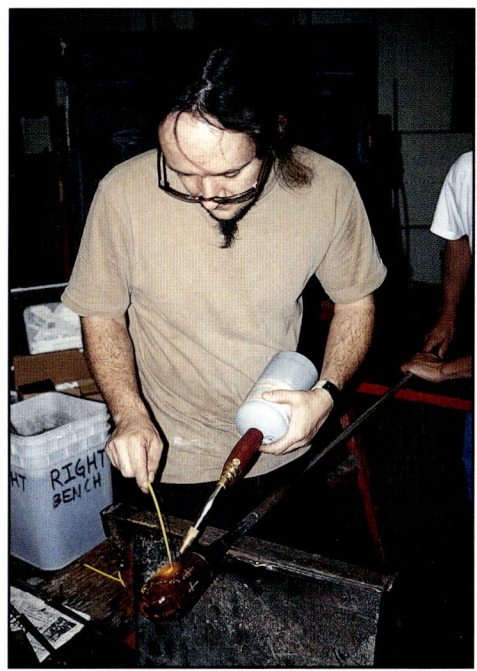

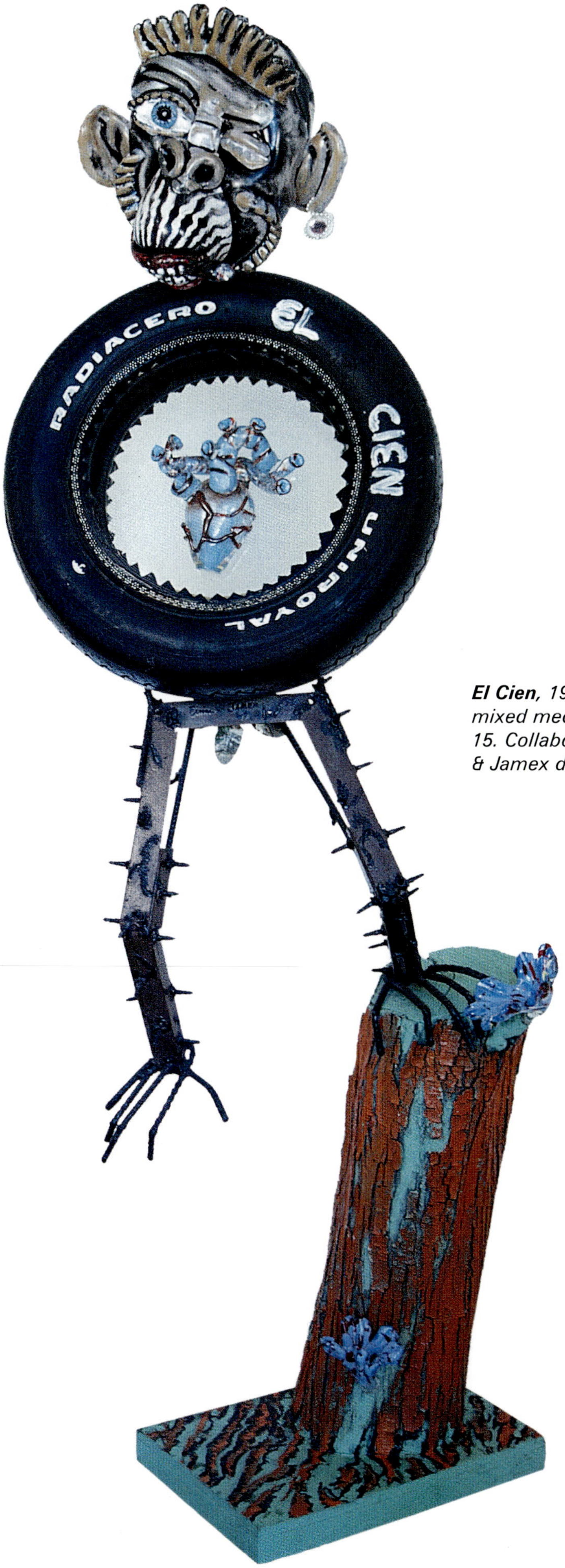

SAN DIEGO, CALIFORNIA

Photos: Nora Moore.

El Cien, 1997. Glass and mixed media, h. 74 x 30 x 15. Collaboration of Einar & Jamex de la Torre.

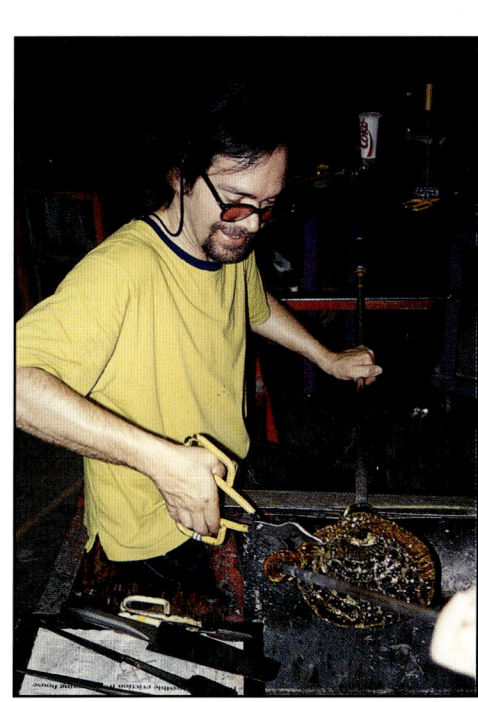

Will Dexter
(b.1952)

BOYERTOWN, PENNSYLVANIA

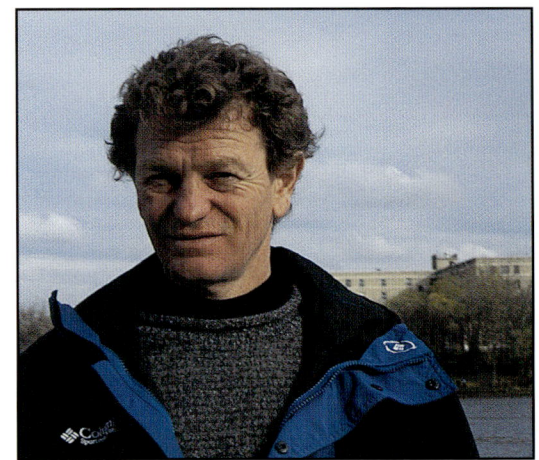

Nest, 1990. Blown glass, polychrome, femo; blown into wood and wet clay, h. 34 x 17 x 9 inches. Collection of Dudley and Lisa Anderson.

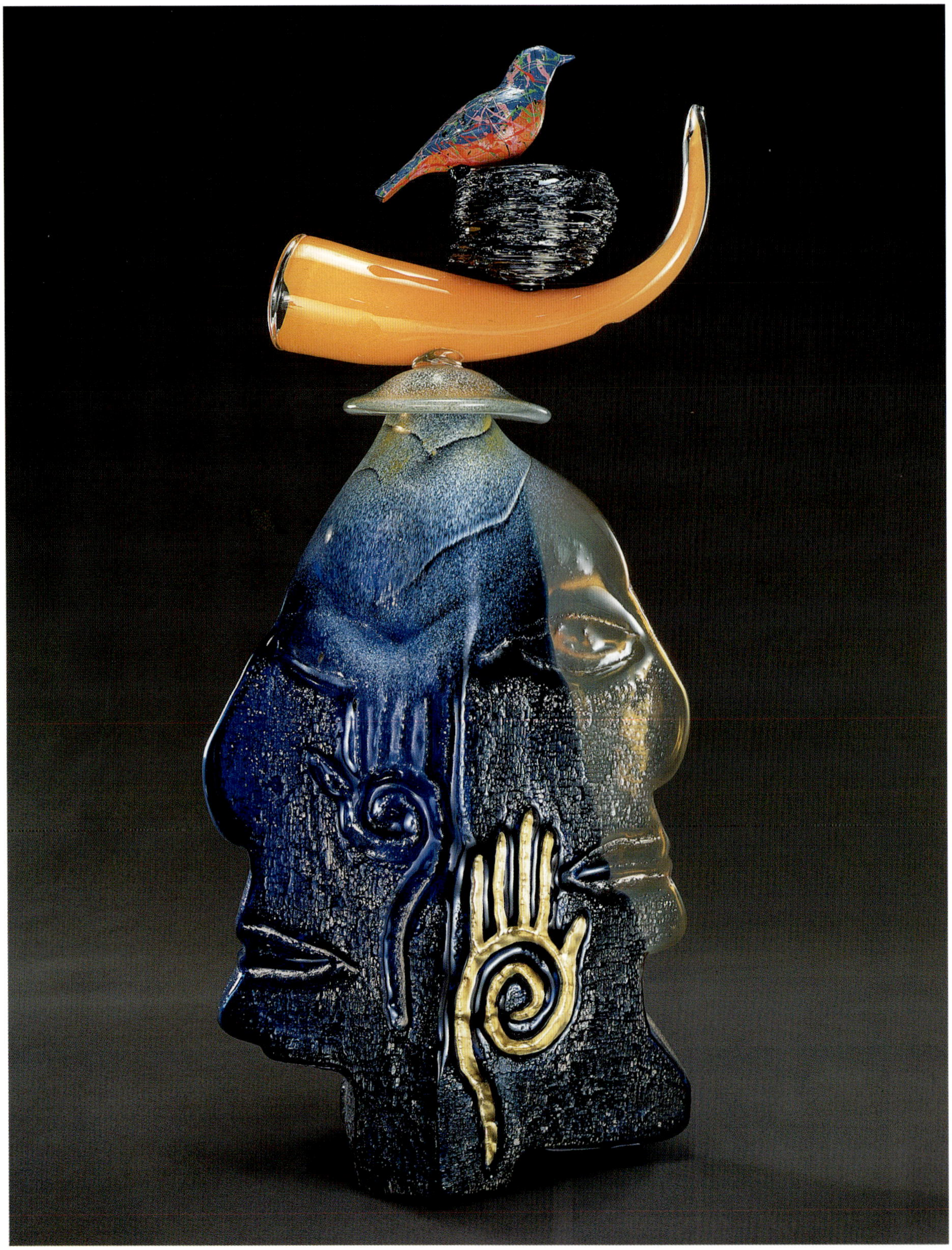

MILLIS, MASSACHUSETTS

Bernard D'Onofrio
(b.1951)

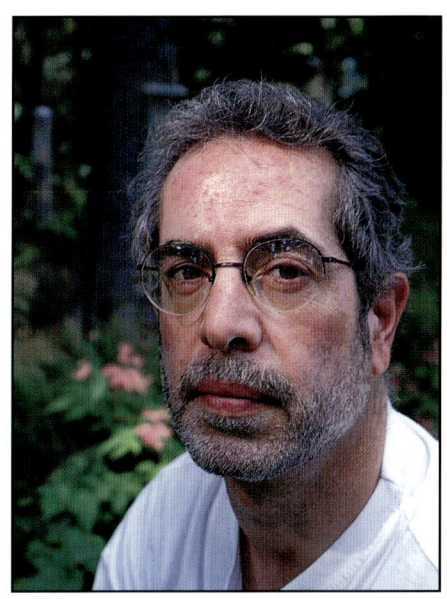

Bottle Still-Life, 1999. Blown glass, powdered colored glasses, etched surface, and black glass base, h. 24 x 24 x 8 inches.

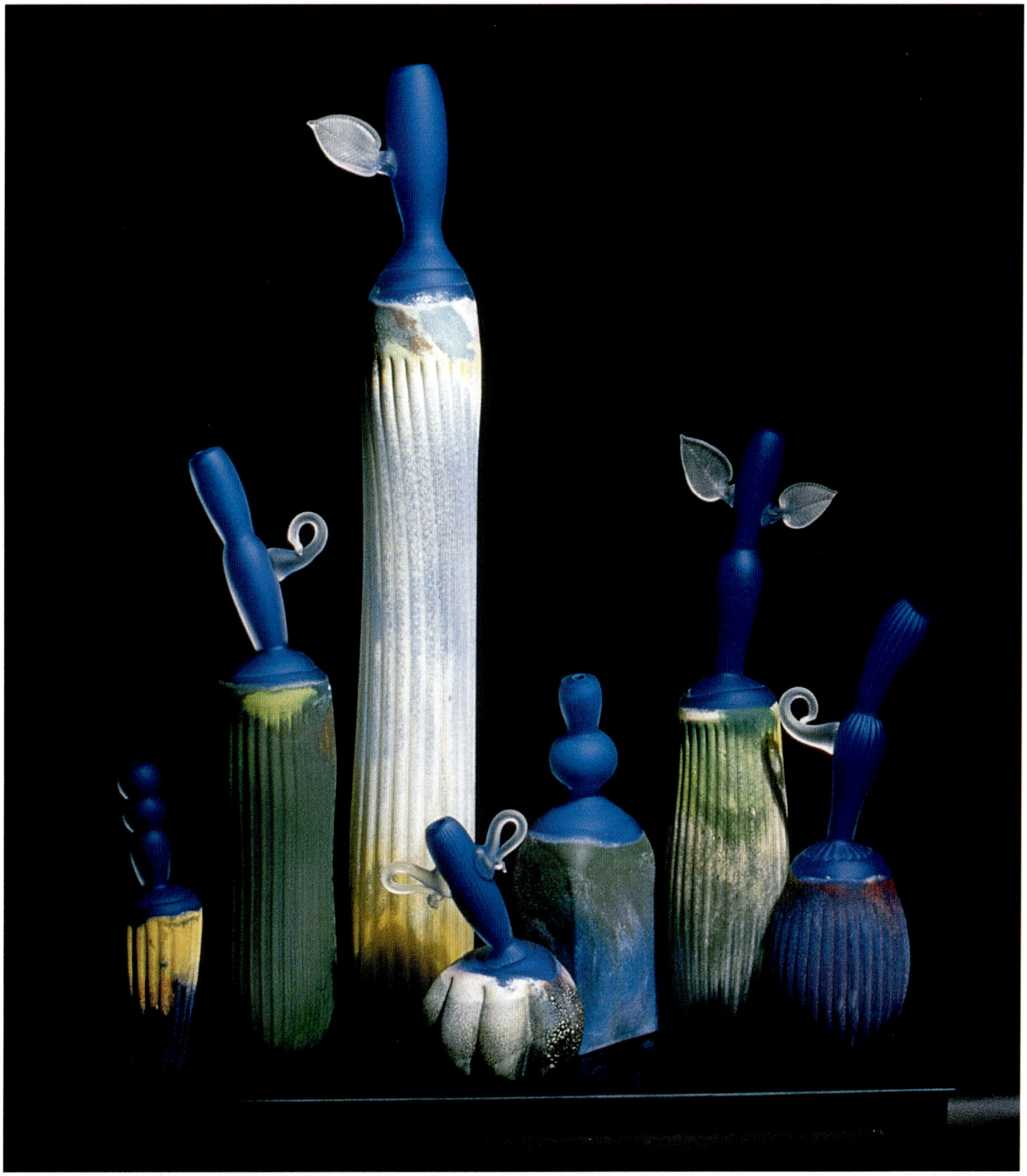

Patti Dougherty
(b.1955)

ELKINS PARK, PENNSYLVANIA

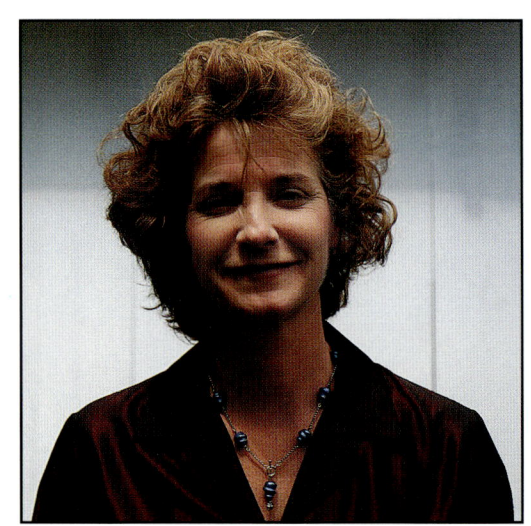

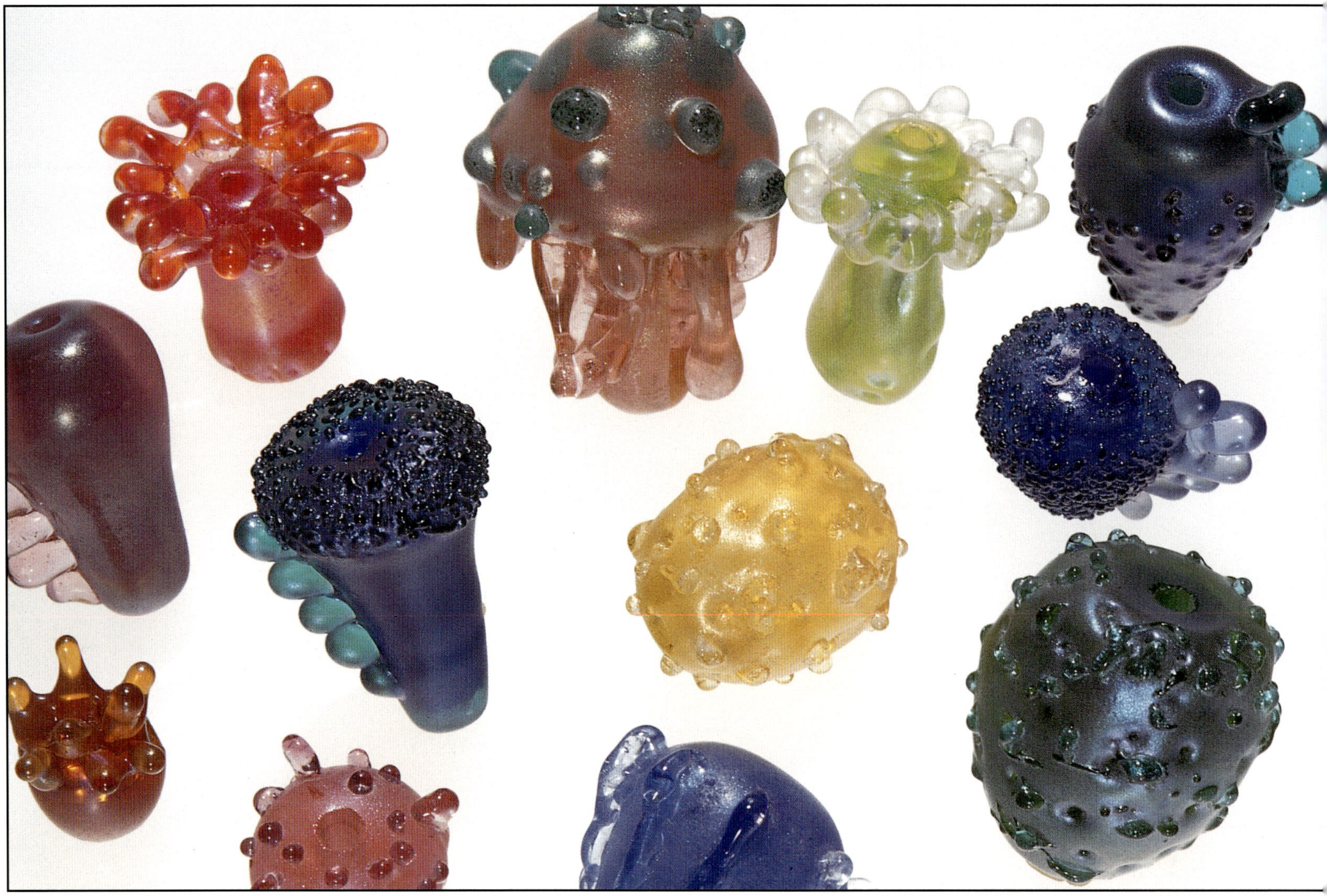

Marine Life Beads, 1999. Lamp worked glass beads with gold and pearlescent enamel, h. 1.5-2.5 inches. Photo: Peter Grosbeck.

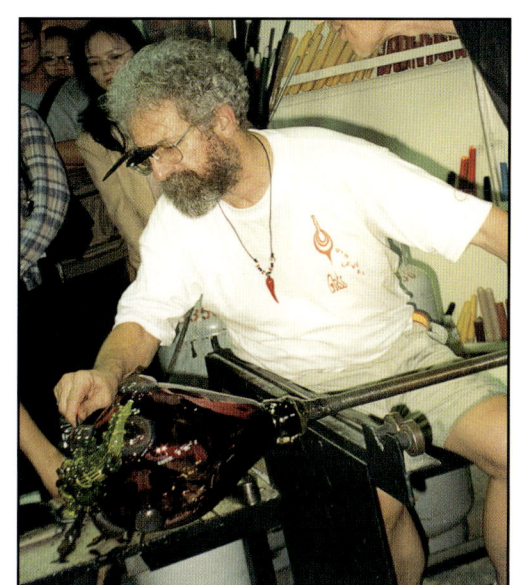

SEATTLE, WASHINGTON

Fritz Dreisbach
(b.1941)

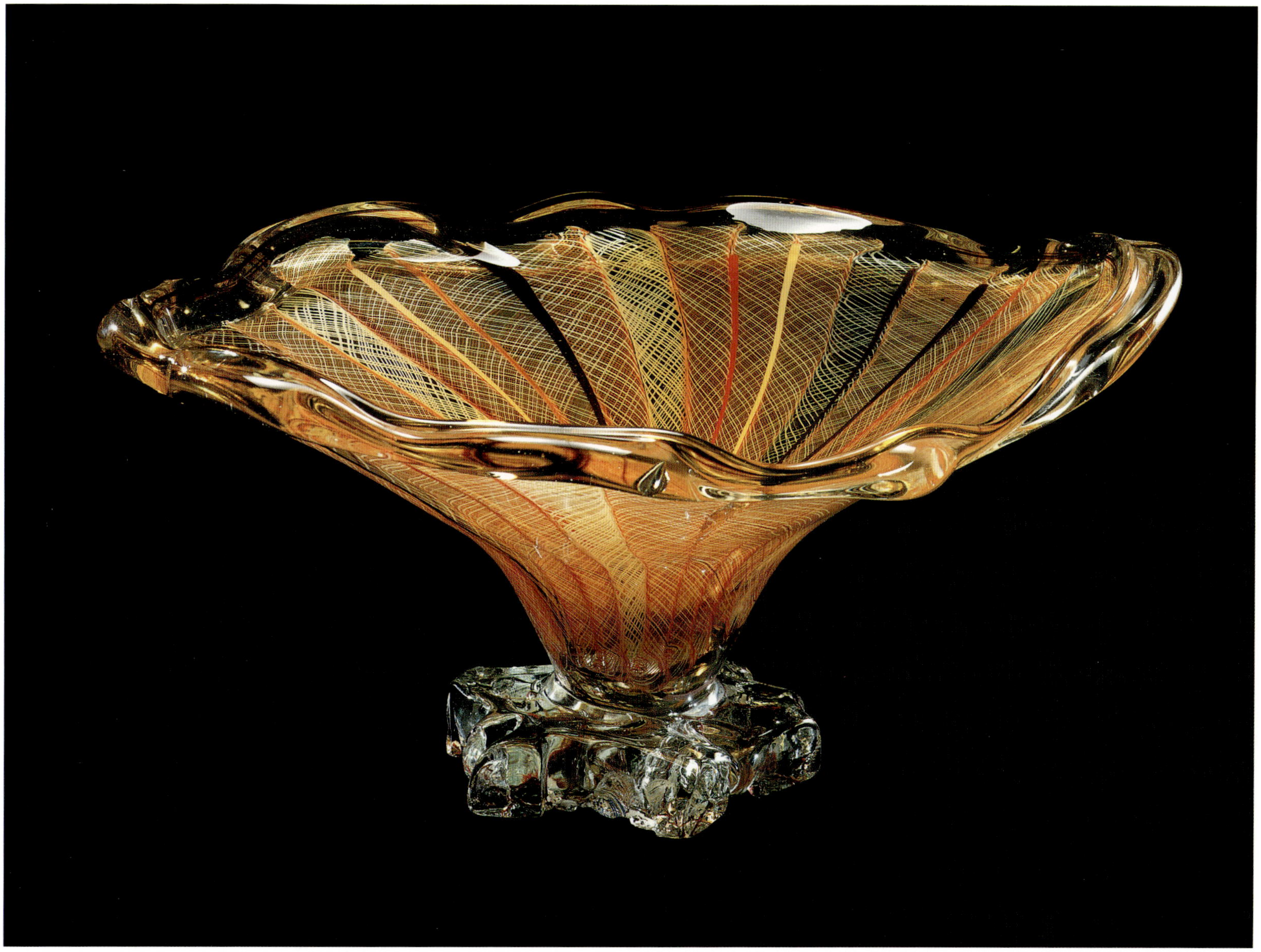

Above:
Golden Mongo Compote with Multi Hue Filagree and Cast Base, 1986. Blown glass, h. 10.5 x 20 x 18 inches. Photo: Mel Schockner.

Following:
Flamingos, Pink Scallop, Sea Shell and Grape Cluster; Fancy Reversible Champagne and Cognac Goblets, 1991-92. Blown glass, h. 14-19 inches. Photo: Roger Schreiber.

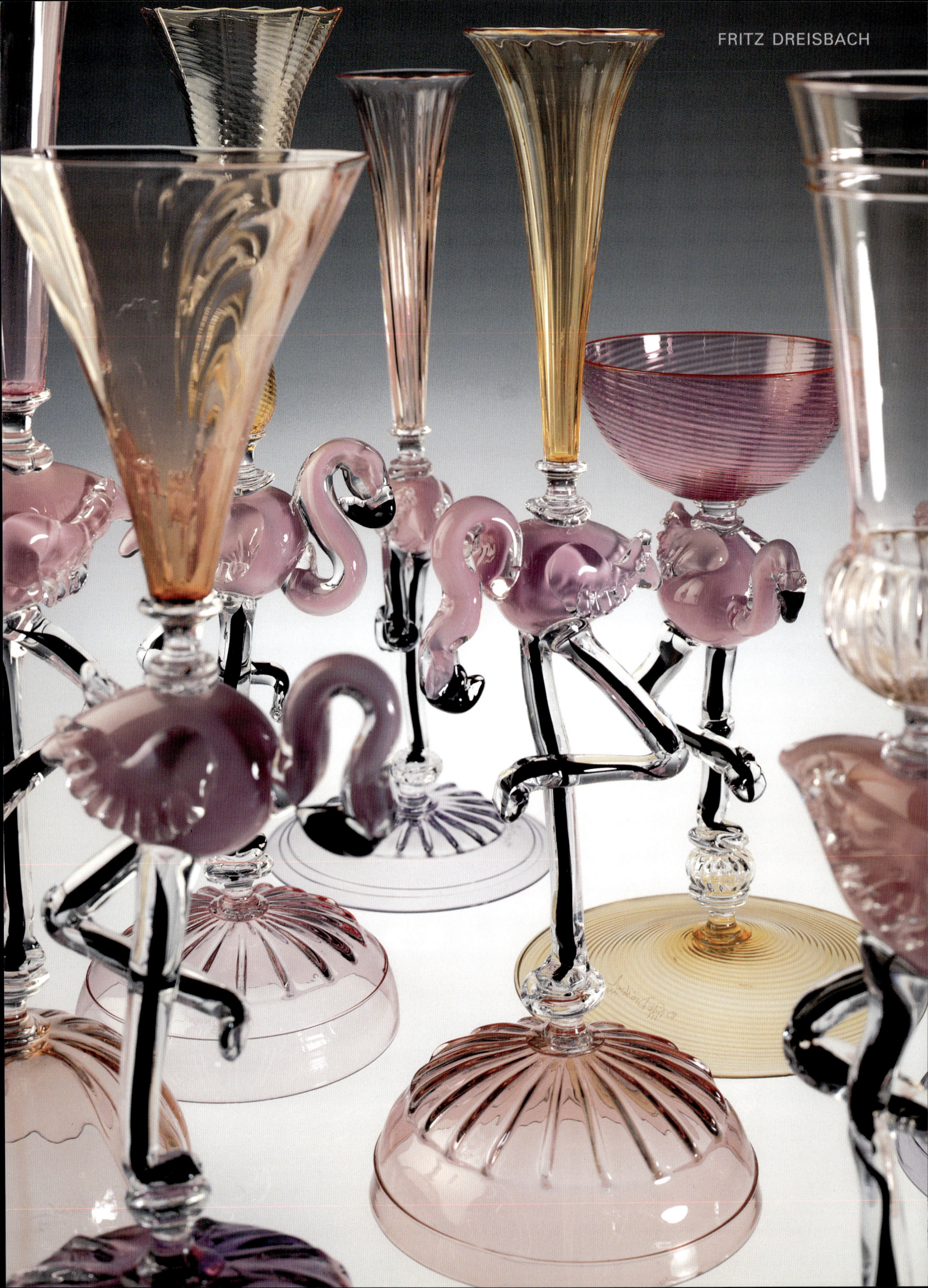

FRITZ DREISBACH

CORNING, NEW YORK

Peter Drobny
(b. 1958)

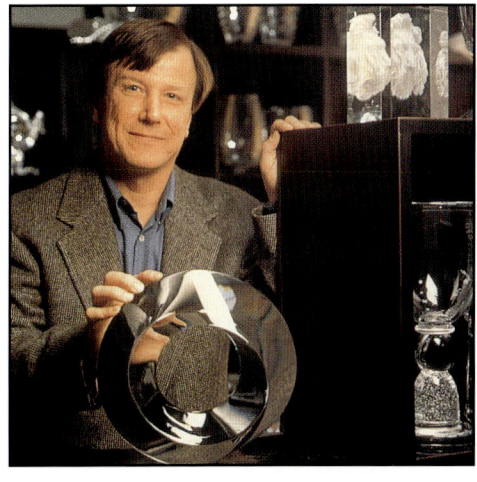

Mobius Prism, 1995. Sag cast Steuben crystal, cut, ground, and polished by hand, and ebonized oak base, h. 11 x 3.5 inches. Courtesy Steuben.

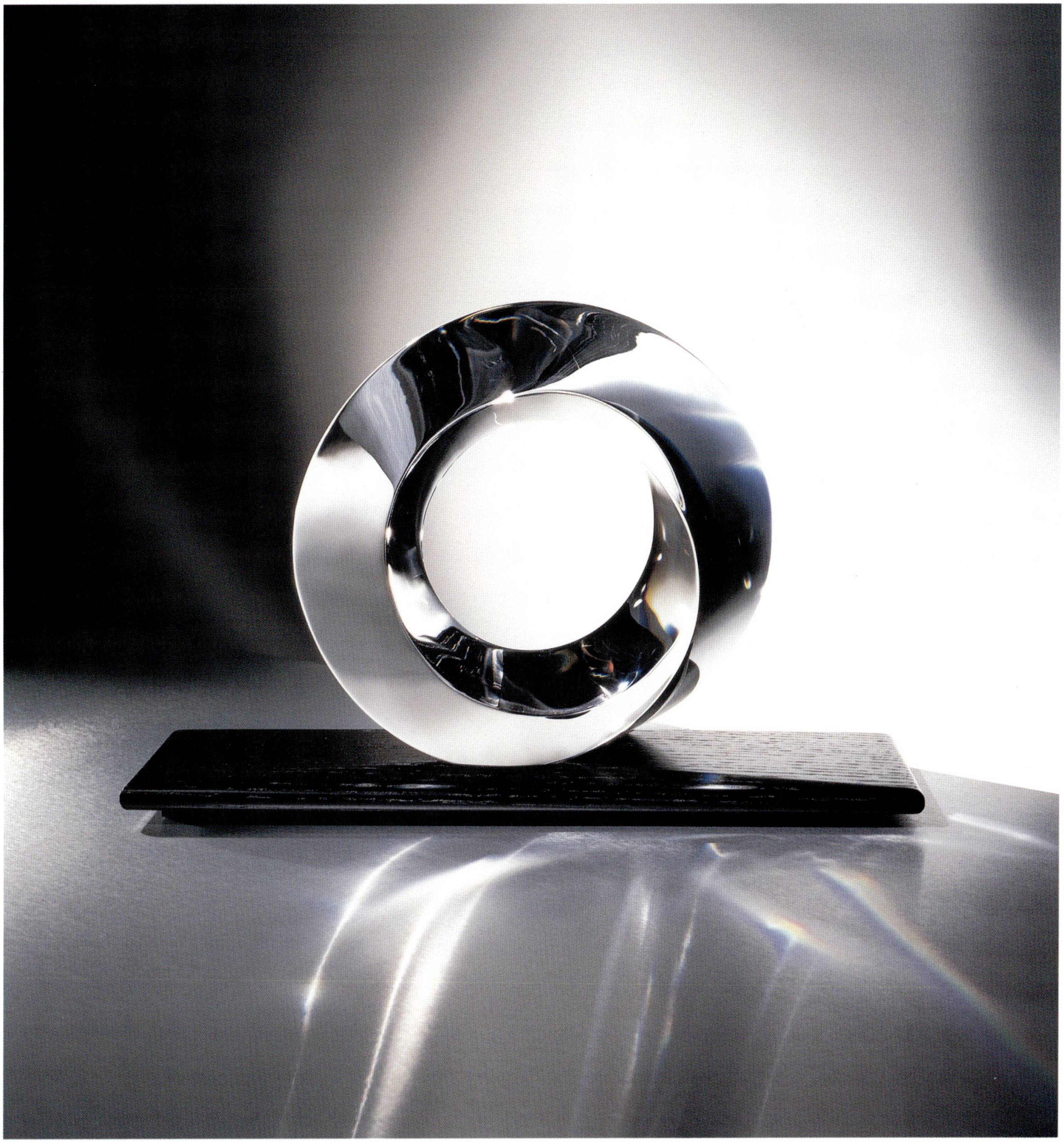

John Drury
(b.1960)

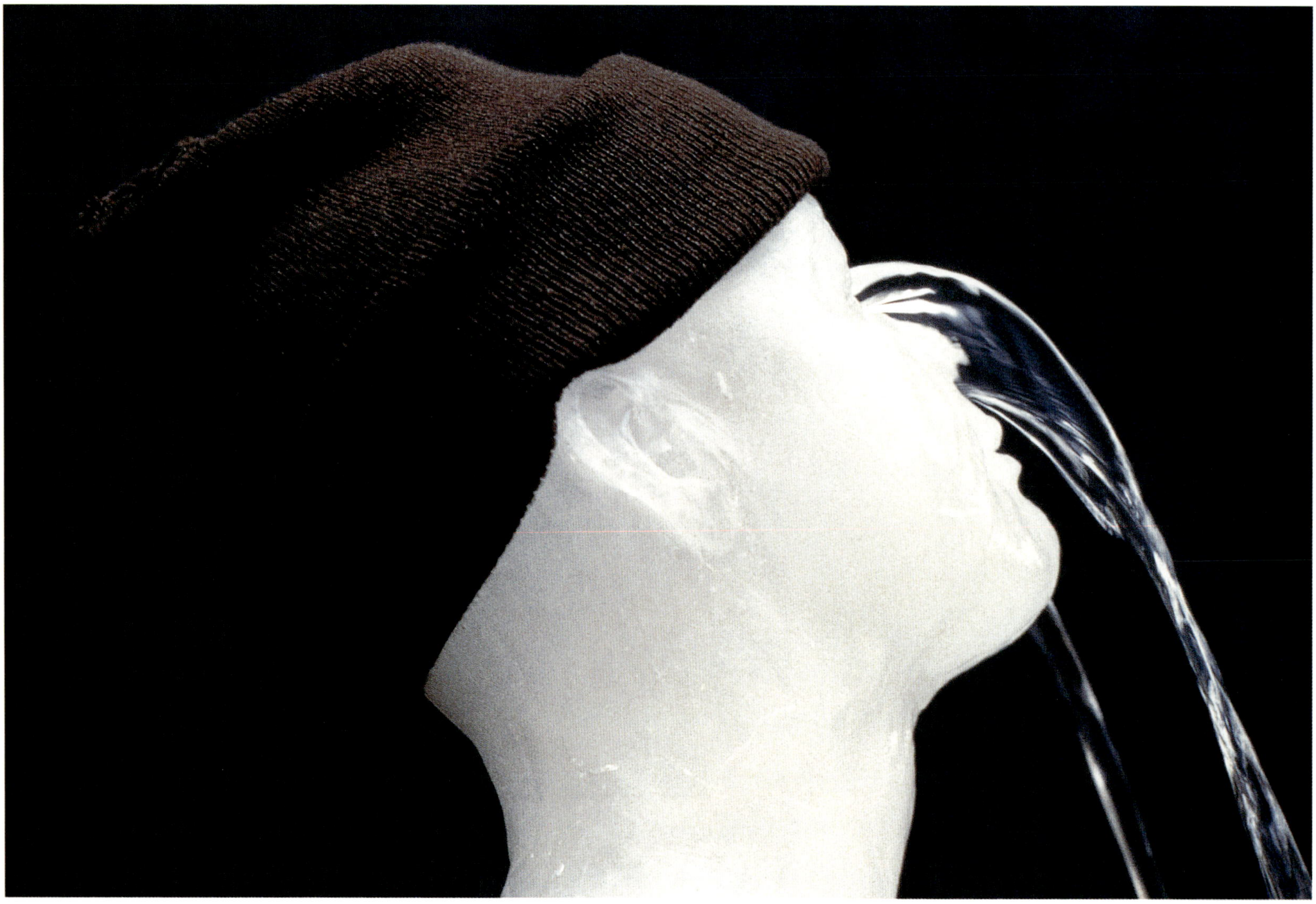

NEW YORK, NEW YORK

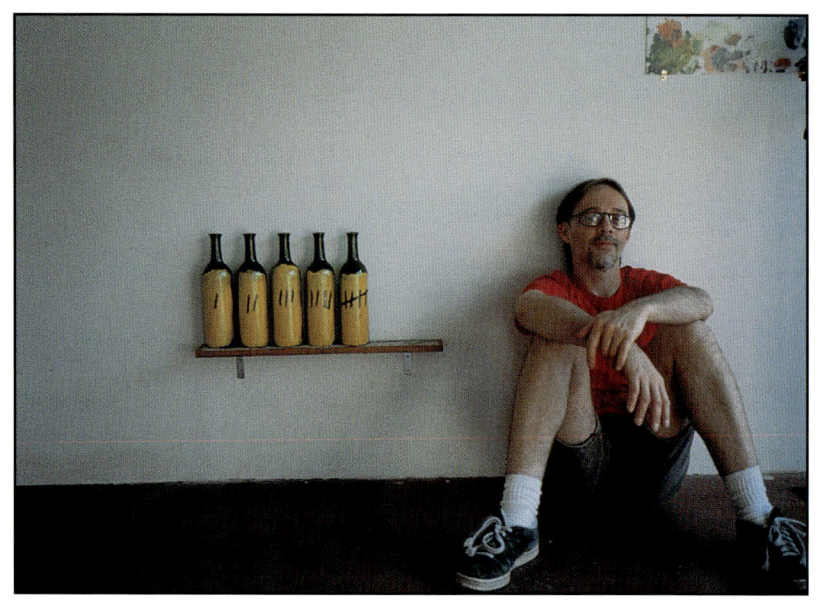

Self Pity Party Portrait, 1996. Glass, knit hat, water, and pump. Life cast bust. Photo: Robbie Miller.

Robert DuGrenier
(b.1955)

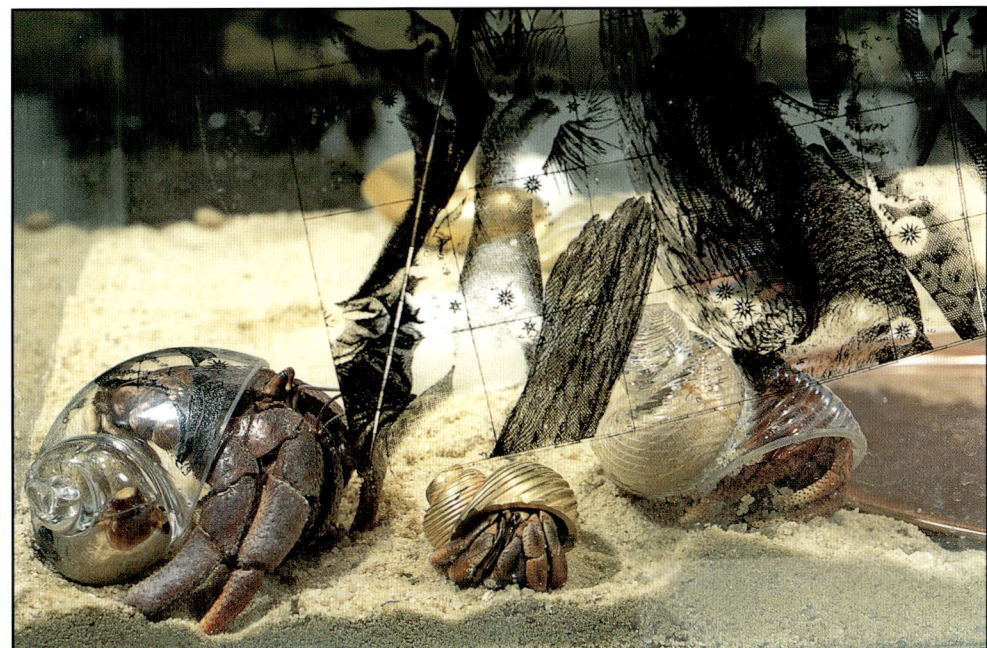

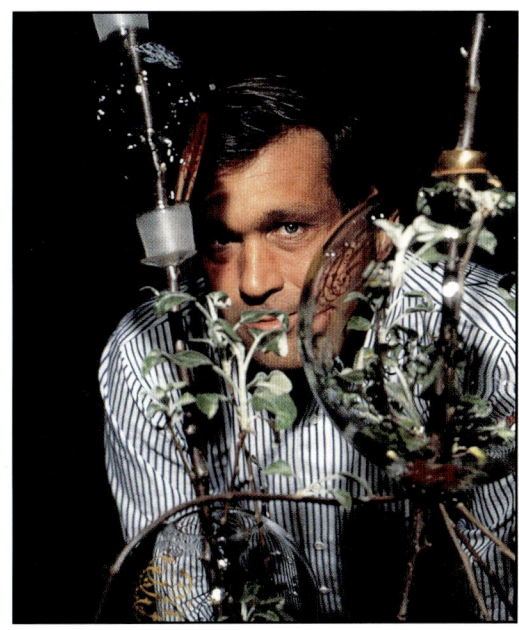

TOWNSHEND, VERMONT

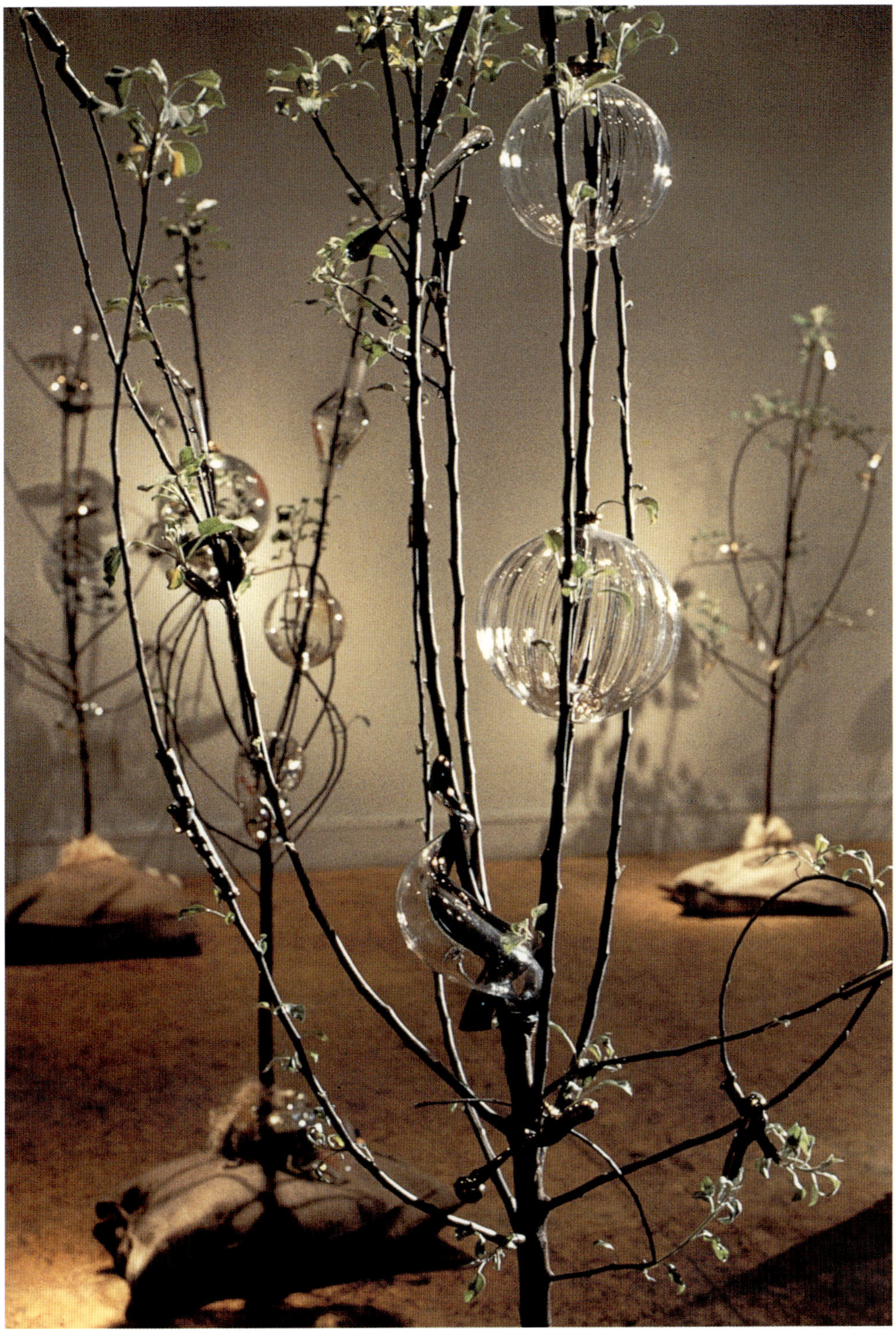

Top:
Hermit Crab; Mobile Home, 1996. Blown glass shell. Life size.

Bottom:
Sculpture 005; Fruit Tree Sculpture, Installation, 1999. Blown glass, metal, and fruit trees, h. 6 x 15 x 20 feet.

Susan Edgerley
(b.1960)

QUEBEC, CANADA

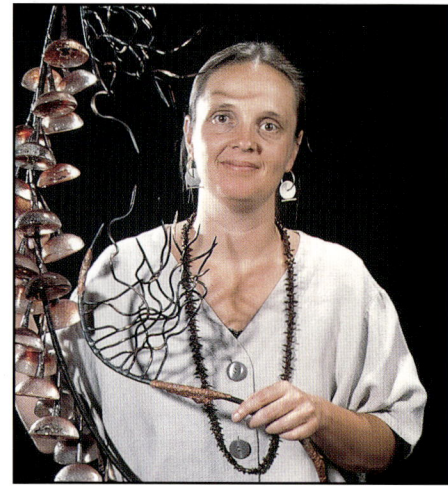

Core II, 1995. Suspended sculpture with 120 glass elements. Sandcast glass, forged steel, copper, and natural fibers, h. 75 x 24 x 15 inches.

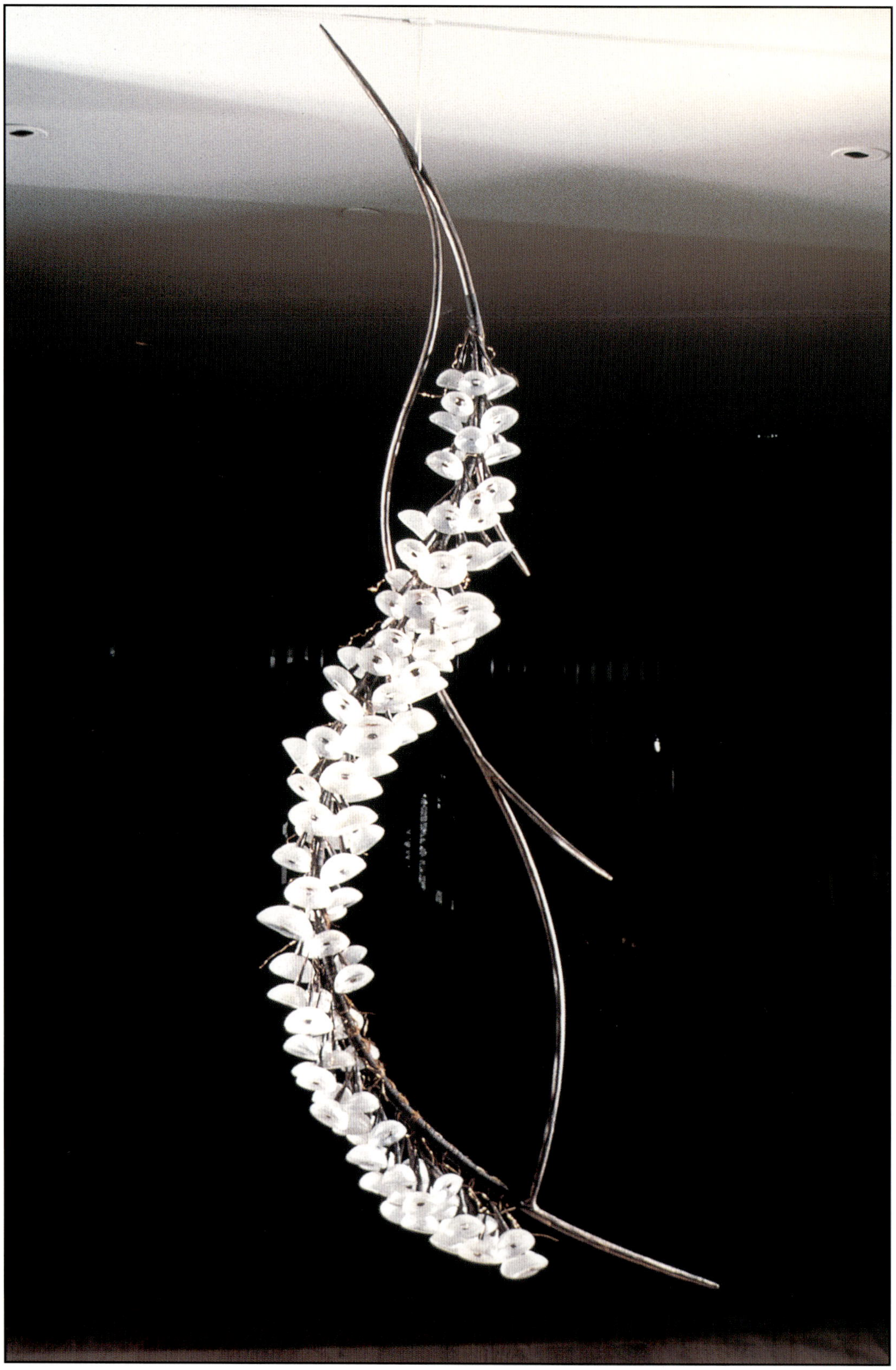

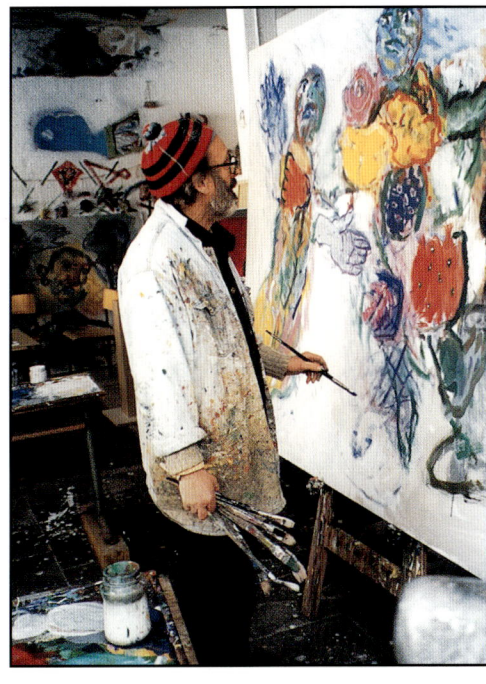

FEDERAL REPUBLIC OF GERMANY

Erwin Eisch
(b.1927)

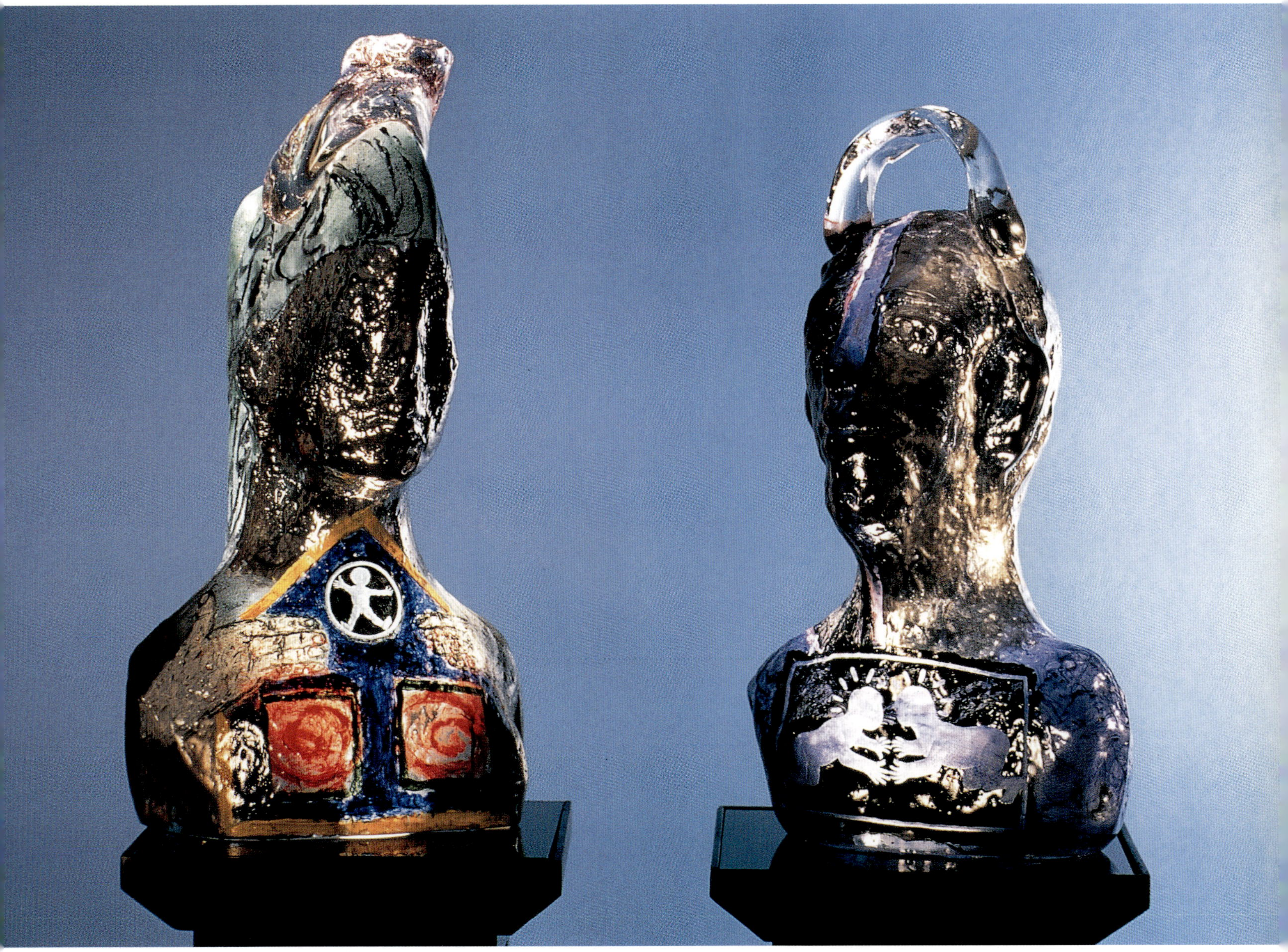

Exchange; Sixteen heads and the Space Between Installation,
1999. Corning Incorporated, Corning, New York. Mold blown glass, paint, and engraving, h. 18 inches each.

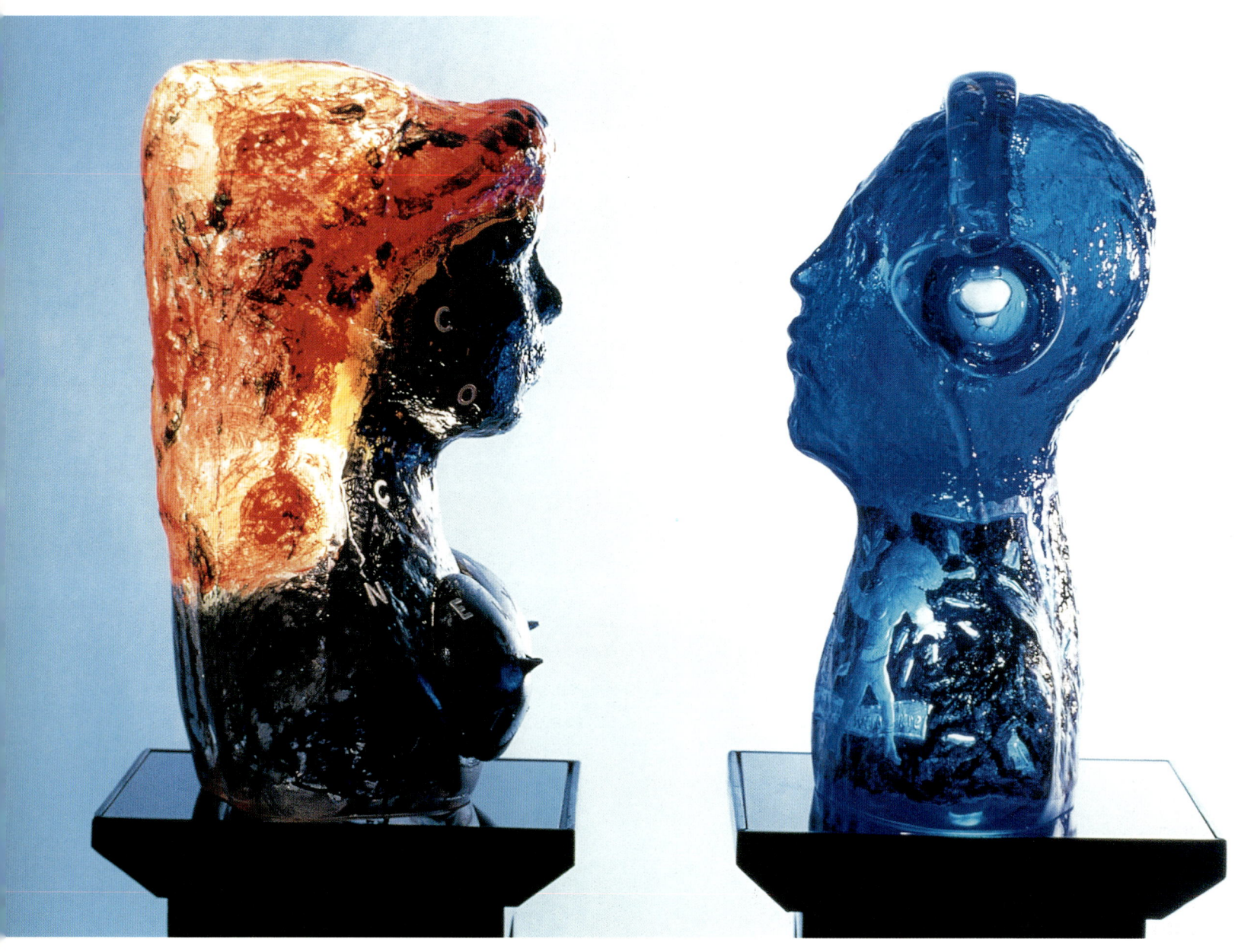

The Music Group; Sixteen Heads and the Space Between Installation, 1999. Corning Incorporated, Corning, New York. Mold blown glass, paint, and engraving, h. 18 inches each.

NEW YORK, NEW YORK

Albins Elskus
(b. 1926)

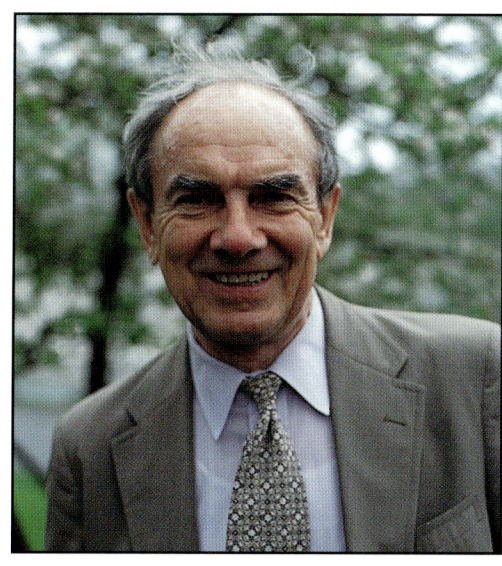

Follow Me and I Will Make You Fishers of Men, 1978. Stained glass window; Hillside United Methodist Church, New Hyde Park, New York.

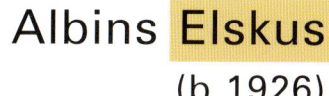

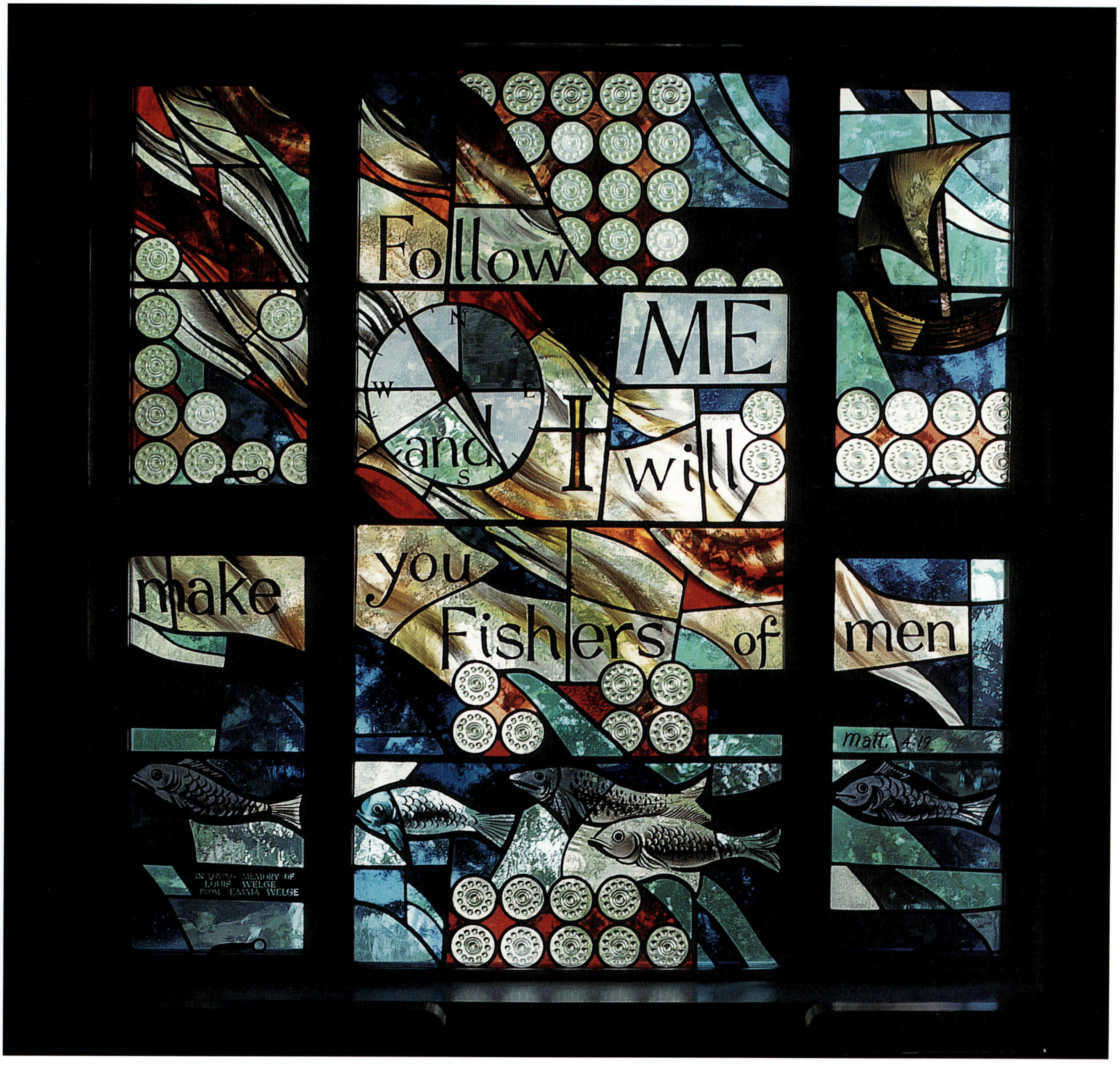

Mark Ferguson
(b.1959

BROOKLYN, NEW YORK

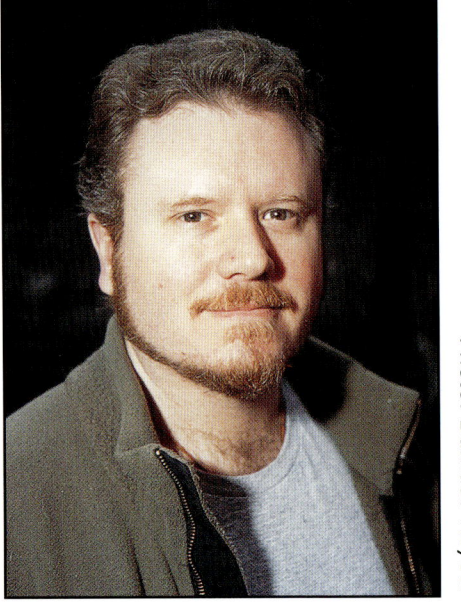
Photo: Damaso Reyes.

Torch, 1999. Cast Glass and metal flashlight, h. 18 x 12 x 6 inches. Collection of Geoffrey J. Isles. Photo: George Erml.

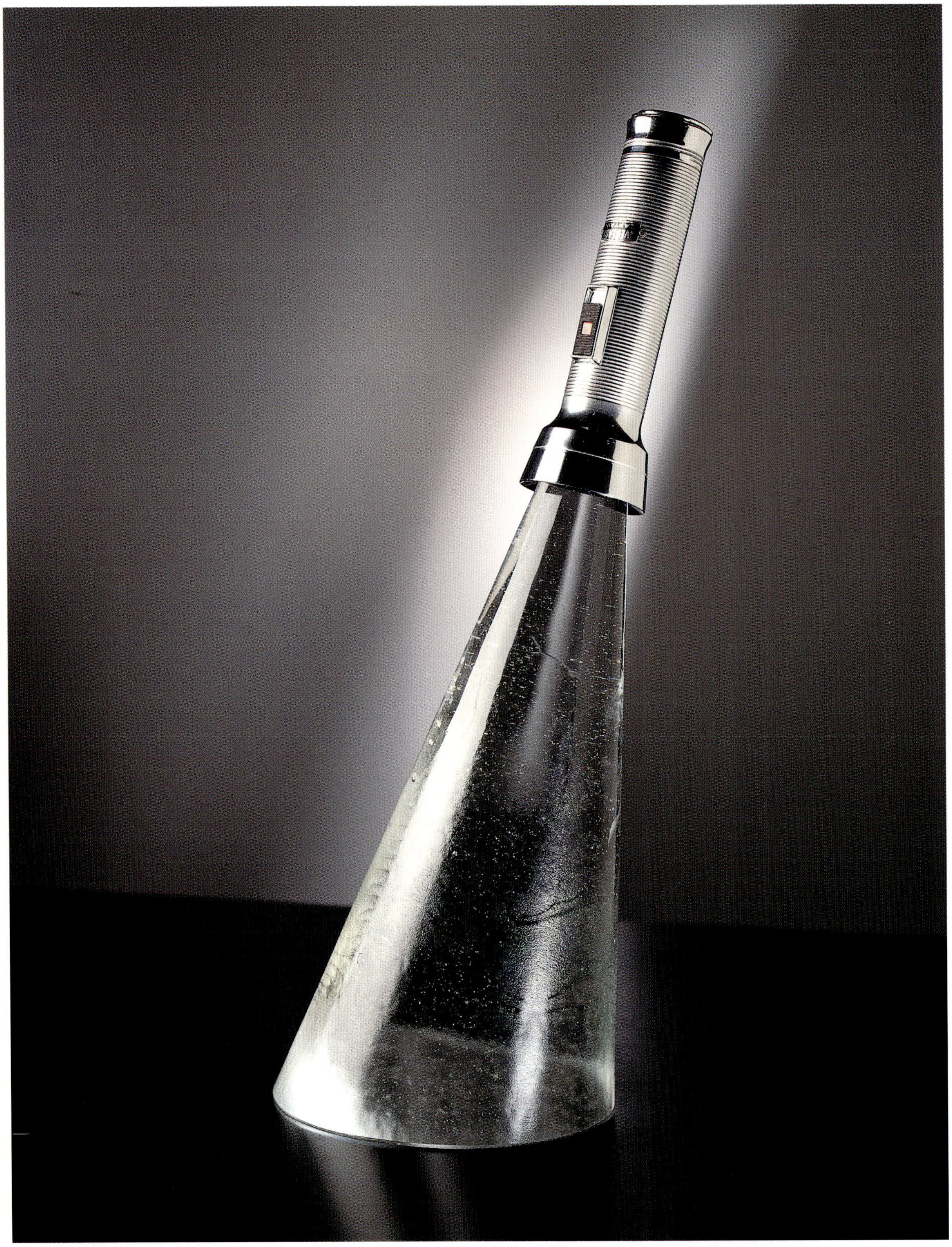

PENLAND, NORTH CAROLINA

Shane Fero
(b. 1953)

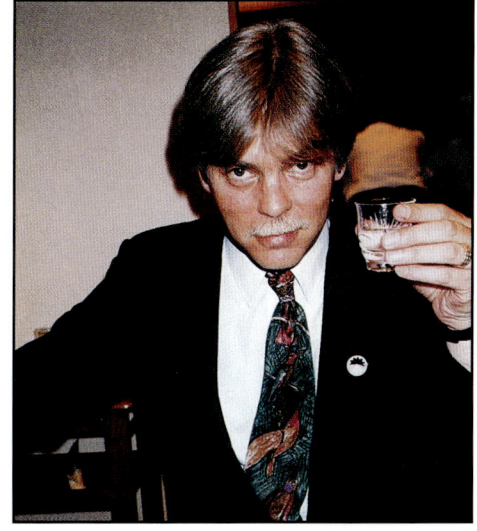

Goddess of The Flame, 1998. Flameworkers glass, and sandblasting, h. 16 x 8.5 x 8.5 inches.

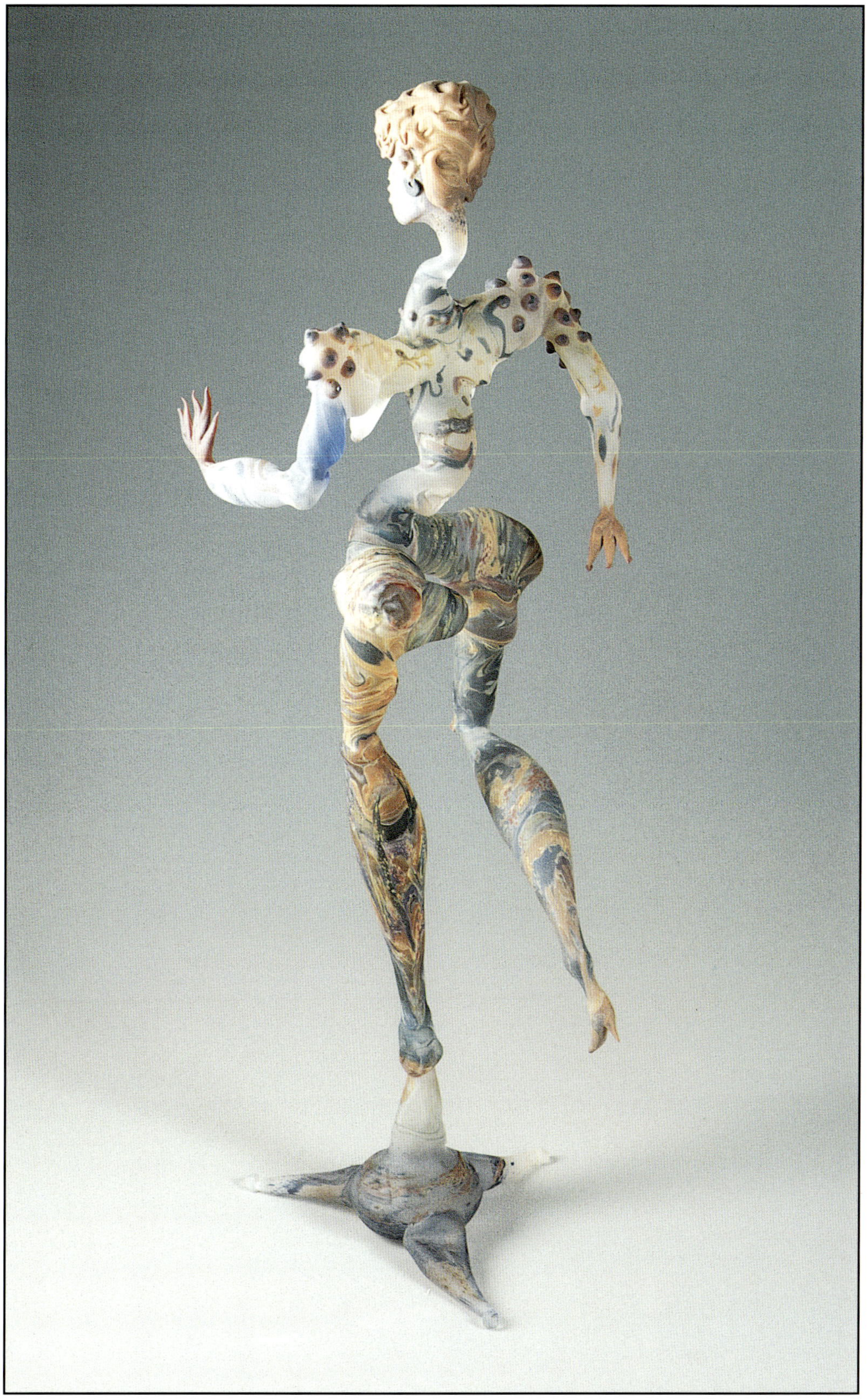

Thomas M. Fleming
(b.1951)

WAUSAU, WISCONSIN

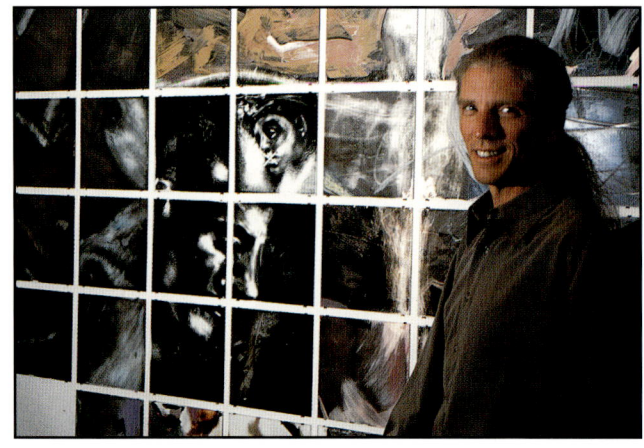

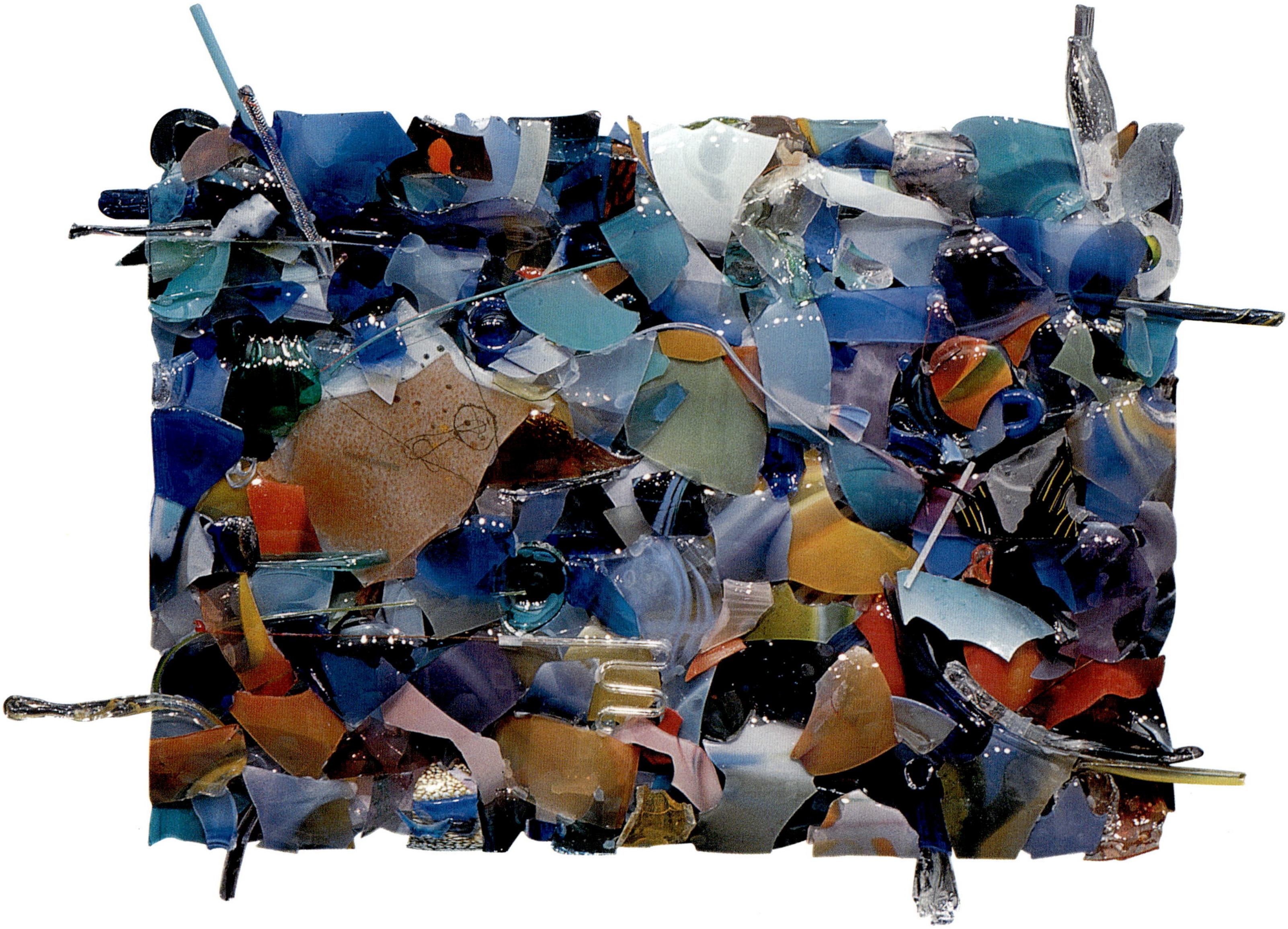

Big Sky Travois, 1991. Recycled glass, painted, and sandblasted, h. 38 x 52 x 2 inches.

NEW YORK, NEW YORK

Hans Frode
(b.1951)

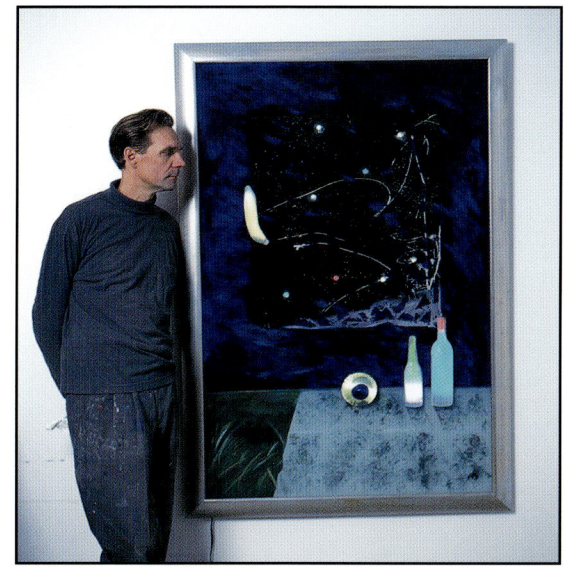

Left:
Expanding Universe, 1999. Painted plate glass, cast glass, and neon behind, h. 64 x 44 inches.

Below:
Universes In 11 Dimensions, 1998. Painted plate glass, cast glass, and neon behind, h. 31 x 27 inches.

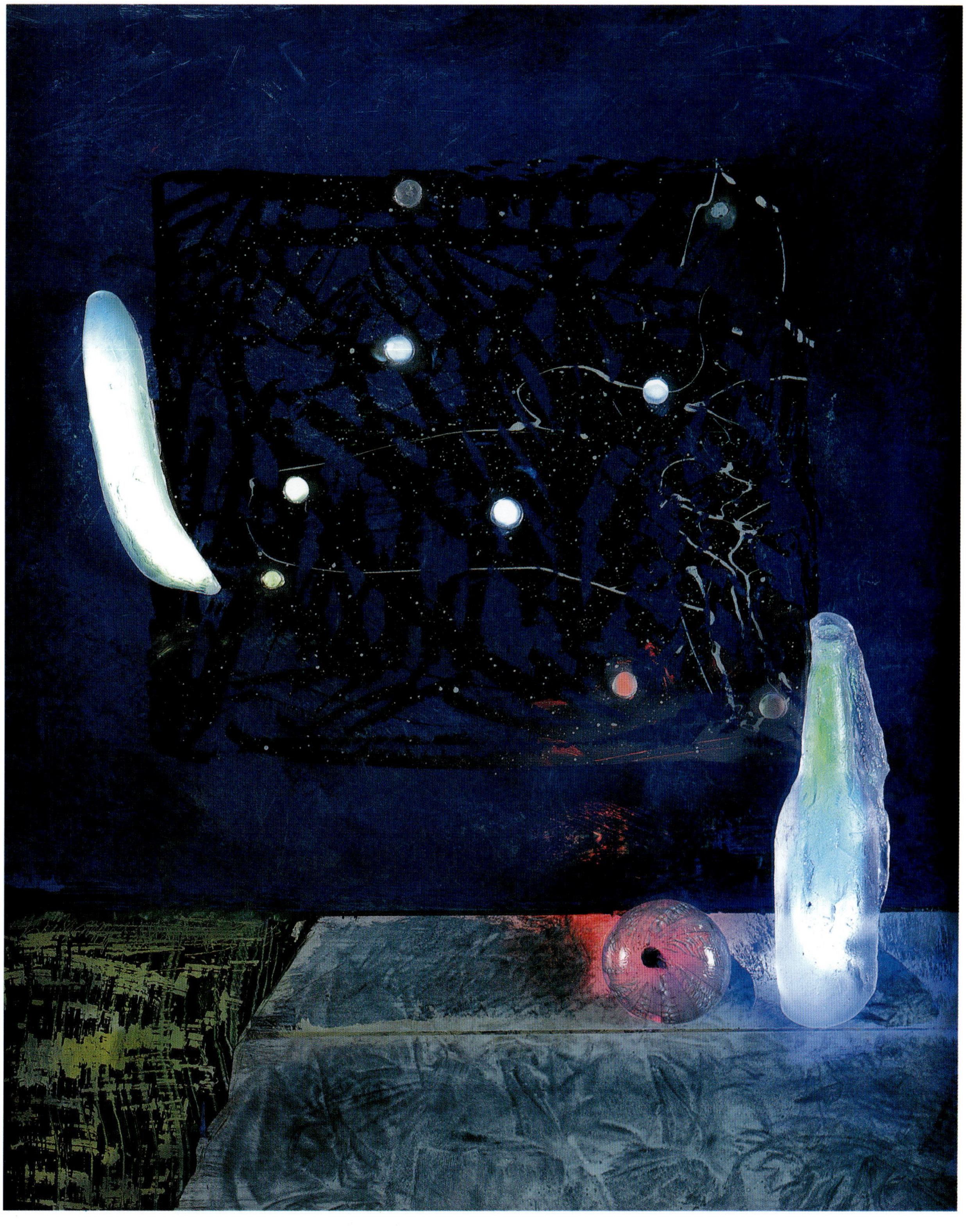

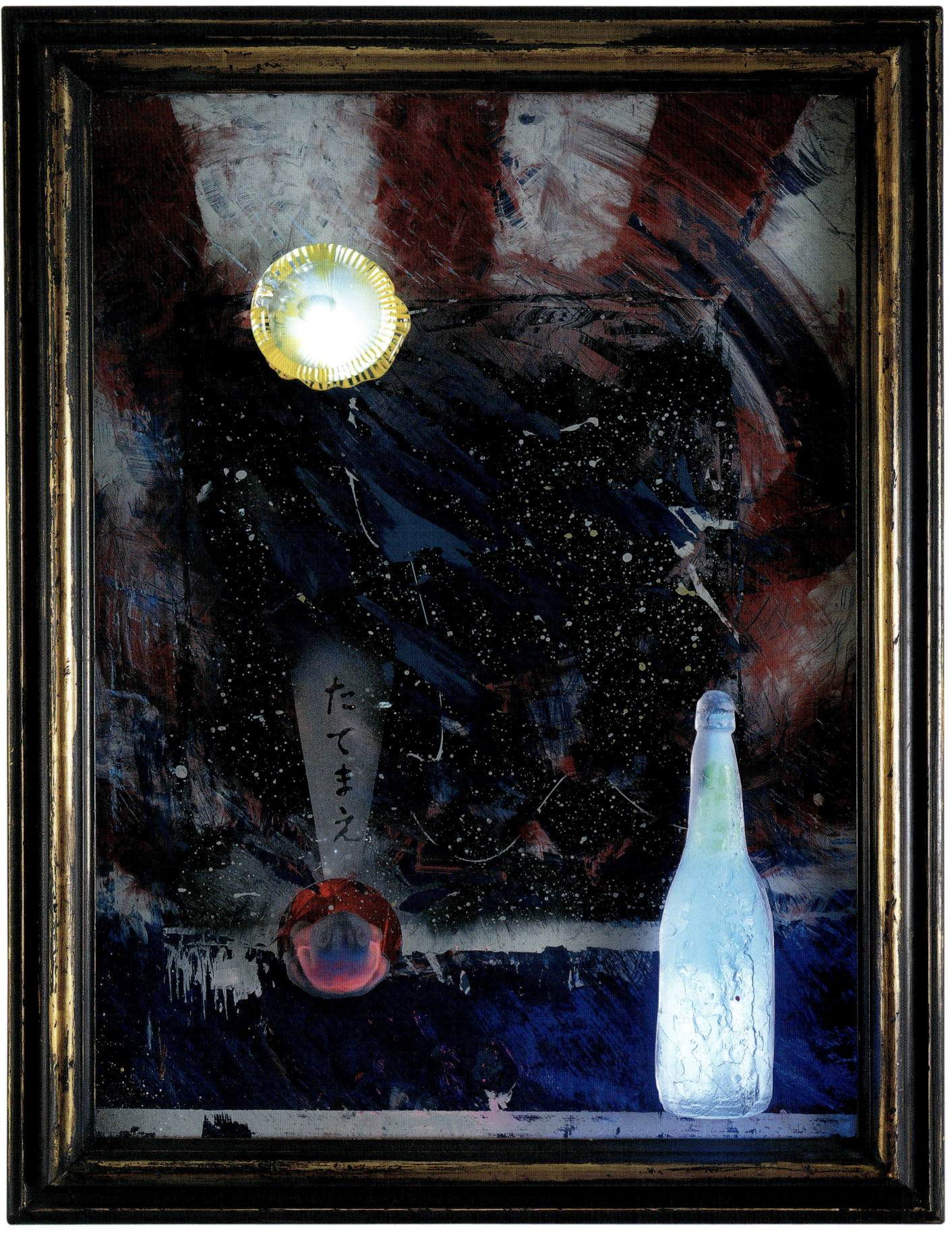

Nippon, (front view) 1999. Painted plate glass, and cast glass, h. 28 x 22 inches.

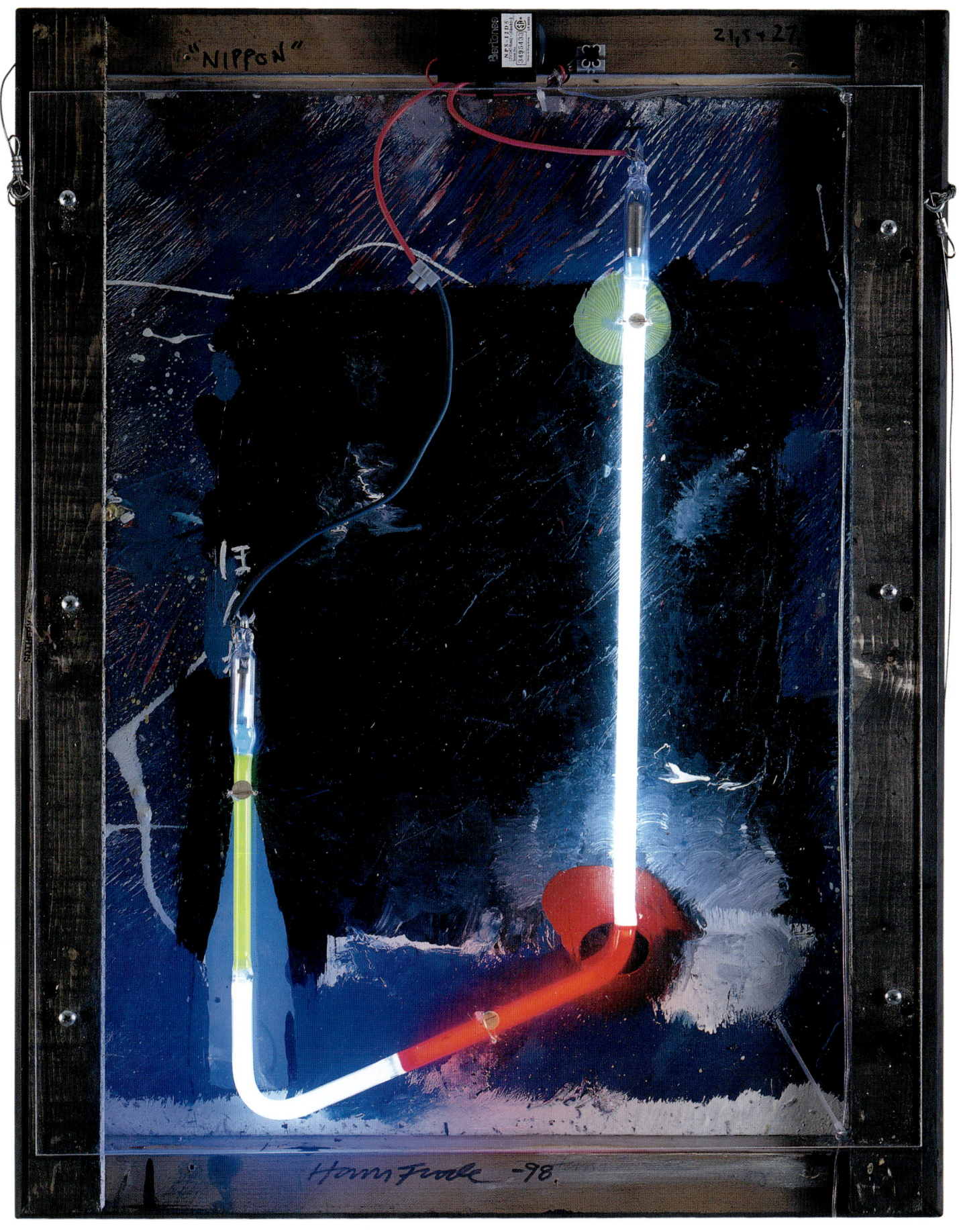

Nippon, (back view) 1999. Painted plate glass, cast glass, and neon tube, h. 28 x 22 inches.

Sandy Gellis
(b.1945)

NEW YORK, NEW YORK

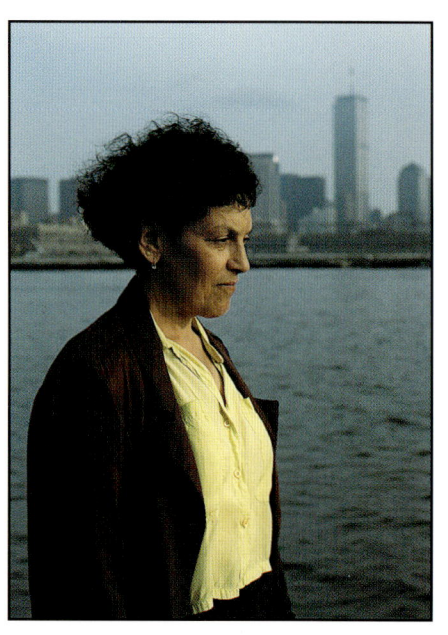

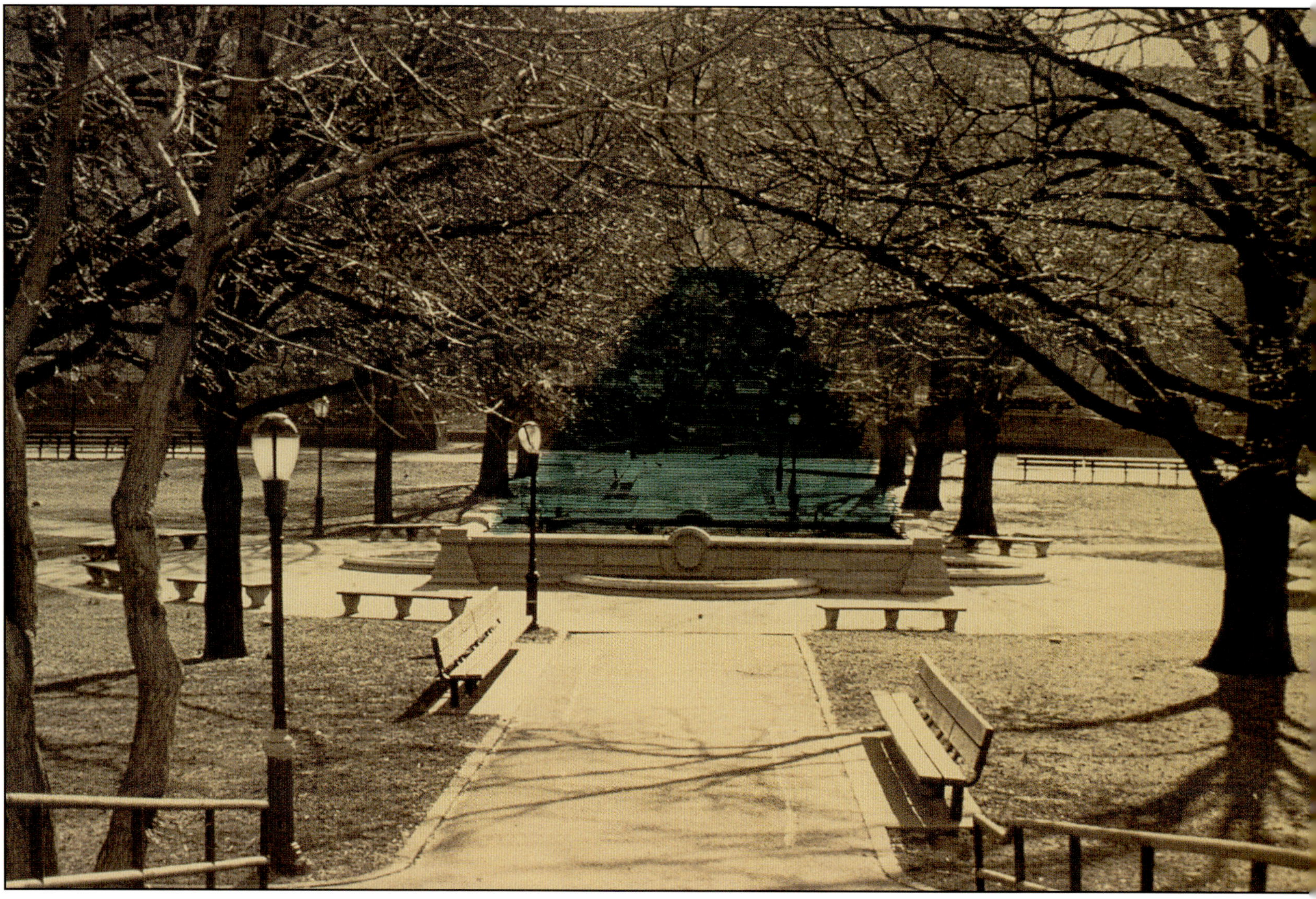

Glass Pyramid; Rain Fountain, (model) 1991. Glass, moss, and rain water, h. 18.75 x 14.5 inches. (proposed scale 1"=1')

REHOBOTH, MASSACHUSETTS # Michael M. Glancy
(b.1950)

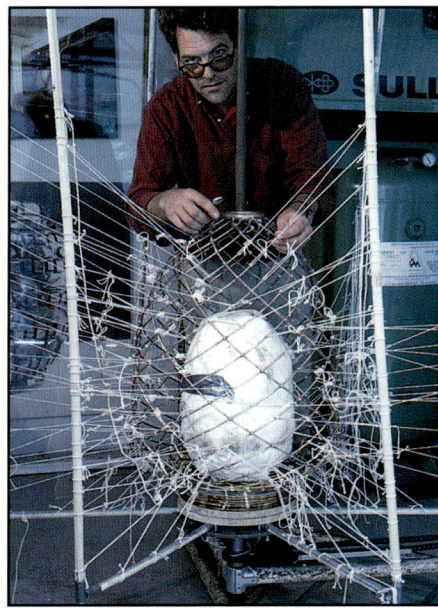

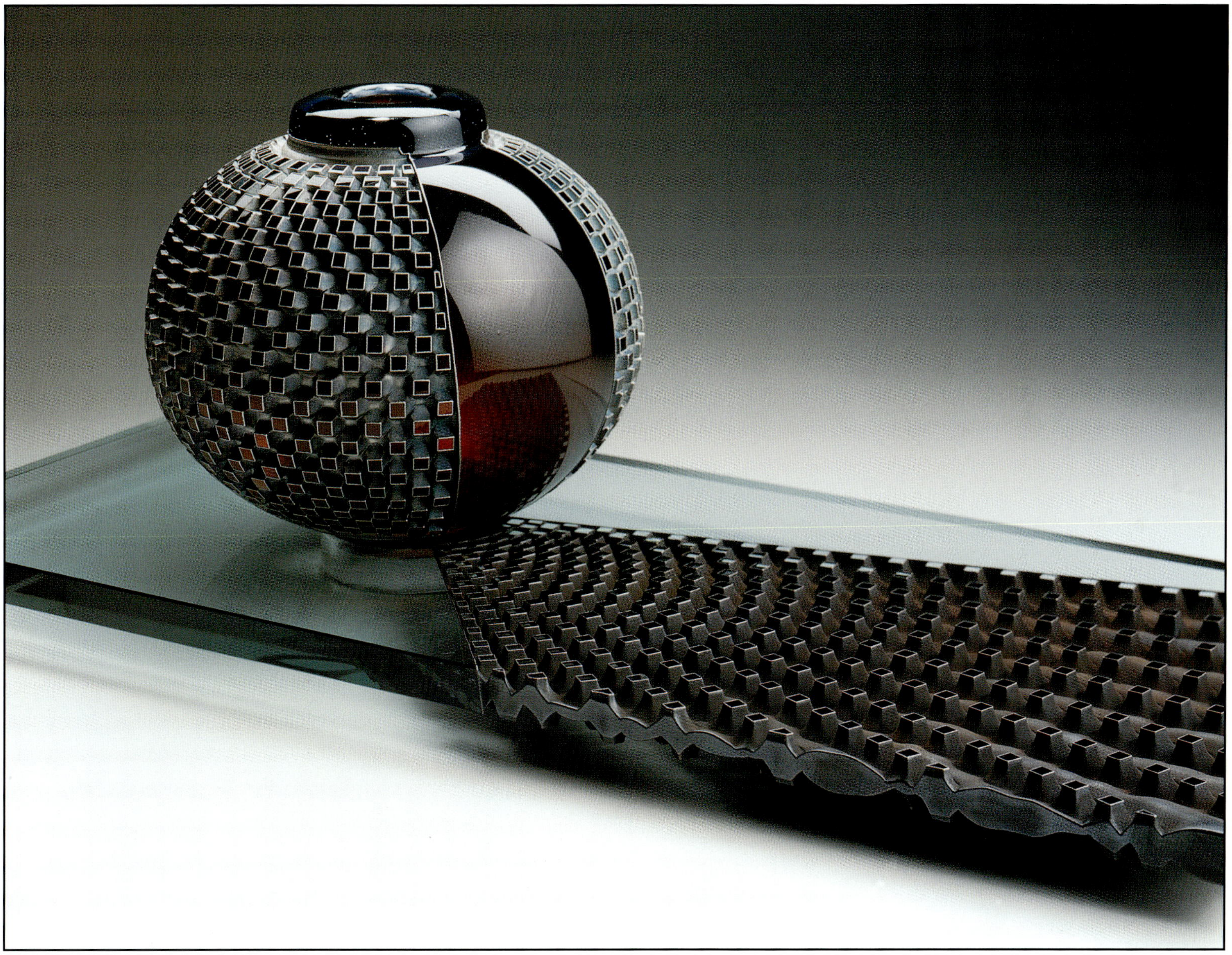

Magna Eclipsed, 1986. Blown glass, industrial plate glass, copper, and silver, h. 8 x 25 x 10 inches. Collection of Daniel Greenberg and Susan Steinhauser. Photo: Gene Dwiggins.

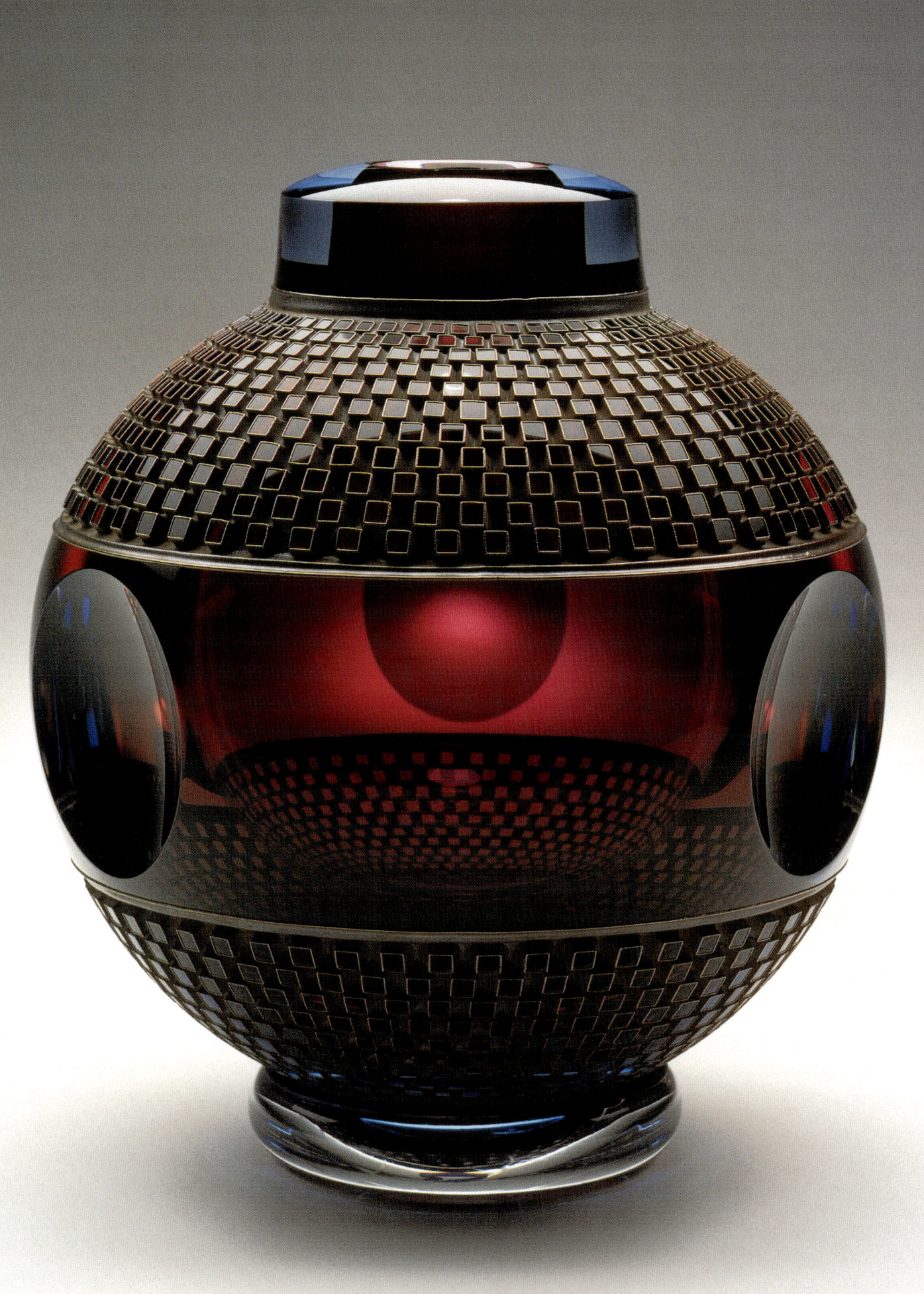

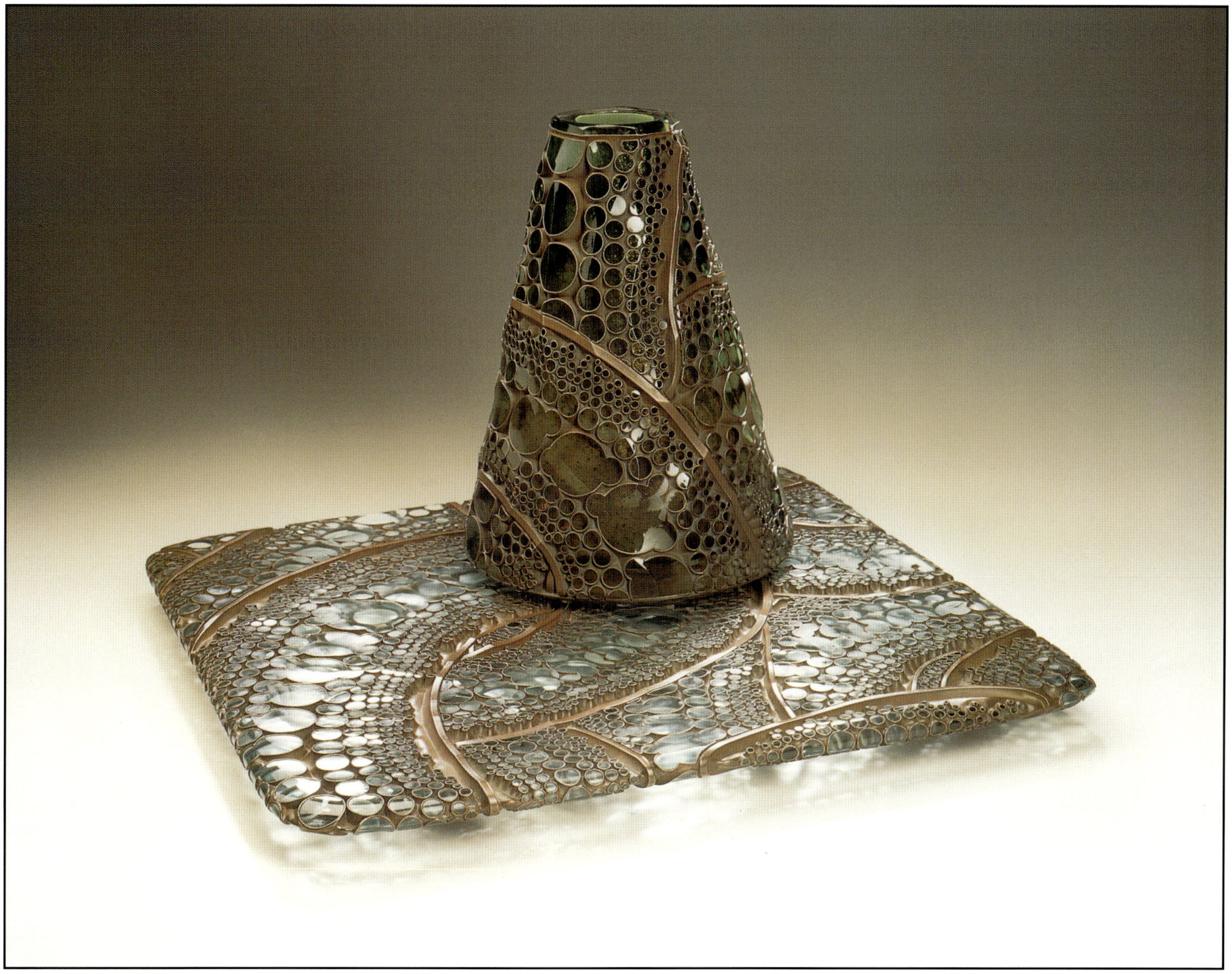

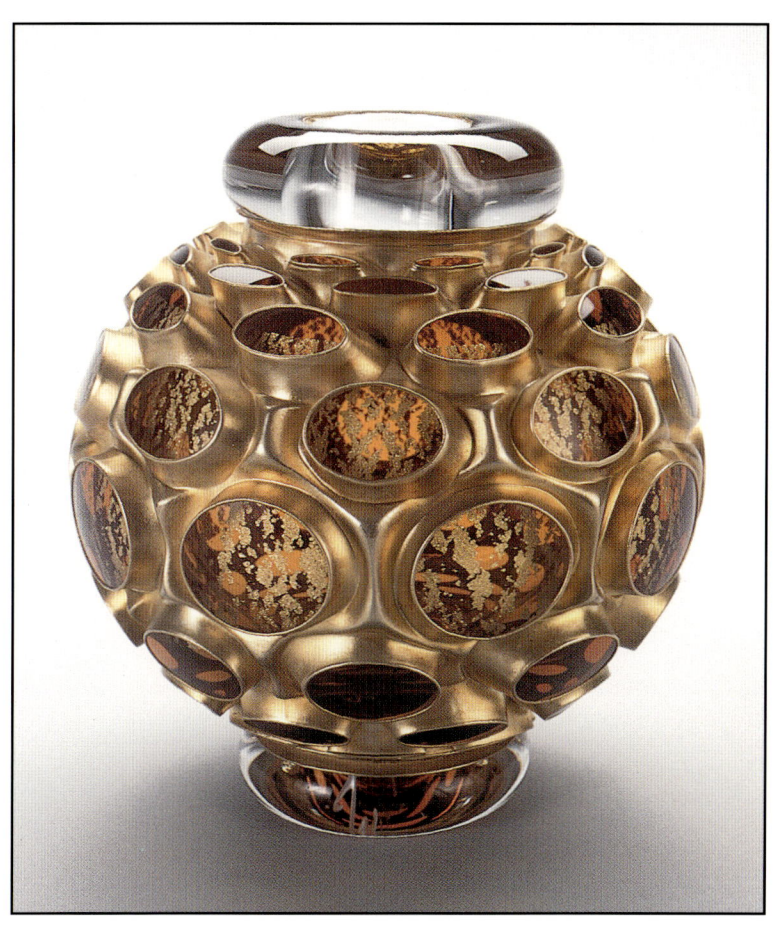

Opposite:
Dichroic Inside Out, 1997. Blown glass, engraved lenses, and copper, h. 9 x 7 x 7 inches. Collection of Barry Friedman.

Above:
Infinite Obsessions, 1999. Deeply engraved (Pompeii cut) blown glass, deeply engraved (Pompeii cut) industrial plate glass, and copper, h. 13 x 18 x 18 inches. Collection of Daniel Greenberg and Susan Steinhauser.

Right:
Golden Enigma, 1992. Blown glass, electroformed copper, and gold electroplating, h. 7 x 6.75 inches. Charles A. Wustum Museum of Fine Arts, Racine, Wisconsin. Gift of Dale and Doug Anderson.

Alan Glovsky
(b.1951)

BROOKLYN, NEW YORK

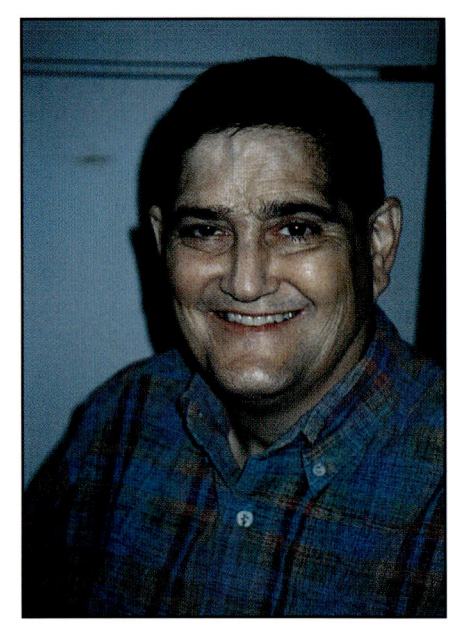

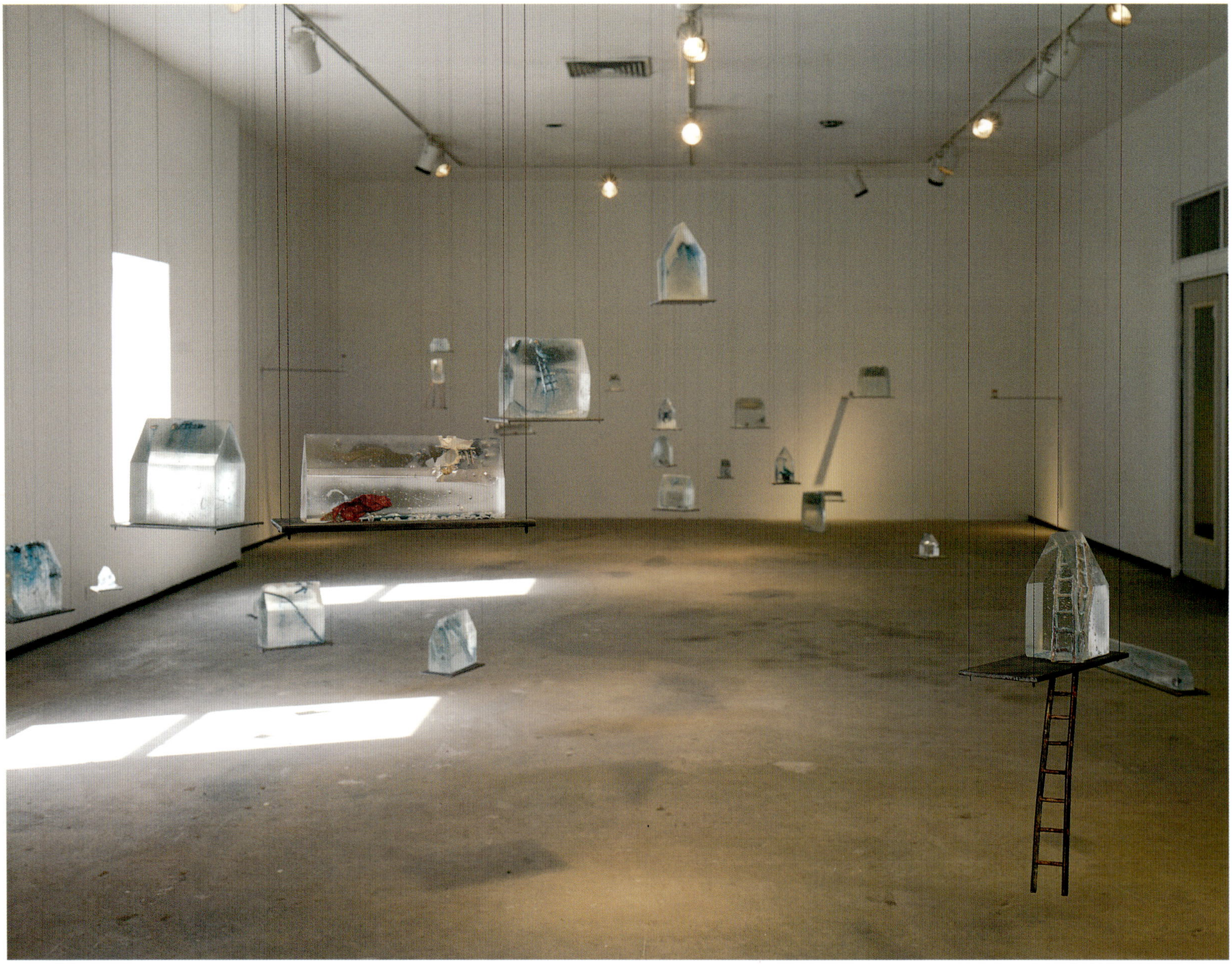

Alan Glovsky

Above:
Mi Casa Es Tu Casa; 1997. Installation, Robert Lehman Gallery, UrbanGlass. Copper elements in cast glass houses, stainless steel cable, shelves, and steel swings. Photo: Kevin Noble.

Opposite:
Jacob's Ladder I, 1997. Copper elements in cast glass house, steel plate, and stainless steel cable, h. 16 x 3 x 3 inches. Collection of Geoffrey J. Isles. Photo: Kevin Noble.

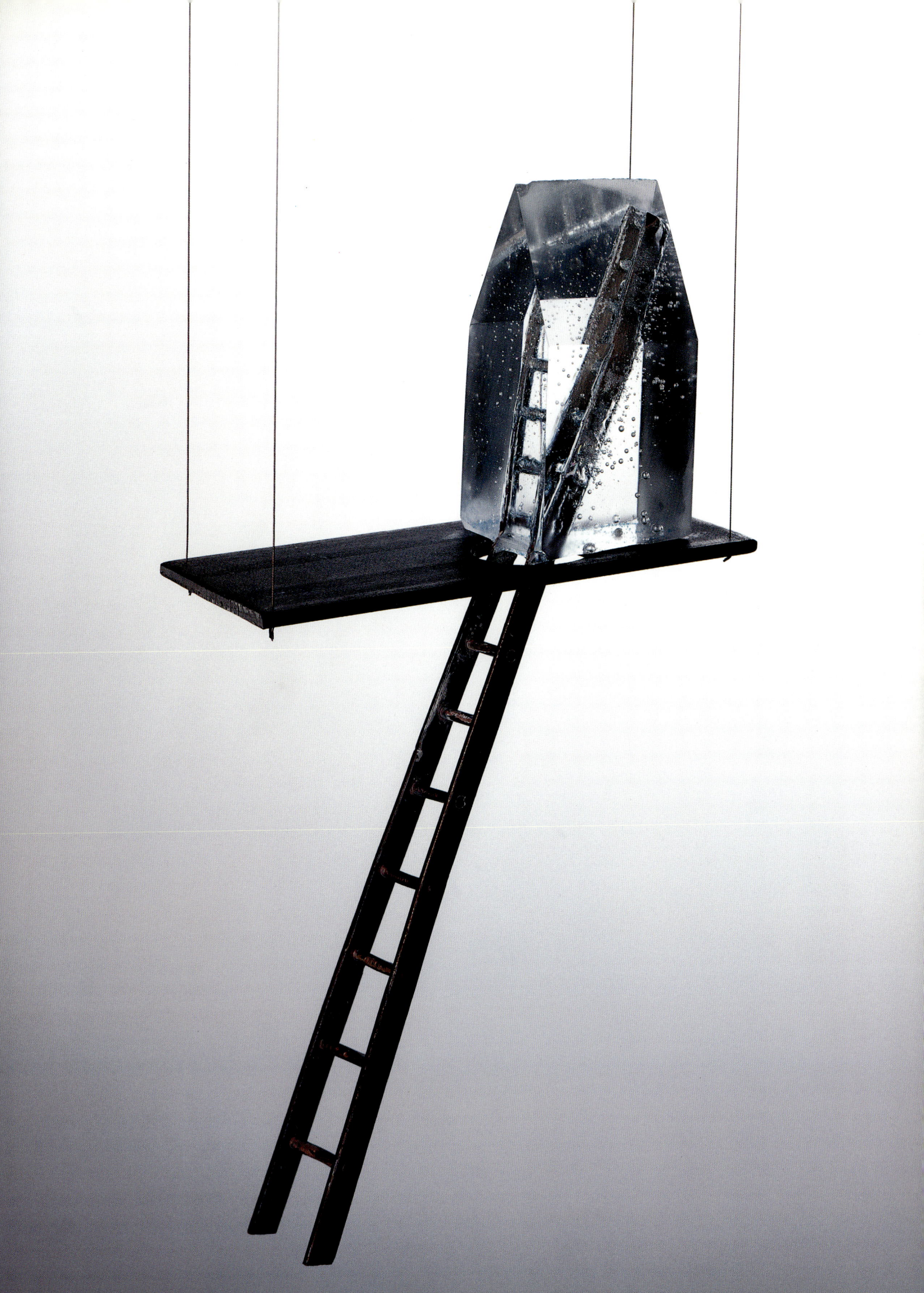

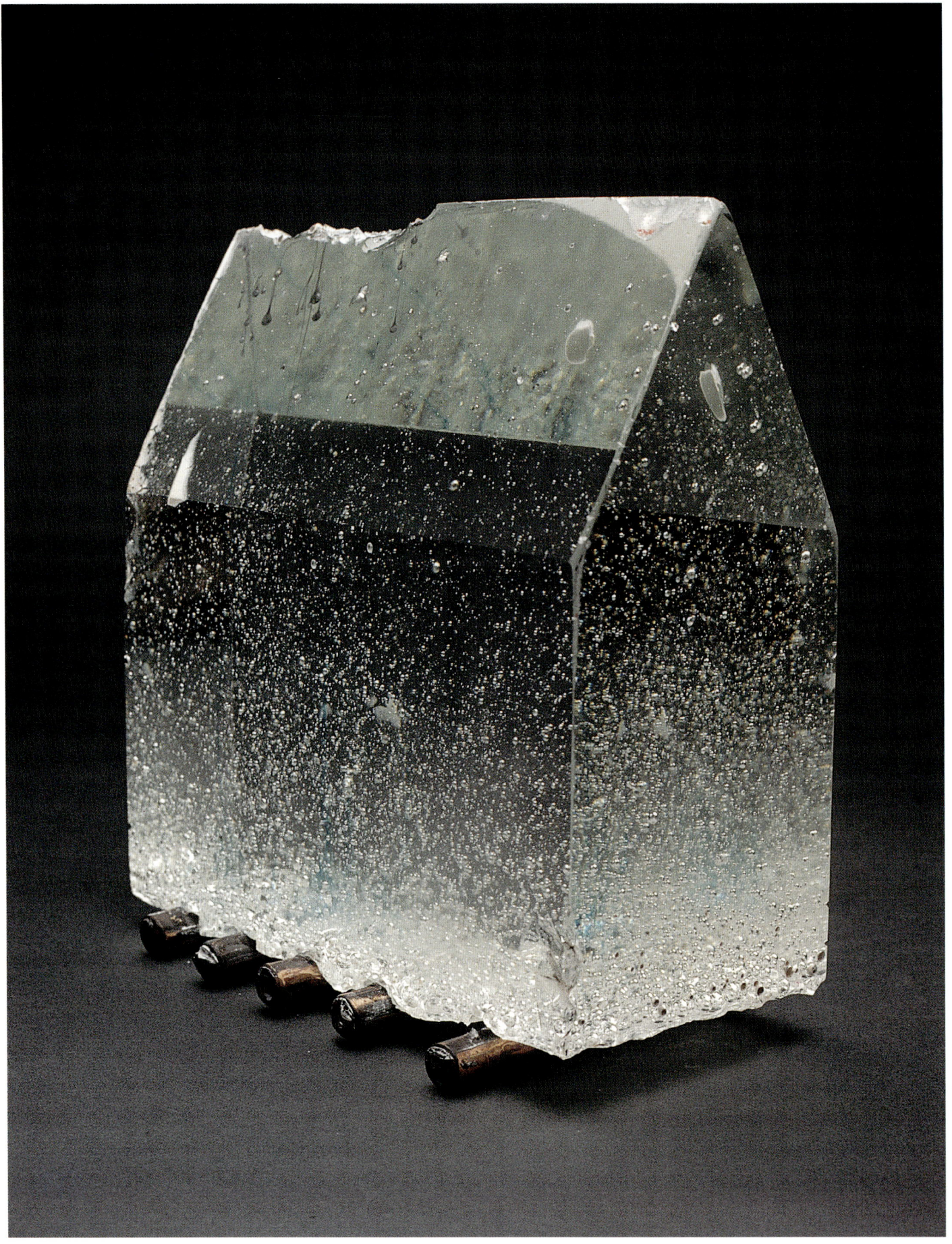

Rolling On, 1998. Copper and silver elements embedded in a cast glass house, h. 8 x 19 x 5 inches. Photo: Kevin Noble.

BURLINGTON, VERMONT

Alan Goldfarb
(b.1959)

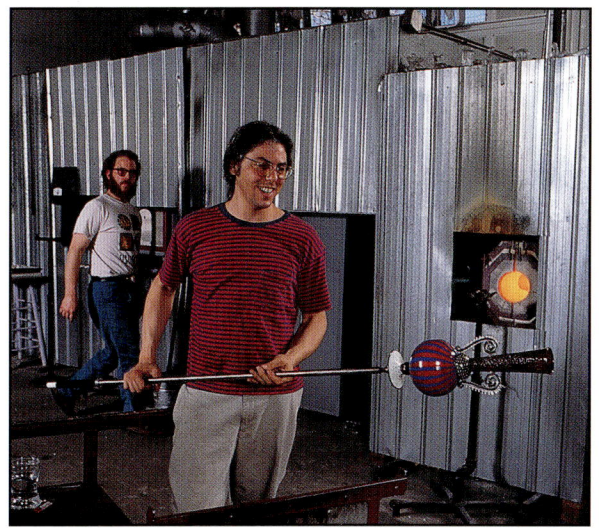

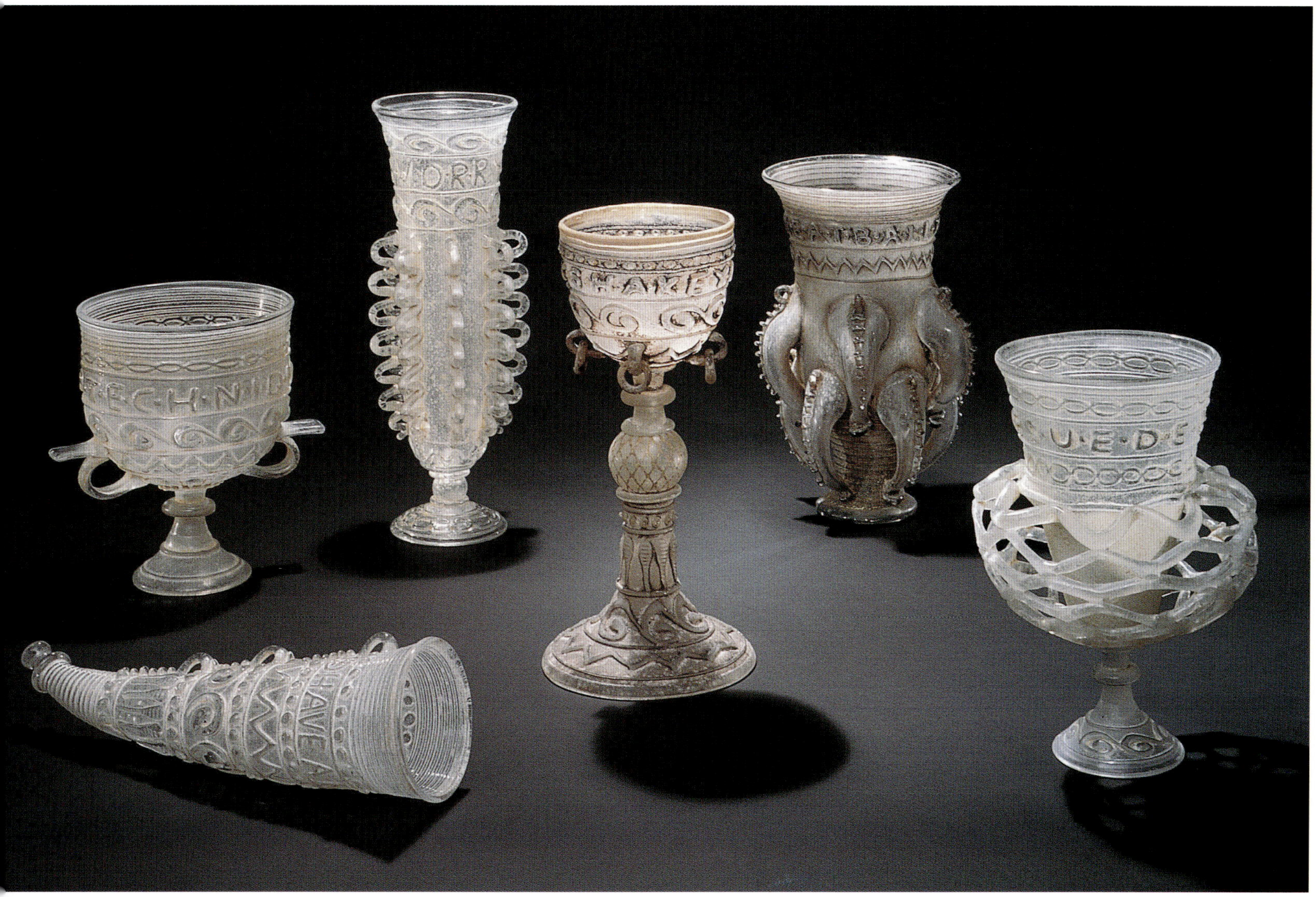

Historical Revisions; Archeo-Pop Series, *1998.*
Blown glass and trailed glass lettering, h. 20 inches.

Robin Grebe
(b.1957)

SOUTH CHATHAM, MASSACHUSETTS

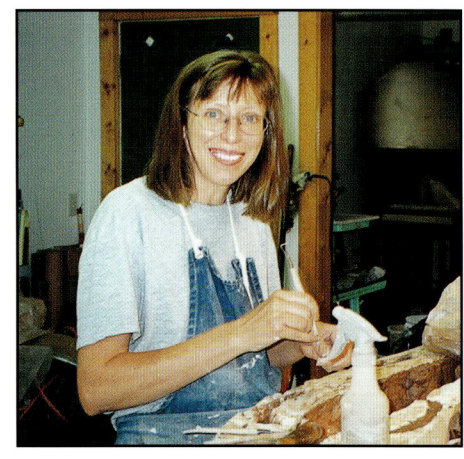

Protector, 1998. Pâte de verre, and mixed media, h. 30 x 15 x 7 inches.

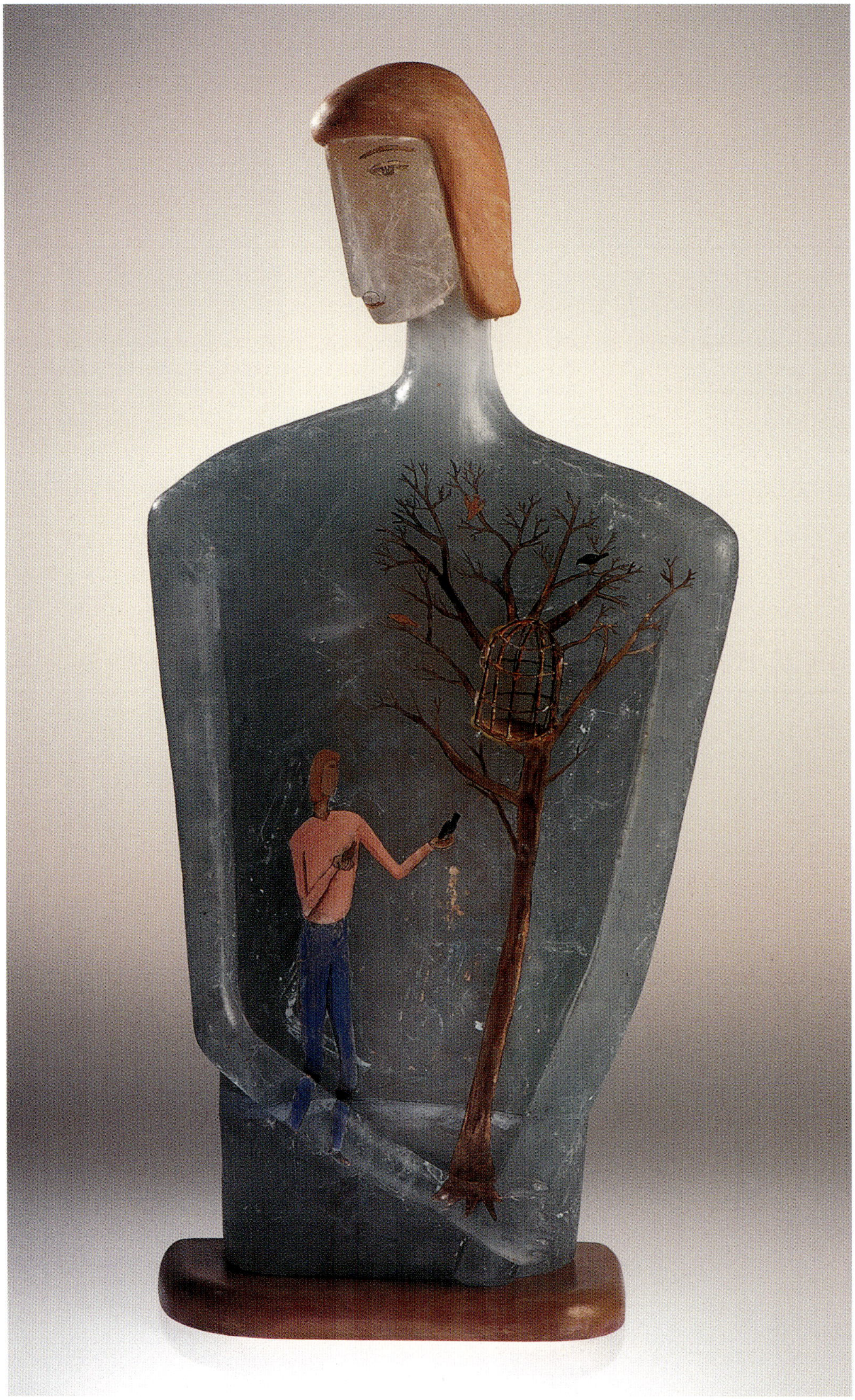

NEW YORK, NEW YORK

Nils Grossien
(b. 1954)

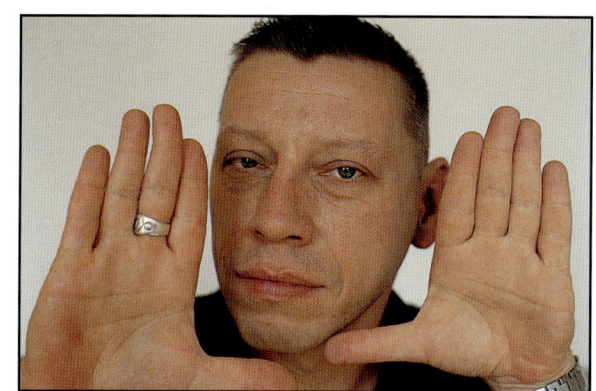

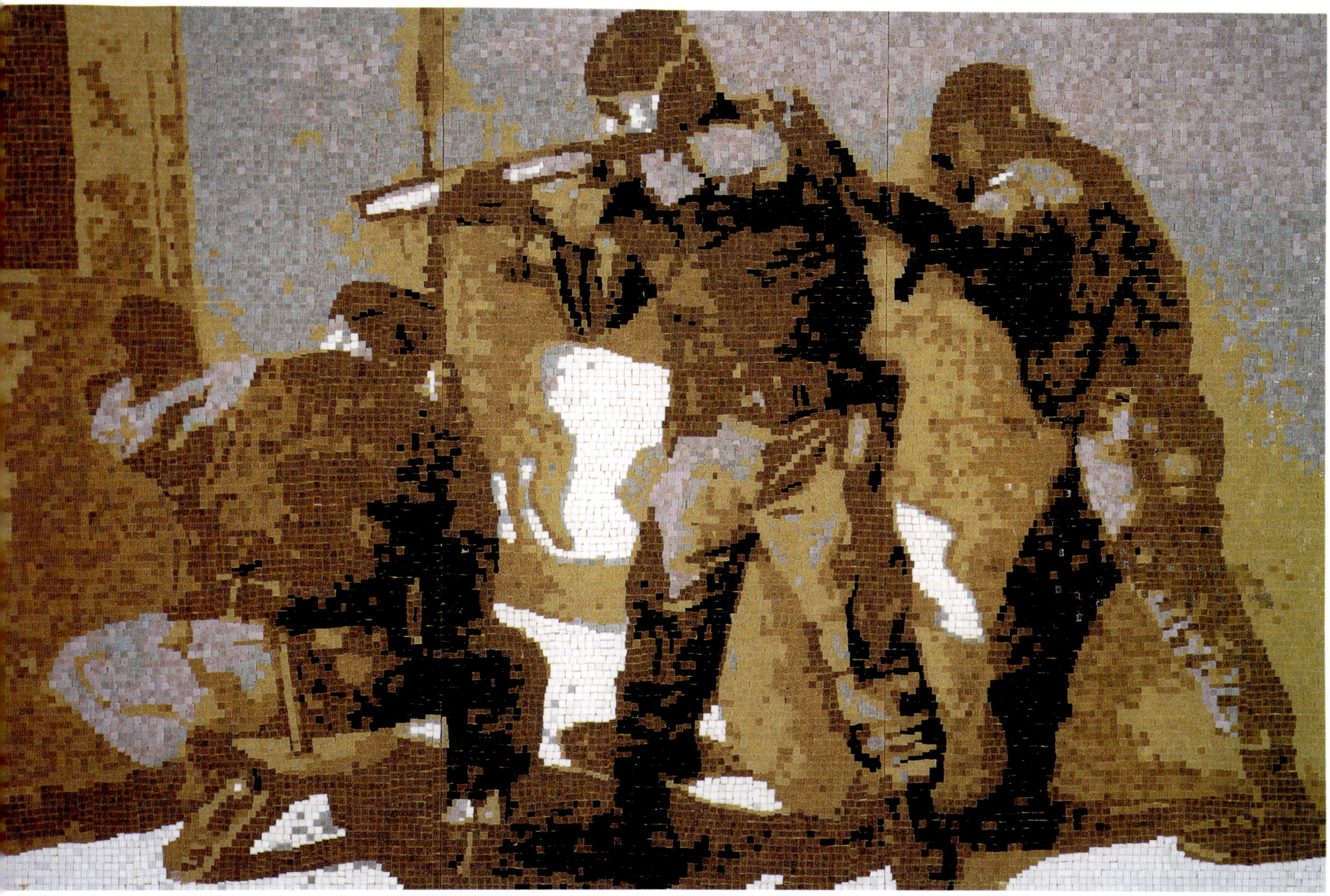

SWAT–Team; News series, *1996. Mexican mosaic glass on wood panel, h. 50 x 72 inches. Photo: Robert Puglisi.*

NILS GROSSIEN

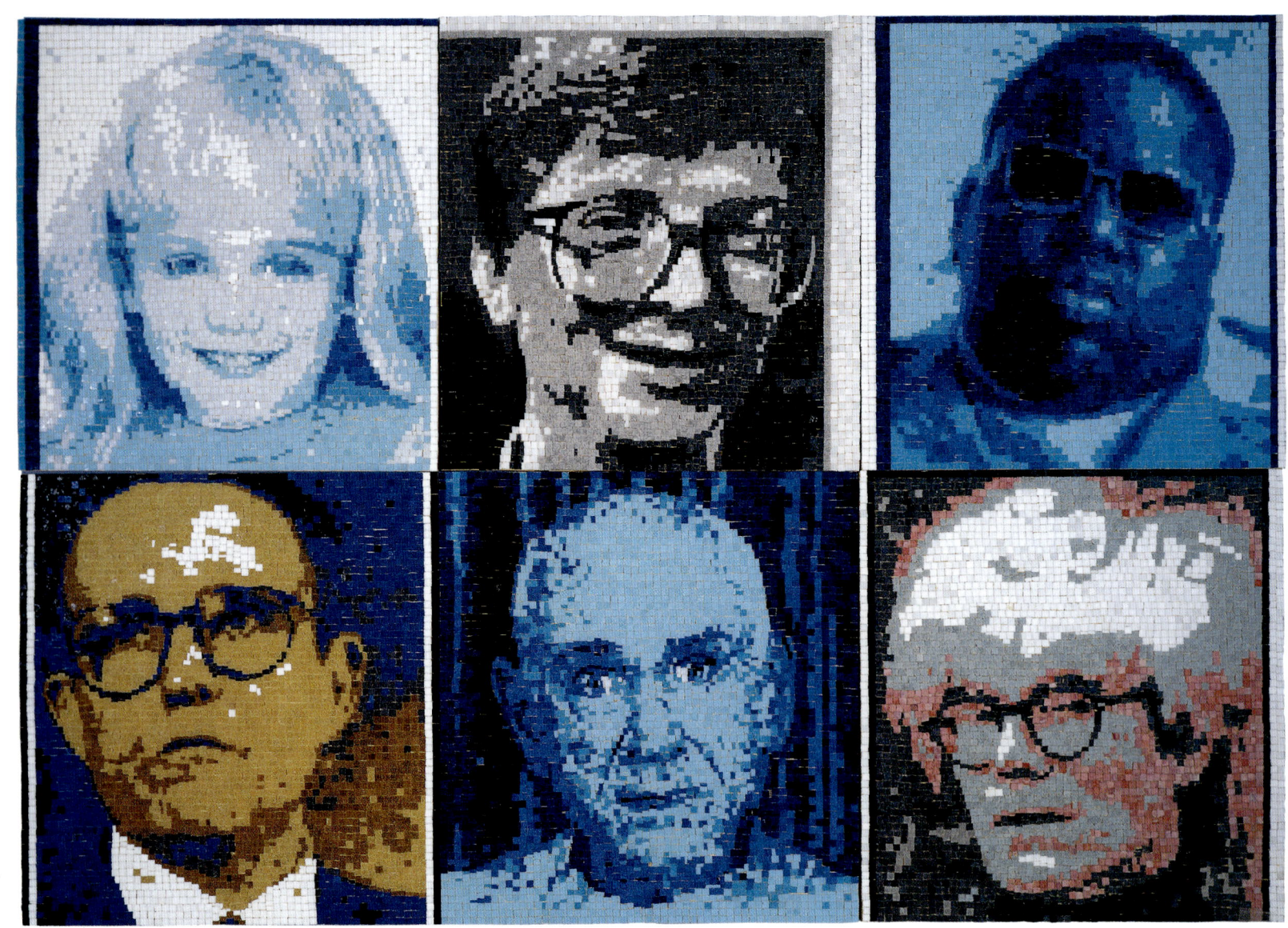

***JonBenet, Bill, B.I.G., Rudy, Do, Andy; American Faces
series***, *1995-98. Mexican mosaic glass on wood panel,
each image h. 25 x 23 inches. Photo: Robert Puglisi.*

CORNING, NEW YORK

William Gudenrath
(b. 1950)

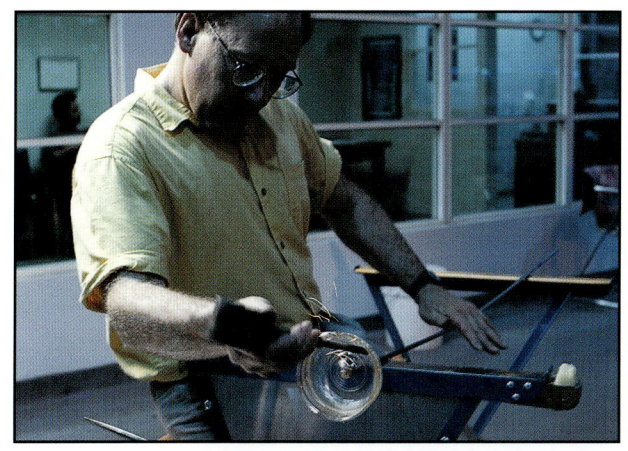

Dragon and Dolphin Stemmed Goblets, 1999.
Blown glass, h. 12 inches. Photo: Nick Williams.

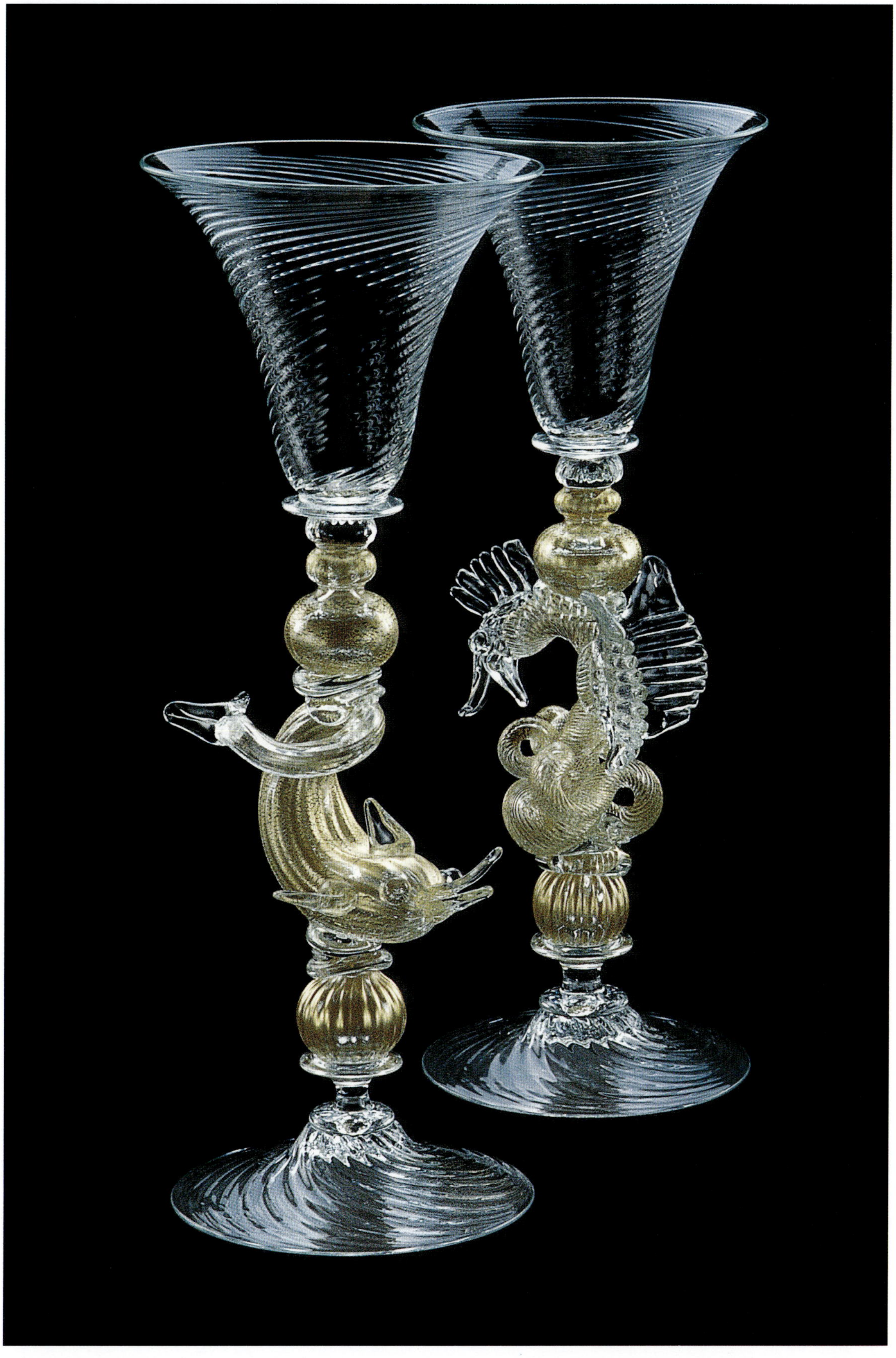

83

Monica Guggisberg & Philip Baldwin
(b. 1955)   (b. 1947)

NONFOUX, SUISSE

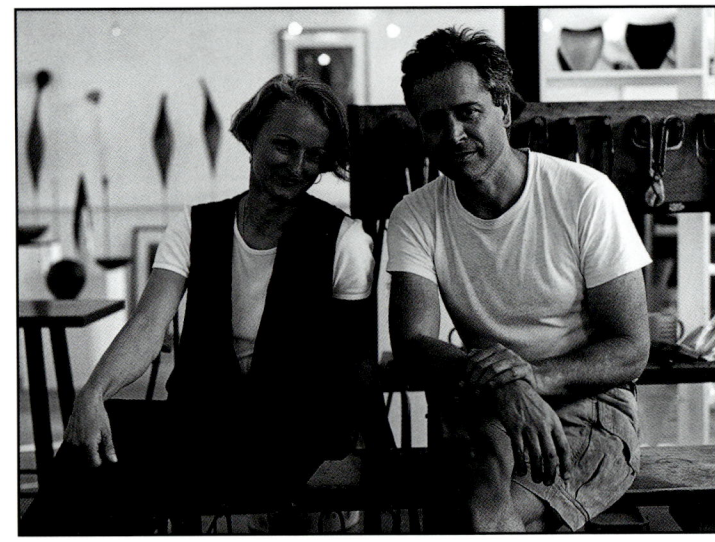

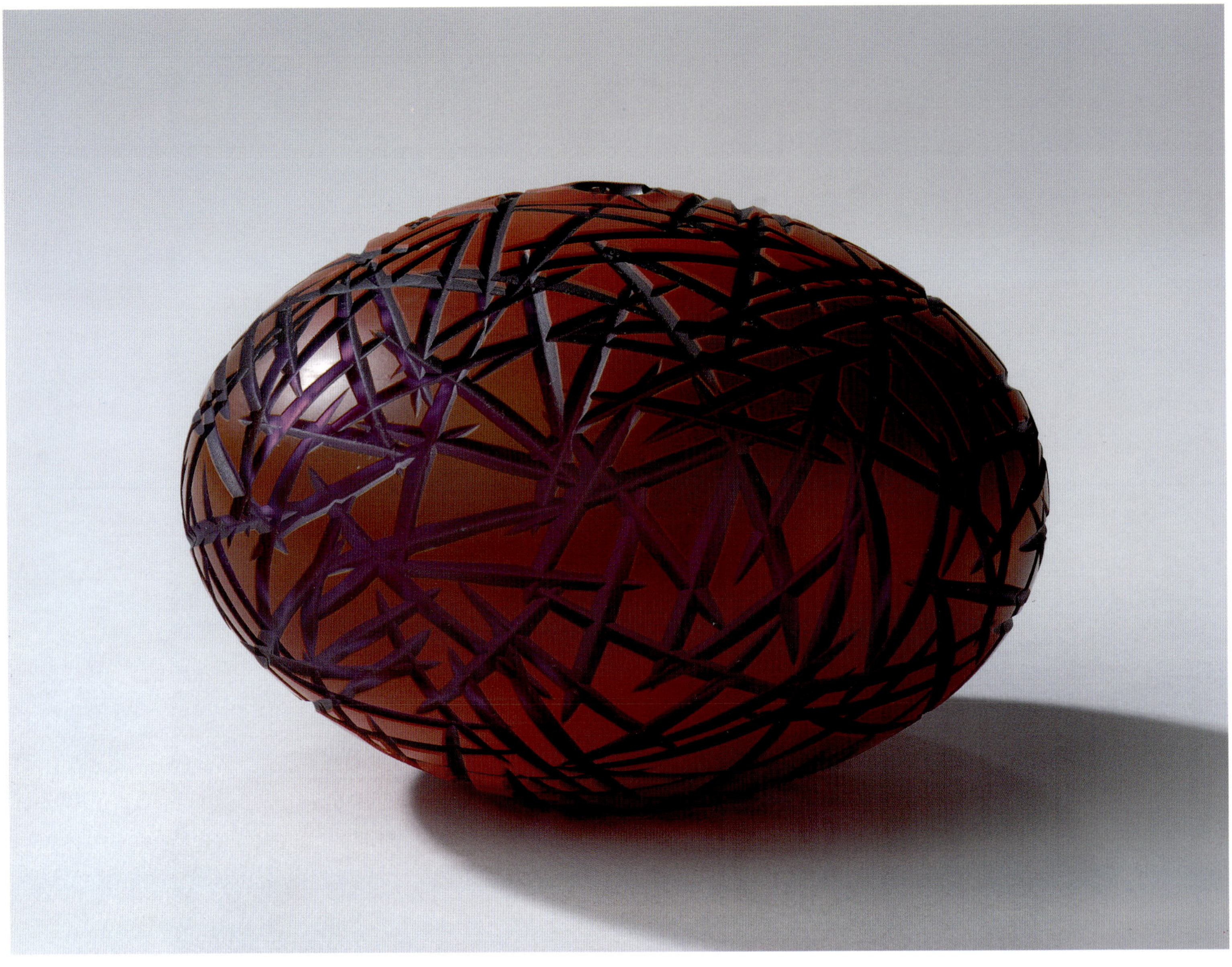

Above:
Red Watcher; Thorn Cuts, 1999. Blown engraved glass, h. 11.2 x 12.8 inches.

Opposite:
Cortigiana Gialla con; Guardiani e Figura, 1998-99. Blown engraved glass, and metal stands, h. 38 x 7.2 inches. Photo: Christophe Lehmann.

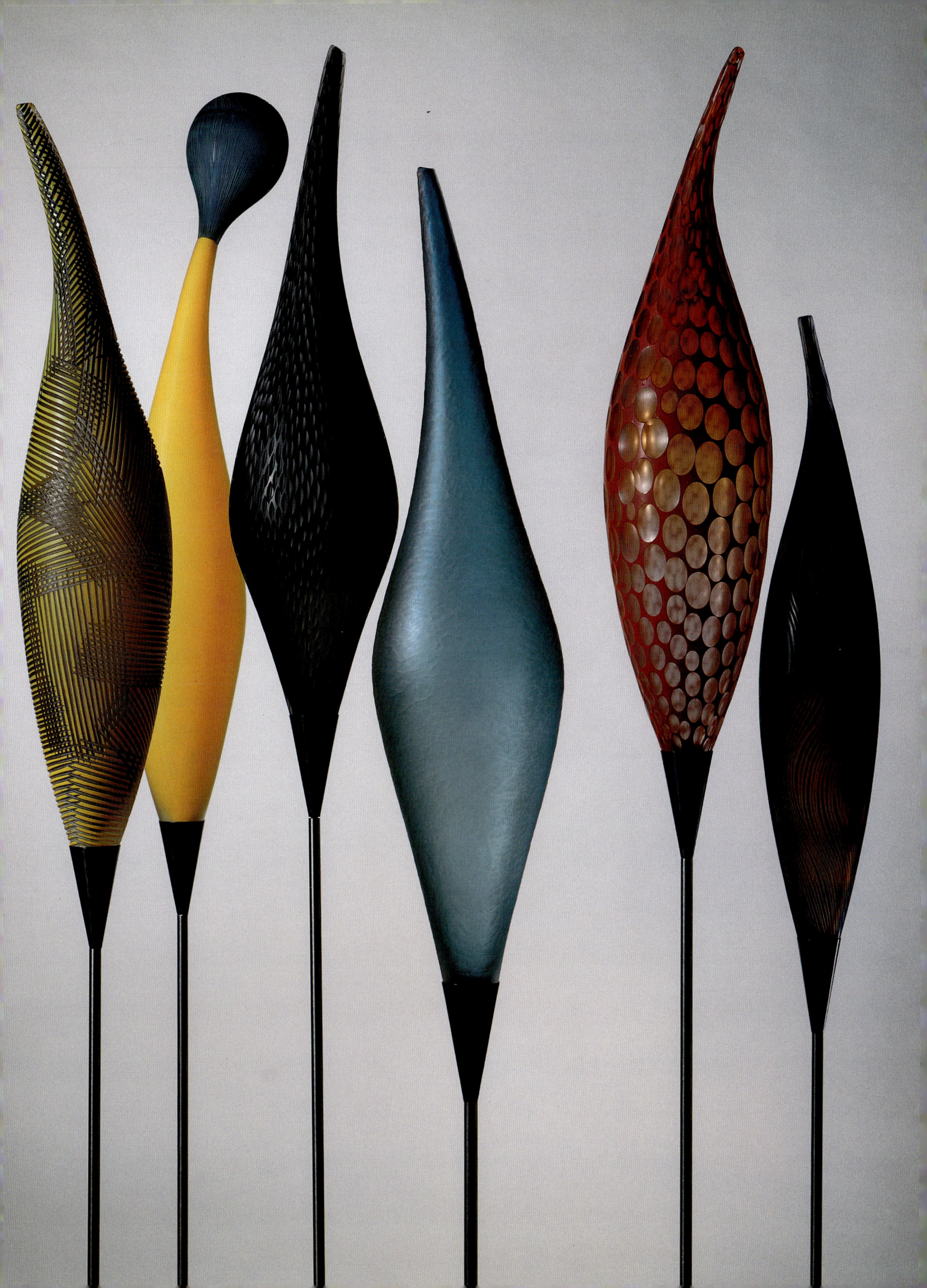

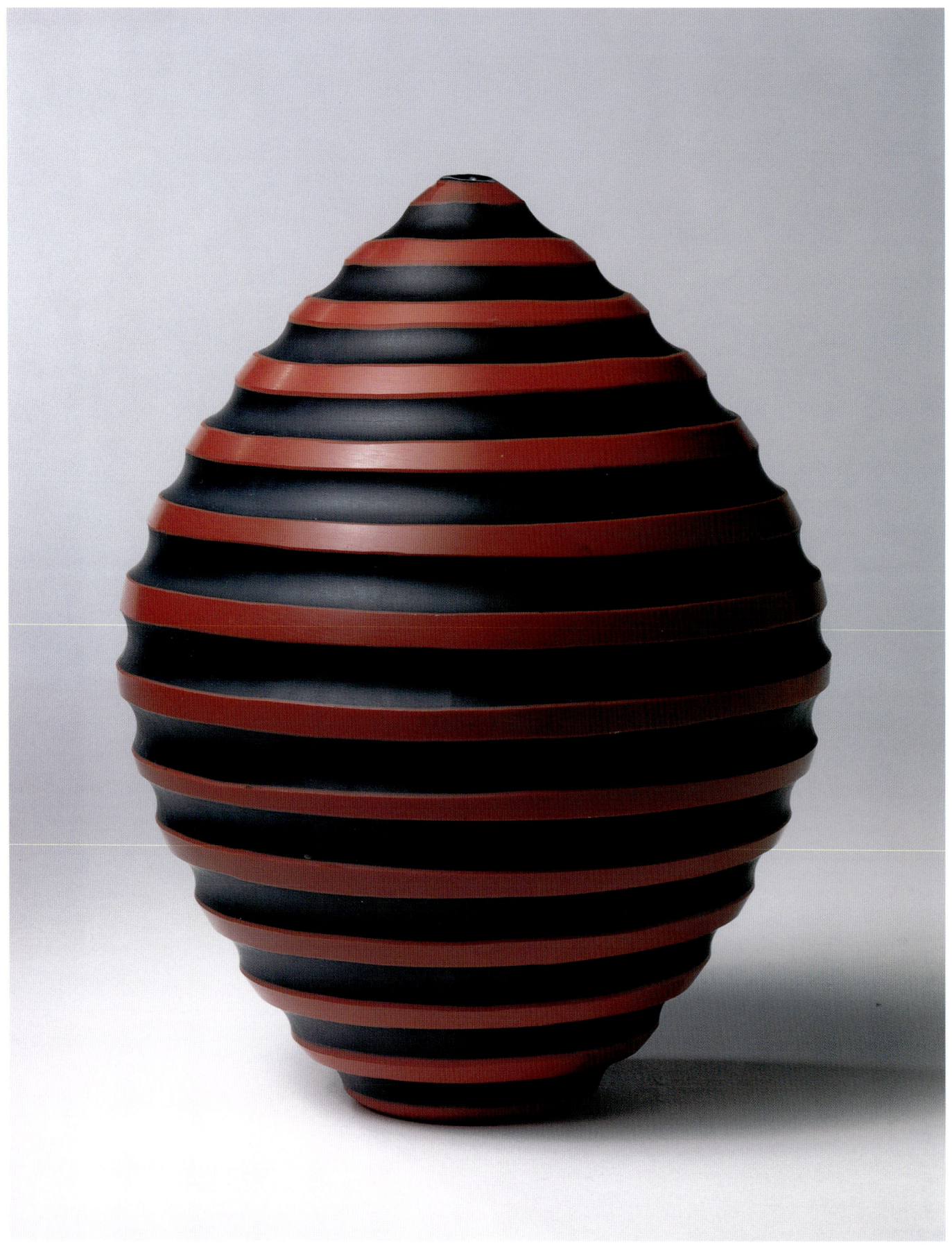

Red + Black Horizontal Sentinel, 1999.
Blown engraved glass, h. 17 x 11.6 inches.

NEW YORK, NEW YORK

Dorothy Hafner
(b.1952)

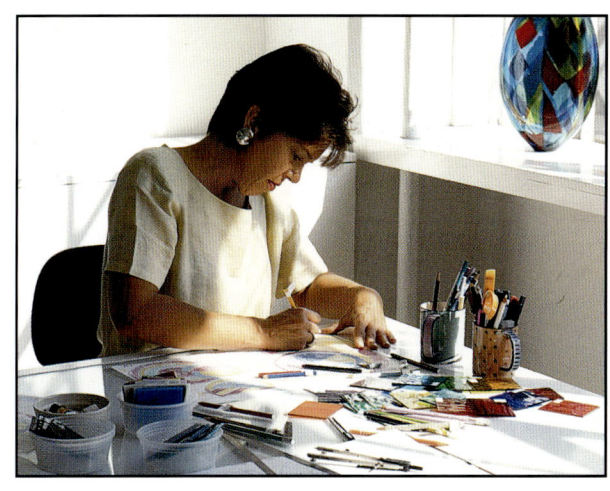

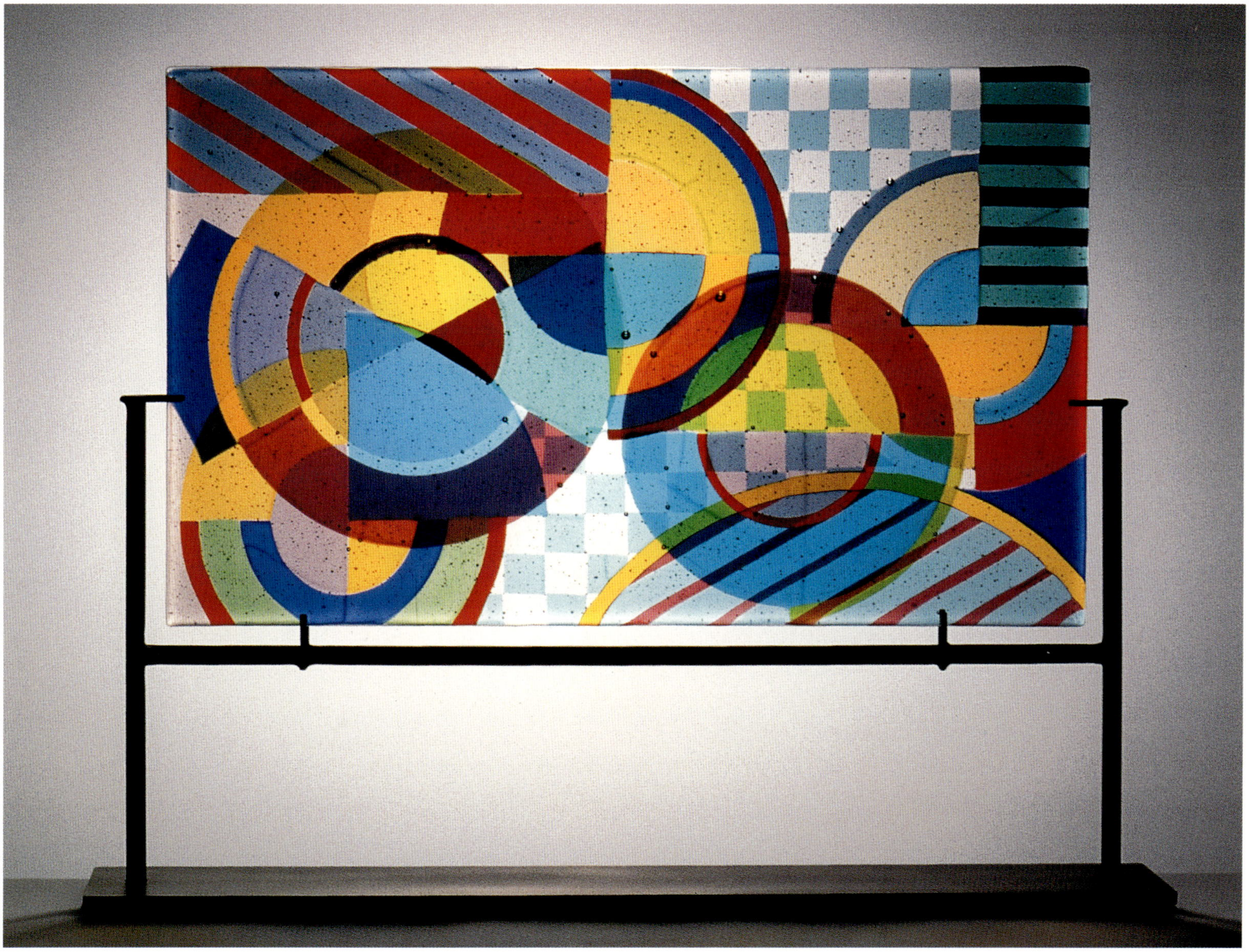

Tantalus, 1998. Six-layer fused glass panel with metal stand, h. 15.5 x 20 inches with stand. Photo: George Erml.

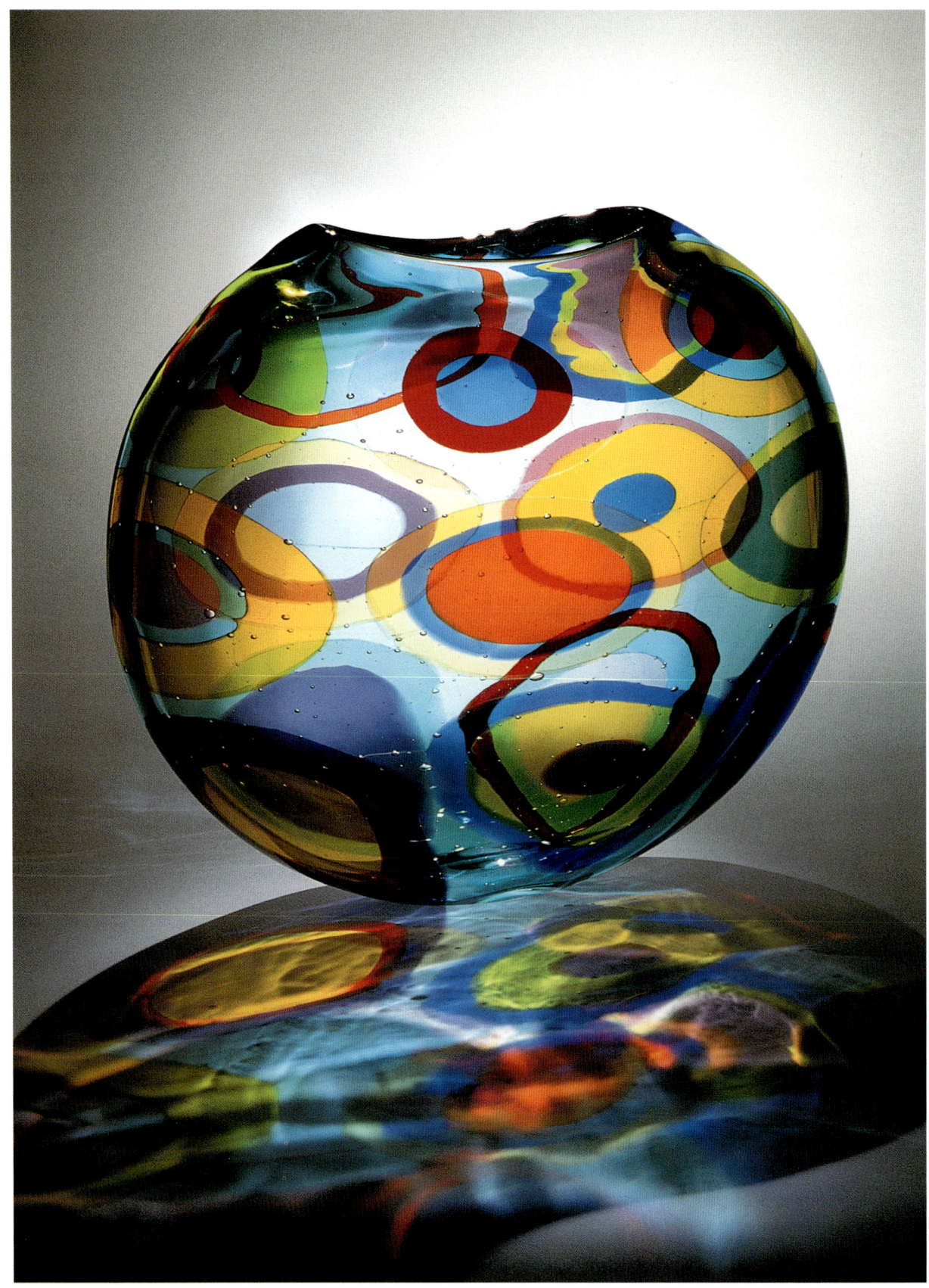

Above:
Agua Bullseyes, 1997. Flat glass cutouts rolled onto clear blown form, h. 12.5 x 13.5 x 5.5 inches. Created with the assistance of Lino Tagliapietra. Photo: George Erml.

Opposite:
Metronome, 1998. Six-layer fused glass panel with metal stand, h. 24.5 x 14.5 inches with stand. Photo: George Erml.

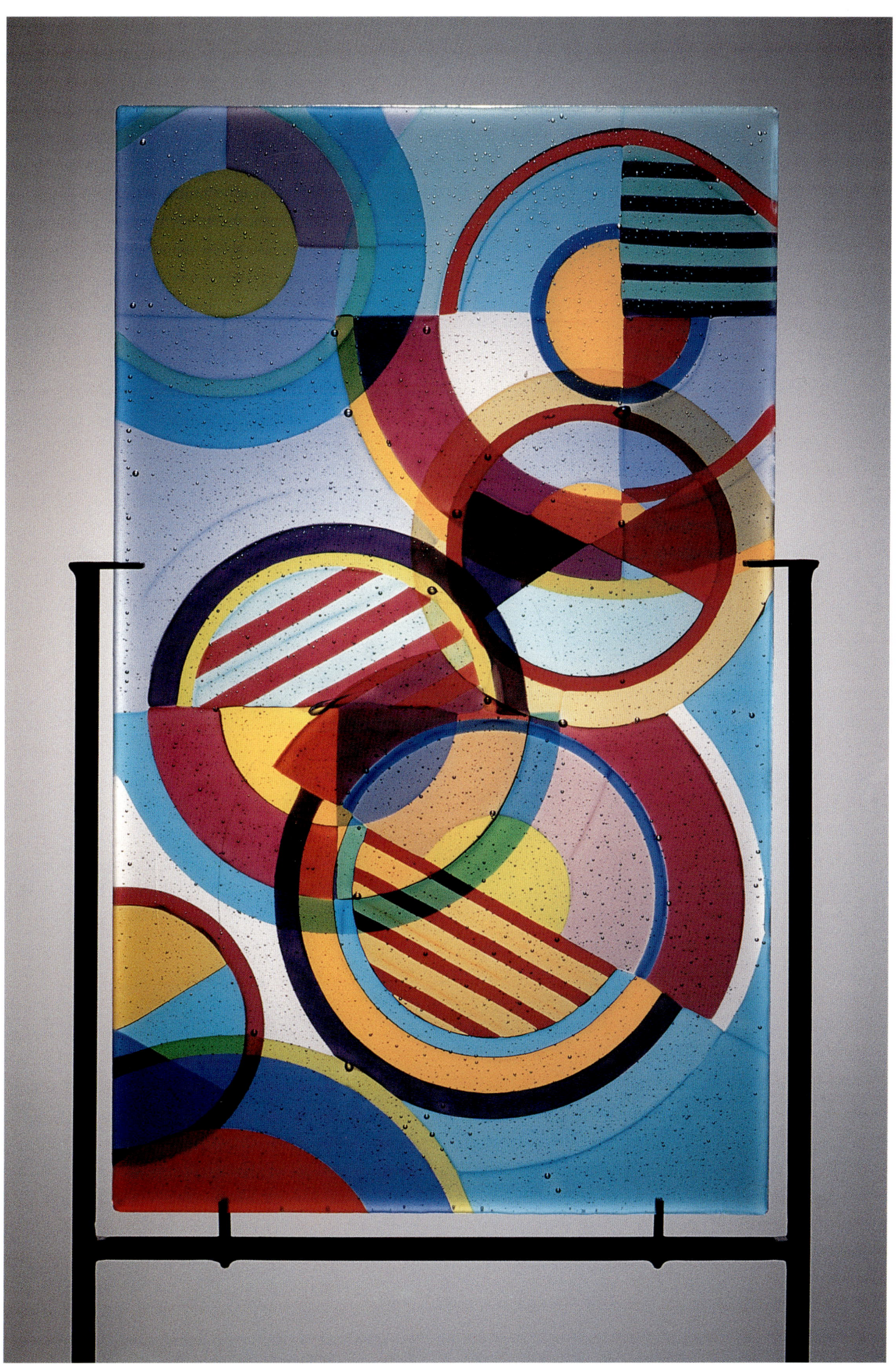

Henry Halem
(b.1938)

KENT, OHIO

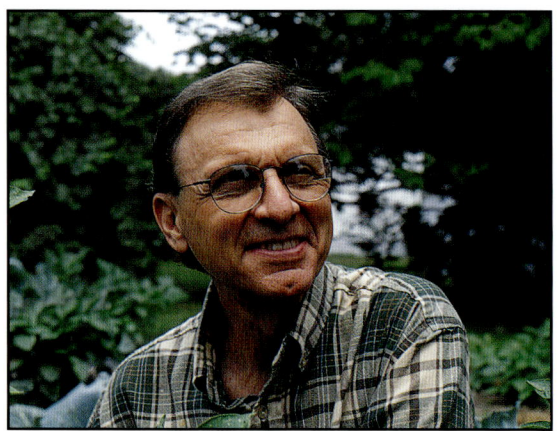

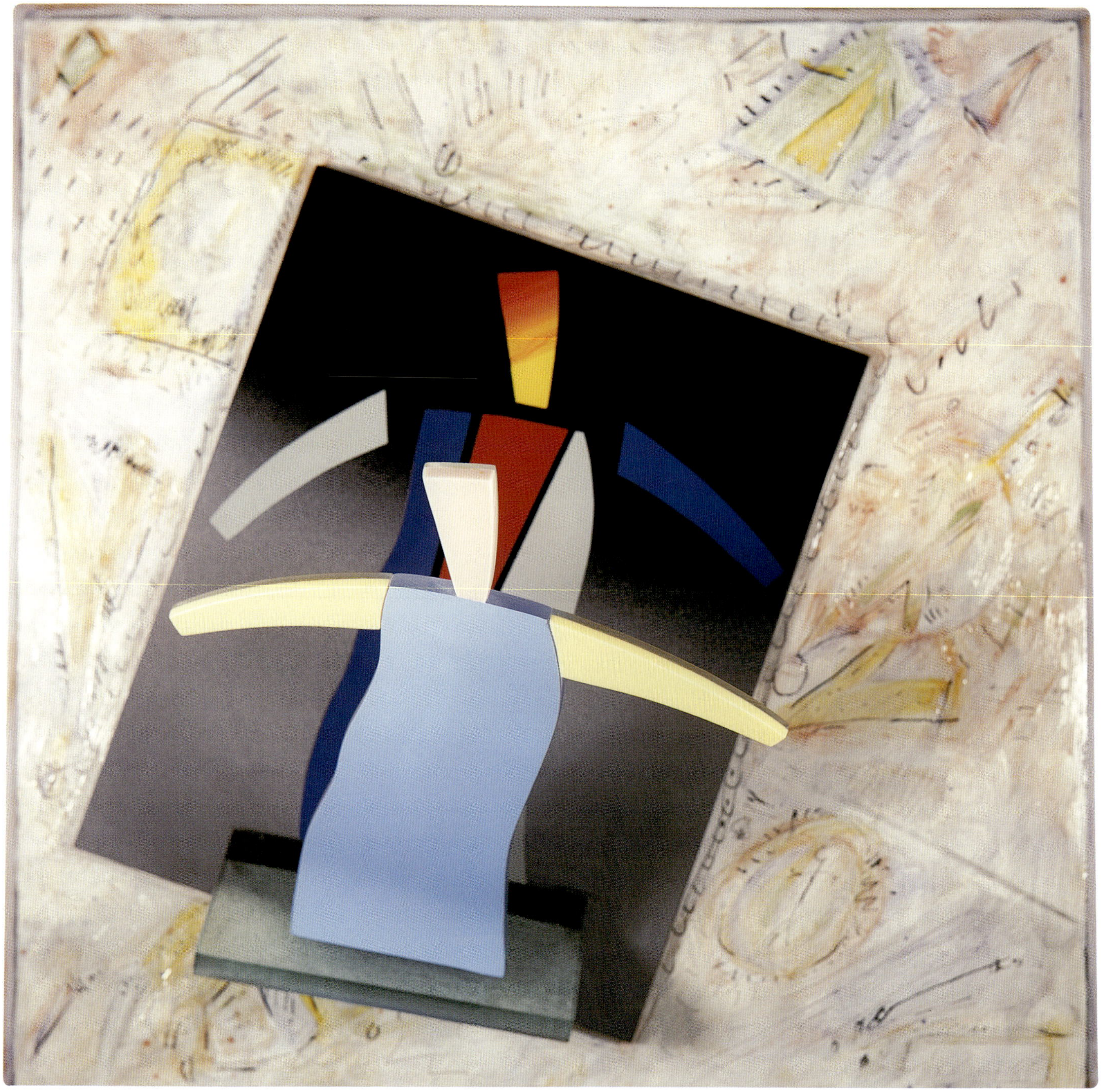

Falling Man, 1992. Cut, polished, assembled and sandblasted structural plate glass, black structural plate glass, and kiln-fired enamels, h. 24 x 24 x 13 inches. Charles A. Wustum Museum of Fine Arts, Racine, Wisconsin. Gift of Dale and Doug Anderson.

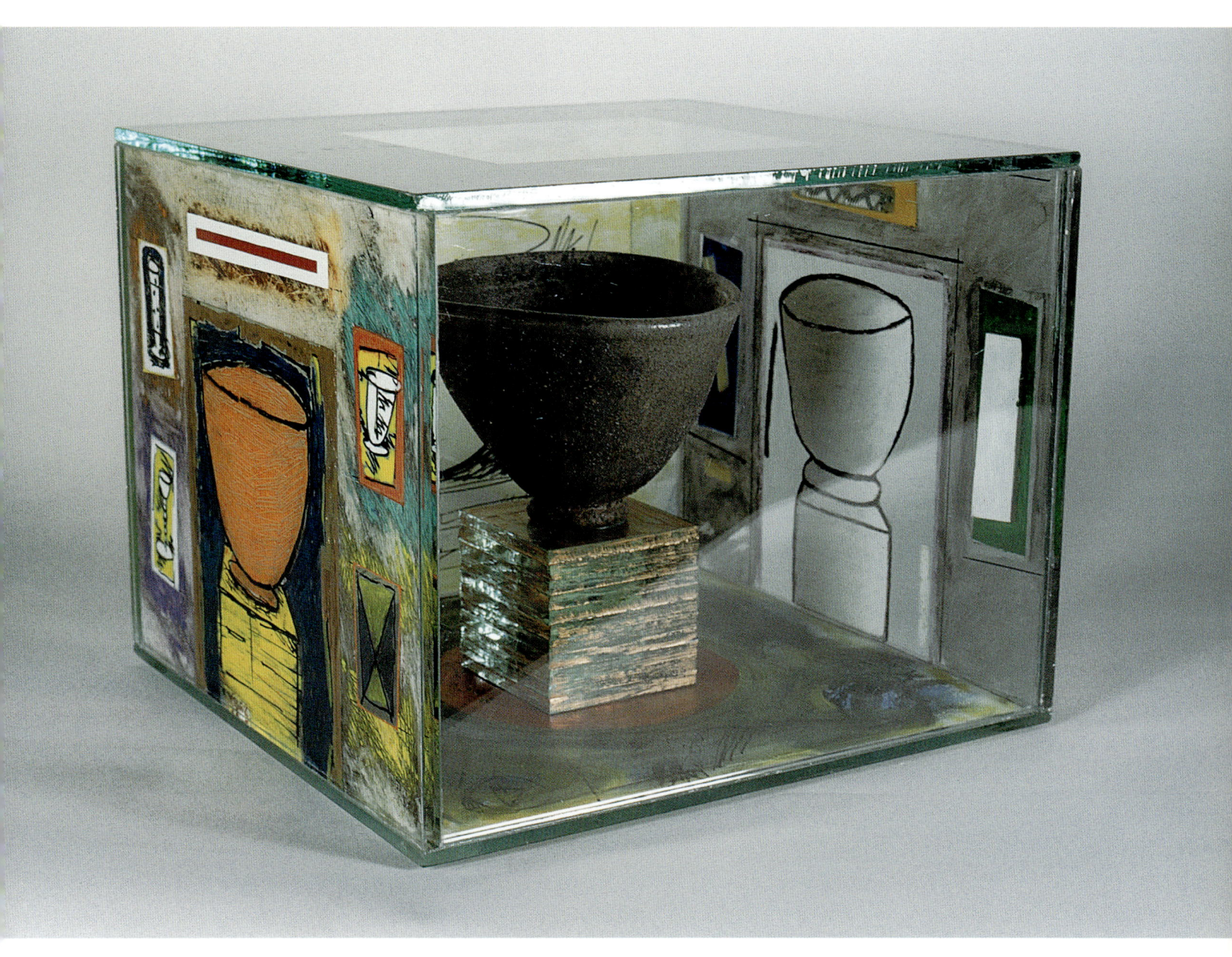

Vessel Three Views, 1997. Ink and acrylic ink reverse glass drawing, h. 12 x 16 inches.

James Harmon
(b.1952)

BARTO, PENNSYLVANIA

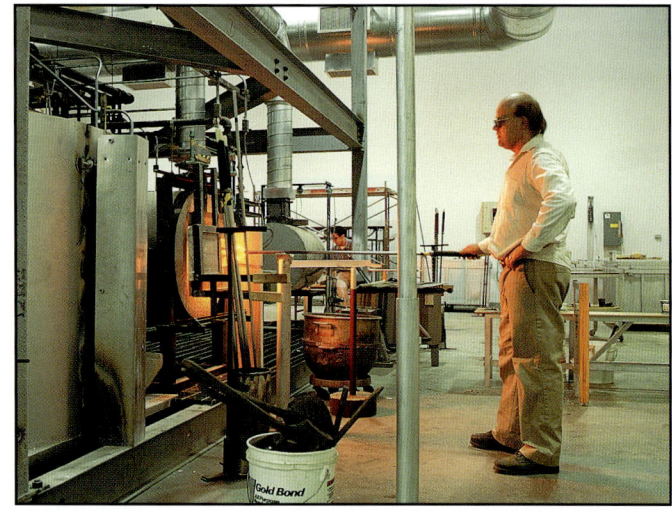

Green Vase, 1982. Blown glass, h. 12 x 15 inches.

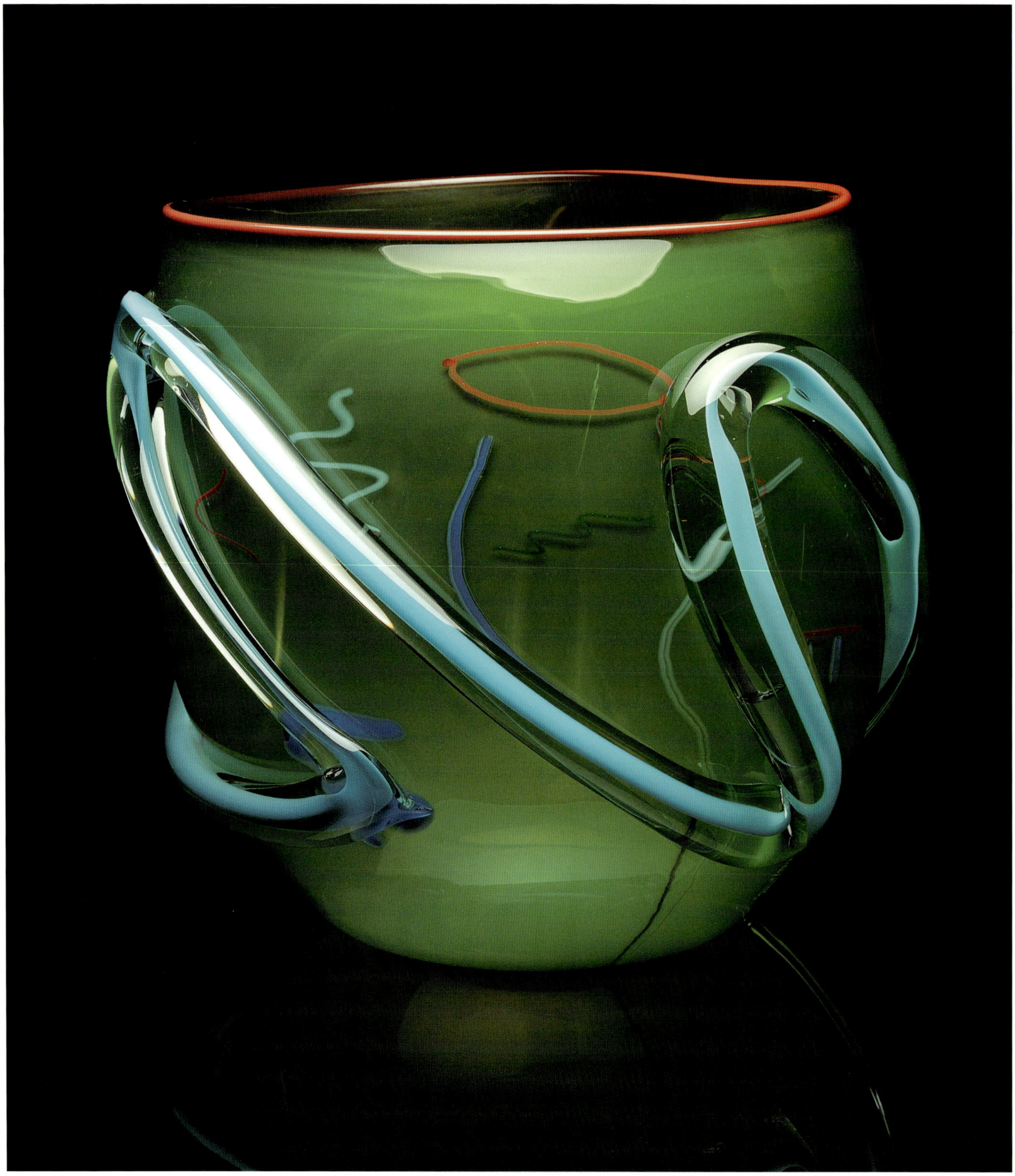

BROOKLYN, NEW YORK # Robert Hickman
(b. 1962)

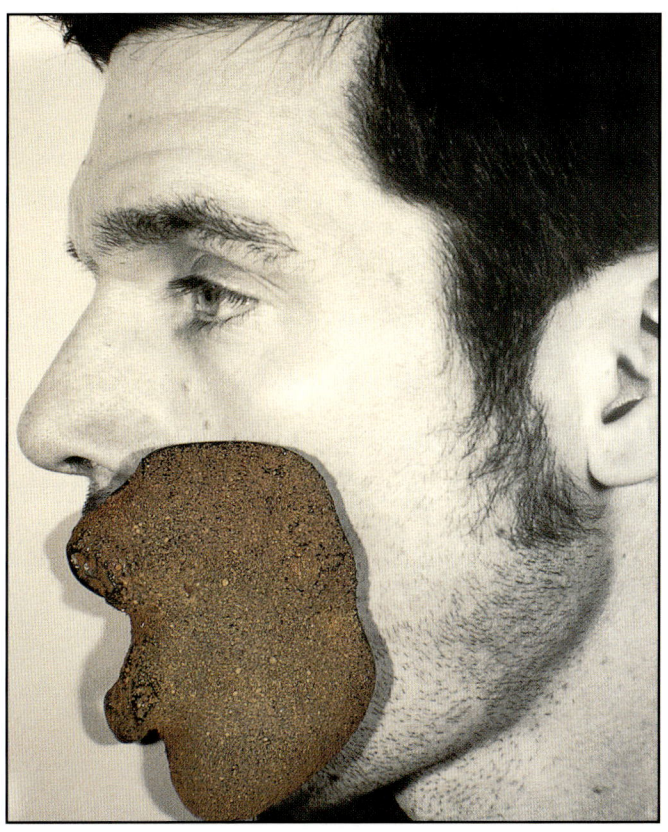

Left:
Giving Lip, 1997. Sandcast glass and B & W photo, h. 10 x 8 inches.

Below:
Convex Disk at Roosevelt Island Station, 1996. 200,000 cut and stratified glass squares, grout, and steel armature, disk h. 75 x 6 inches. New York Metropolitan Transportation Authority with the Sculpture Center. Photo: Mike Kamber.

Next:
Convex Disk at Roosevelt Island Station; Detail, 1996.

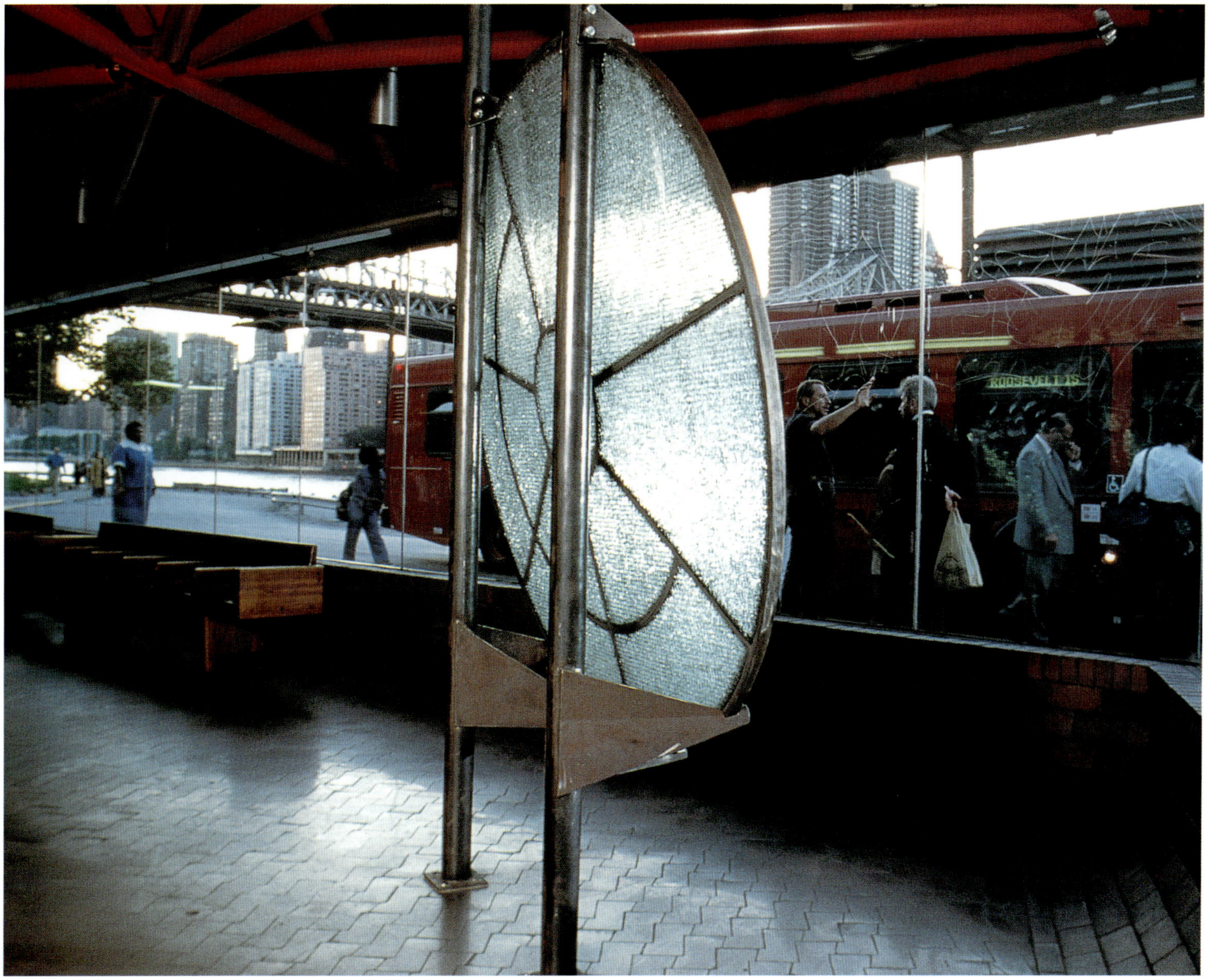

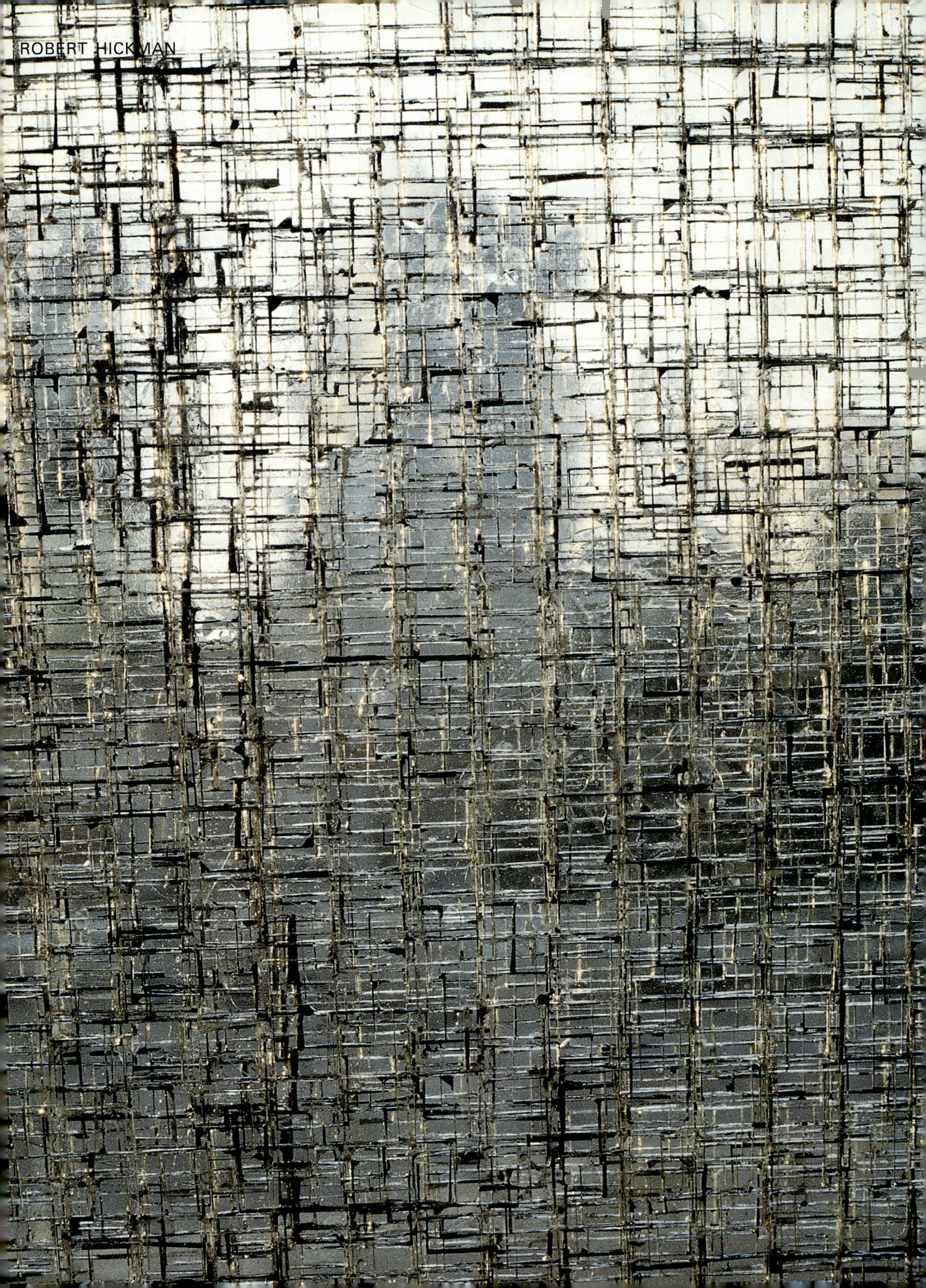

PARADISE, CALIFORNIA

David Hopper
(b.1946)

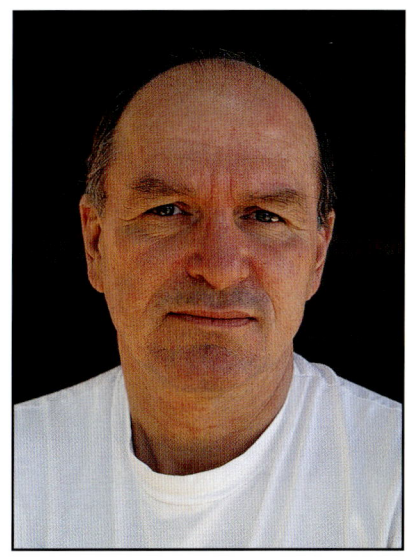

His Game, 1993. Hot worked, sand carved body parts, high temperature enamels, and poliergold, h. 18 x 10 x 7 inches.

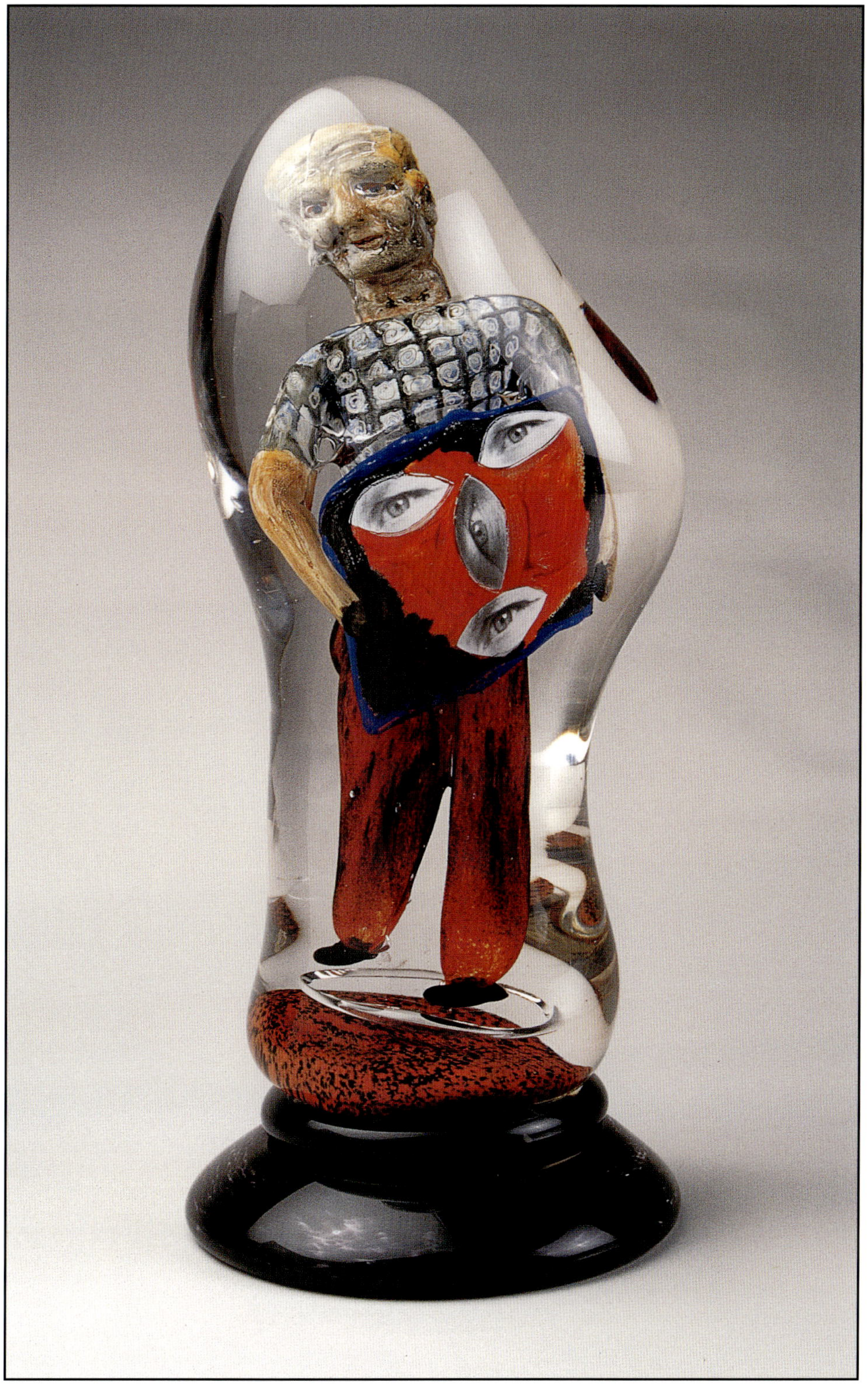

Shari Maxson Hopper
(b. 1949)

PARADISE, CALIFORNIA

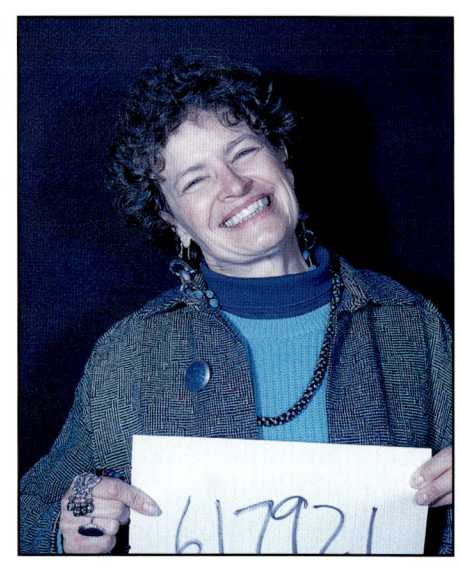

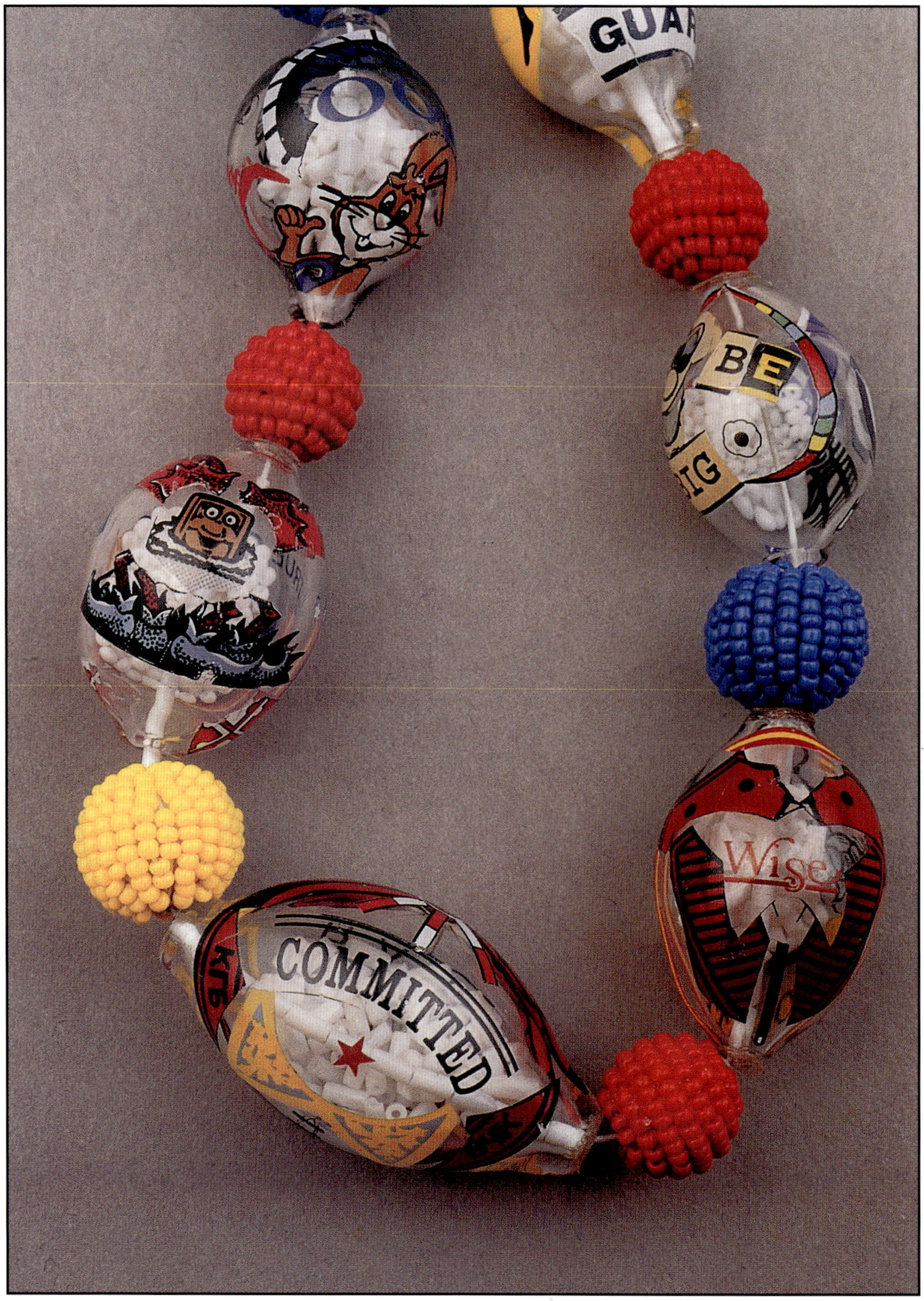

Browser's Dictionary, 1998. Lamp blown neon and borosillicate glass, enamel and photographic detail fired on.

BROOKLYN, NEW YORK

Arlan Huang
(b.1948)

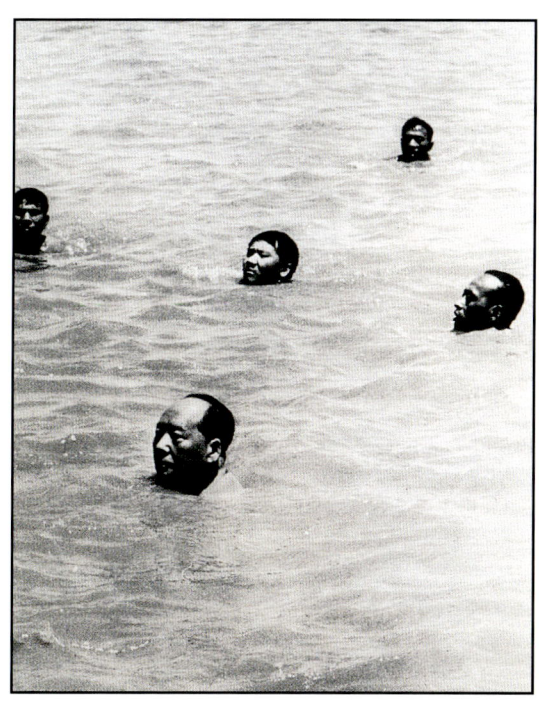

Left:
Swimming With Friends: A summation of my years during the genesis of the Glass Workshop from 4 Great Jones to Mulberry Streets. I learned to swim again then JB introduced me to glass in 1990.

Below:
American Origins; Red Wall. Permanent Installation at PS 152, Brooklyn, New York, 1996. Blown glass in glass blocks, and sandblasted, h. 56 x 128 inches. A Percent For Arts Project. Photo: Michael Moran.

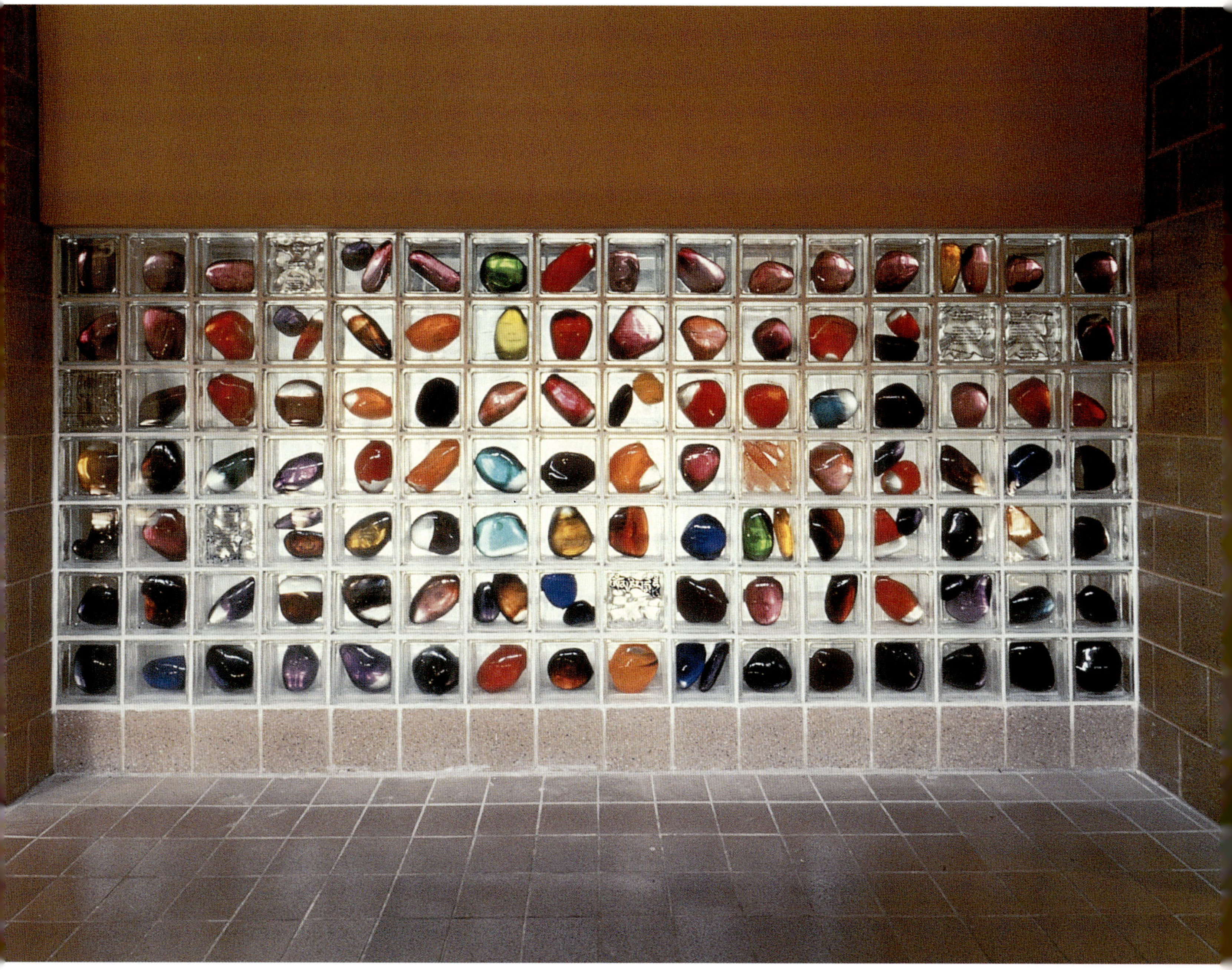

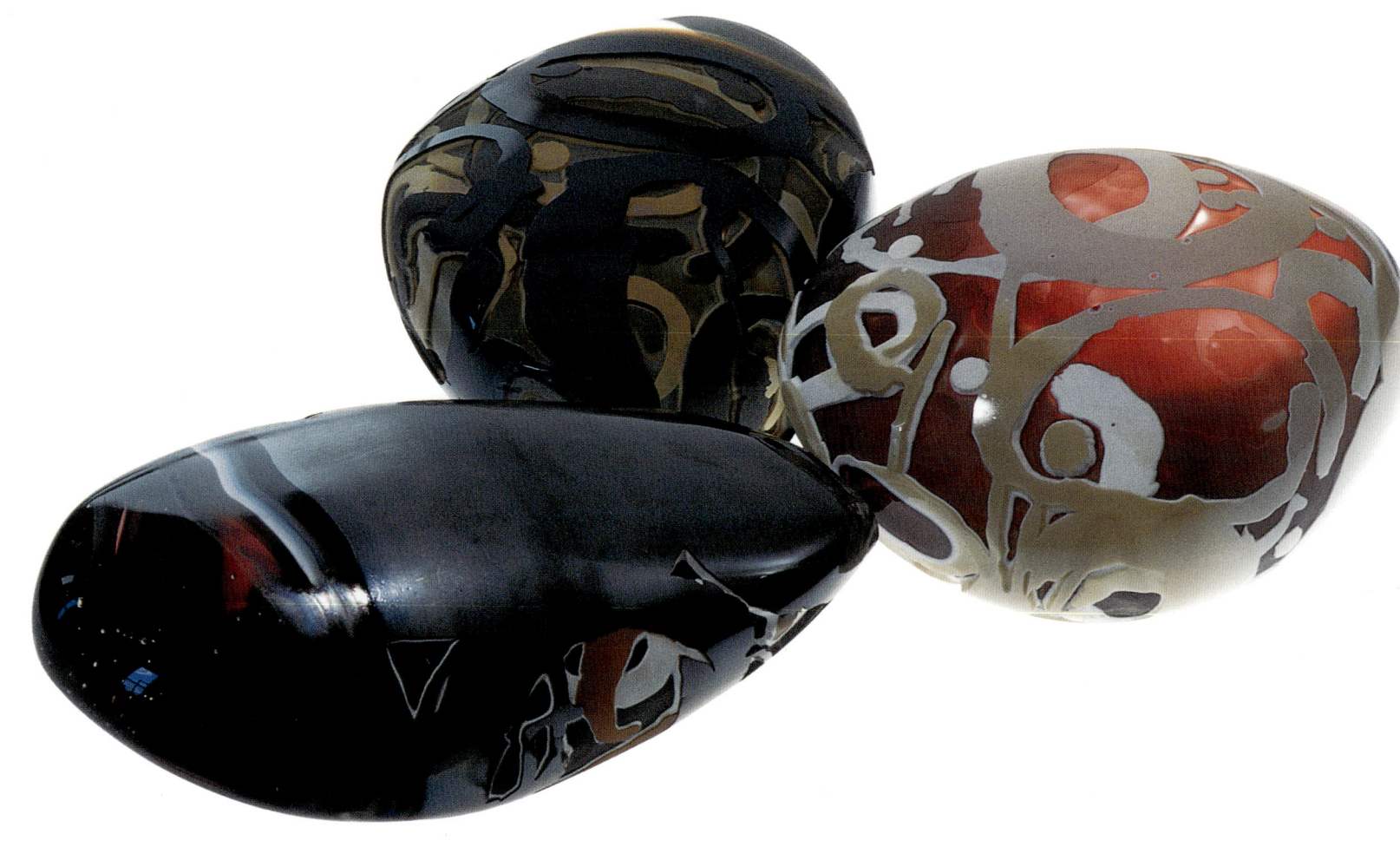

Jade Mountain D–Tour, 1999. Blown sandblasted glass, h. 6 x 10 x 5 inches each. Photo: Robert Puglisi.

SEATTLE, WASHINGTON

David Huchthausen
(b.1951)

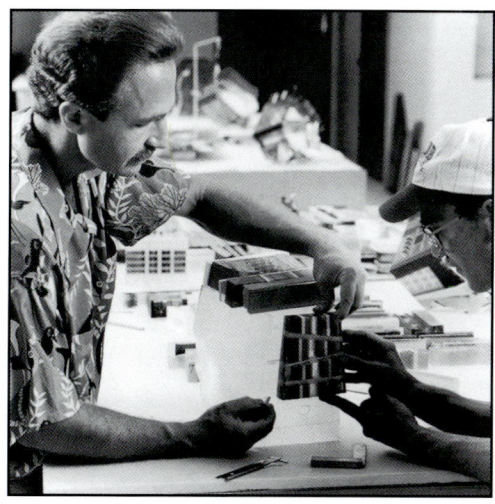

Fire Echo, 1997. Fractured, laminated, and polished glass with projected light, h. 11 x 16 x 8 inches. Photo: Rob Vinnedge.

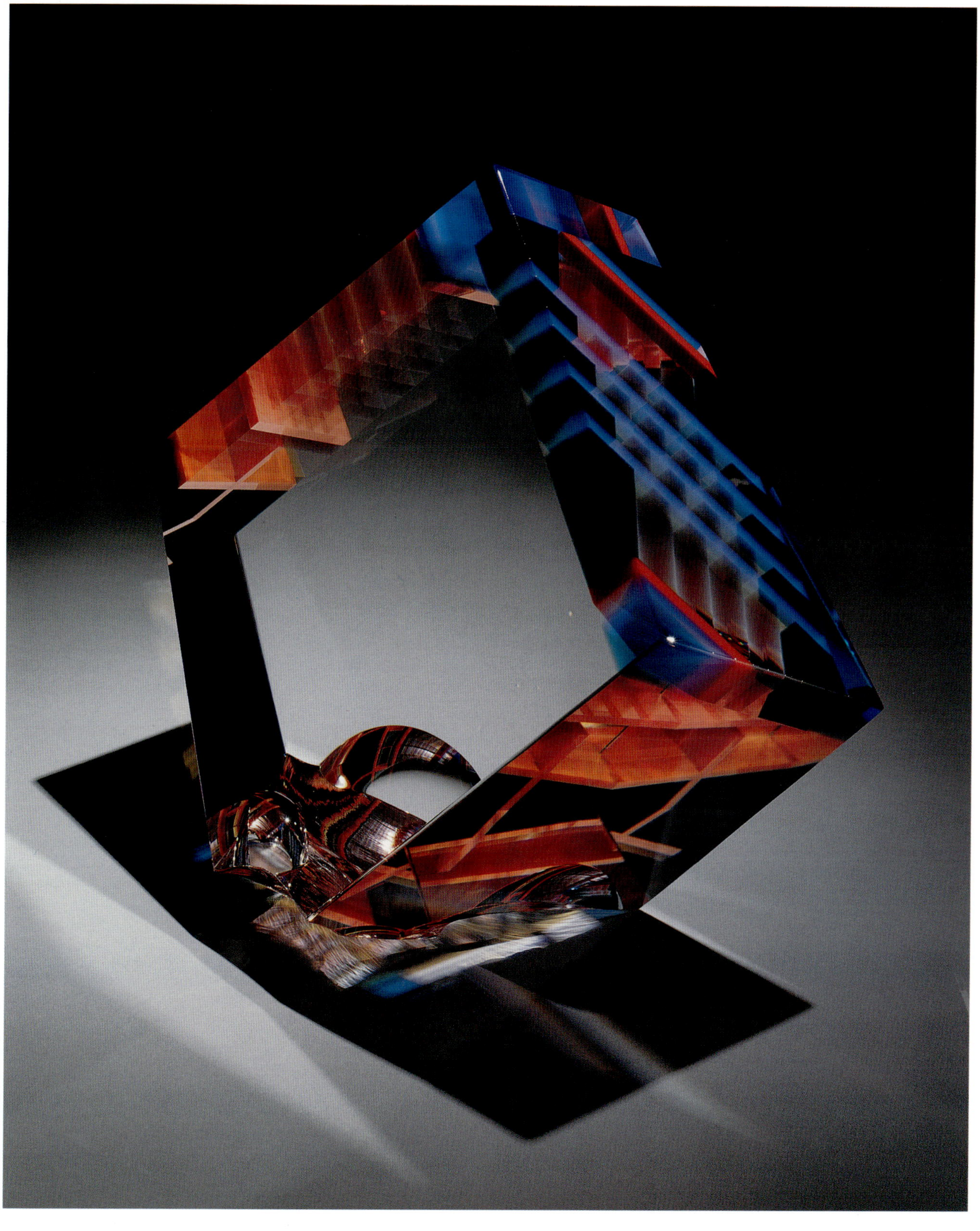

Ulrica Hydman-Vallien
(b.1938)

ERIKSMALA, SWEDEN

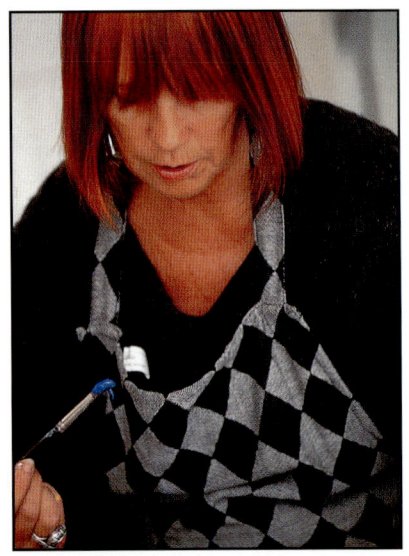

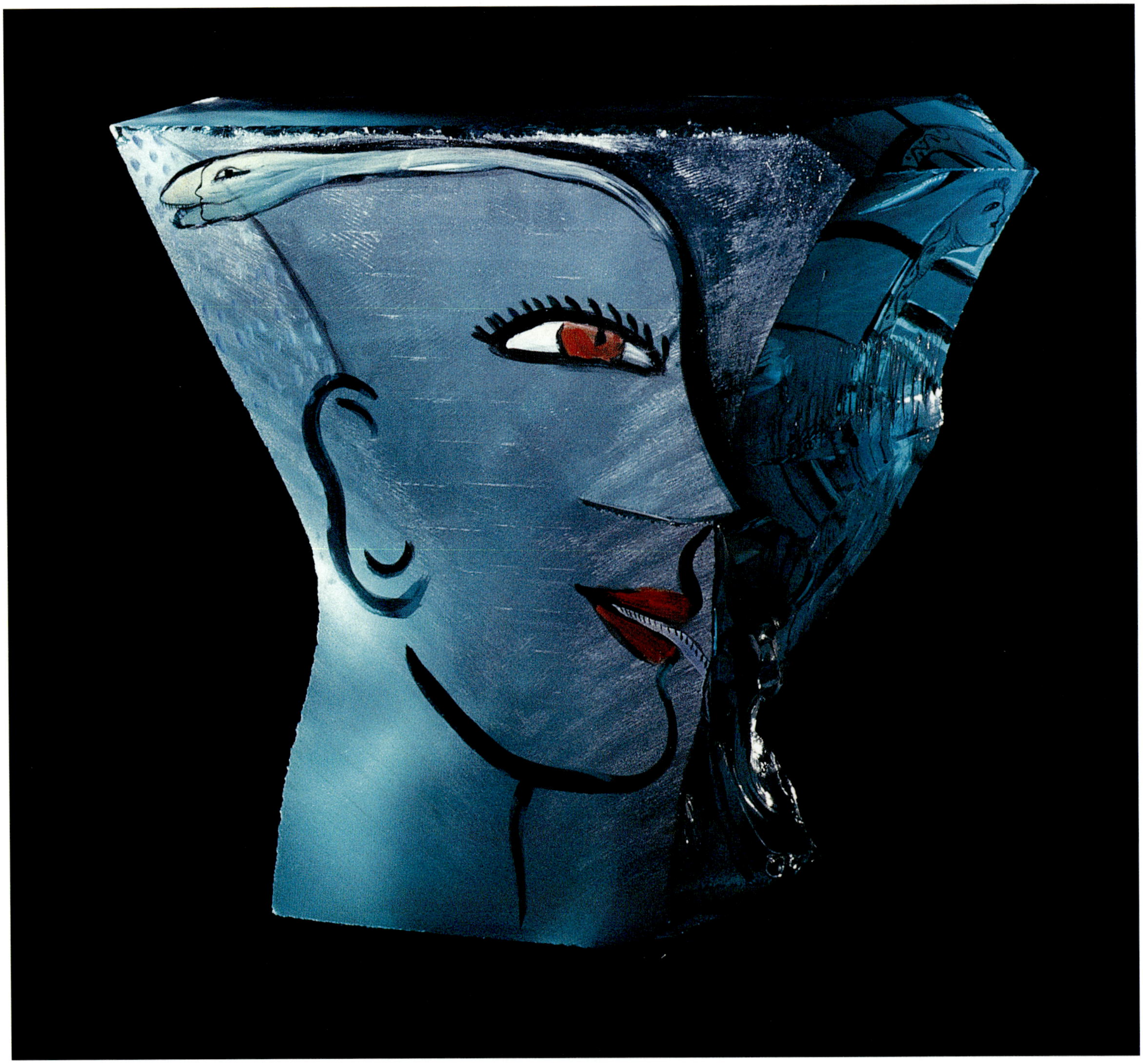

He and Me, 1987. Solid crystalblock, paint, and mixed media, h. 16 x 14 inches. Photo: Ola Terje.

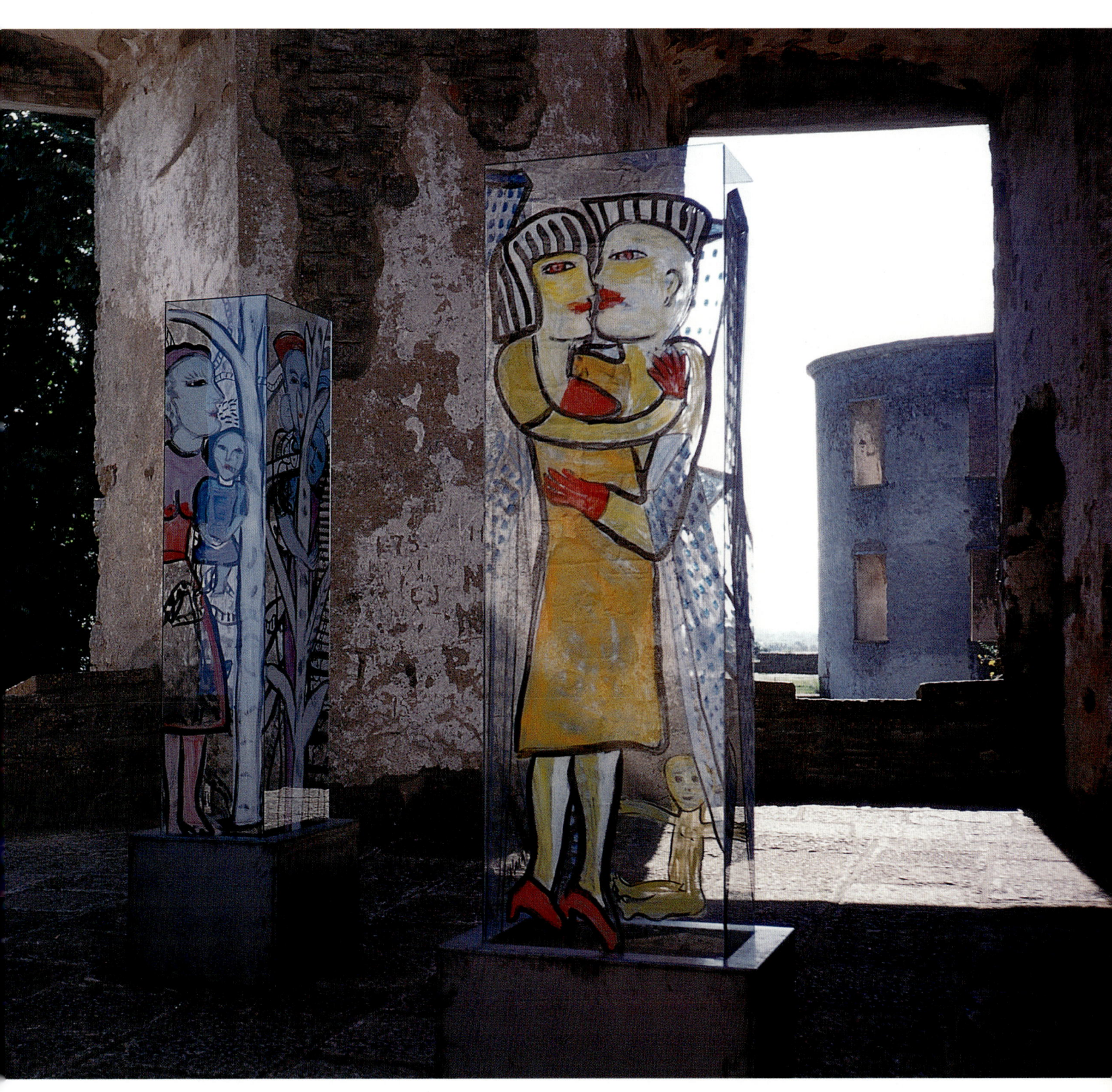

Family Life; Installation, Global Art Exhibition, Borgholm, Sweden, 1999. Painted Glass, and mixed media, h. 24 x 16 x 104 inches.

Tokiko Ishiguro
(b.1974)

NEW YORK, NEW YORK

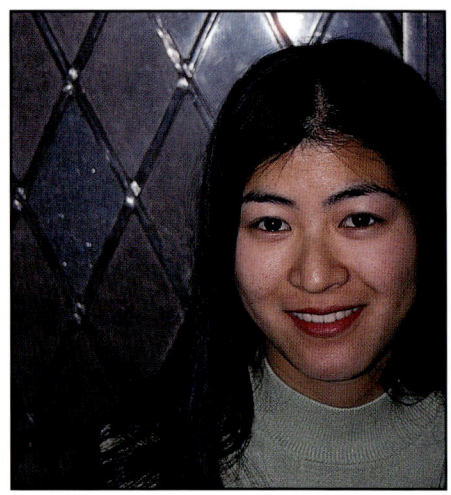

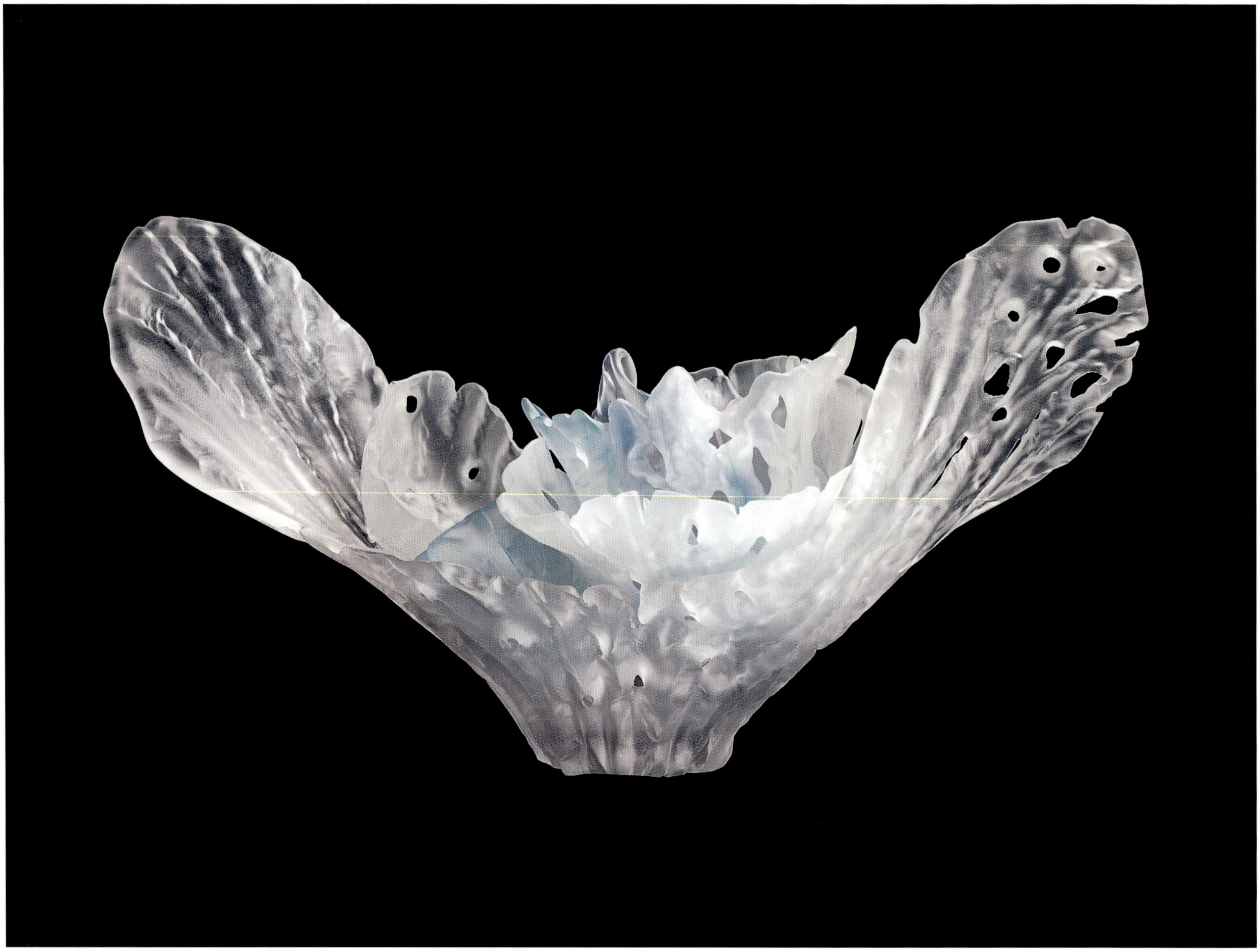

Above:
Sea Form, 1999. Sandblasted blown glass, h. 7 x 19 x 10 inches.

Opposite:
Natural Growth, 1999. Sandblasted blown glass, and lampworked glass, h. 10 x 9 x 6 inches.

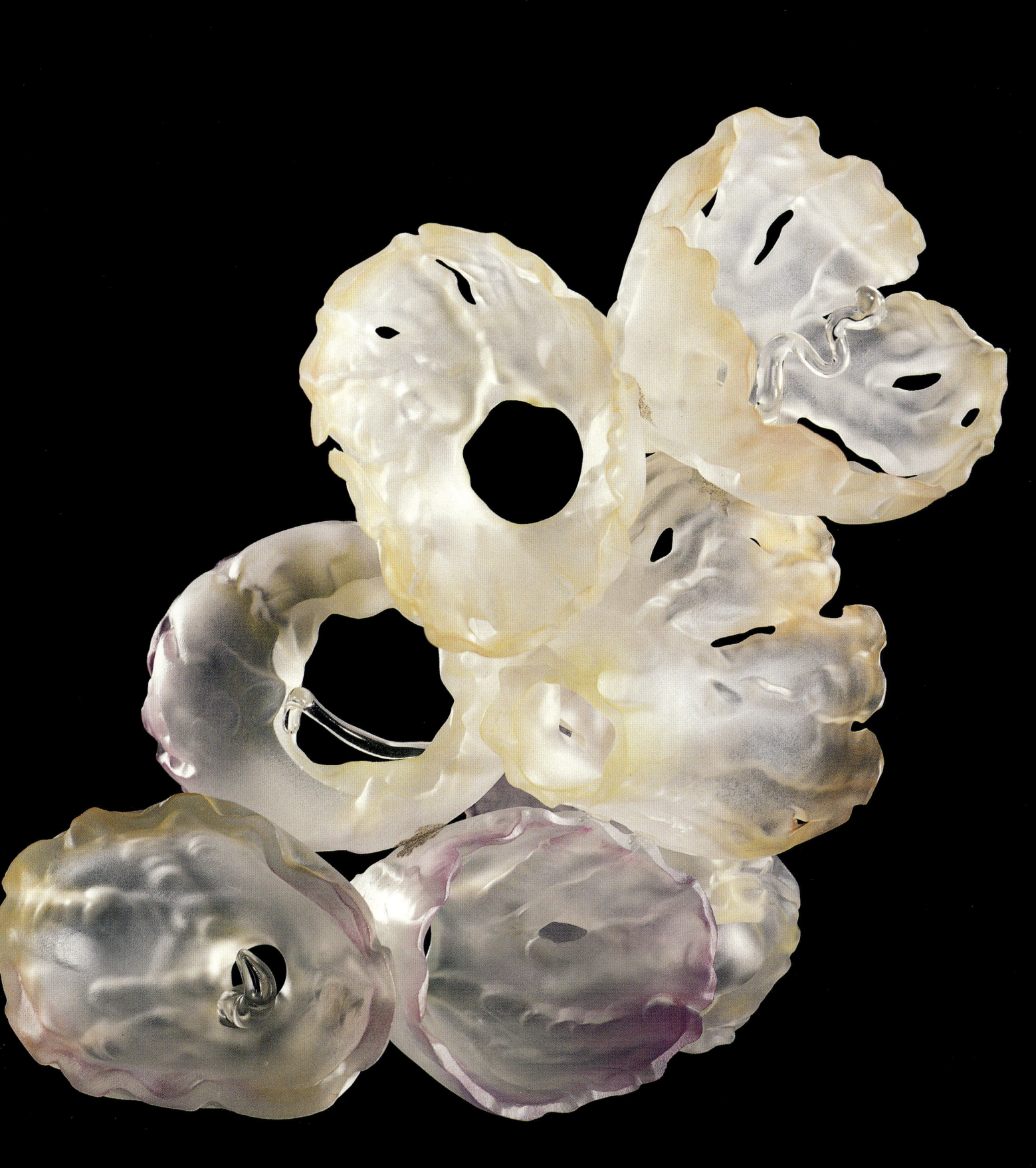

Geoffrey J. Isles
(b.1960)

NEW YORK, NEW YORK

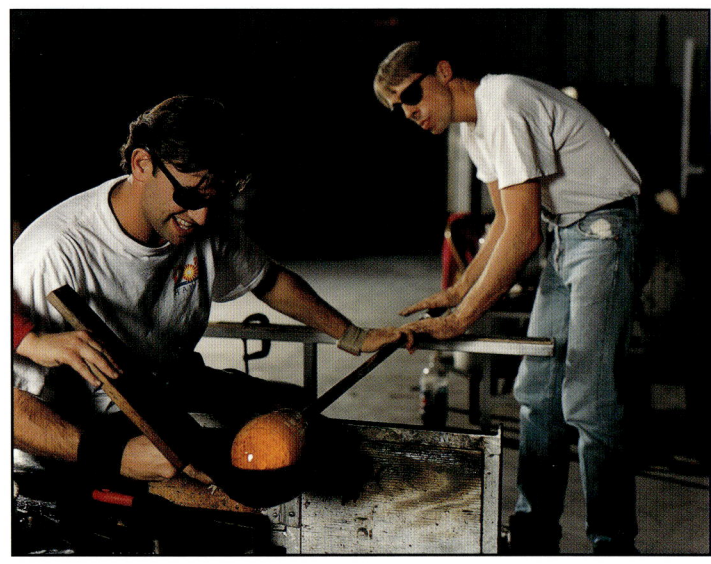
Photo: Tina Barney

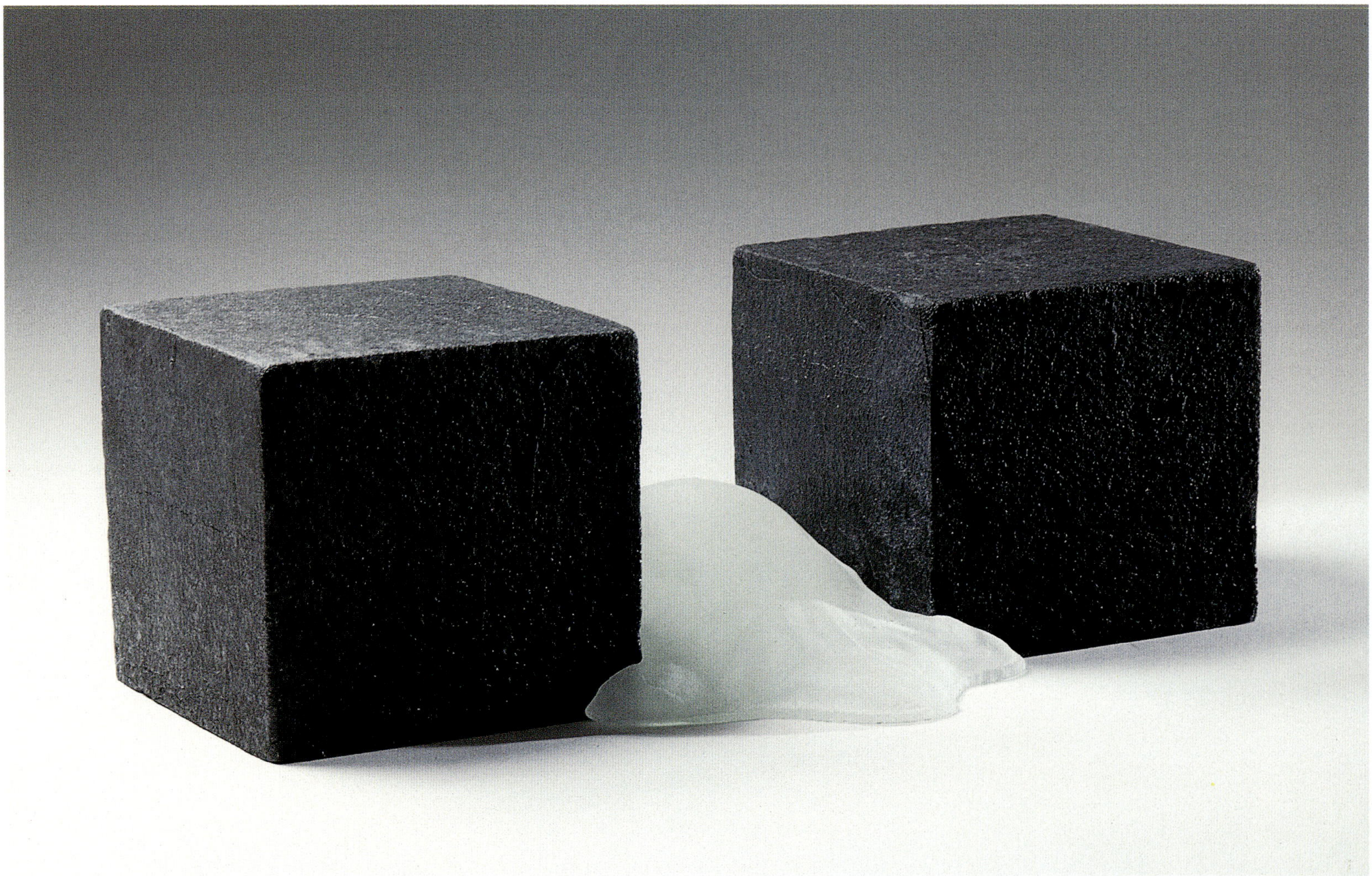

Above:
***Flow: Cubes**, 1995. Kilncast glass with ceramic stains, sandblasting, and acid etching, h. 8 x 21 x 23 inches.*

Opposite:
***Flow: Columns**, 1994. Kilncast glass with ceramic stains, sandblasting, and acid etching, h. 11 x 8 x 8 inches.*

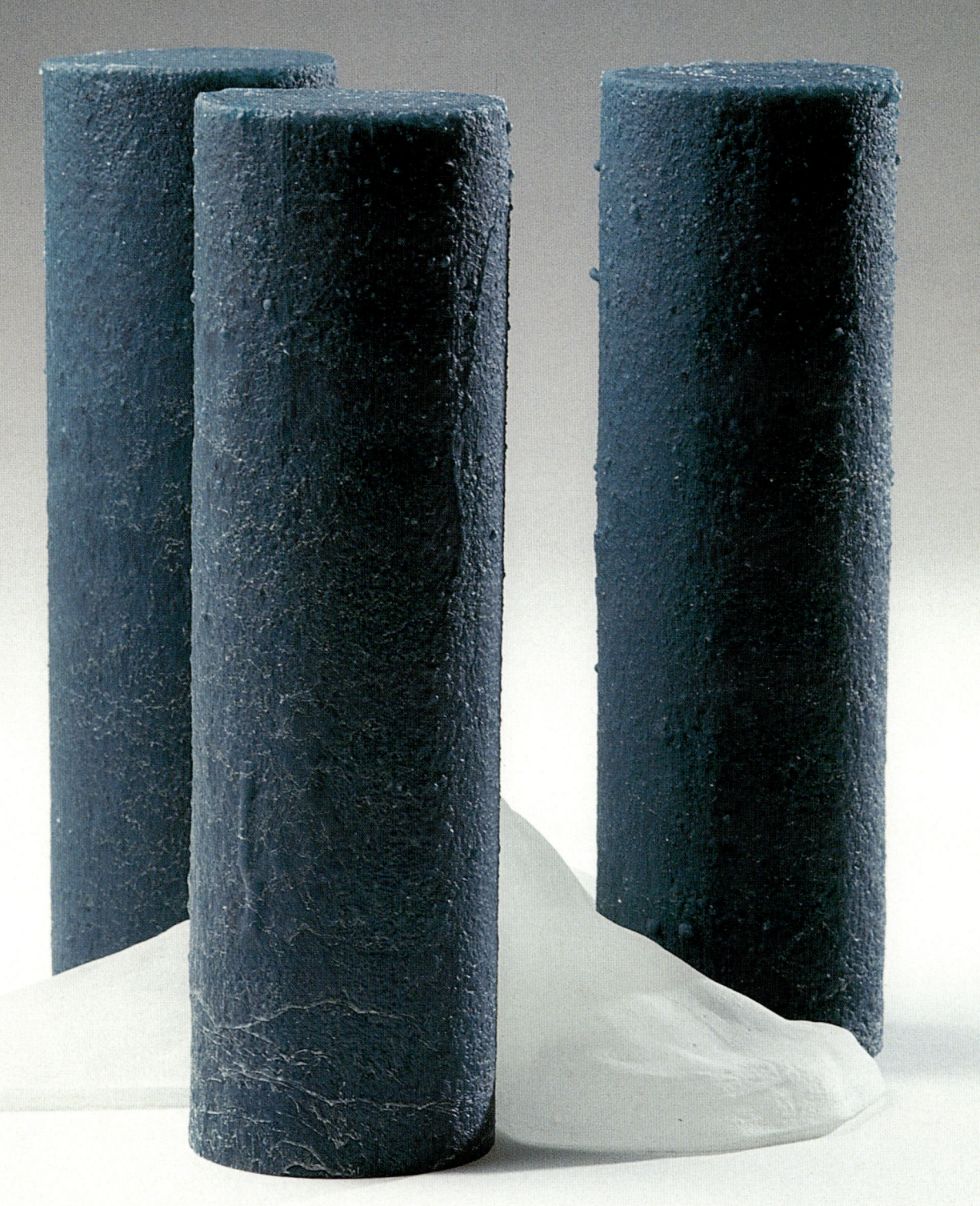

GEOFFREY J. ISLES

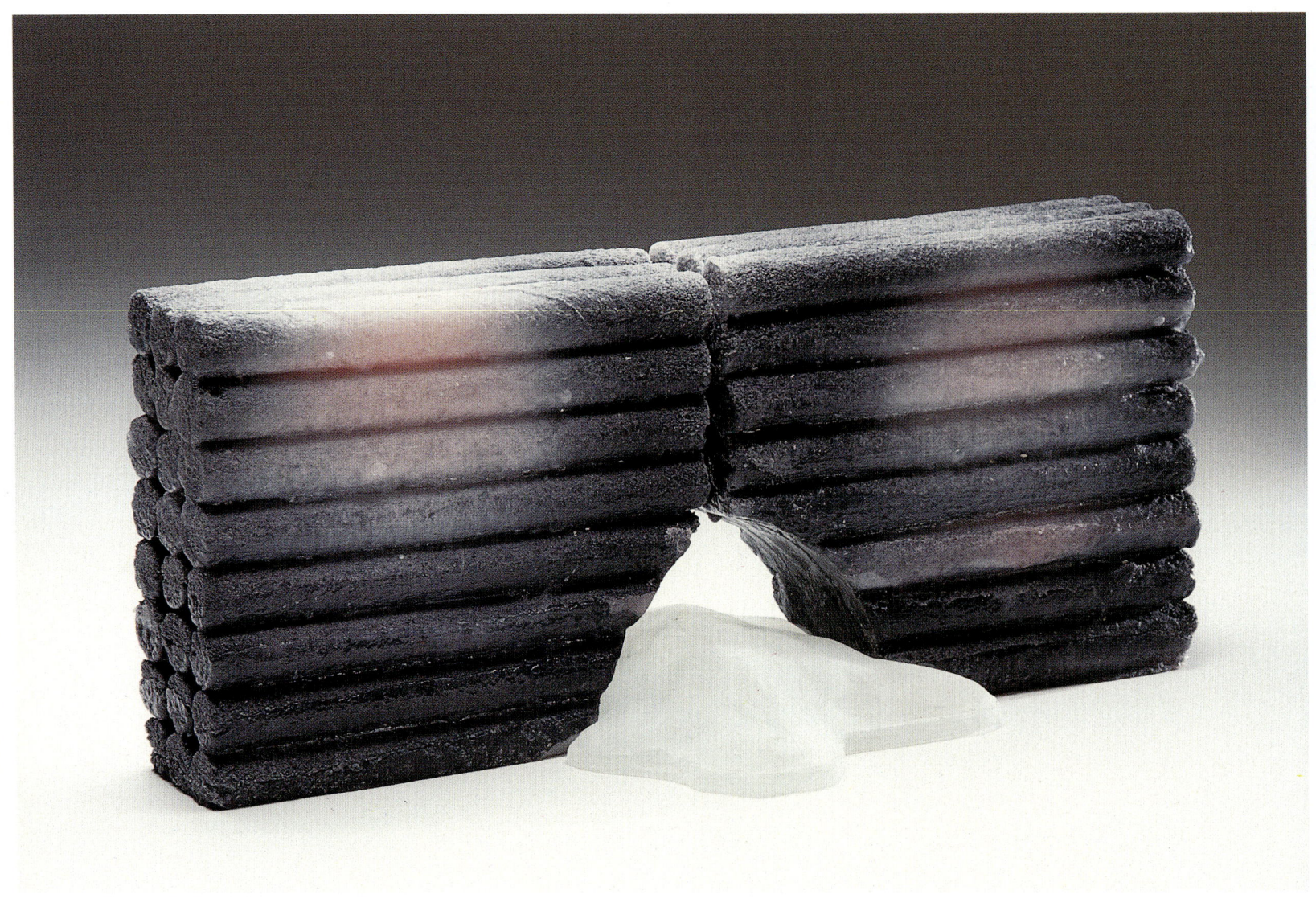

Flow: Bridge, 1994. Kilncast glass with ceramic stains, sandblasting, and acid etching, h. 8 x 20 x 6 inches.

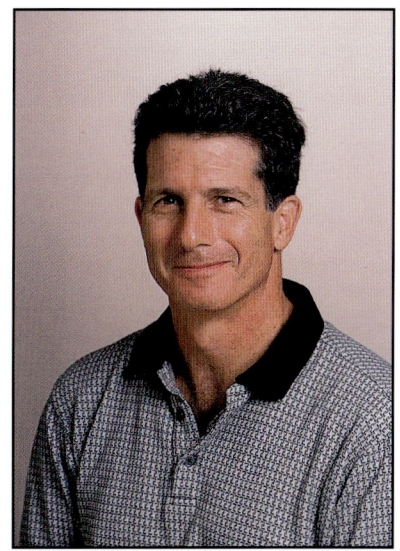

WHITE PLAINS, NEW YORK

David Jacobson
(b.1952)

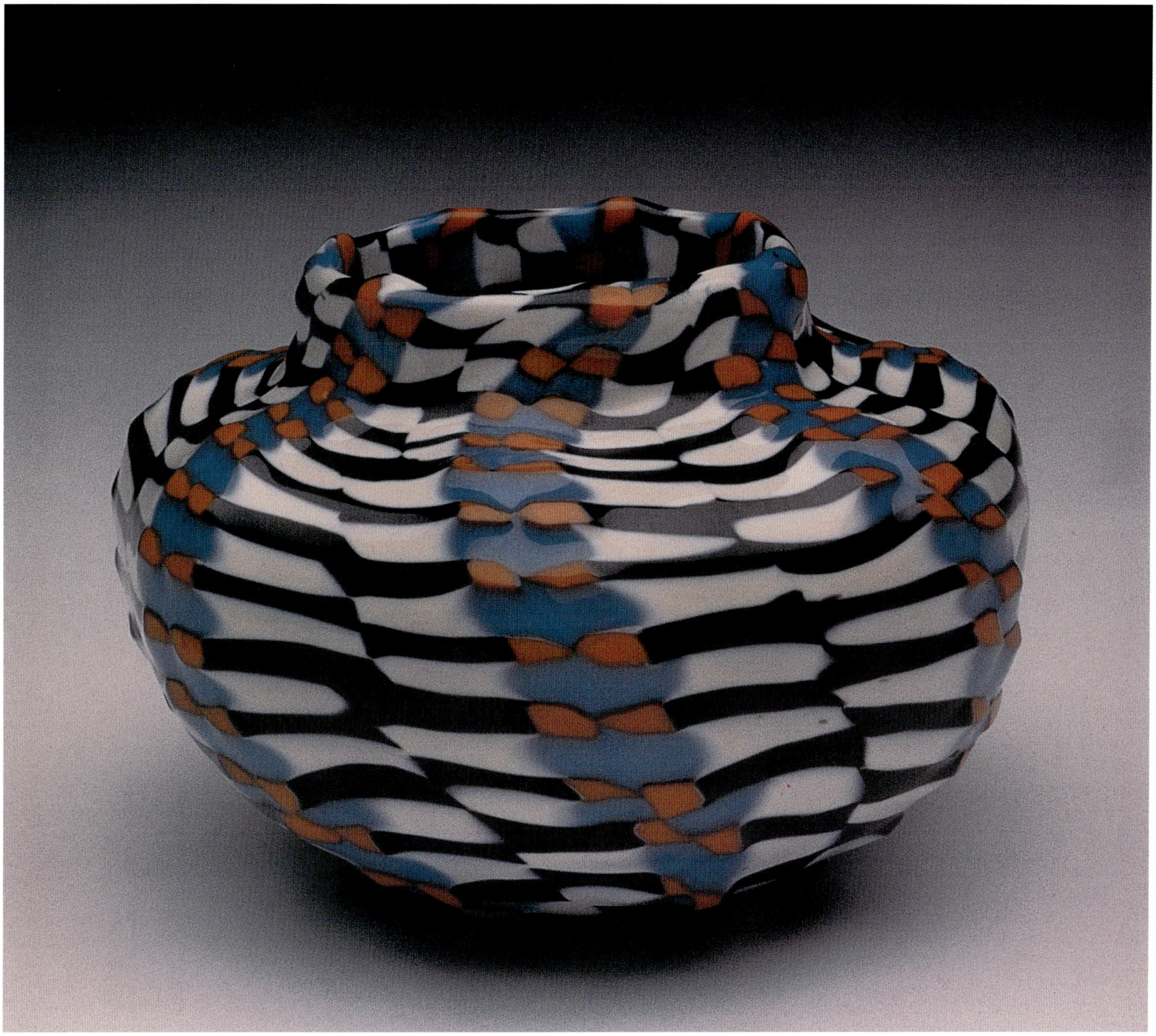

Untitled, 1998. Blown glass with murrini, h. 3 x 3.5 inches.

Eileen Jager
(b. 1958)

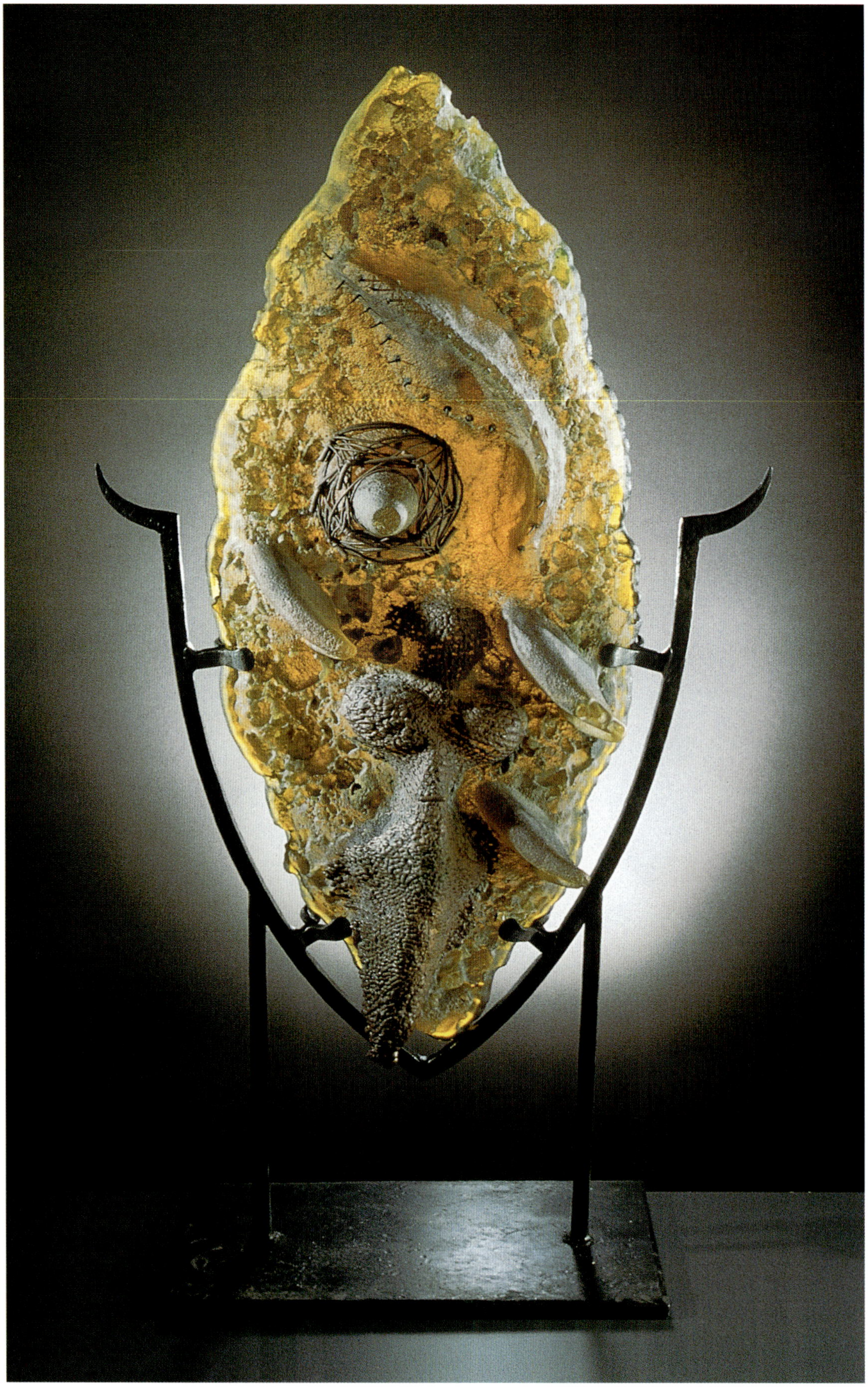

EASTHAMPTON, MASSACHUSETTS

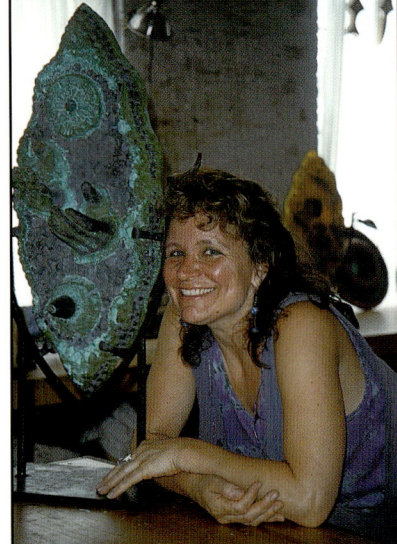

Kurgan, 1999. Amber sandcast glass, electroplated copper with metal stand, h. 33 x 18 x 8 inches. Photo: Tommy O. Elder

AUSTIN, TEXAS

Judy Jensen
(b. 1953)

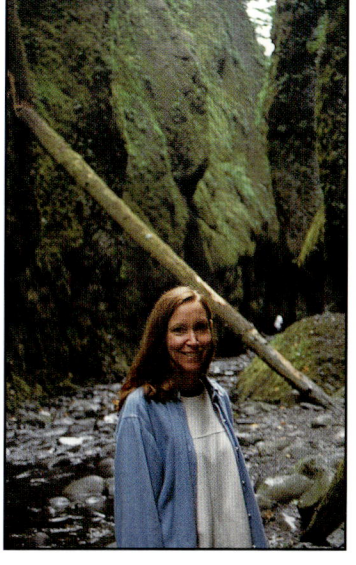

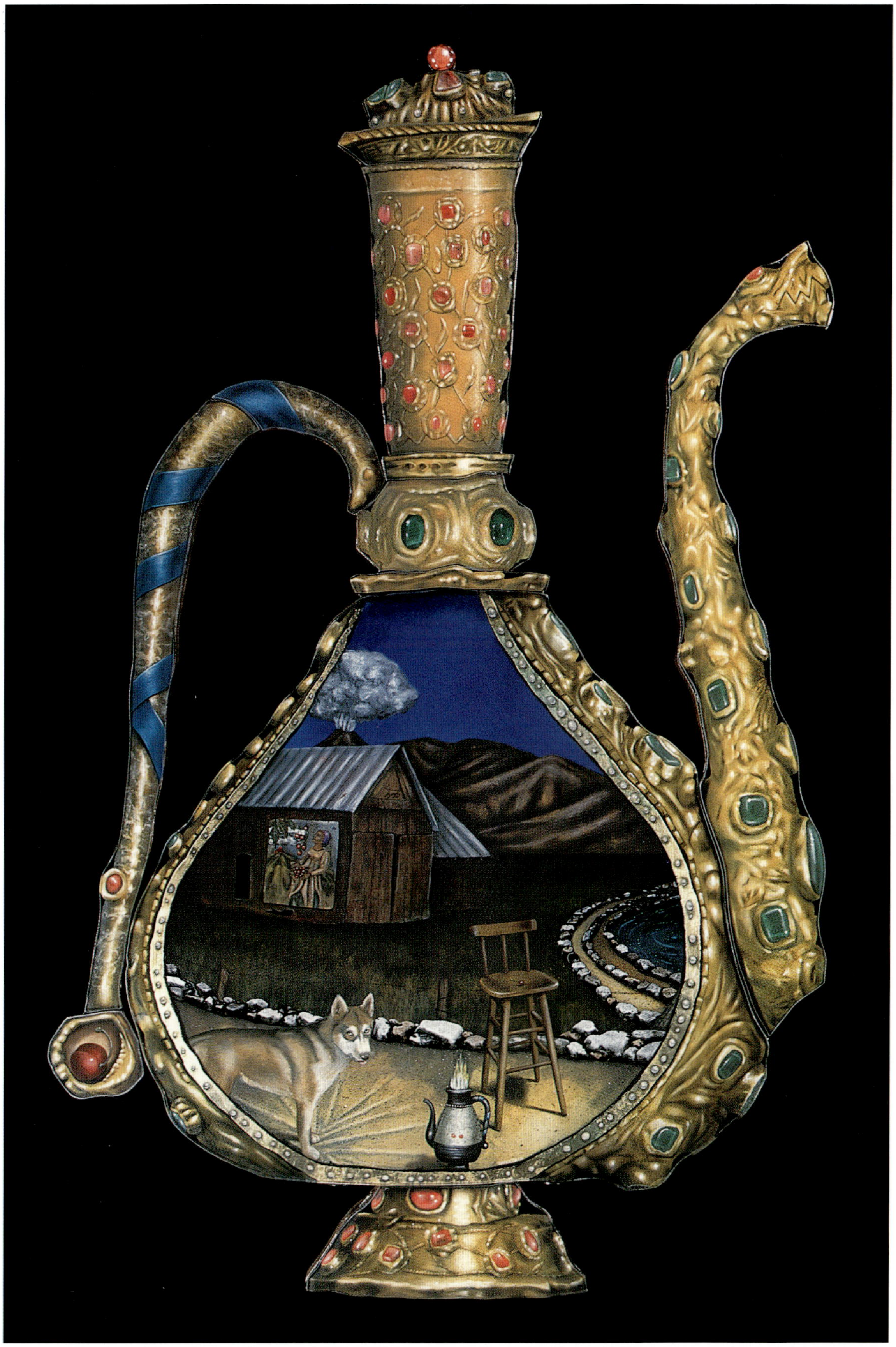

Disparities, 1995. Reverse painting and drawing on glass and mixed media, h. 37 x 22 inches. Photo: Emil Vogely.

Richard Jolley
(b. 1952)

KNOXVILLE, TENNESSEE

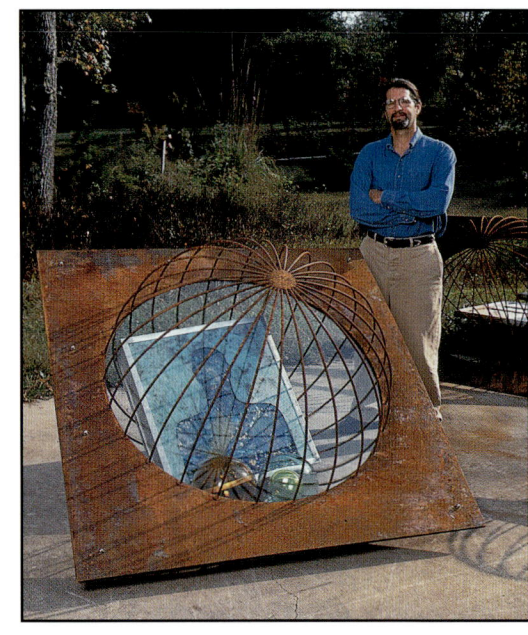

Polarity, 1998. Glass, copper, and aluminum, h. 29 x 28 x 8 inches. Photo: Charles Brooks.

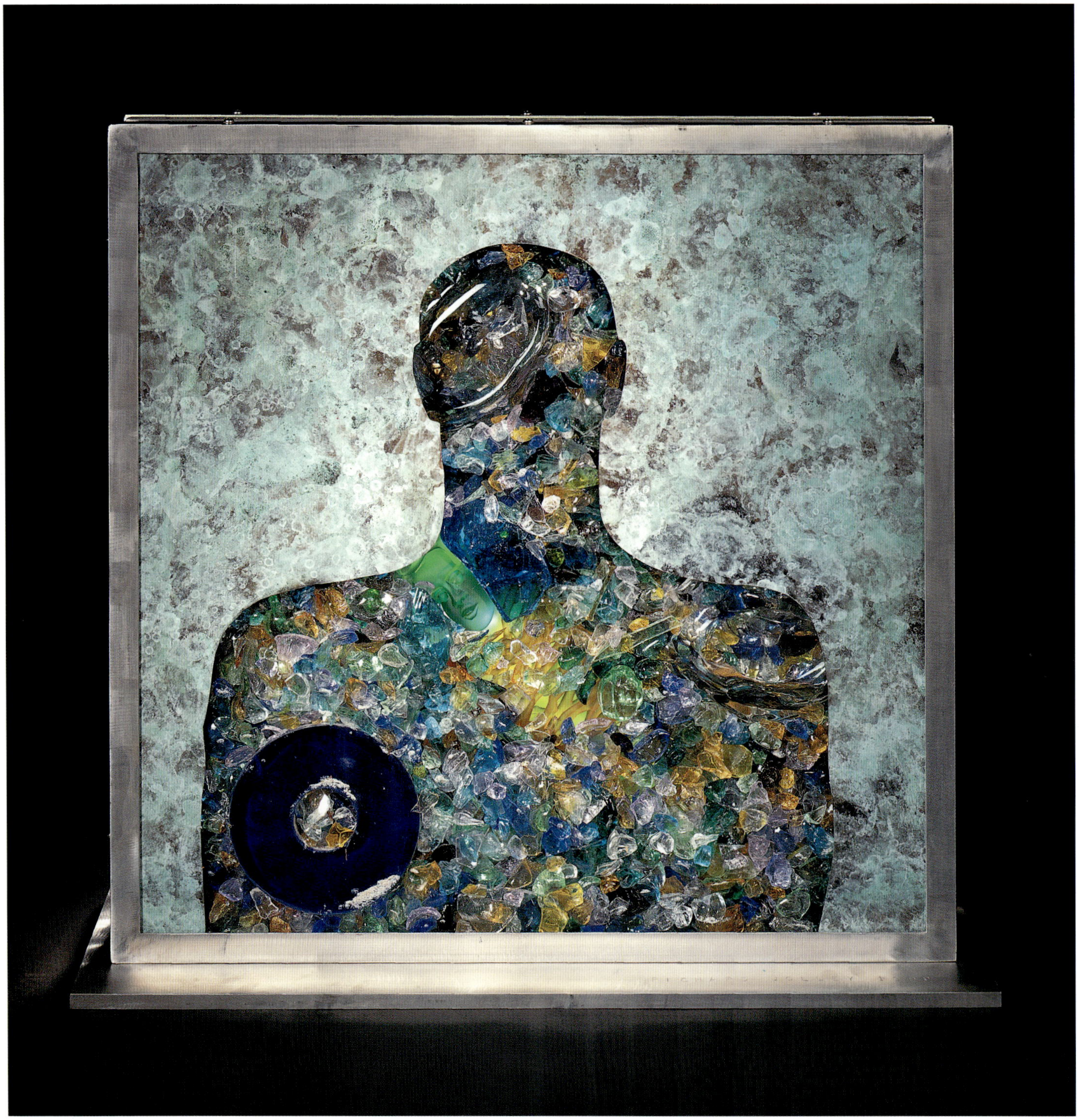

CZECH REPUBLIC

Marian Karel
(b.1944)

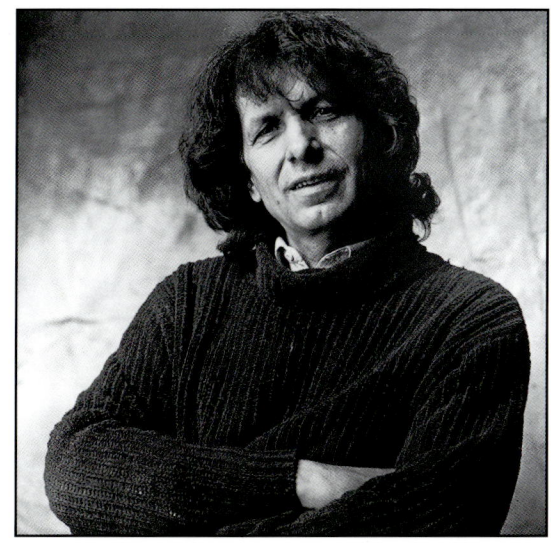

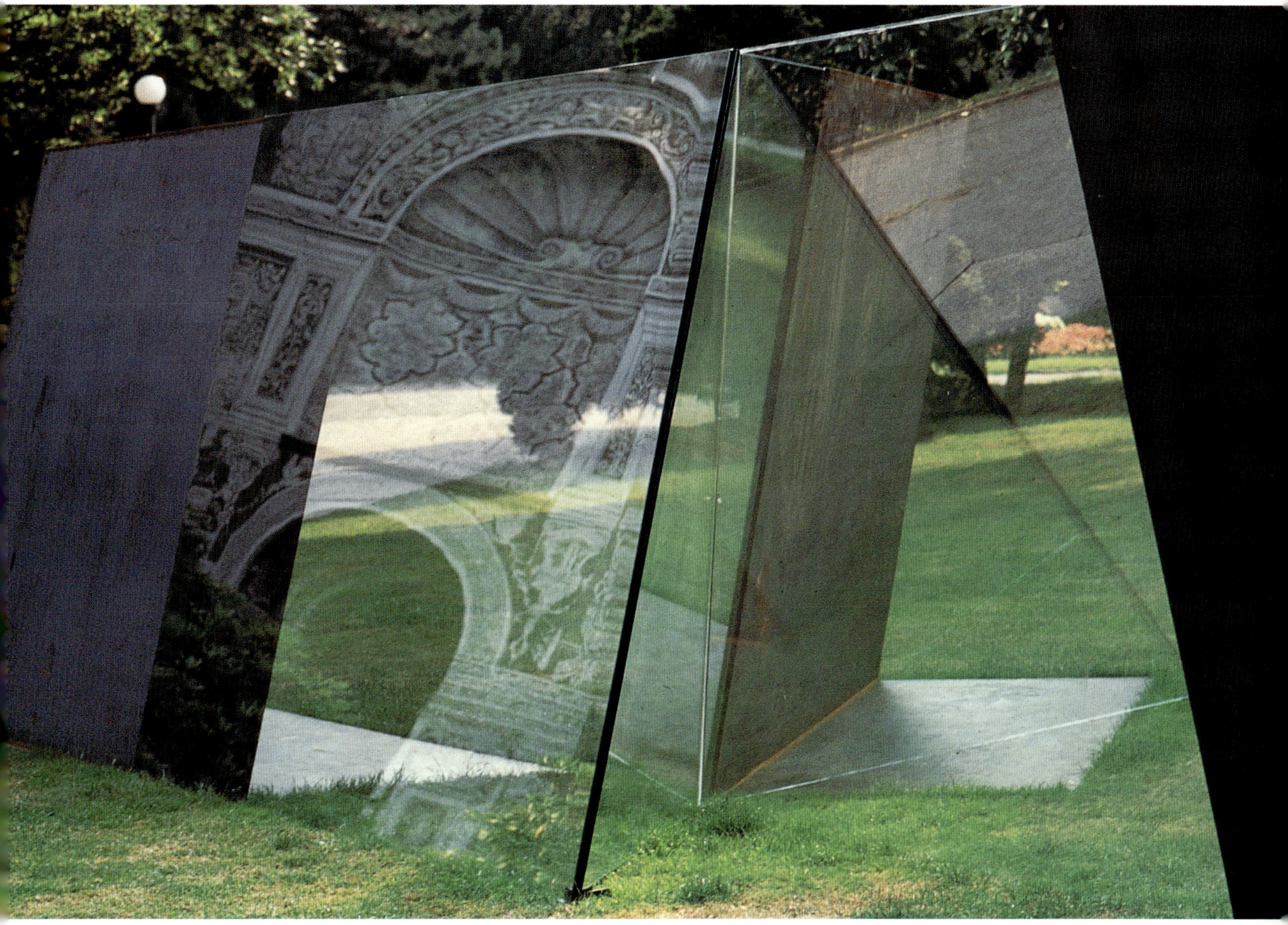

Encounter; Royal Gardens, Prague Castle, 1995.
Flat glass and steel, h. 6.5 x 39.3 x 13.7 feet.

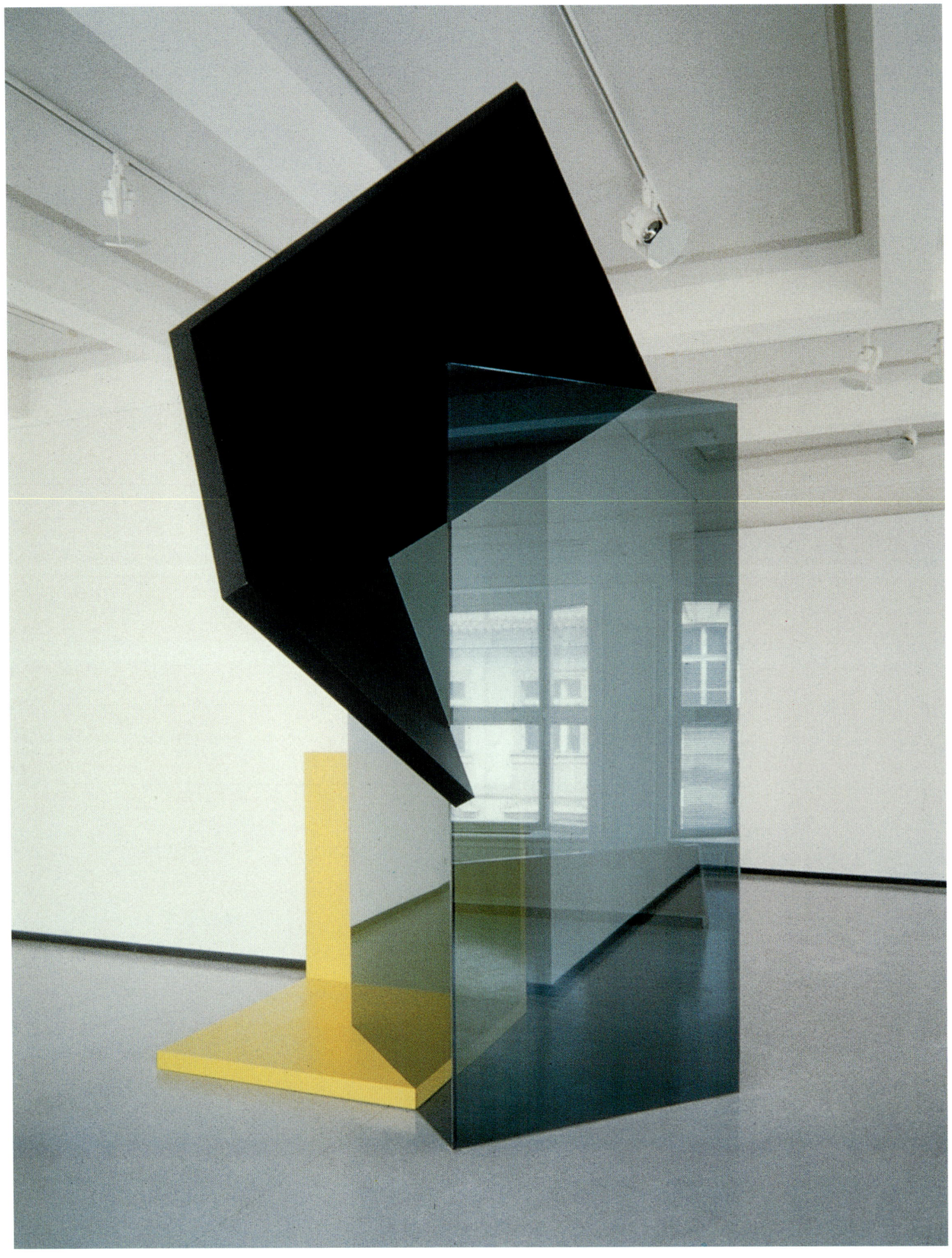

Prism; Cubist House of The Black Madonna, Prague, 1998. Flat glass and steel, h. 13.7 x 8.8 x 7.2 feet.

BERKELEY, CALIFORNIA

Robert Kehlmann
(b.1942)

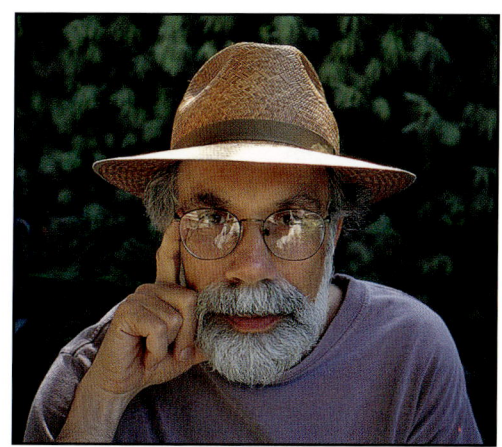

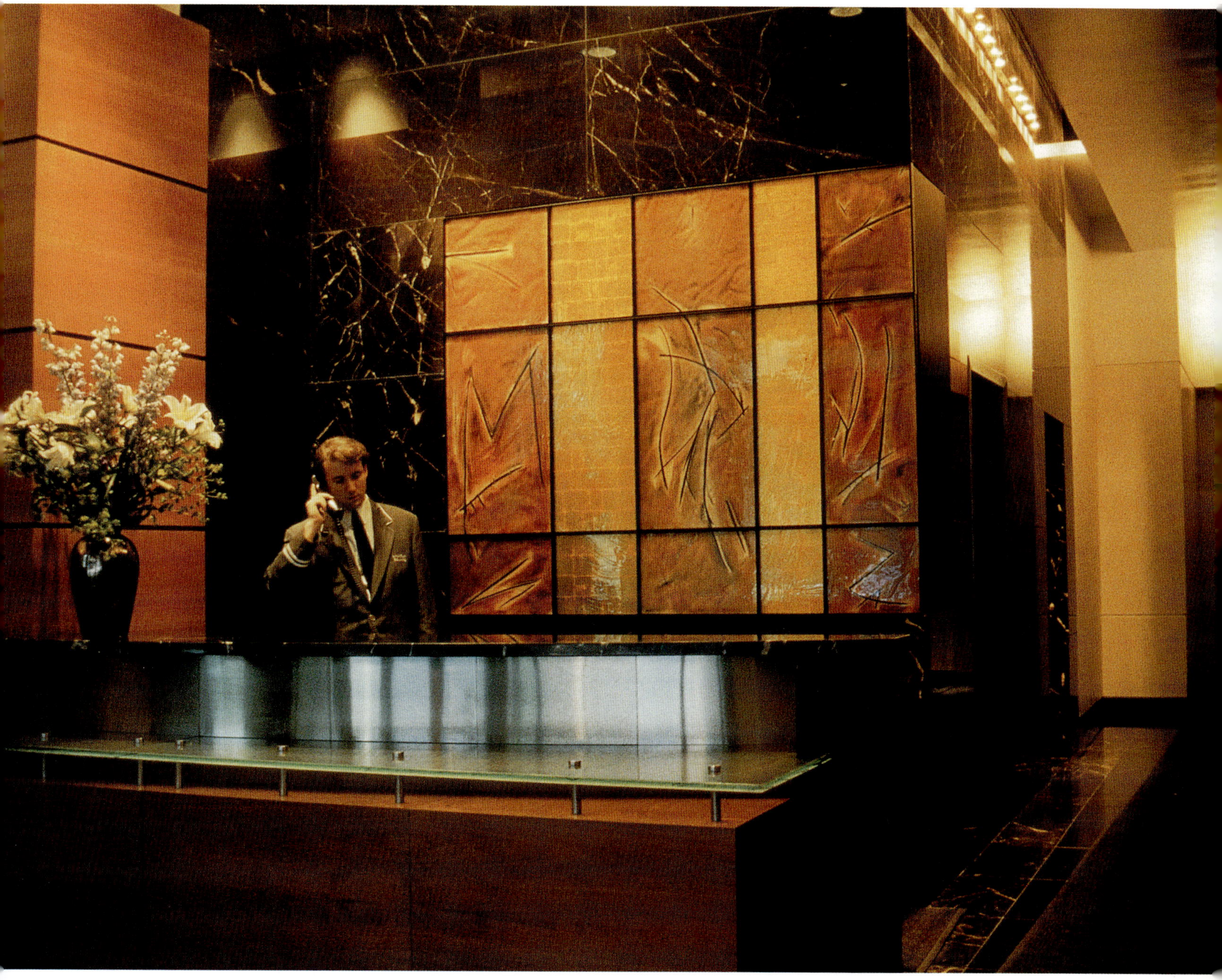

Millennium Byoubu, Lobby: 111 West 67th Street, New York City, 1994. Sandblasted glass, and mixed media on board, h. 68 x 79 inches.

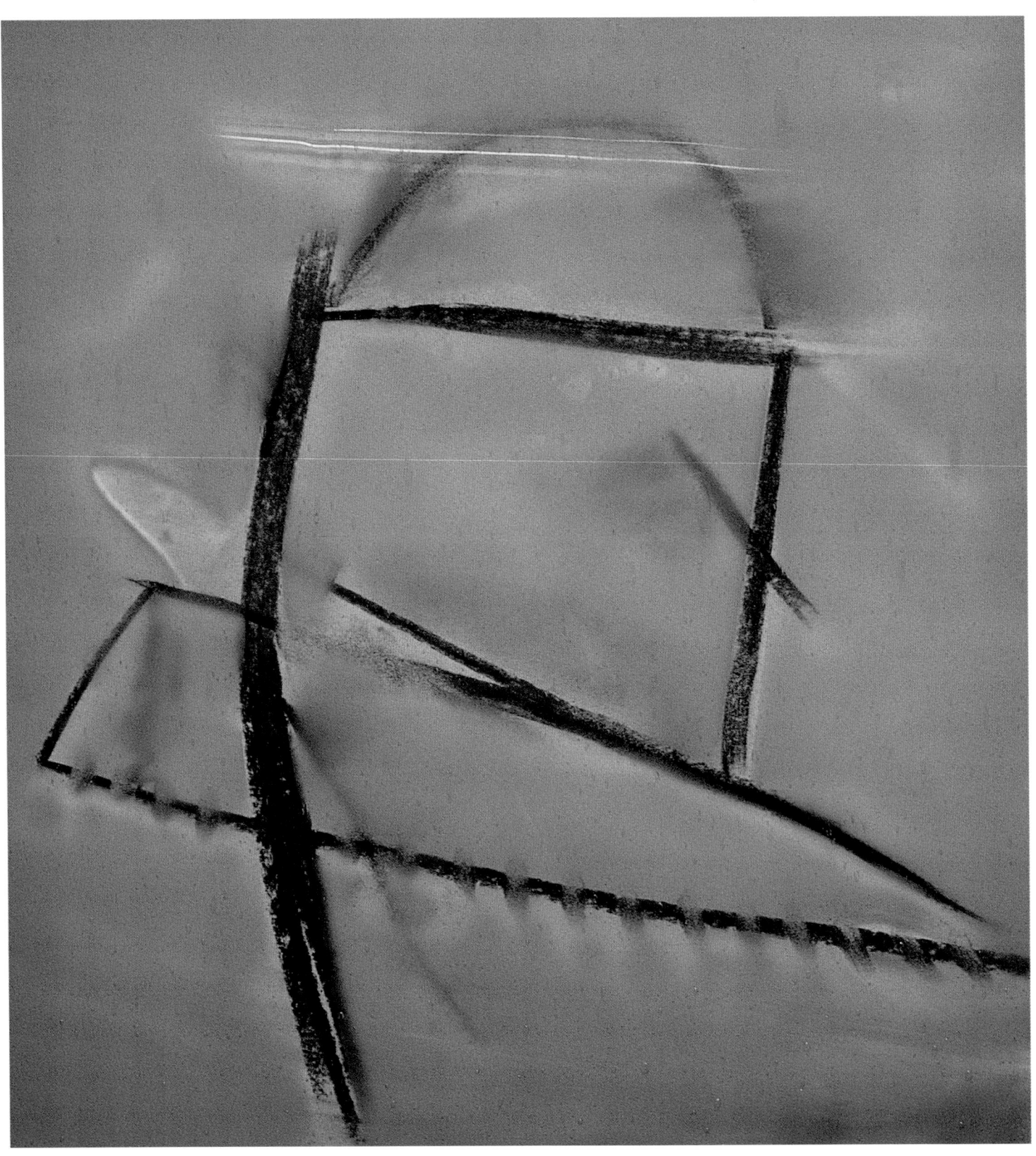

Palimpsest III, 1992. Sandblasted glass and charcoal on board, h. 9.5 x 8.5 inches. Collection of Peter and Judy Mollica.

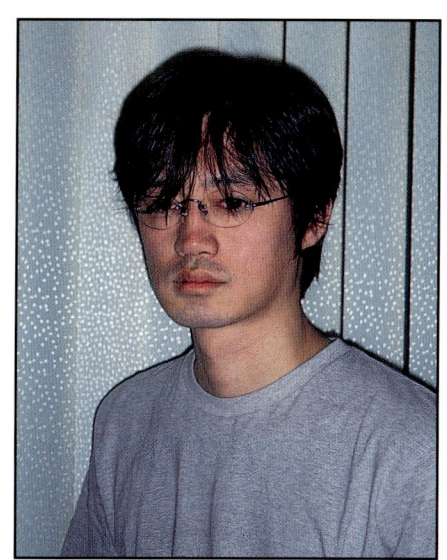

SEOUL, SOUTH KOREA

Chang Hyeon Kim
(b.1968)

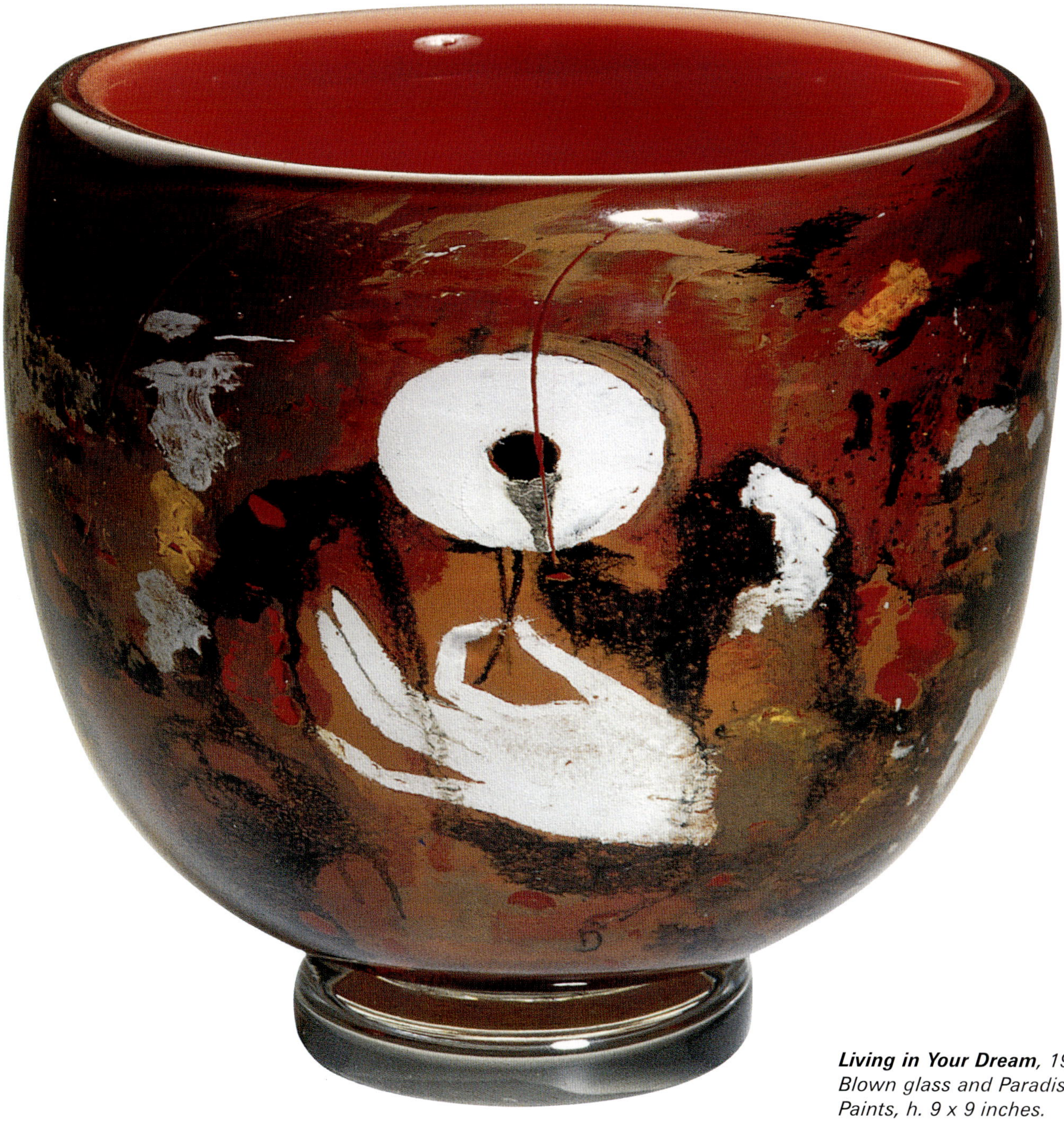

Living in Your Dream, 1999,
Blown glass and Paradise
Paints, h. 9 x 9 inches.
Photo: Eva Heyd.

Ray King
(b.1950)

PHILADELPHIA, PENNSYLVANIA

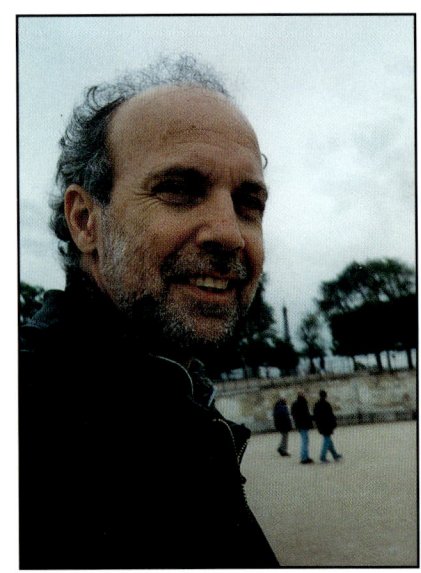

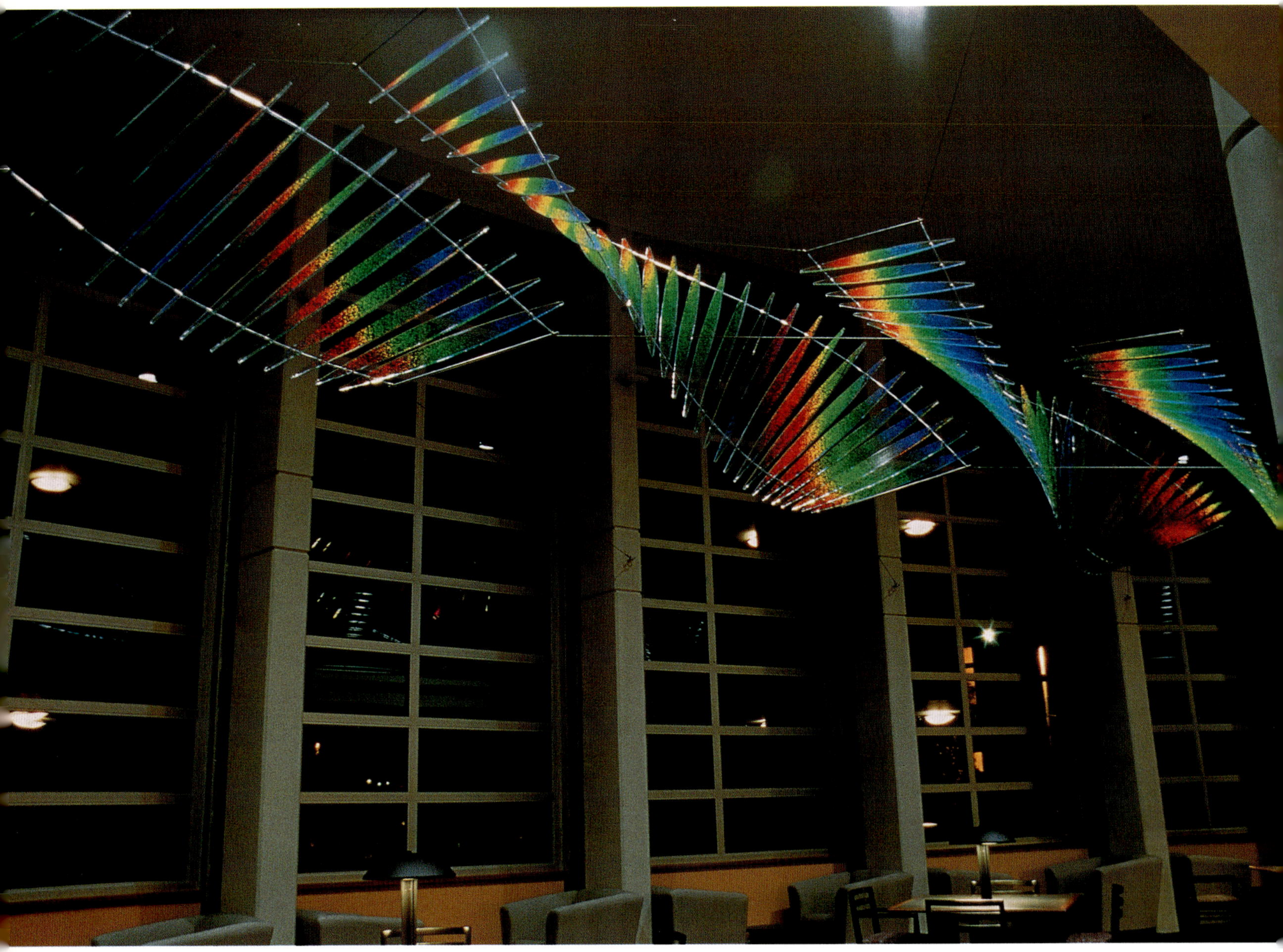

Above:
Light Wave; Student health Center, Iowa Sate University, Ames, 1994. Suspended series of four helices made of laminated, light refractive glass, holographic film, and stainless steel cable, h. 4 x 46 x 4 feet.

Opposite:
Elliptic Lens; Center for Research in Electro-Optic, and Laser Building, University of Florida, Orlando, 1998. Laminated holographic glass and stainless steel cable, h. 26 x 16 feet.

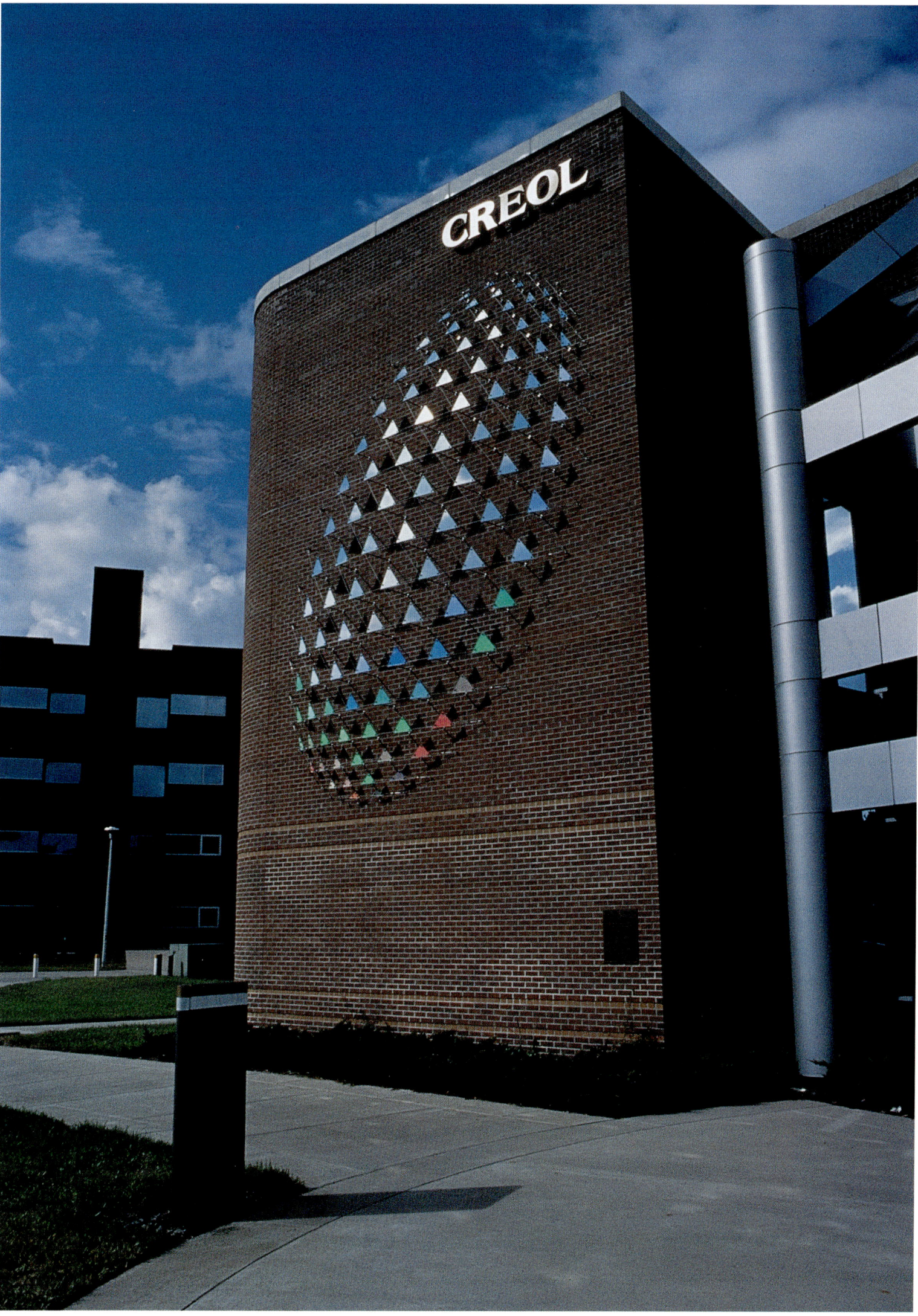

Ruth King
(b.1958)

COLUMBUS, OHIO

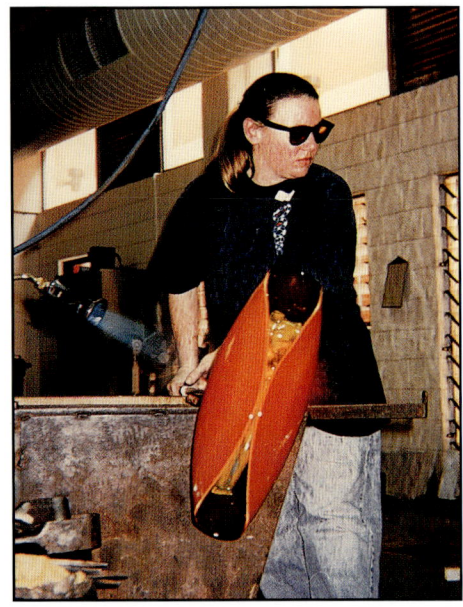

Falling Bodies; Detail, 1999. Blown and coiled glass, and mirror, (figure) h. 15 inches. Photo: Russell Johnson.

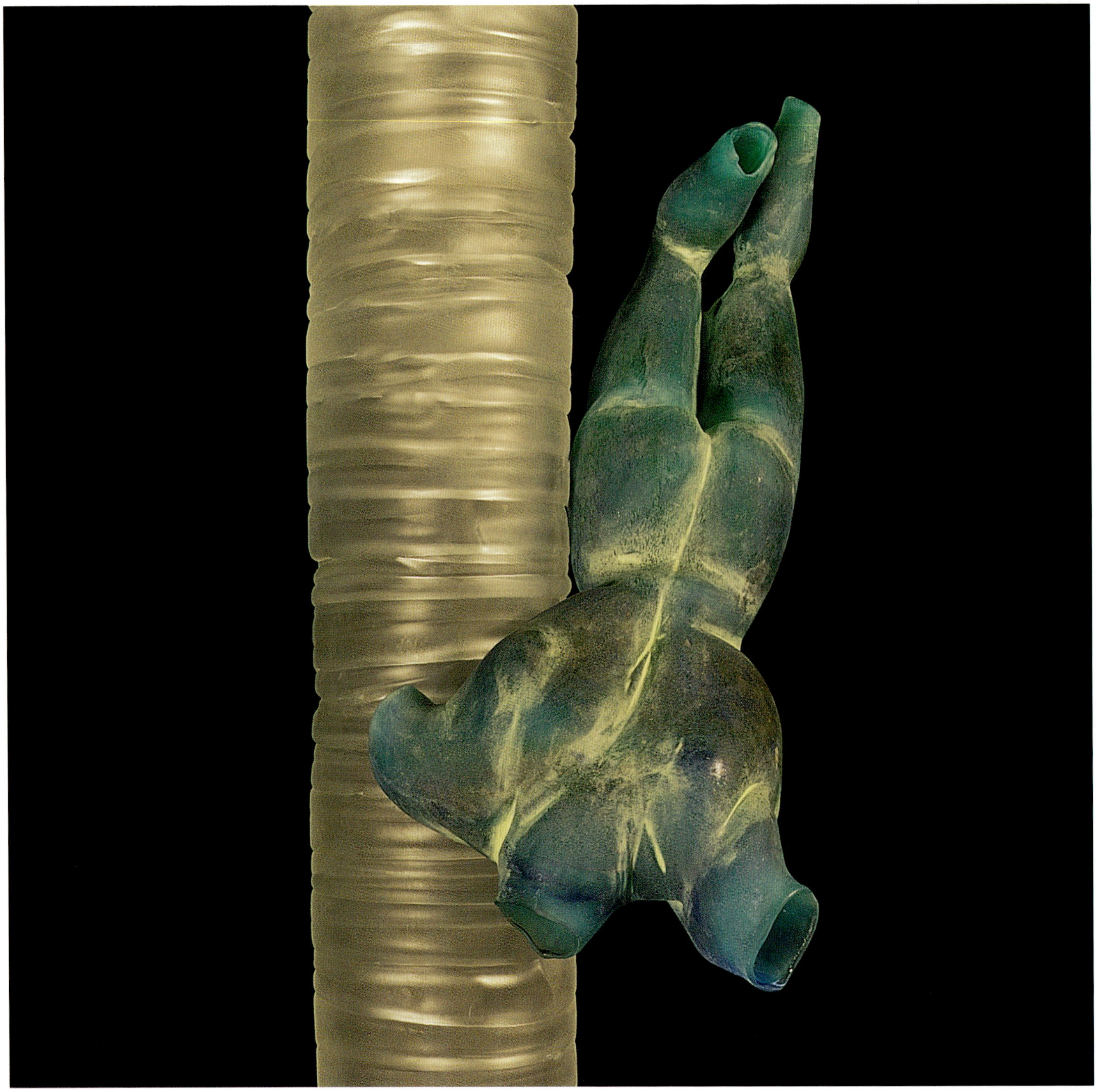

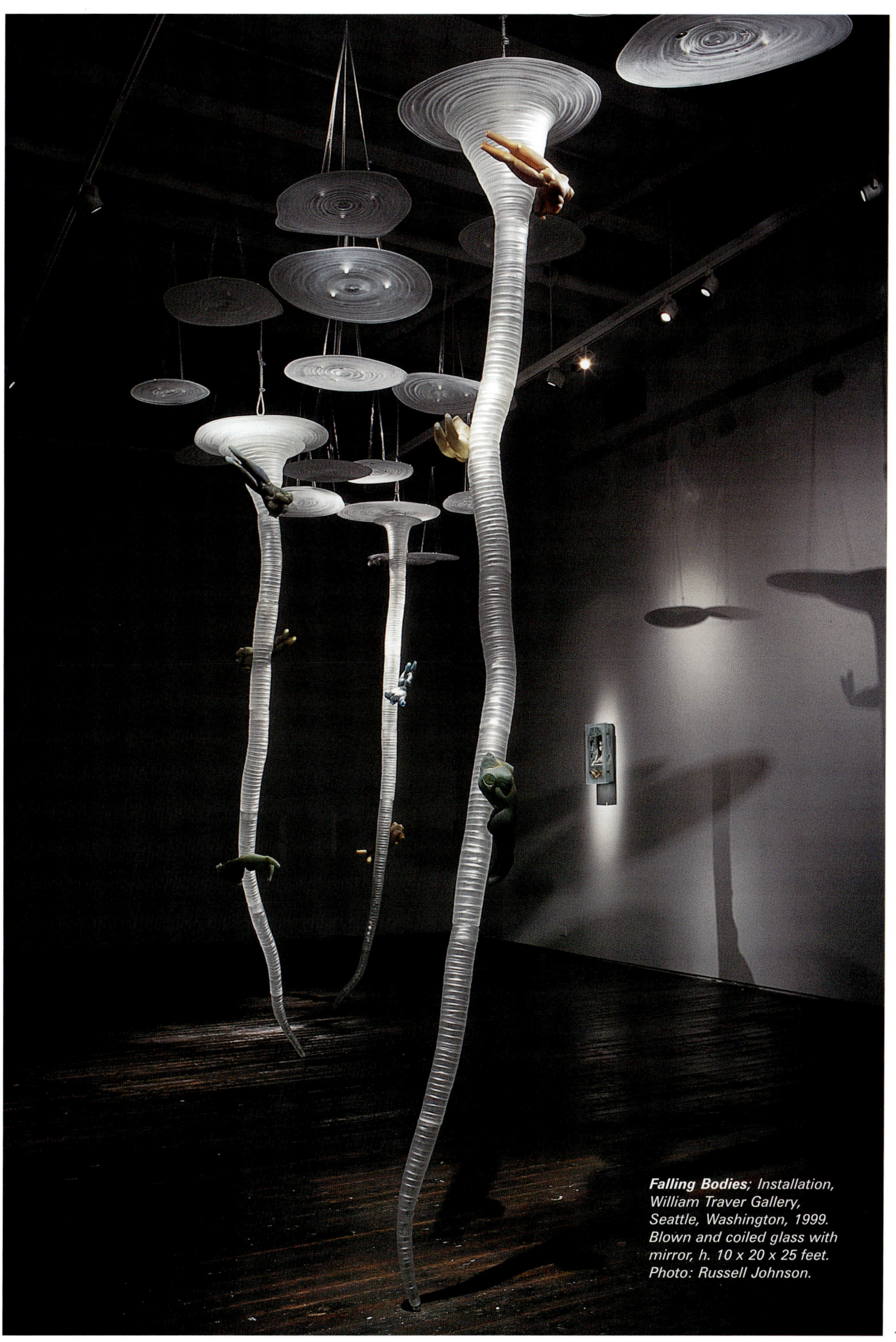

Falling Bodies; Installation, William Traver Gallery, Seattle, Washington, 1999. Blown and coiled glass with mirror, h. 10 x 20 x 25 feet. Photo: Russell Johnson.

Joey Kirkpatrick & Flora C. Mace
(b.1952) (b.1949)

SEATTLE, WASHINGTON

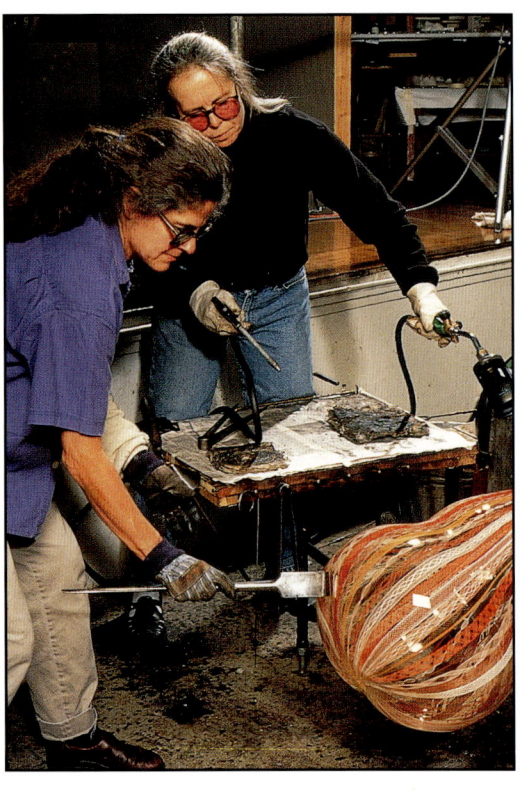

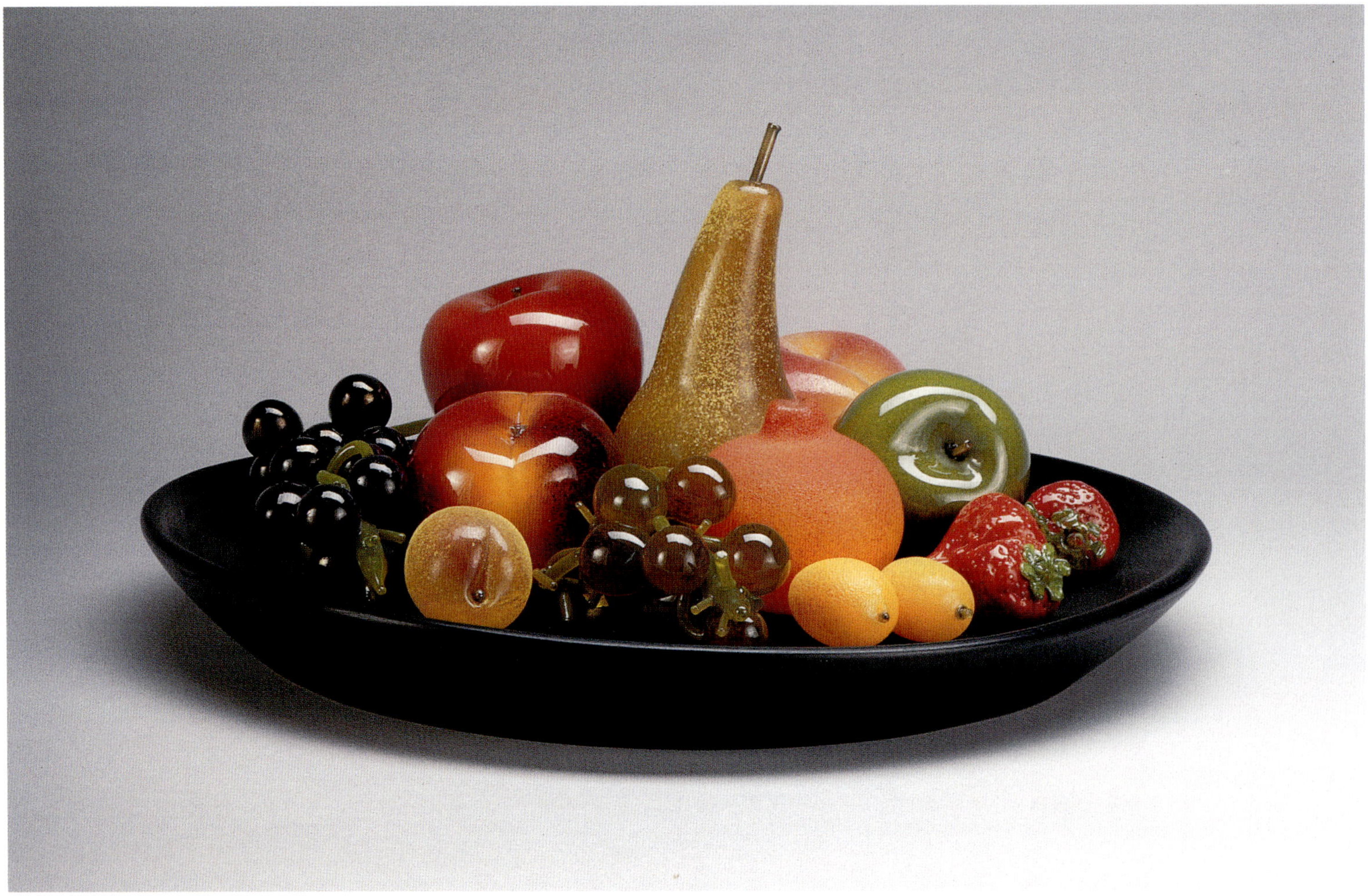

***Fruit Still Life**, 1990. Off hand blown glass, and hand turned alder wood, h. 7.75 x 15.25. Collection of Charles A. Wustum Museum of Fine Arts, Racine, Wisconsin. Gift of Dale and Doug Anderson. Photo: Jon Bolton.*

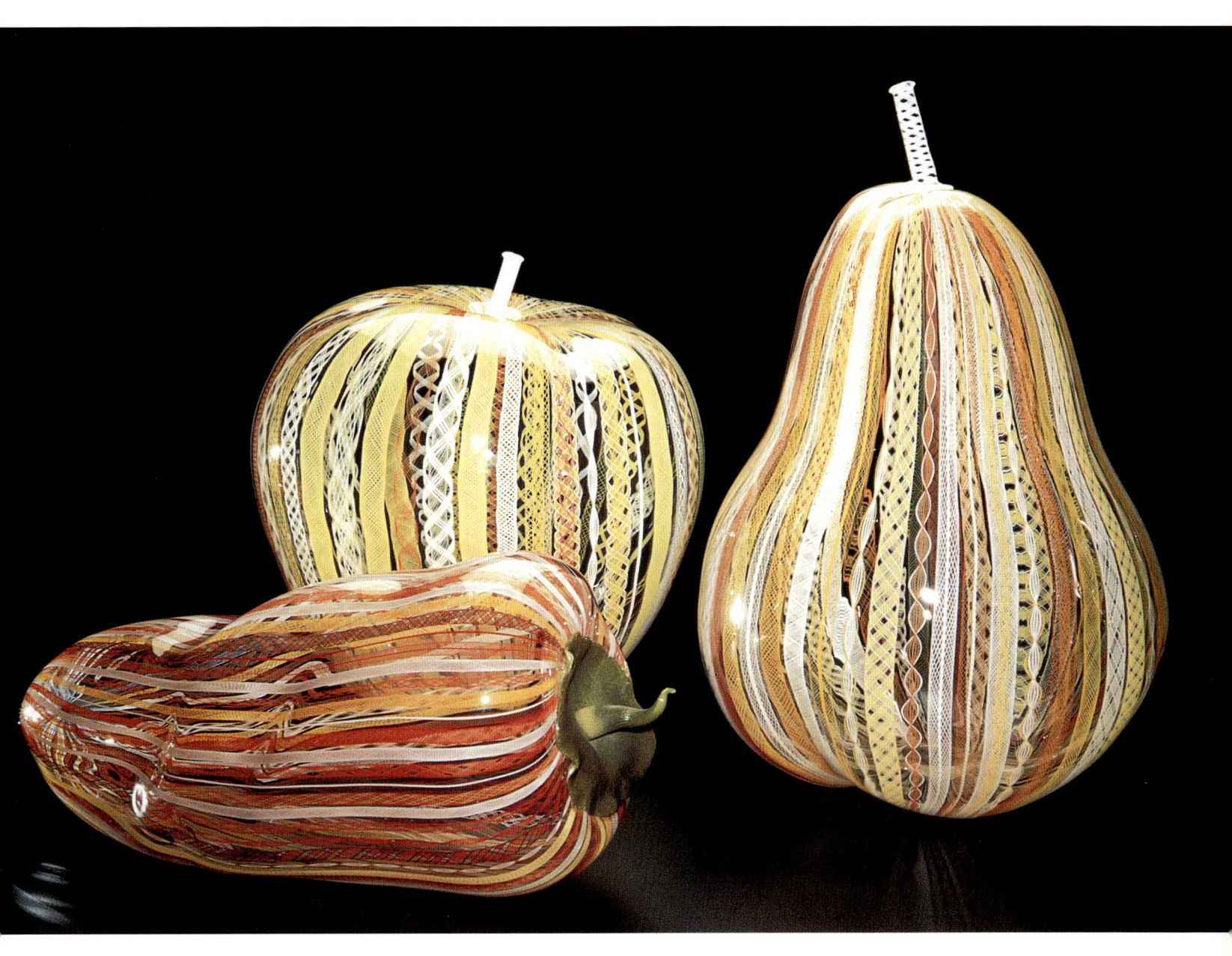

Zanfirico Still Life, 1996. Hand blown glass with Zanfirico cane pick-ups, (pear) h. 27 inches.

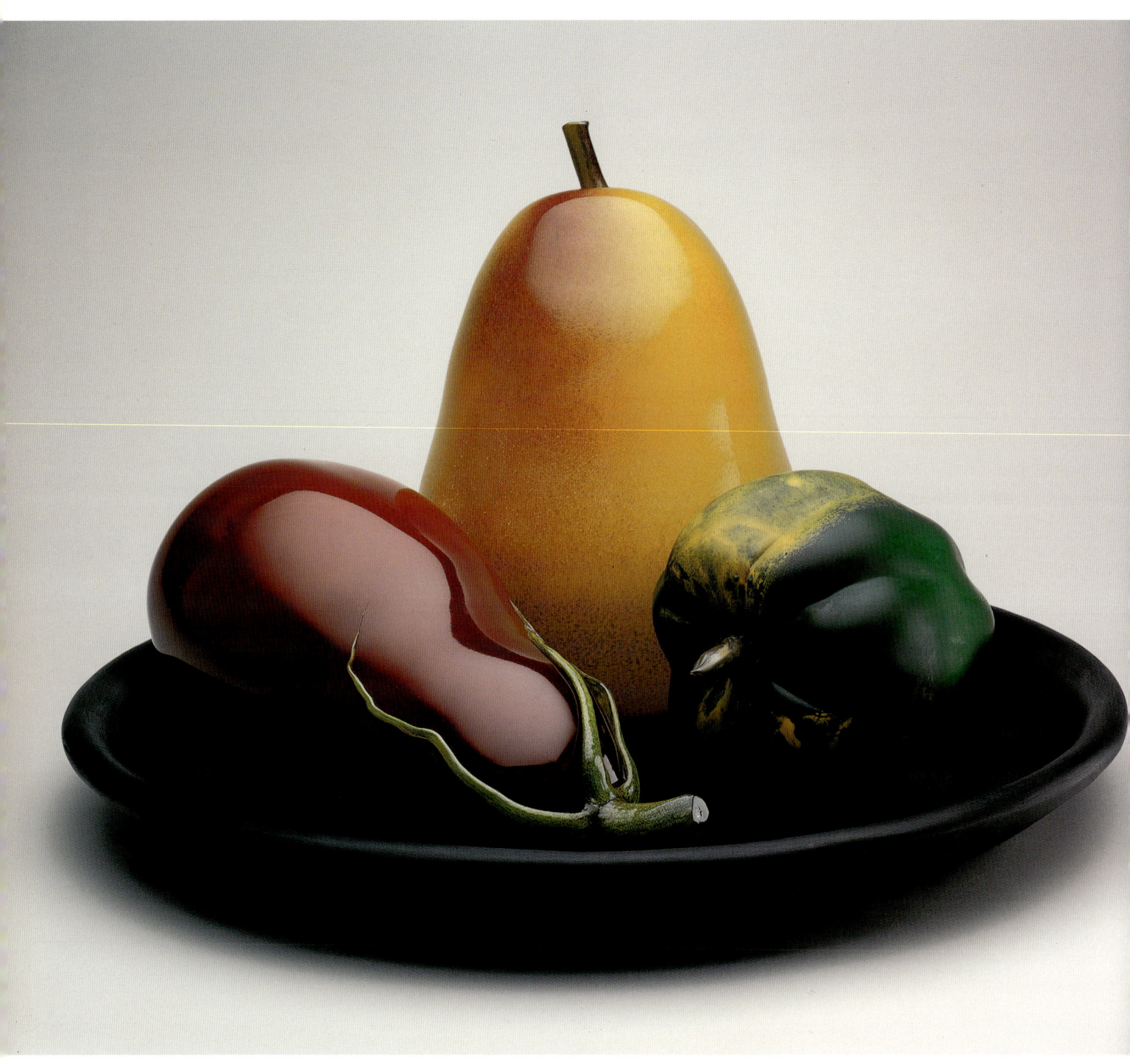

Still-Life with Pear, 1994. Hand blown glass and stained alder wood, h. 28 x 45 inches. Collection The Toledo Museum of Art, Ohio. Gift of Dale and Doug Anderson in honor of Dorothy and George Saxe. Photo: Tim Thayer.

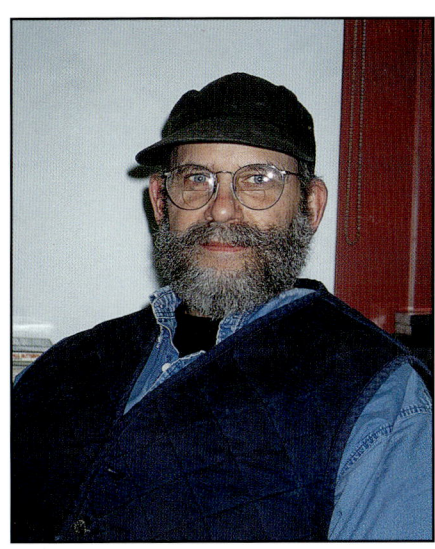

ARLINGTON, MASSACHUSETTS

Alan Klein
(b.1947)

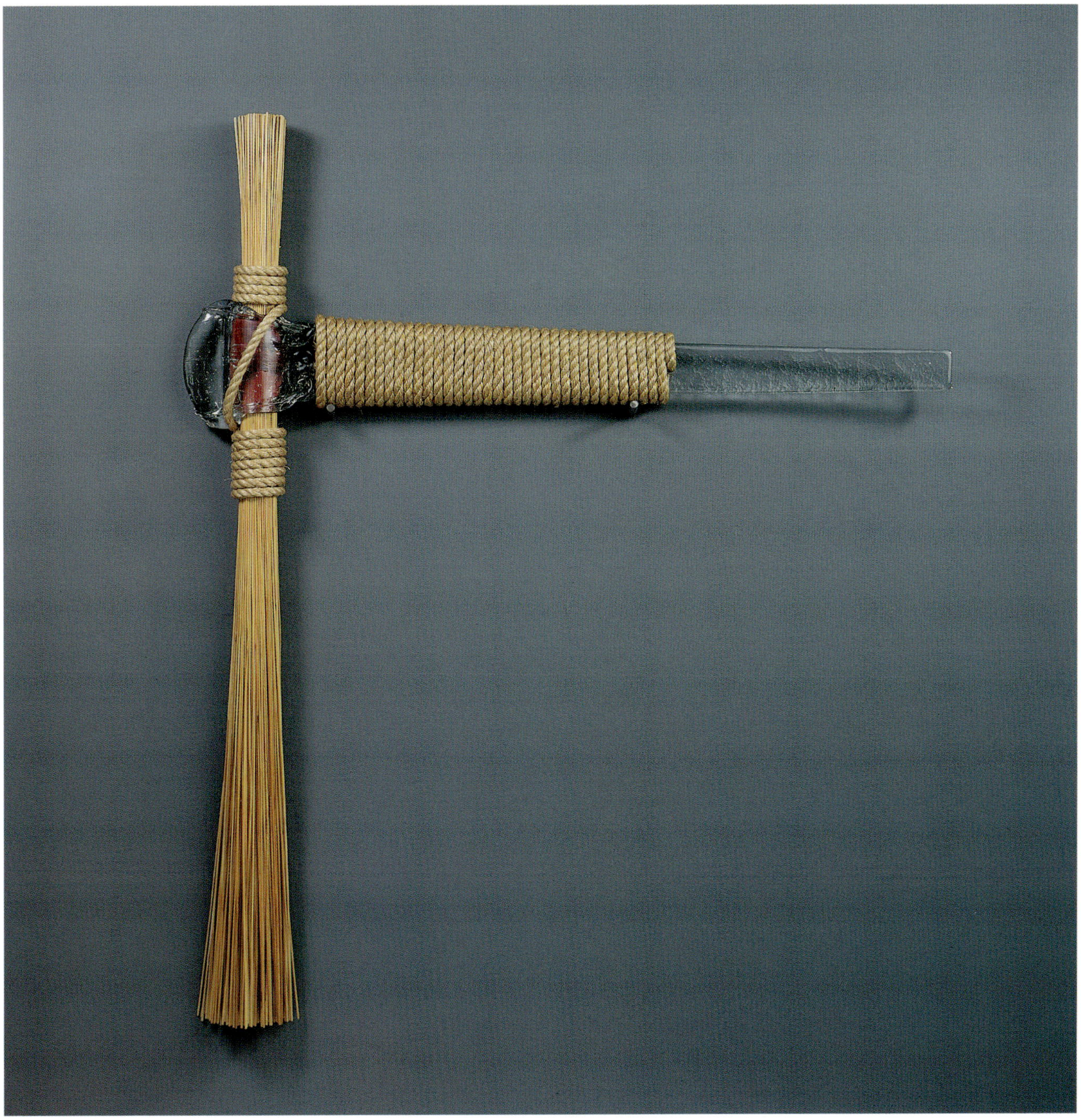

Bound Brush, 1995. Cast glass, tape, and bamboo, h. 48 x 48 x 3 inches.

Gene Koss
(b.1947)

NEW ORLEANS, LOUISIANA

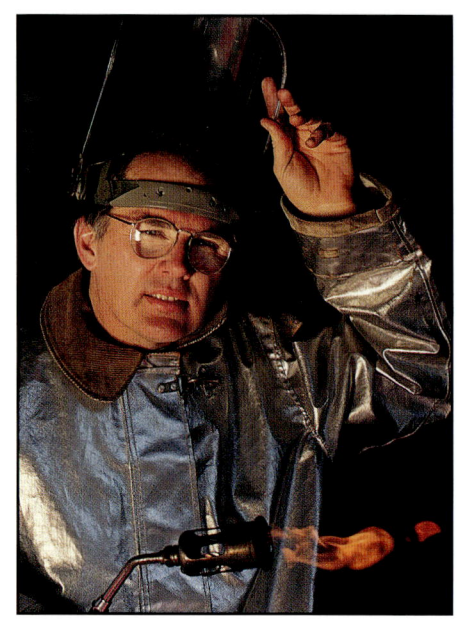

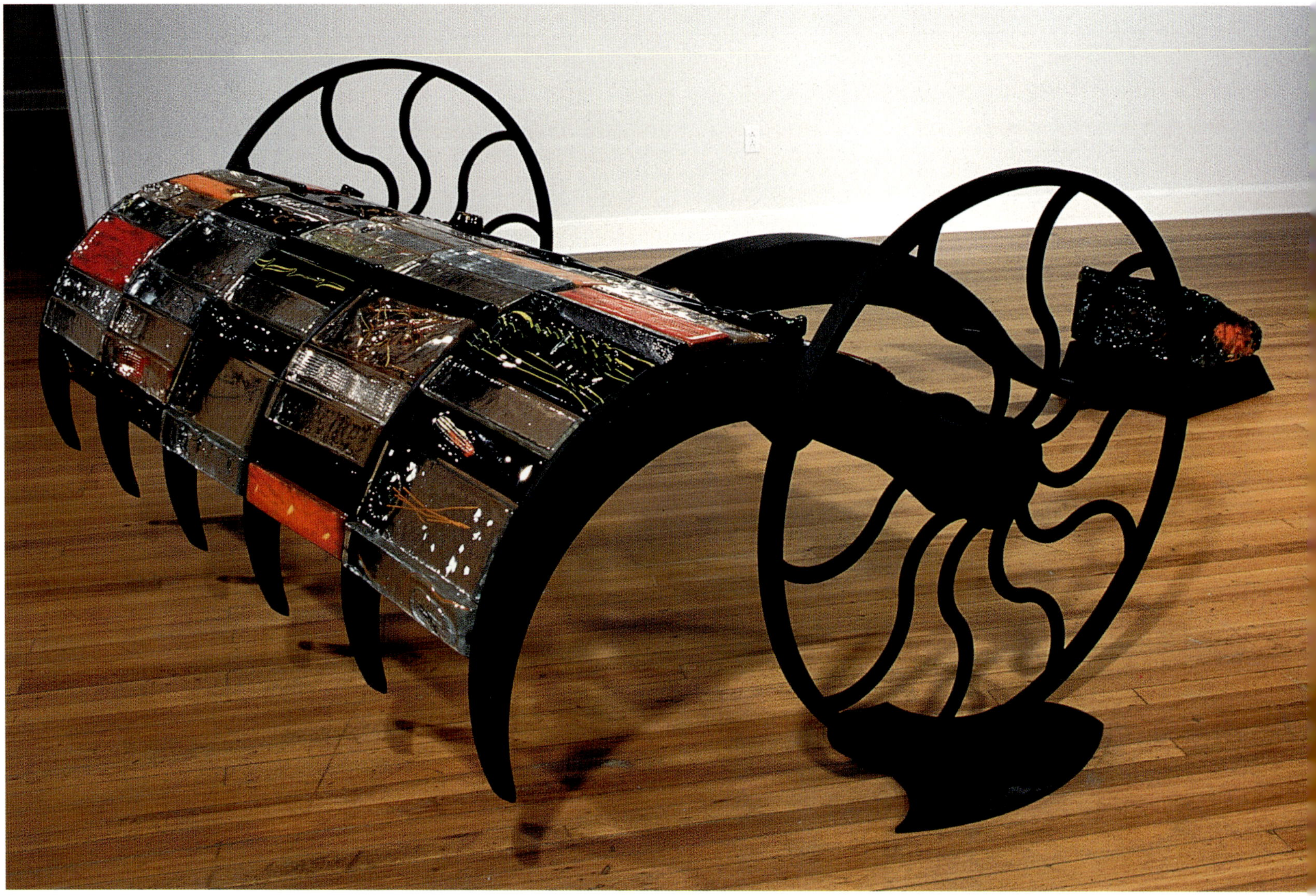

Amish, 1995. Cast glass, and steel, h. 4.5 x 8 x 15 feet. Photo: Dana Sherman.

BROOKLYN, NEW YORK

Andi Kovel
(b.1969)

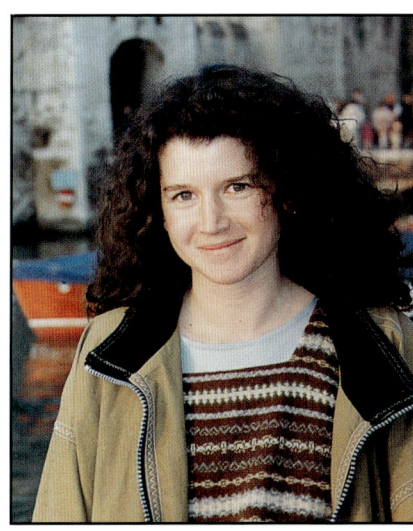

Trophies, 1997. Glass, wood and, rubber, h. 65 x 3 inches.

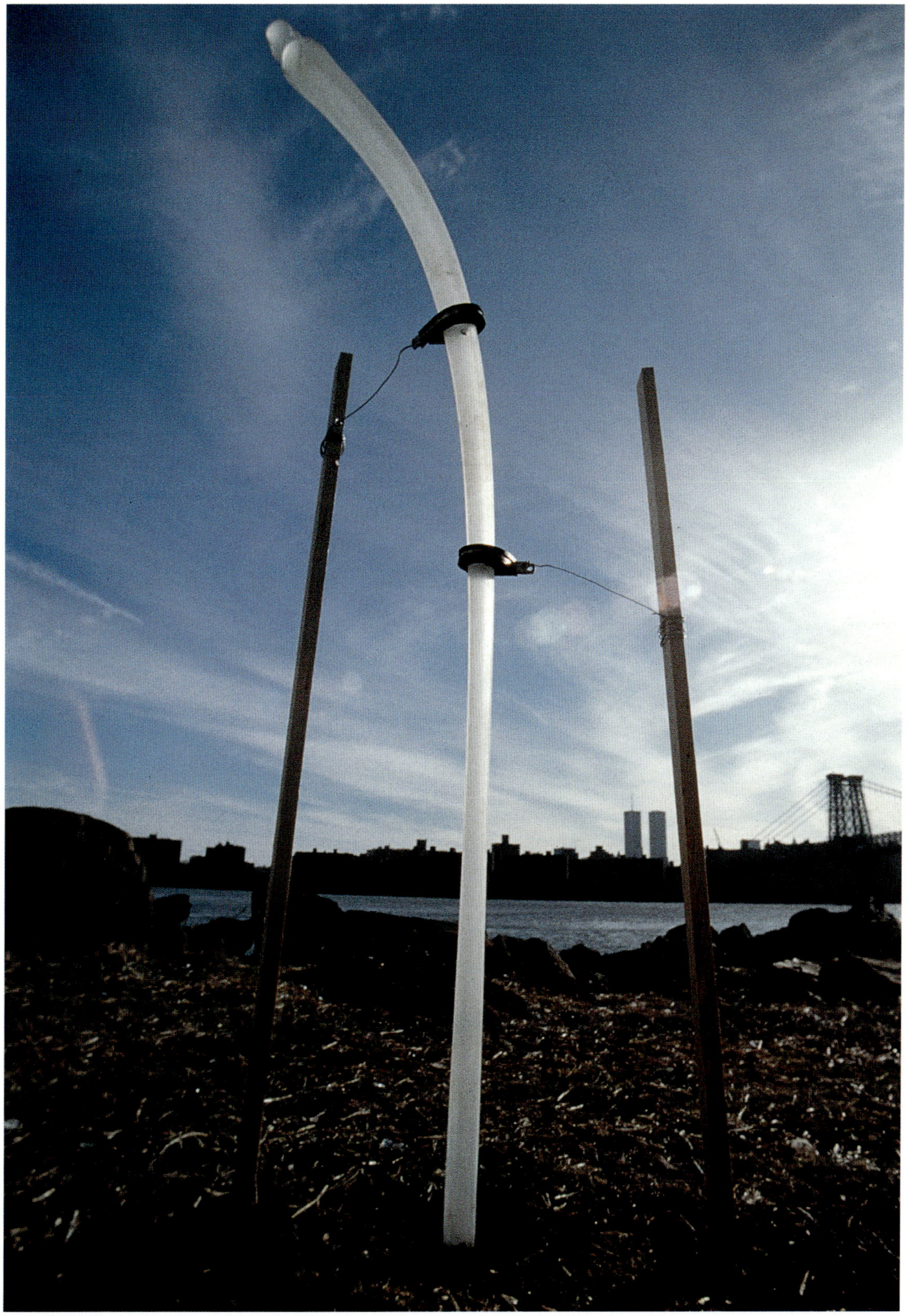

125

Niho Kozuru
(b.1968)

HONOLULU, HAWAII

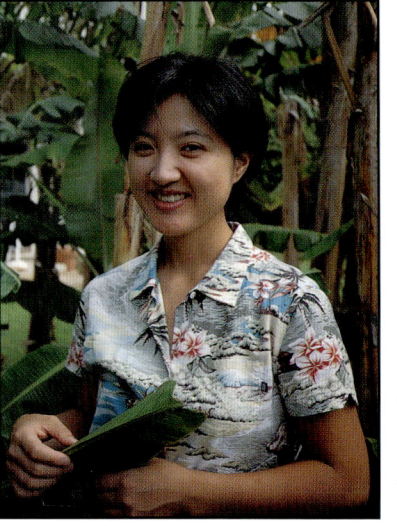
Photo: Jeffrey H. Hayes

Celebration of Spirit; Installation, Forest Hills, Boston, 1998. Mold blown glass, h. 9 x 15 x 40 feet.

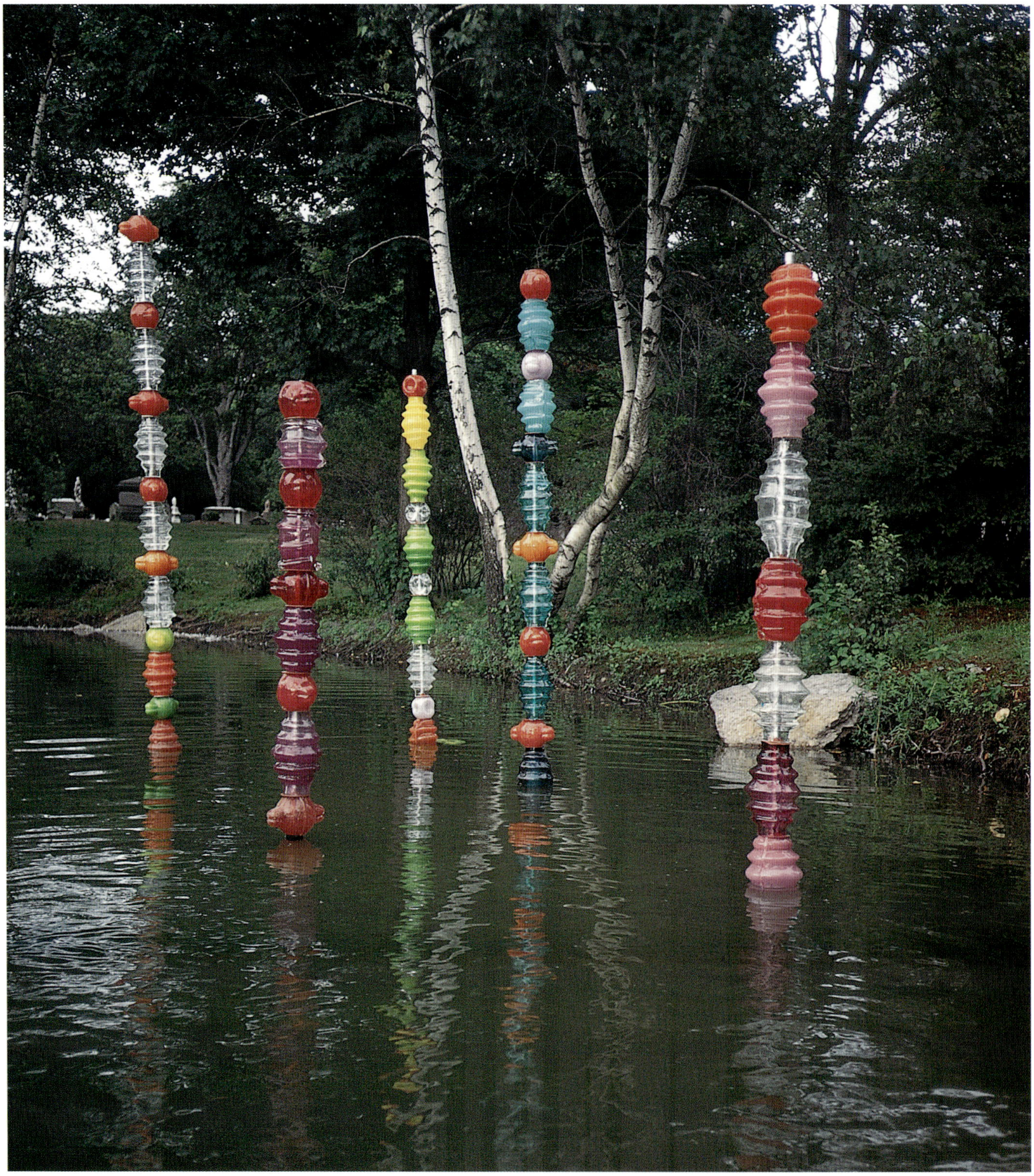

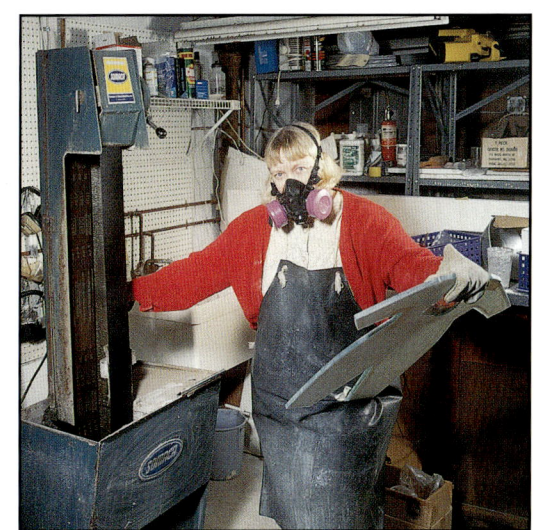

SILVER SPRING, MARYLAND

Susie Krasnican
(b.1954)

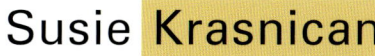

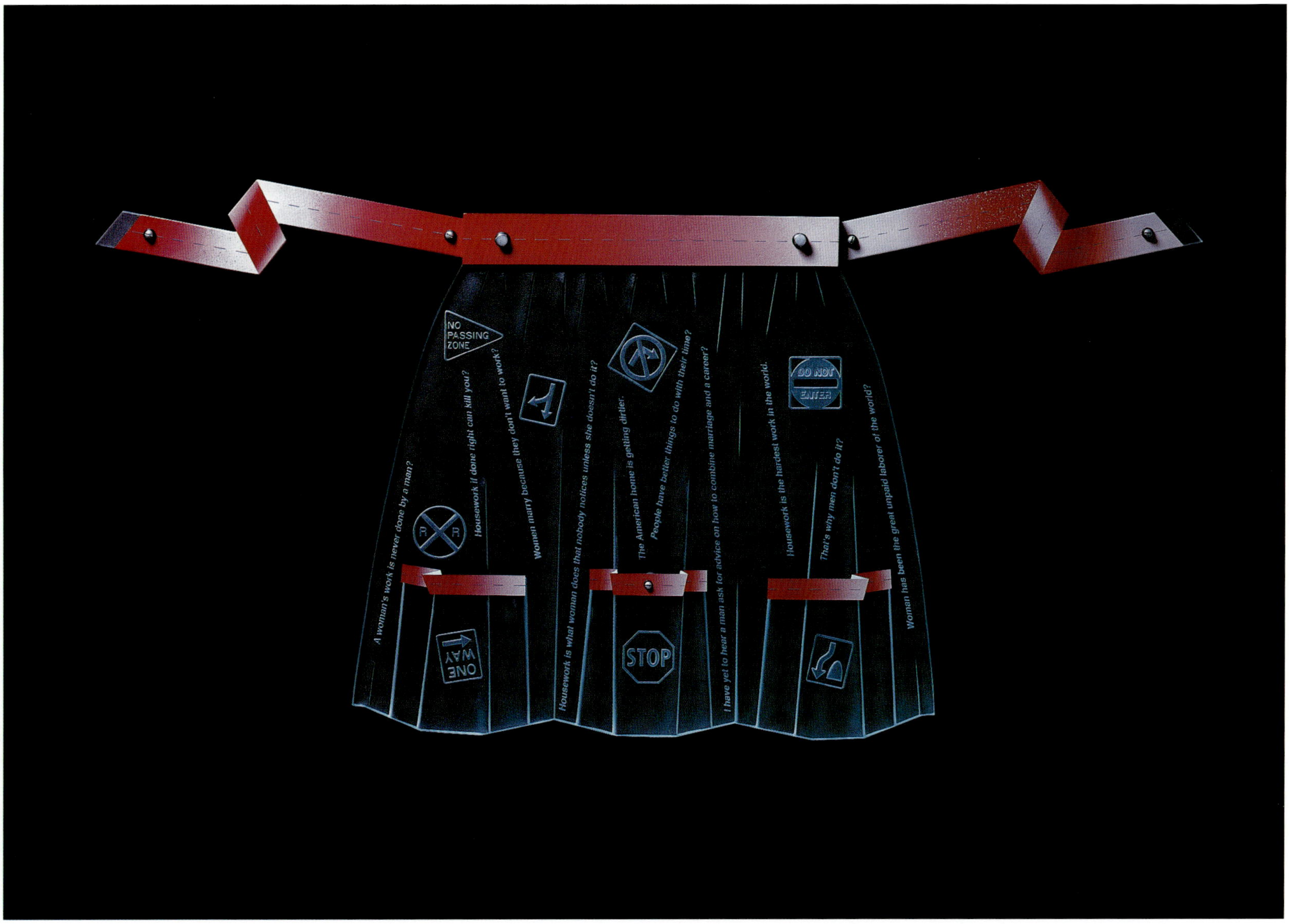

Stop, Look, Listen, 1998. Words courtesy of (reading left to right):
1. Saying; 2. John Skow; 3. Unknown; 4. Evan Estar; 5. Mary
Ellen Pinkham; 6. Gloria Steinem; 7. Edna Ferber; 8. Elizabeth
Cady Staton, Susan B. Anthony and Matilda J. Gage. Sandblasted
and enameled glass, h. 20 x 40 x .5 inches. Photo: Mark Gulezian.

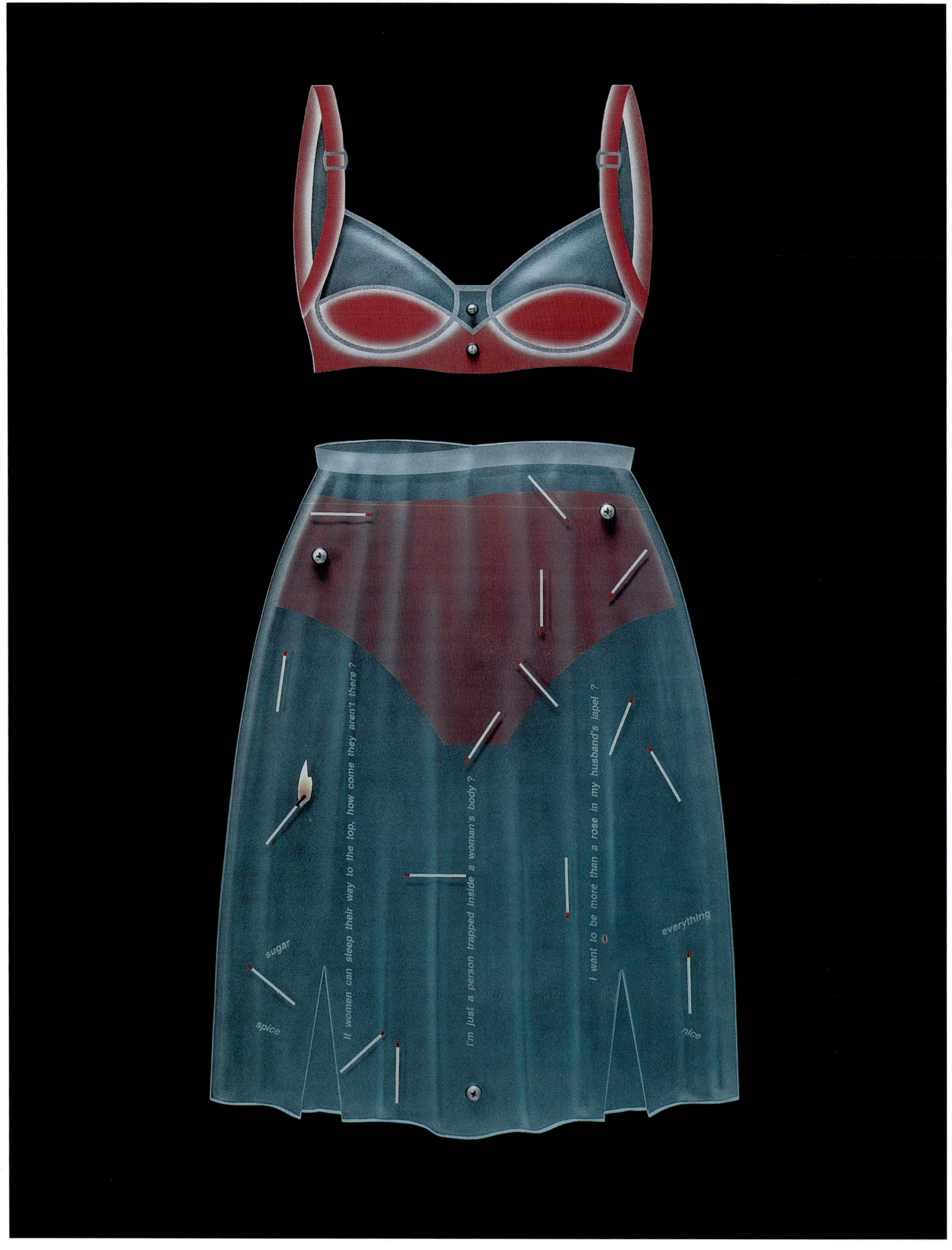

Sugar, Spice & Everything Nice, 1998. Words courtesy of (reading left to right): 1. Ellen Goodman; 2. Elayne Boosler; and 3. Margaret Trudeau. Sandblasted and enameled glass, h. 35.3 x 16.5 x .5 inches overall. Photo: Mark Gulezian.

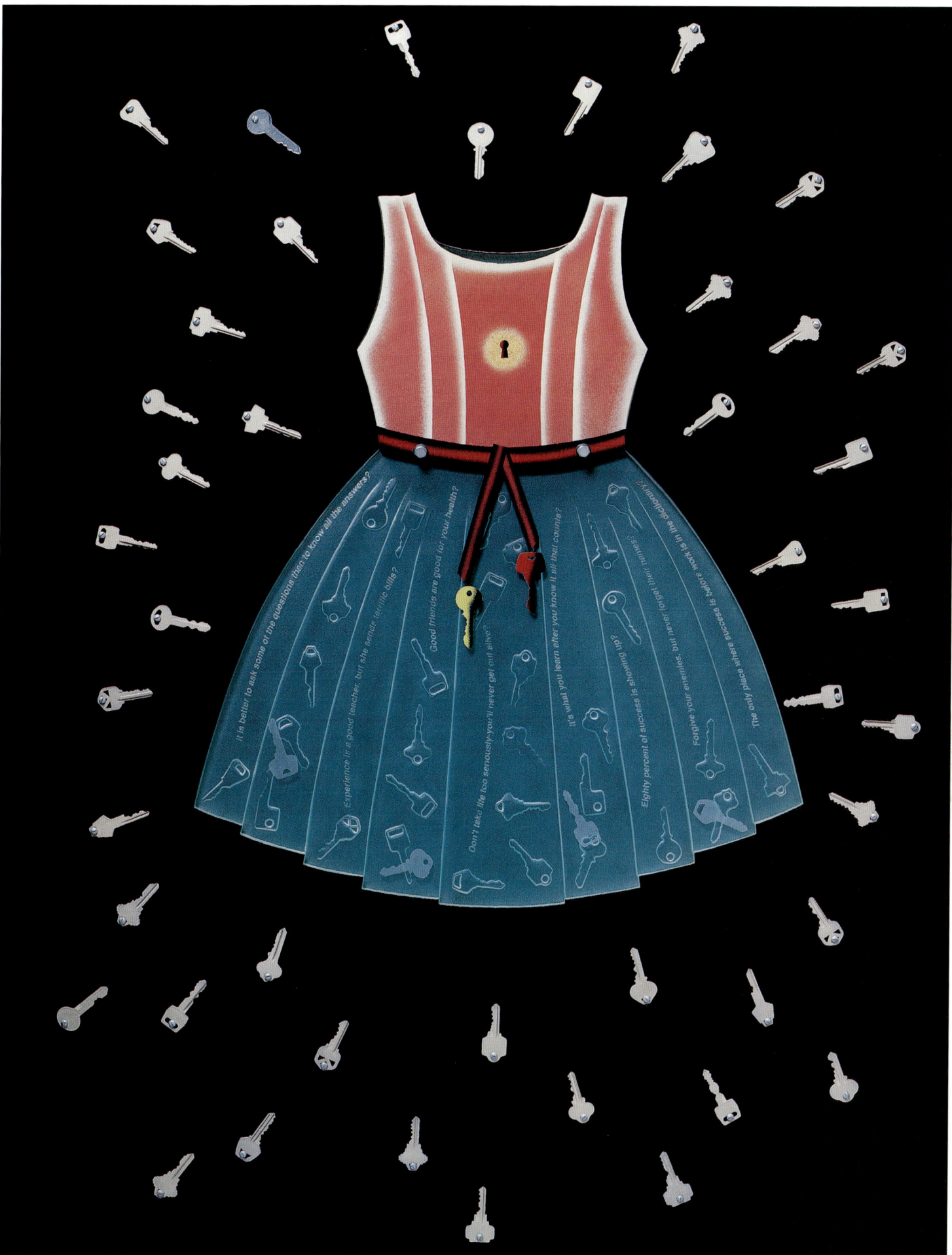

Dress For Success, 1997. Words courtesy of (reading left to right): 1. James Thurber; 2. Minna Antrim; 3. Irwin Sarason; 4. Elbert Hubbard; 5. John Wooden; 6. Woody Allen; 7. Attributed to John F. Kennedy; and 8. Vidal Sassoon. Sandblasted and enameled glass, h. 26.5 x 20 x .5 inches. National Museum of American Art, Smithsonian Institution. Gift of Anne and Ronald Abramson, Vera and Robert Loeffler, Elmerina and Paul Parkman, and Maurine Littleton Gallery. Photo: Mark Gulezian.

Karen La Monte
(b.1967)

CZECH REPUBLIC

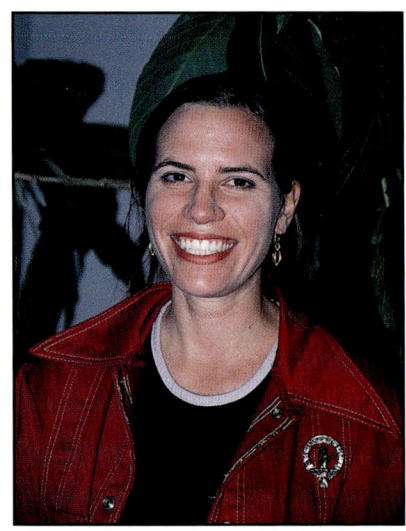

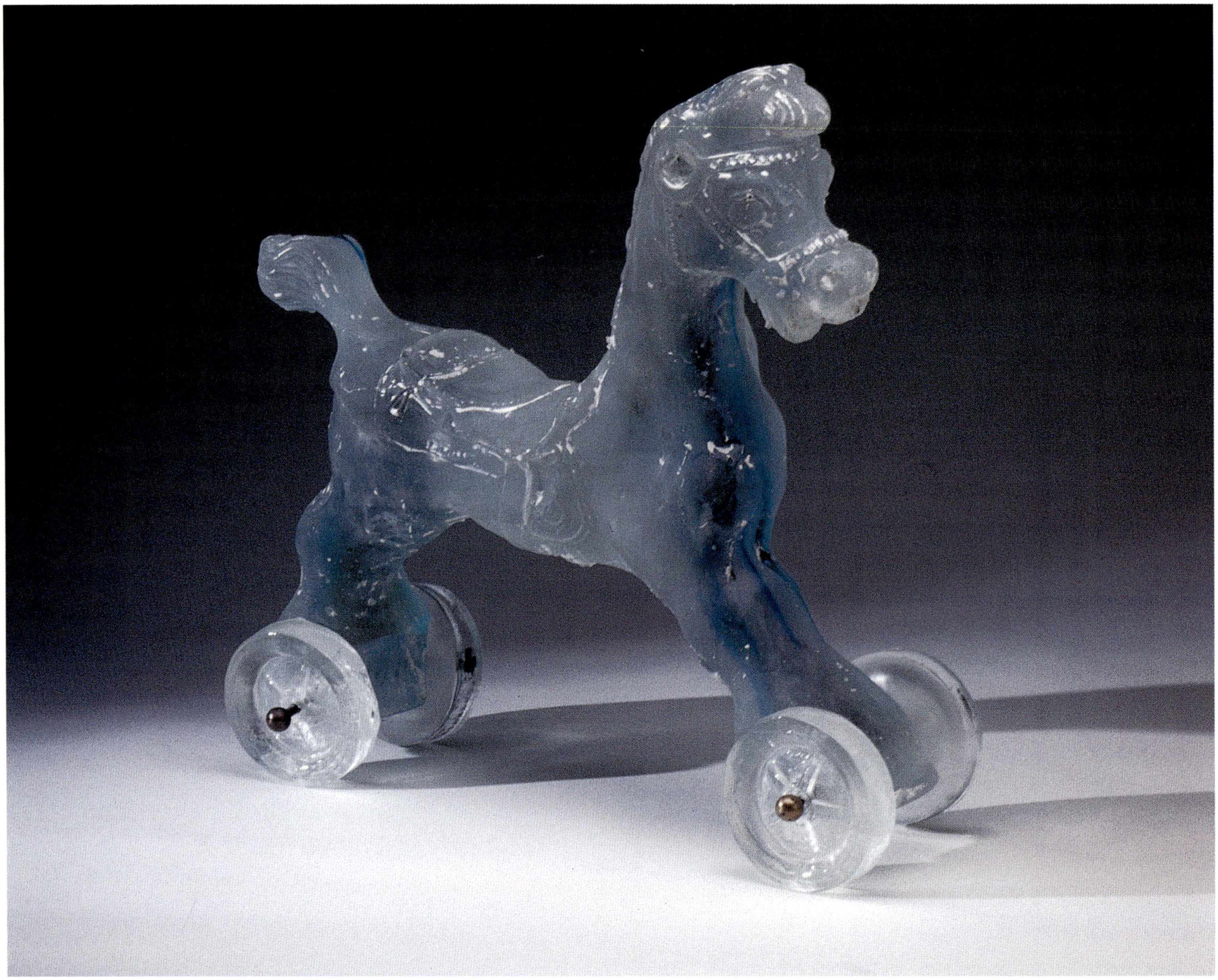

Untitled, 1995. Cast glass and brass, h. 18 x 18.5 x 5.75 inches.
Charles A. Wustum Museum of fine Arts, Racine, Wisconsin.
Gift of Dale and Doug Anderson. Photo: Jon Bolton.

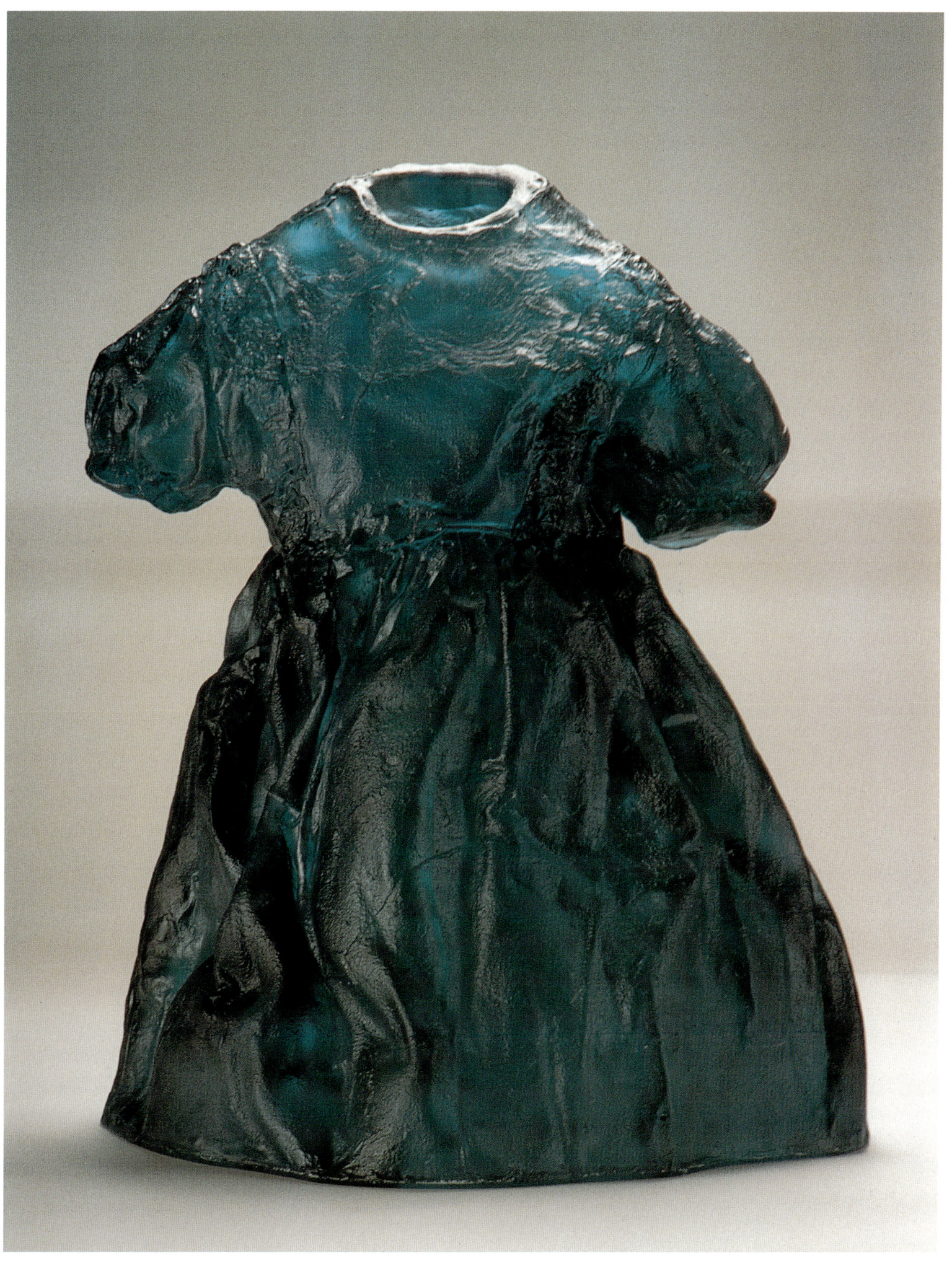

Dress Blue, 1998. Cast glass, h. 18 x 16 x 16.

Andrée Laramée
(b.1956)

BROOKLYN, NEW YORK

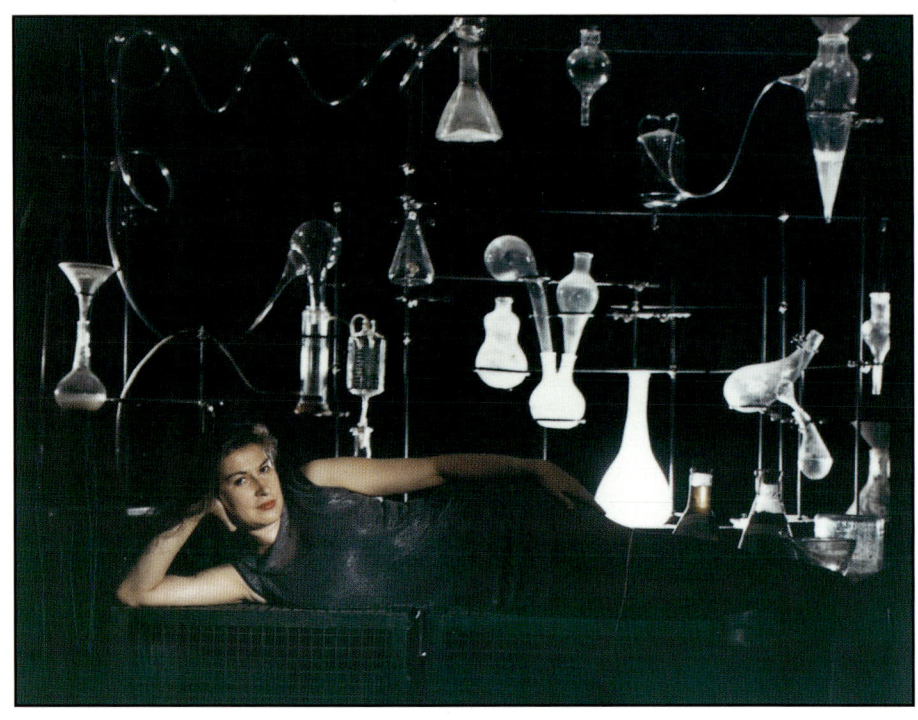

Queen of the Laboratory, *Photo: Jason MacConnathy.*

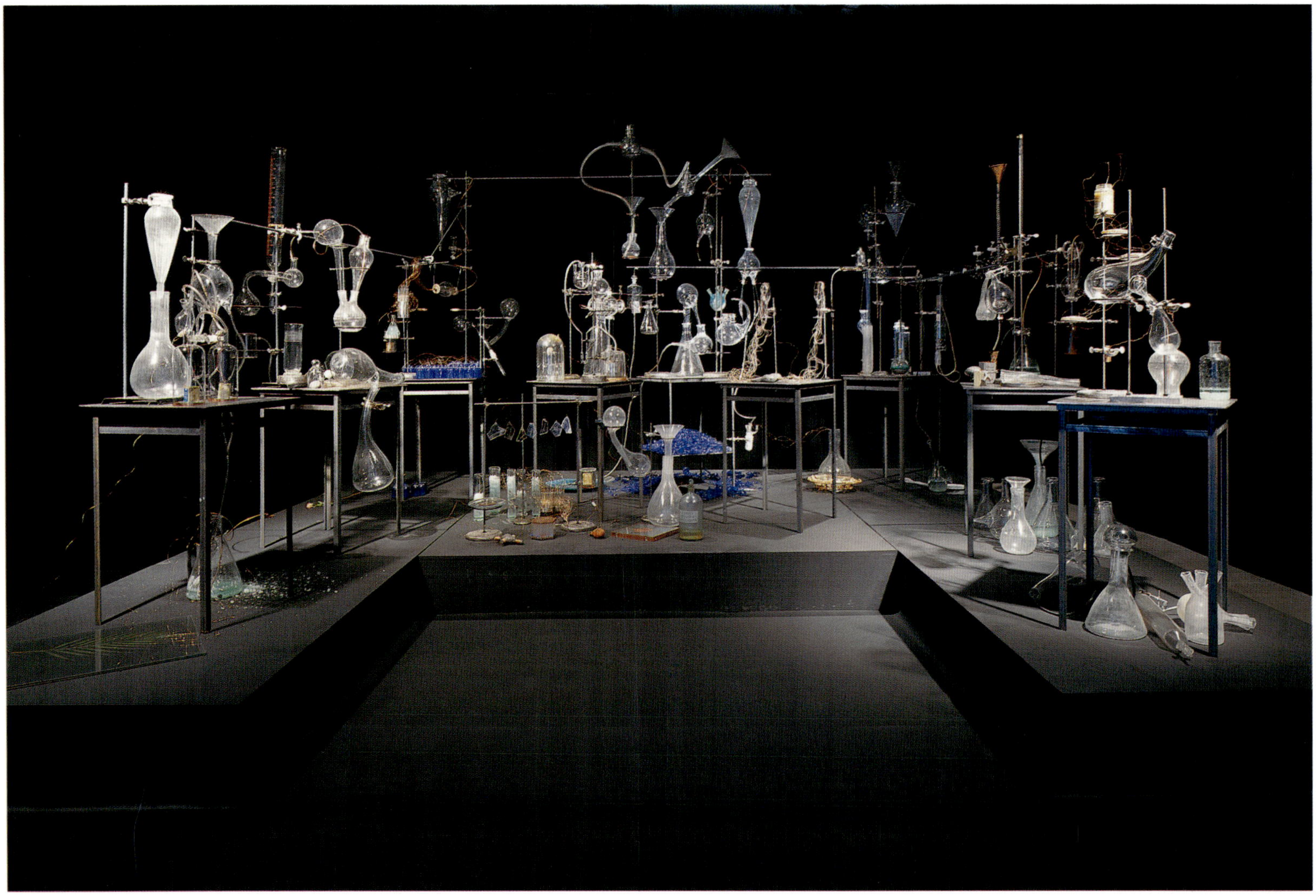

Above:
The Science of Approximation; Installation, Robert Lehman Gallery, UrbanGlass, 1991. Handblown glass, laboratory glass sandblasted with text, copper, steel, fresh flowers, salt, and water, h. 10 x 20 x 14 feet. Photo: Eve Heyd.

Opposite:
The Science of Approximation; Installation Detail.

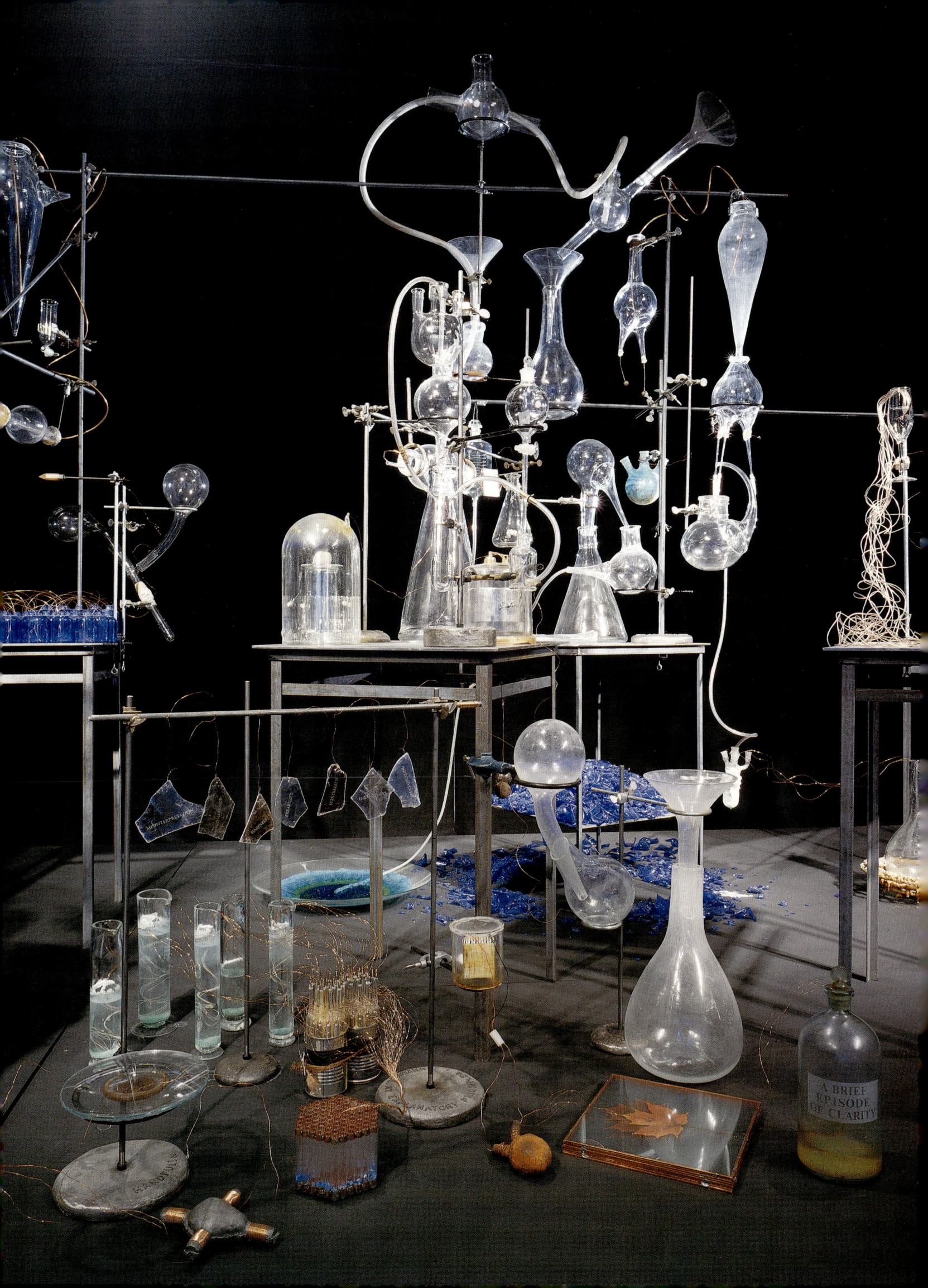

Antoine Leperlier
(b.1953)

CONCHES EN OUCHE, FRANCE

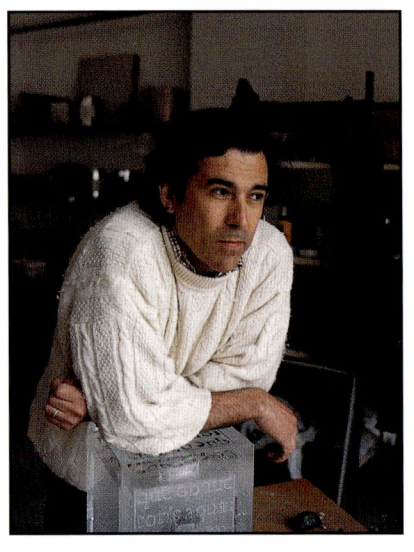

Photo: Dicki Goupy

Still Life/Still Alive XII, 1998. Crystal Pâte de Verre, enameled text, steel frame with black patina and engraved text. h. 30 x 22 x 9 inches. Courtesy Habatat Galleries. Photo: Douglas Schaible.

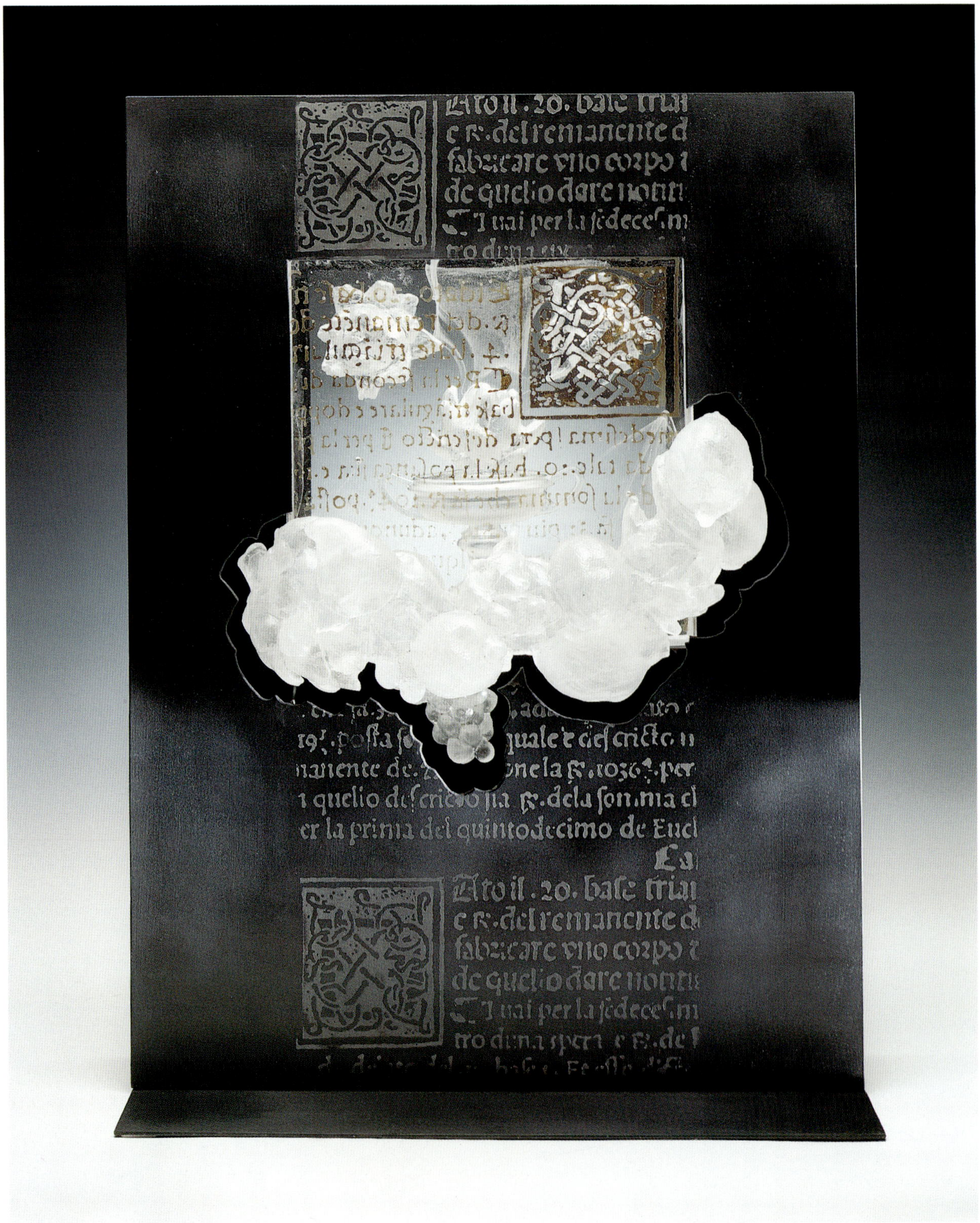

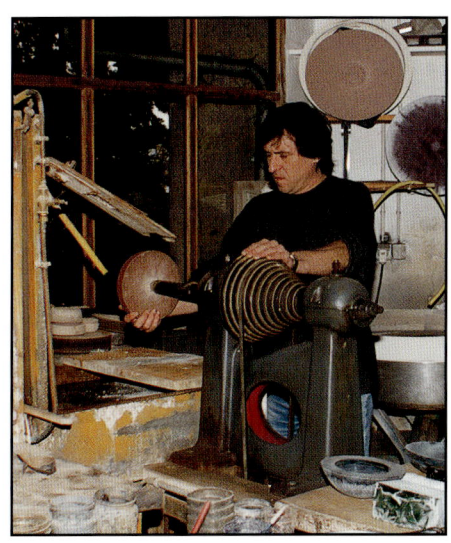

CONCHES EN OUCHE, FRANCE

Etienne Leperlier
(b.1952)

Anatomie D'Ombre II, 1998. Crystal Pâte de Verre, h. 24 x 8 inches. Collection of the Detroit Institute of Arts. Gift of Jack and Aviva Robinson. Photo: Courtesy Habatat Galleries.

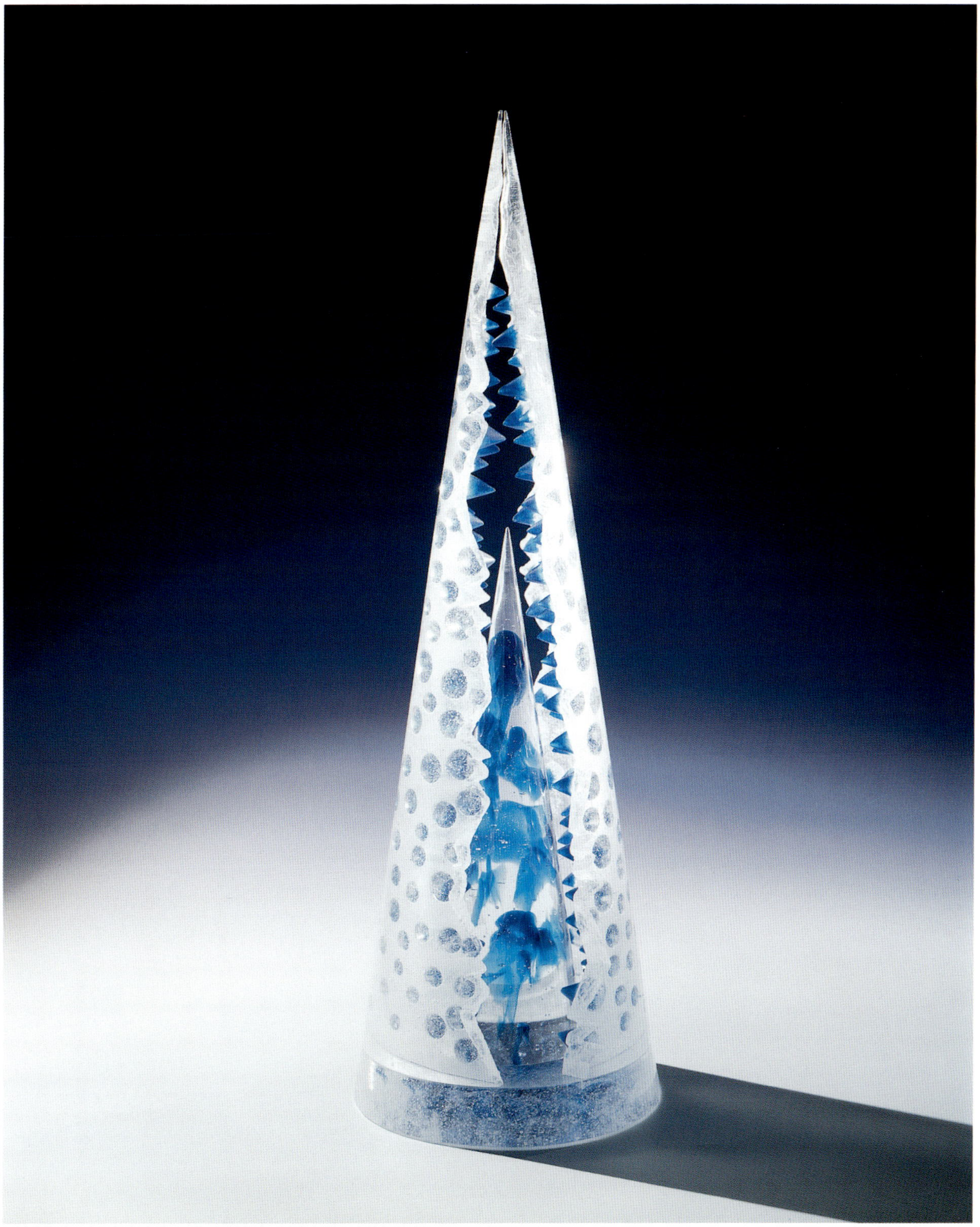

Marc Leuthold
(b.1962)

POTSDAM, NEW YORK

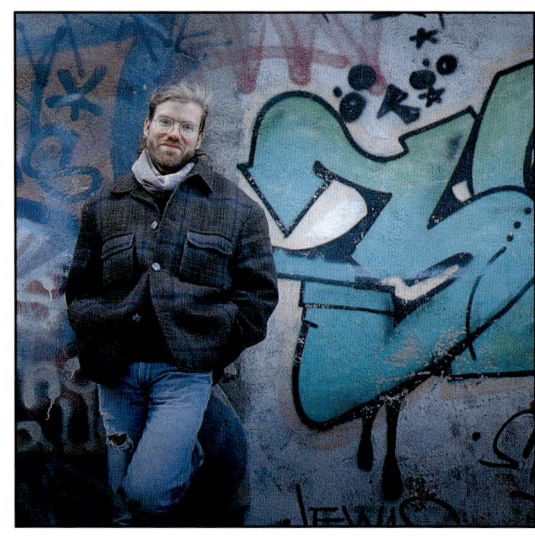

Untitled 52, 1998 Lead crystal pâte de verre, h. 11.5 x 2 inches. Photo: Eva Heyd

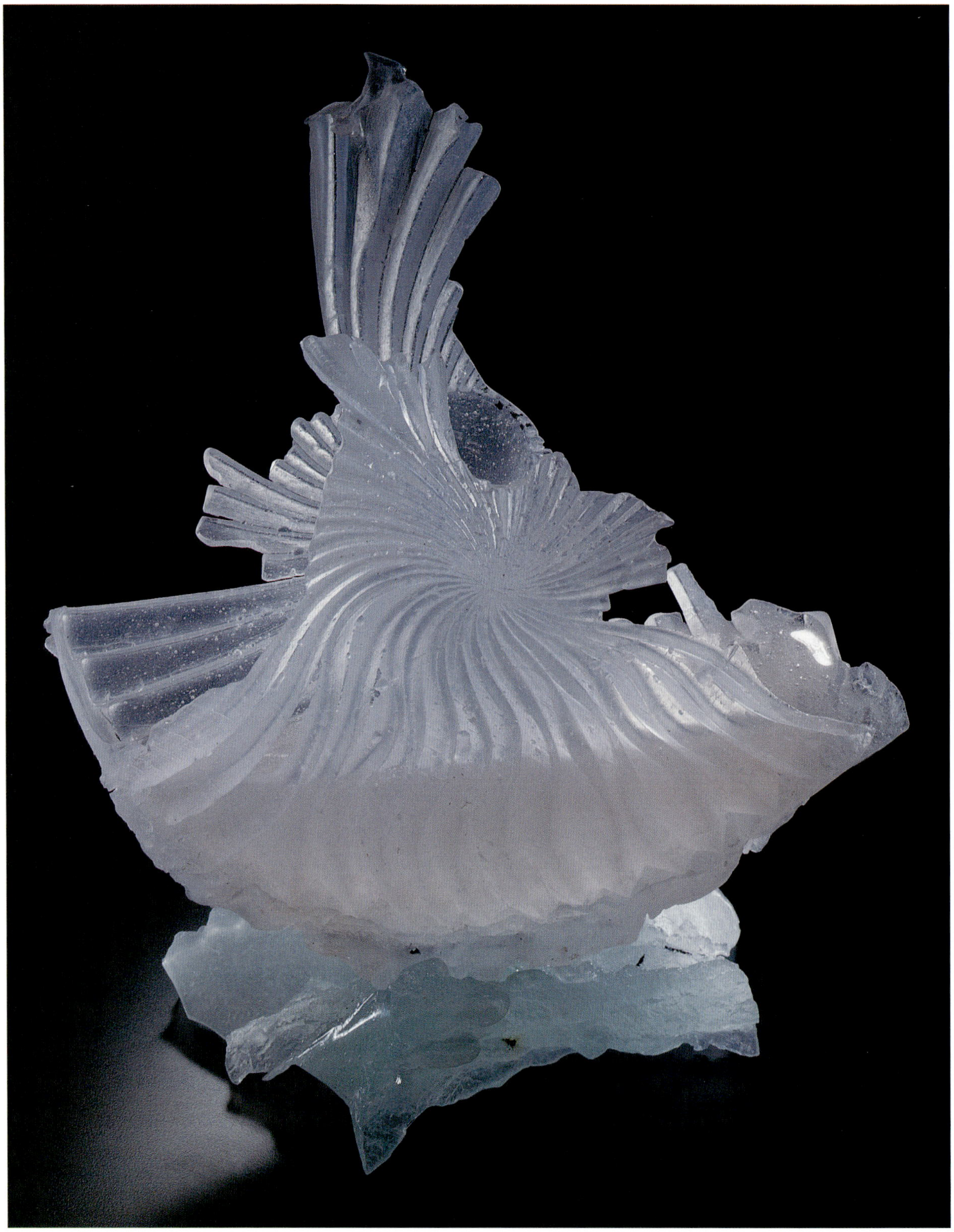

CZECH REPUBLIC

Stanislav Libensky & Jaroslava Brychtova
(b.1921) (b.1924)

Photo: Russell Johnson

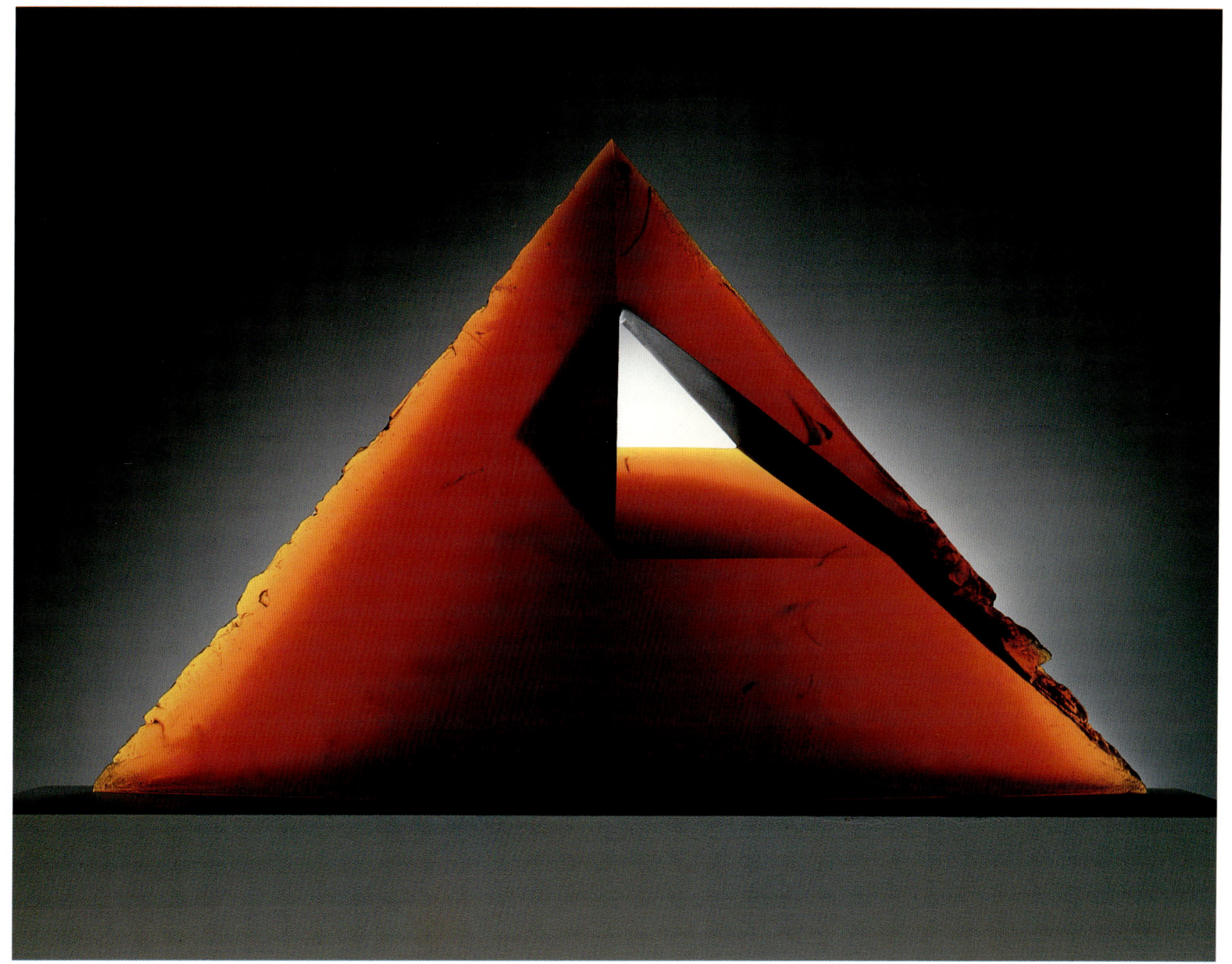

***Triangle in a Triangle**, 1990-91. Cast glass, h. 12 x 51.6 x 10 inches. Courtesy Habatat Galleries. Photo: Doug Schaible.*

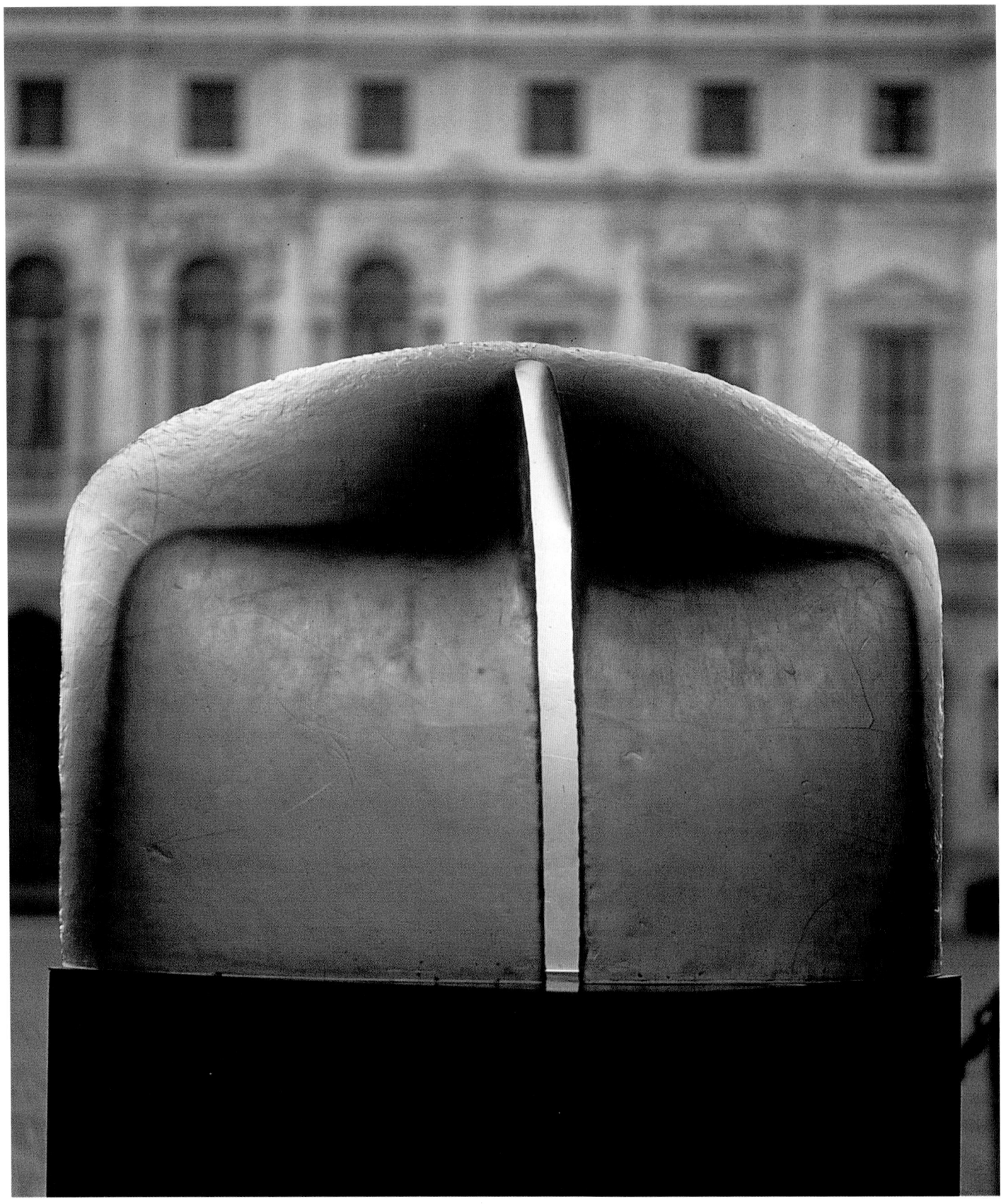

Above:
Imprint of an Angel II, 1996-97. Cast glass, h. 30.7 x 42.9 x 10.24 inches. Private collection. Photo: Martin Polak.

Opposite:
Crystal Wall; Old Town Hall, Prague, 1983-90. Cast glass in metal structure, h. 322.8 x 287.4 inches. Courtesy Heller Gallery. Photo: George Erml.

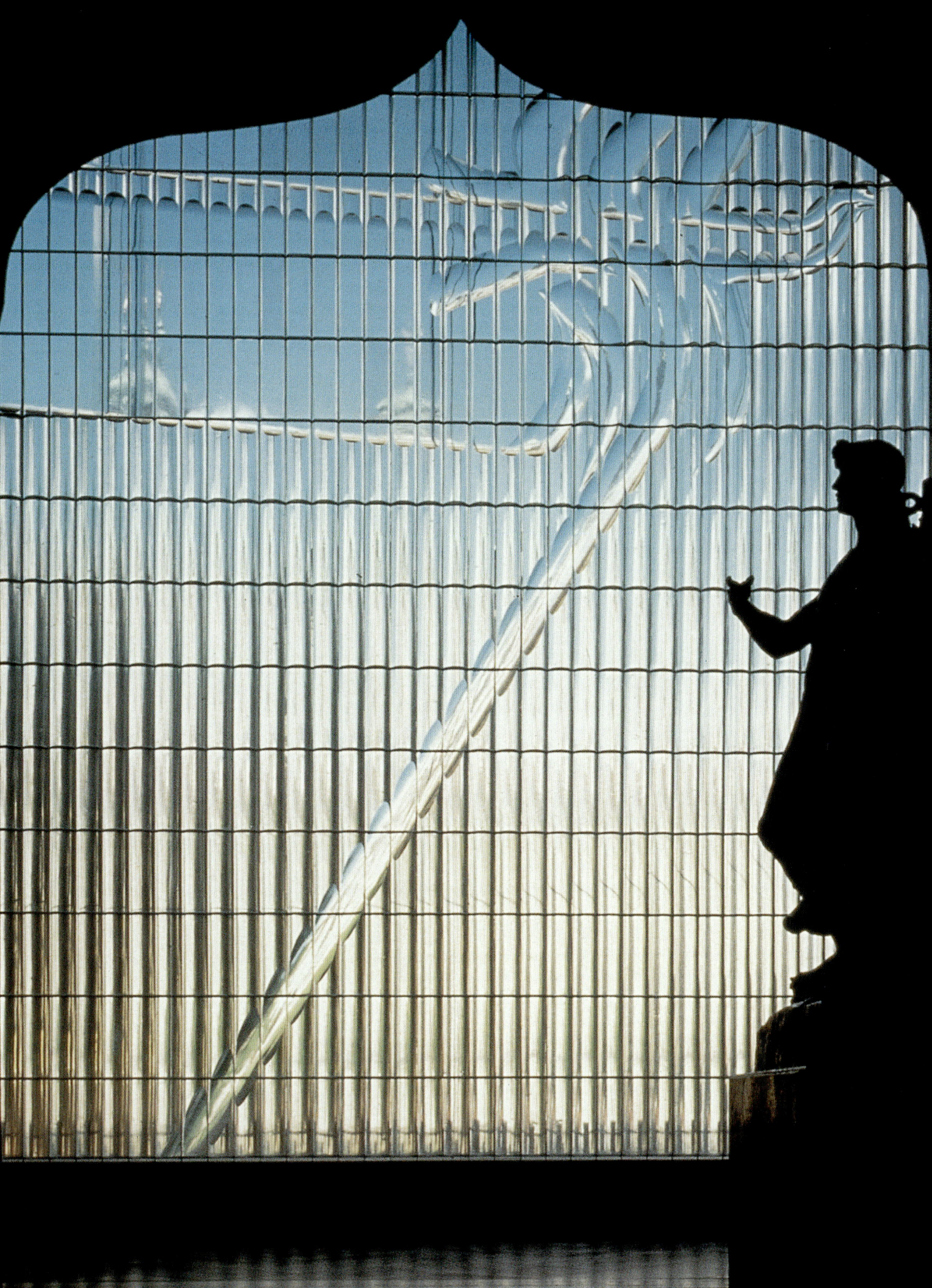

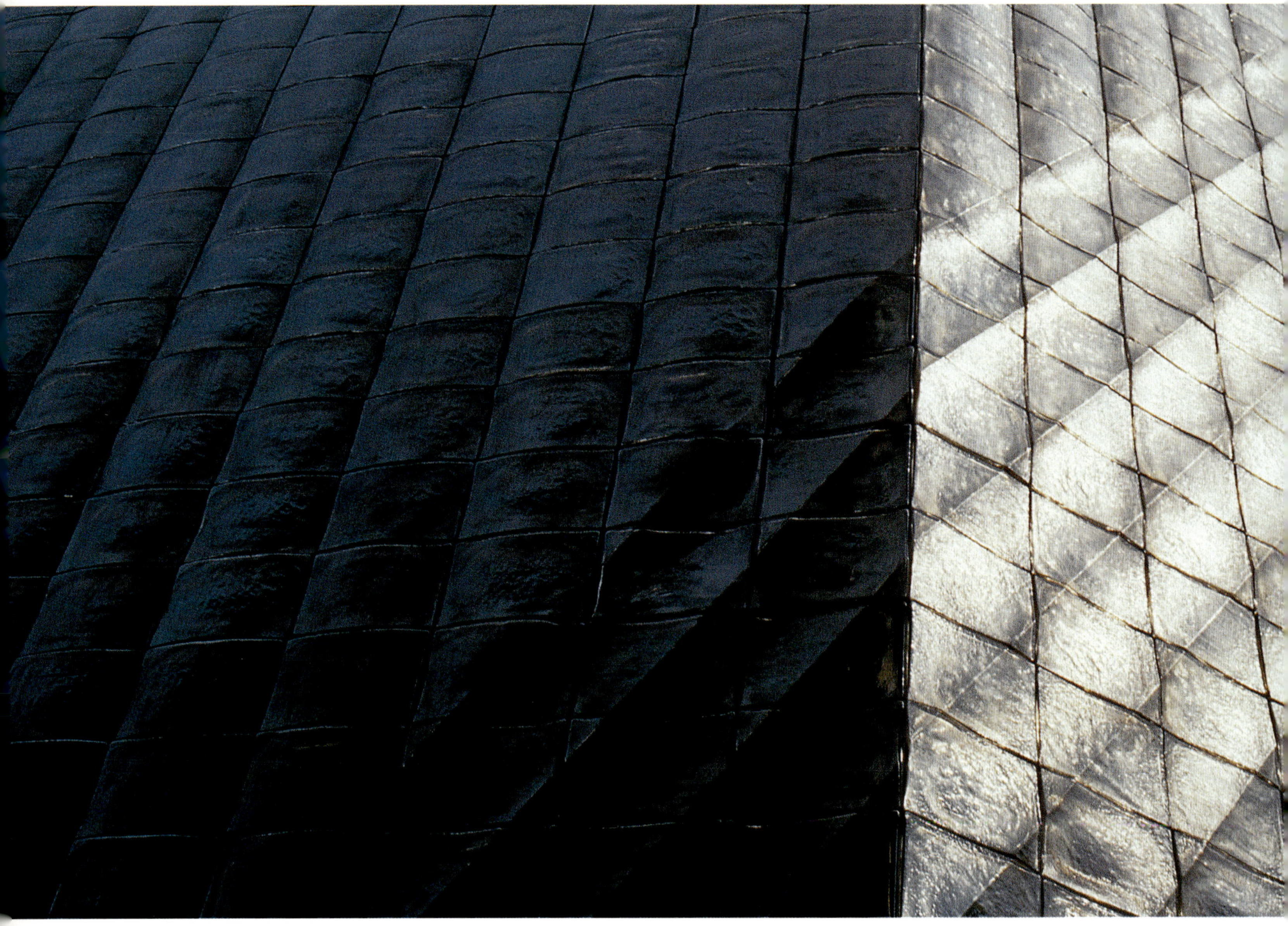

STANISLAV LIBENSKY & JAROSLAVA BRYCHTOVA

Above:
Façade of National Theater's New Stage; Detail, Prague, Czech Republic, 1982. Cast glass, h. 15.7 x 19.7 inches each block. Courtesy Heller Gallery. Photo: George Erml.

Right:
Silhouettes of the Town, 1998-89. Cast dichroic glass, h. 16.5 x 28 inches. Collection of Cynthia and Jeffrey Manocherian. Photo: Eva Heyd.

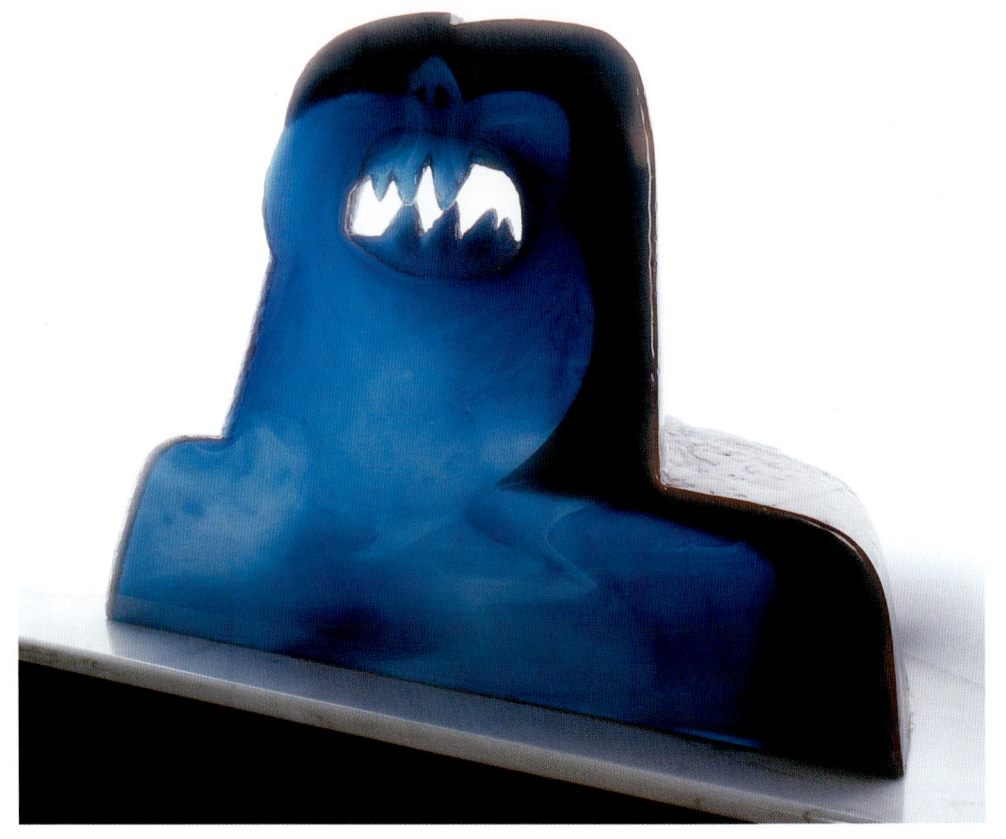

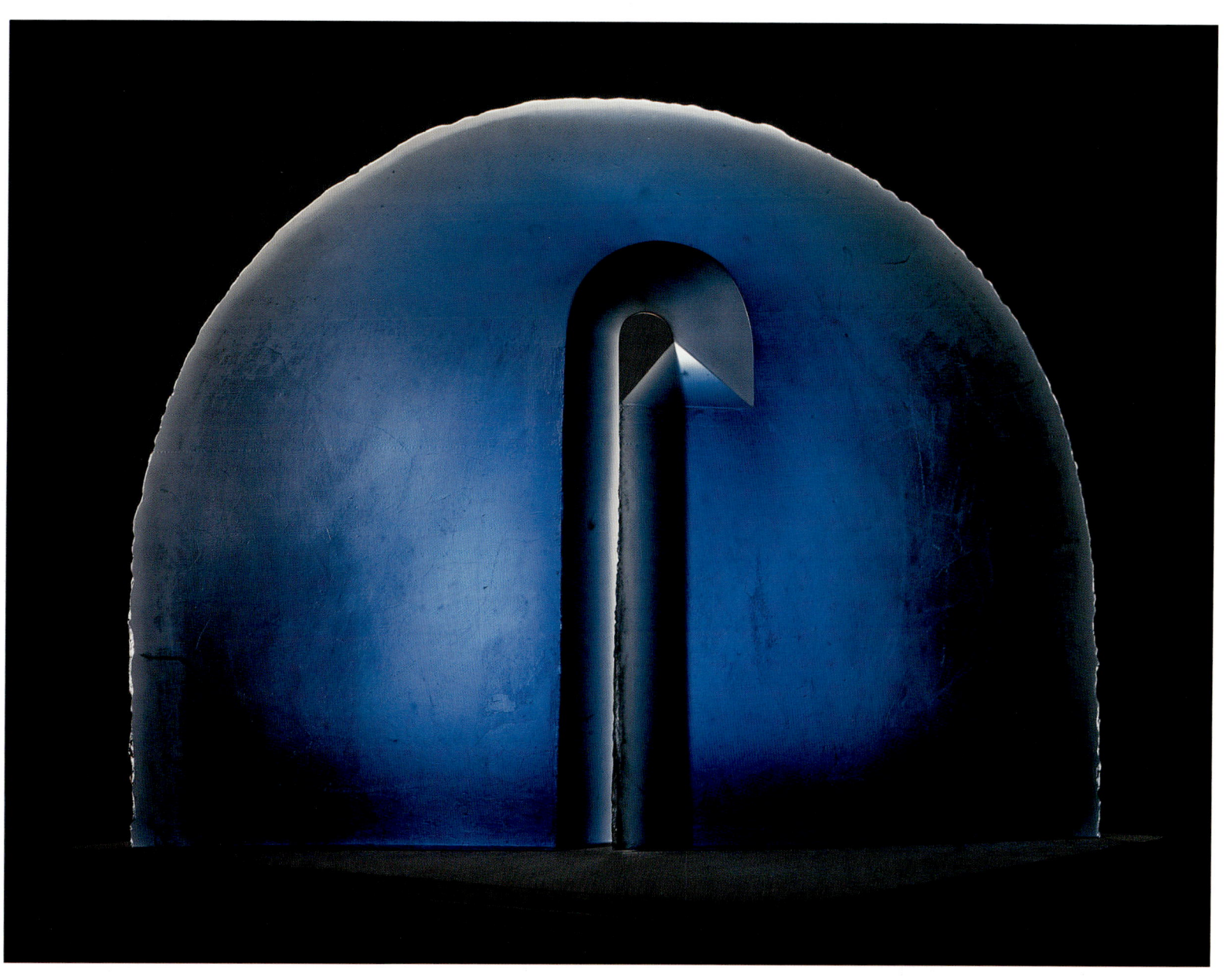

Arcus I, 1990-91. Cast glass, h. 30 x 39.2 inches.
Courtesy Habatat Galleries. Photo: Doug Schaible.

Walter Lieberman
(b.1954)

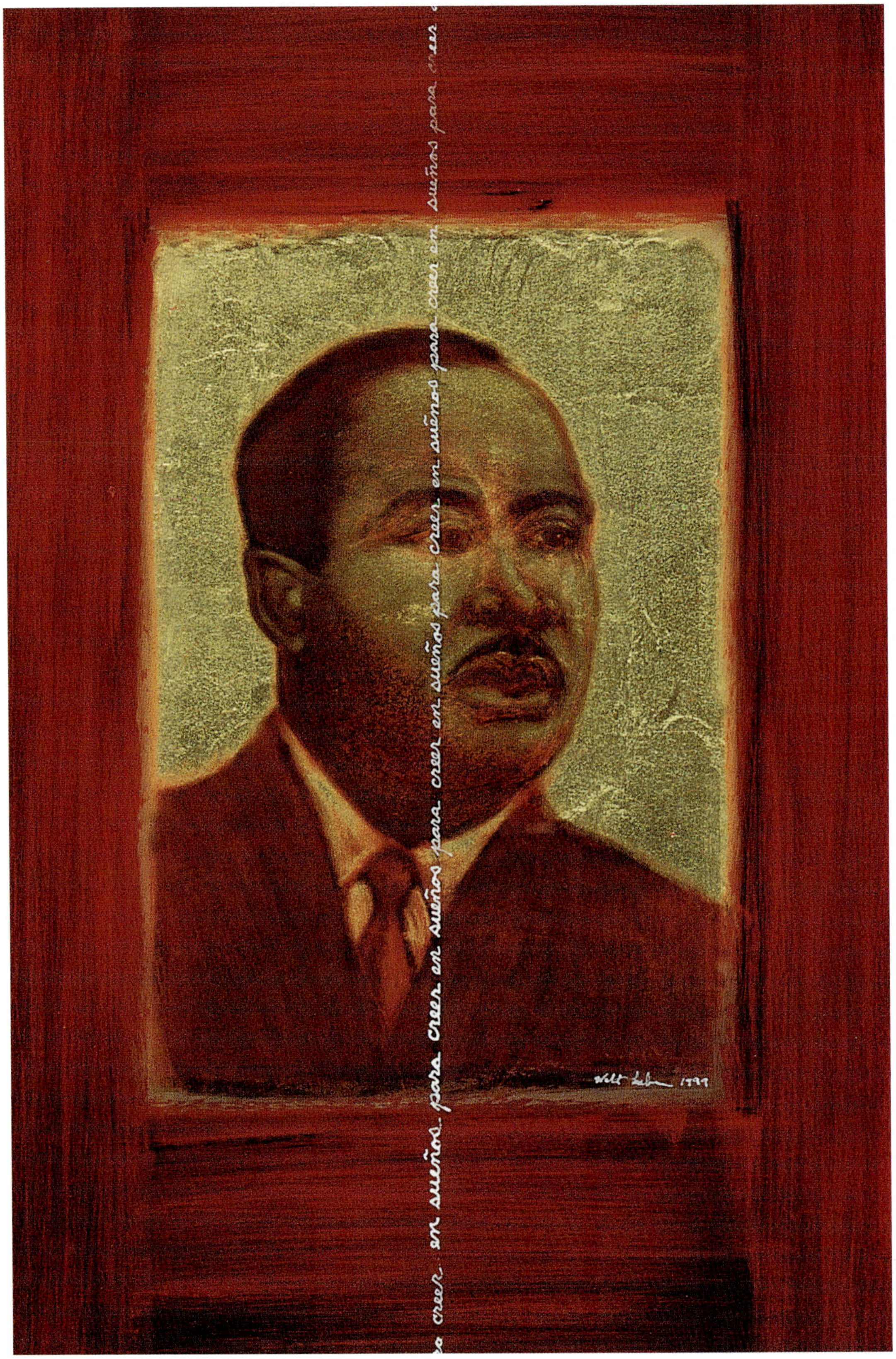

SEATTLE, WASHINGTON

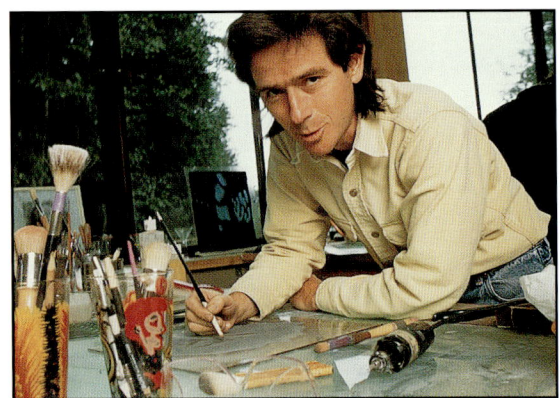

Red, Dream, King, 1999. Reverse painted enamel fired on glass, and gold leaf, h. 17 x 14 inches. Photo: Ivey Seright.

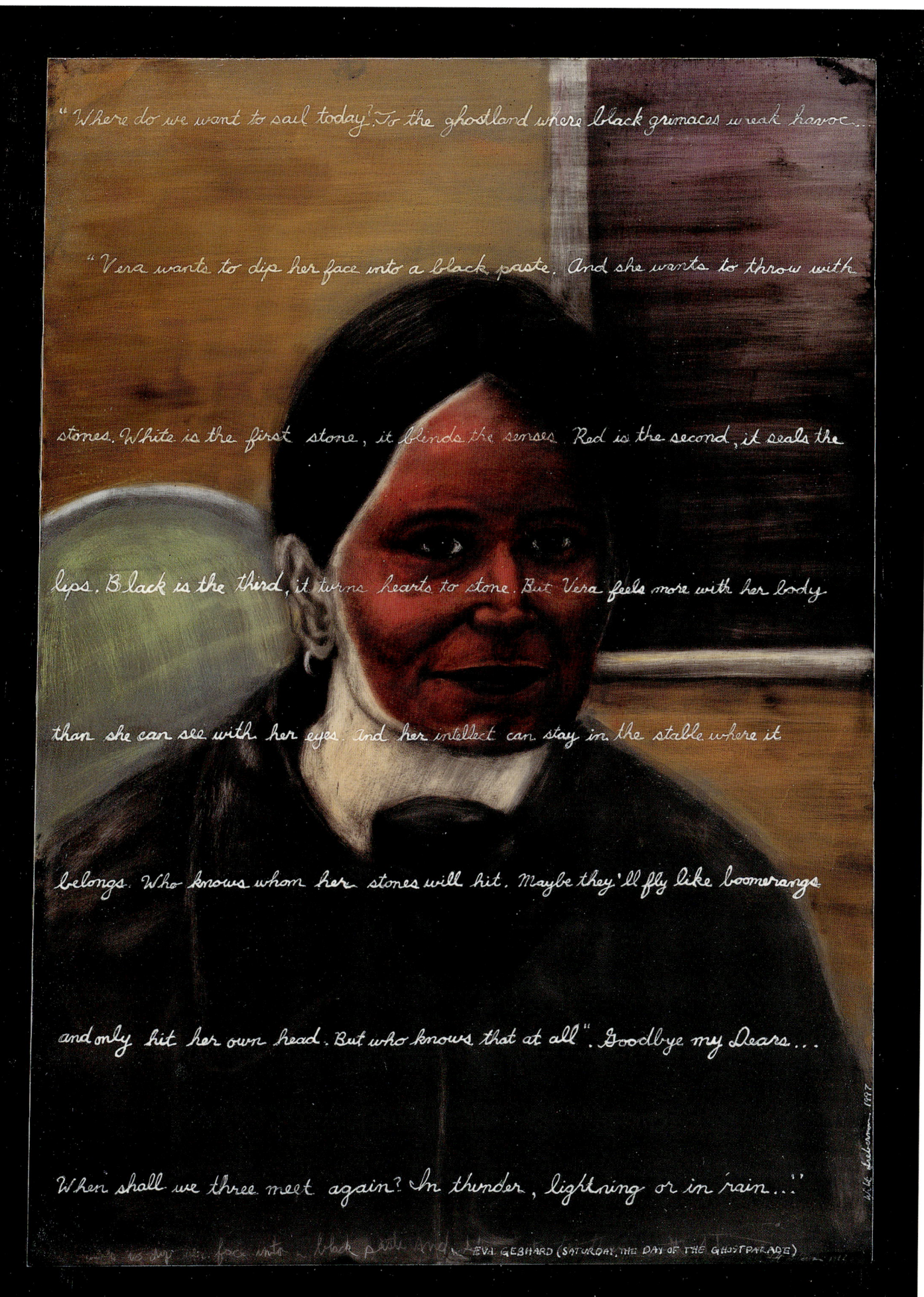

The Third Stone, 1997. Reverse painted enamel fired on glass, h. 24.5 x 19.5 inches. Photo: Roger Schreiber.

Beth Lipman
(b.1971)

BROOKLYN, NEW YORK

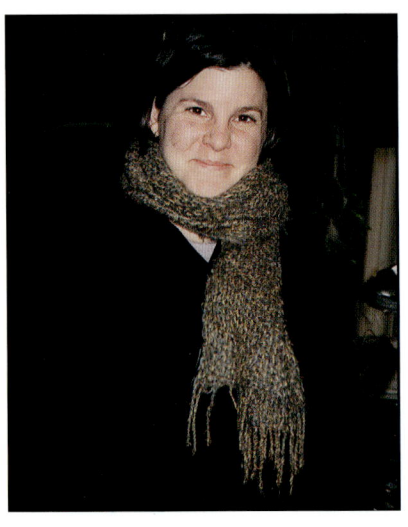

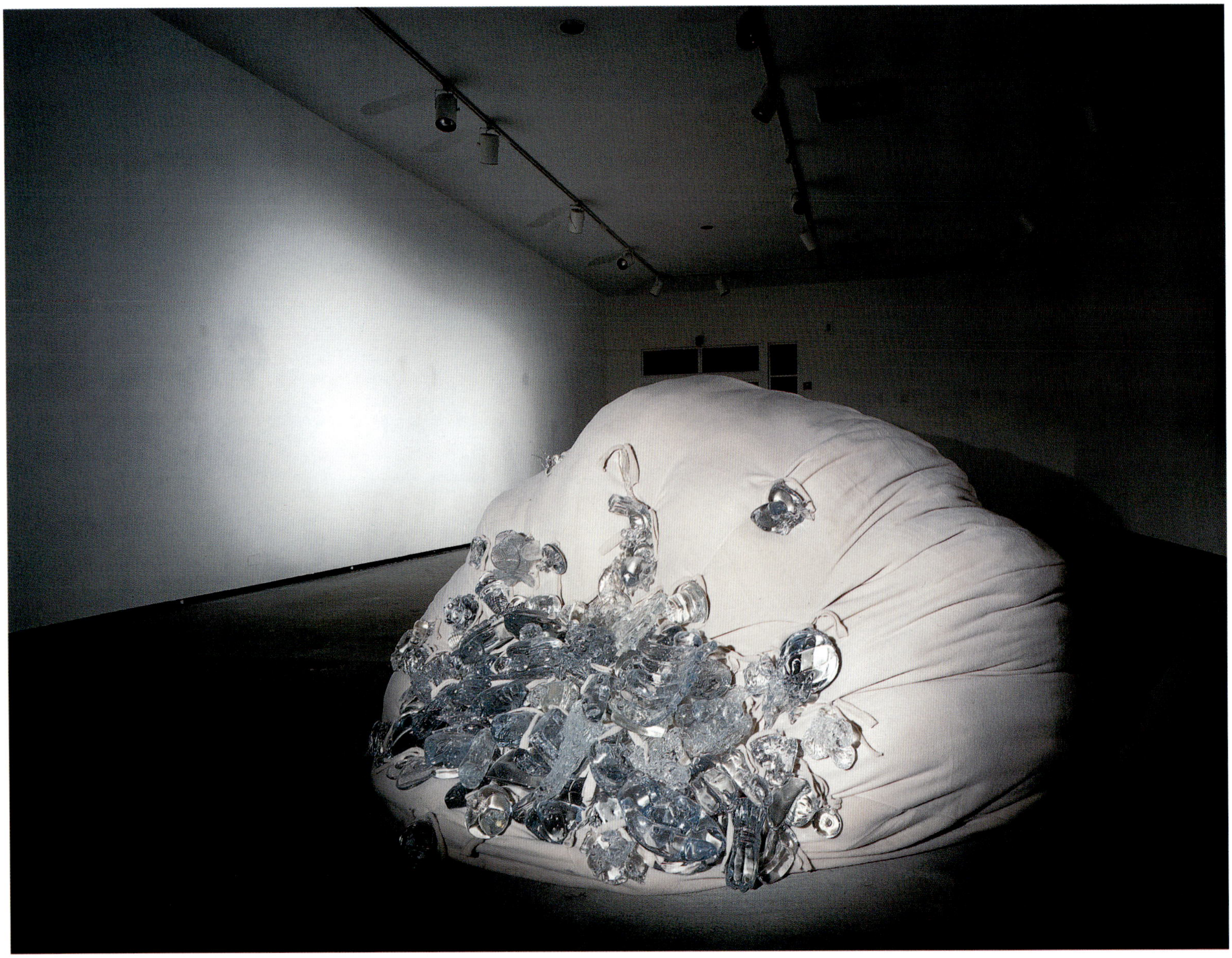

Untitled; Installation, Robert Lehman Gallery, UrbanGlass, 1996. Blown glass, and mixed media, h. 4 x 6 feet.

BERKELEY, CALIFORNIA

Marvin Lipofsky
(b.1938)

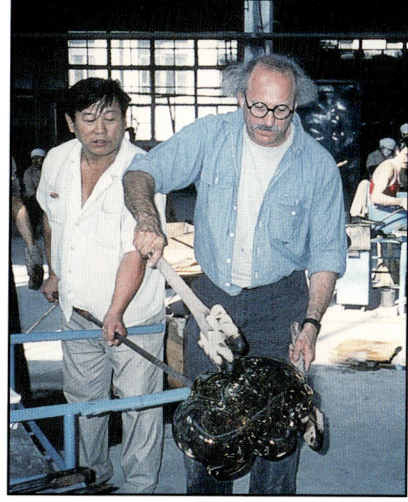

Lipofsky and Glassmaster Wang Cheng Yun at Daliar Glassware Factory, China, October 1996.

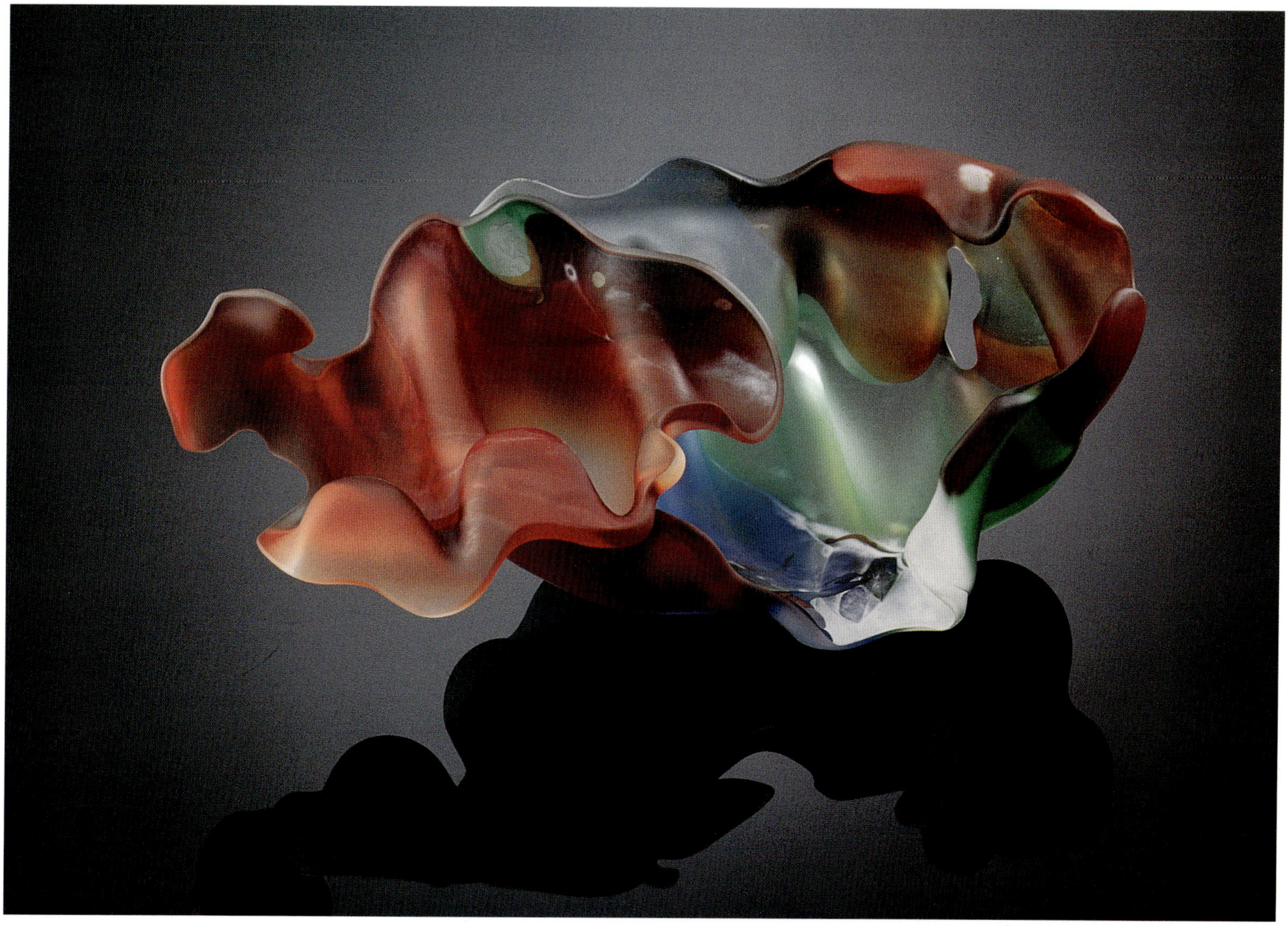

Lauscha Group; 1997-98, #8, Lauscha, Germany. Glass blown into handmade wooden forms, cut, ground, sandblasted, and acid polished by the artist in his studio. Made at Farblashüttle, Lauscha, Germany with help from Rainer Bock & Frhnk Ficht-Müller. Photo: M. Lee Fatherree.

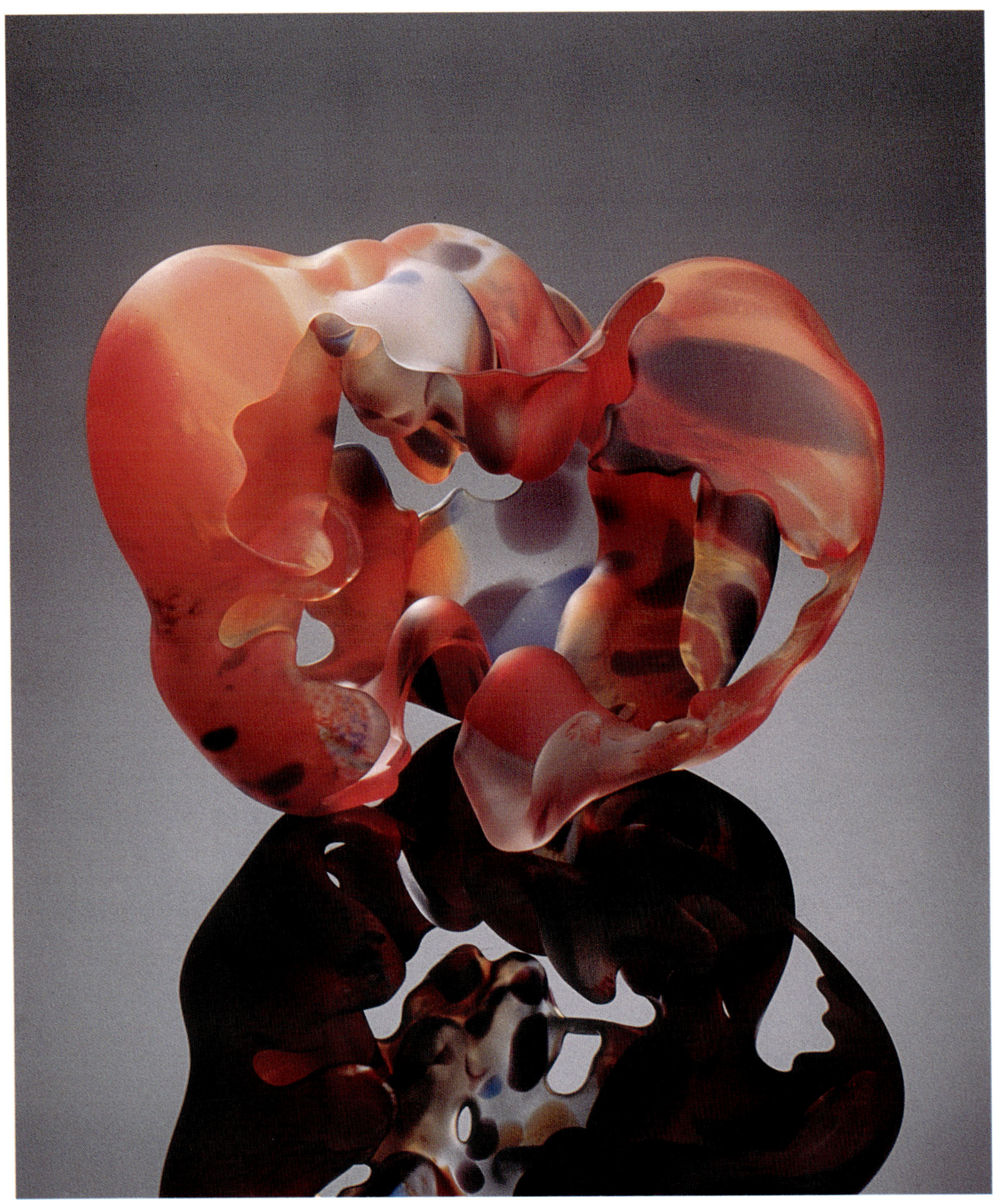

China Group, 1996-97 #2. Glass blown into handmade wooden forms, cut, ground, sandblasted, and acid polished by artist in his studio. Made at Dalian Glassware Factory, China, with help from Glassmaster Wang Cheng Yun. Private collection. Photo: M. Lee Fatherree.

SAG HARBOR, NEW YORK

Donald Lipski
(b.1947)

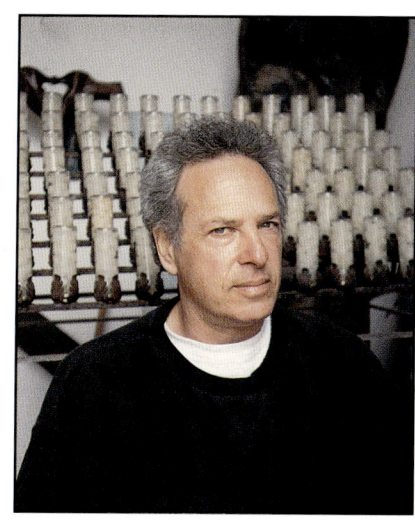

Poxabogue Pond No.32, 1995. Glass, lemons, preservative solution, and hardware, h. 21.3 x 13.2 x 6 inches. Collection of Terri Hyland.

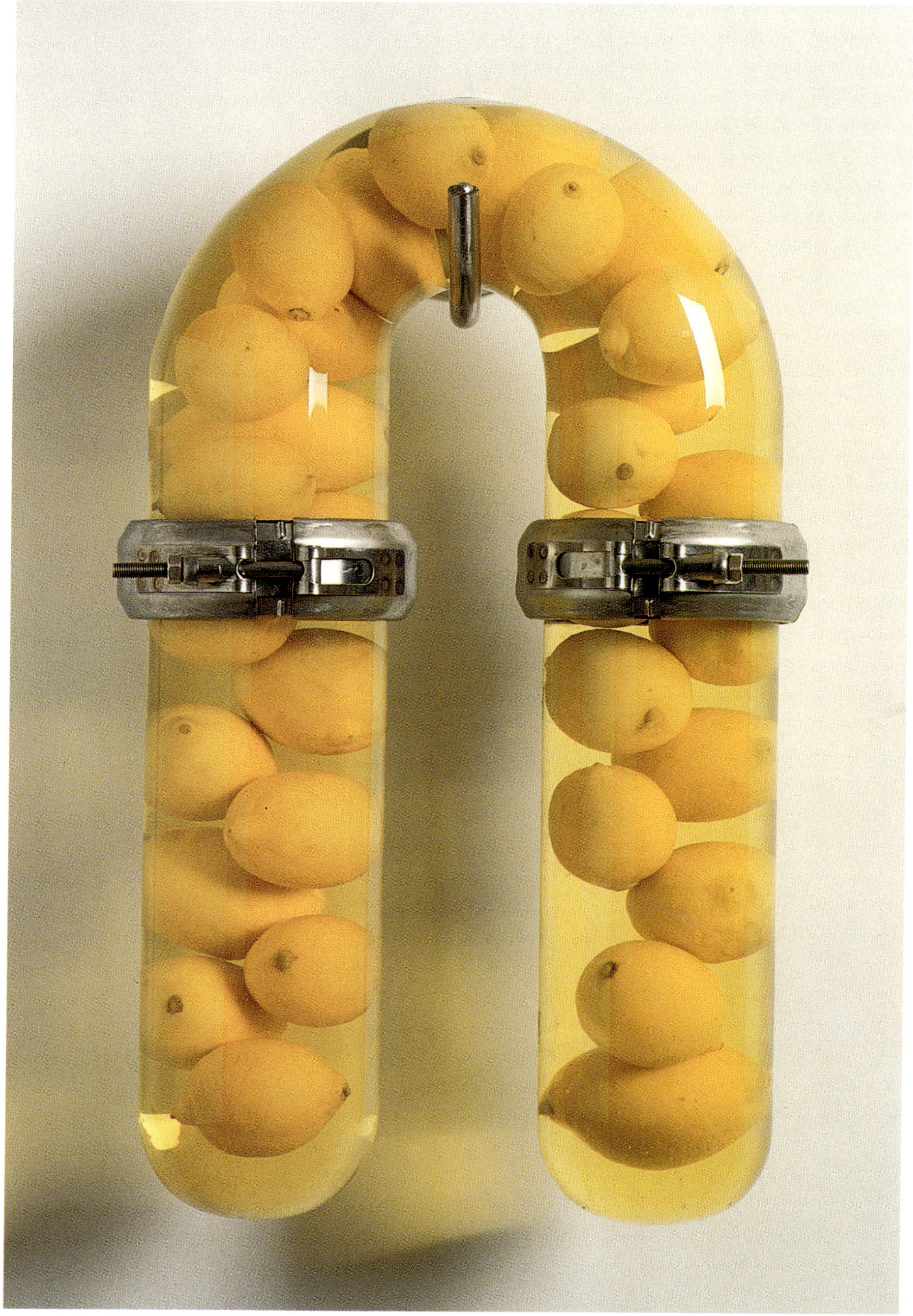

DONALD LIPSKI

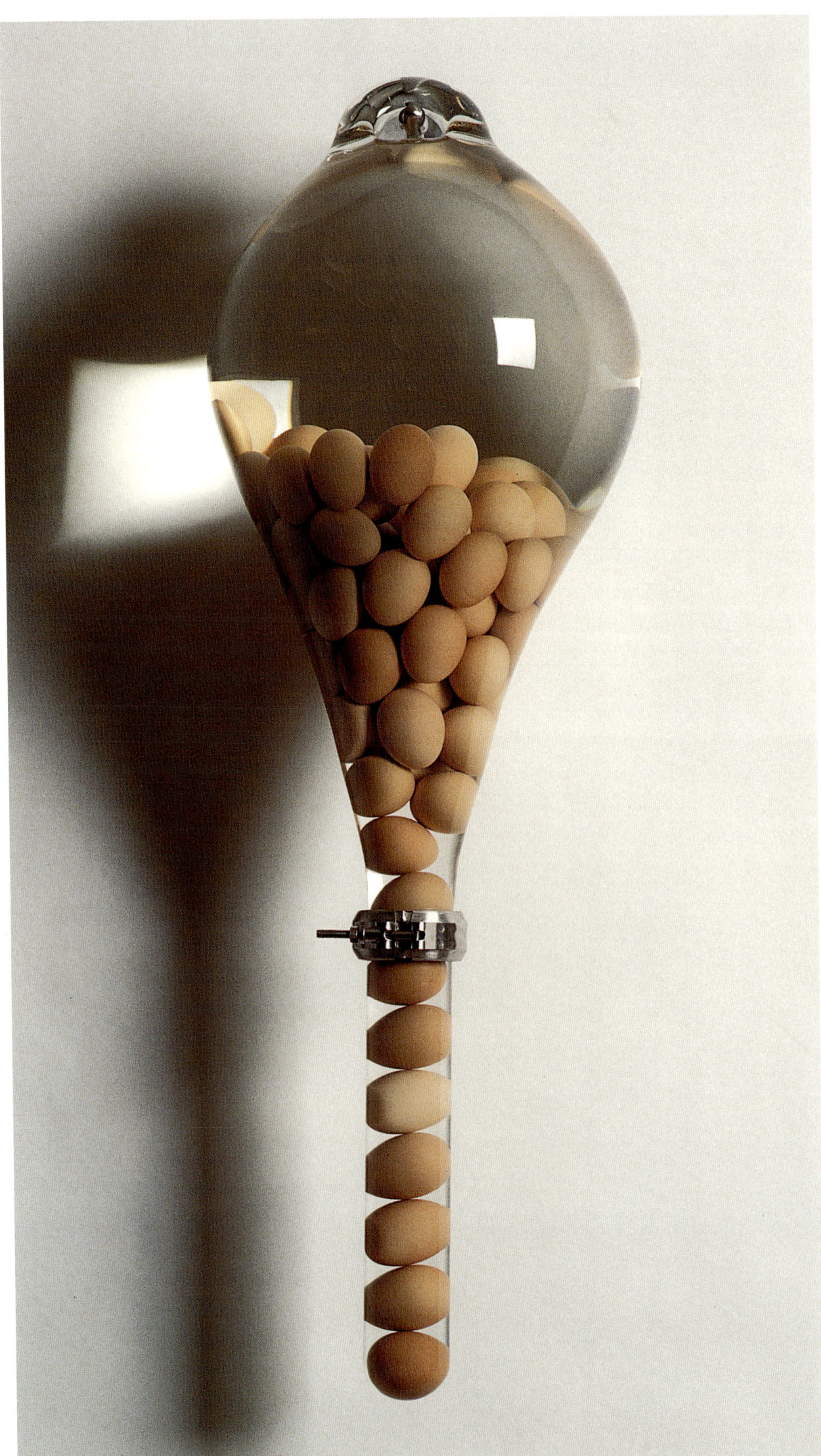

Poxabogue Pond No. 29*, 1995. Glass, eggs, preservative solution, and hardware, h. 36 x 12 x 12 inches. Hot blown glass by Michael Scheiner.*

SPRUCE PINE, NORTH CAROLINA

Harvey Littleton
(b.1922)

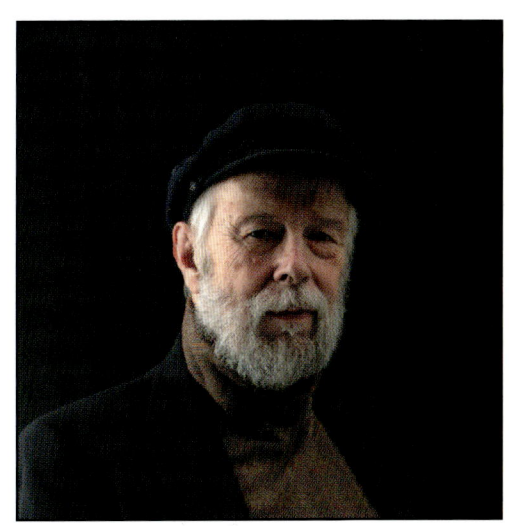

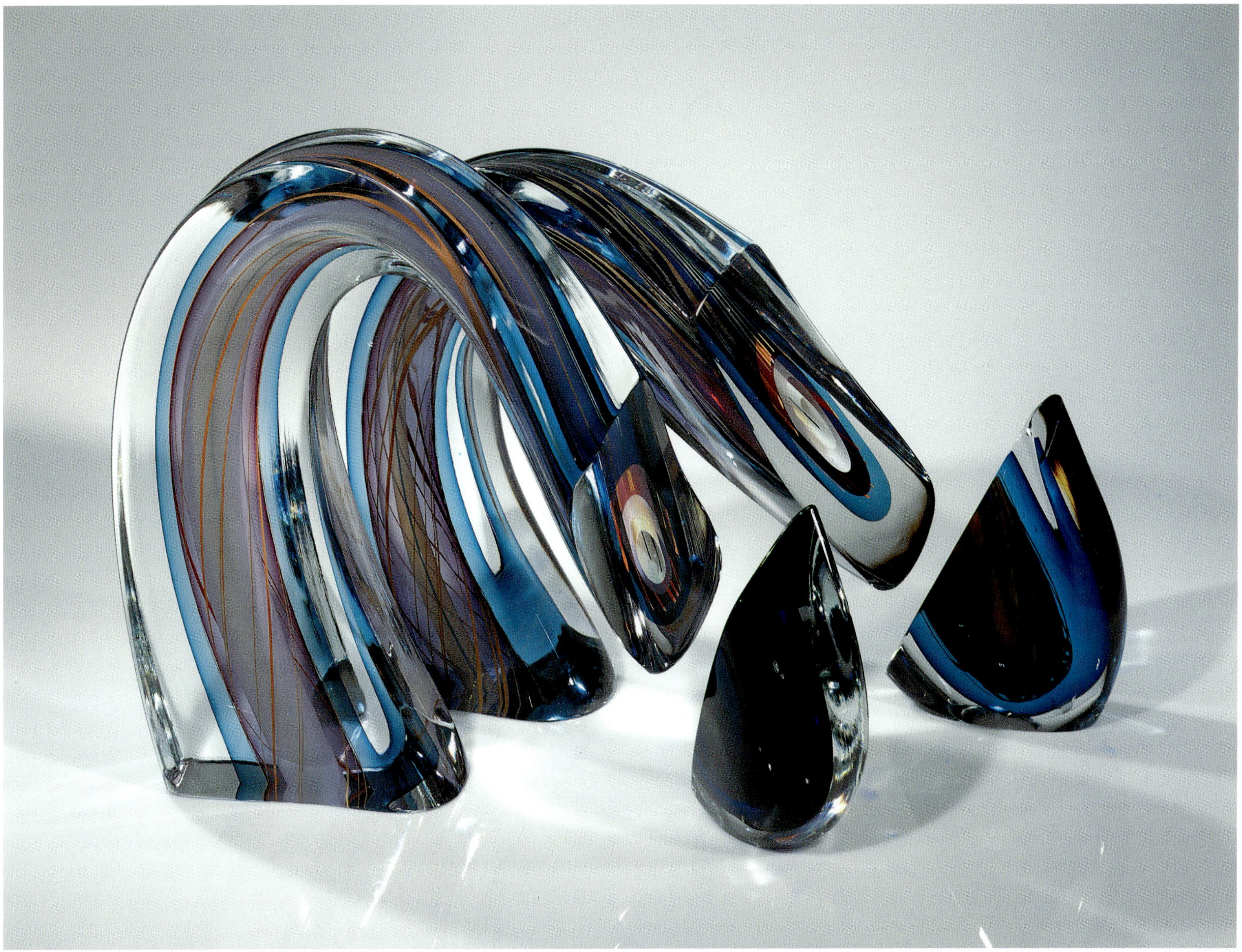

Pair of Blue Sliced Descending Forms, 1990. Blown glass, cut, and polished, h. 12 x 16 x 9 inches. Courtesy Maurine Littleton Gallery.

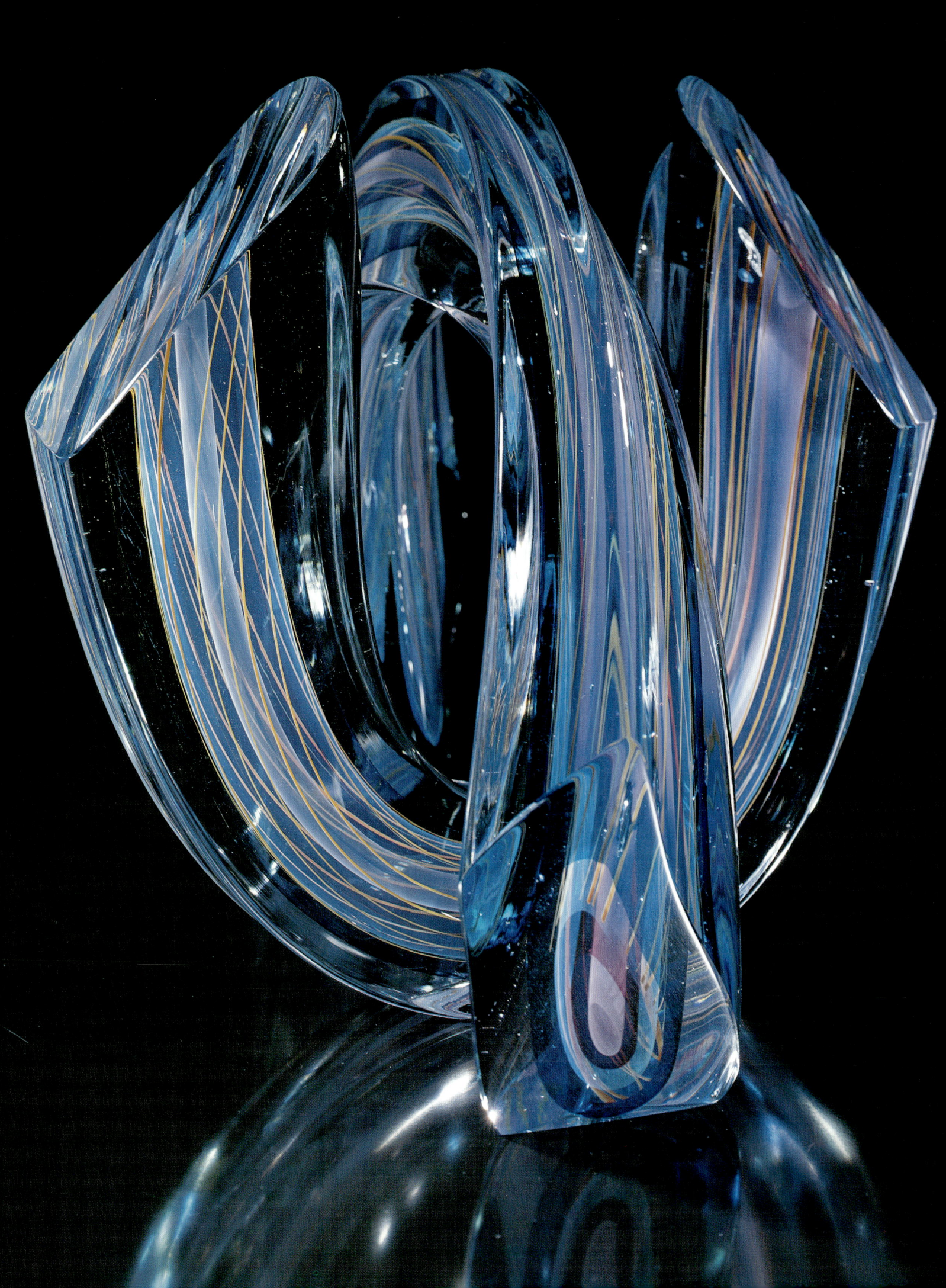

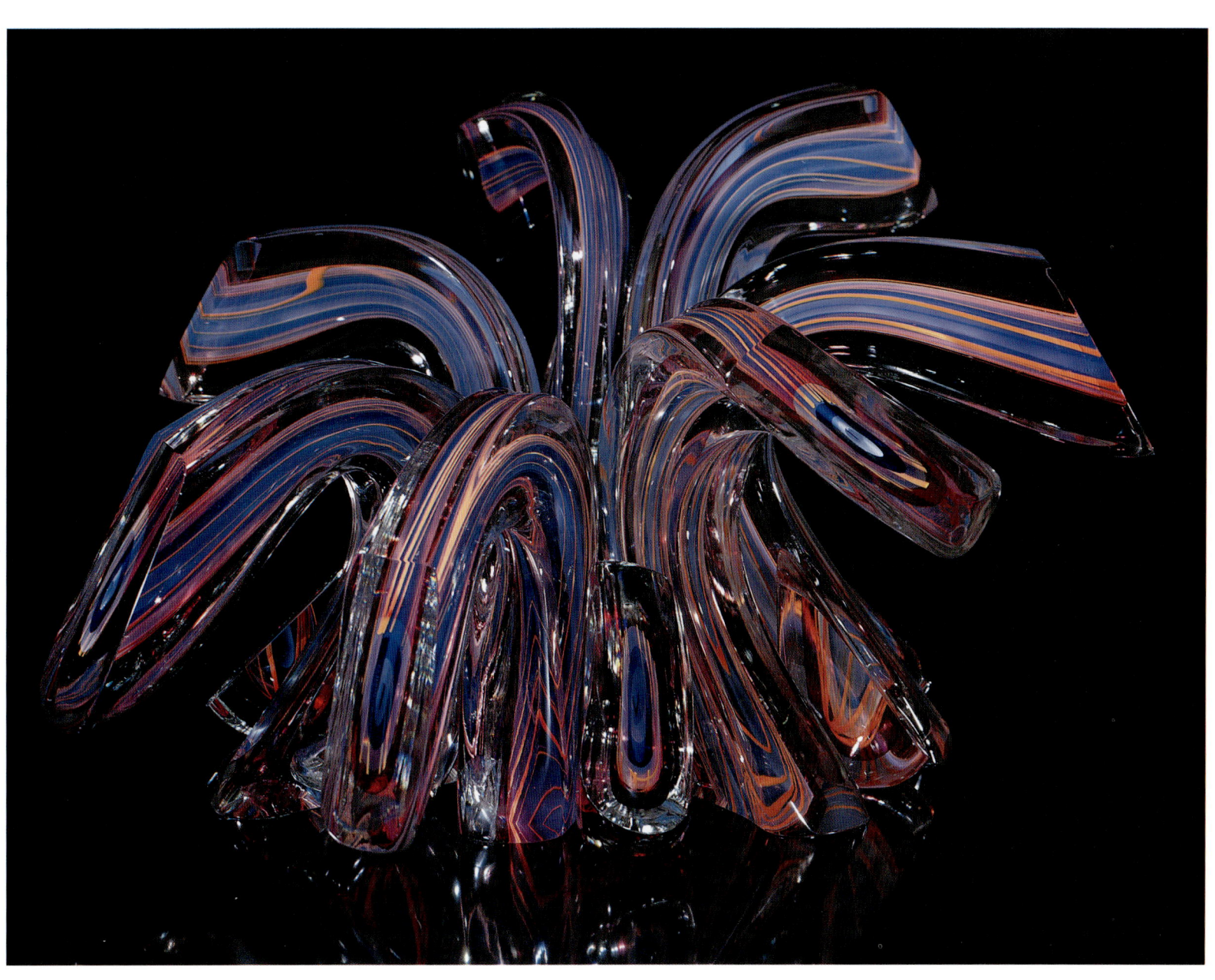

Opposite:
Blue Crossed Form, 1989. Blown glass, cut, and polished, h. 15 x 12.75 x 14 inches.

Above:
Ruby Spray, 1990. Blown glass, cut, and polished, 14 parts, h. 17.25 x 30 x 30 inches.

Kristina Logan
(b.1964)

PORTSMOUTH, NEW HAMPSHIRE

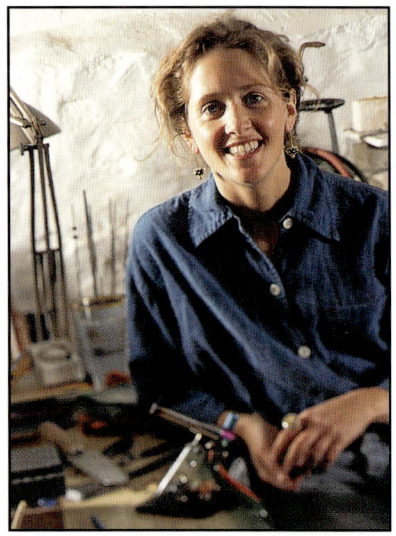

Below:
Olive Cactus Bead. 1997. Lampworked soda-lime glass, h. 1.75 x 1.75 x 1.75 inches. Photo: Paul Avis.

Next:
Collection of Beads, 1997-99. lampworked soda lime glass. Longest bead, h. 2.75 inches. Photo: Paul Avis.

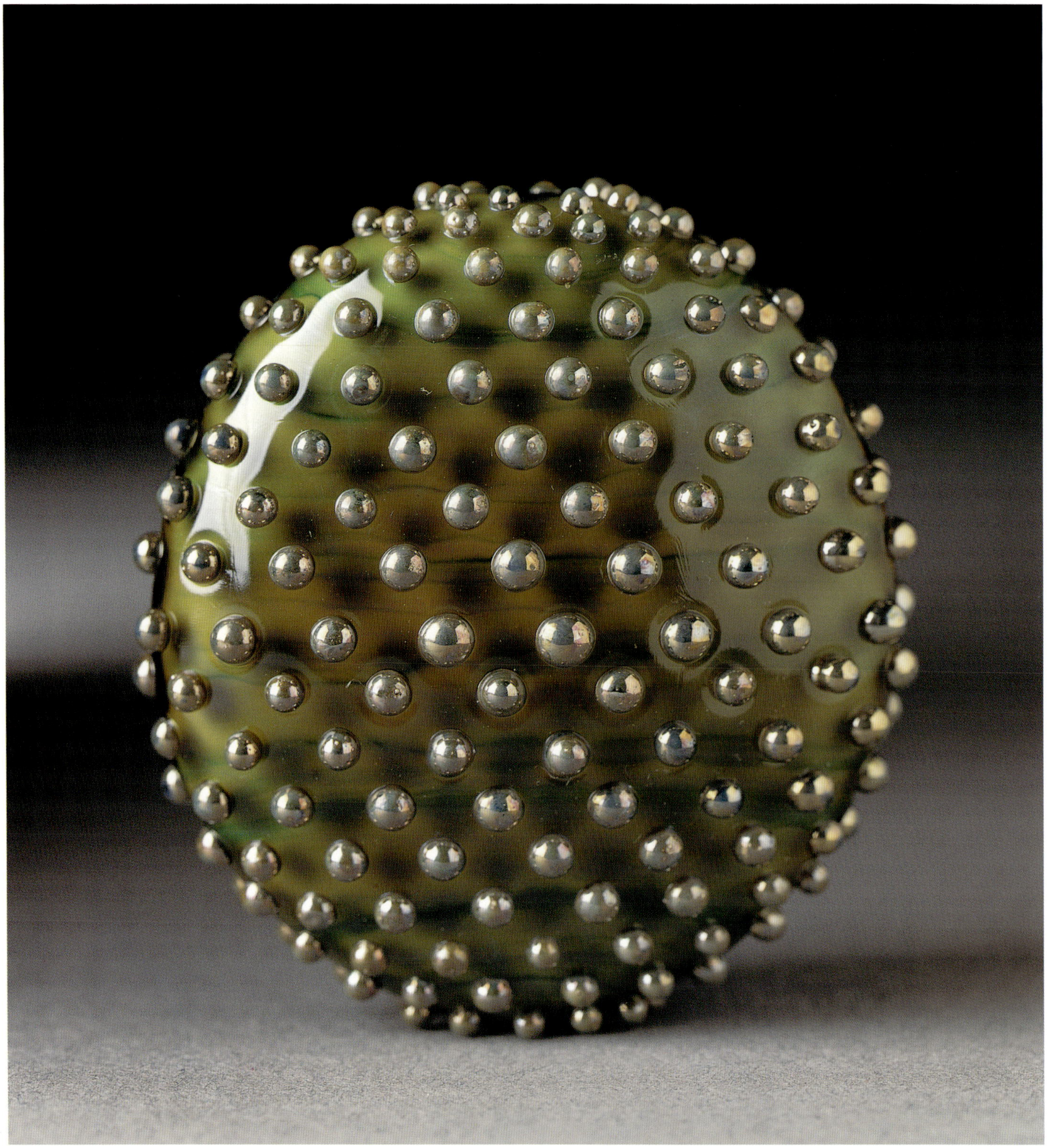

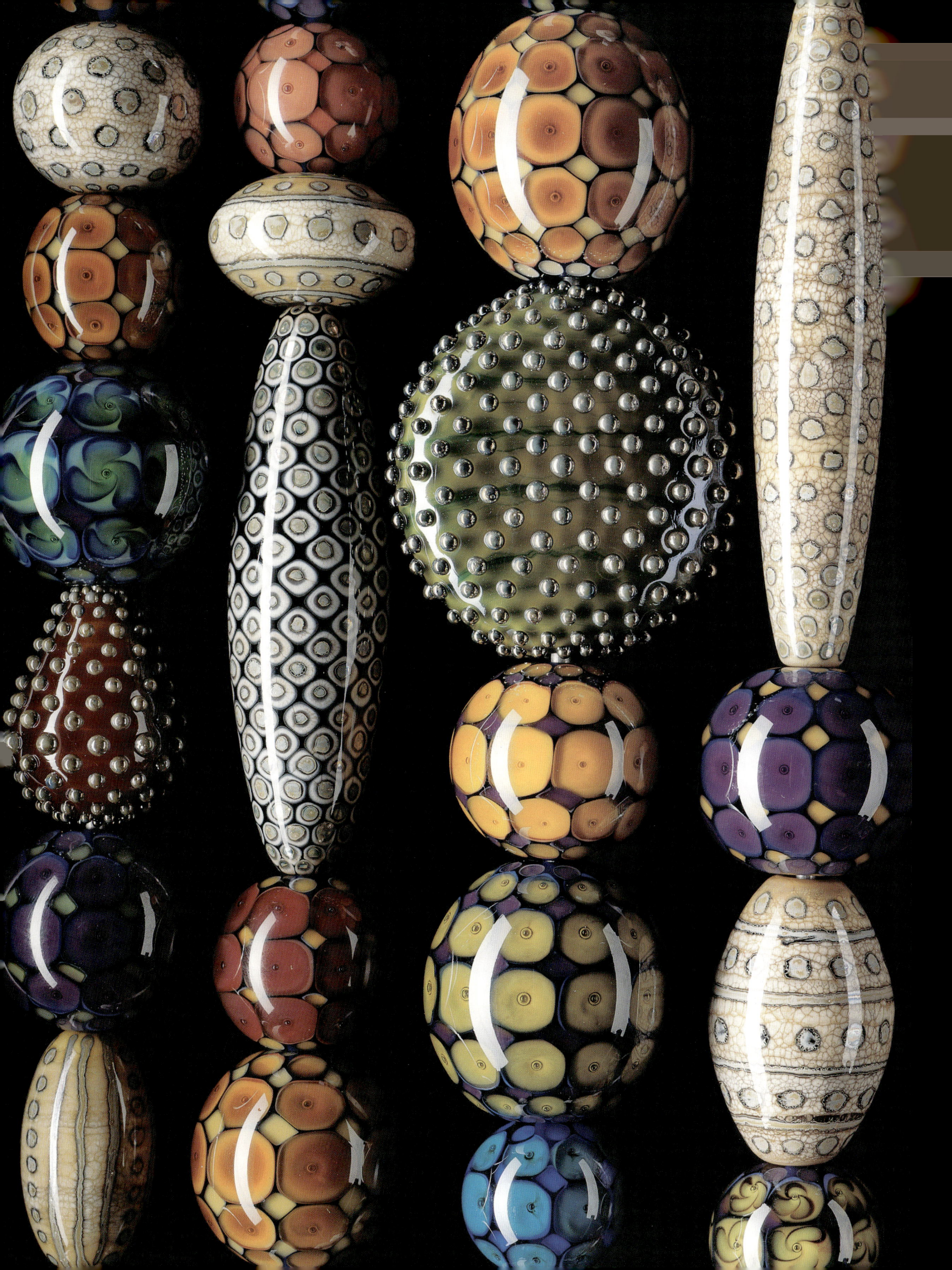

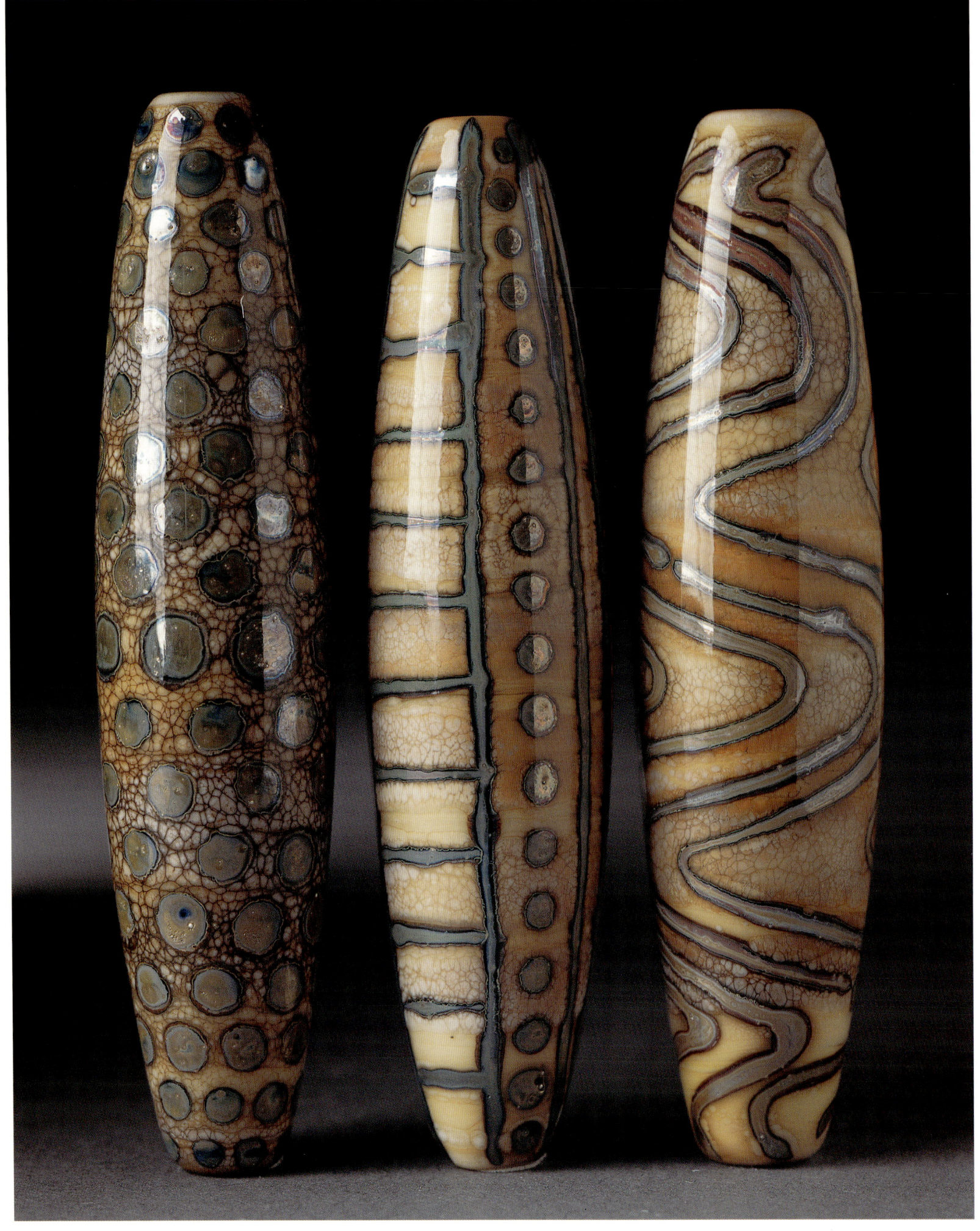

Ivory Totem Beads, 1998. Lampworked soda-lime glass, h. 2.75 x 2.75 inches. Photo: Paul Avis.

KENSINGTON, NEW HAMPSHIRE

Linda MacNeil
(b.1954)

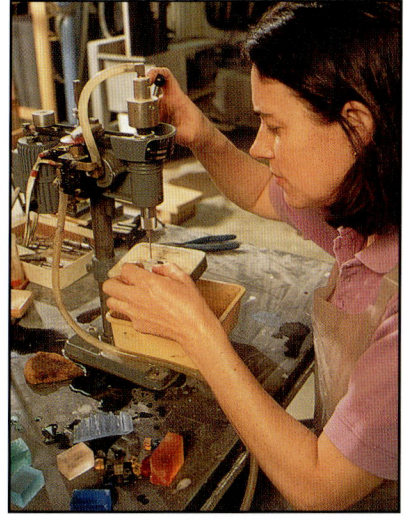

Photo: Russell Johnson

Mesh Necklace, 1996. 24K gold plated brass, clear acid polished glass, mirrored detail, (pendant) h. 2 inches. Private Collection. Photo: Bill Truslow.

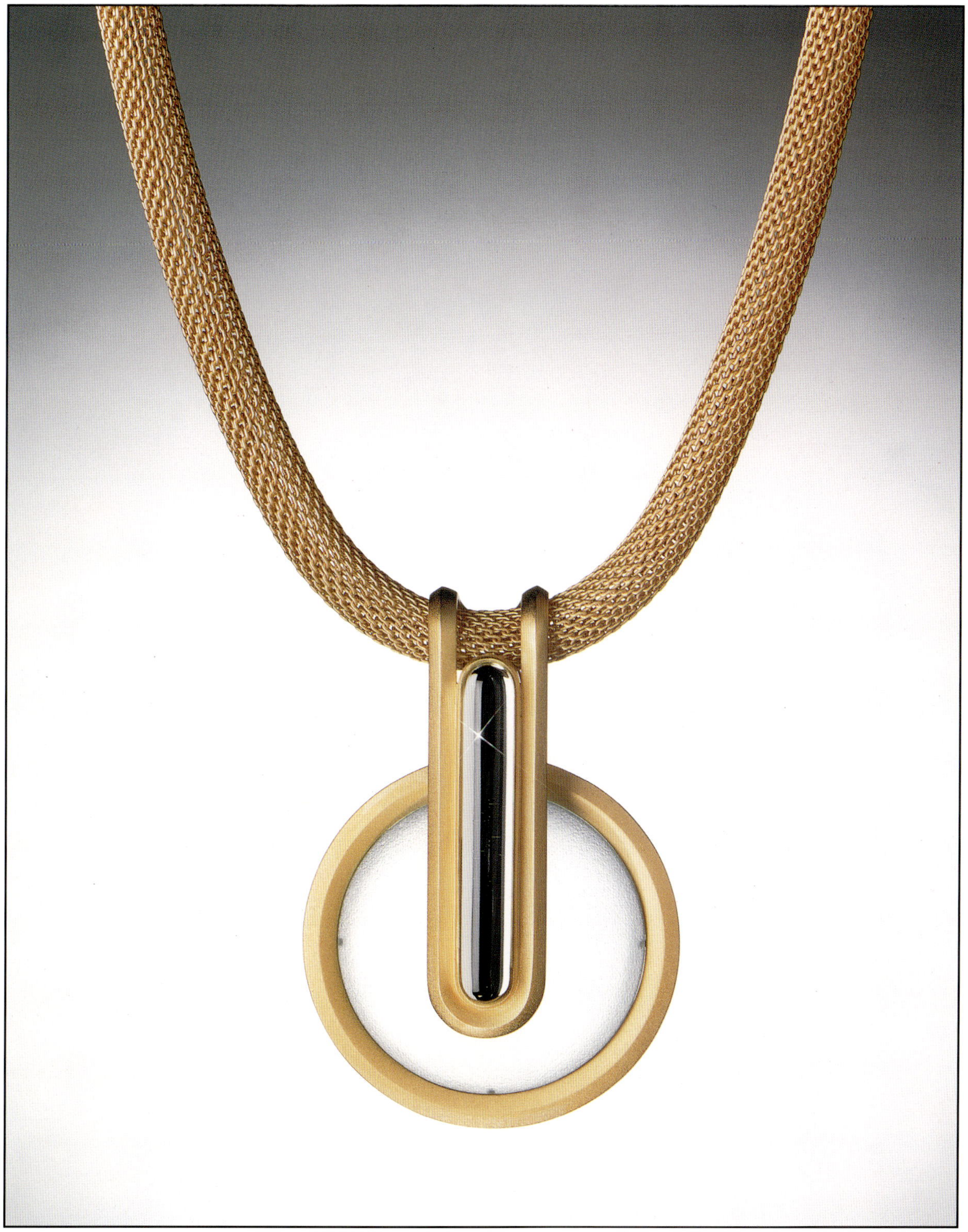

Terence Main
(b.1954)

BROOKLYN, NEW YORK

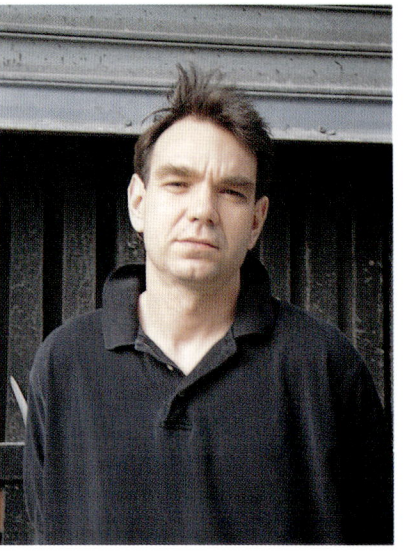

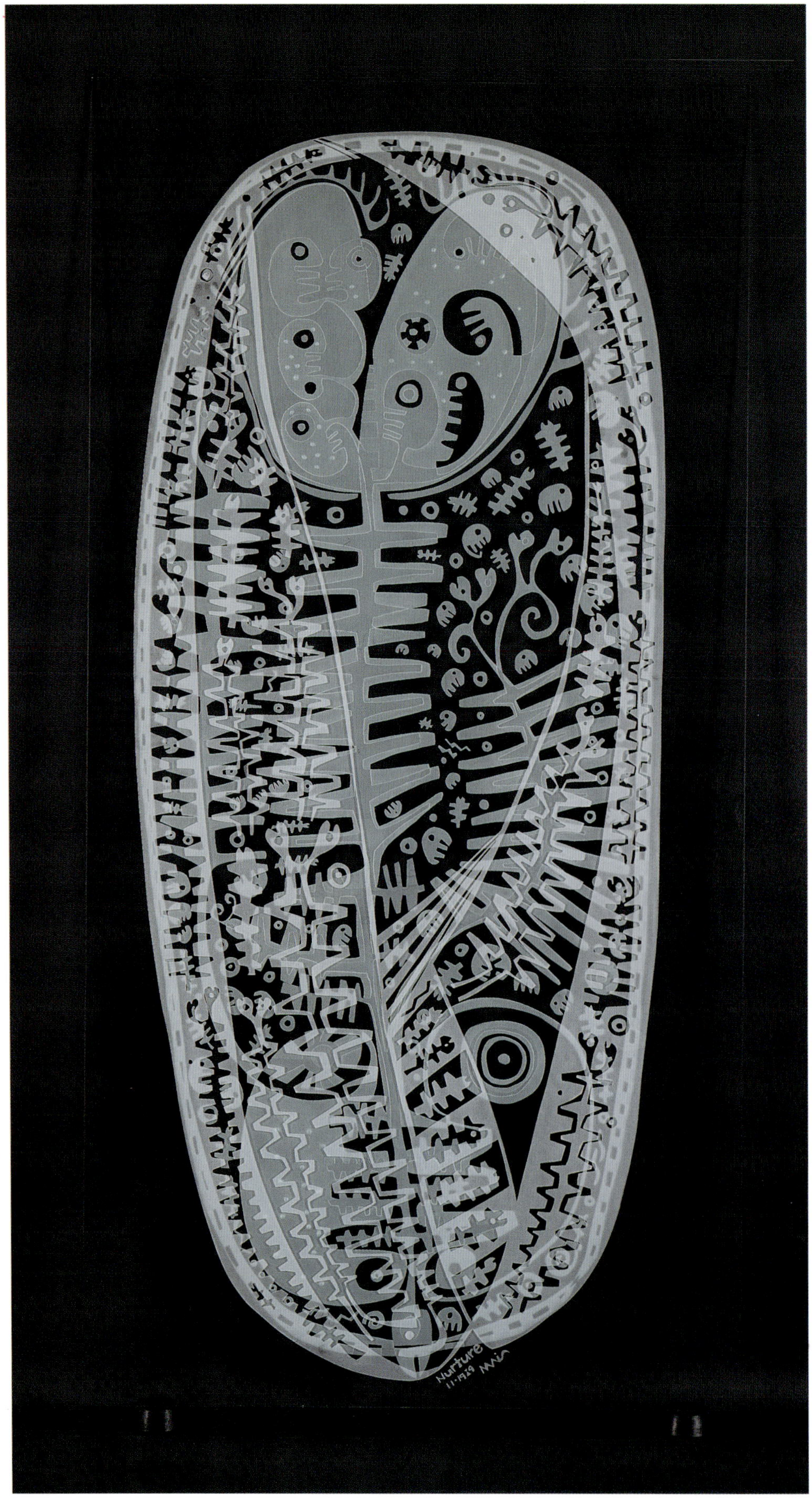

Nurture, 1989. Carved glass, h. 96 x 48 x .4 inches. Photo: Joseph Coscia Jr.

SEATTLE, WASHINGTON

Dante Marioni
(b.1964)

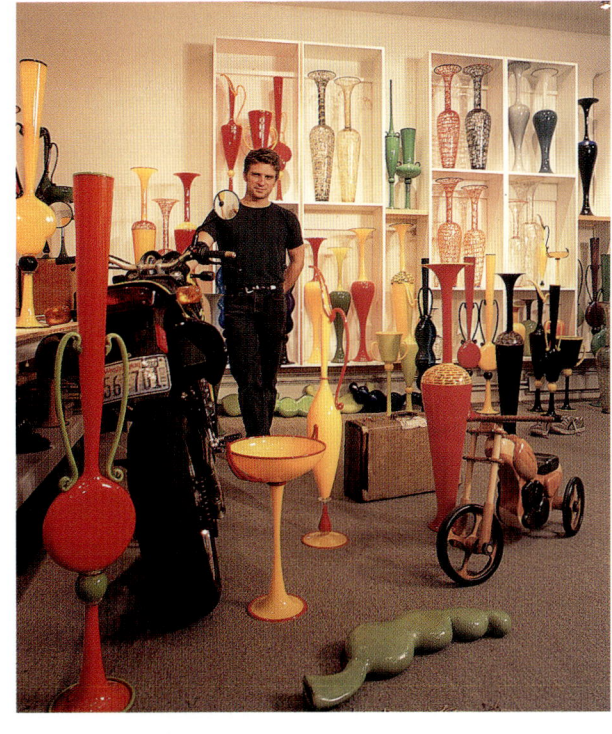

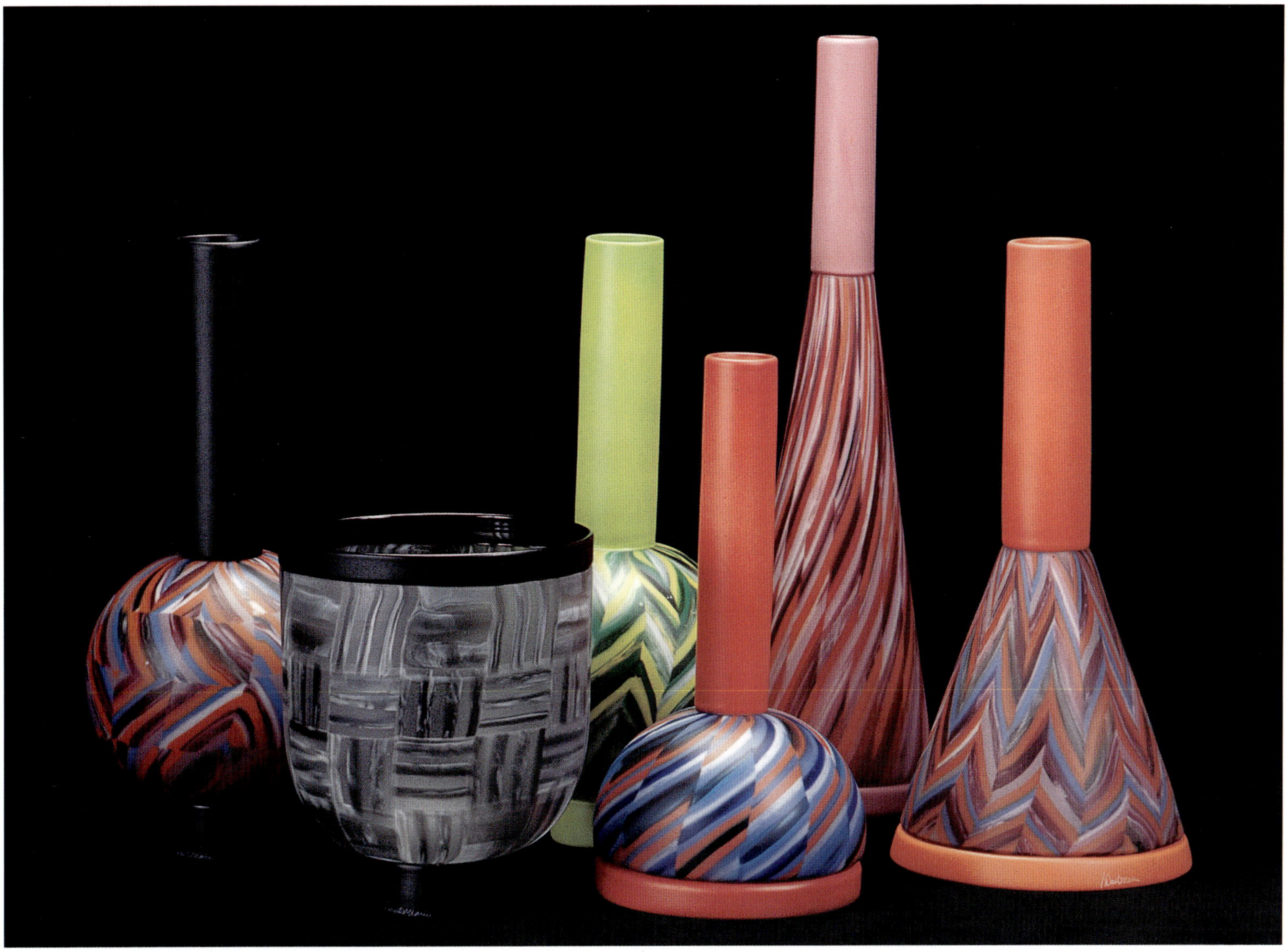

Photo: Russell Johnson

Moje Meets Marioni, 1993. Blown glass, (tallest) h. 12 inches.

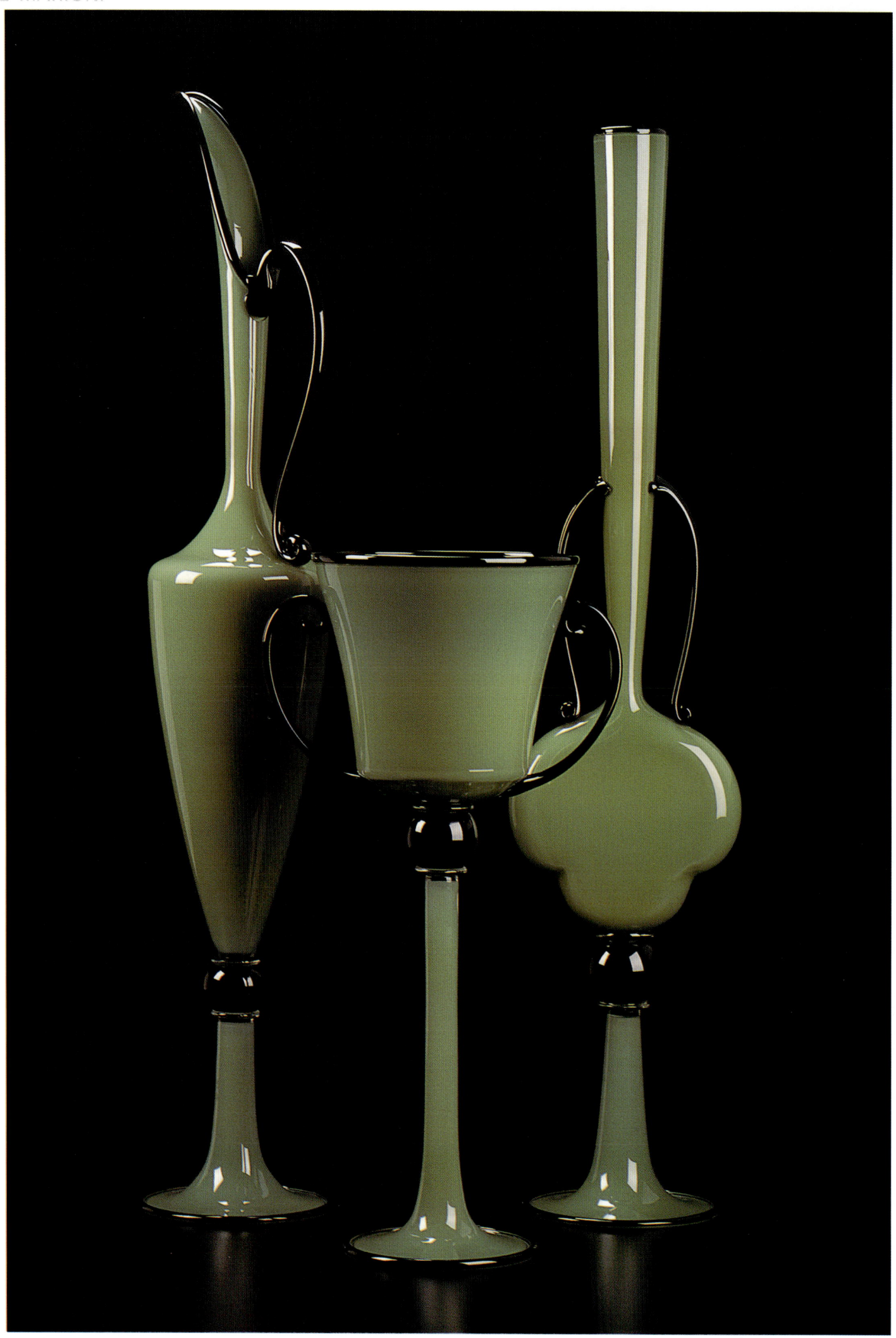

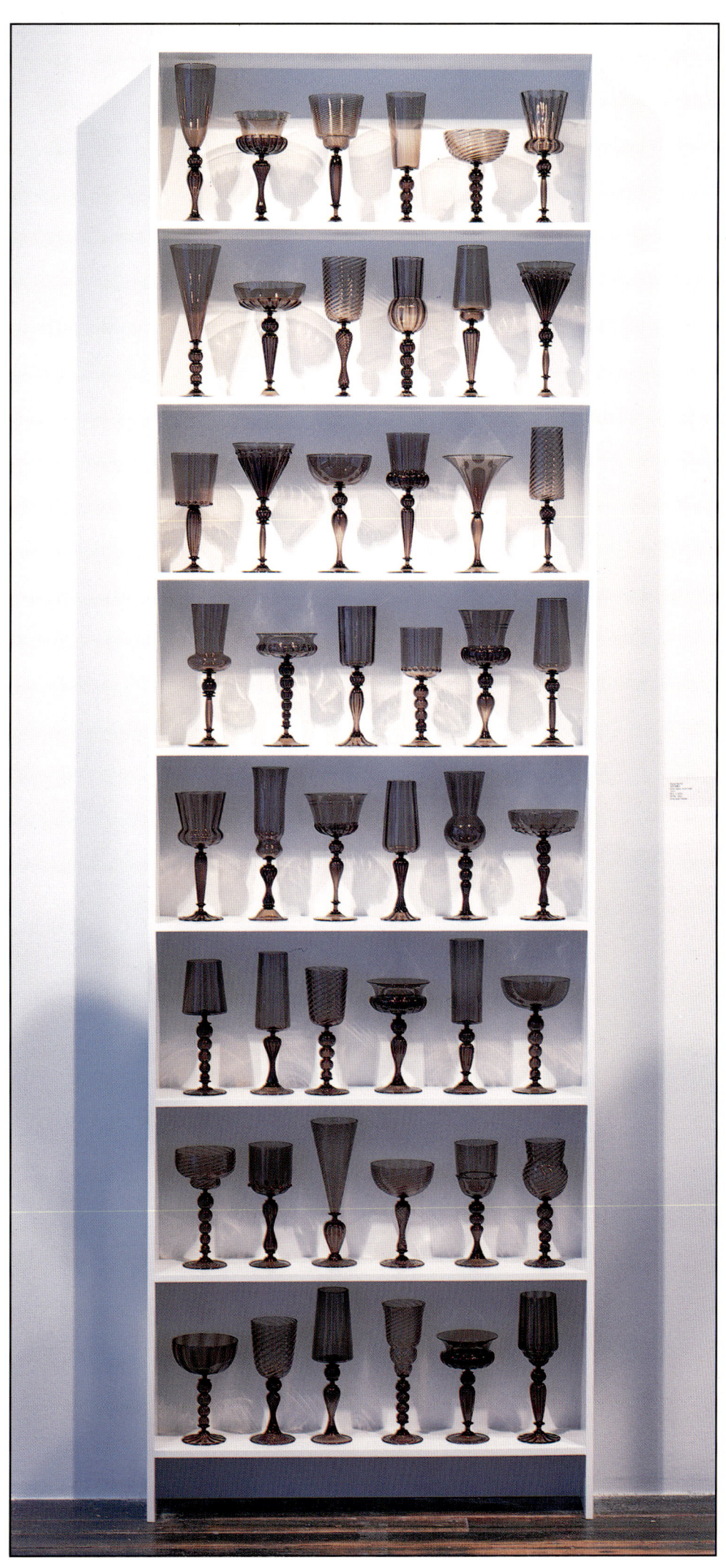

Opposite:
***Moss Green Group**, 1999. Blown glass, h. 25.5–40.5 inches. Photo: Roger Schreiber.

Left:
***Cup Box**, 1999. Blown glass, h. 8 x 2 feet overall. Private Collection. Courtesy William Traver Gallery

Paul Marioni & Ann Troutner
(b.1941)   (b.1958)

SEATTLE, WASHINGTON

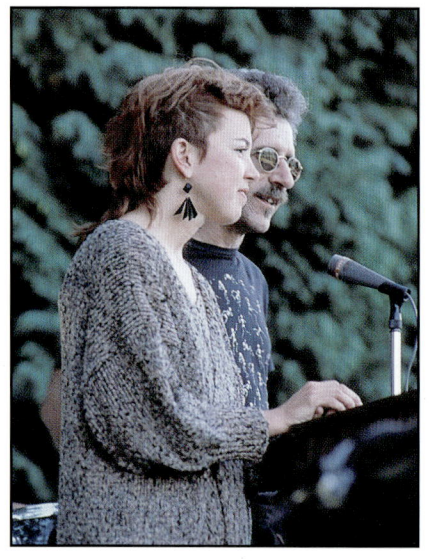
Photo: Roger Schreiber

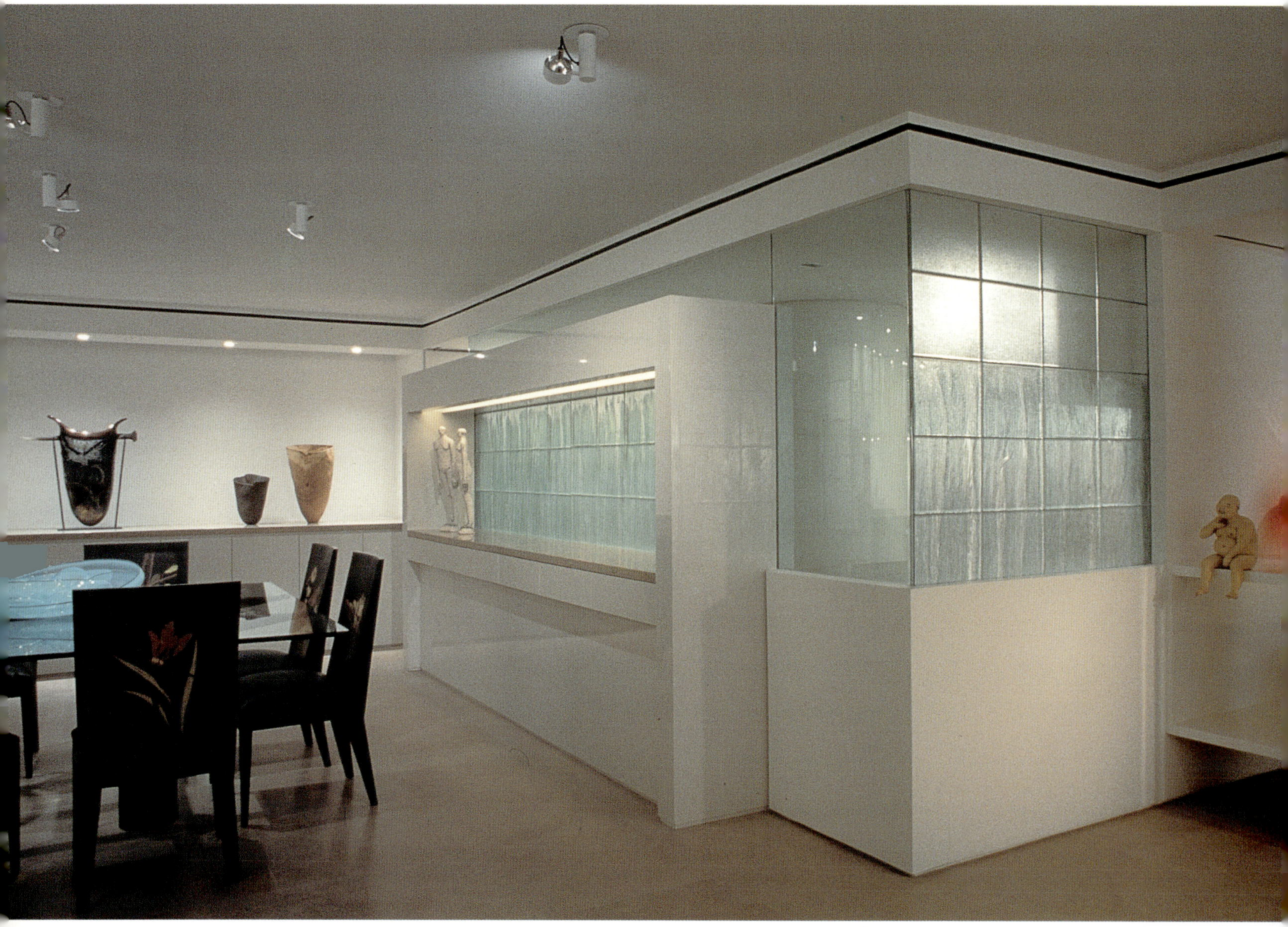

Above:
Sea Grass; Dining room installation, Dale and Doug Anderson residence, Palm Beach, Florida, 1998. Cast glass, (left) h. 3.5 x 12 and (right) h. 4.5 x 6.5 feet. Photo: Russell Johnson

Opposite:
Sea Grass; Dining room installation detail.
Photo: Russell Johnson

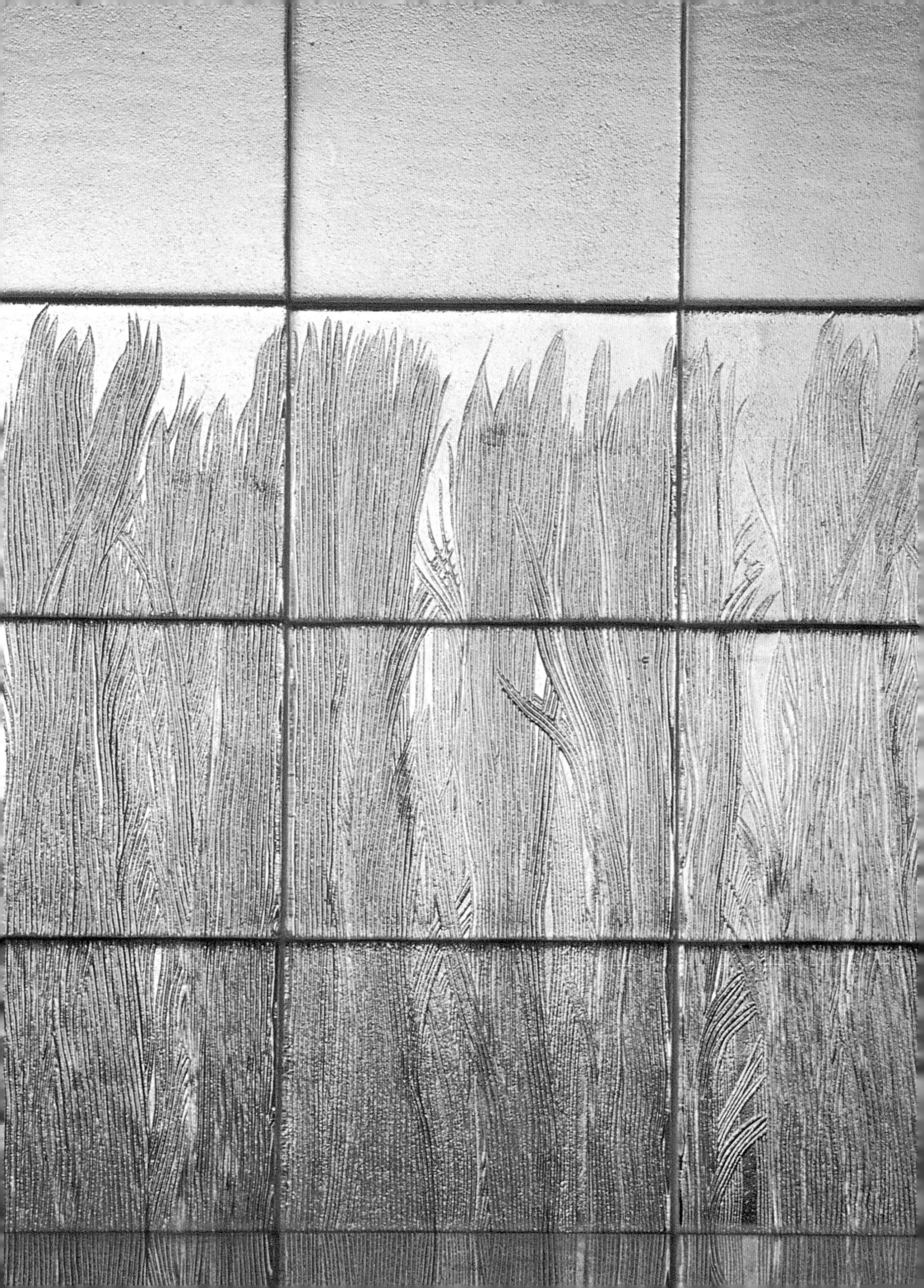

PAUL MARIONI & ANN TROUTNER

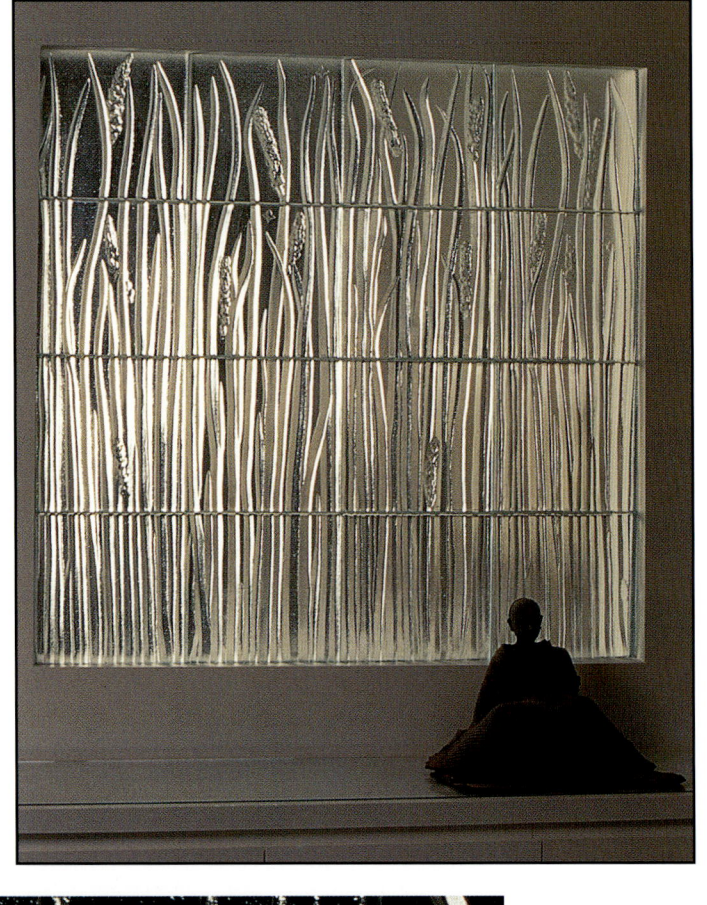

Right:
River Grass; *Bedroom installation, Dale and Doug Anderson residence, Palm Beach, Florida, 1998. Cast glass, h. 3.5 x 3.5 feet. Photo: Russell Johnson*

Below:
River Grass; *Bedroom installation detail. Photo: Russell Johnson*

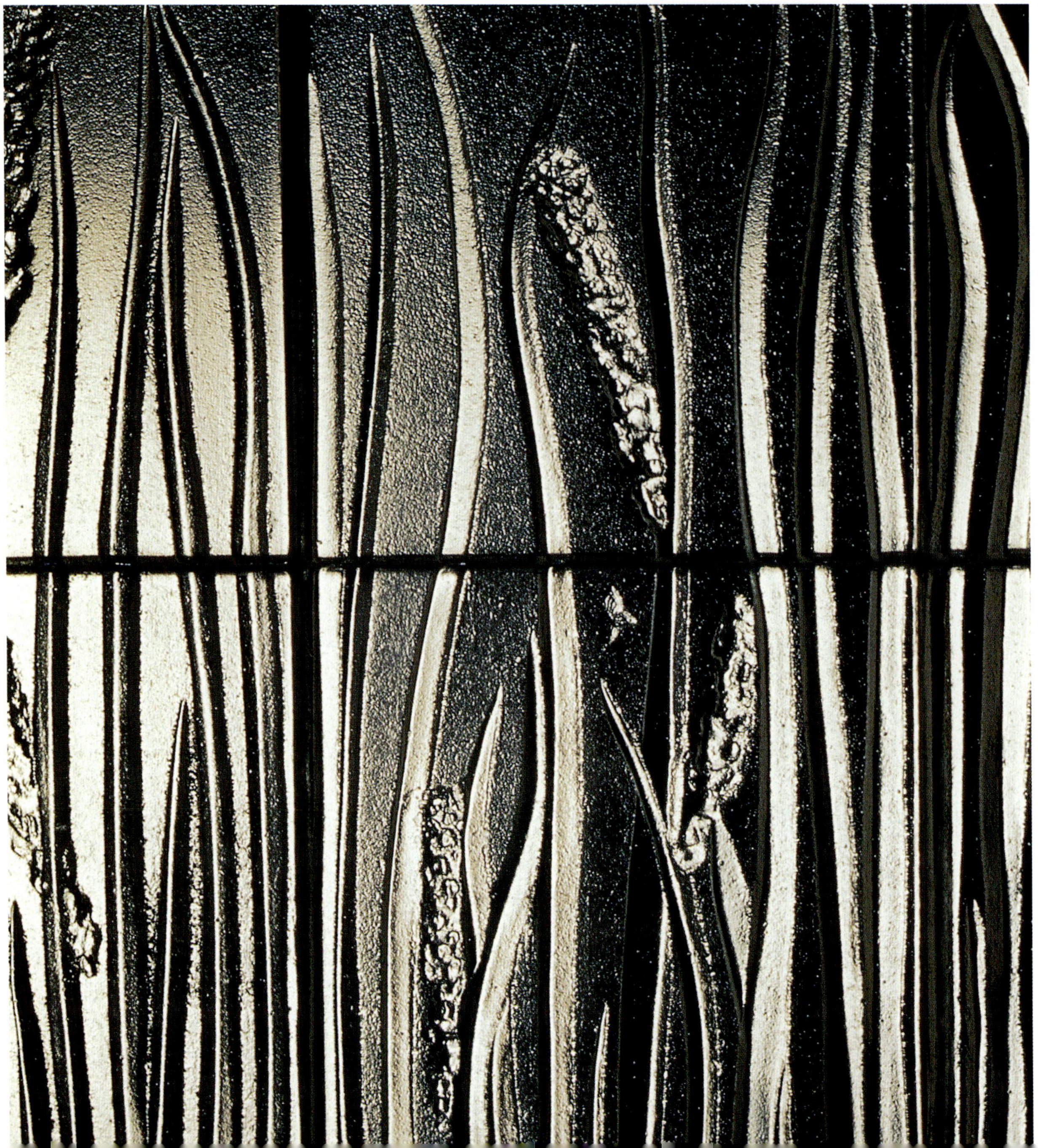

BERKLEY, CALIFORNIA

Richard Marquis
(b.1945)

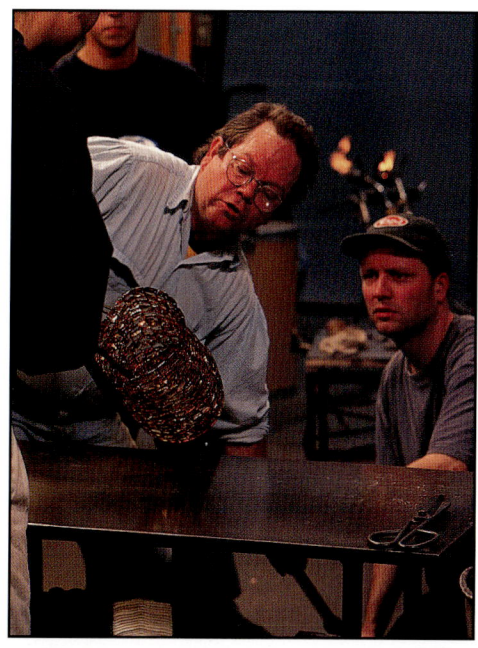

Marguiscarpa #99-5, 1999 Fused, slumped, blown glass, and carved silhouette murrine, h. 6.5 x 9.25 x 5 inches. Courtesy of Elliott Brown Gallery.

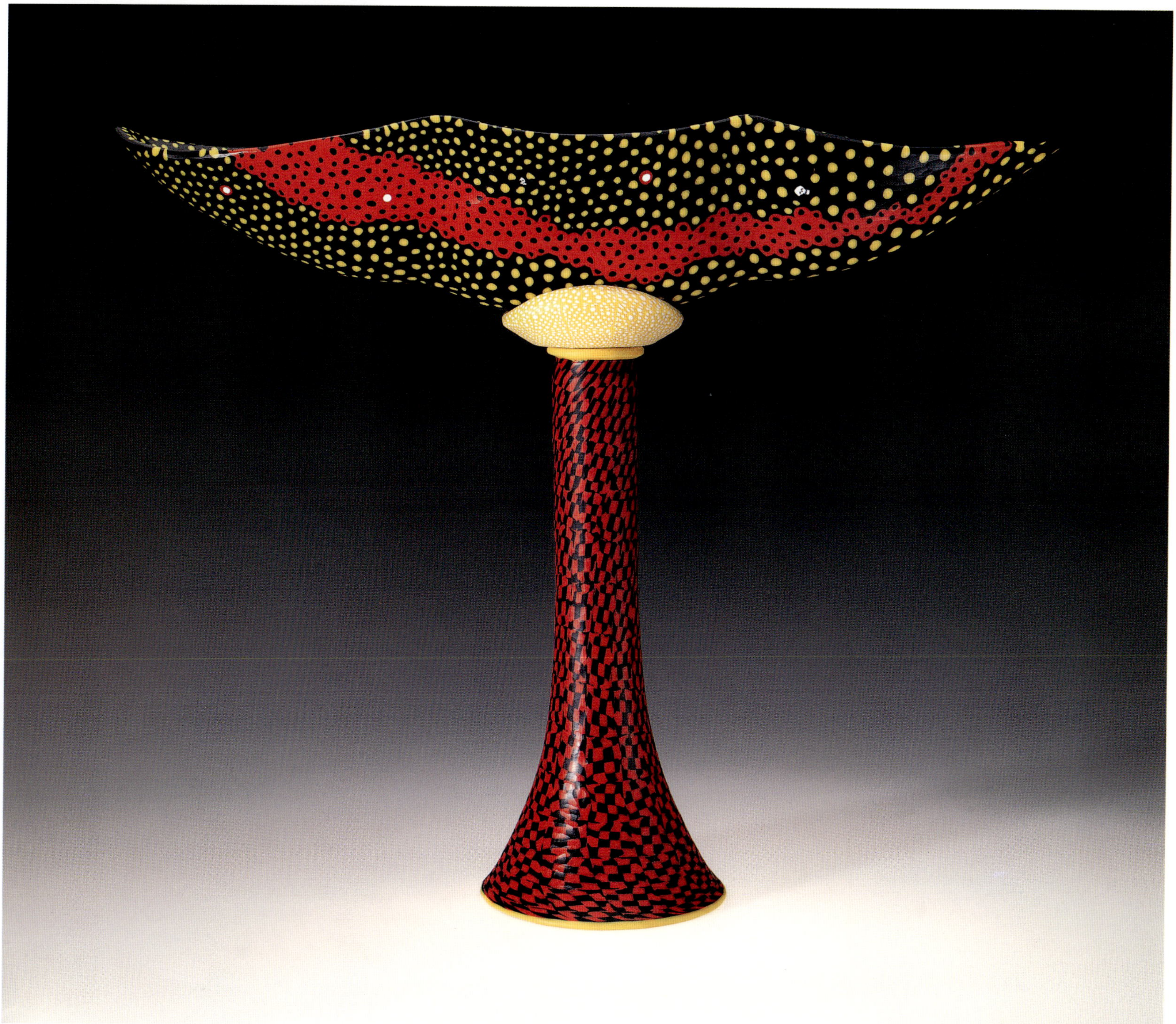

163

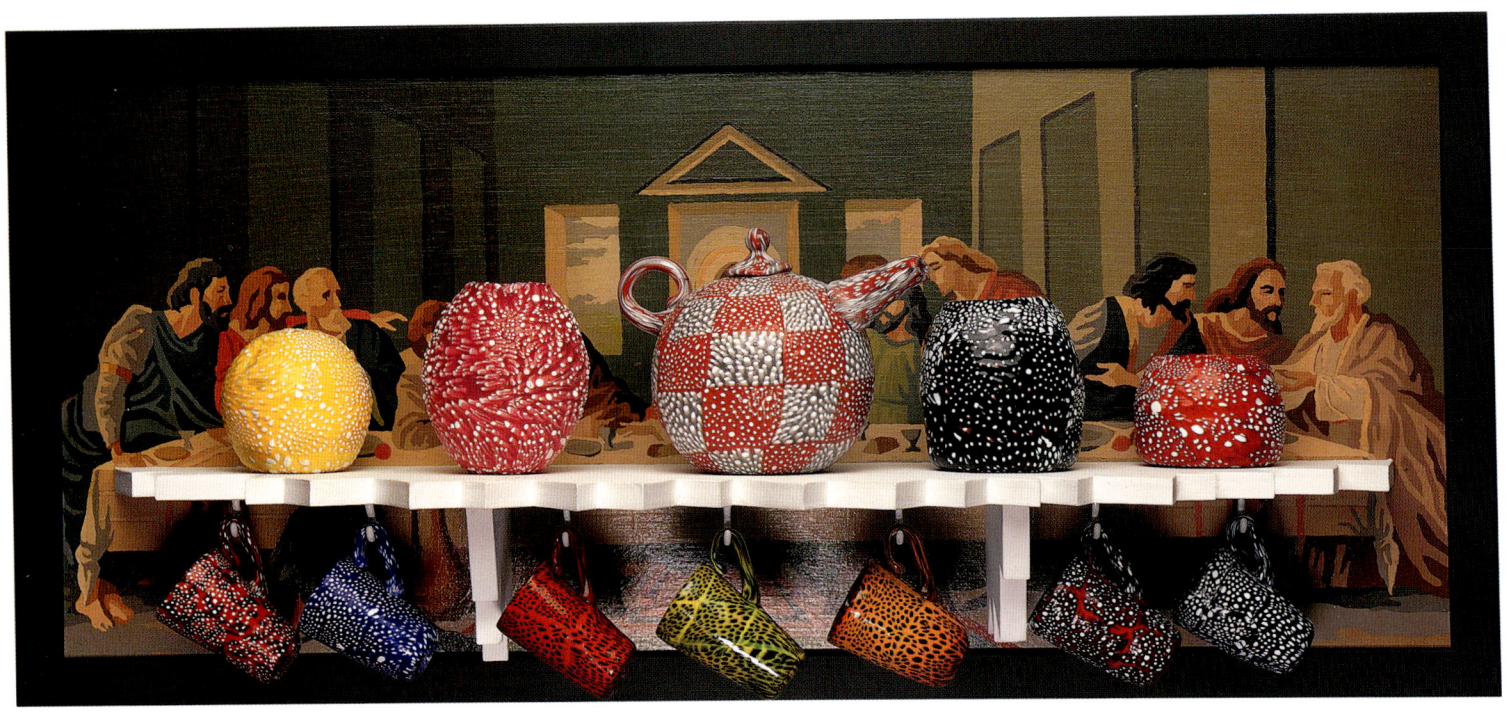

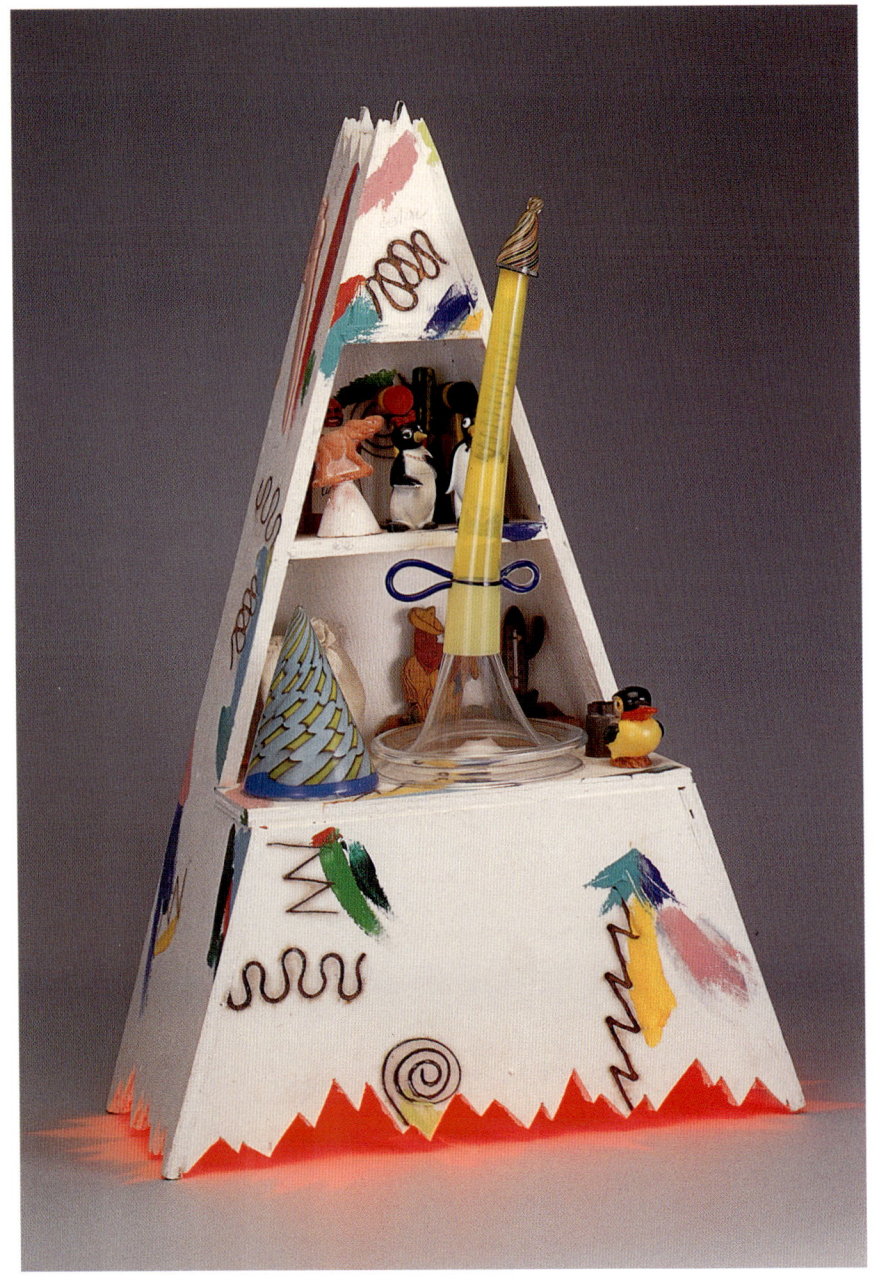

Above:
Lumpyware Shelf Unit—The Last Supper, 1998. Glass, wood, and mixed media, h. 14.5 x 34.25 x 9 inches. Courtesy Franklin Parrasch Gallery.

Right:
Personal Archive Unit—Yellow Spring, 1981. Blown glass, assembled and painted wood, found ceramic and plastic objects, h. 30 x 12.5 x 8.75. Charles A. Wustum Museum of Fine Arts, Racine, Wisconsin. Gift of Dale and Doug Anderson. Photo: Jon Bolton.

RICHARD MARQUIS

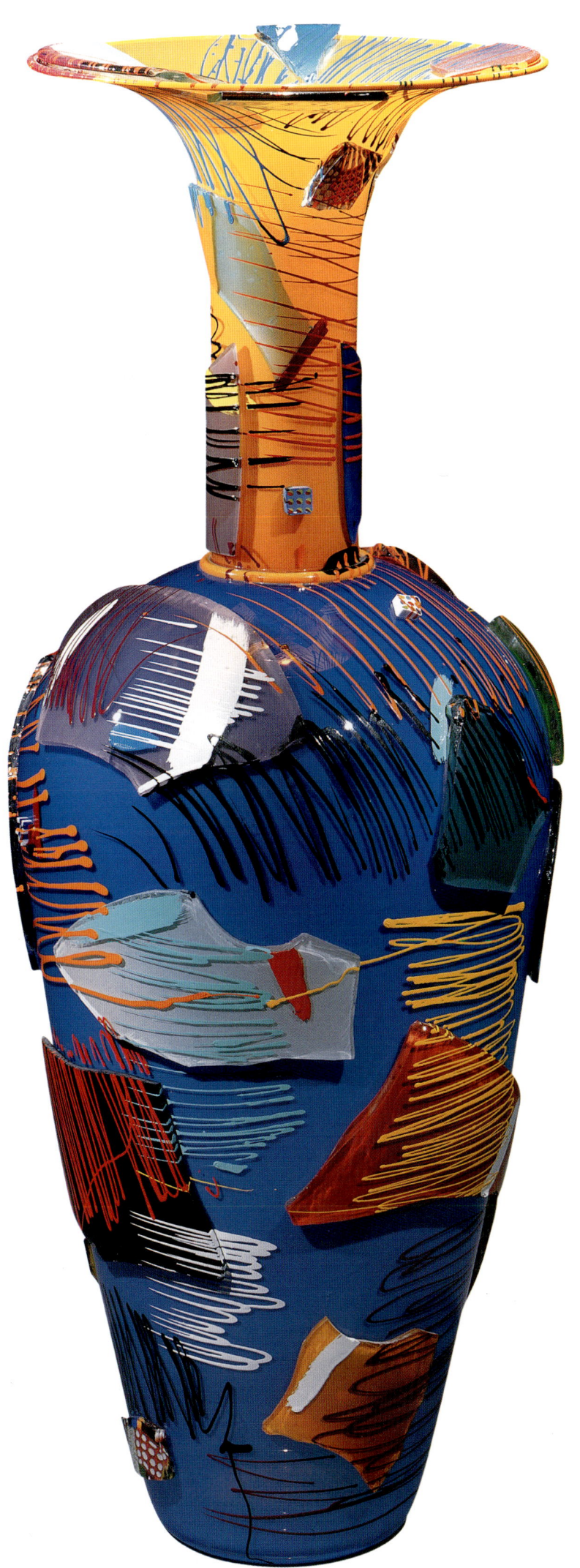

Shard Whopper; Blown by Dante Marioni in 1992, and altered by Richard Marquis in 1995. Blown glass and glass shards, h. 28 x 10.25 inches. Tampa Museum of Art, Florida. Collection of Dale and Doug Anderson. Photo: Bill Sanders.

Duncan McClellan
(b.1955)

TAMPA, FLORIDA

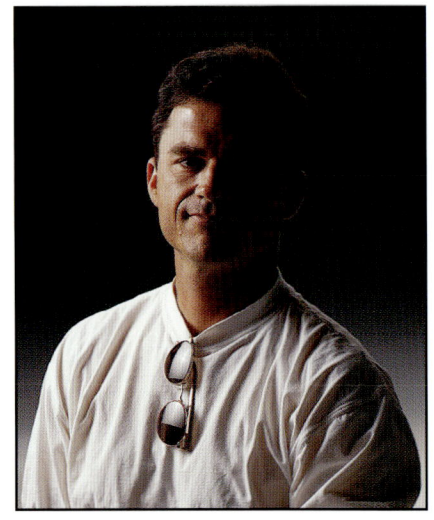

50th Cousins, 1998. Glass, overlay technique, sand carved, and steel, h. 26 x 21 x 9 inches. Photo: Randall Smith.

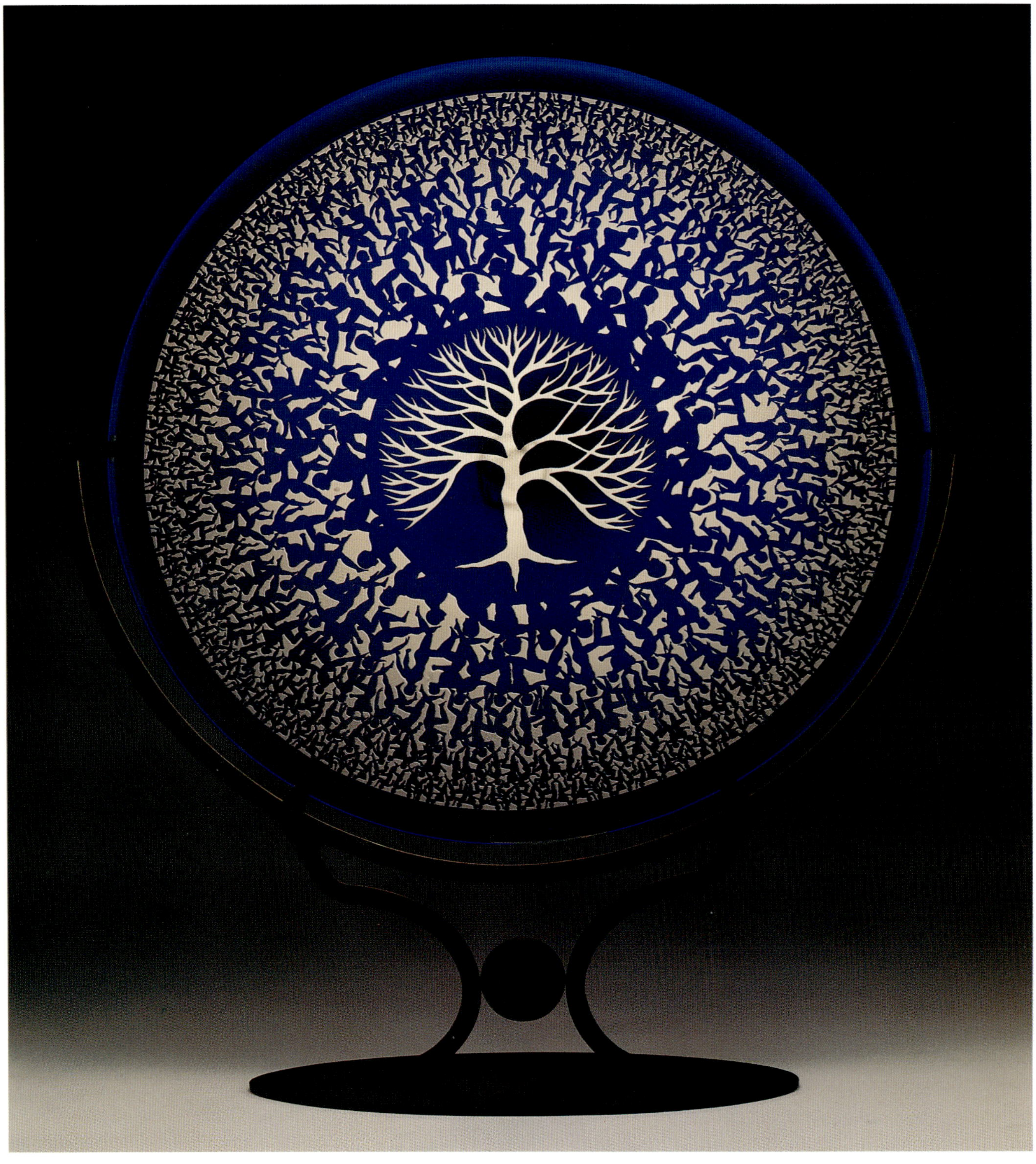

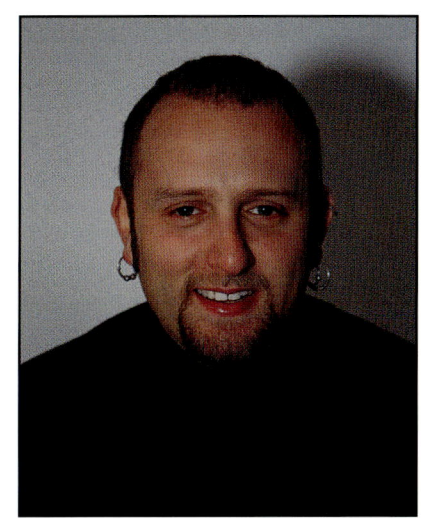

BROOKLYN, NEW YORK

Zesty Meyers
(b.1969)

White Bread, 1996. Slumped glass, and mixed media, h. 18.5 x 14 x 4 inches.

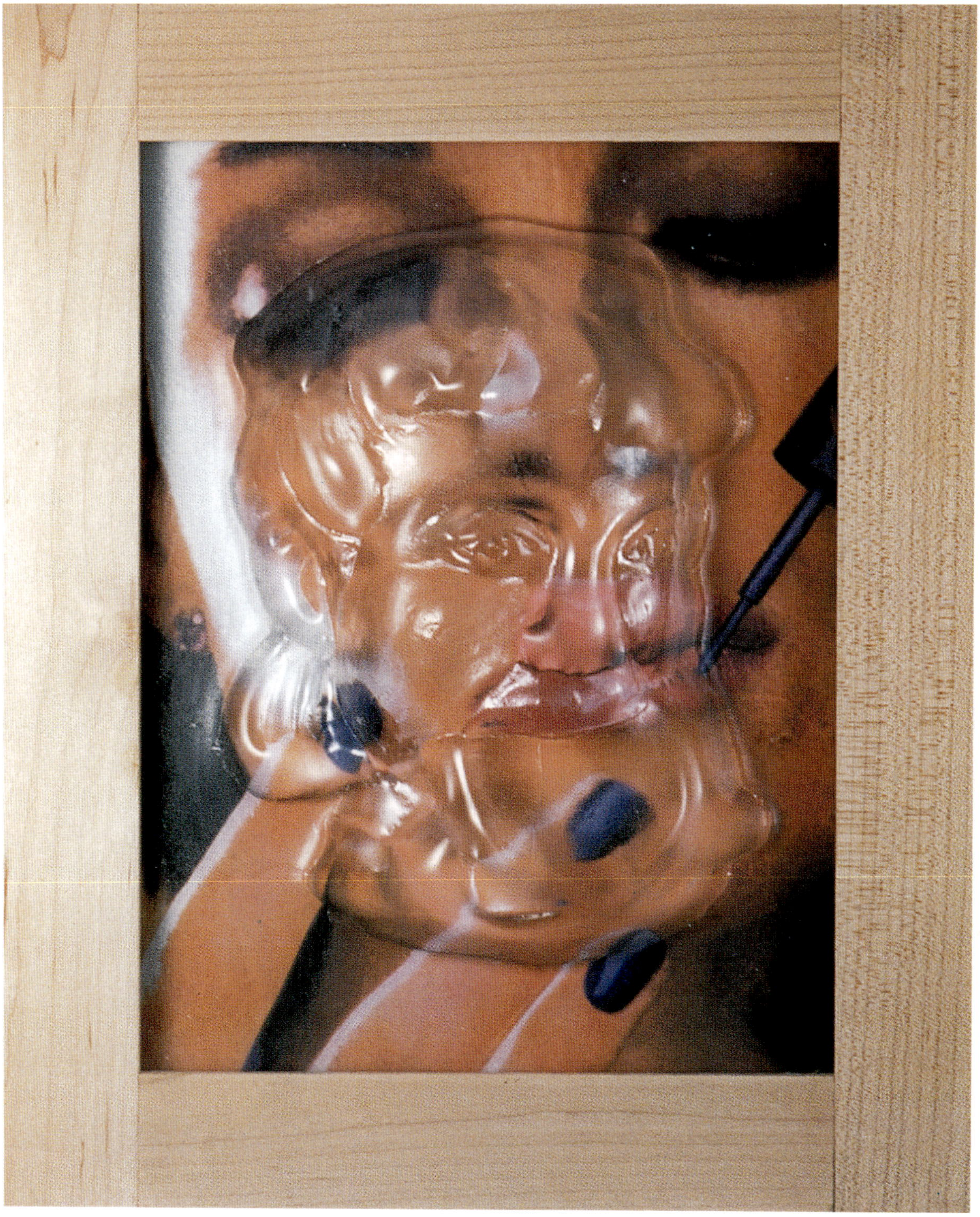

ZESTY MEYERS

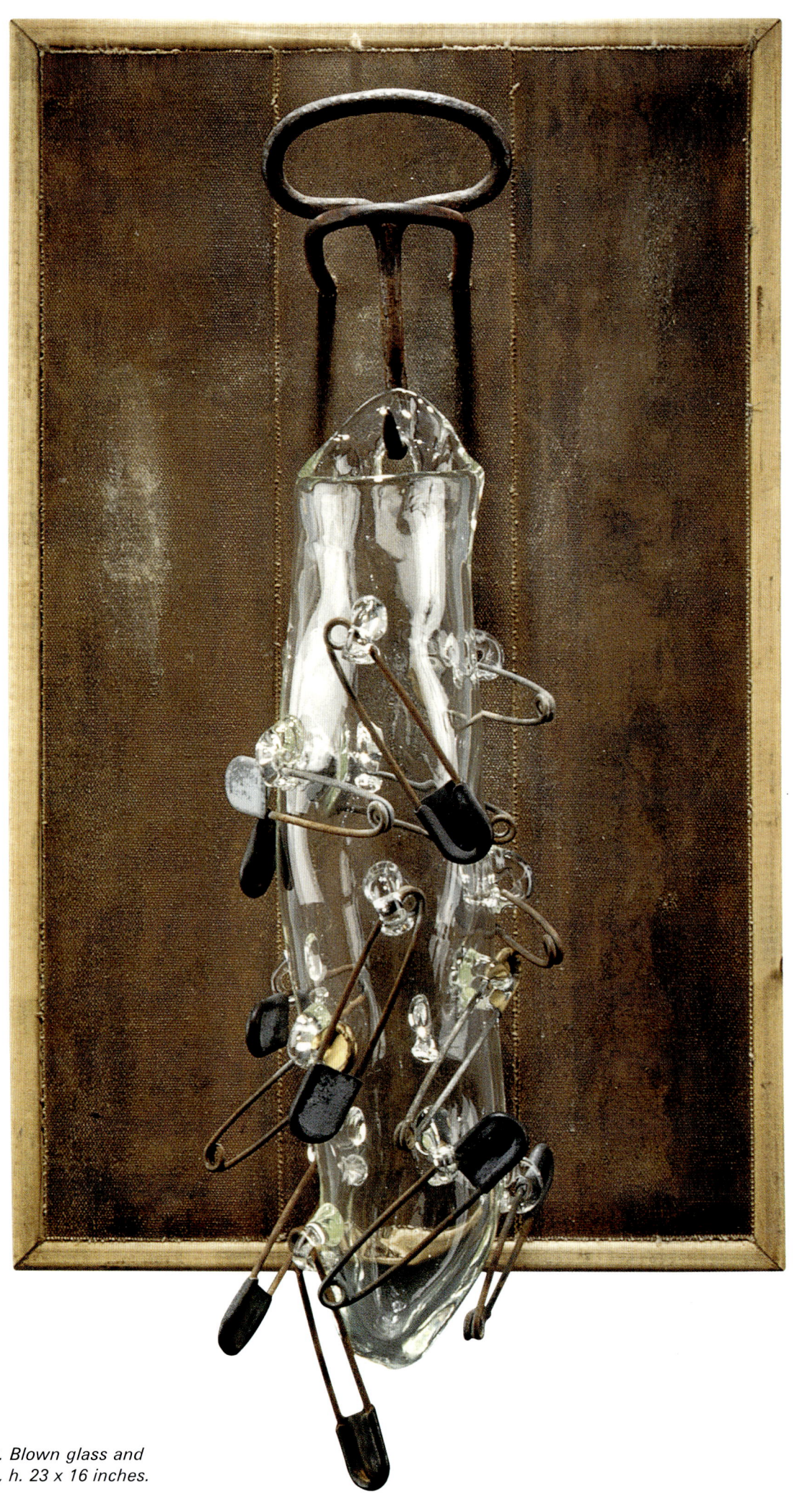

Untitled, 1993. Blown glass and found objects, h. 23 x 16 inches.

SEATTLE, WASHINGTON

James Minson
(b. 1970)

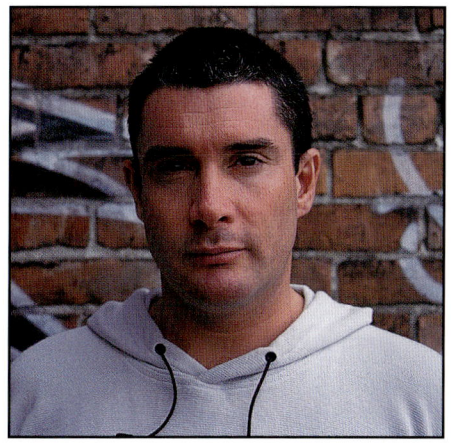

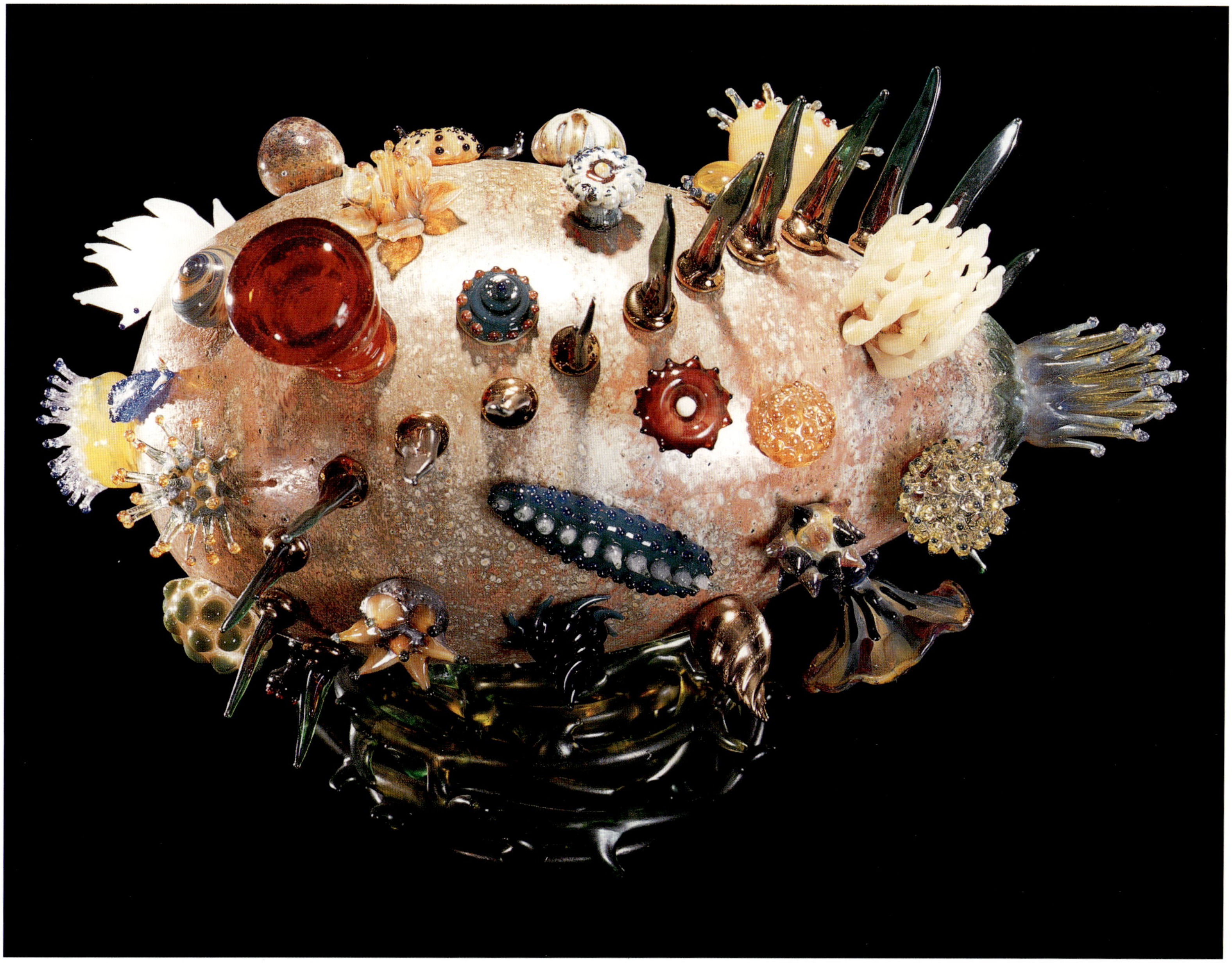

Encrusted Egg, 1995. Blown and flameworked glass, h. 6 x 7 x 9 inches.

Klaus Moje
(b.1936)

TANJA, AUSTRALIA

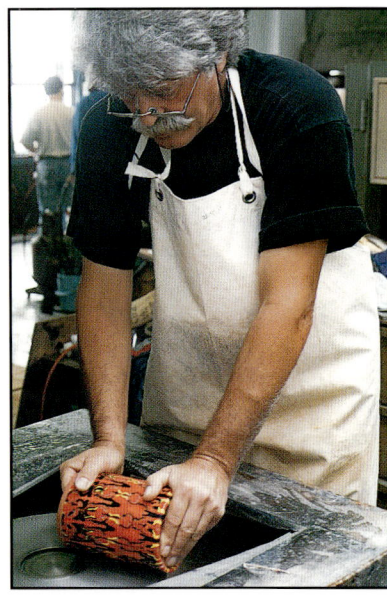

Song Lines, 1989. Fused glass, h. 17.2 x 17.2 x 3 inches.

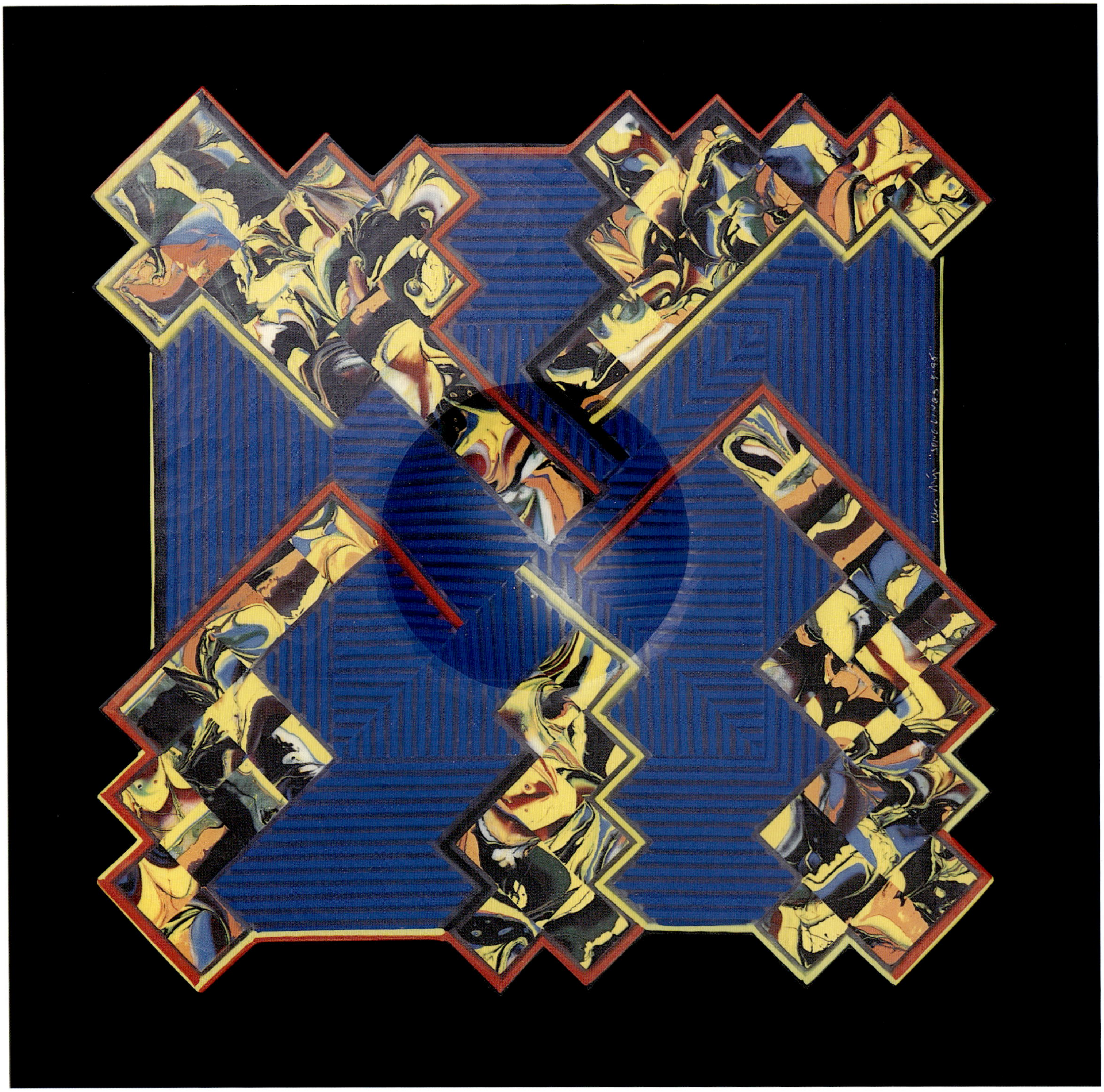

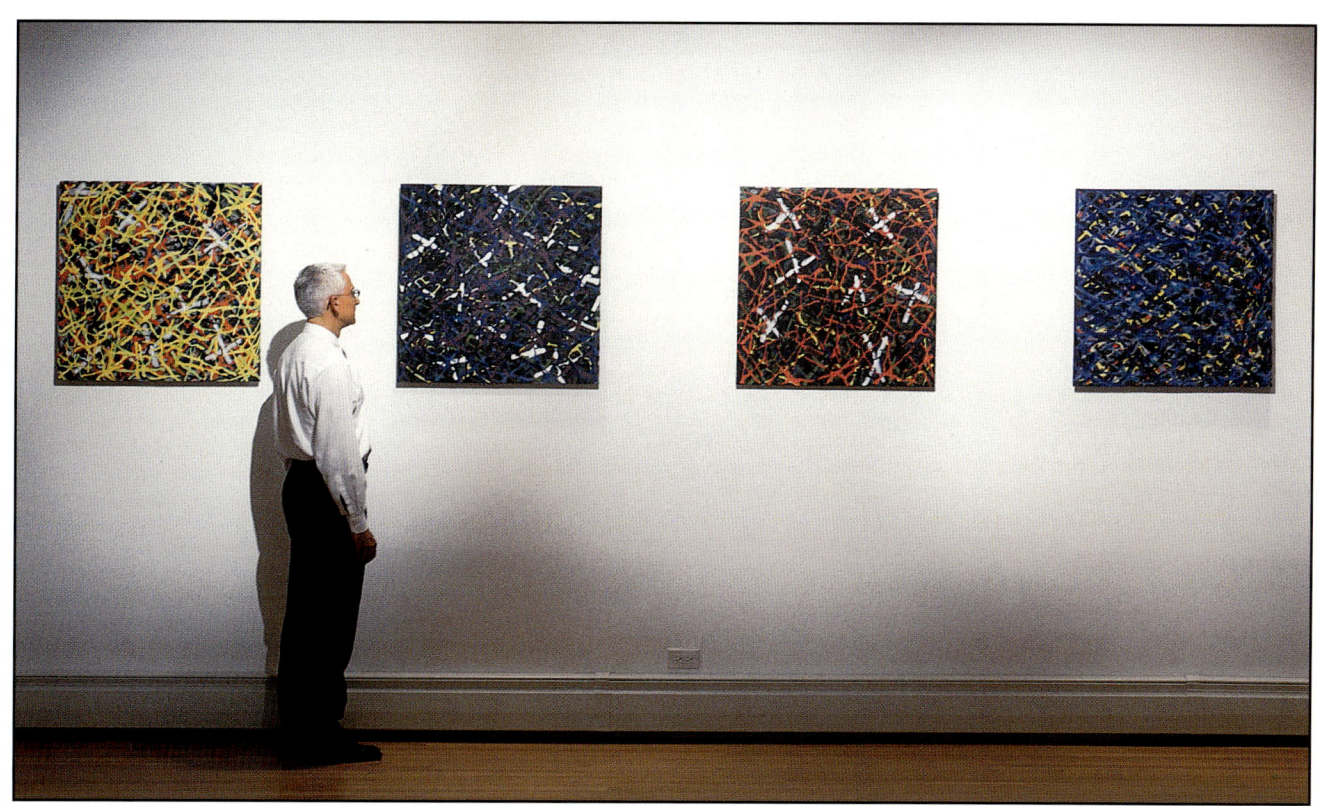

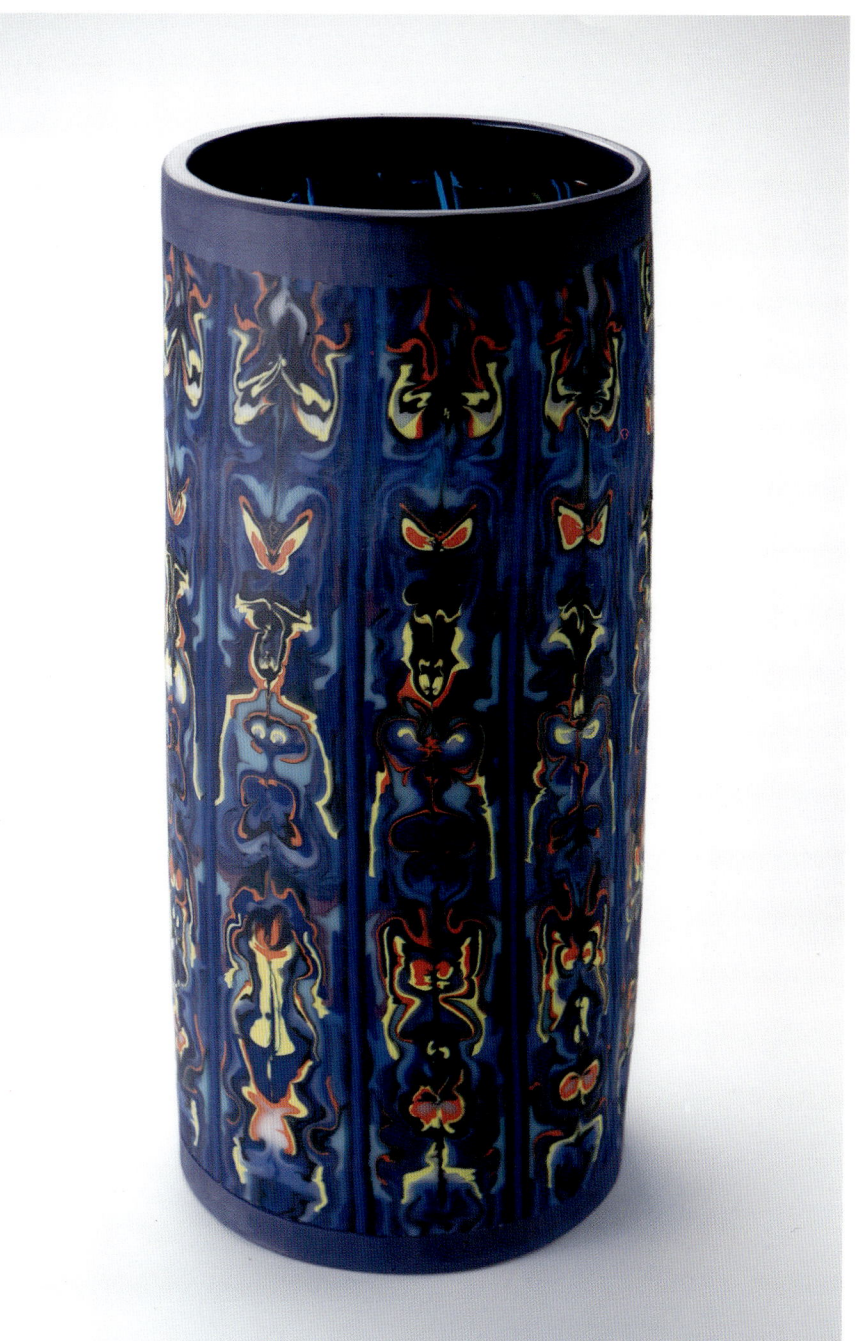

Above:
Wall Panels; Installation Shot, Heller Gallery, New York City. Fused glass, h. 28.8 x 28.8 inches.

Left:
Niljima Vessel Series #7, 1999. Fused and hotformed glass, h. 16.25 x 7.5 inches. Collection of Cynthia and Jeffrey Manocherian. Photo: Eva Heyd.

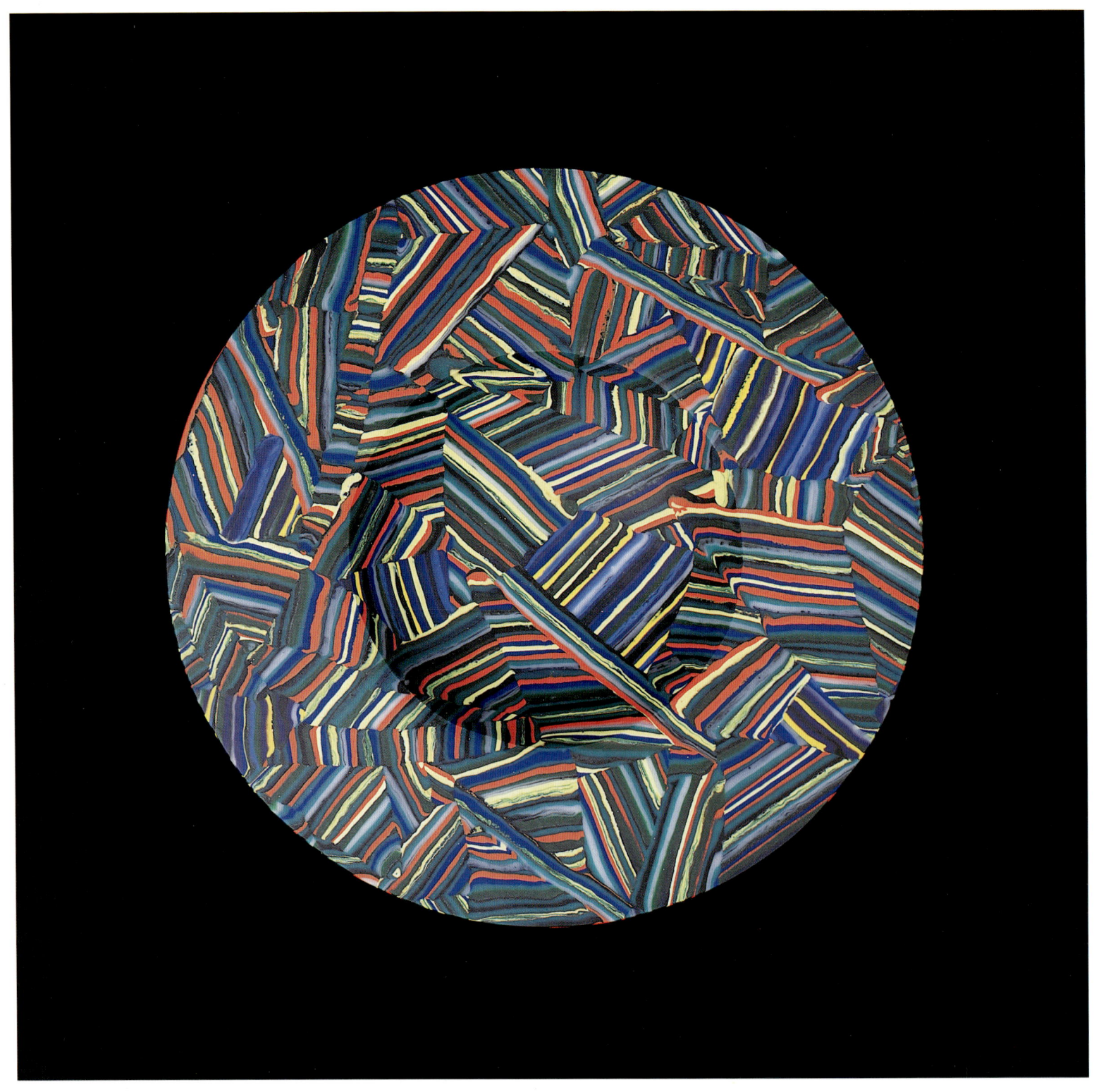

1-1999, 1999. Fused glass, h. 21.2 x 21.2 x 3 inches.

STANWOOD, WASHINGTON

William Morris
(b. 1957)

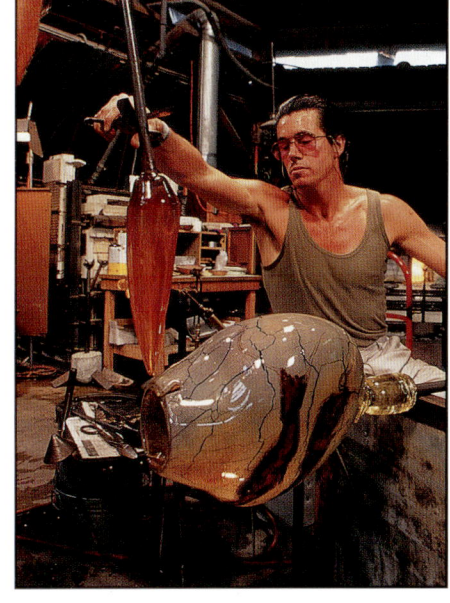
Photo: Russell Johnson

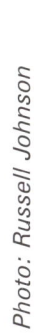

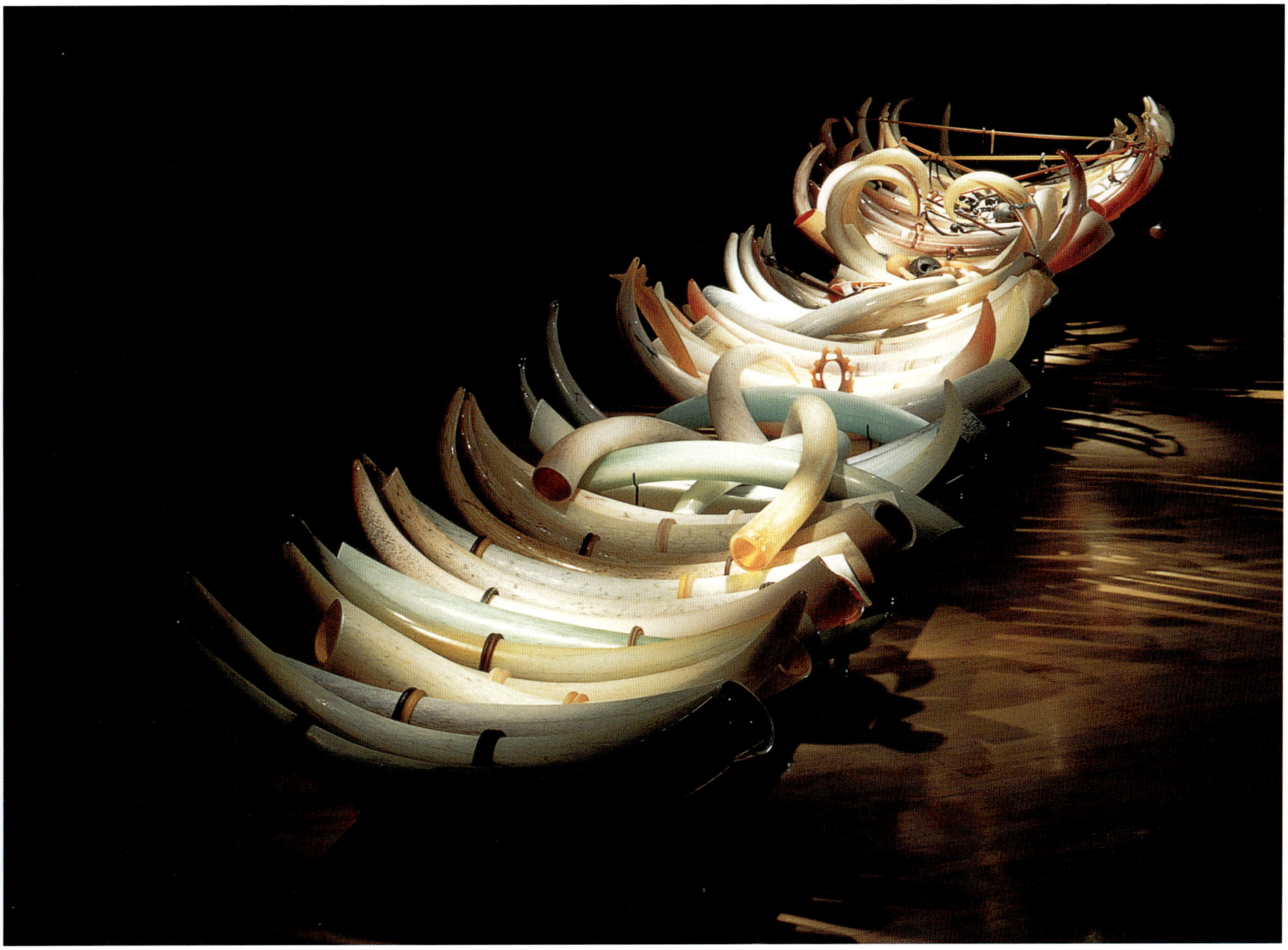

Installation; American Craft Museum, *New York City, 1993. Blown glass, metal, and wood, h. 5 x 36 x 6 feet.*

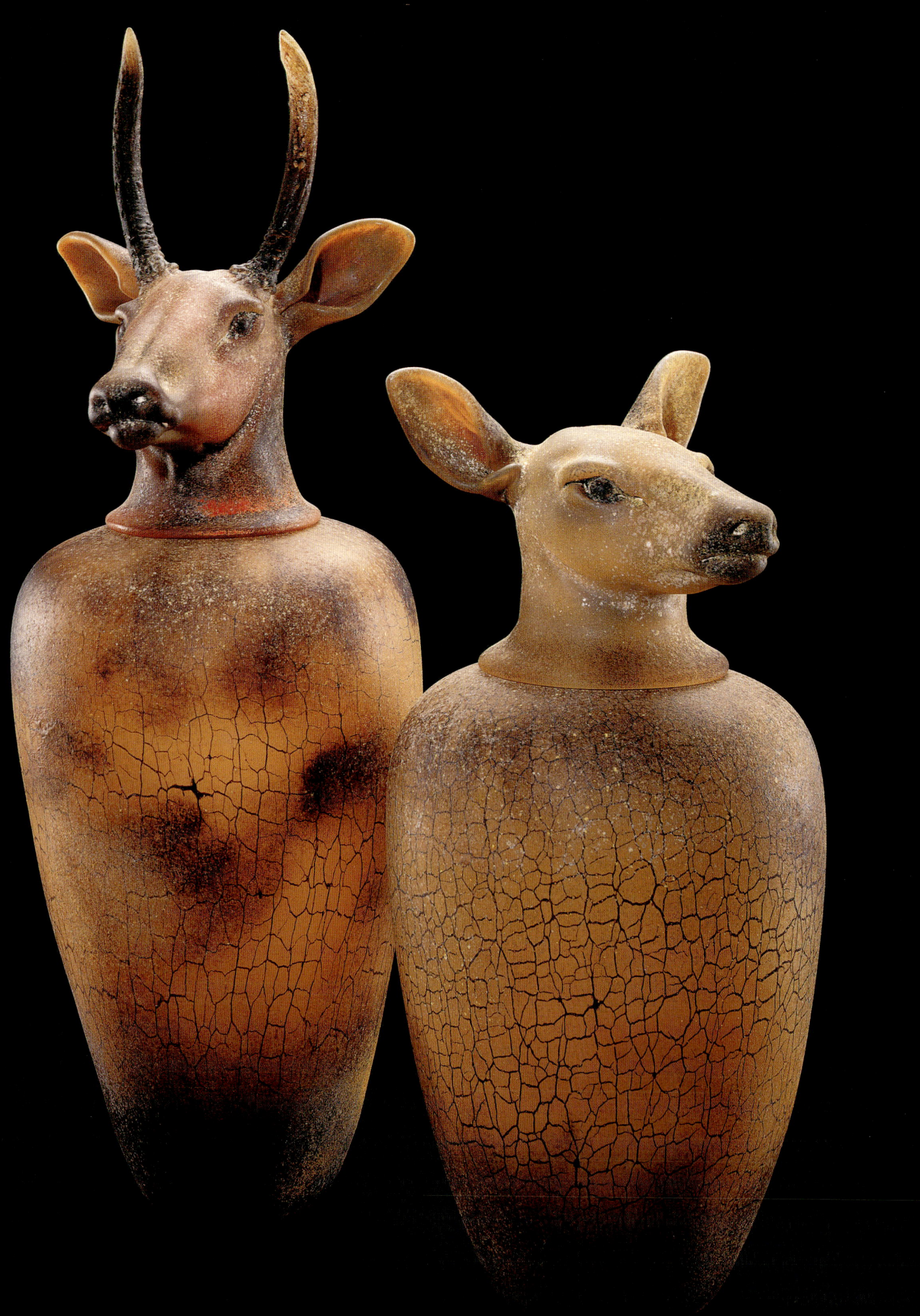

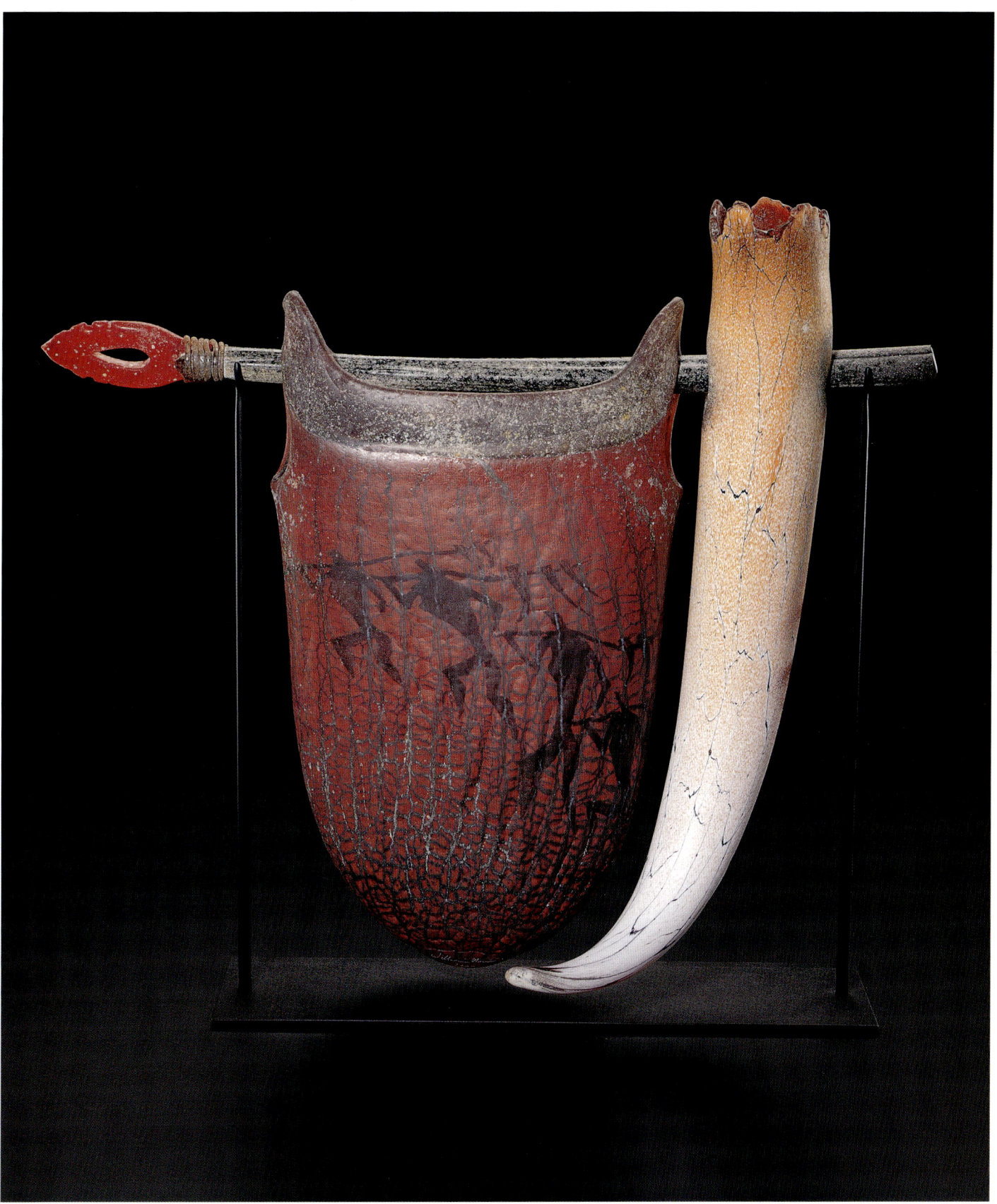

Opposite:
Canopic Jar: Elk (Cow and Spike), 1993. Blown glass, left to right: h. 39 x 13 and h. 28 x 12 inches. The Metropolitan Museum of Art. Gift of Dale and Doug Anderson. Photo: Rob Vinnedge.

Above:
Suspended Artifact, 1993. Blown glass and steel stand, h. 24 x 26 x 7 inches. The Metropolitan Museum of Art. Gift of Dale and Doug Anderson. Photo: Rob Vinnedge.

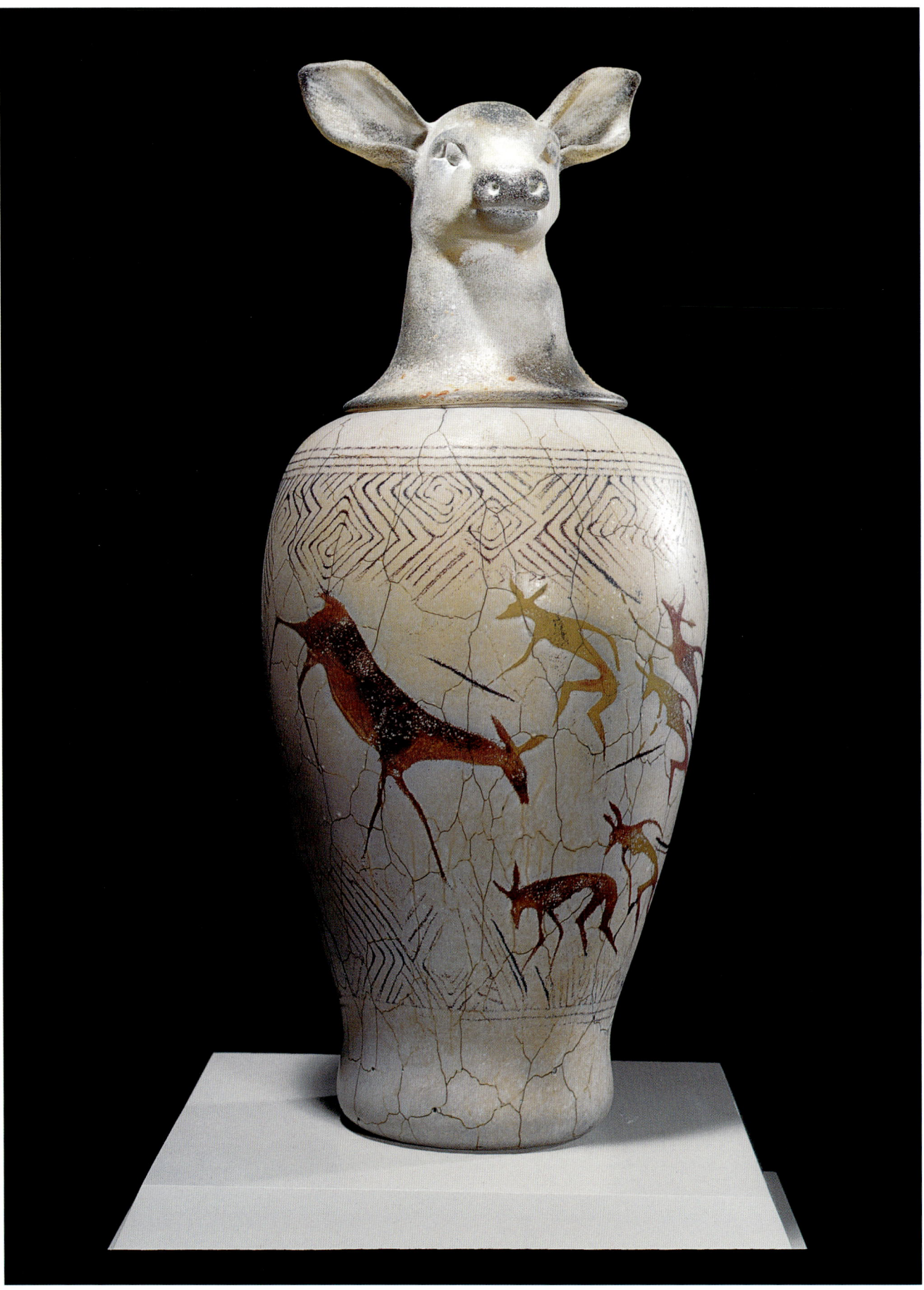

Canopic Jar: Fawn, 1992. Blown glass, h. 27 x 11 inches. Norton Museum of Art, West Palm Beach, Florida. Gift of Dale and Doug Anderson.

BERKELEY, CALIFORNIA

Jay Musler
(b.1949

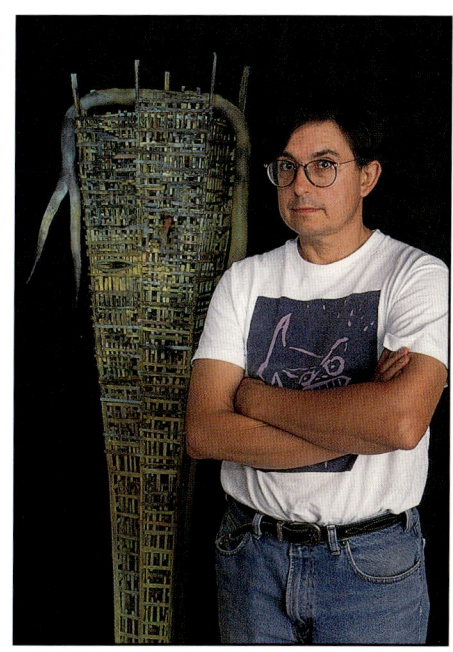

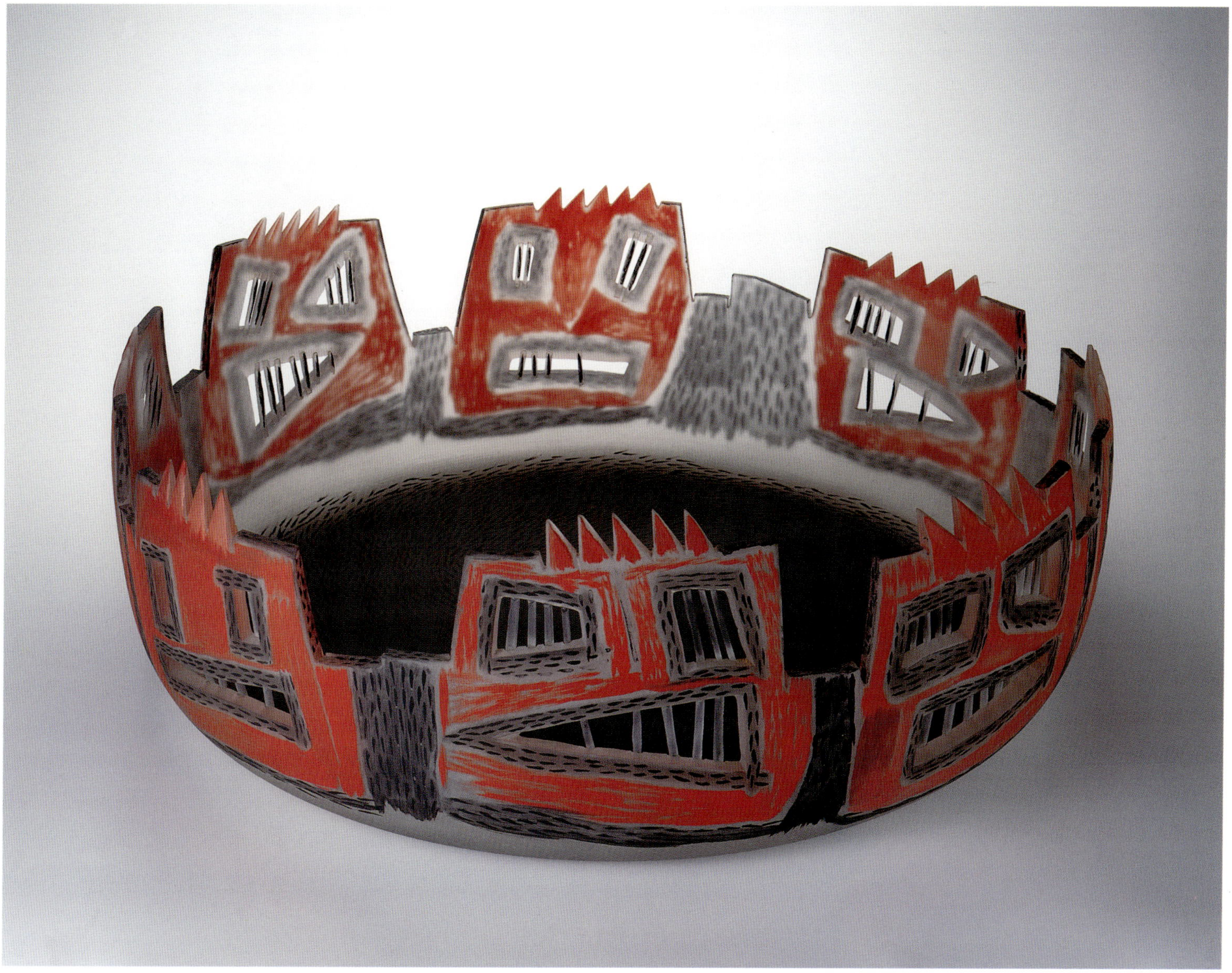

The Image, 1984. Blown sandblasted glass and oil paint, h. 6 x 17 inches. Collection of Cynthia and Jeffrey Manocherian. Photo: Eva Heyd.

JAY MUSLER

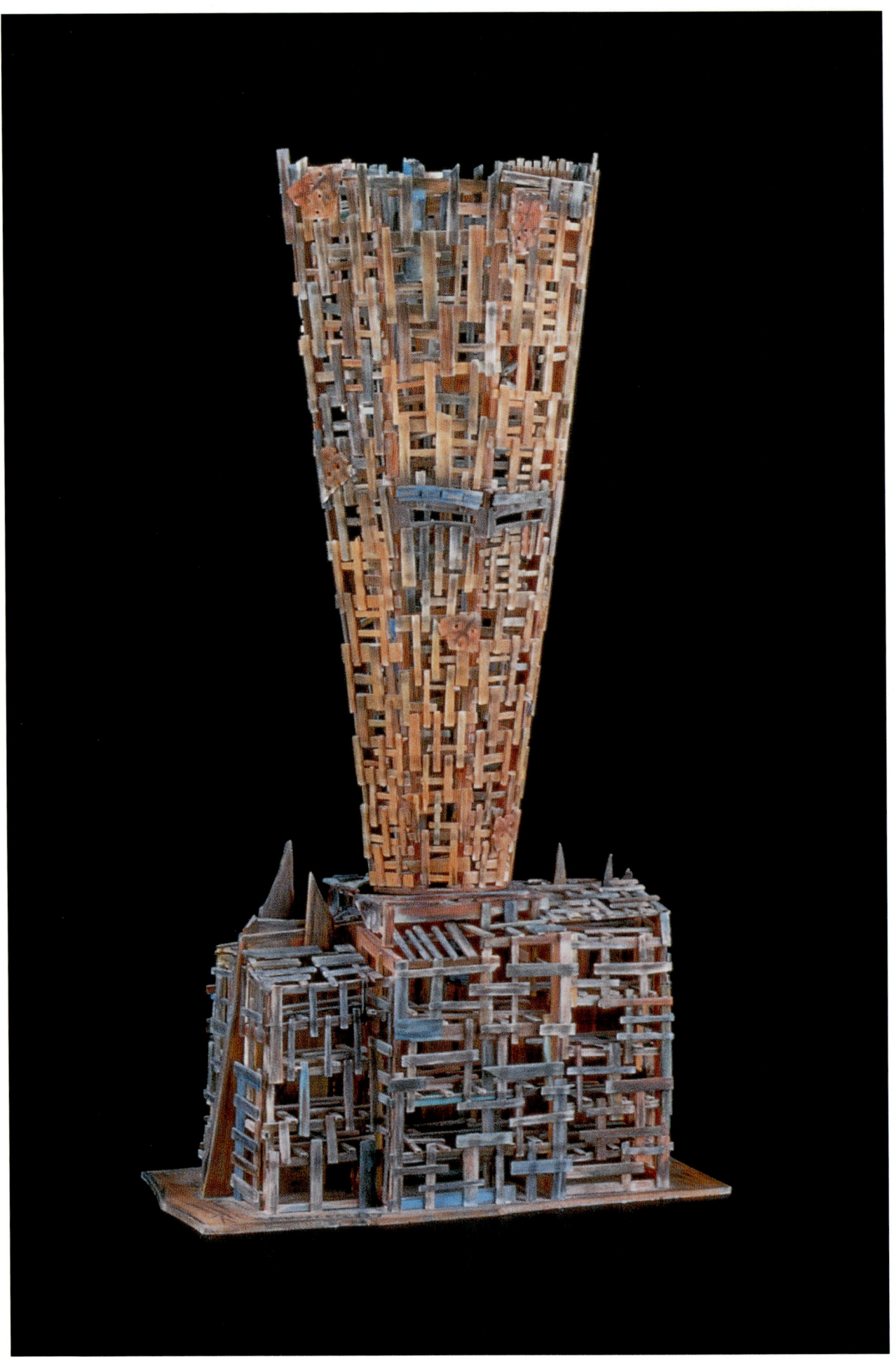

Above:
Mask House, 1987. Plate glass, cut, sandblasted, and oil paint, h. 30 x 16 x 7 inches. The Metropolitan Museum of Art. Gift of Dale and Doug Anderson. Photo: Courtesy Slide Library, Museum of Fine Arts, Boston.

Right:
Speechless, 1999. Plate glass, and oil paint, h. 47 x 20 x 8.5 inches. Courtesy Heller Gallery. Photo: Sibila Savaga.

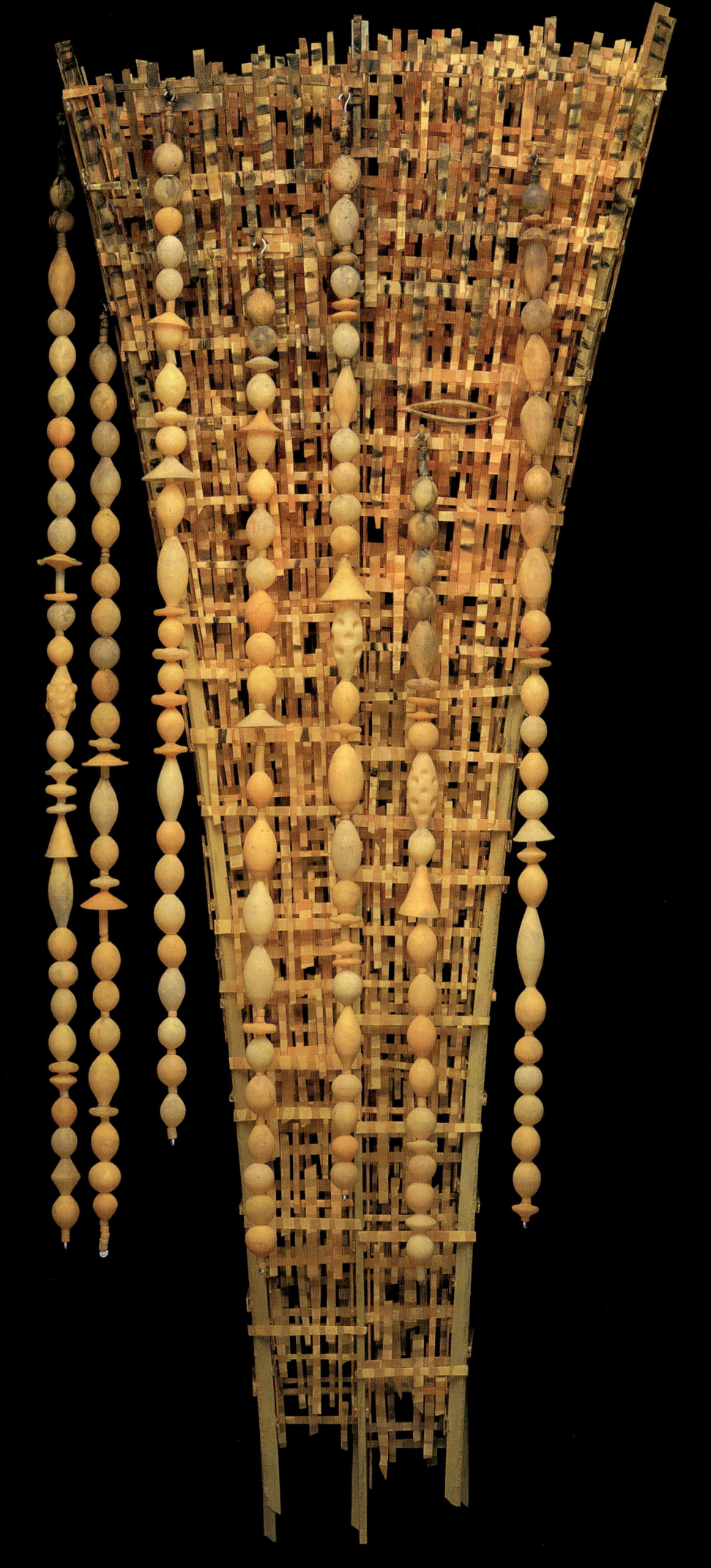

JAY MUSLER

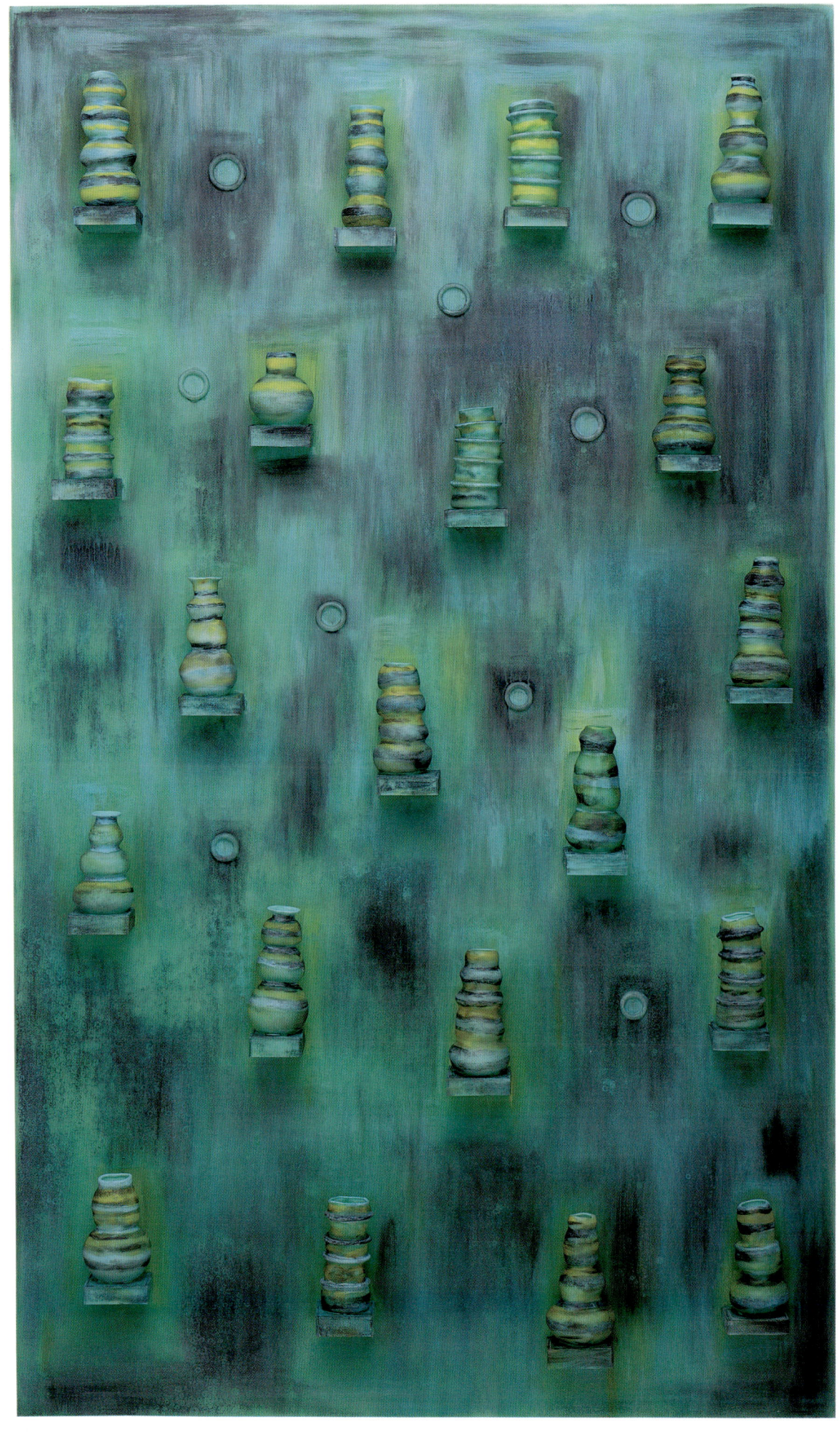

Midnight Calling, 1999. Glass and oil paint, h. 43 x 25 x 3 inches.
Courtesy Heller Gallery. Photo: Sibila Savaga.

MARIETTA, PENNSYLVANIA

Joel Philip Myers
(b. 1934)

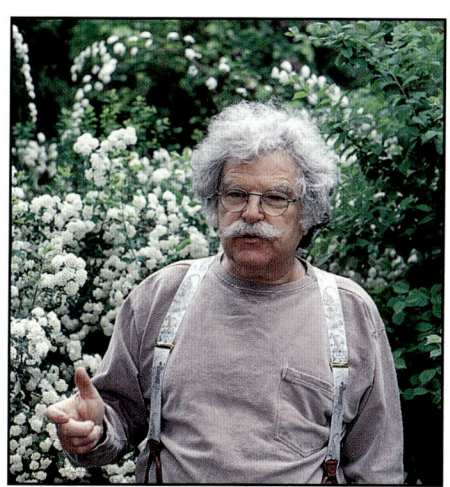

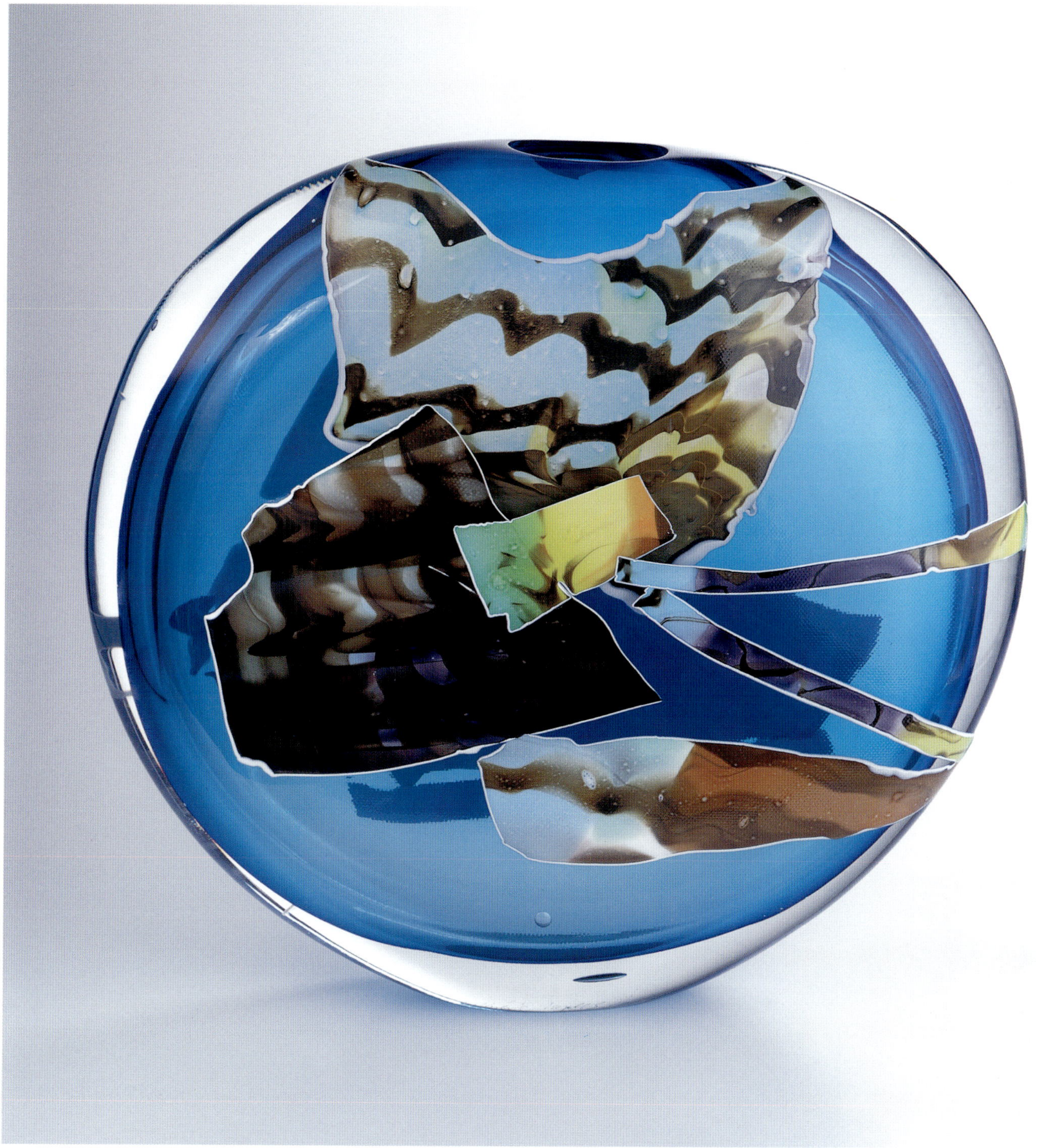

Kaleidoscope Blue X, 1990. Blown glass with applied elements, h. 16.25 x 15 x 4 inches. Courtesy Barry Friedman Ltd., New York. Photo: Eva Heyd

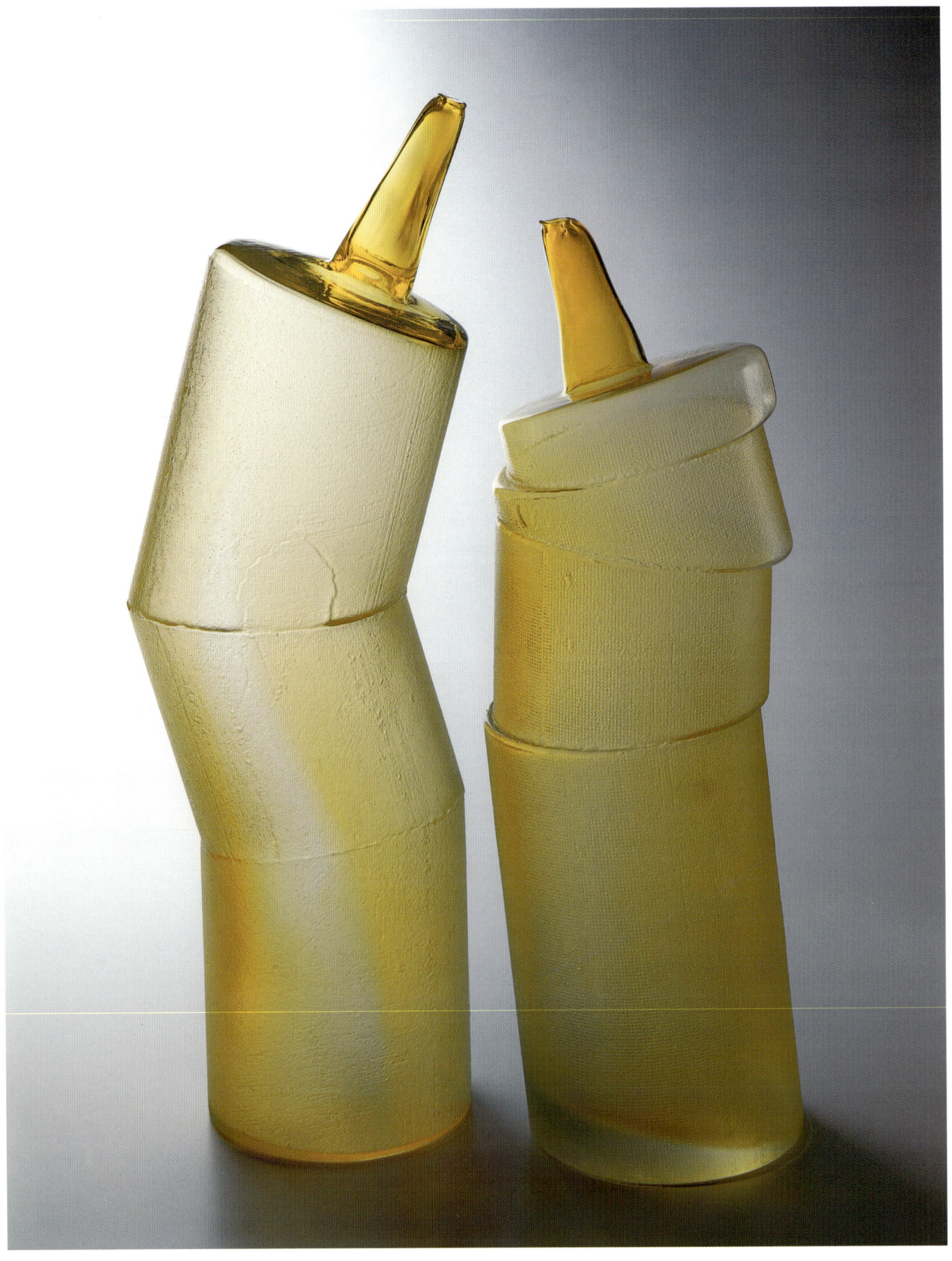

Dialogue #17, 1999. Blown glass, (left) h. 20.75 and (right) h. 18.5 inches. Courtesy Barry Friedman Ltd., New York. Photo: Eva Heyd.

BROOKLYN, NEW YORK

Doug Navarra
(b.1954)

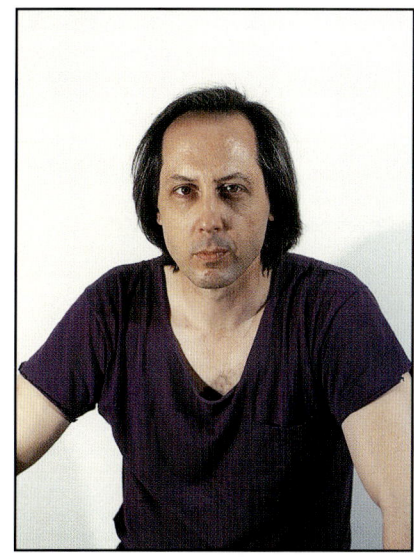

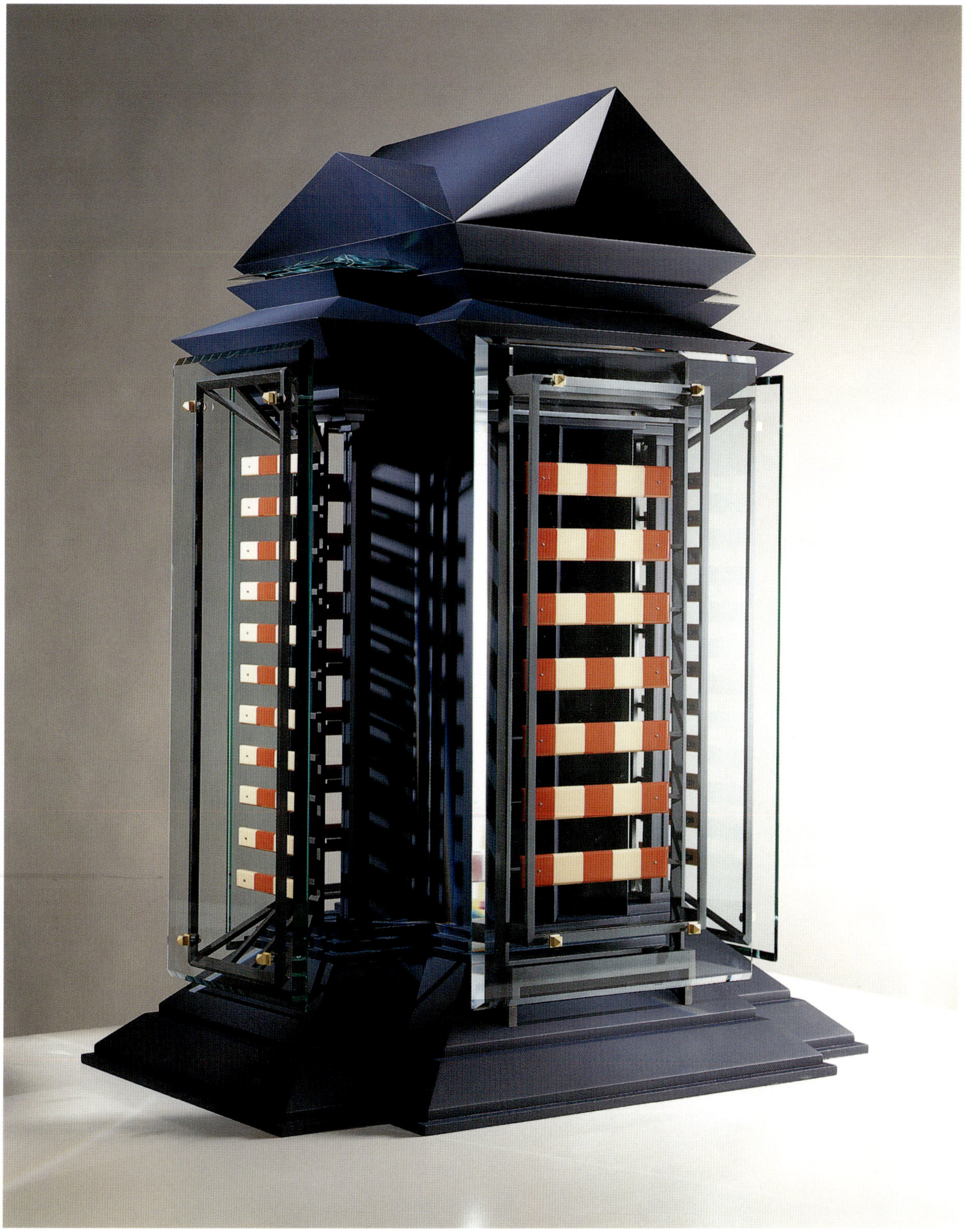

Palazzo, 1999. Carrara glass and mixed media, h. 41 x 28 x 22 inches. Photo: George Erml.

Trinh Huu Nguyen
(b.1975)

BROOKLYN, NEW YORK

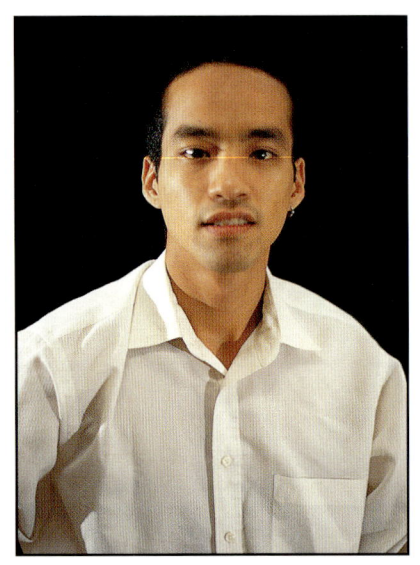

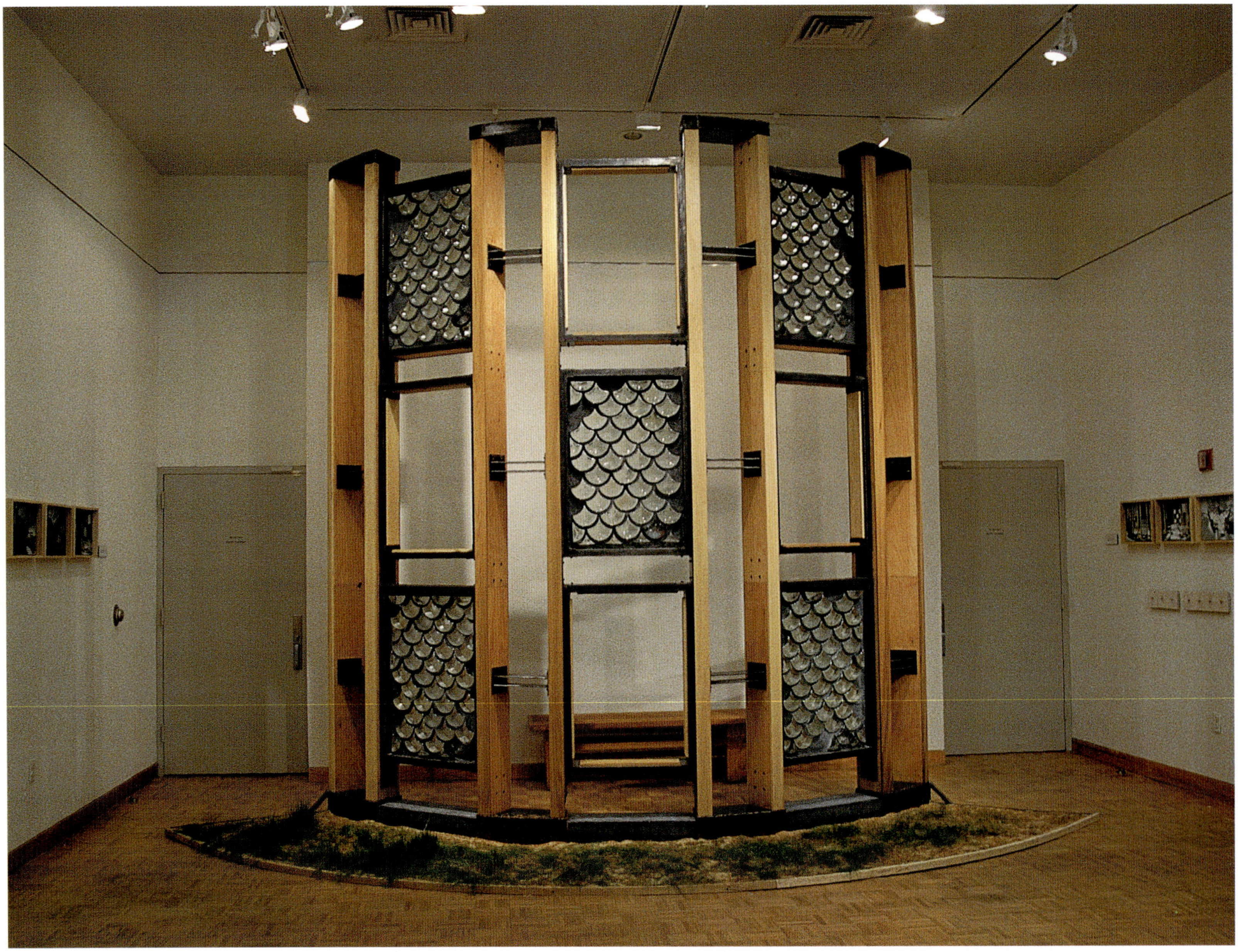

Architectonic Form; *Modular Component For Public Art Proposal, Installation, 1999. Aronson Galleries, Parsons School of Design, New York City.*

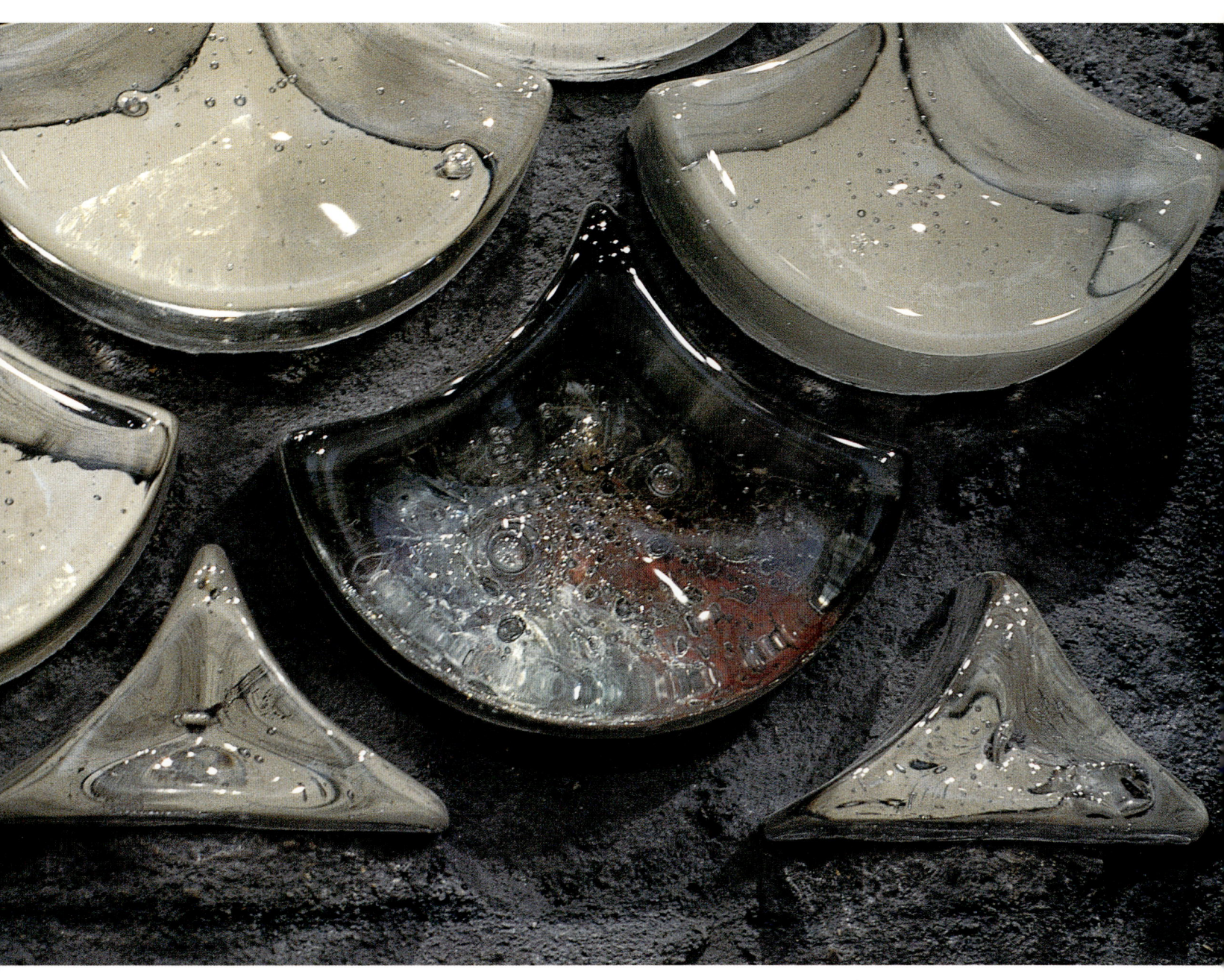

Architectonic Form; Modular Component For Public Art Proposal, Detail, 1999. Cast glass fish-scale bricks, steel, pigmented cement, wood, copper, sand, and wheat grass. Installation, h. 13.5 feet. Fish-scale bricks, h. 5.5 inches.

Himiko Ohta
(b.1972)

JERSEY CITY, NEW JERSEY

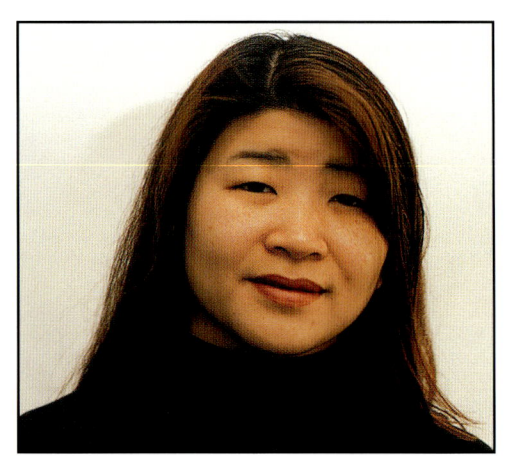

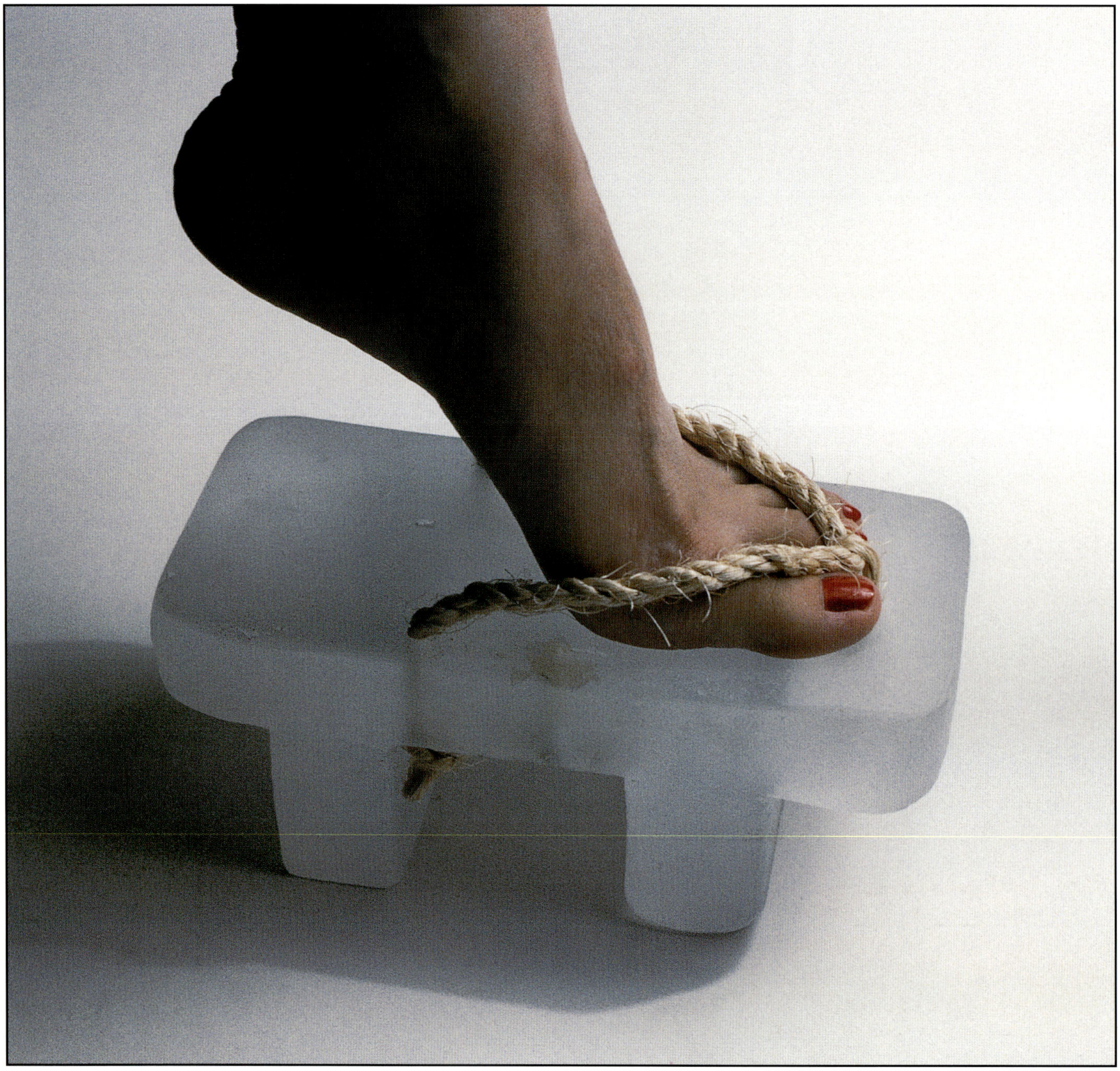

Geta, 1998. Cast glass Japanese slipper and rope, h. 2 x 9 x 8 inches.

NEW YORK, NEW YORK

Dennis Oppenheim
(b. 1938)

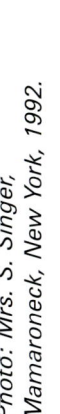
Photo: Mrs. S. Singer, Mamaroneck, New York, 1992.

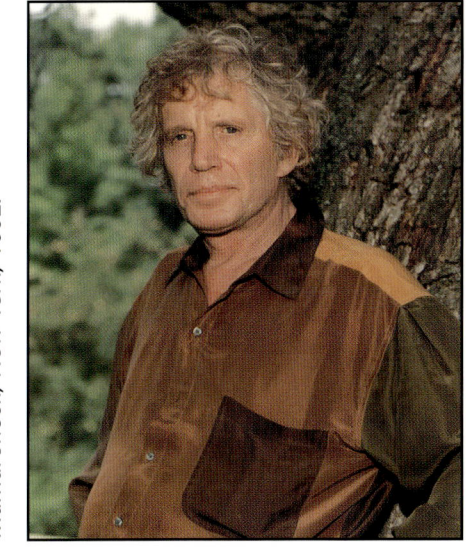

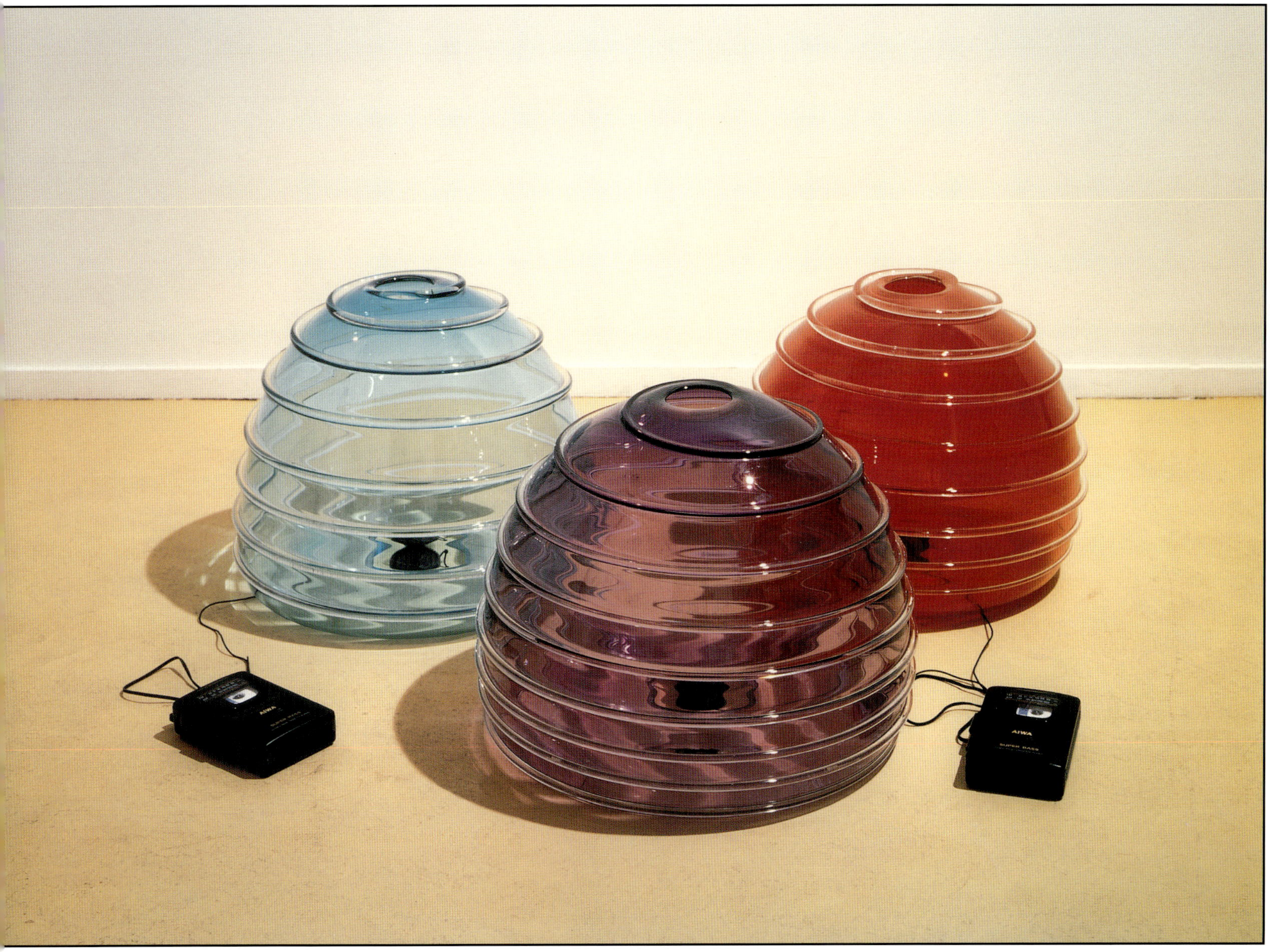

Beehive—Volcano, 1979. Blown glass, audiotape with sounds from a beehive, and tape player, h. 2 x 3 x 3 feet. Photo: Yvon Lambert.

DENNIS OPPENHEIM

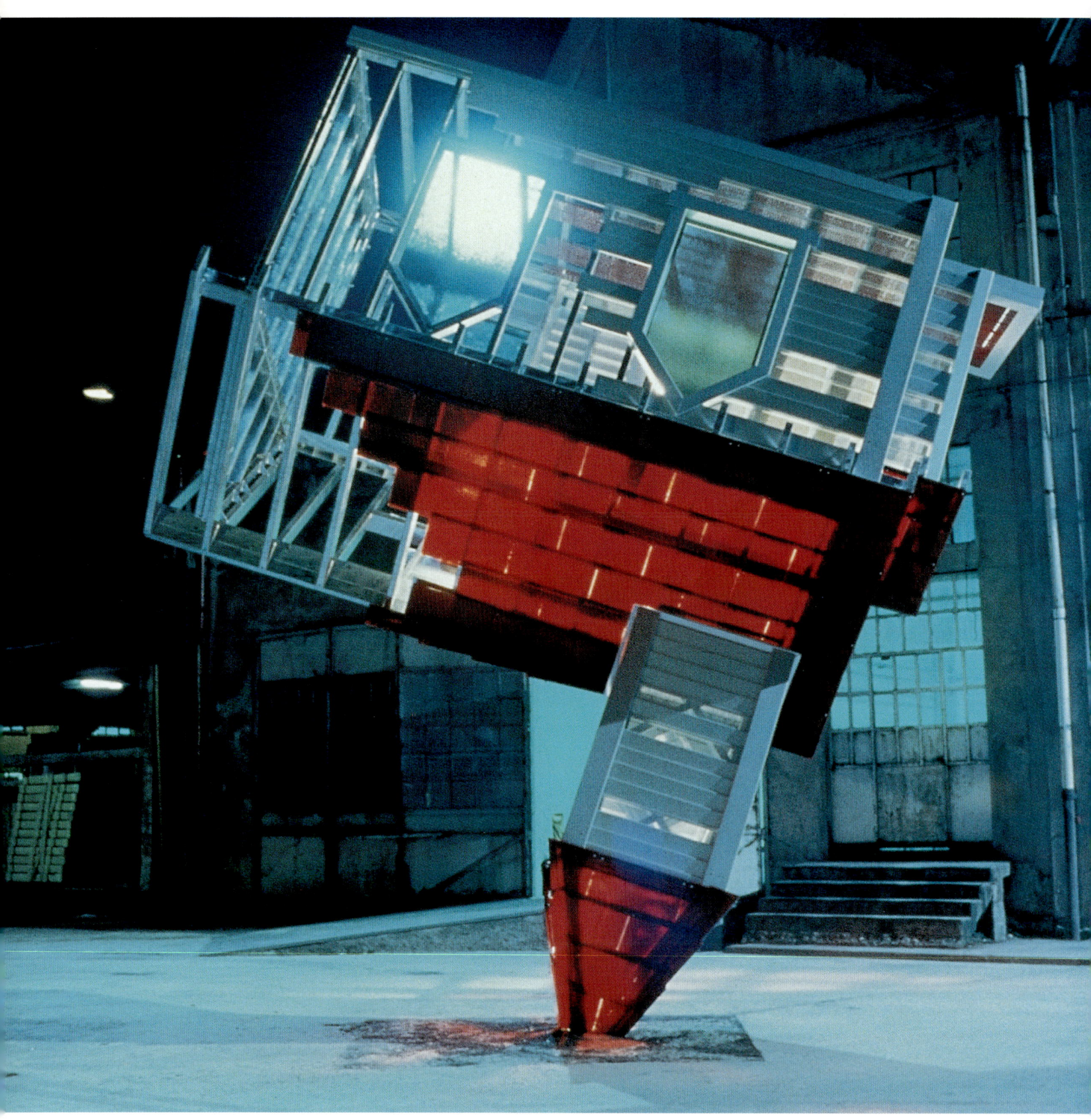

Device to Root Out Evil; Project for Venice Biennale, 1997. Galvanized structural steel, anodized perforated aluminum, transparent red Venetian glass, and concrete foundations, h. 20 x 15 x 8 feet. Denver Art Museum. Gift of Ginny Williams. Photo: Edward Smith, Venice, Italy.

PAWTUCKET, RHODE ISLAND

Libby Pace
(b. 1968)

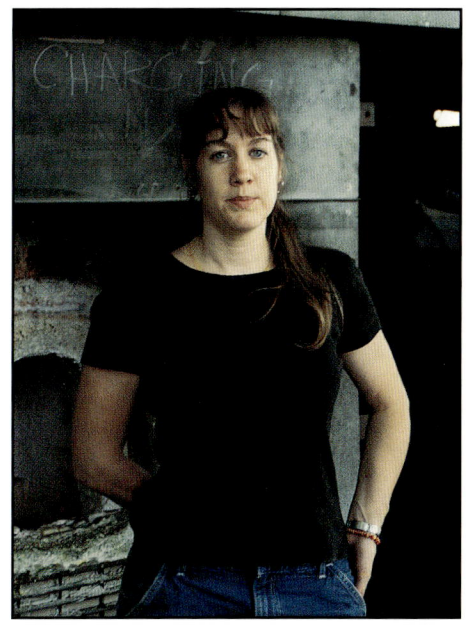

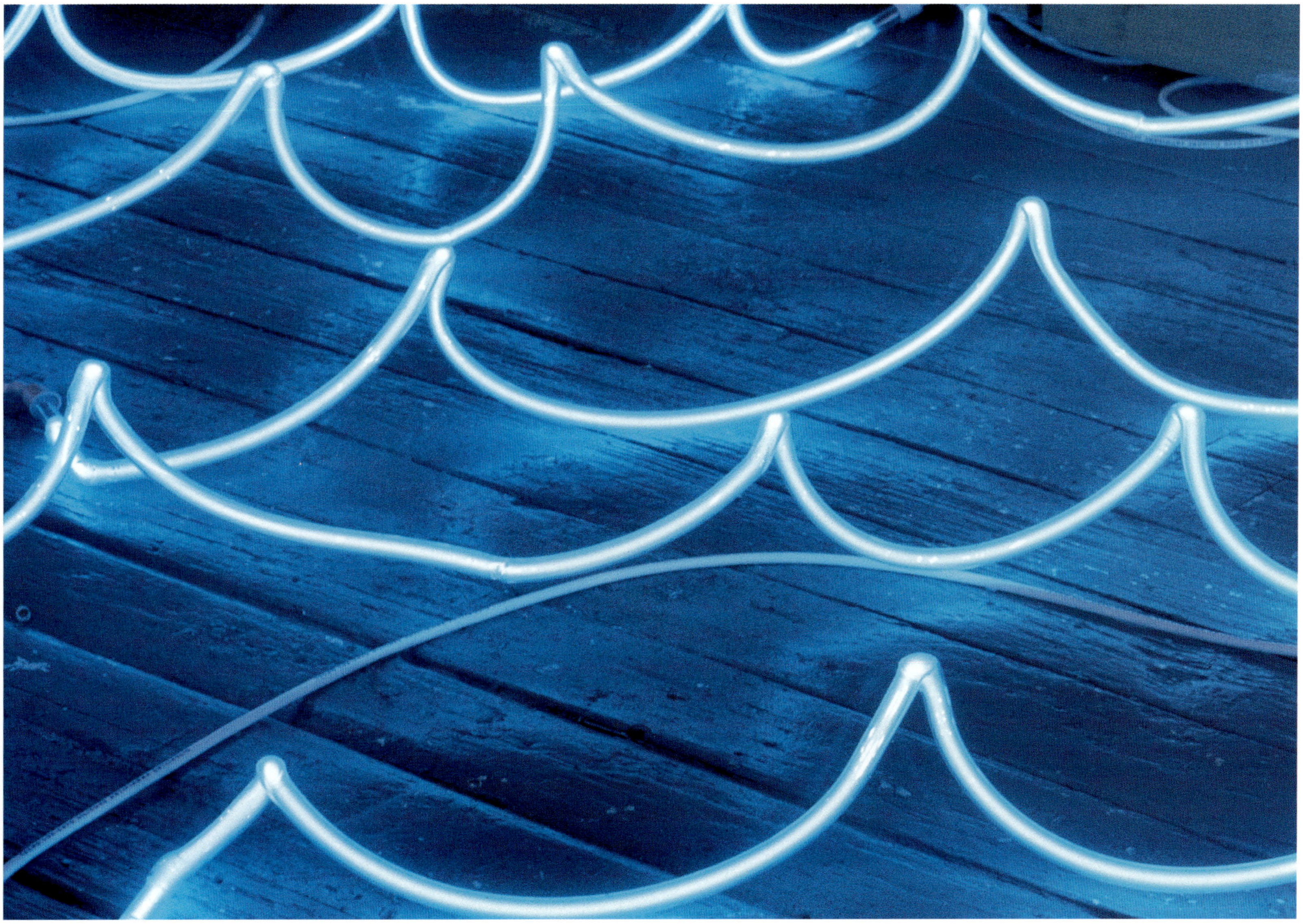

Wave II; Detail, 1998. Neon, h. 1 x 6 x 6 feet.
Photo: Eva Heyd.

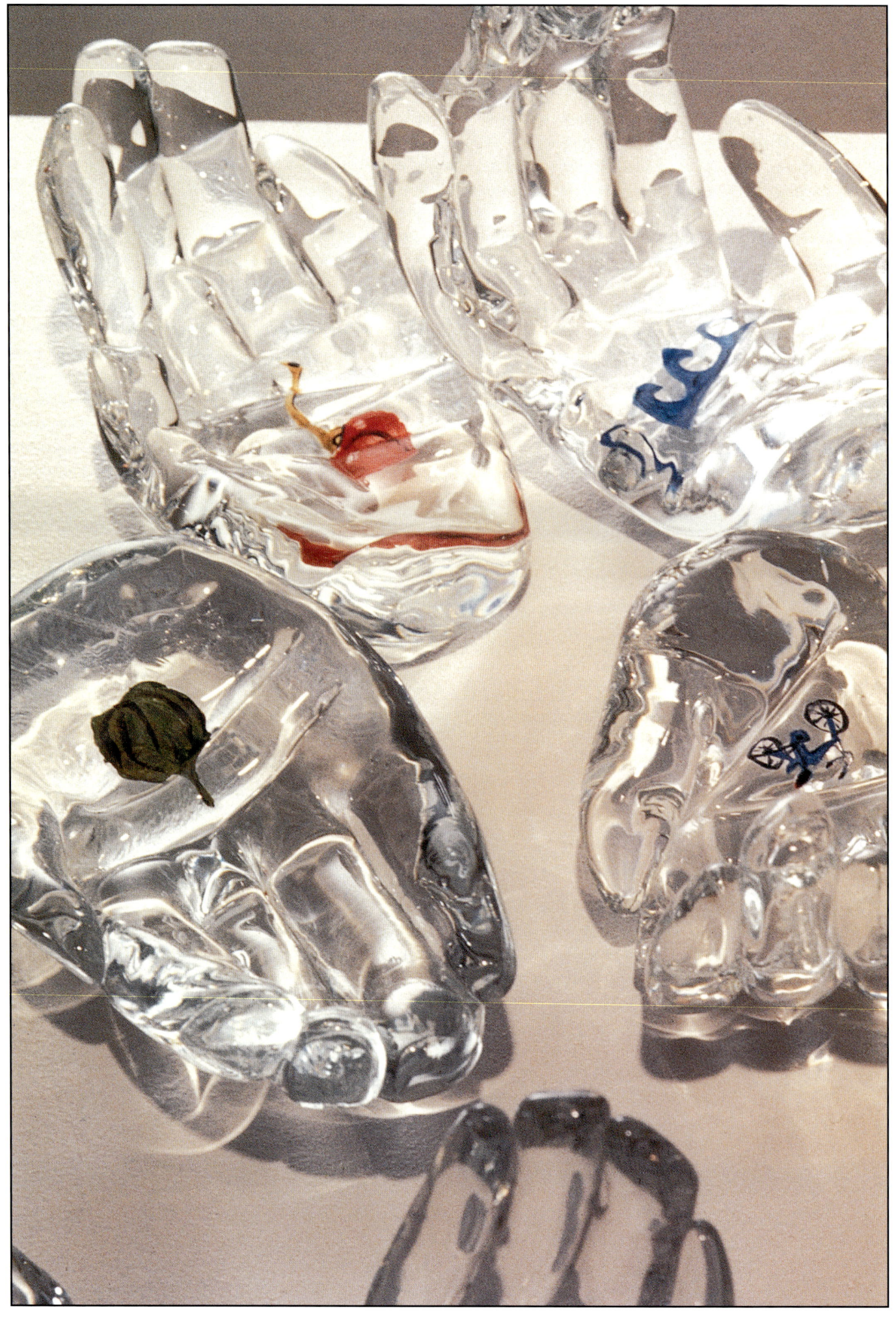

Hands with Mnemonic Devices; Detail, 1998. Glass and oil paint, h. 6 x 36 x 36 inches. Photo: Eva Heyd.

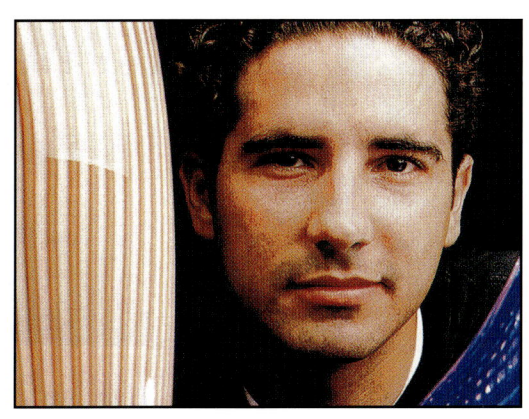

BROOKLYN, NEW YORK

Joseph Pagano
(b. 1965)

Untitled, 1999. Blown glass, h. 16 x 7 inches.

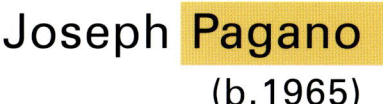

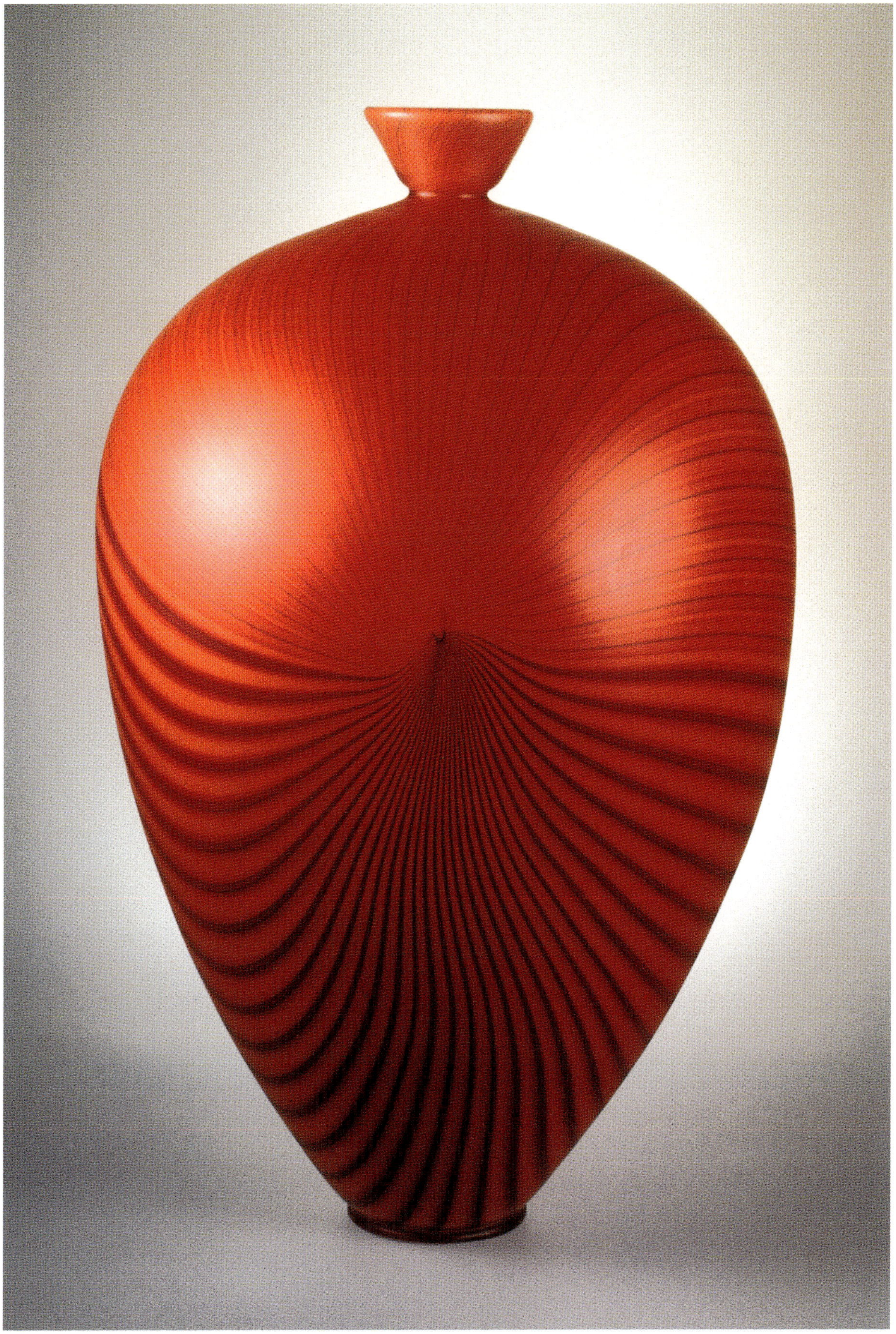

Justin Parker
(b.1972)

BROOKLYN, NEW YORK

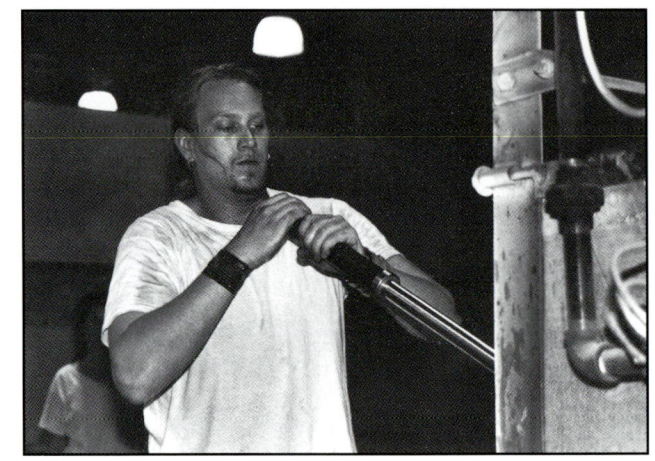

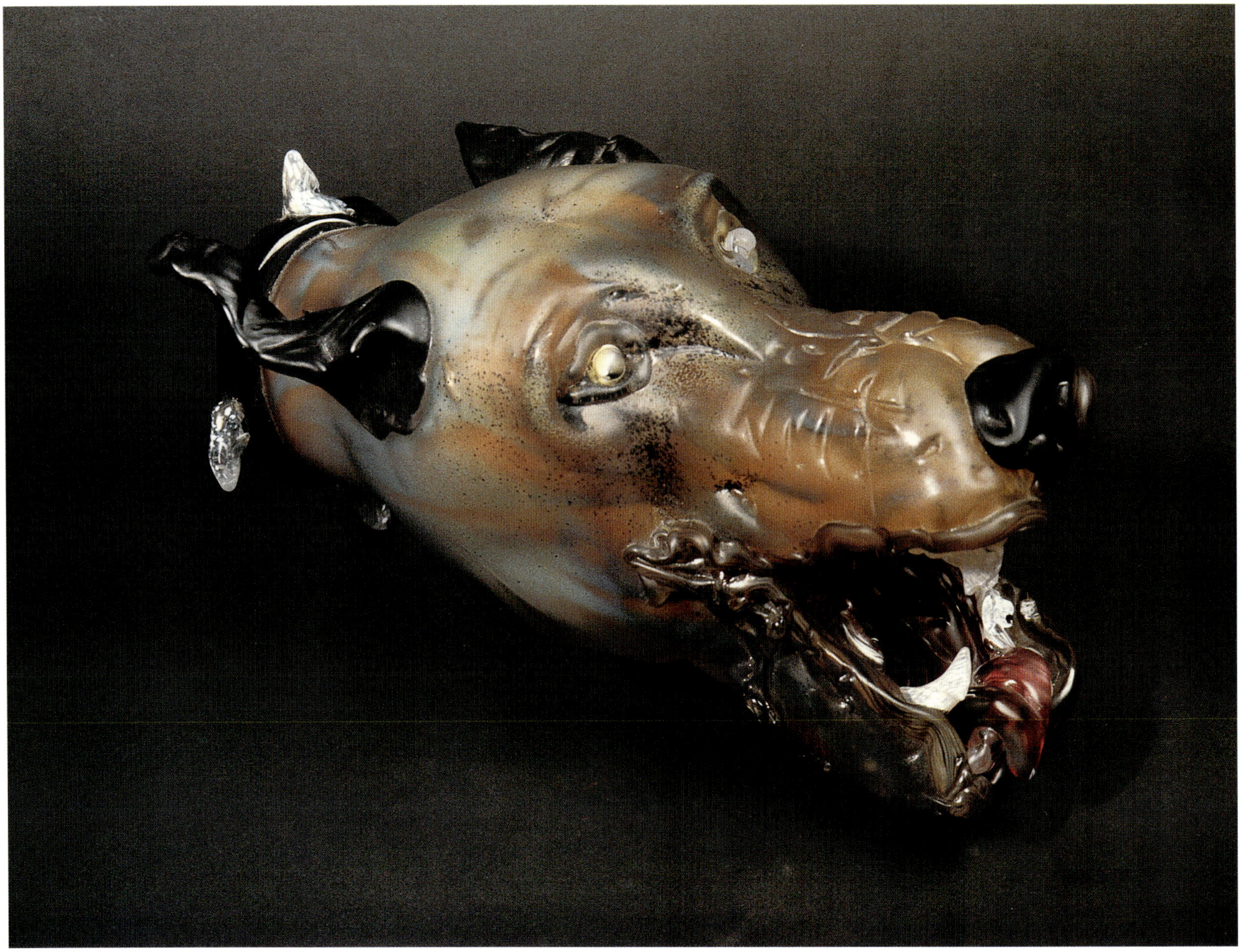

Mad Dog, 1996. Blown glass, h. 6 x 14 x 8 inches.

Izhar Patkin
(b.1955)

NEW YORK, NEW YORK

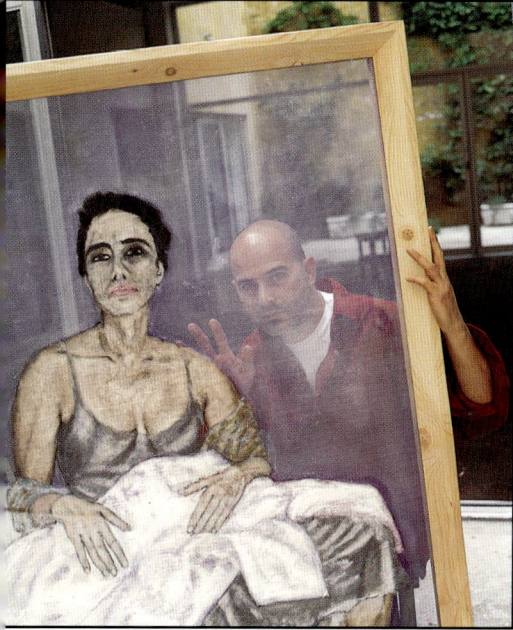

Above:
Untitled, Oil on wire mesh. Photo: Courtesy the Artist and Holly Solomon Gallery.

Right:
Where Each is Both, 1992-93. Blown glass and steel, h. 168 x 84 x 84 inches. Solomon R. Guggenheim Museum. Gift, Annie Laurie Aitken Charitable Trust. Photo: David Heald, ©The Solomon R. Guggenheim Foundation, New York.

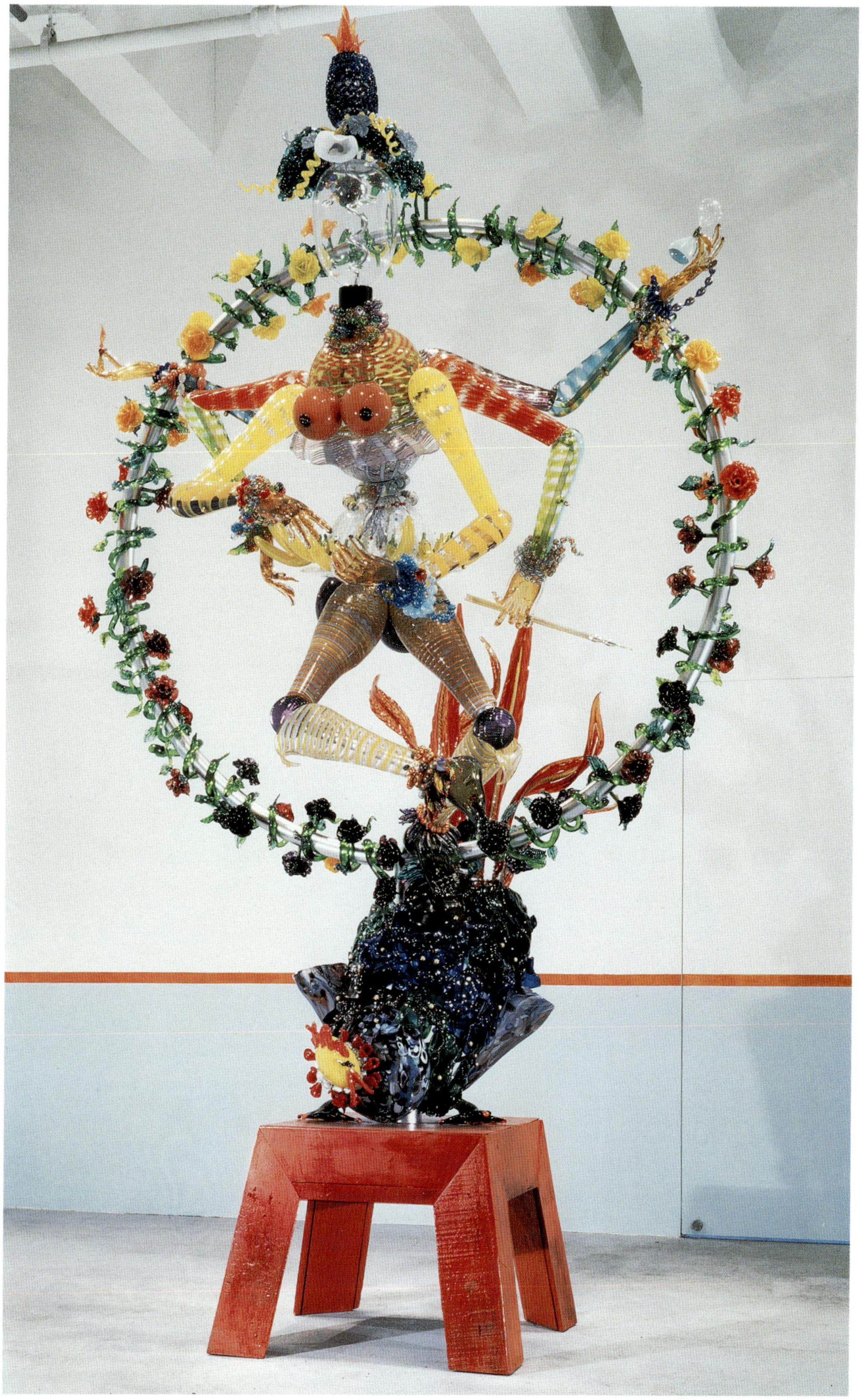

Tom Patti
(b.1943)

PITTSFIELD, MASSACHUSETTS

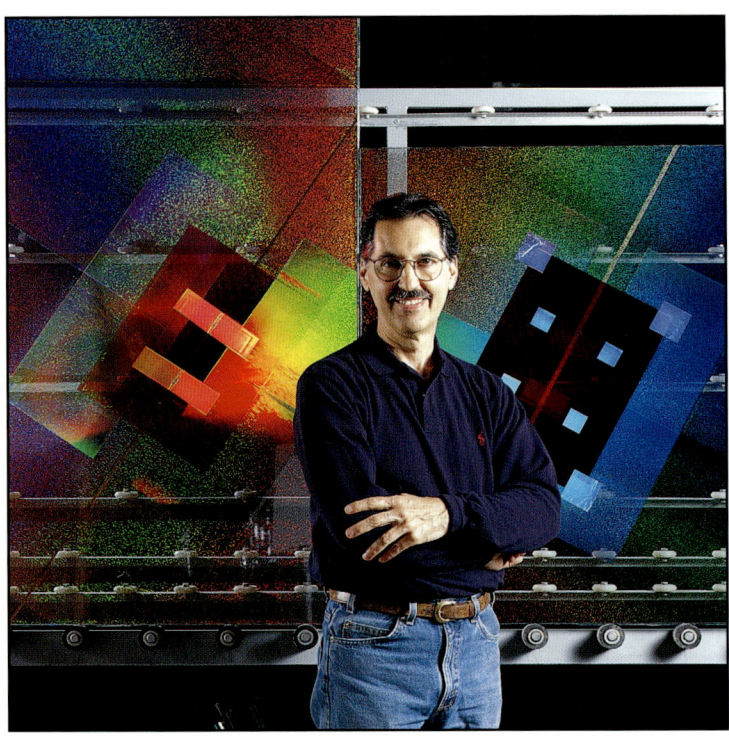

Mint Museum; Installation Detail, *1998.*

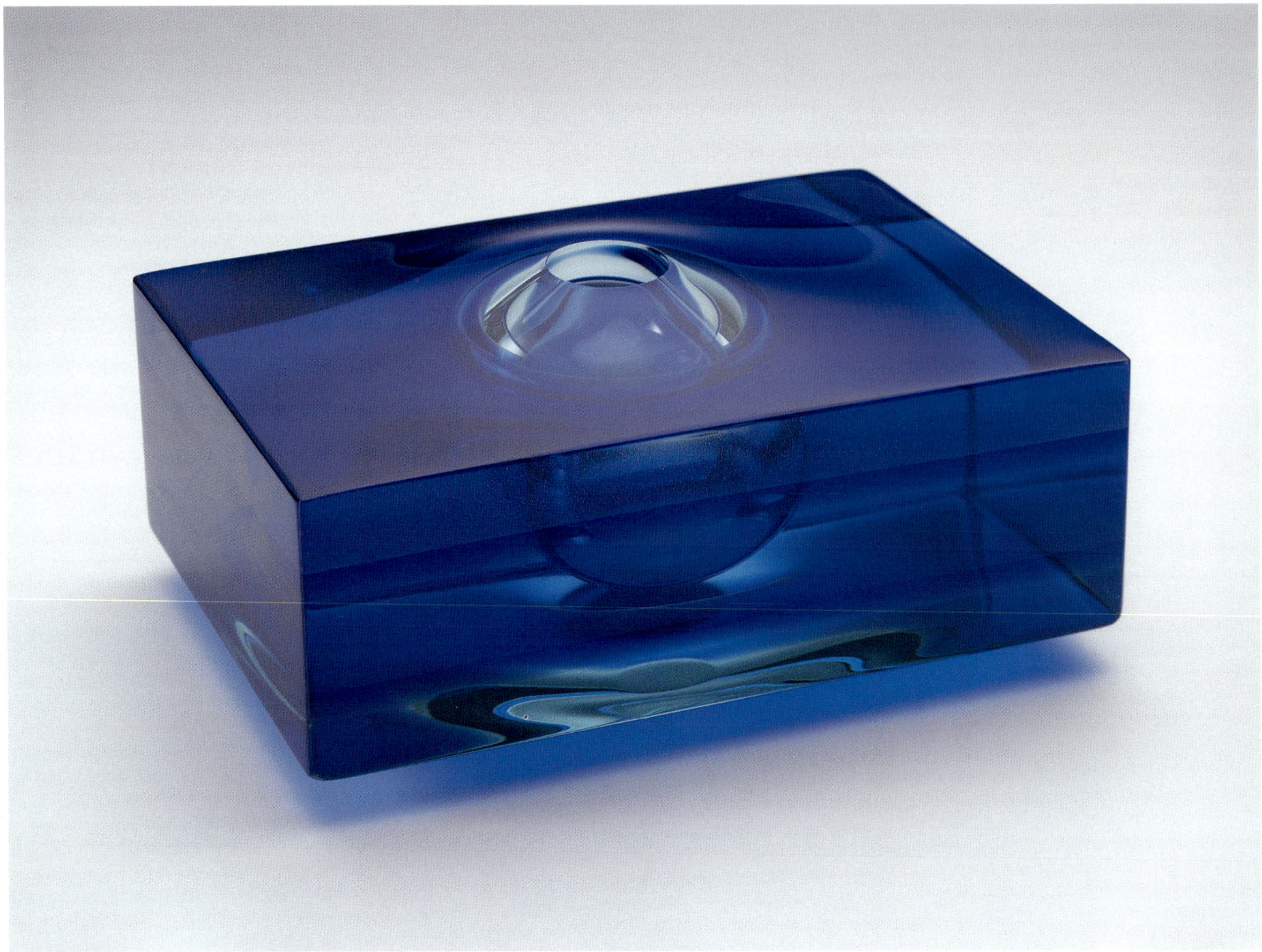

Compacted Horizontal Solarized Blue, *1986.* Fused, hand-shaped, ground, and polished glass, h. 2.5 x 5.25 x 3.75 inches. Collection of Cynthia and Jeffrey Manocherian. Photo: Eva Heyd.

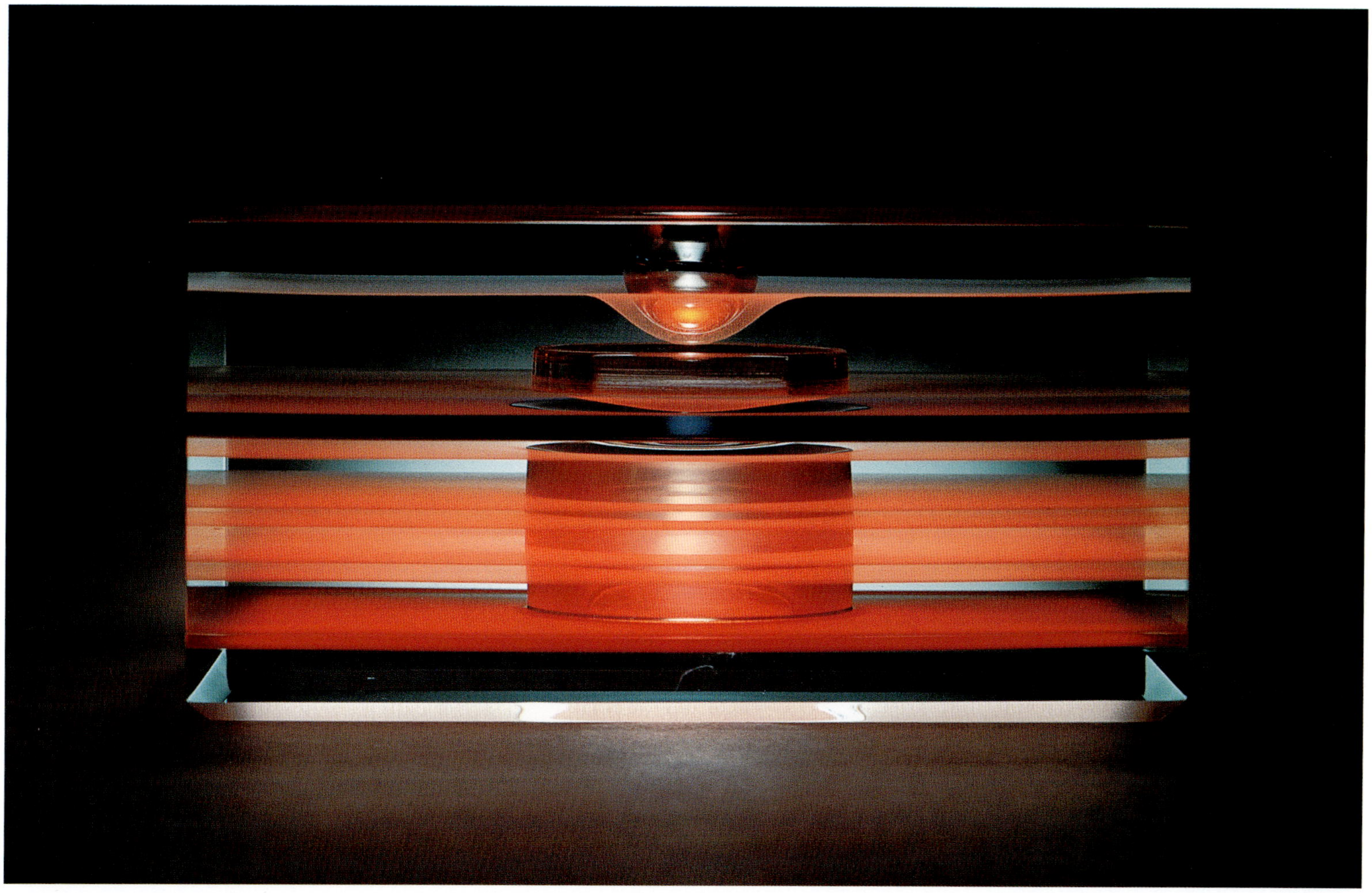

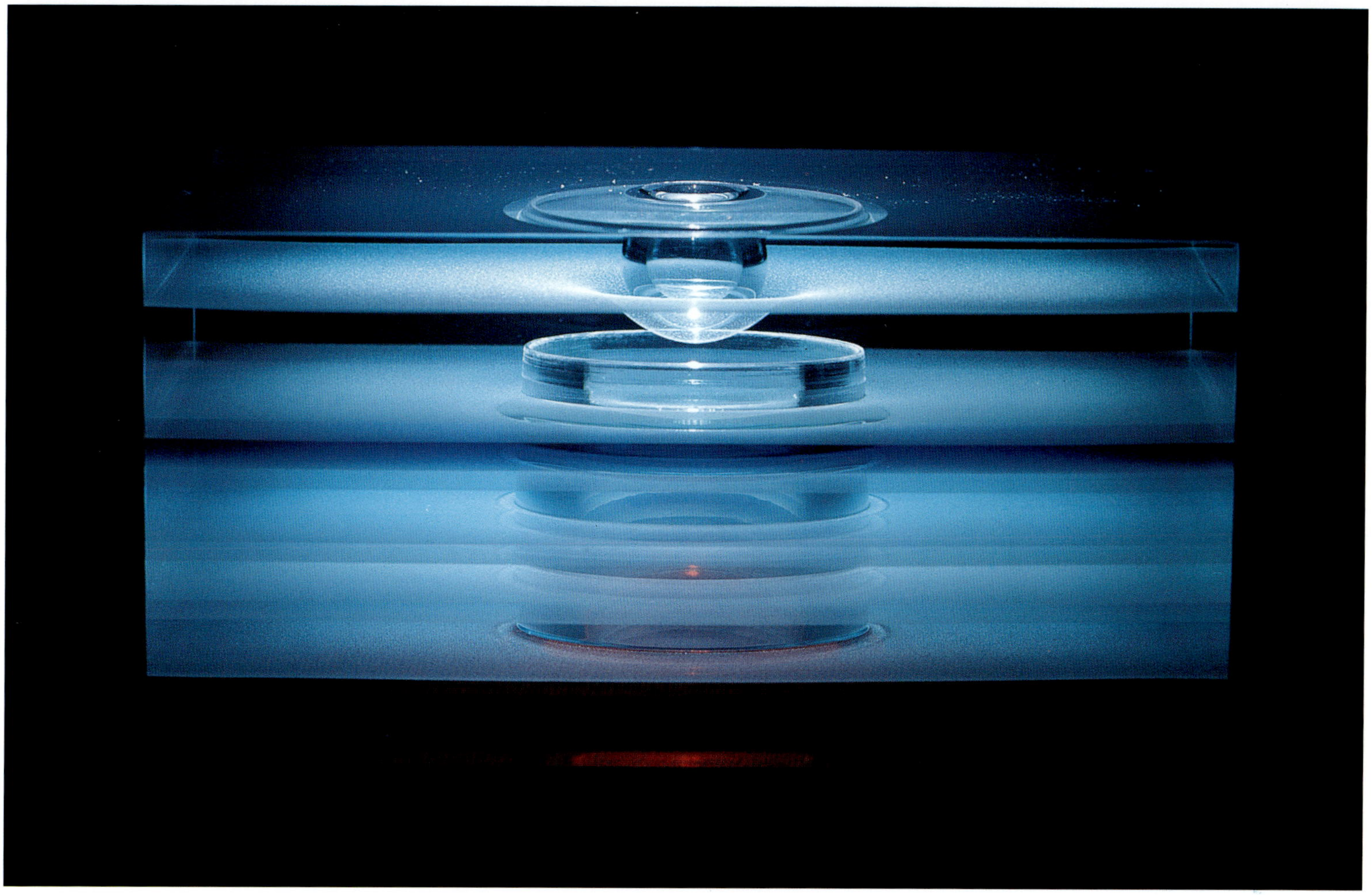

Top:
Solarized Red Lumina Echo, 1990. (bottom lighting) Fused, hand formed, and polished glass. h. 3.2 x 6.3 x 4.5 inches. Collection of Milton and Joan Baxt. Photo: Tom Patti

Bottom:
Solarized Red Lumina Echo, 1990. (top lighting)
Photo: Tom Patti

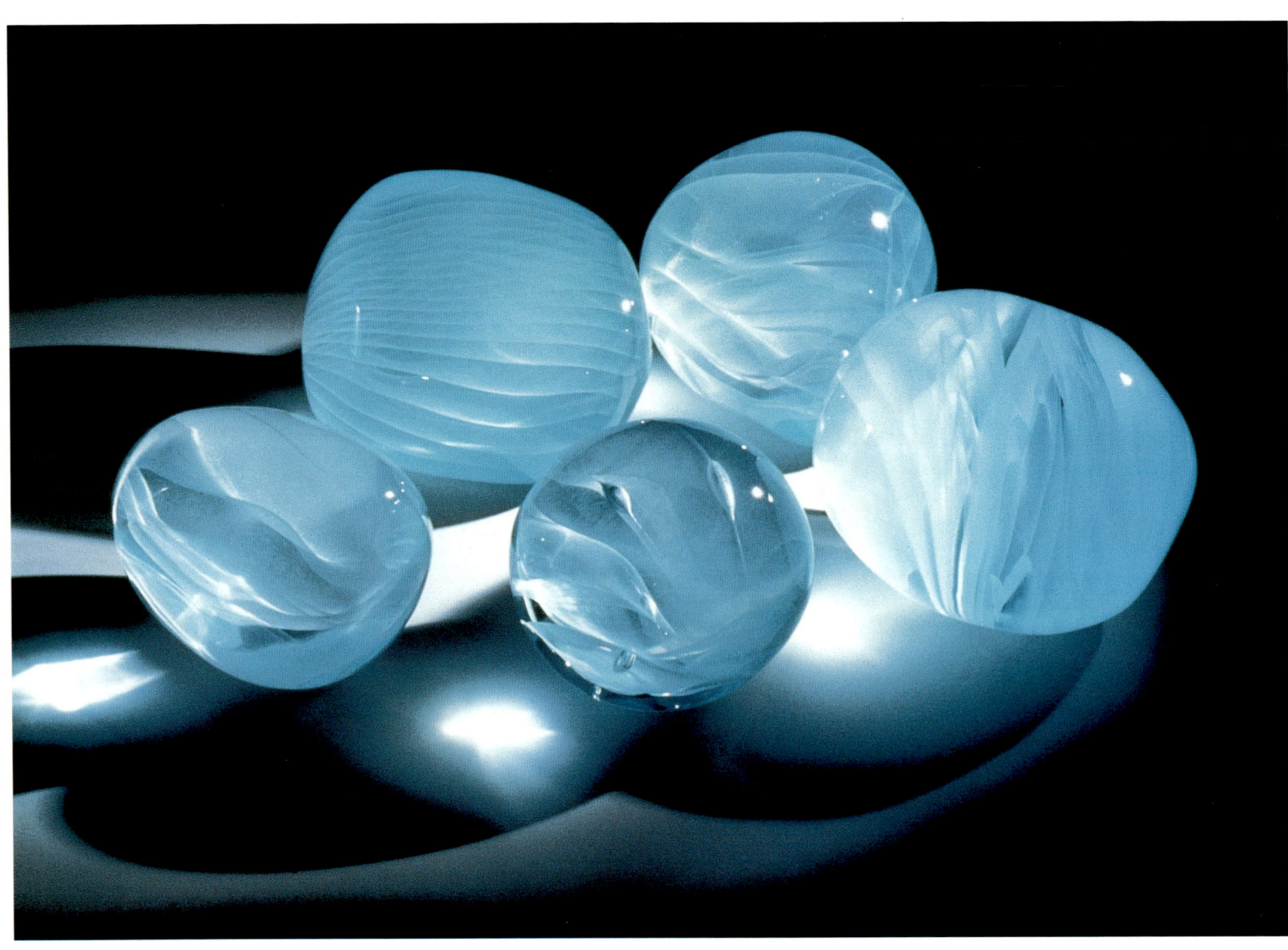

Above:
Division of Fifty Illuminated Particles for Doug, 1990. Fused, hand formed, and polished glass, (tallest) h. 6.35 inches, (widest) w.5.8 inches. Collection of Dale and Doug Anderson. Photo: George Erml.

Opposite top:
Spectral Boundary; Installation, Mint Museum of Craft and Design, 1998. Glass, h. 25 x 40 feet. Photo: Paul Rocheleau.

Opposite bottom:
Owens Corning World Headquarters; Commission, Toledo, Ohio, 1994-96. Glass and fiberglass, h. 10 x 22 feet. Photo: Marco Lorenzetti.

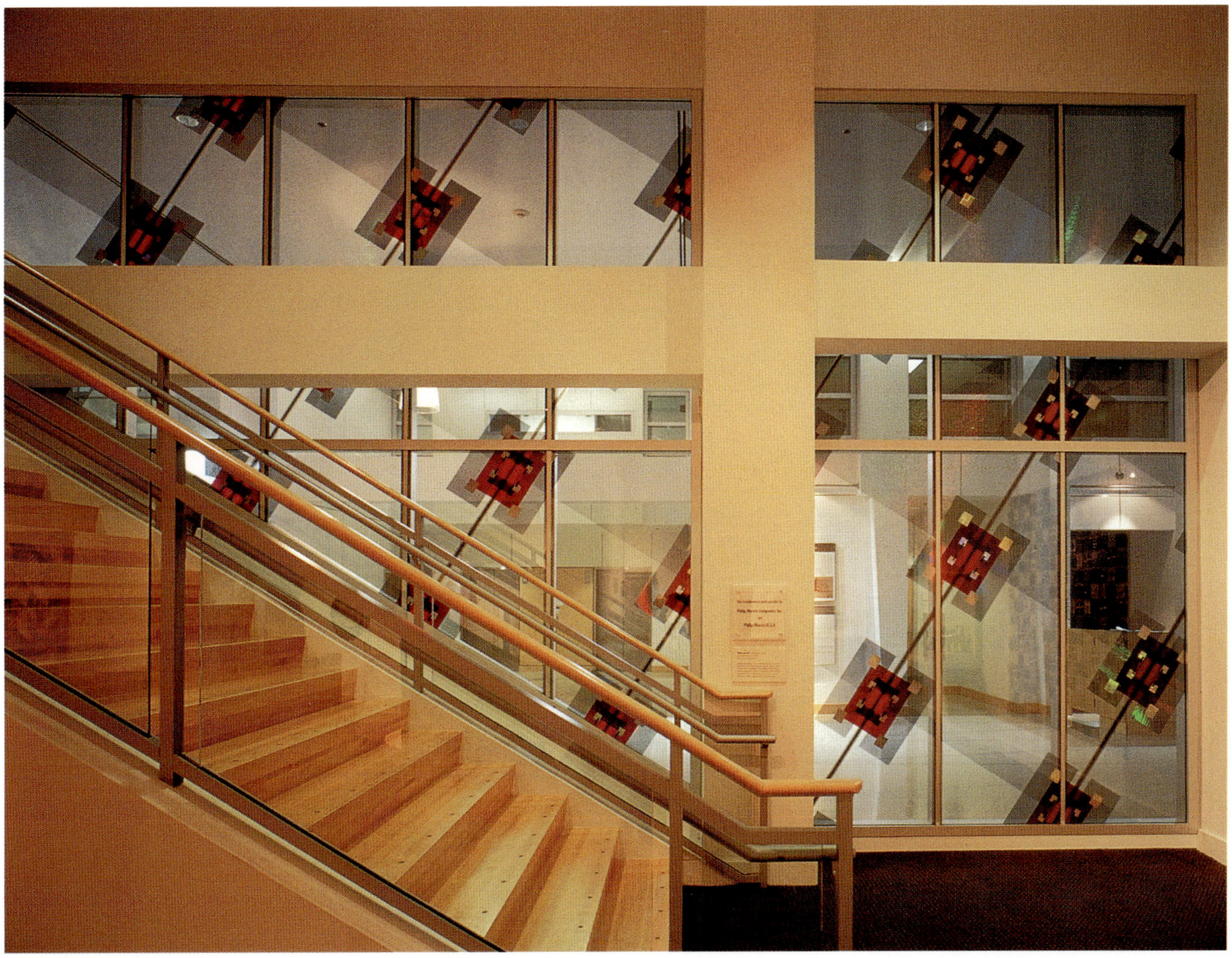

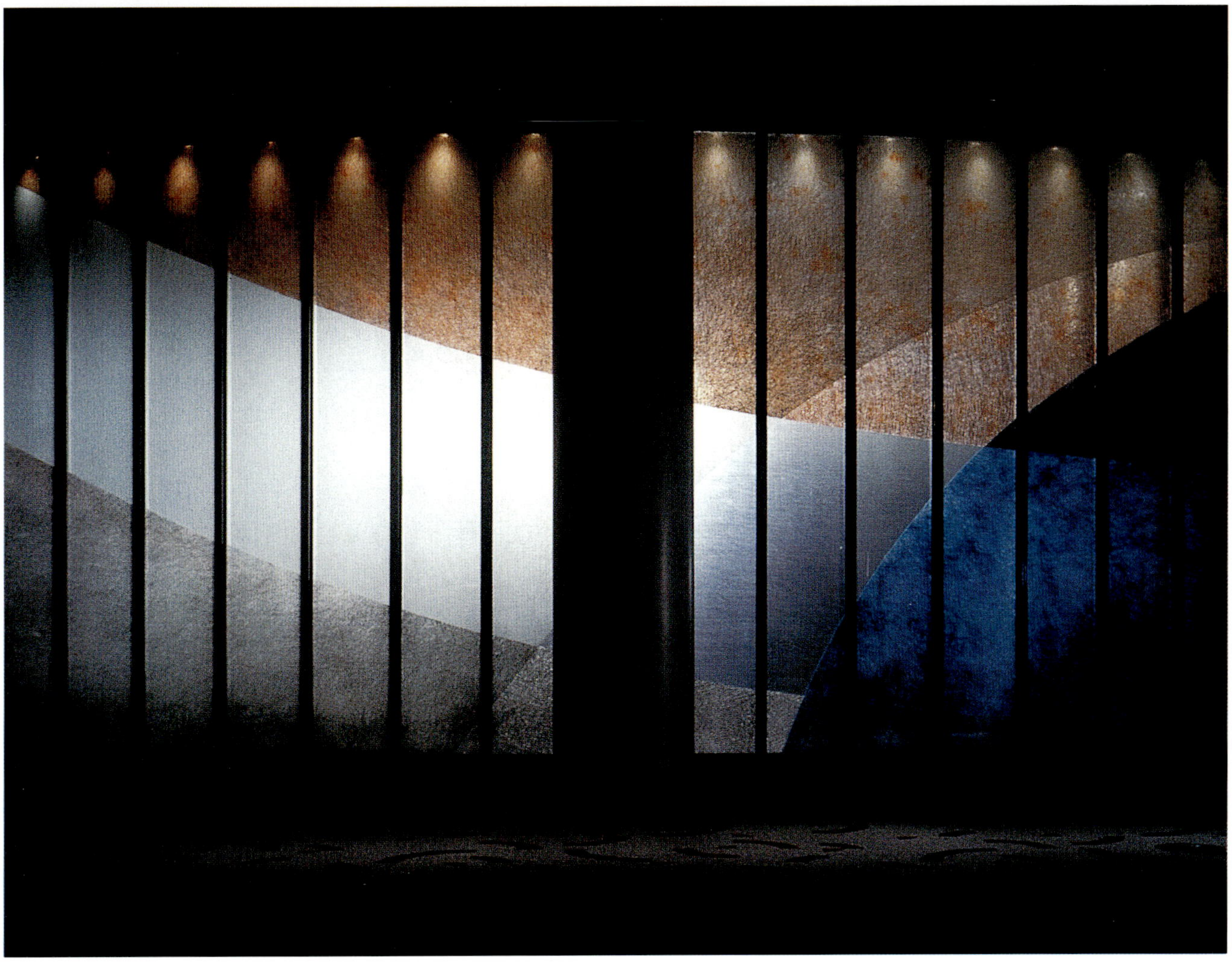

TOM PATTI

Kim Petro & Andy Stenerson
(b. 1967)   (b. 1963)

BROOKLYN, NEW YORK

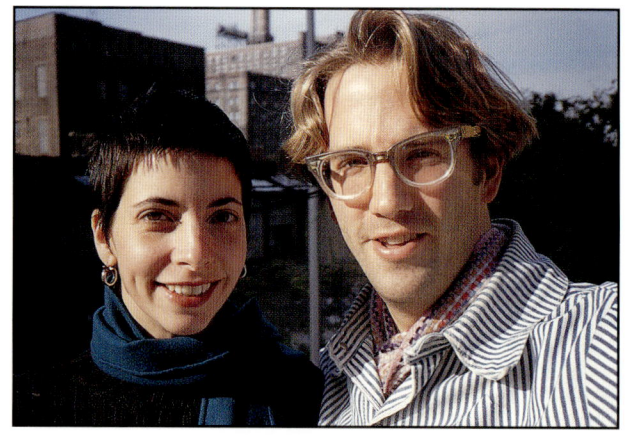

Untitled, 1998. Blown glass, (overall) h. 12 x 24 inches.
Photo: Courtesy Happy Medium.

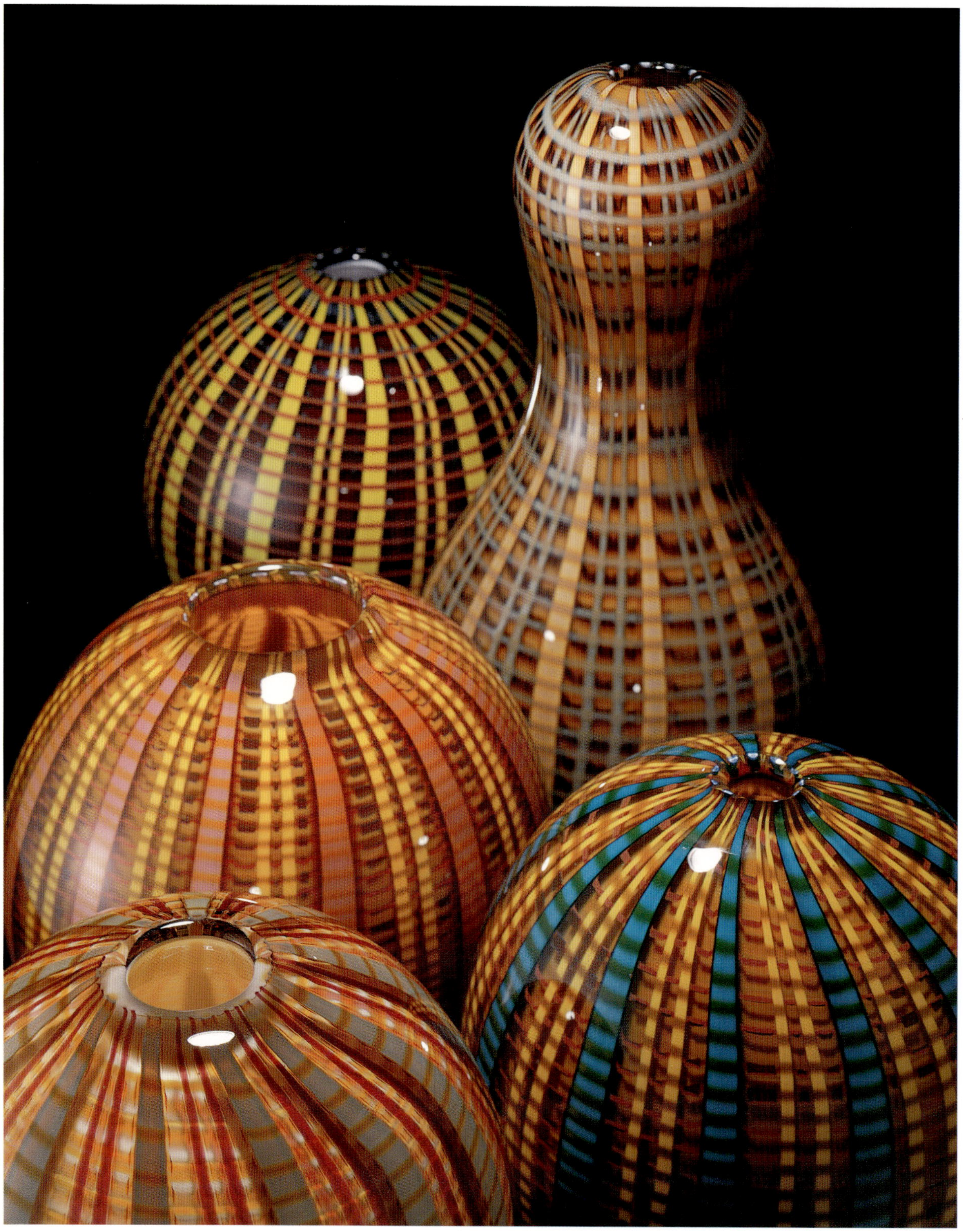

BROOKLYN, NEW YORK

Ernest Porcelli
(b.1945)

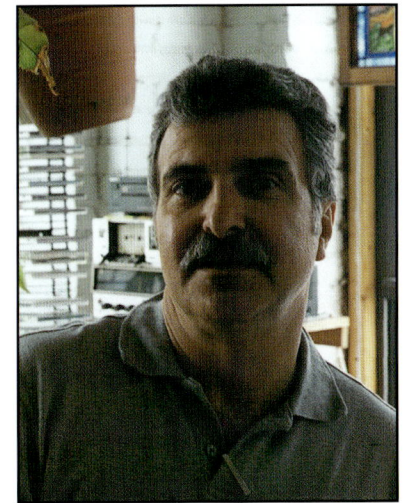

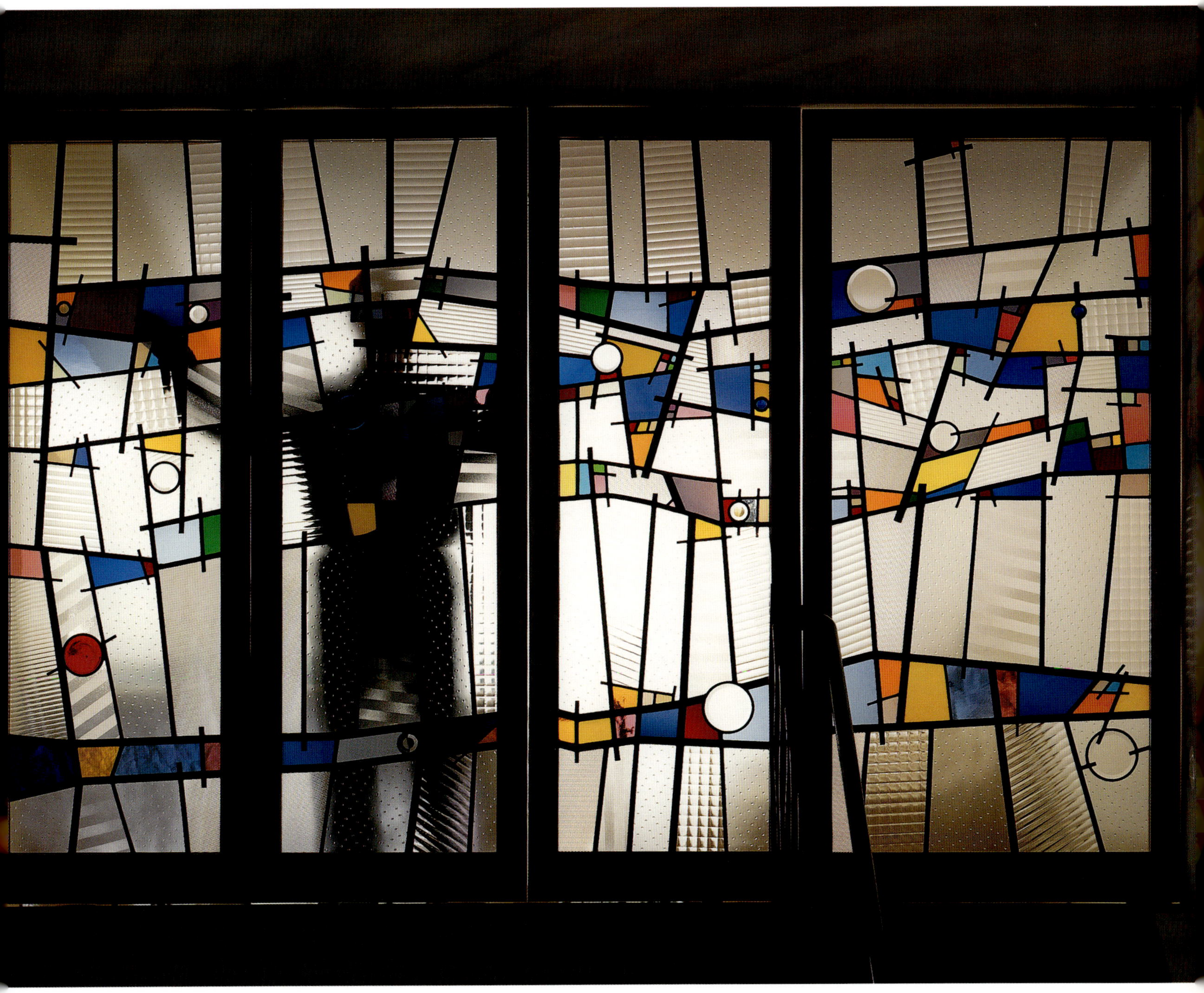

Lead Glass Wall; Commission, 1999. Colored glass sheet, and lead came, h. 6 x 8 feet.

Richard Posner
(b.1948)

WITTEN, FEDERAL REPUBLIC OF GERMANY

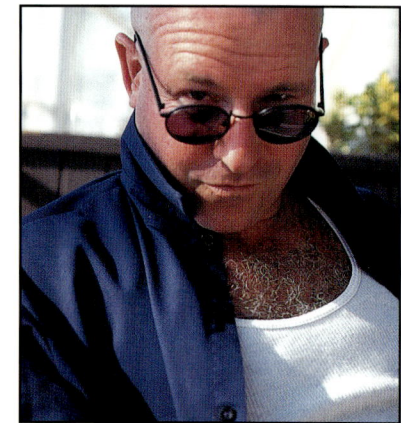

The Bottle Hymn of The Republic; *Detail of scale model, 1996. Soda, beer, wine bottles, (bottlenecks face outward to catch the wind) and cement, h. 18 x 60 feet. Made in collaboration with architect Rick Gooding and landscape architect Lili Merck. Photo: Benny Chan.*

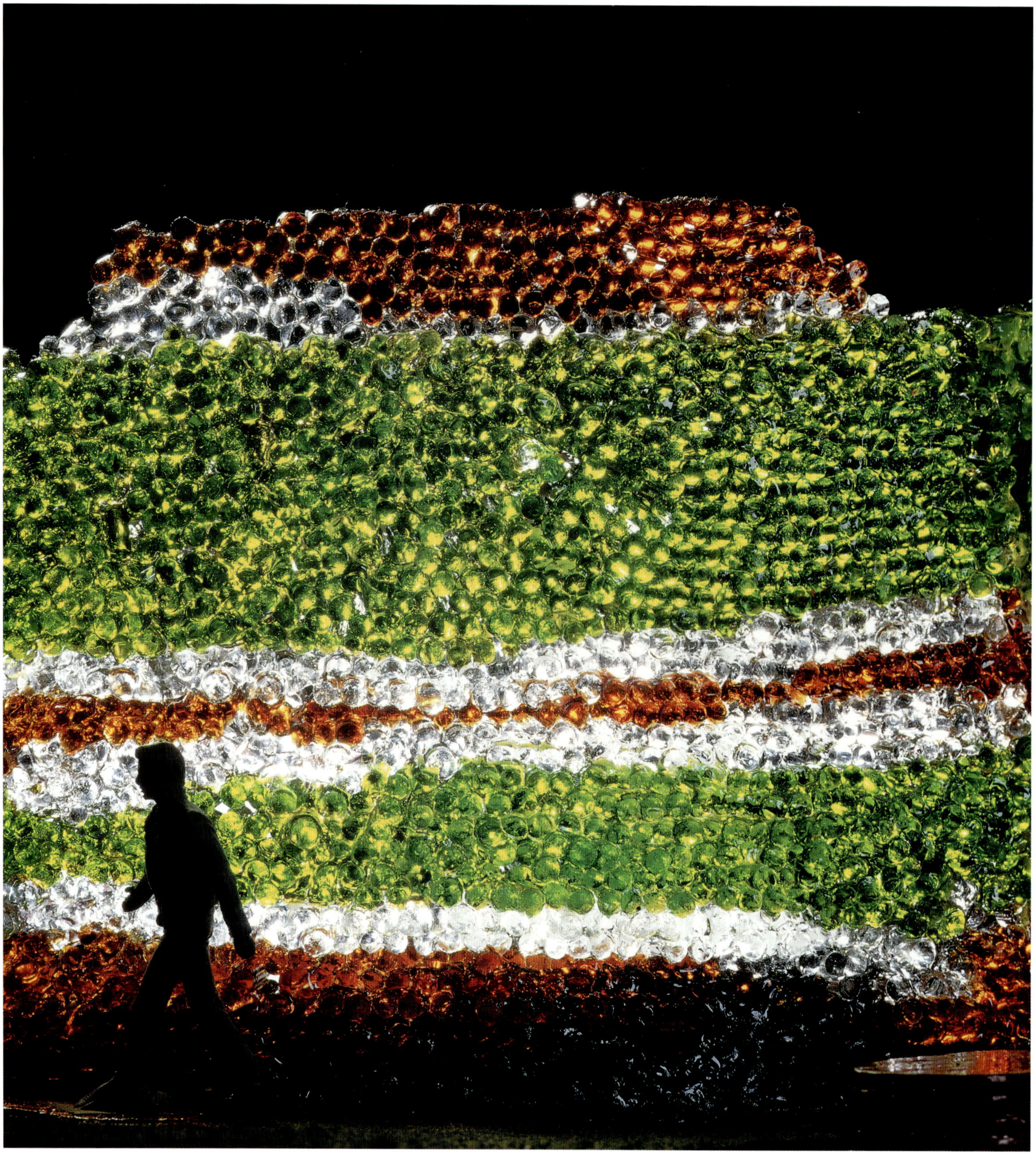

DANVILLE, KENTUCKY

Stephen Rolfe Powell
(b.1951)

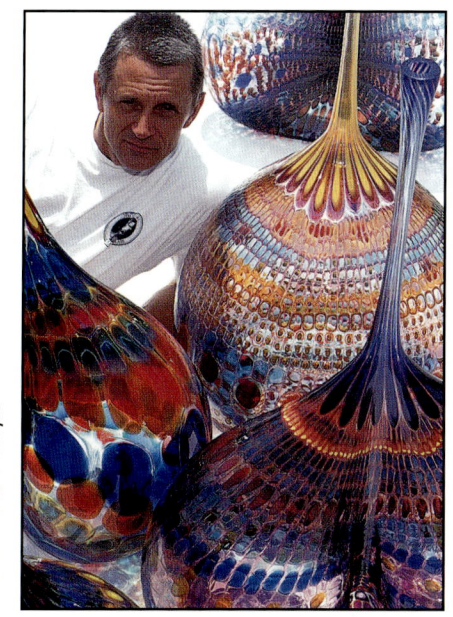

Photo: Kate Philips

Persimmon Jupiter Johnson; Detail, 1999. Blown glass, h. 49 x 19 x 19 inches. Assisted by: Chris Bohach, Paul Hugues, Che Rhodes, Nathan Watson, and Brook white. Collection of Sophia Markovitz.

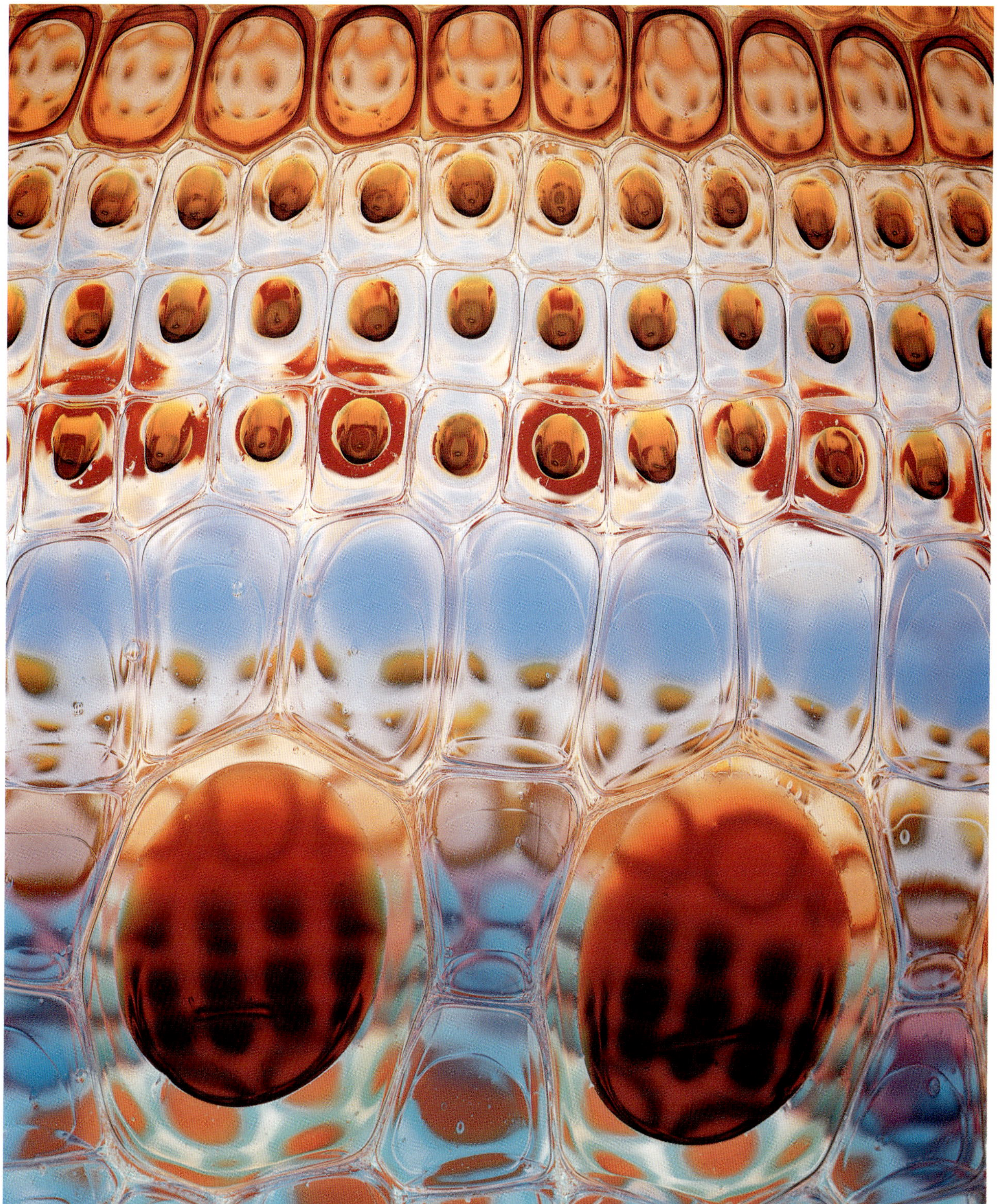

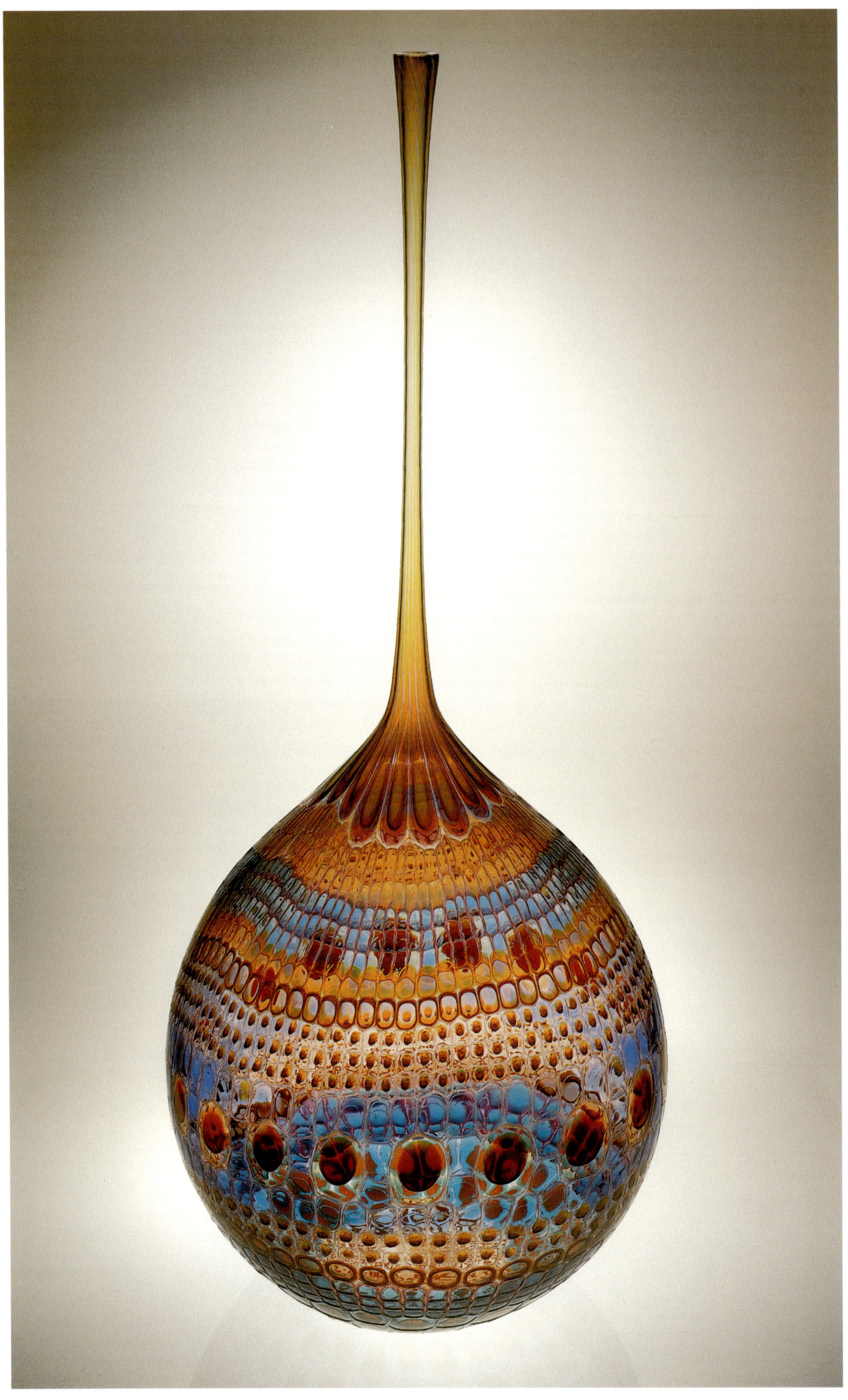

Persimmon Jupiter Johnson, *1999.*

STANWOOD, WASHINGTON

Pike Powers
(b.1956)

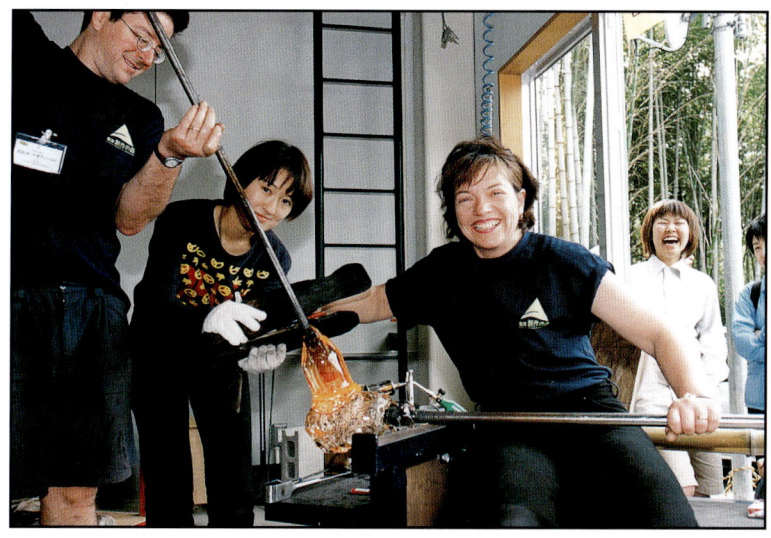

Solid Pack Carrot Boy, 1994.
Blown glass, h. 11 x 5 inches.

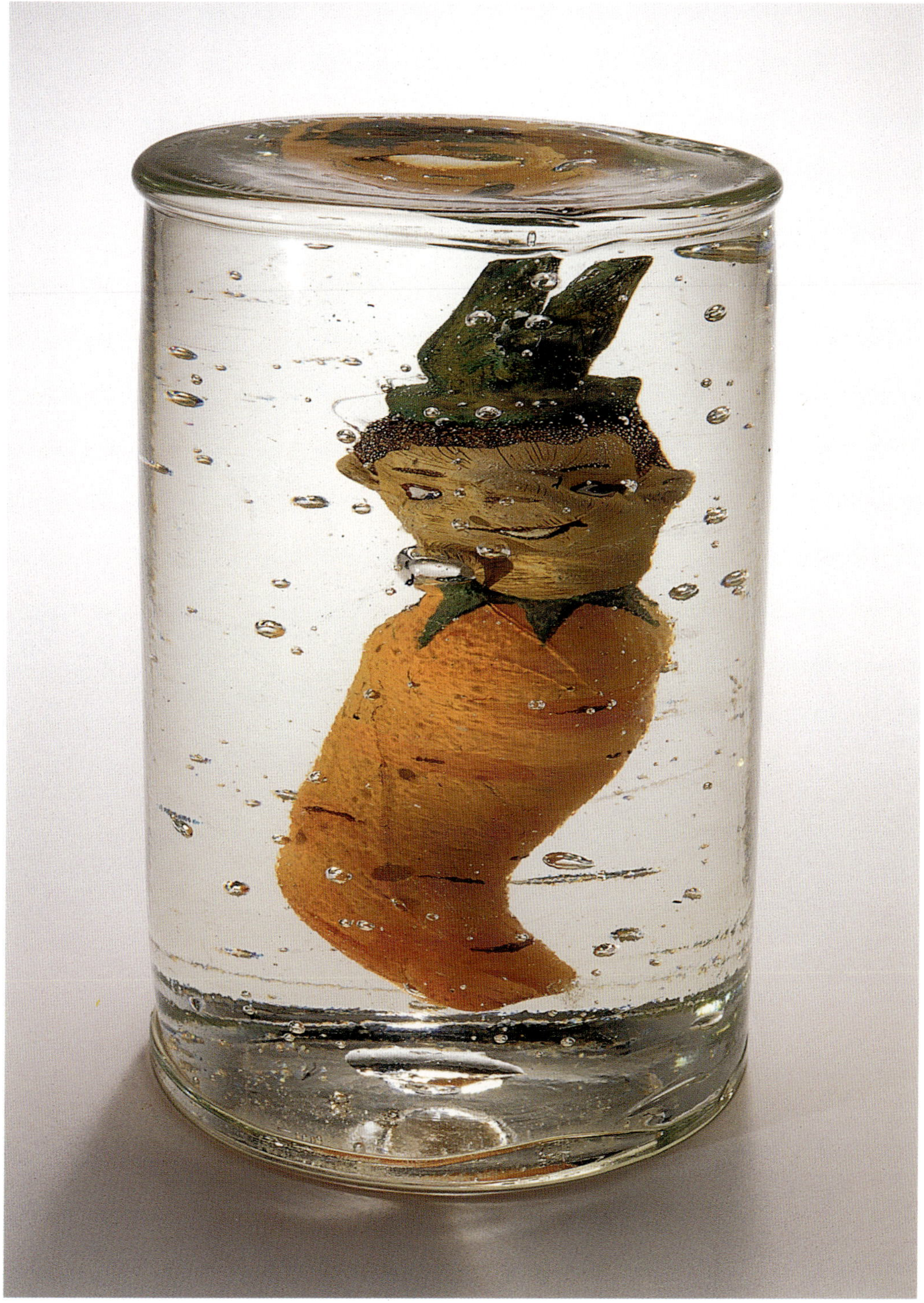

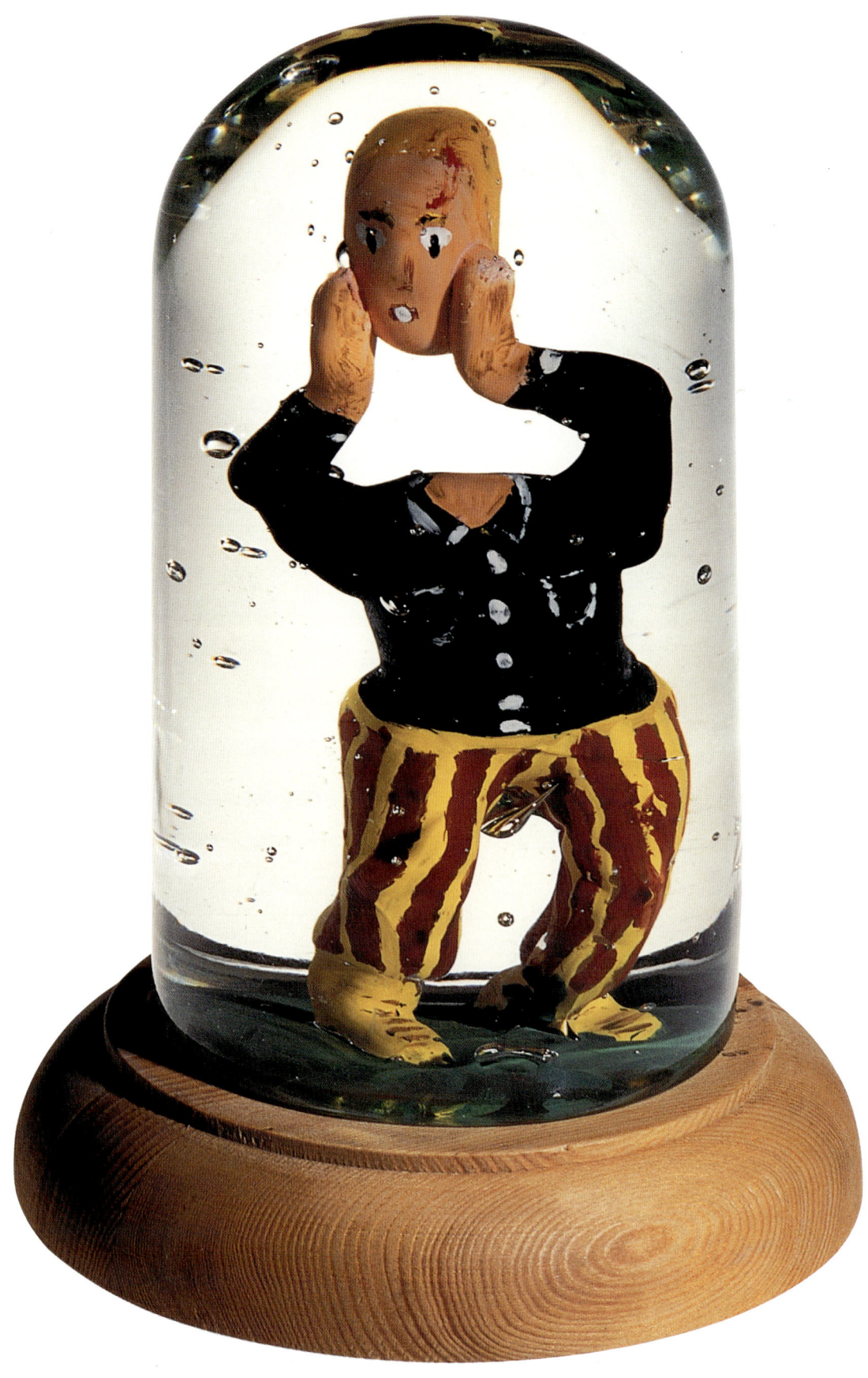

Heads Off, 1997. Blown glass, h. 11 x 5 inches.

MONTAGUE, MASSACHUSETTS

Sally Prasch
(b.1957)

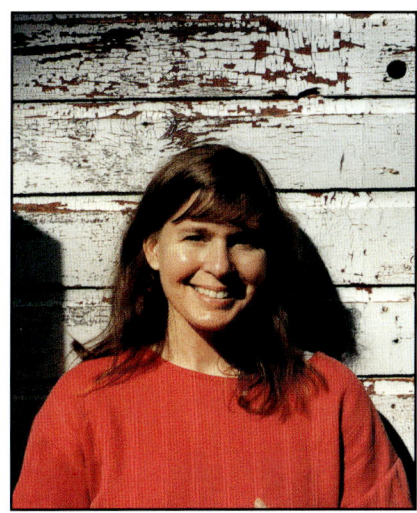

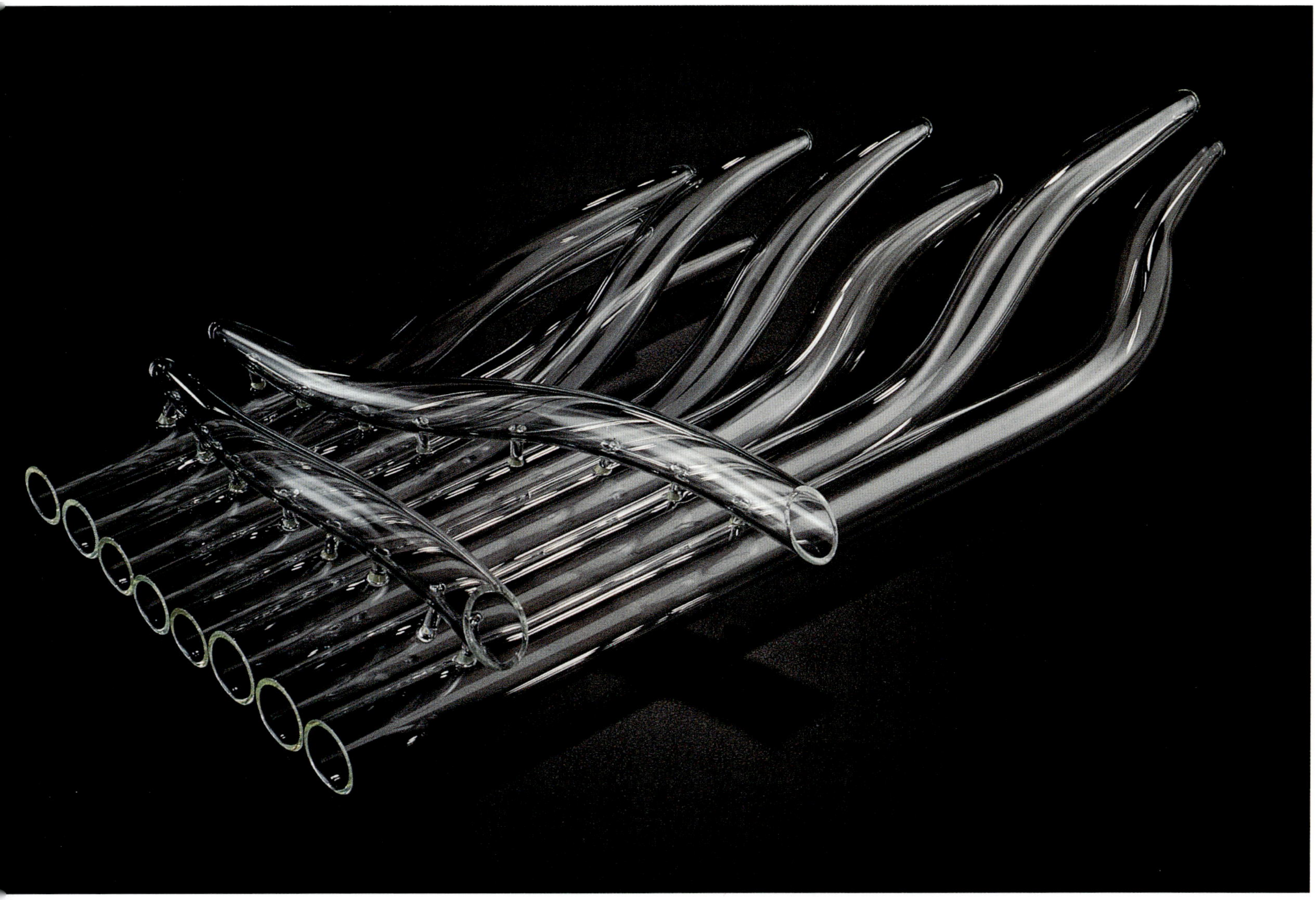

Pan Pipes; C Scale, 1999. Lampworked glass, h. 12 x 8 inches.

Clifford Rainey
(b. 1948)

NAPA, CALIFORNIA

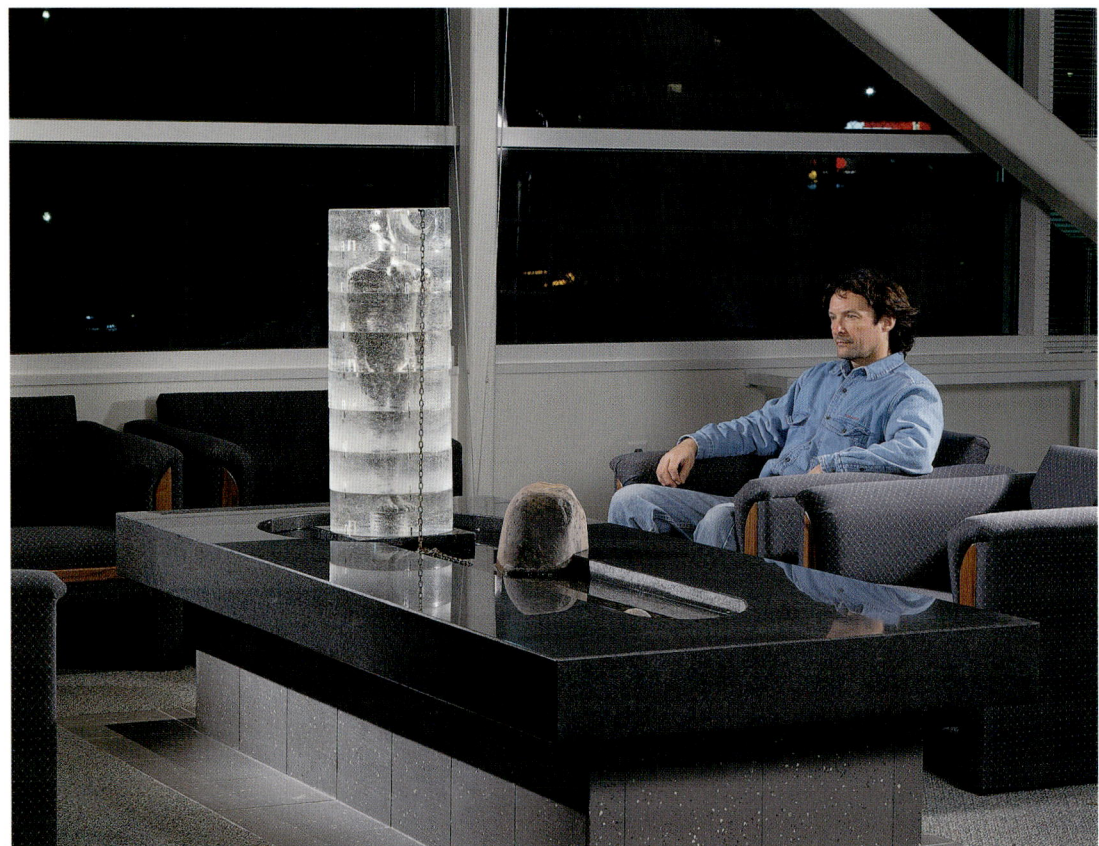

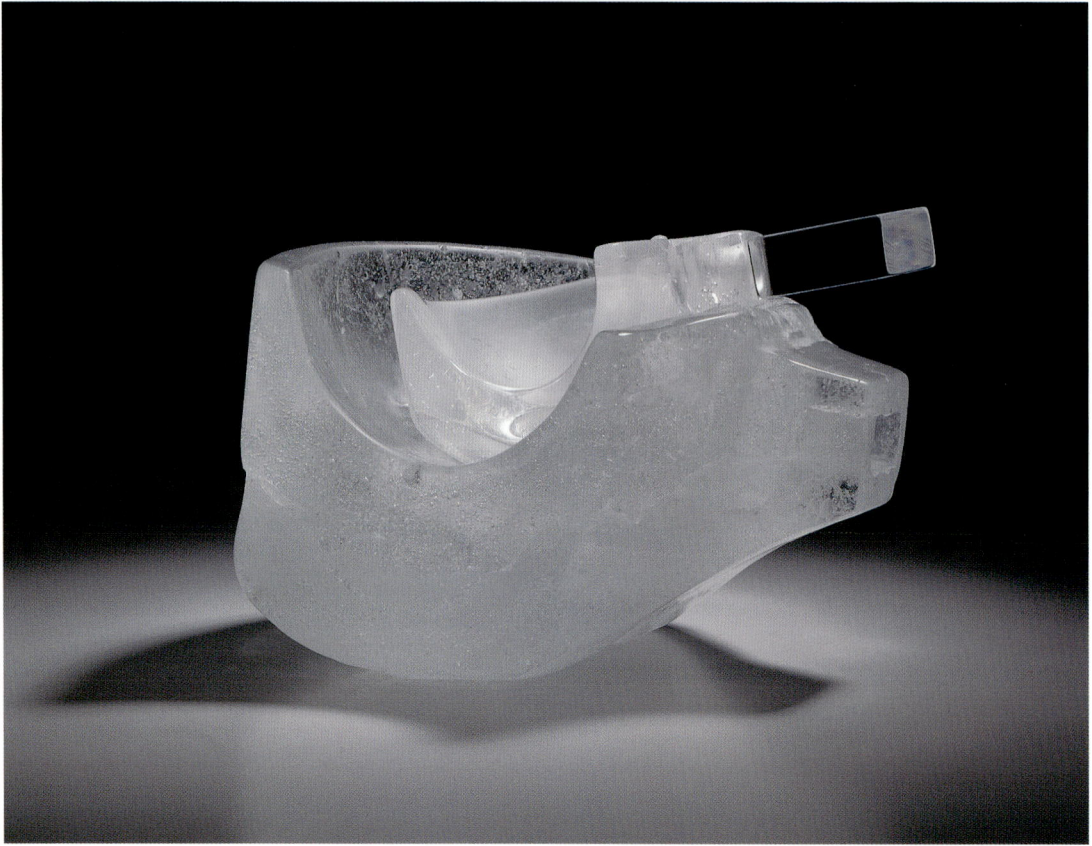

Top:
Water Table; Commission, 911 Emergency Communications Center, San Francisco. San Francisco Art Commission. Cast glass in eight sections, black granite, chain, river stones, and running water, h. 60 x 96 x 40 inches. Photo: Lee Fatherree.

Bottom:
Blocking, 1996. Cast glass in three sections, h. 12 x 14 x 12 inches. Collection of Bradford and Arabella Georges. Photo: Lee Fatherree.

Opposite:
The Kiss, 1996. Cast optical glass, and bronze, h. 18 x 8 x 8 inches. Collection of George and Dorothy Saxe. Photo: Lee Fatherree.

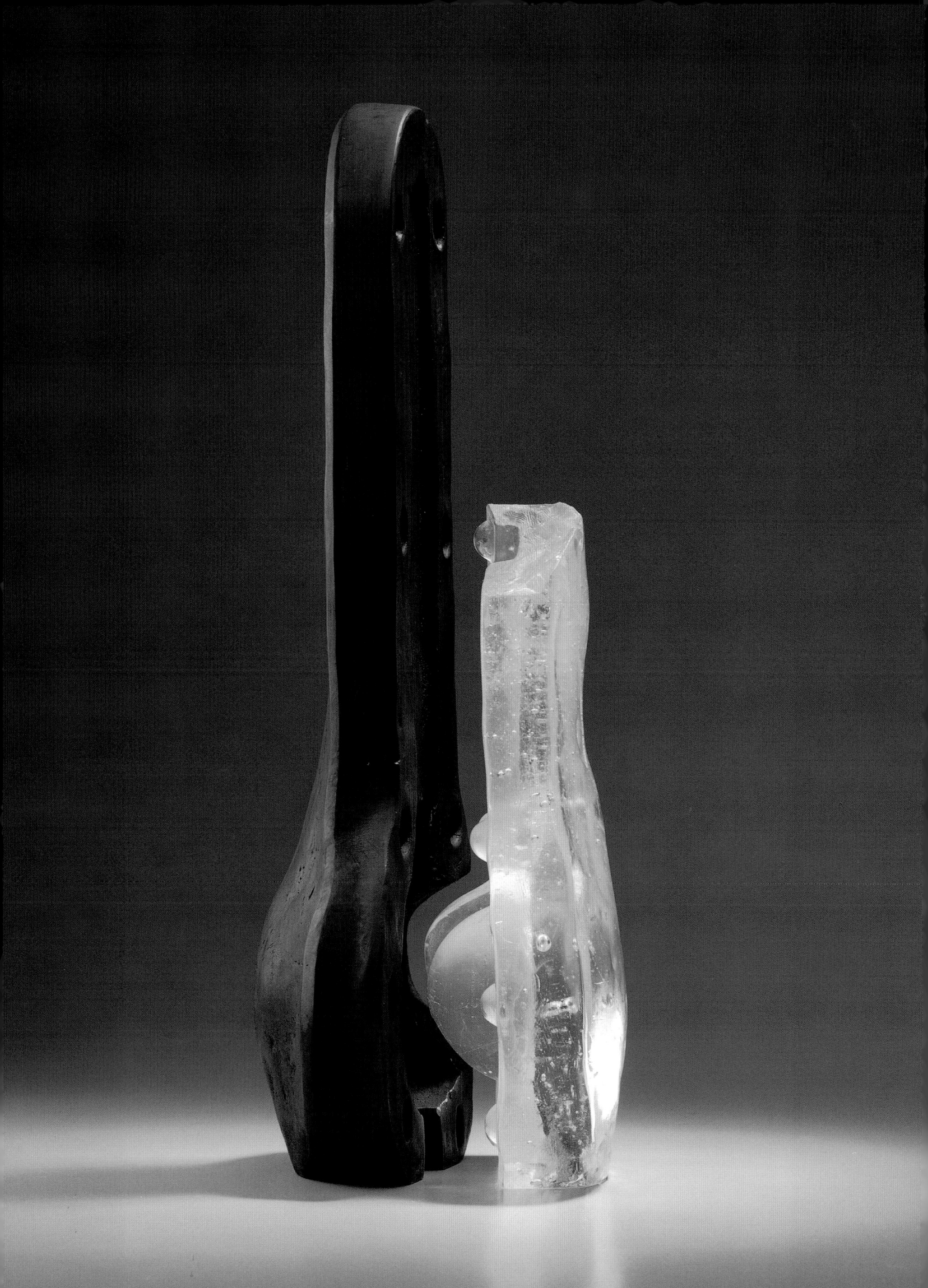

Seth Randal
(b.1942)

LOS ANGELES, CALIFORNIA

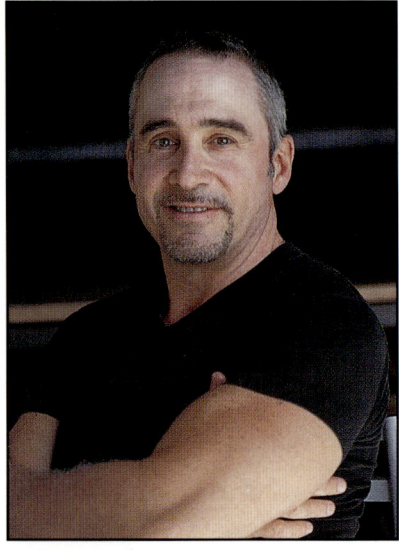

Below:
Mesopotamia, 1995. Cast glass, h. 24 x 14 inches. Courtesy Leo Kaplan Modern.

Opposite
Crown of Fire, 1996. Cast glass, h. 25 x 17 inches. Courtesy Leo Kaplan Modern.

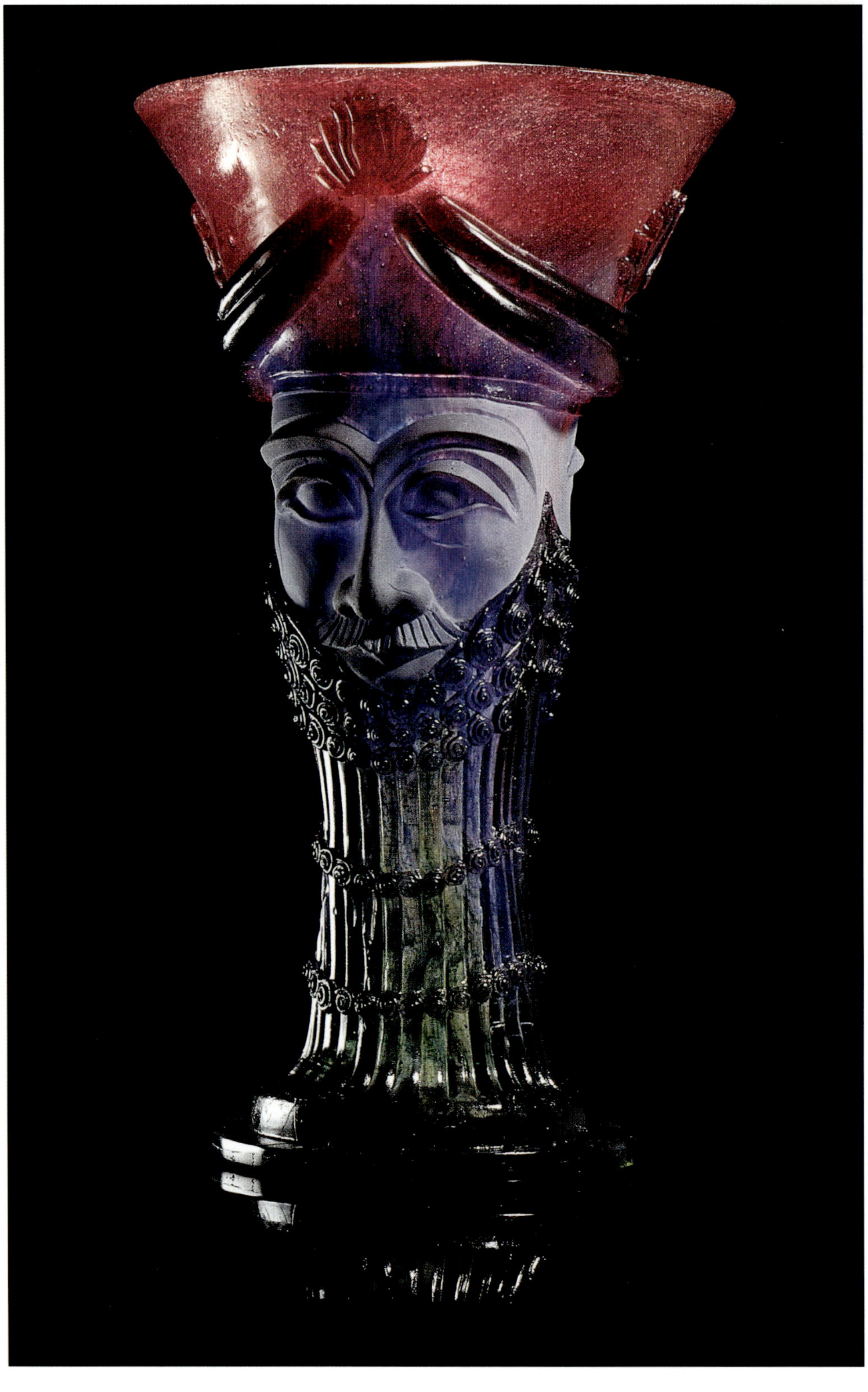

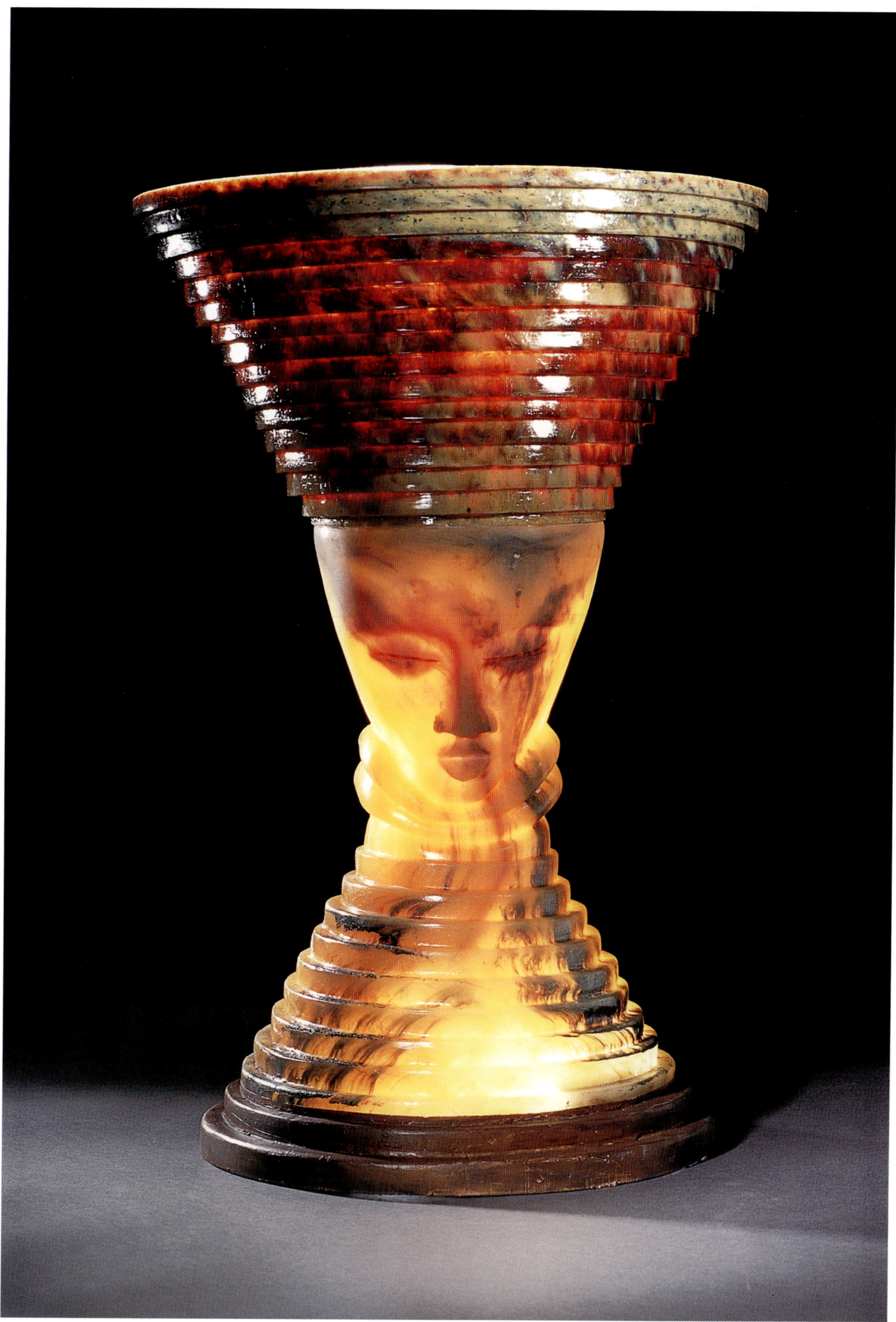

209

SETH RANDAL

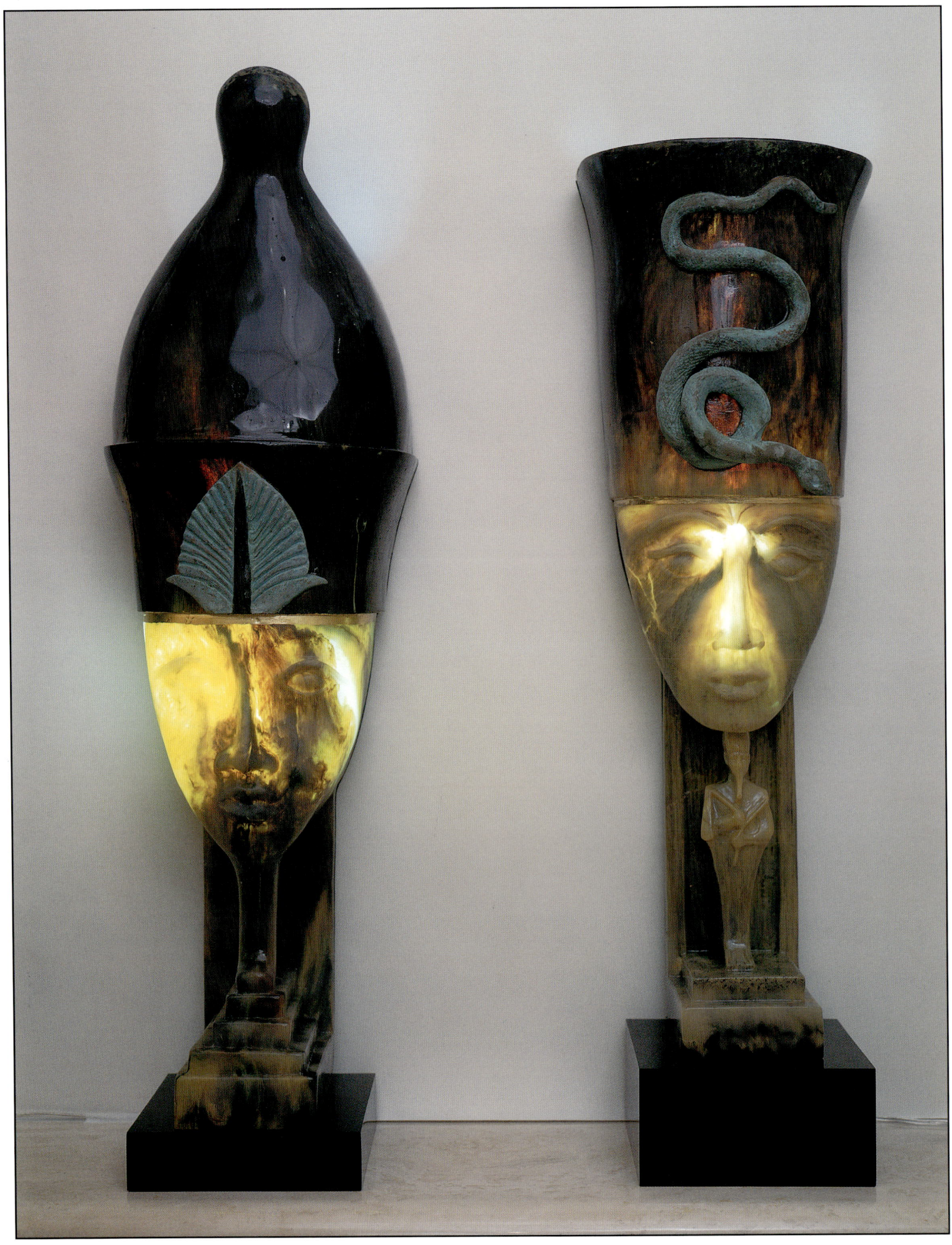

Fit for a Queen, 1999. Cast crystal, and electroformed copper, (left) h. 32 x 12 and (right) h. 38 x 12 inches. Collection of Anne and Marvin H. Cohen.

CAPTIVA, FLORIDA

Robert Rauschenberg
(b.1925)

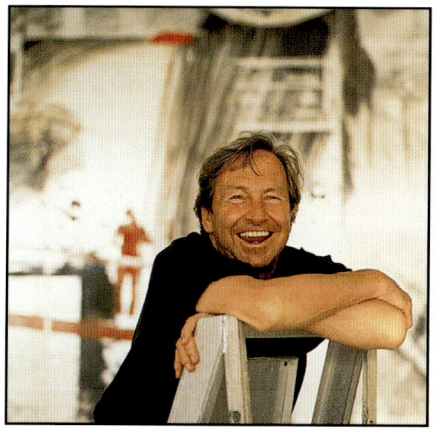

Photo: Ed Chappell

Untitled, glass tires; Installation view of the Robert Rauschenberg exhibition, Solomon R. Guggenheim Museum, 9/19/97–1/7/98. Mold blown glass, and silver-plated steel. Life size. Photo: Ellen Labenski. ©The Solomon R. Guggenheim Foundation, New York.

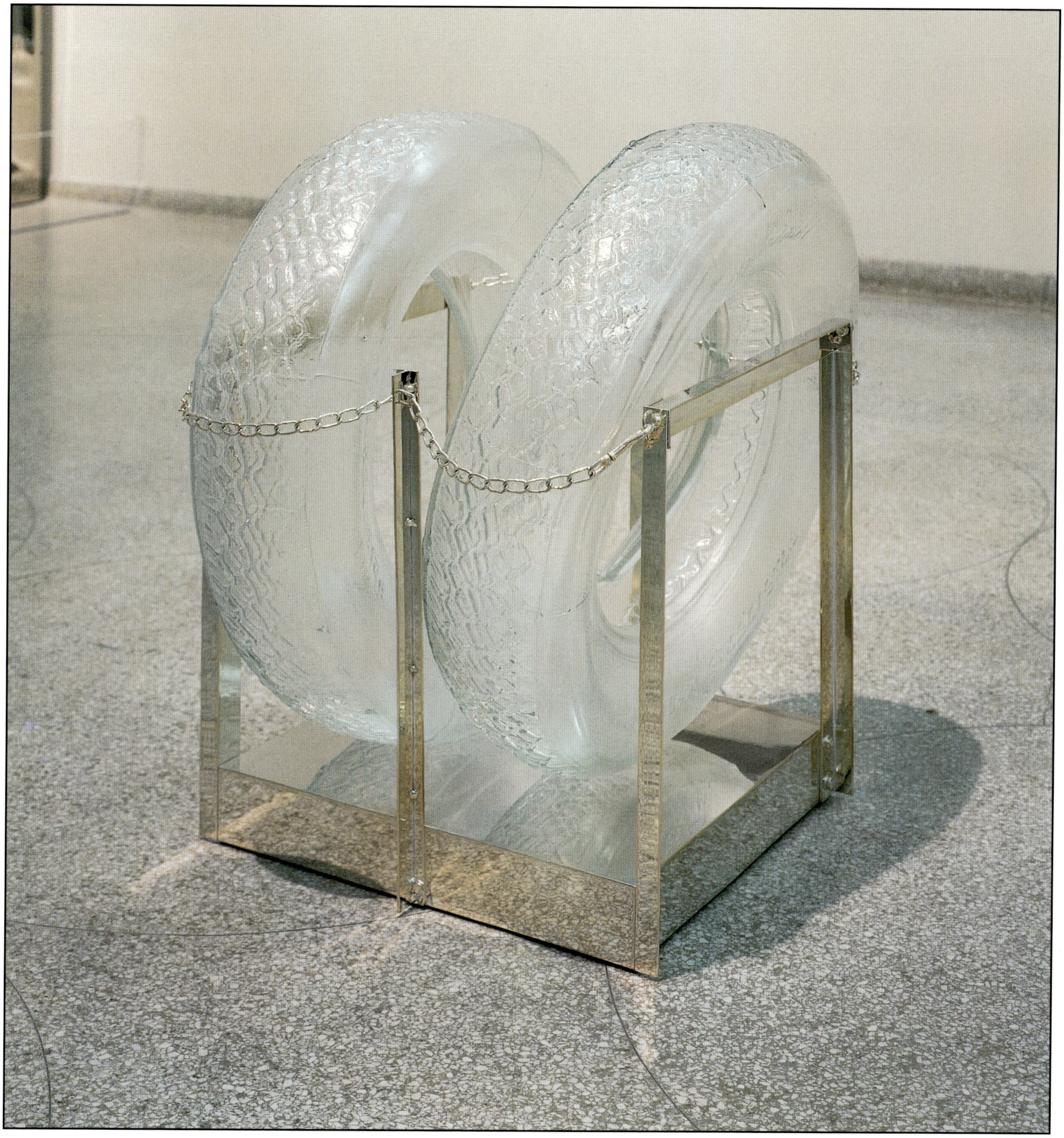

Colin Reid
(b.1953)

GLOUCESTERSHIRE, UNITED KINGDOM

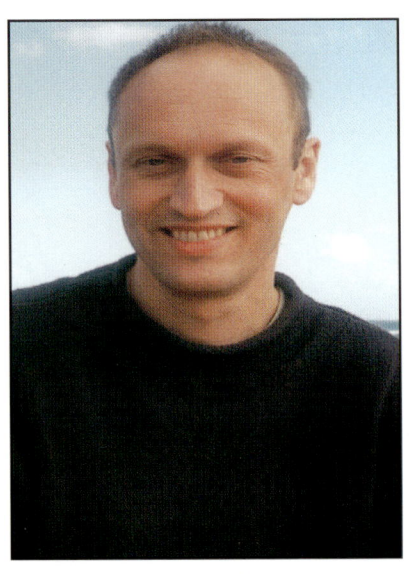

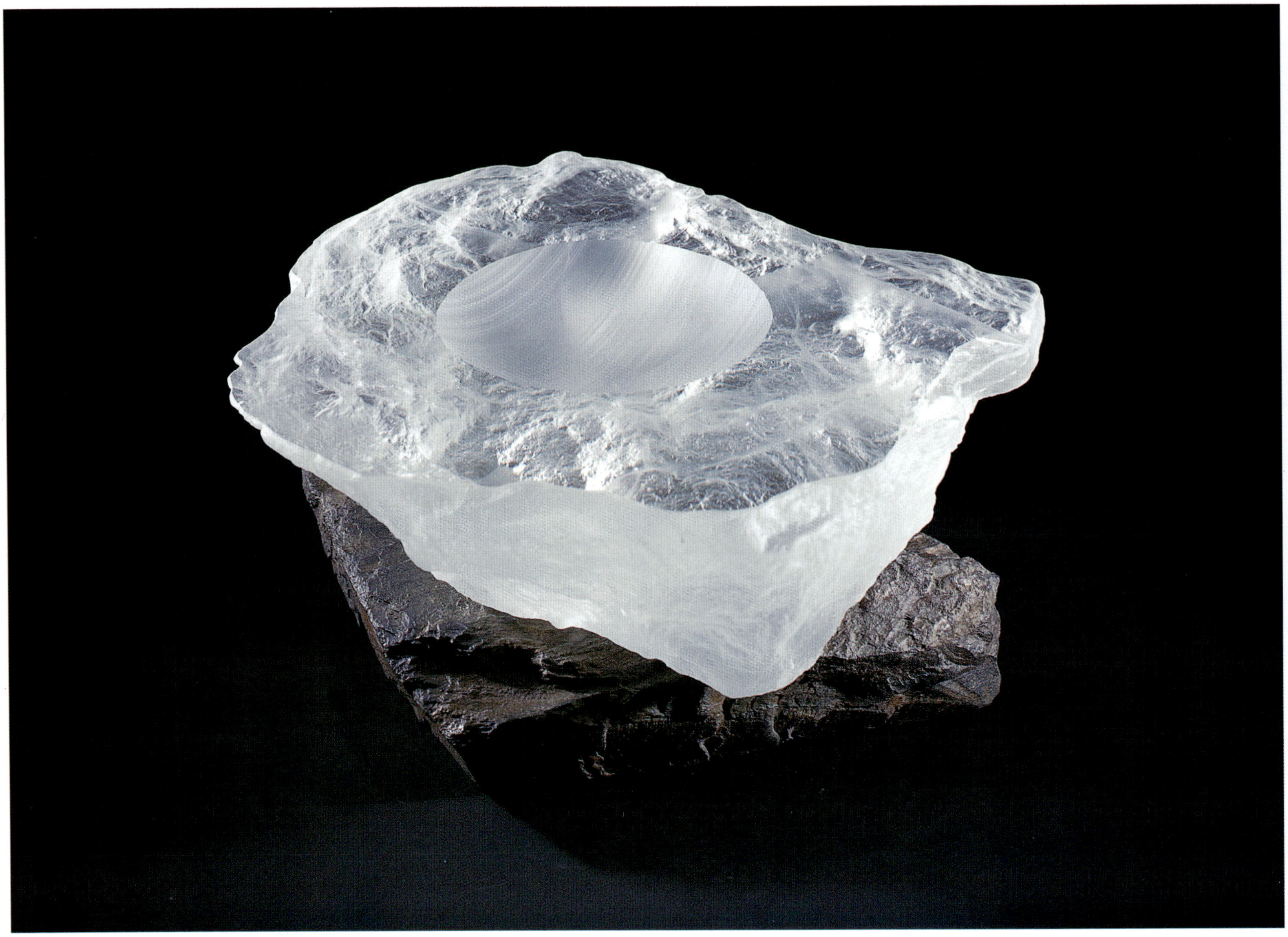

Untitled #R853, 1999. Cast optical glass, slate, and lost wax kilncast, h. 9 x 14.5 x 15 inches. Courtesy Miller Gallery.

SEATTLE, WASHINGTON

Kait Rhoads
(b. 1968)

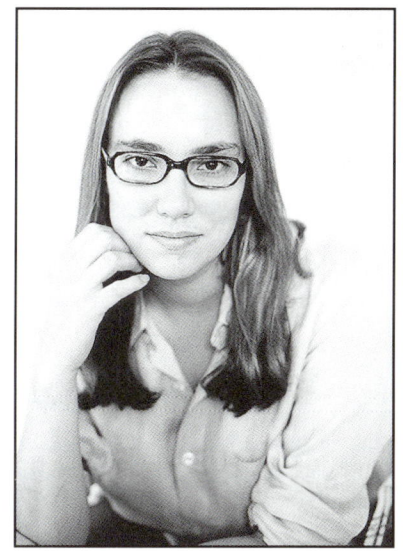

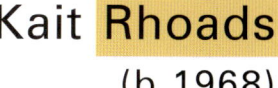

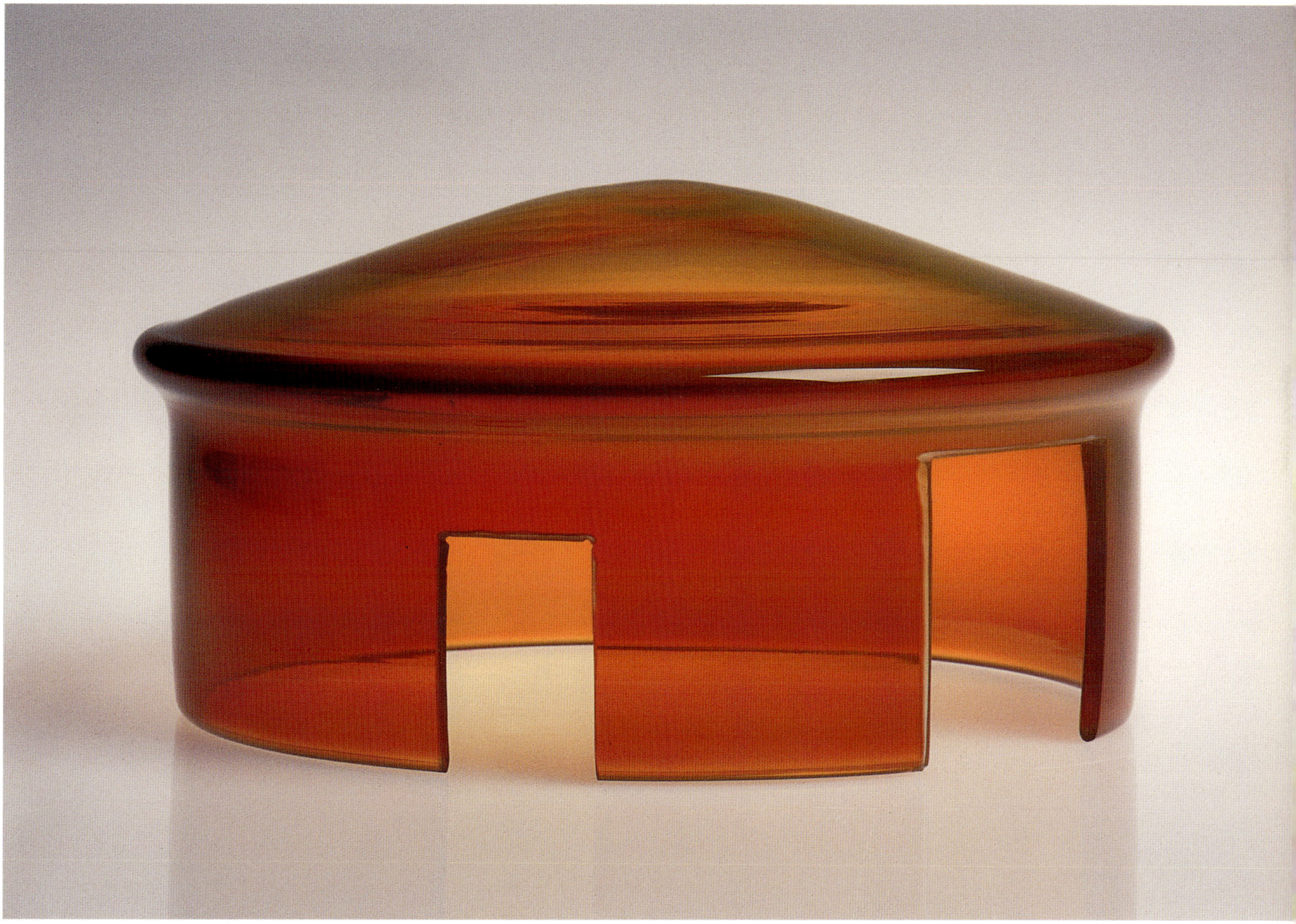

Shorty George, 1999. Blown glass, cut, and ground, h. 4.5 x 9 inches.

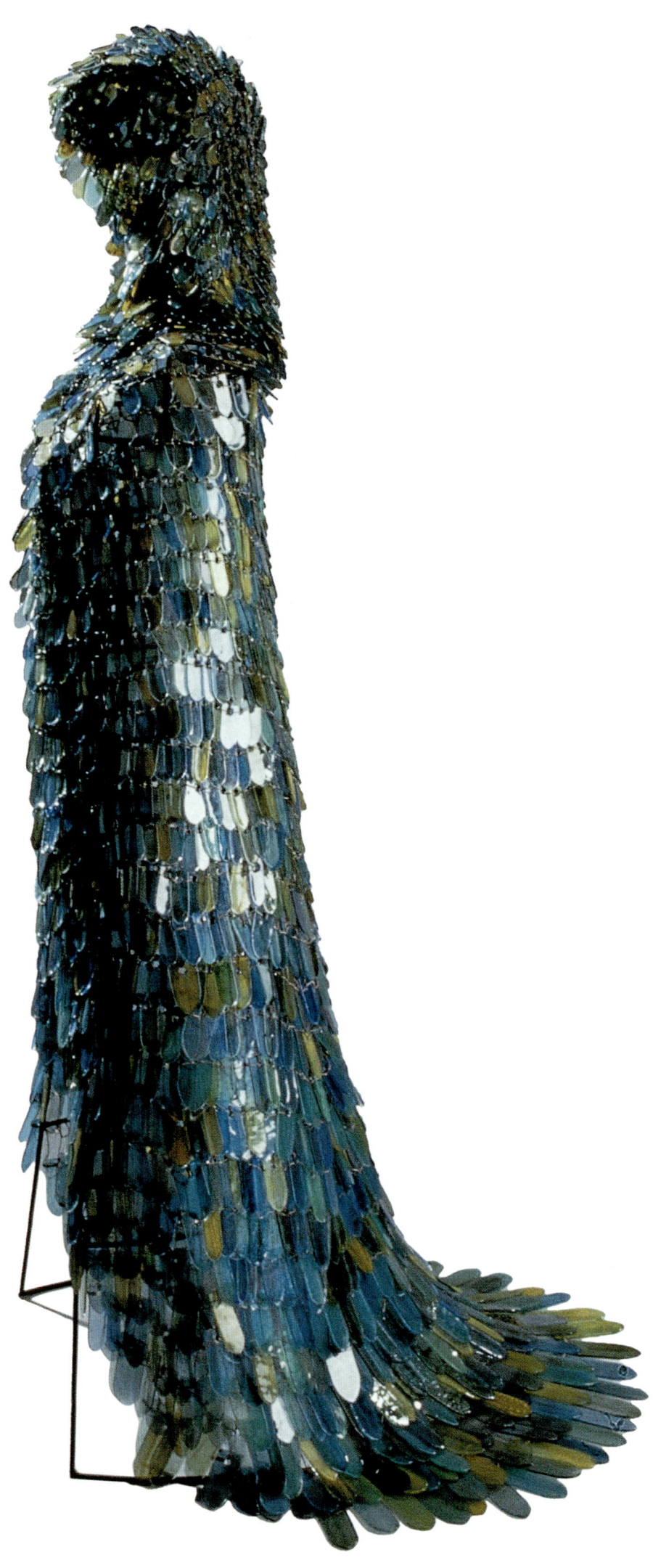

Selkie's Skin, 1998. Glass, waxed linen, and steel, h. 28 x 17 x 5 inches.

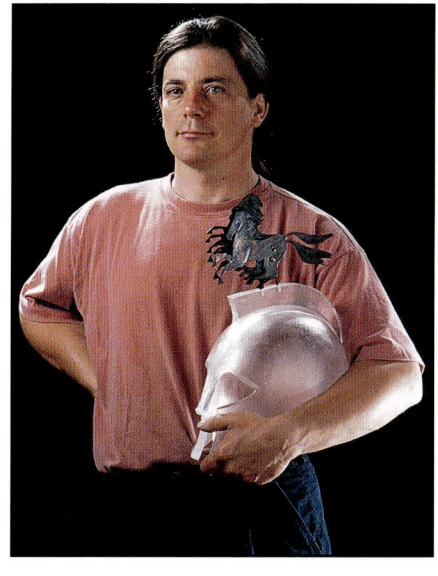

Photo: Jocelyn Blais

QUEBEC, CANADA

Donald Robertson
(b.1952)

The Charge; The Warrior Series, *1991. Cast crystal, lost wax, cut, polished, and copper, h. 15.6 x 7.2 x 10.8 inches. Courtesy Galerie Elena Lee, Montreal.*

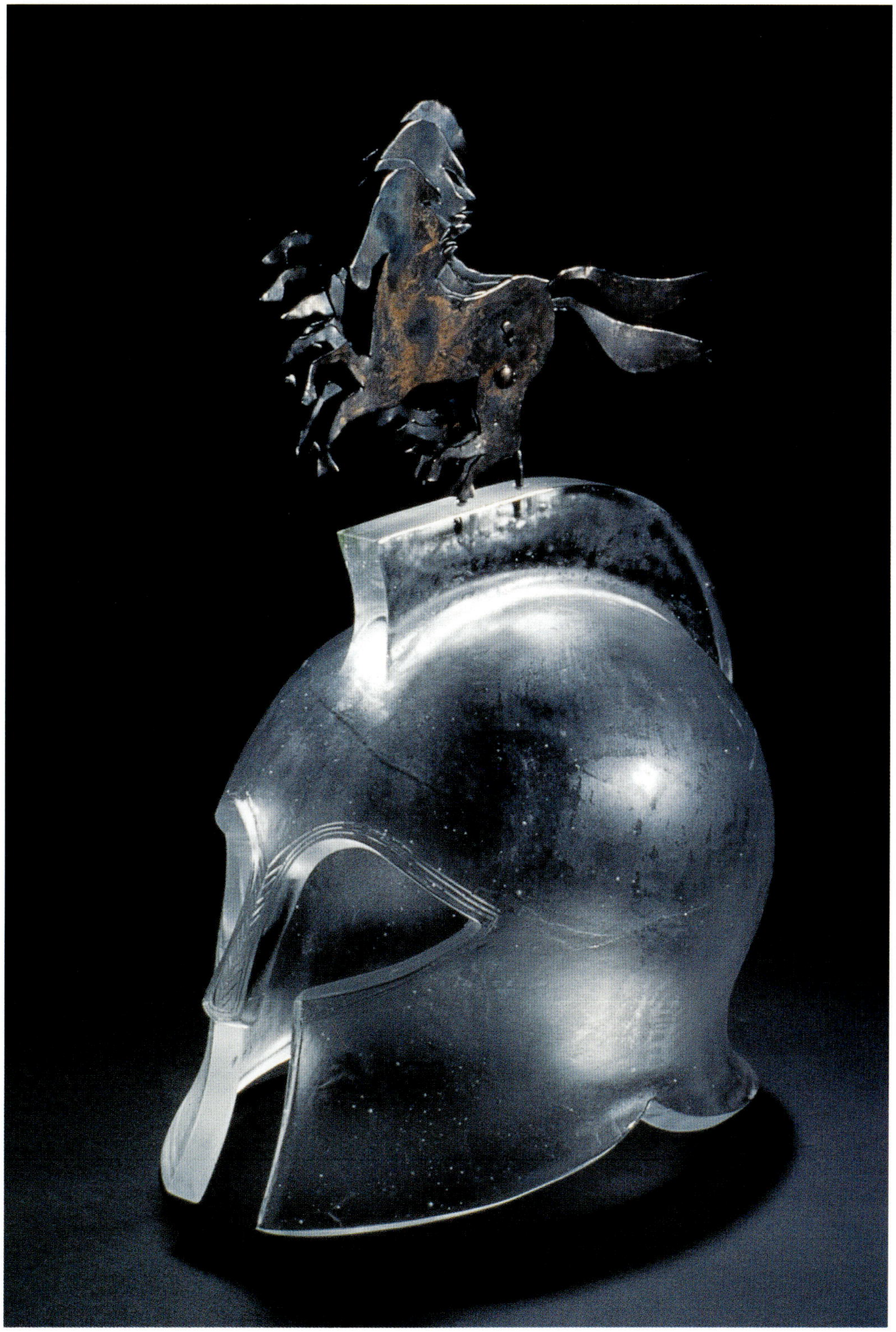

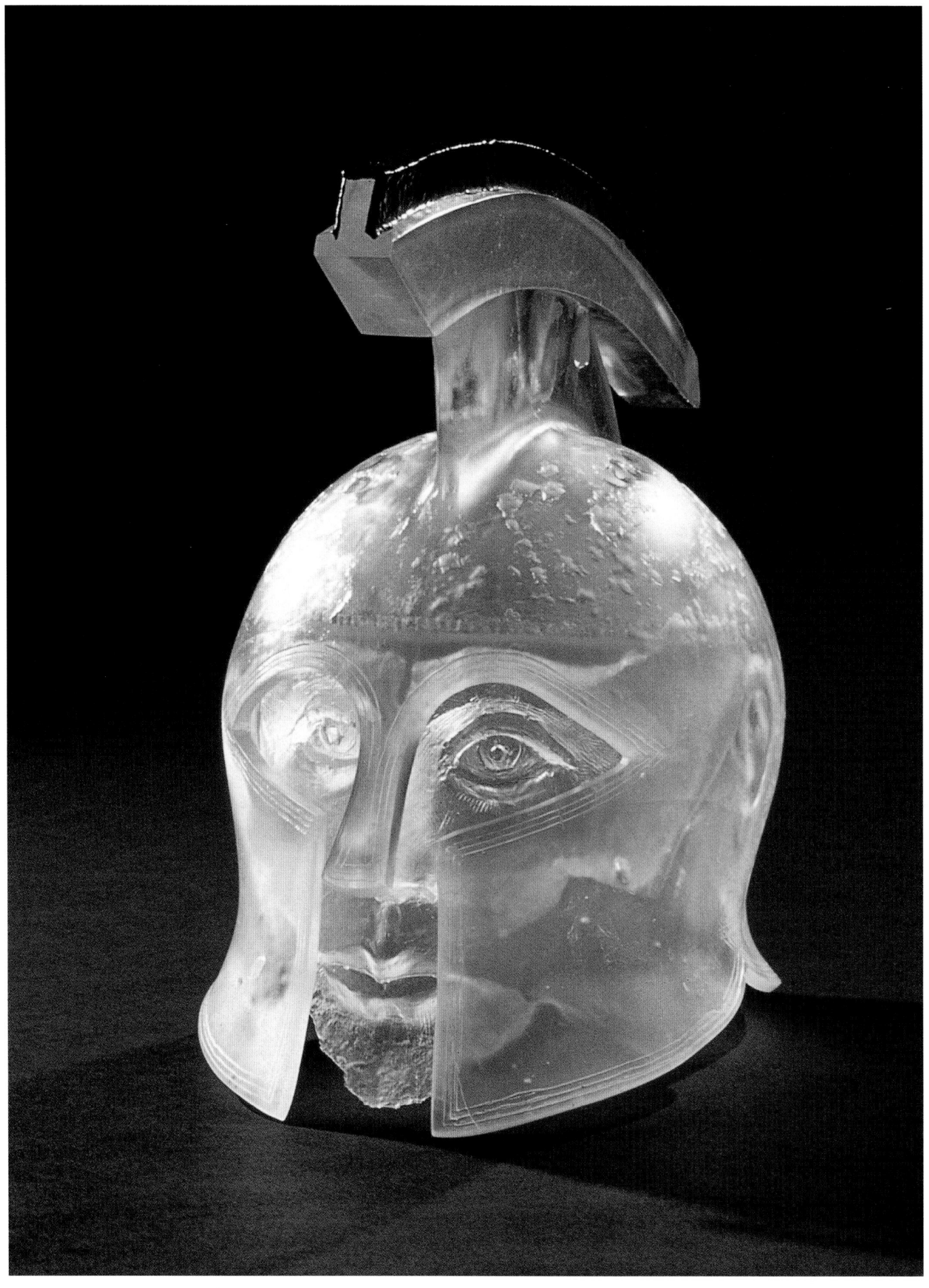

Memory; The Warrior Series, 1992. Cast crystal, lost wax, cut, polished, and lead, h. 12 x 14.8 x 7.2 inches. Courtesy Galerie Elena Lee, Montreal.

SUNNYSIDE, NEW YORK

Gerald Rose
(b.1958)

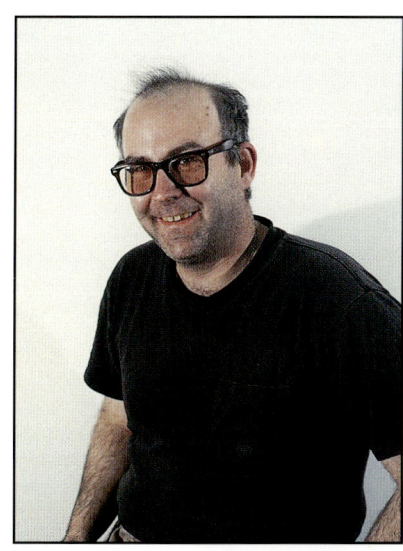

Untitled, 1999. Neon, h. 44 x 32 inches.

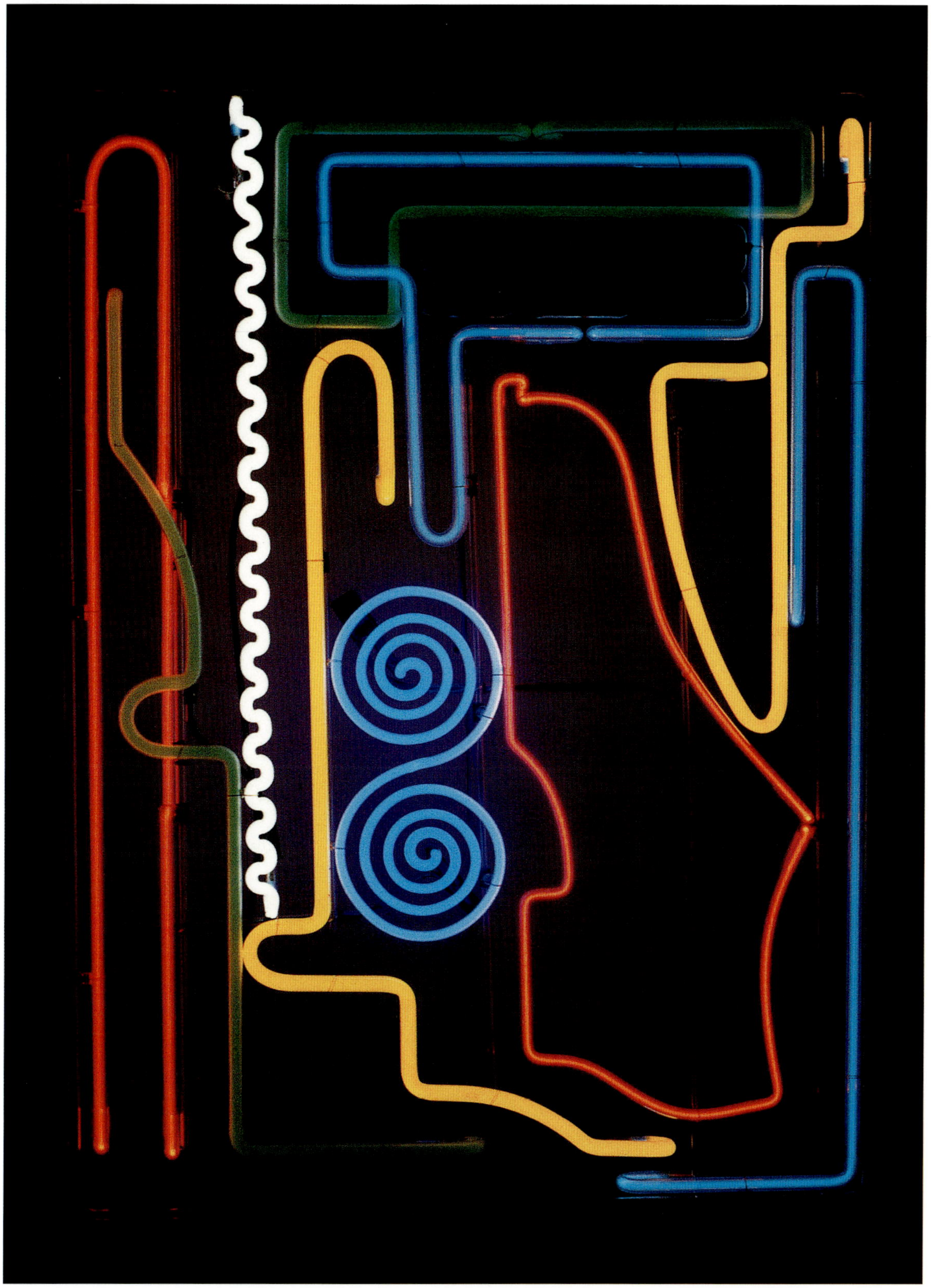

Linda Ross
(b.1957)

BOSTON, MASSACHUSETTS

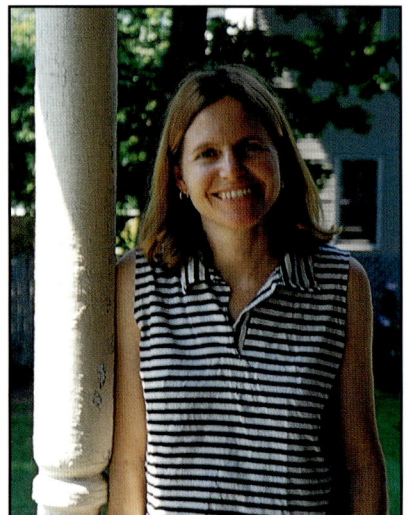

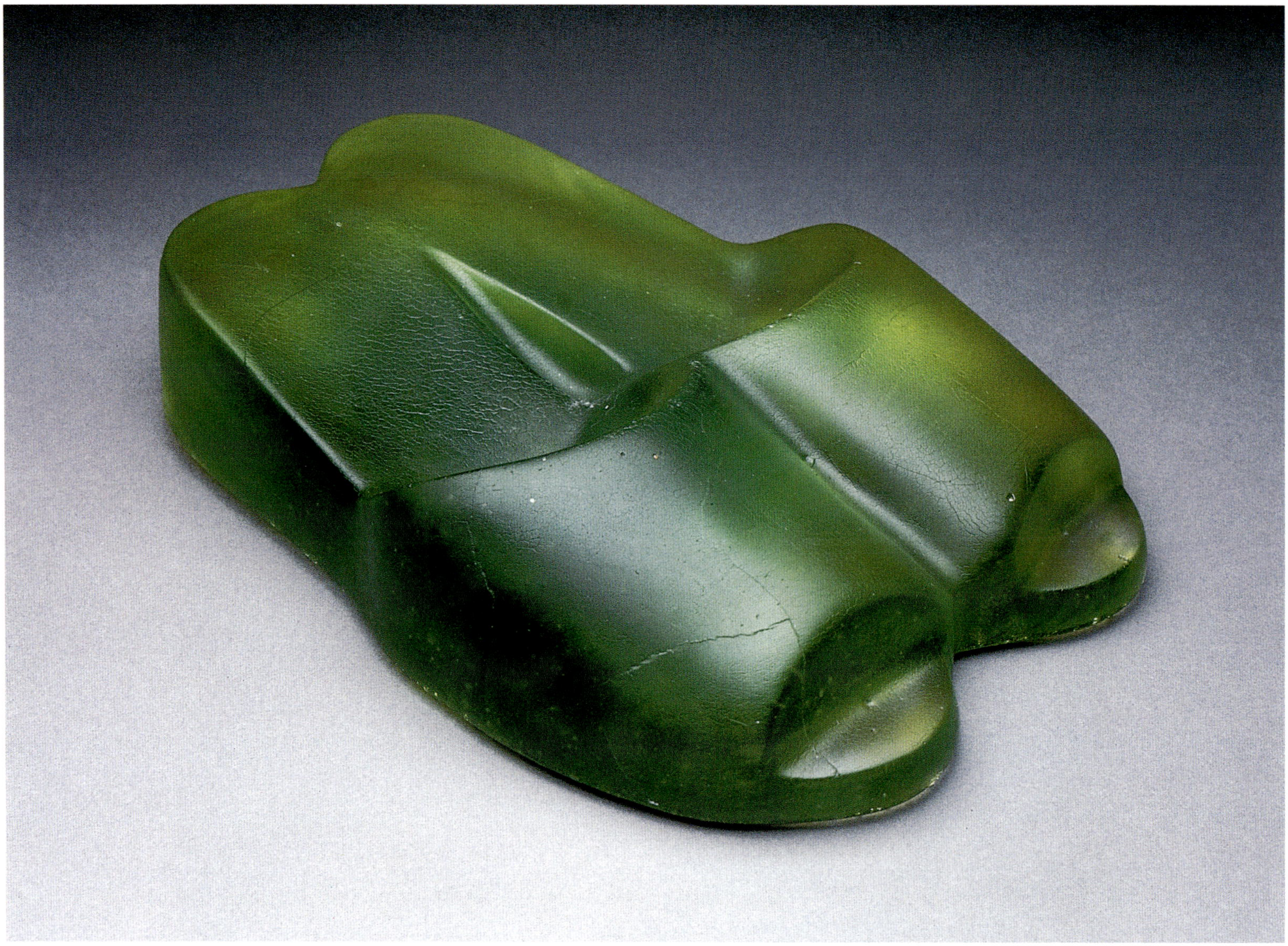

Fairy Shoes; Olive Slippers, 1998.
Cast glass, h. 3 x 8 x 6 inches.

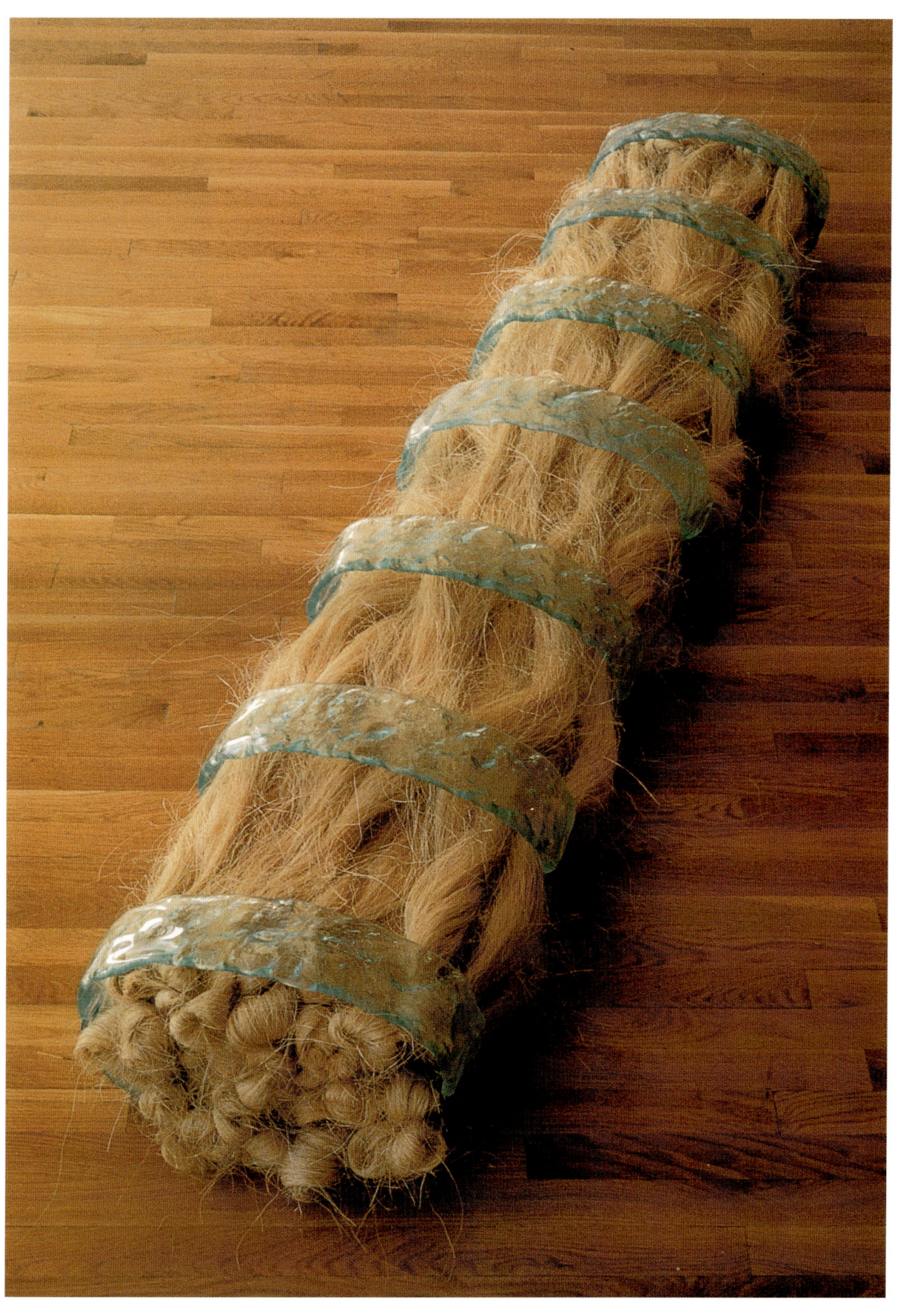

Rapunzel's Ladder, 1996. Glass and hemp, h. 12 x 86 x 14 inches.

Daniel A. Rothenfeld
(b.1953)

BRATENAHL, OHIO

Below:
Love is Joy, 1999. Cut plate glass with lazerfoil inclusions and UV adhesive, h. 18 x 12 inches. Photo: Barney Taxel.

Opposite:
Chrysalis, 1983. Individually sculpted plates of ½-inch clear float glass, layered and bonded with adhesive, h. 22 x 9 x 6 inches. The Cleveland Museum of Art. Photo: ©The Cleveland Museum of Art.

Photo: Greg Bruce.

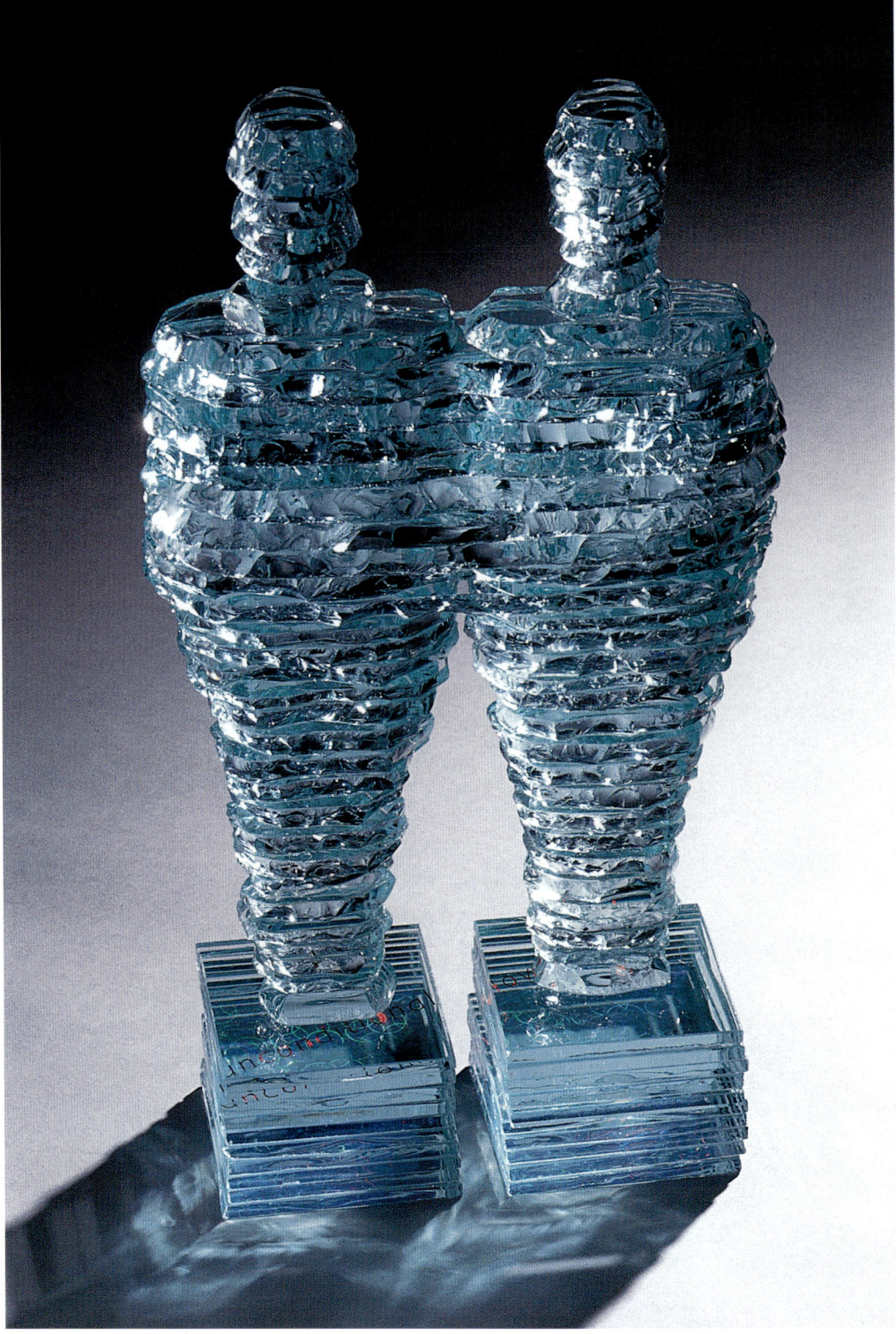

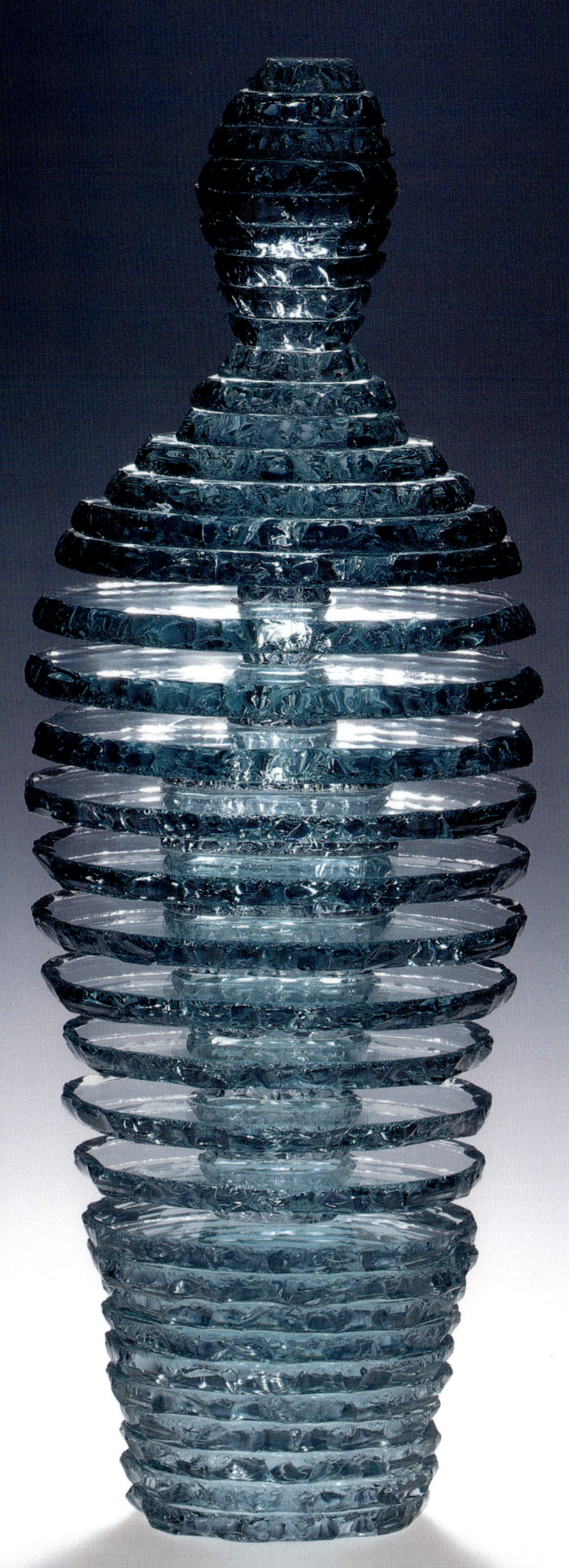

Eric Rubinstein
(b.1956)

BROOKLYN, NEW YORK

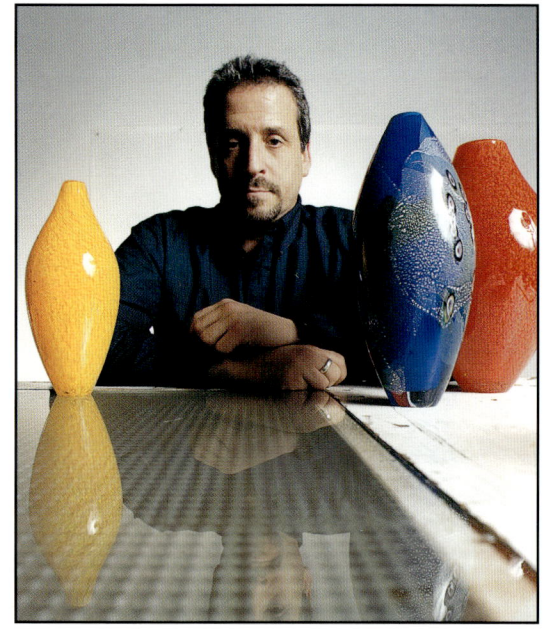

Pointillism Series; *Vessels,* 1999. Blown glass, (left to right) h. 10 x 4, h. 12.5 x 4.5, and h. 11.5 x 8.5.

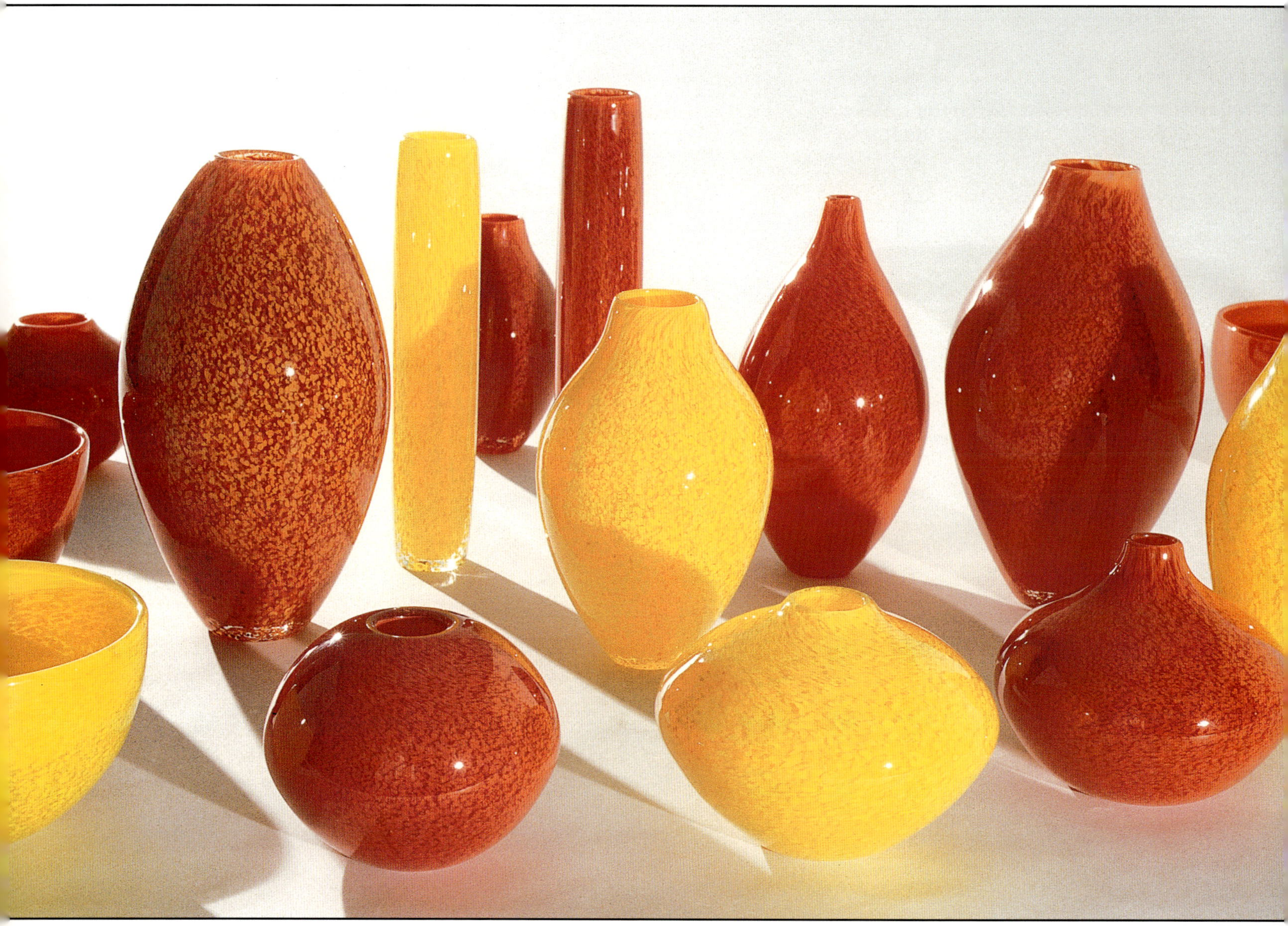

Pointillism Series; *Vessels,* 1999. Blown glass, (largest) h. 8 x 6 inches and (smallest) h. 4 x 3 inches.

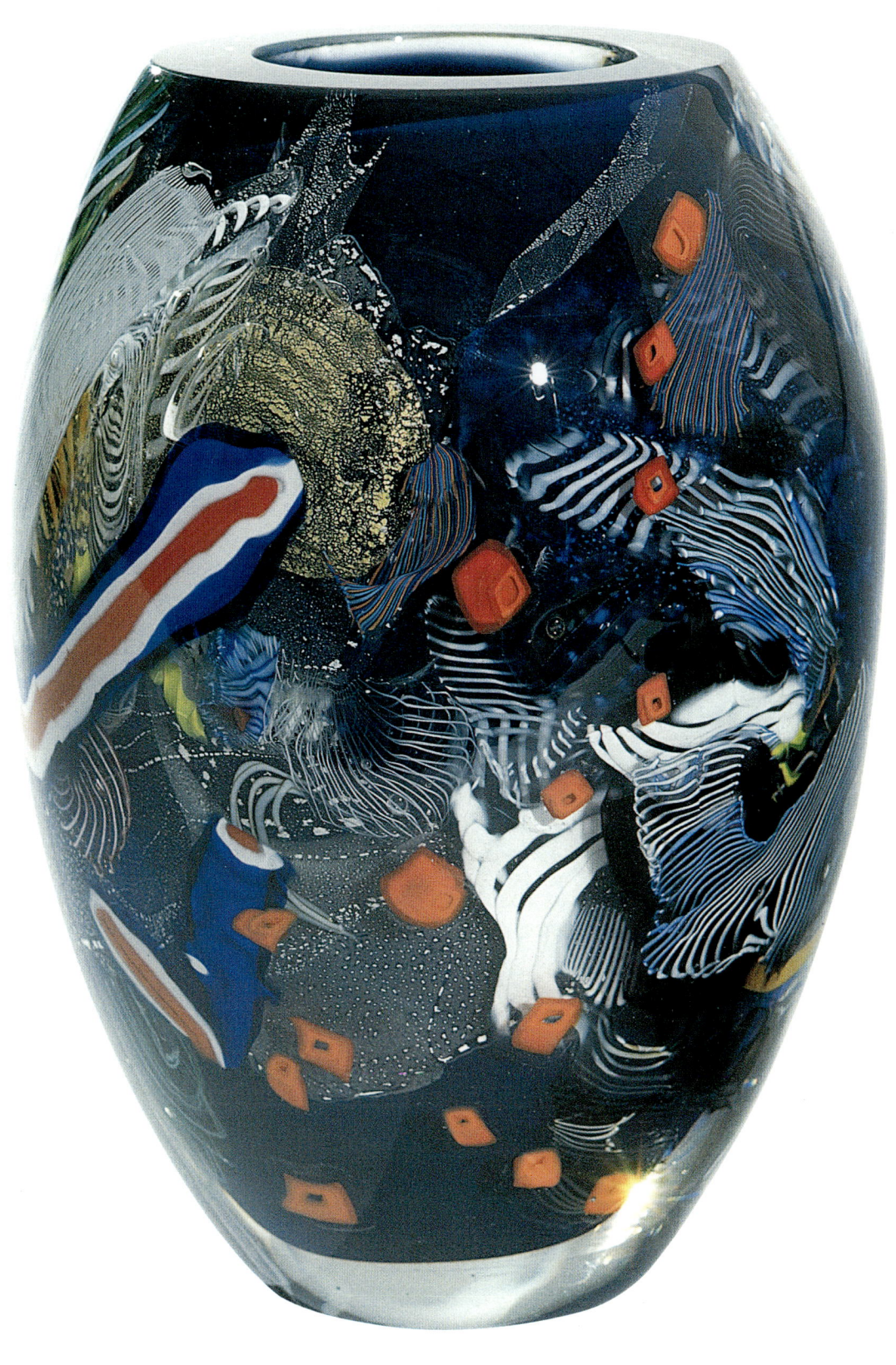

Seascape Series; Vessel, 1999.
Blown glass, h. 8 x 6 inches.

Ginny Ruffner
(b.1952)

SEATTLE, WASHINGTON

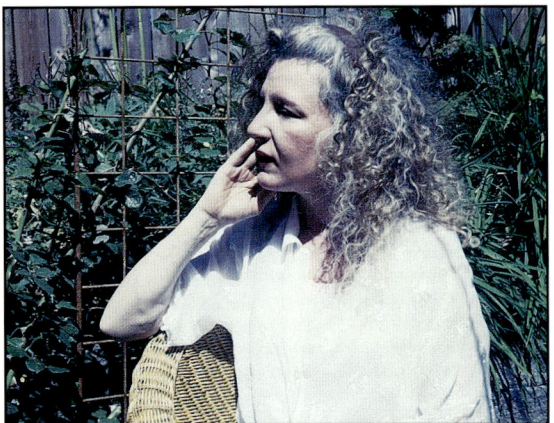

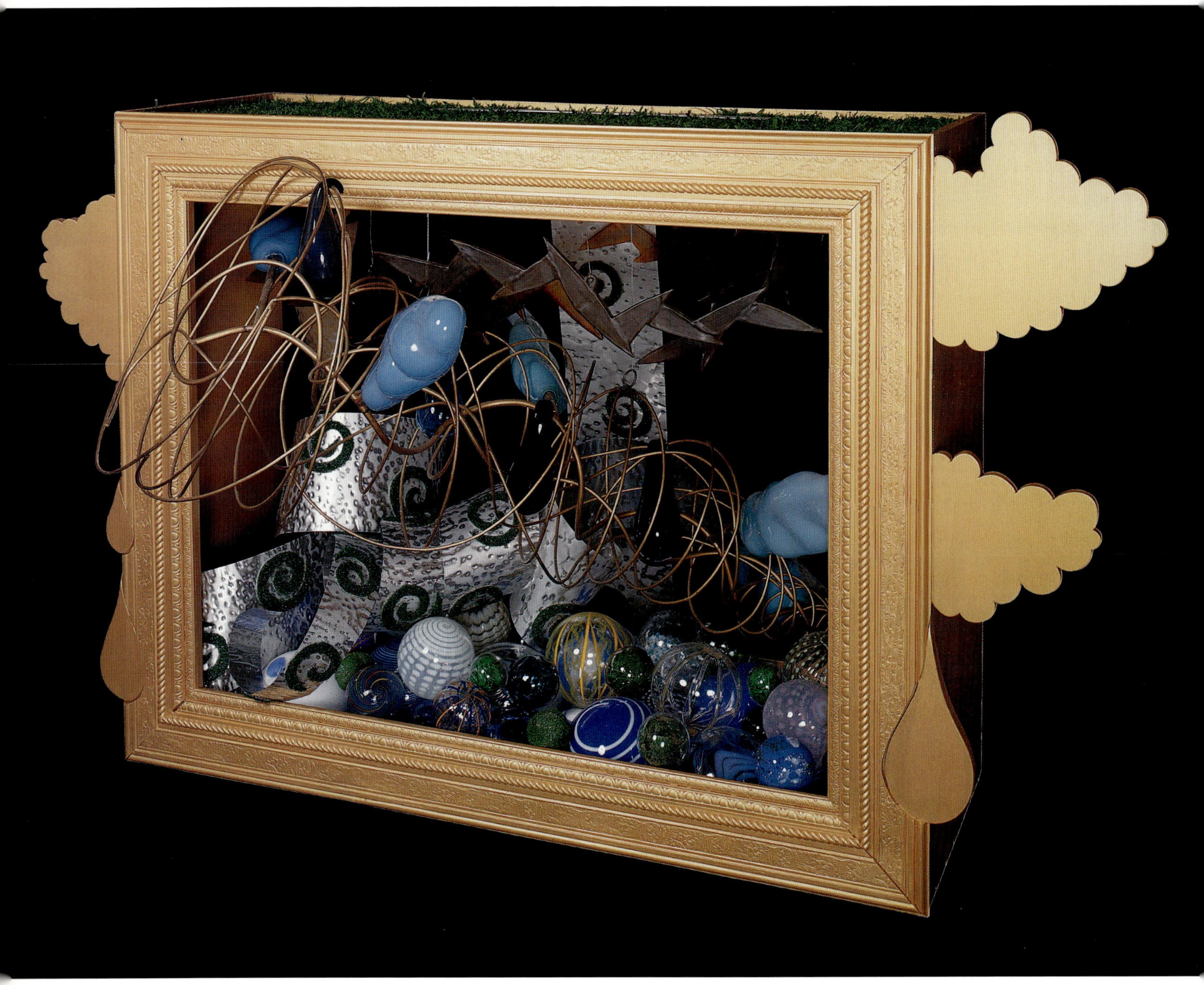

Above:
Growing Beautiful Weather; Large Conceptual Narratives Series, 1997. Glass and mixed media, h. 56 x 90 x 45 inches.

Opposite:
Fruit and Flowers, 1995. Lampworked glass and glass enamel paint, h. 25 x 14 x 13 inches. Charles A. Wustum Museum of Fine Arts, Racine, Wisconsin. Gift of Dale and Doug Anderson. Photo: Jon Bolton.

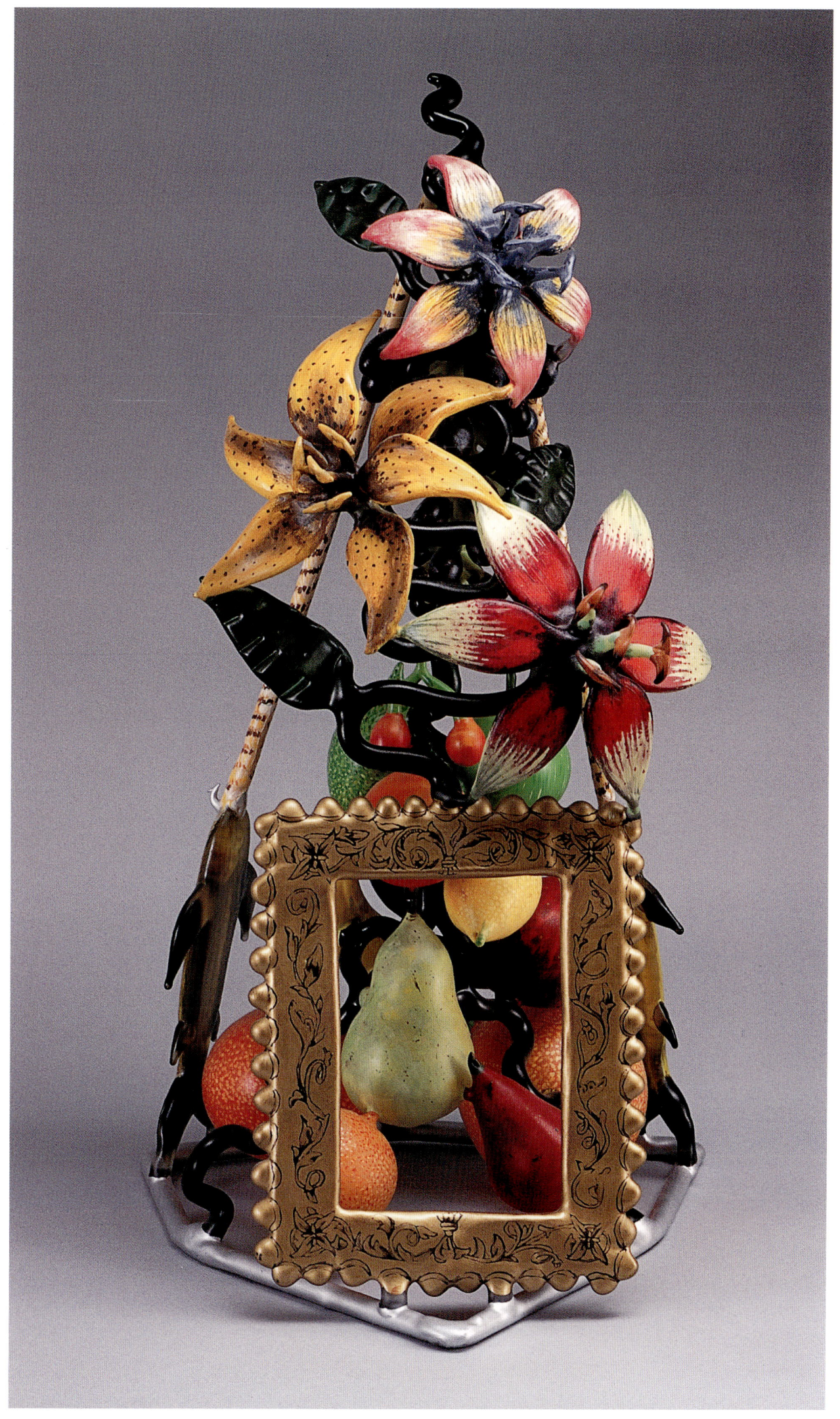

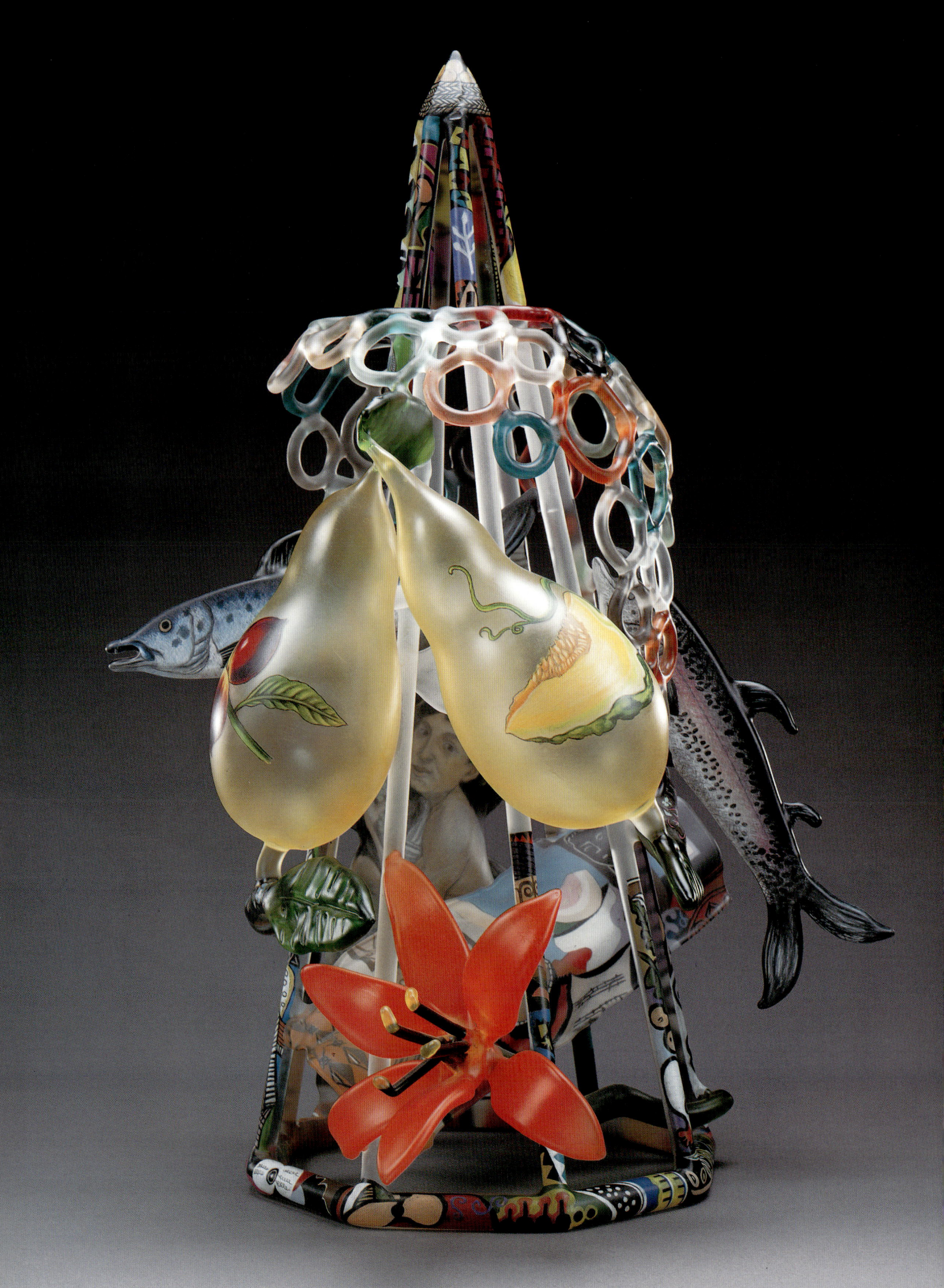

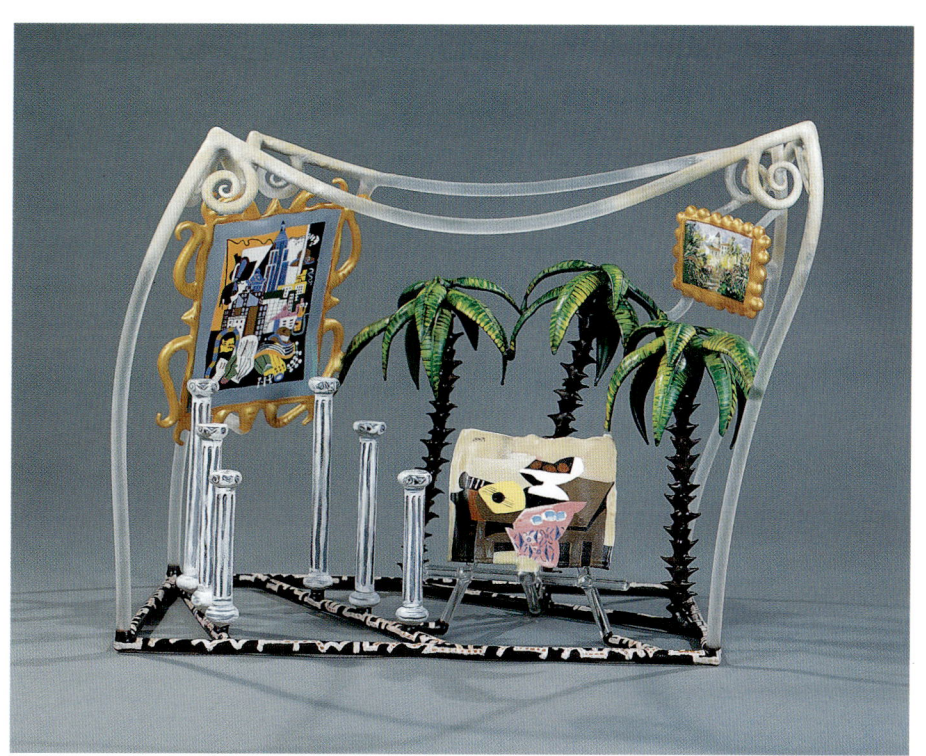

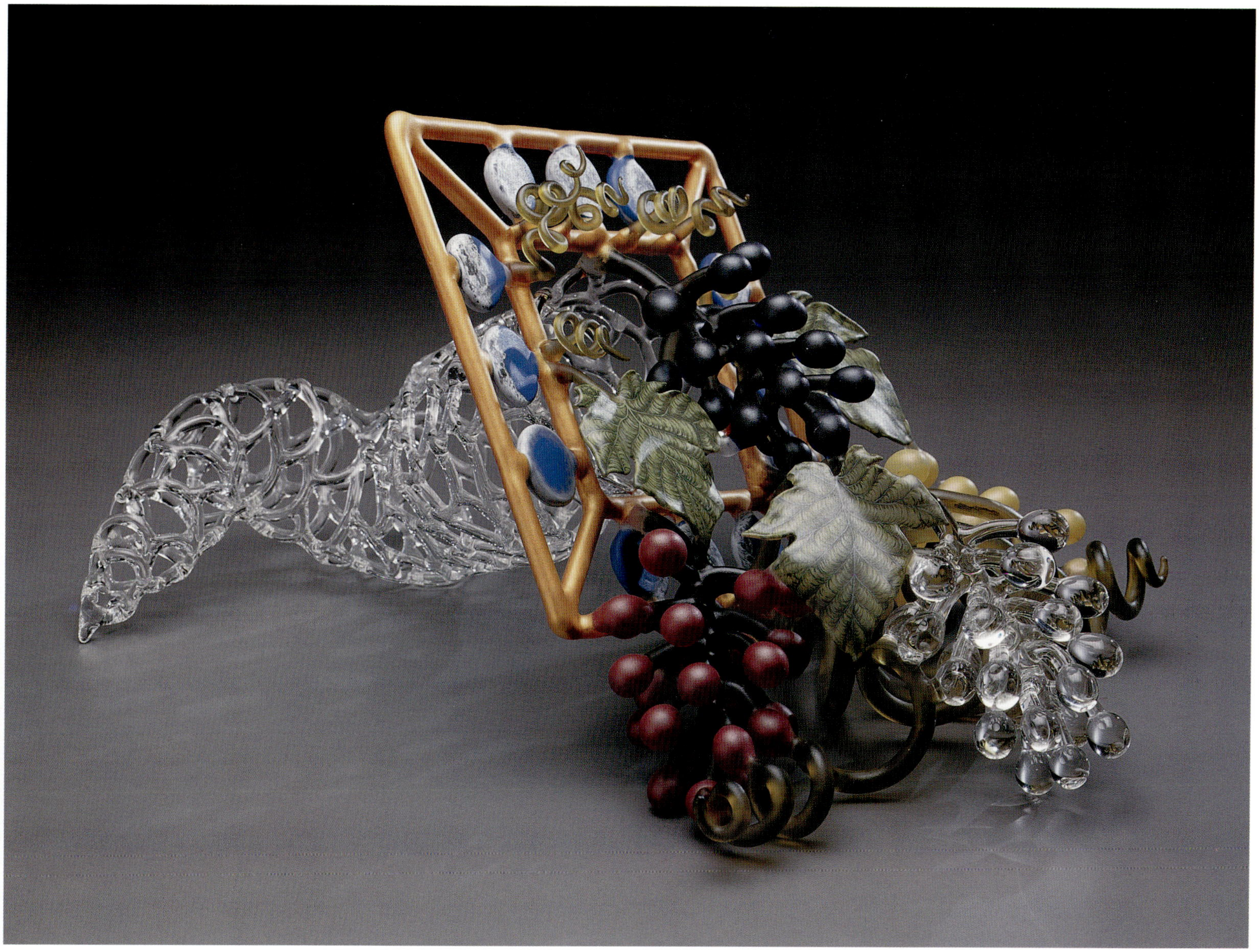

Opposite:
What a Pear, 1992. Lampwork, painted glass, h. 27 x 18 inches. The Metropolitan Museum of Art. Gift of Dale and Doug Anderson, 1994. Photo: The Metropolitan Museum of Art, 1995

Top:
Norton Palm Trees, 1997. Painted glass sculpture, h. 17 x 21 x 16 inches. Norton Museum of Art, West Palm Beach, Florida. Gift of Dale and Doug Anderson.

Bottom:
Plenty of Moonlight, 1998. Glass and mixed media, h. 12 x 15 x 23 inches.

Peet Sasaki
(b. 1970)

SEATTLE, WASHINGTON

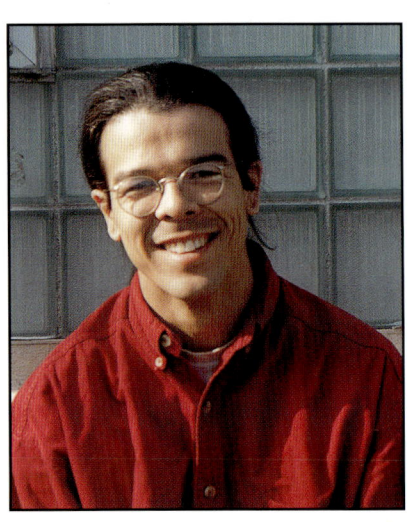

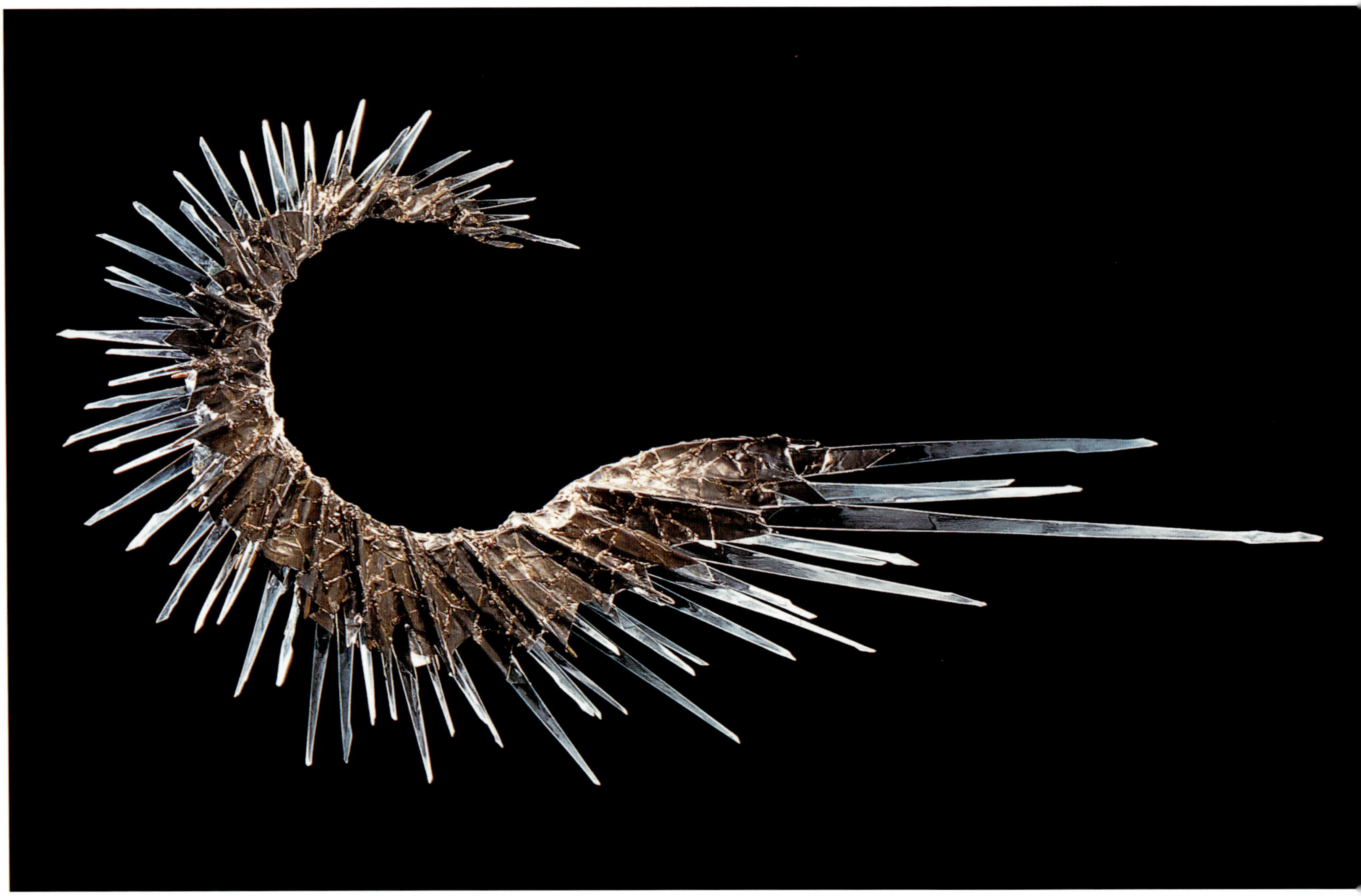

Carapace 1, 1999. Glass, lead, and steel,
h. 13 x 36 x .5 inches.

NEW YORK, NEW YORK

Kevin Scanlan
(b.1951)

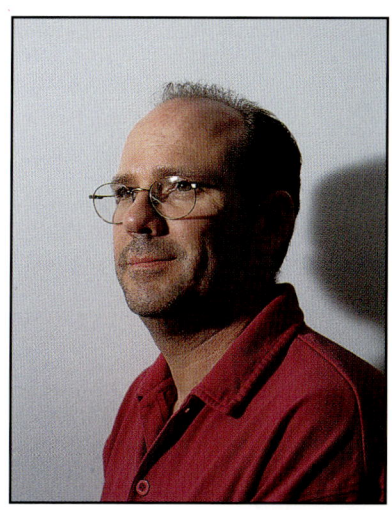

Standing Figure, 1999. Cast and hot worked glass, h. 16.5 x 6 inches.

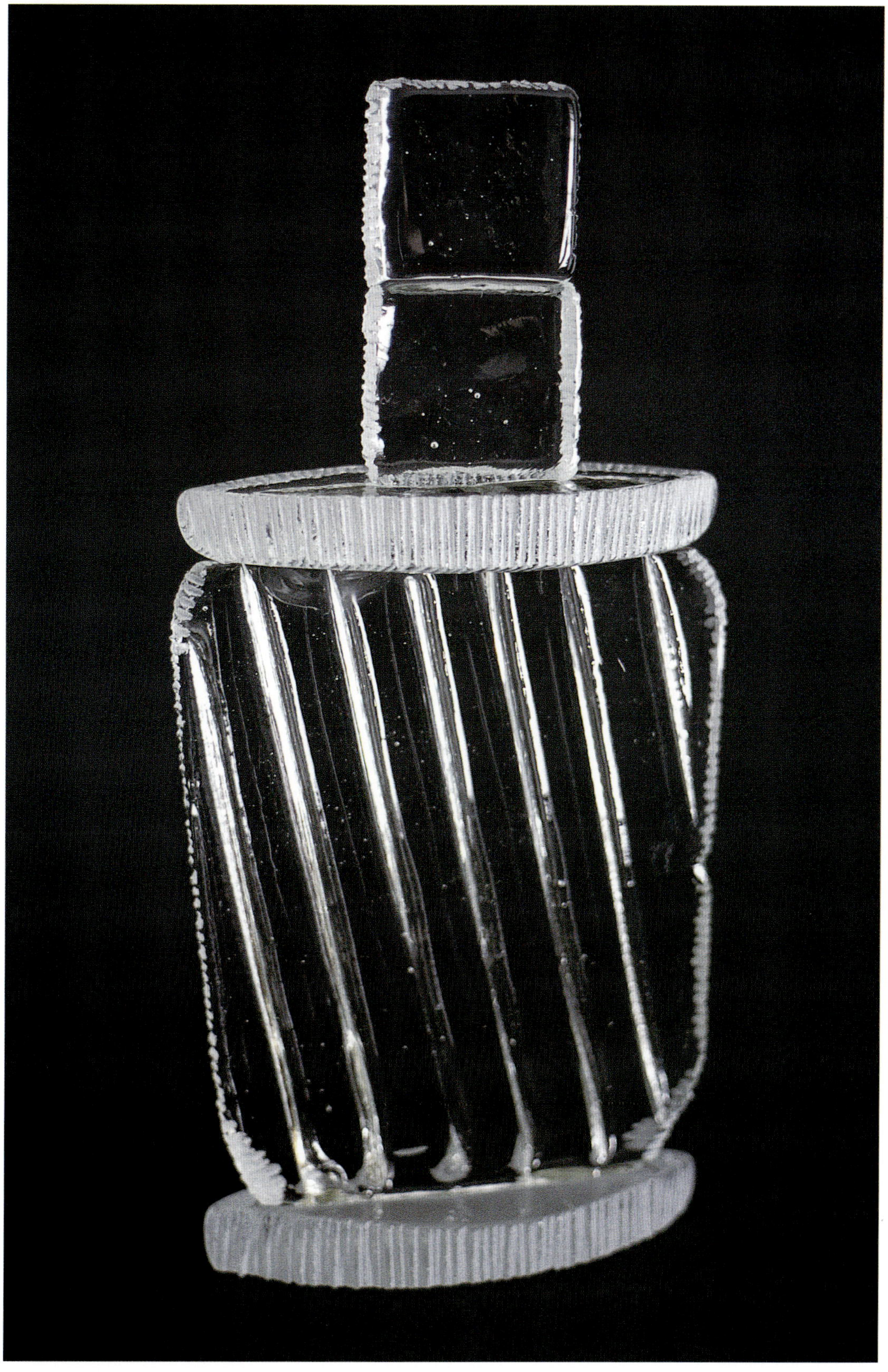

Judith Schaechter
(b. 1961)

PHILADELPHIA, PENNSYLVANIA

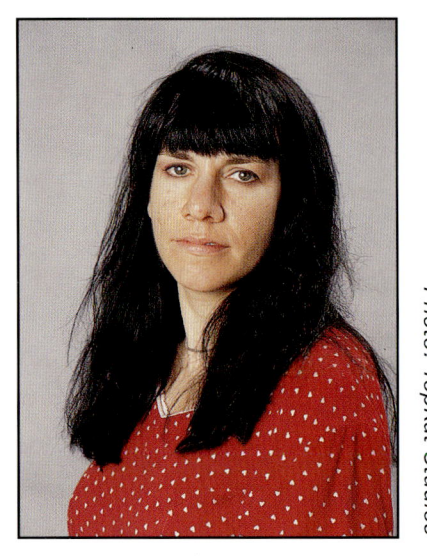

Photo: TopKat Studios

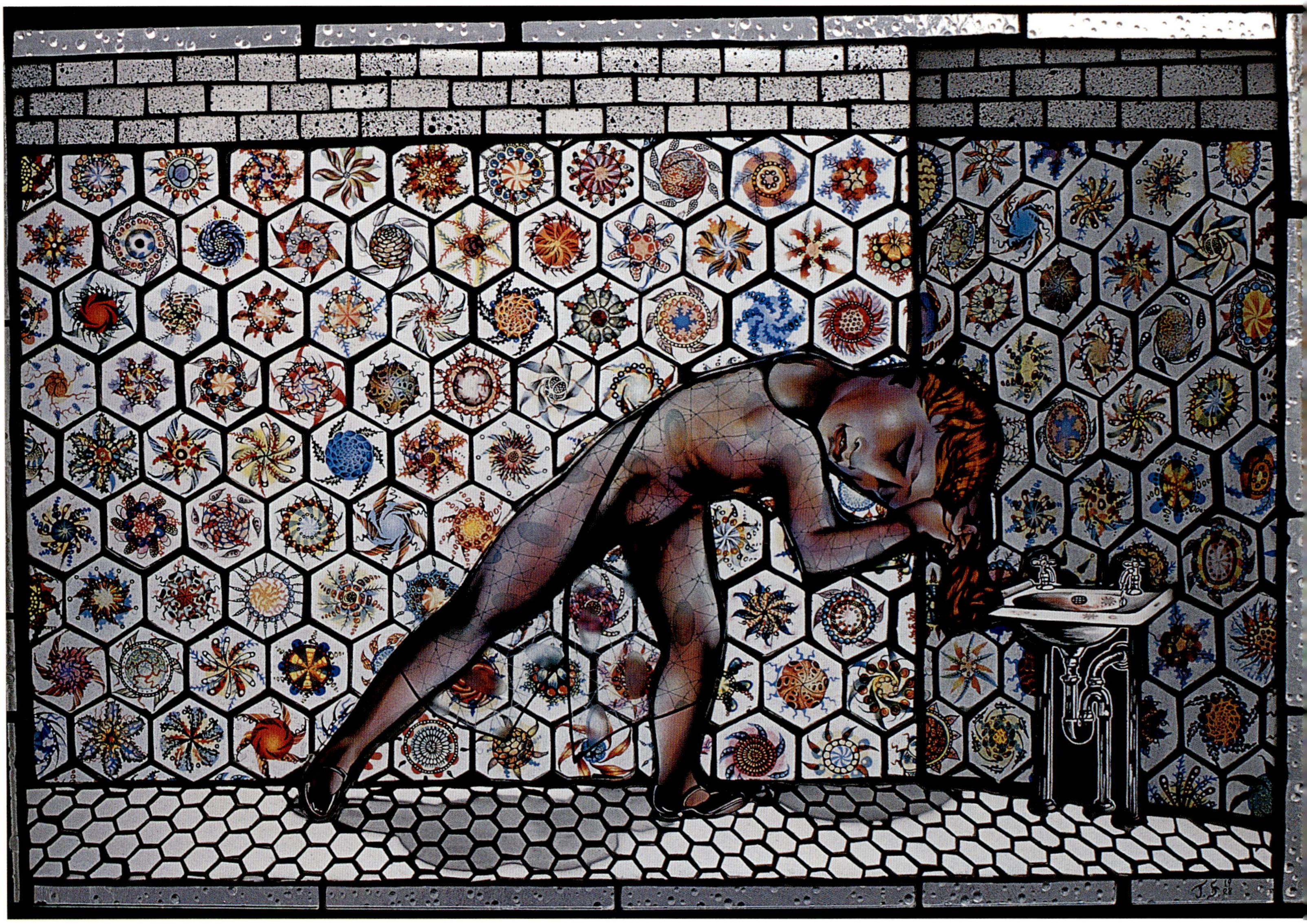

Girl Dyeing Hair, *1998. Cut flat glass, enameled and leaded, h. 19 x 28 inches.*

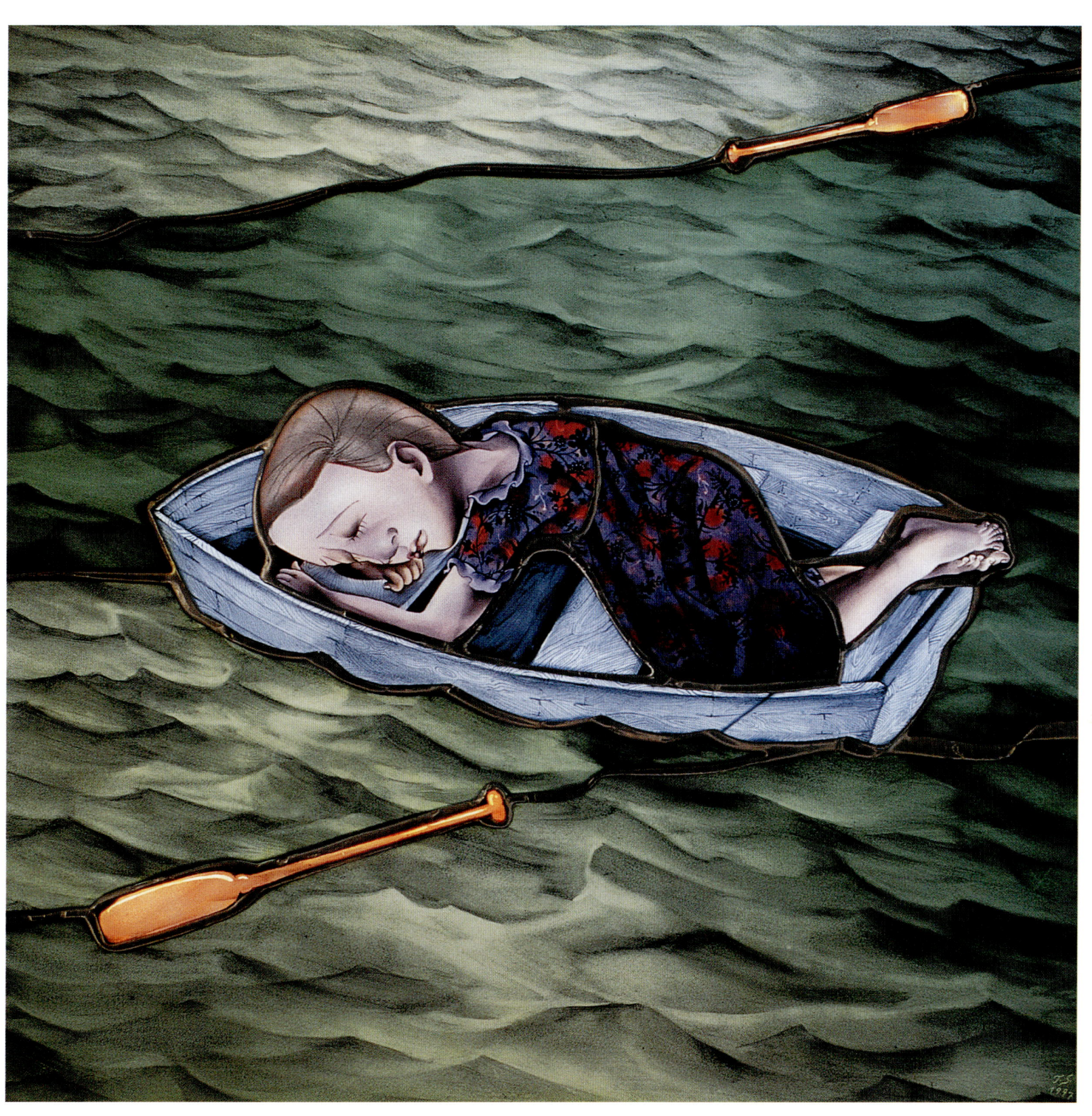

Asleep/Adrift, 1997. Cut flat glass, enameled, and leaded, h. 22 x 23 inches.

Michael Scheiner
(b.1956)

CENTRAL FALLS, RHODE ISLAND

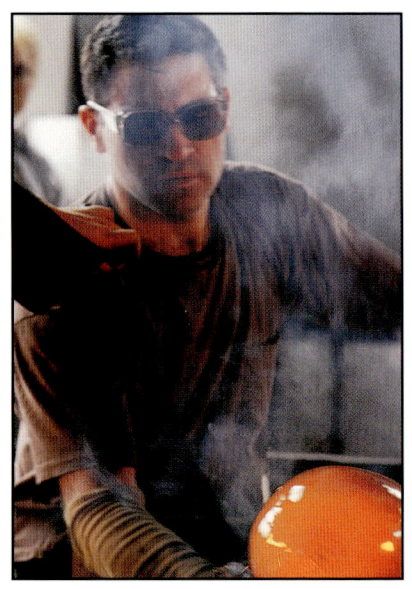

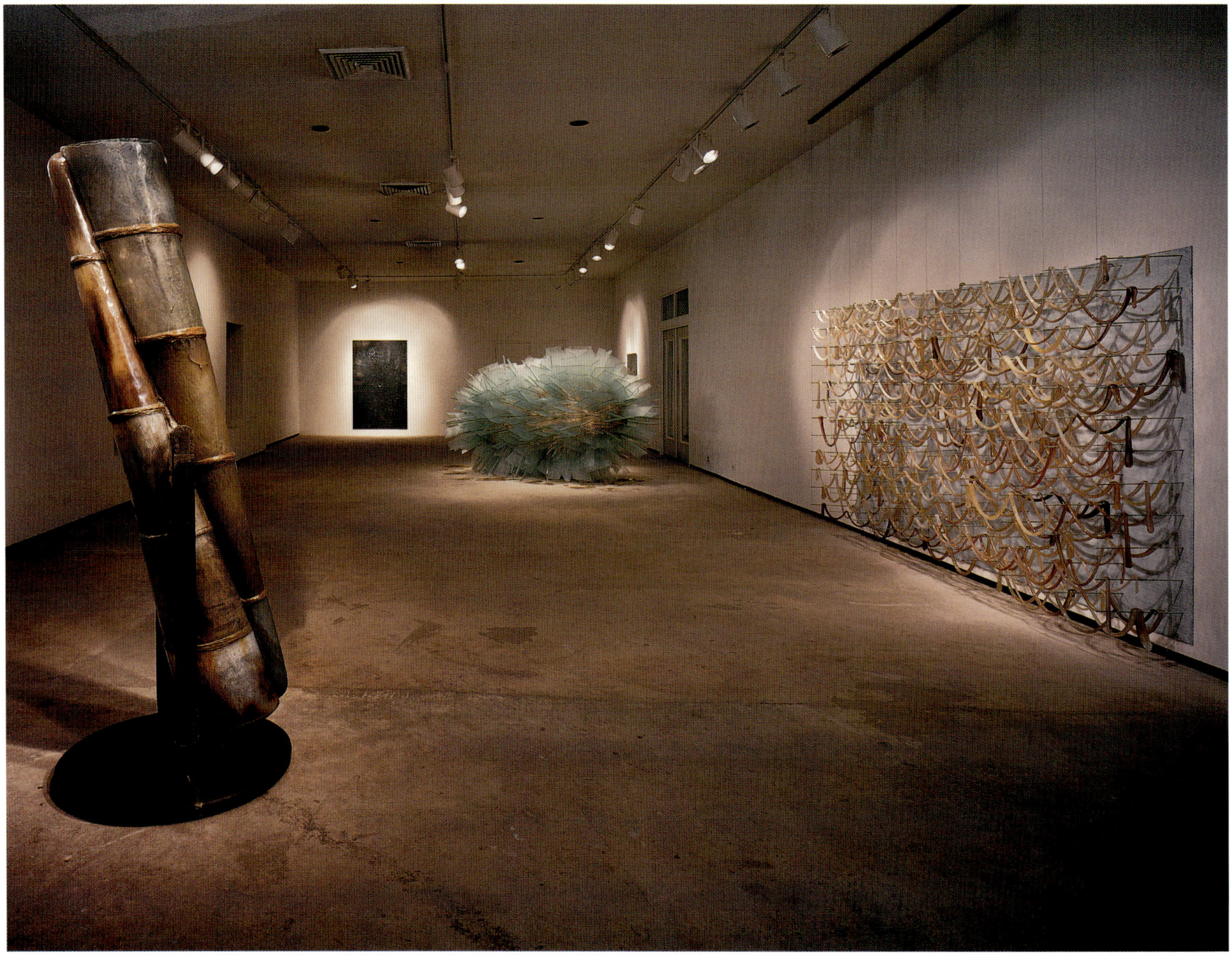

Installation: Robert Lehman Gallery, UrbanGlass, 1993. Left to right: Telescope, Event Horizon, Shimmer, and Curtain. Glass and mixed media, h. 10 x 20 x40 feet. Photo: David Lubarski.

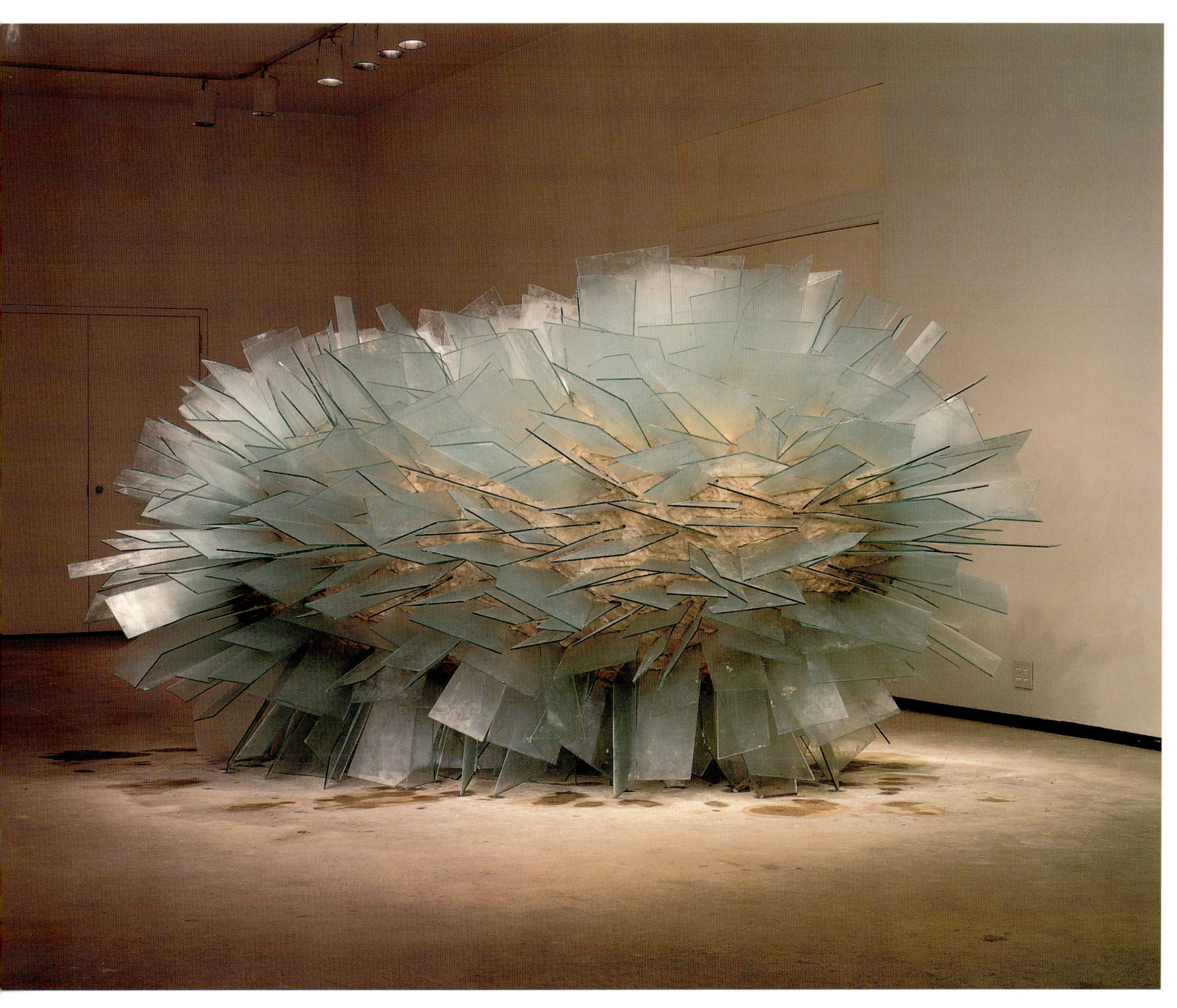

Shimmer; *installation detail, 1993. Glass and clay, h. 69 x 141 inches. Photo: David Lubarski.*

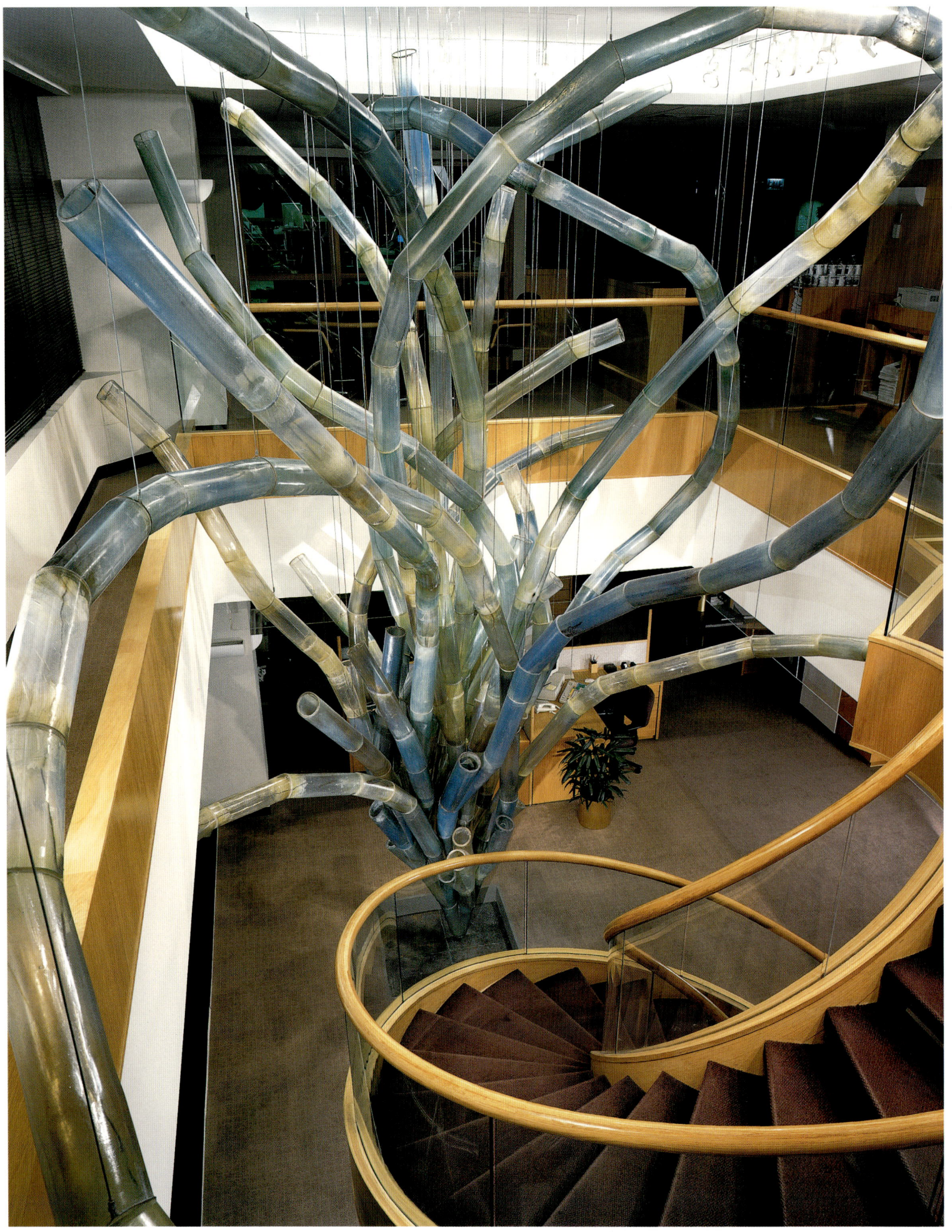

Natural Progression; Commission, Bloomberg LP. Glass, fiberglass, epoxy, and copper wire, h. 23 x 45 x 22 feet. David Lubarski.

TOLEDO, OHIO

Jack Schmidt
(b.1945)

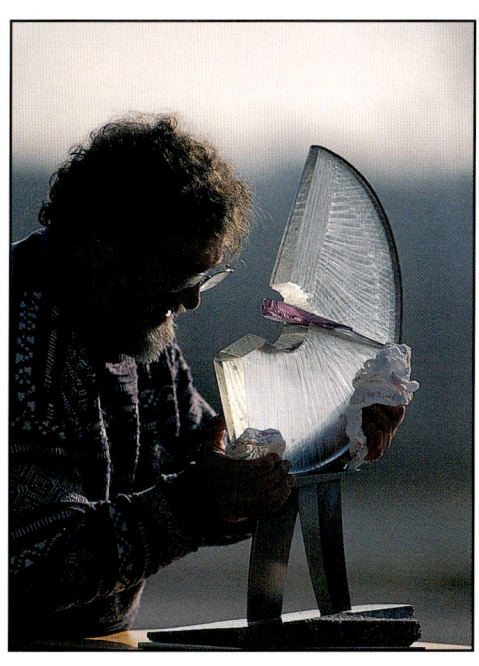

Left:
Bust IIX, Cast cut and polished glass, stainless steel and black granite. h. 24" x 8". Photo: Mark Packo.

Below:
Sarah's Stone (left) and Homage to Drummond (right), 1998. Toledo Botanical Gardens, Ohio. Blown and stacked glass, mild and stainless steel, (left) h. 5 x 3 feet, and (right) h. 3 x 2 feet. Photo: Mark Packo.

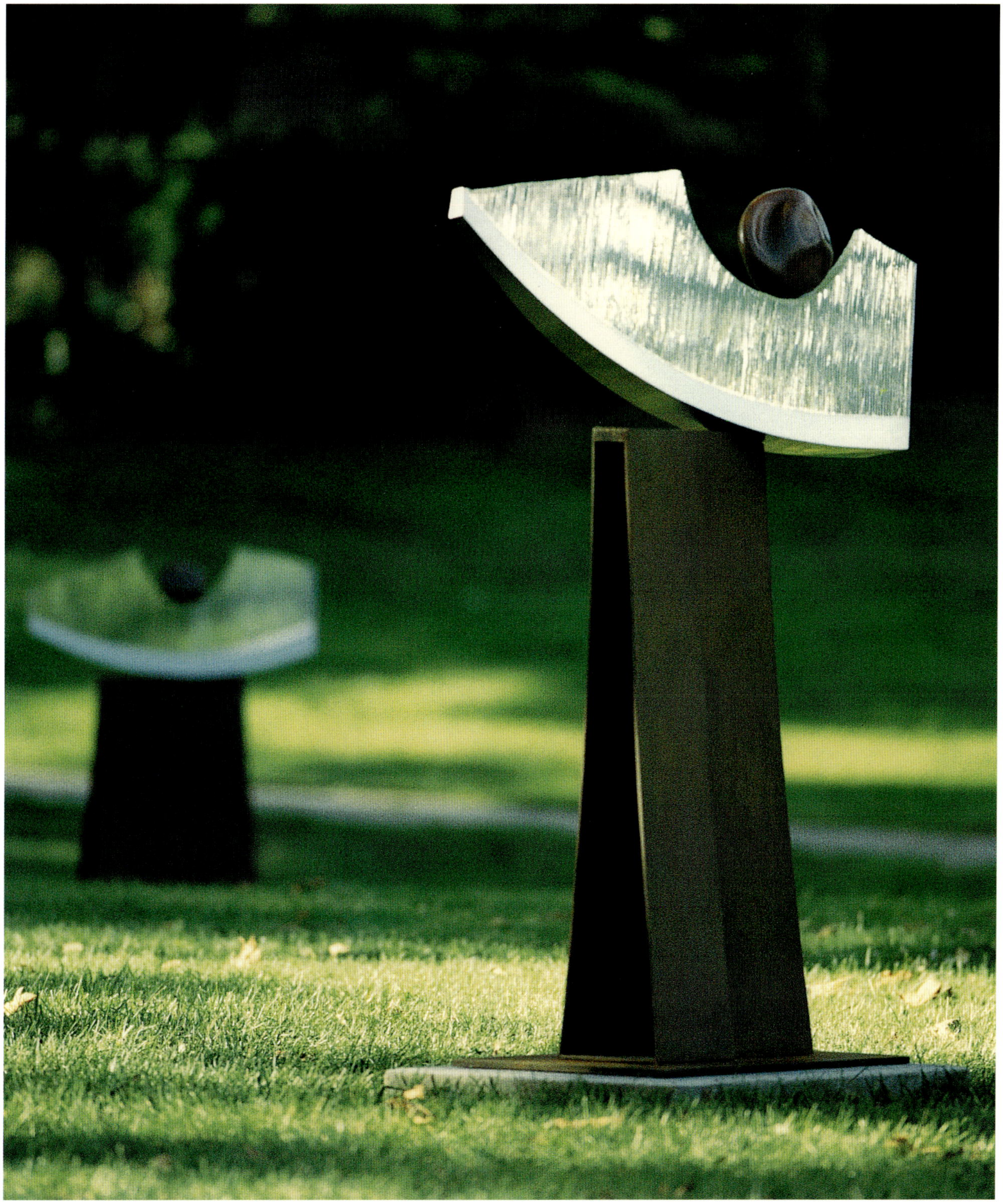

Paul Seide
(b.1949)

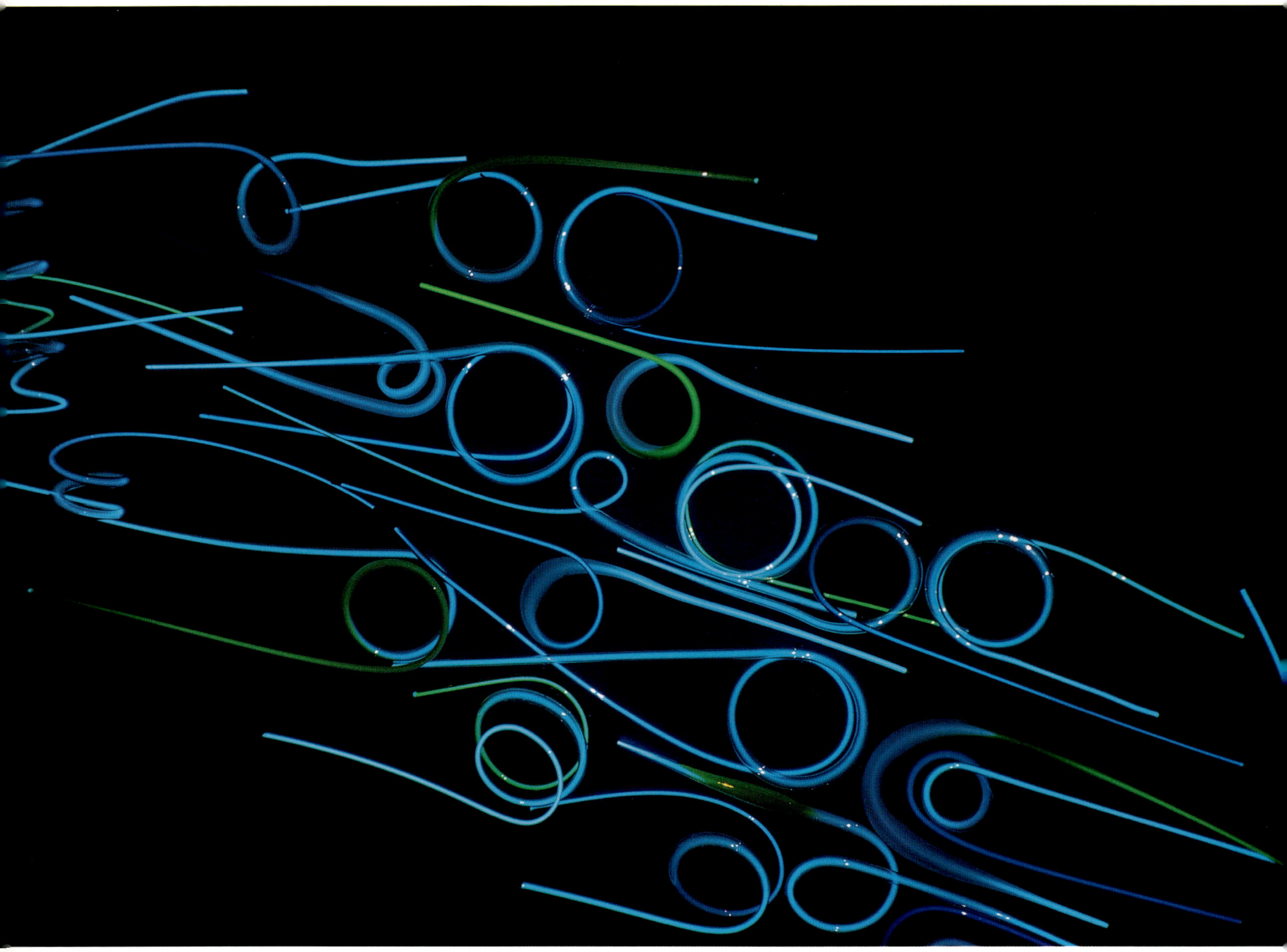

NEW YORK, NEW YORK

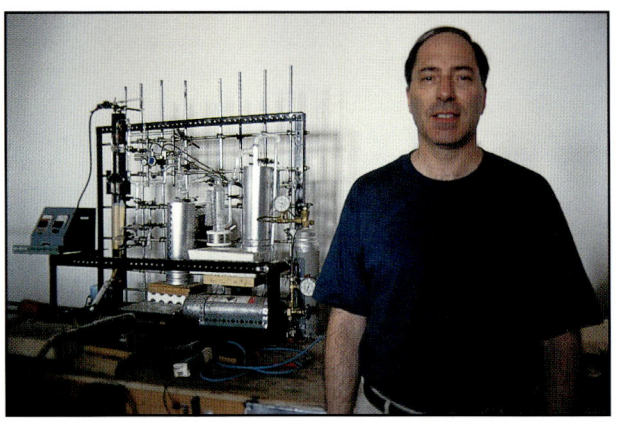

Crystal Calligraphy; Detail of Commission for Swarovski, Wattens, Austria, 1996. Neon, h. 25 x 45 x 2 feet.

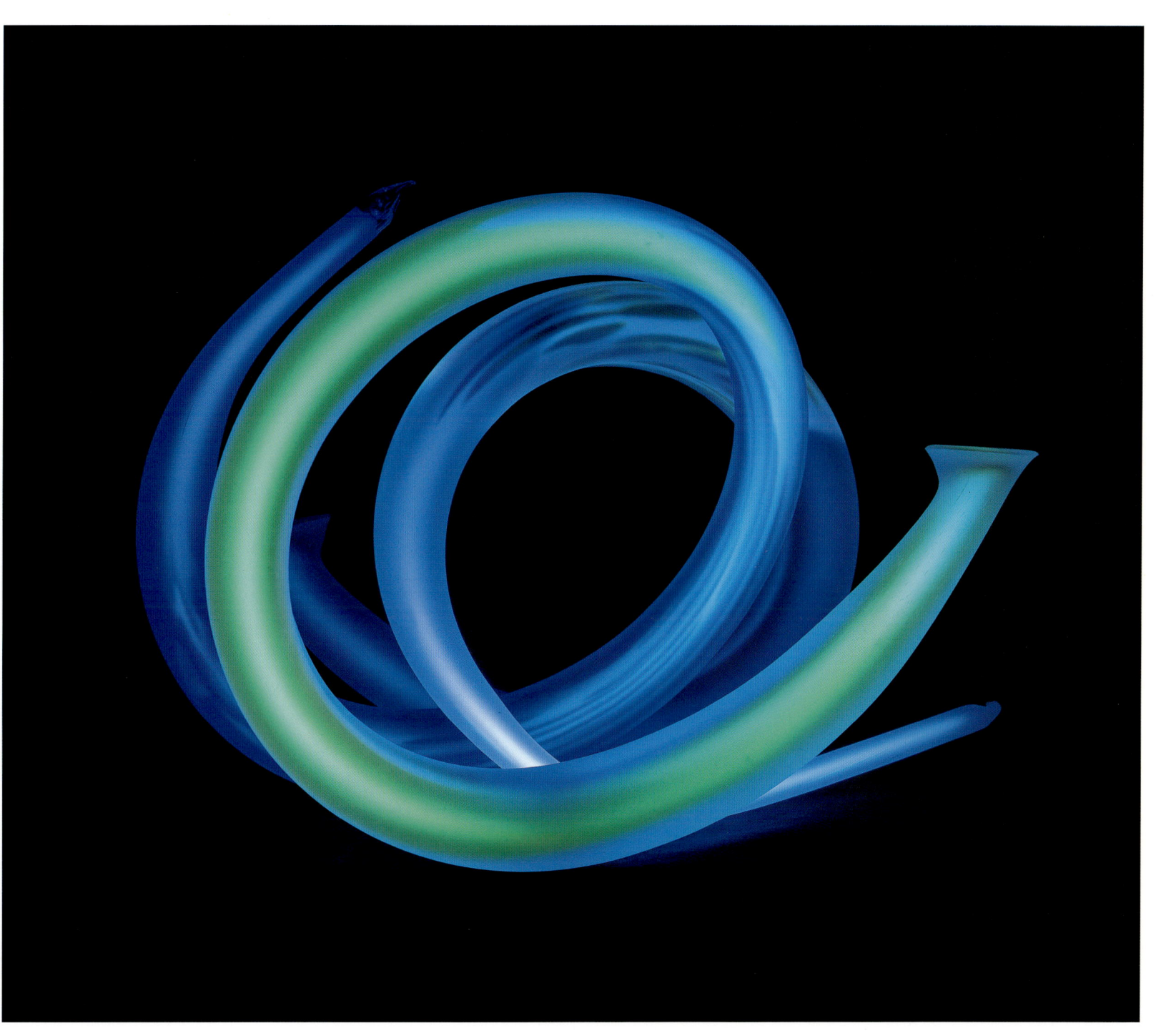

Fractal Nature, 1997. Blown glass, and neon, h. 15 x 20 x 20 inches.
Courtesy Leo Kaplan Modern.

Mary Shaffer
(b.1947)

MARFA, TEXAS

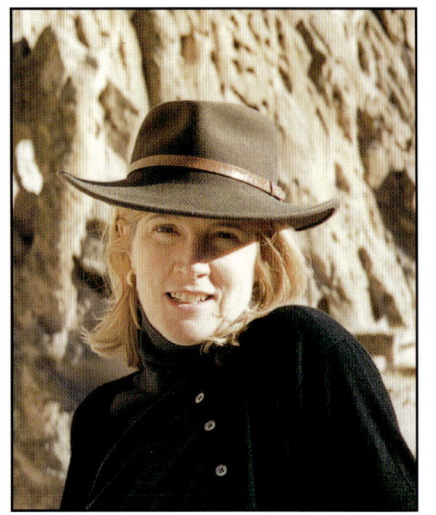
Photo: Ishan Clemente

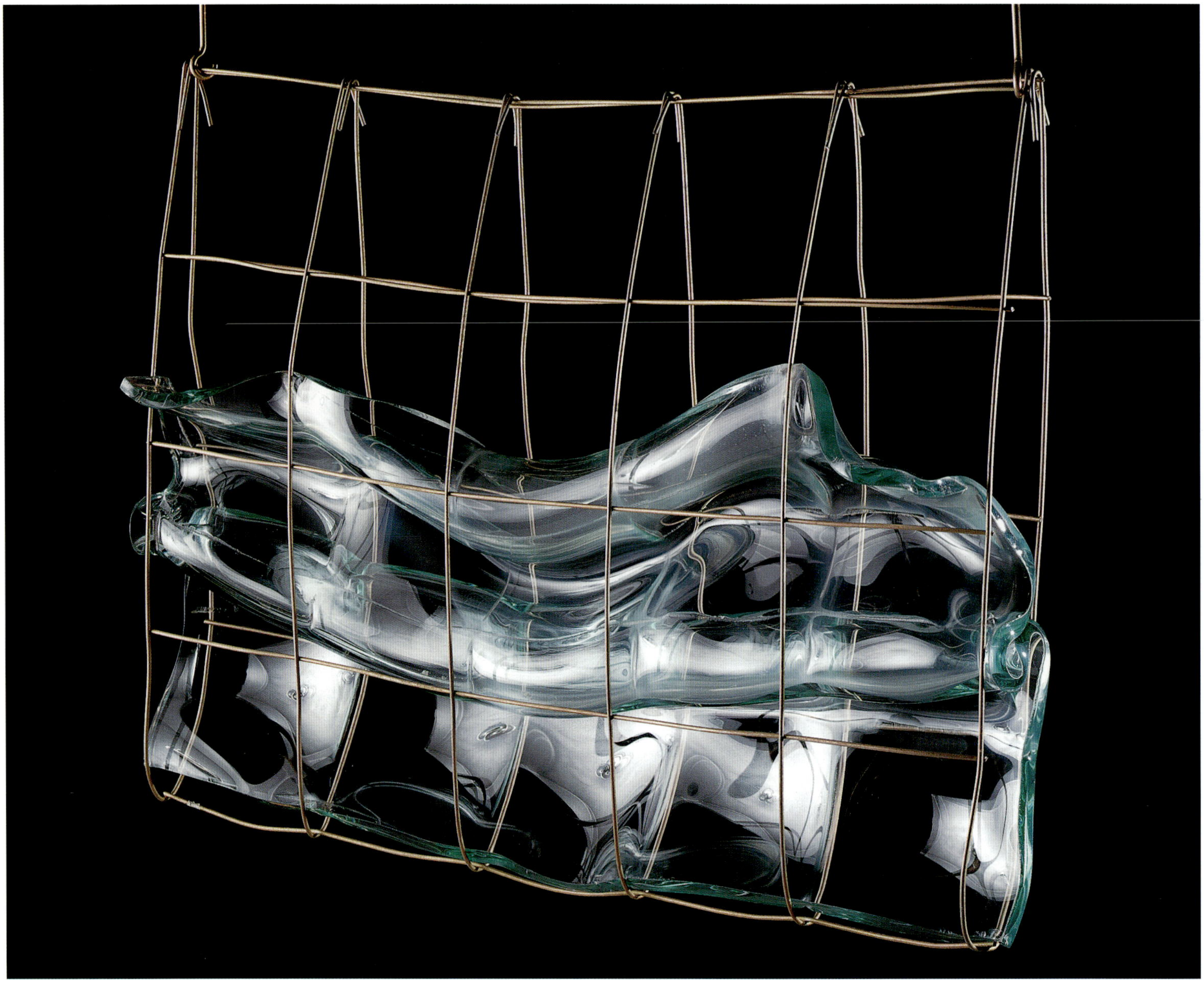

Above:
Hanging Series #10, 1990. Slumped glass and wire, h. 24 x 30 x 8 inches. Courtesy Habatat Galleries. Photo: Doug Schaible.

Opposite:
Center Cube, 1992. Slumped glass, and bronze, (together) h. 32x12x33 inches. Courtesy Habatat Galleries. Photo: Doug Schaible.

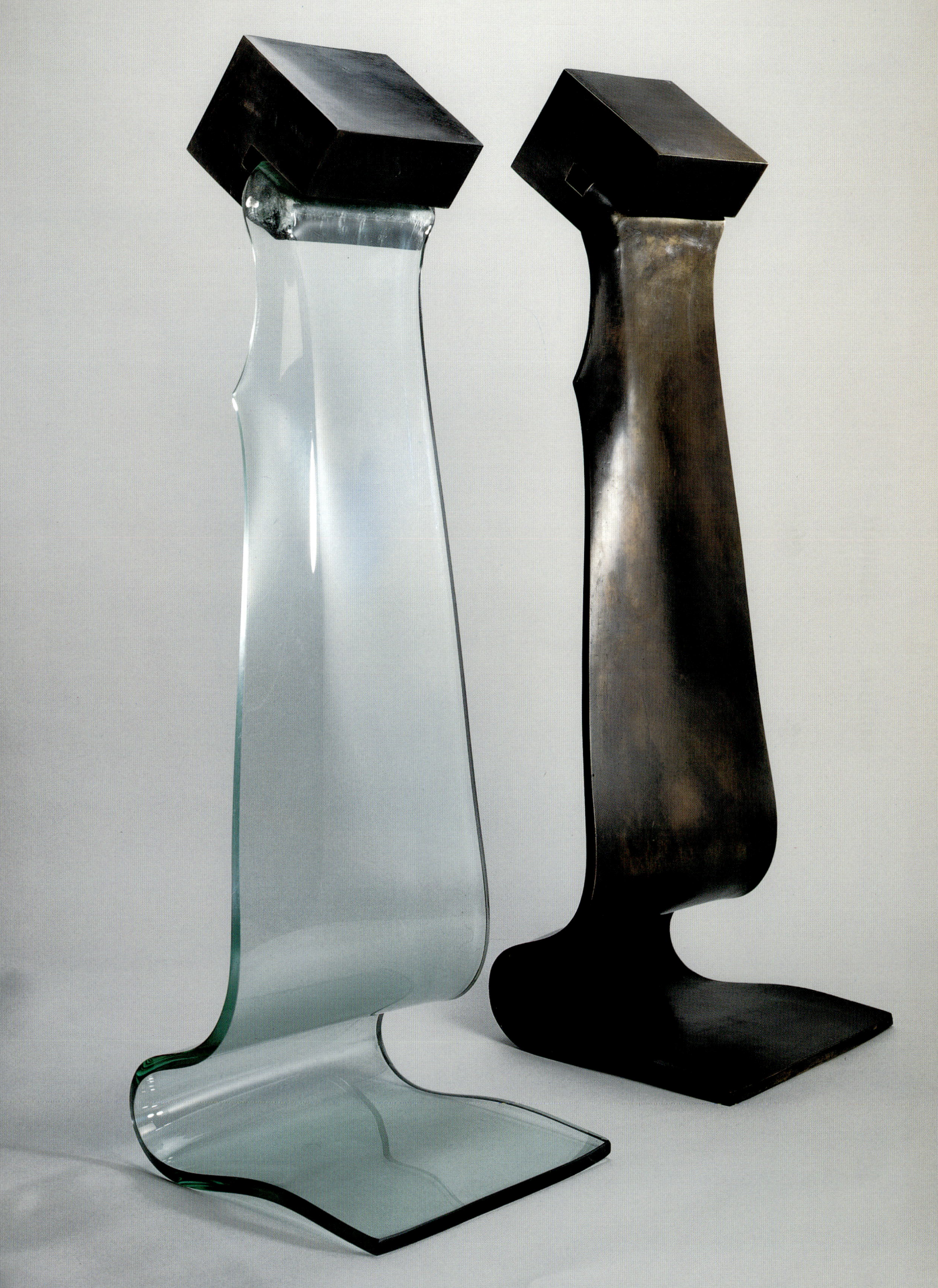

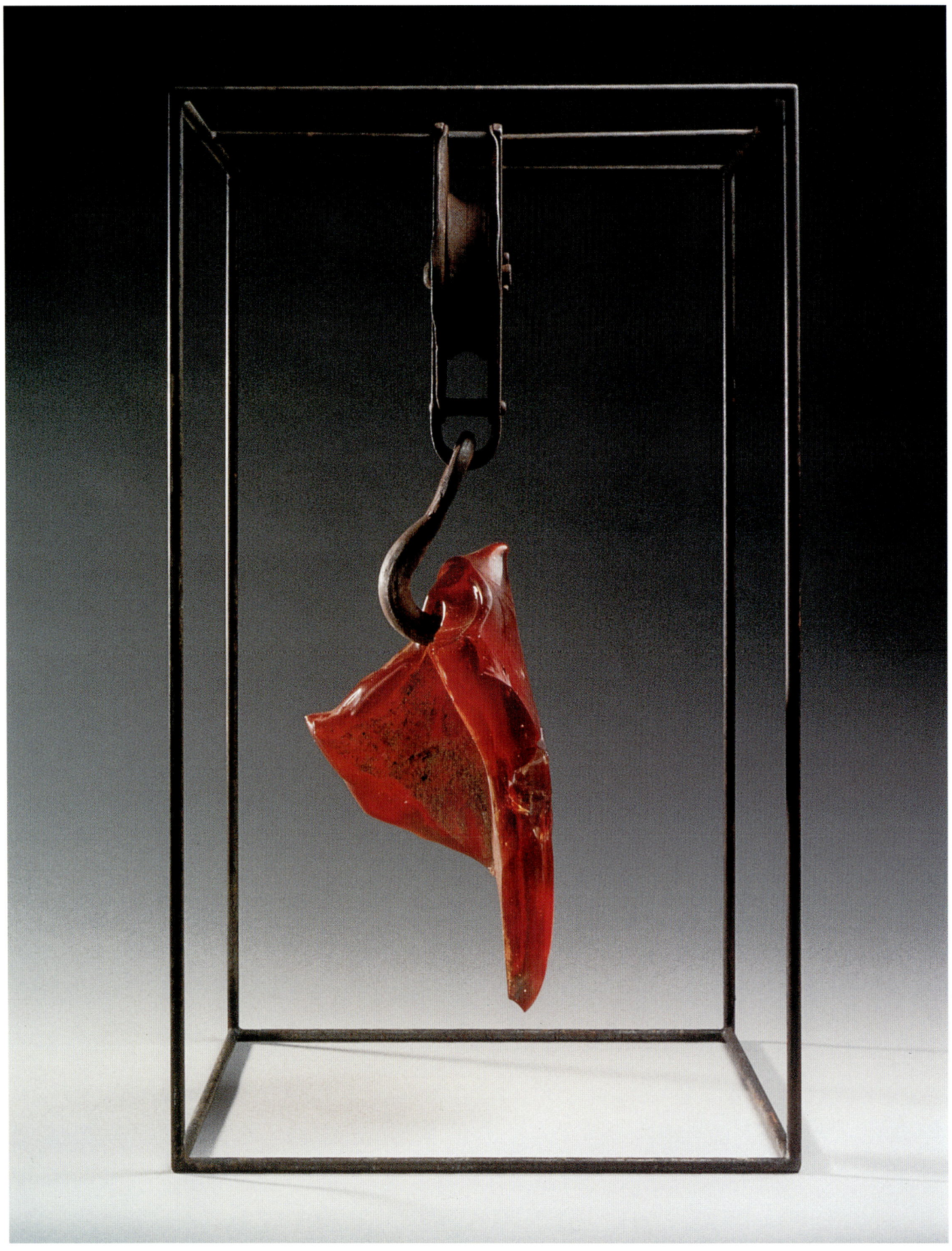

Red Square, 1999. Slumped glass, and steel, h. 28 x 16 x 16 inches. Courtesy Heller Gallery.

NEW YORK, NEW YORK

Maura Sheehan
(b. 1955)

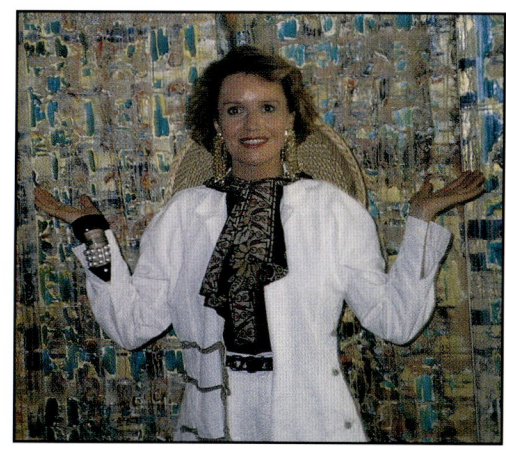

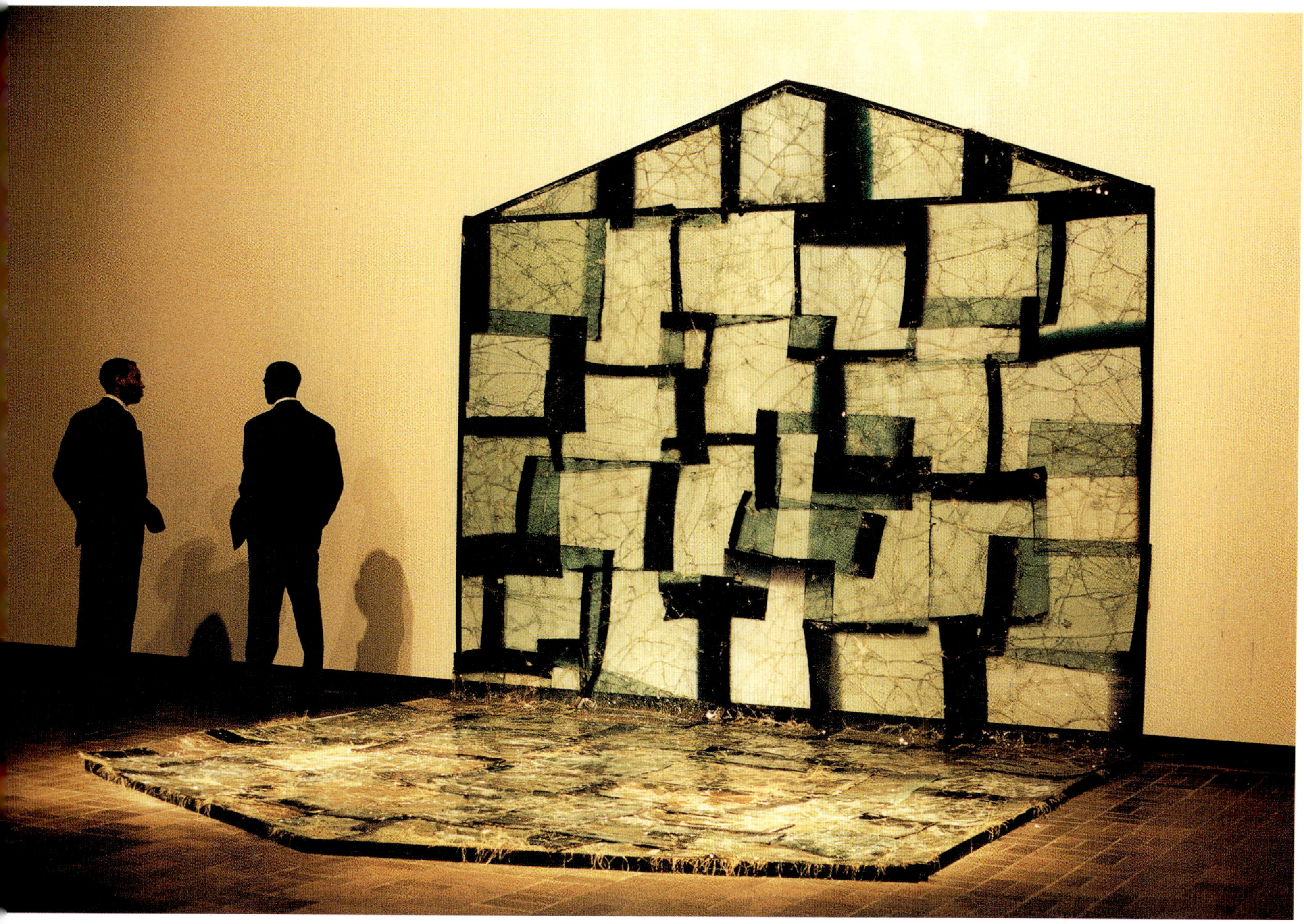

***Ice House; Installation, Neuberger Museum**, Purchase, New York, 1998. Automobile windshields nailed to the wall, and grass and glass on the floor, h. 12 x 12 feet.*

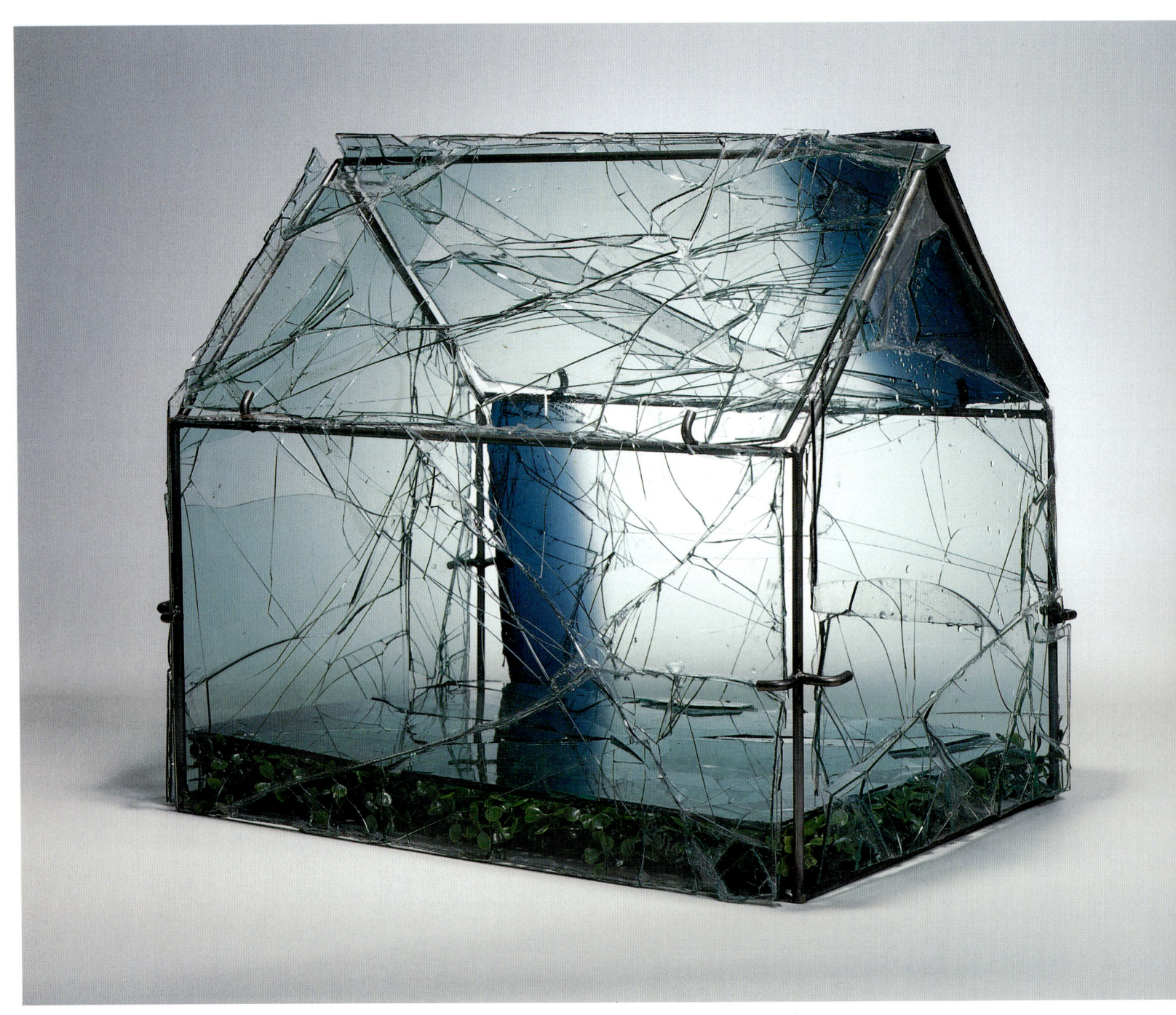

The Glass House, 1998. Laminated glass with welded steel structure, h. 18 x 24 x 16 inches.

IRELAND

Ruth Shortt
(b.1972)

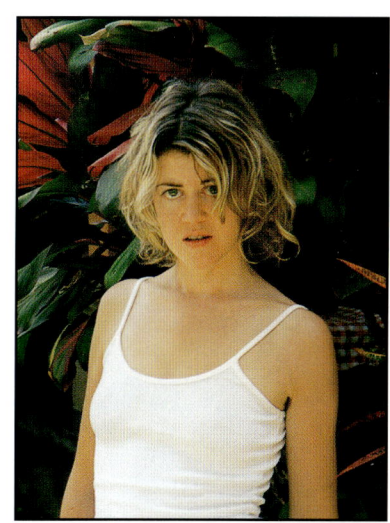

Fluids, 1996. Glass, resin, and steel, h. 60 x 28 inches.

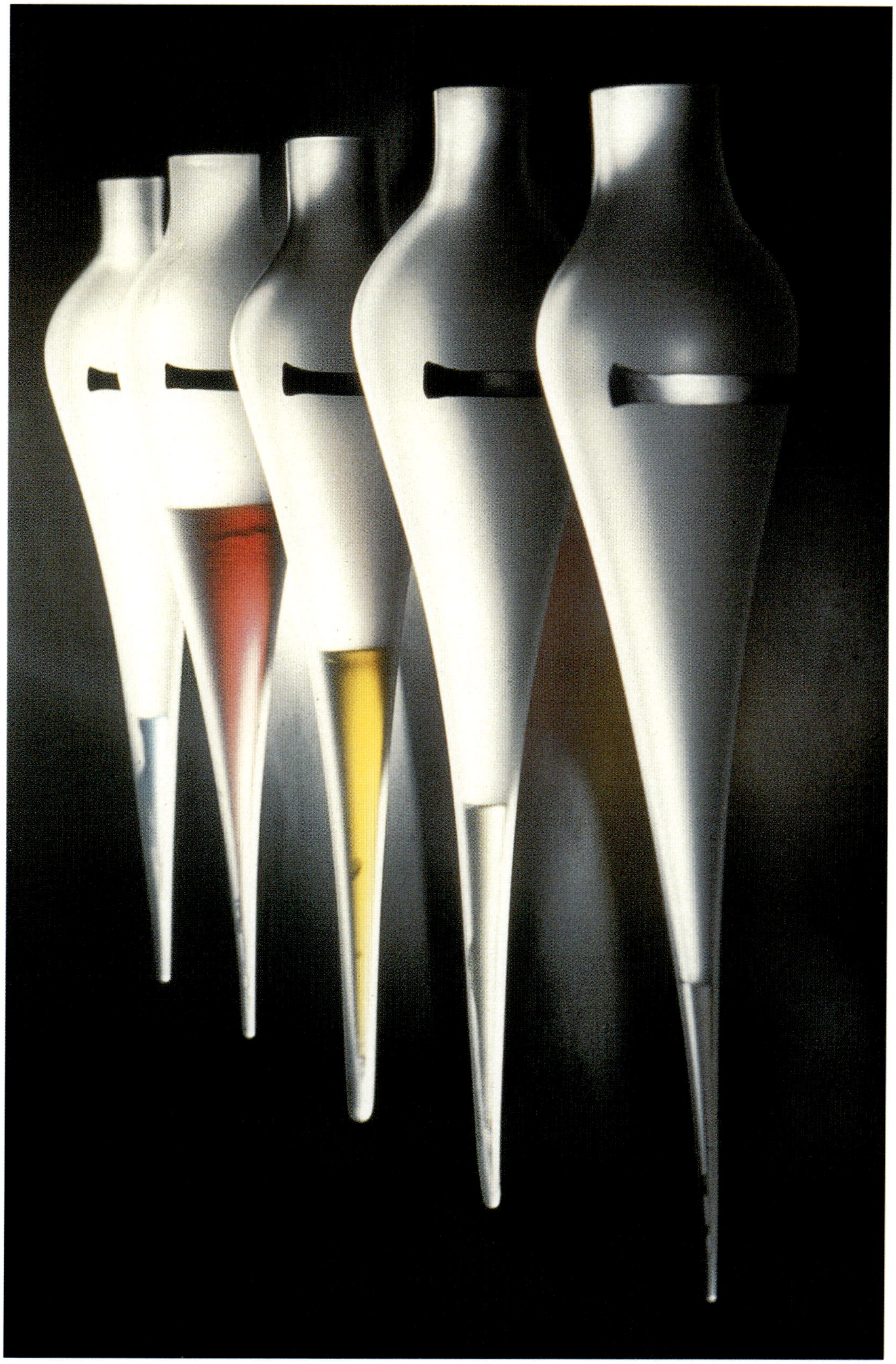

Josh Simpson
(b.1955)

SHELBURNE, MASSACHUSETTS

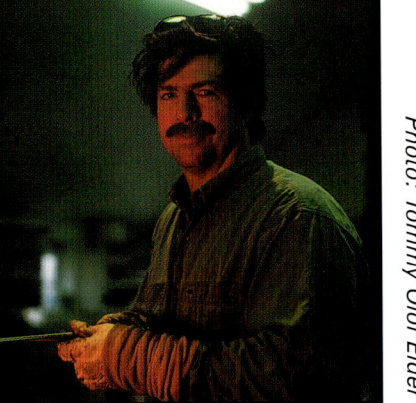

Photo: Tommy Olof Elder

Many Megas, 1999, Multi-layered silver reactive glass with preformed inclusions, (largest) h. 10 inches. Photo: Tommy Olof Elder.

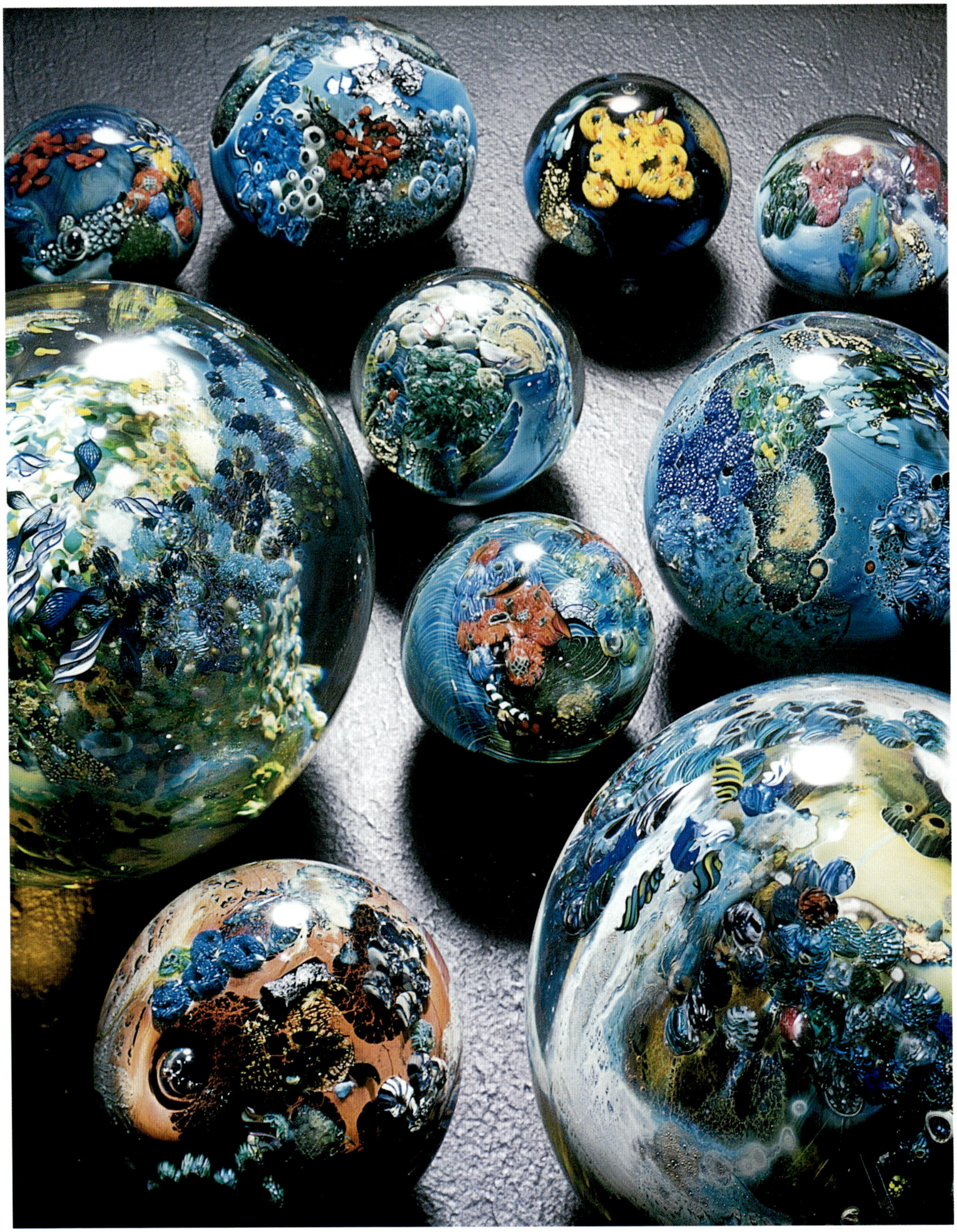

NEW YORK, NEW YORK

Kiki Smith
(b. 1954)

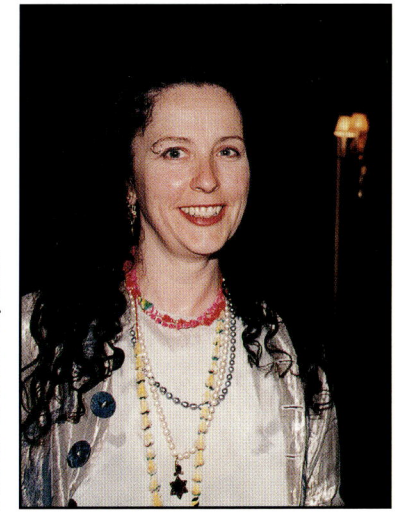
Photo: Jeanne Wyshak

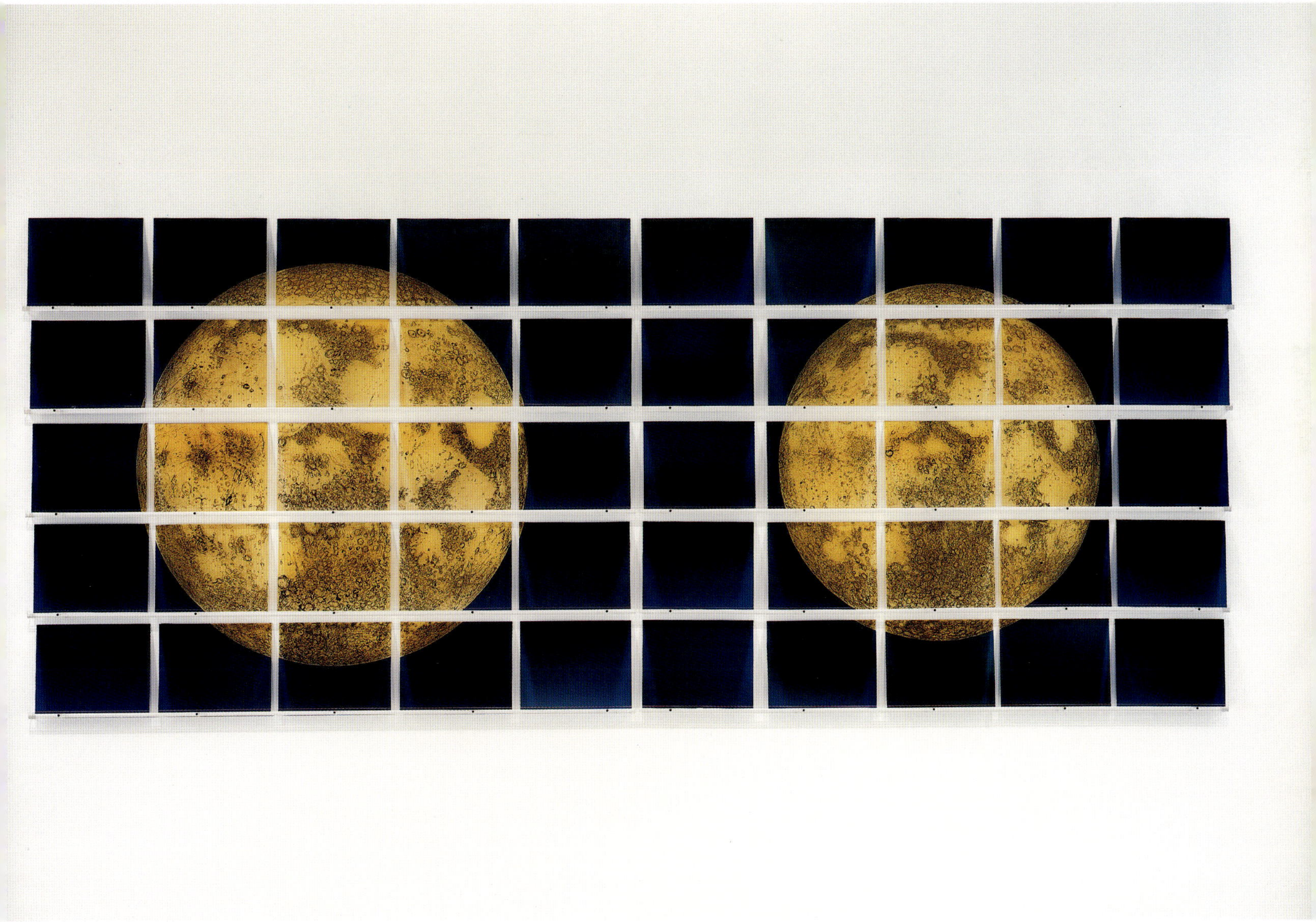

Yellow Moon, 1998. Lead paint on glass, 50 units, each h. 12 x 15 inches.
Courtesy PaceWildenstein, New York. Photo: Ellen Page Wilson. ©Kiki Smith

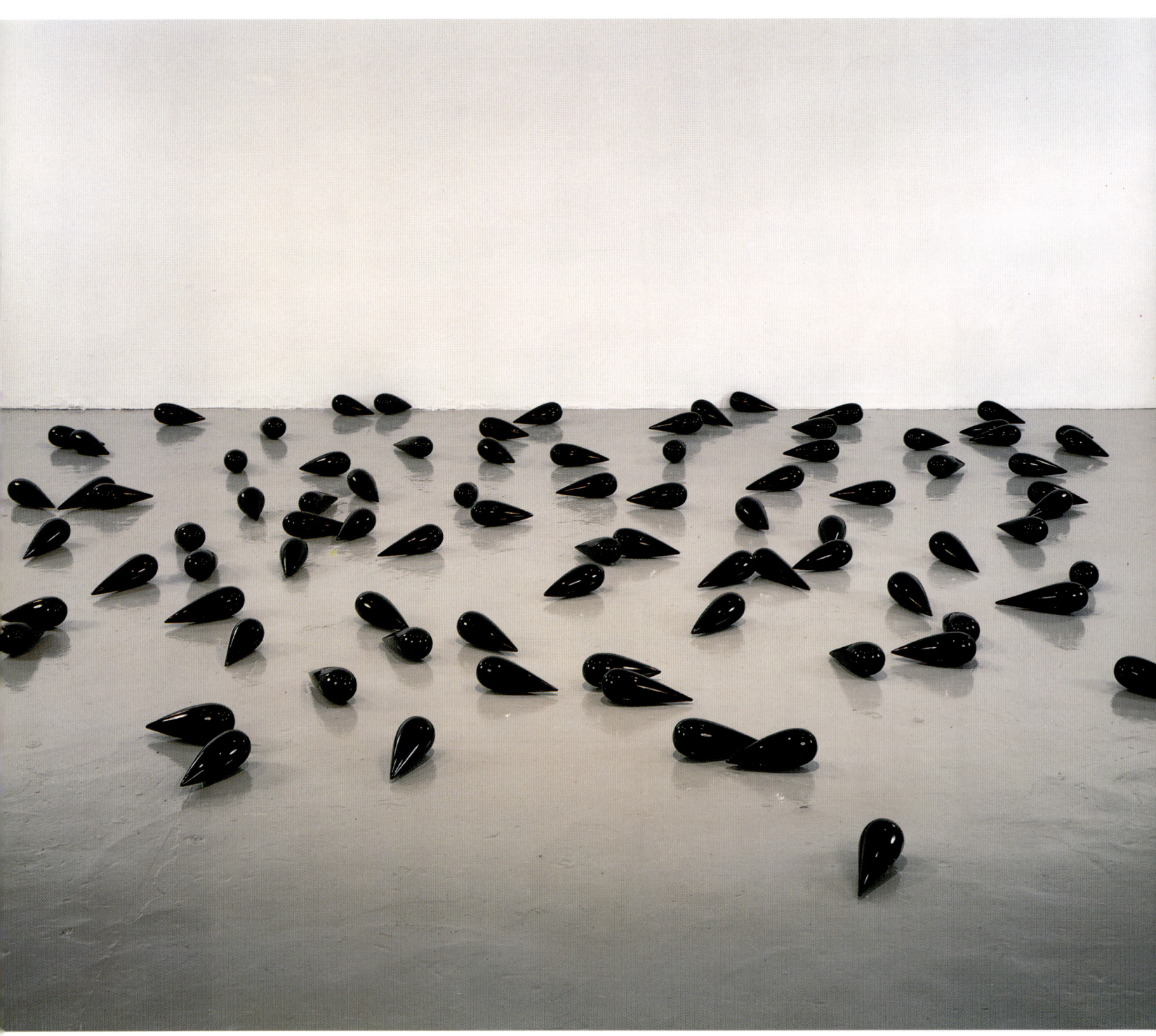

Black Rain, 1998. Glass, 85 units, each h. 7 x 2.5 x 2.5 to h. 10 x 4 x 4 inches. Courtesy PaceWildenstein, New York. Photo: Ellen Page Wilson. ©Kiki Smith

BROOKLYN, NEW YORK

Evan Snyderman
(b.1970)

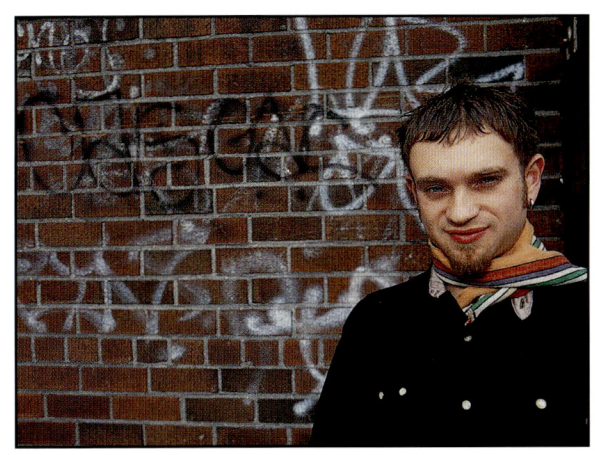

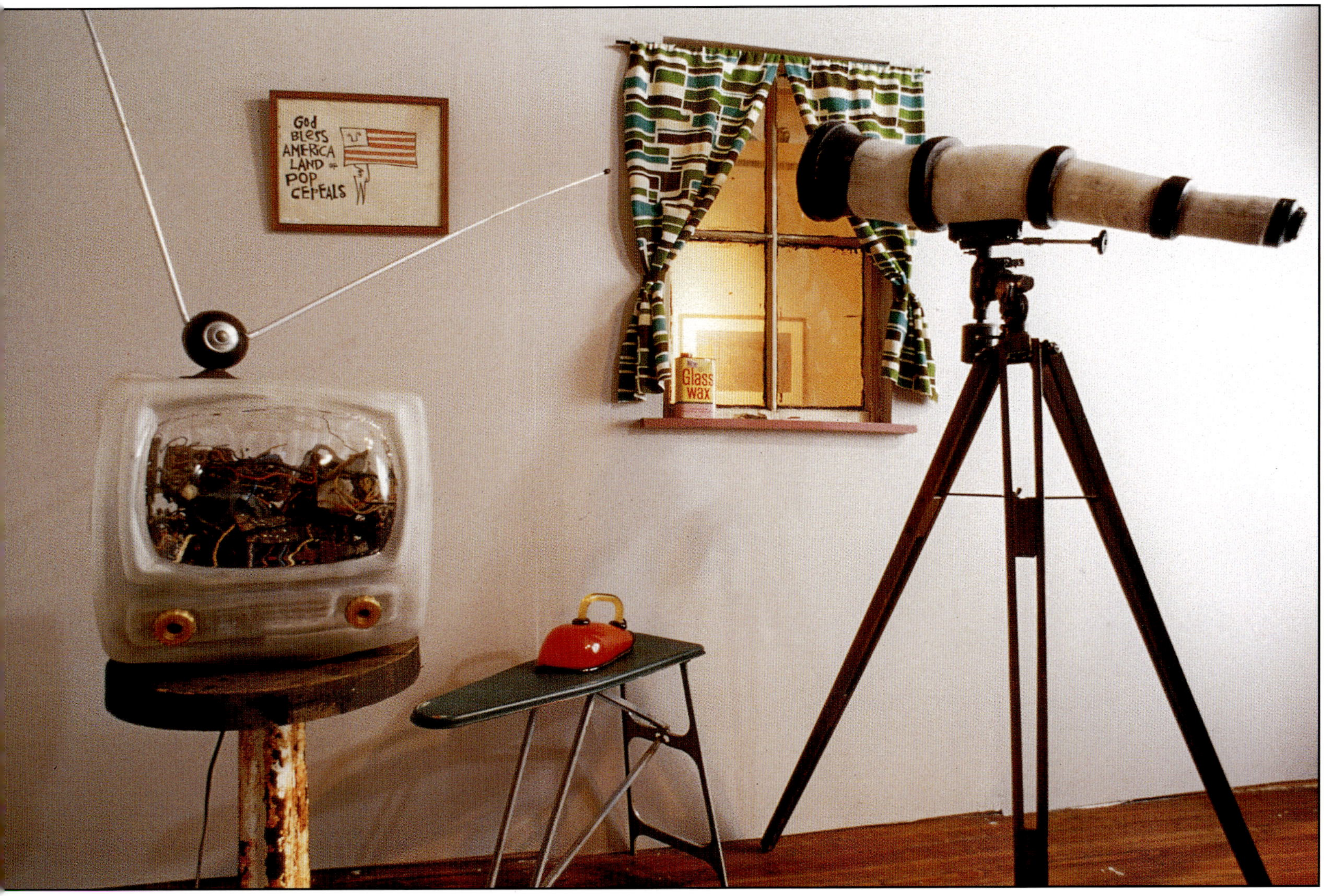

Room With A Skew; Installation *(Interior View), Rosenfeld Gallery, Philadelphia, 1996. Glass and mixed media, h. 12 x 12 feet.*

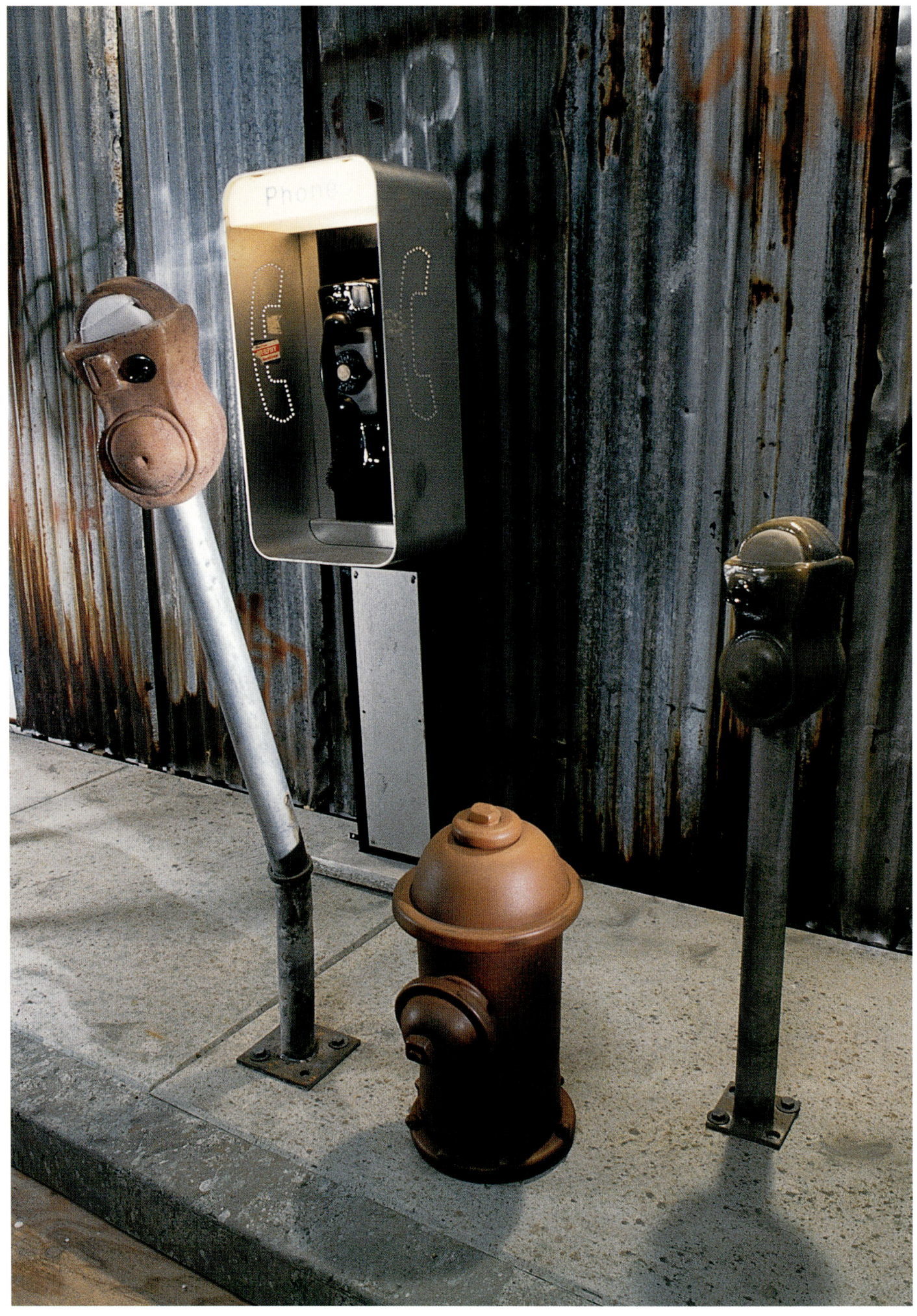

Street; Installation Detail, *Rosenfeld Gallery, 1998-99.*
Glass and mixed media, h. 10 x 25 x 4 feet.

ROME, ITALY

Vanessa Somers
(b.1940)

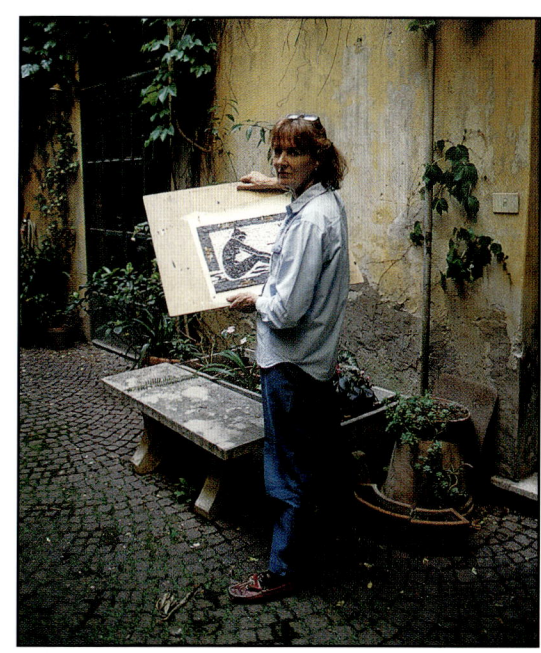

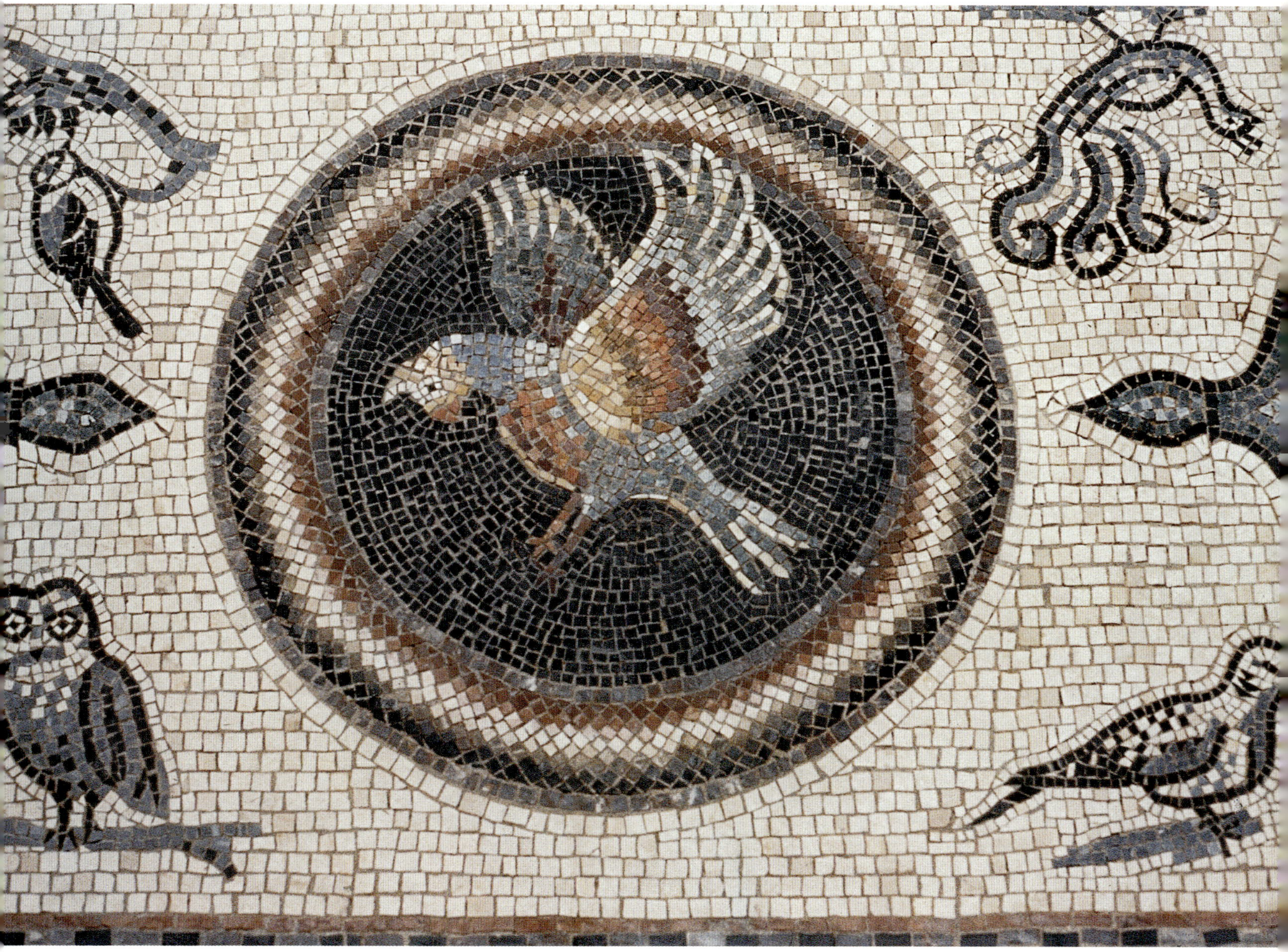

7 Virtues, *(detail) 1995. Glass and marble mosaic, h. 27 x 47 inches.*

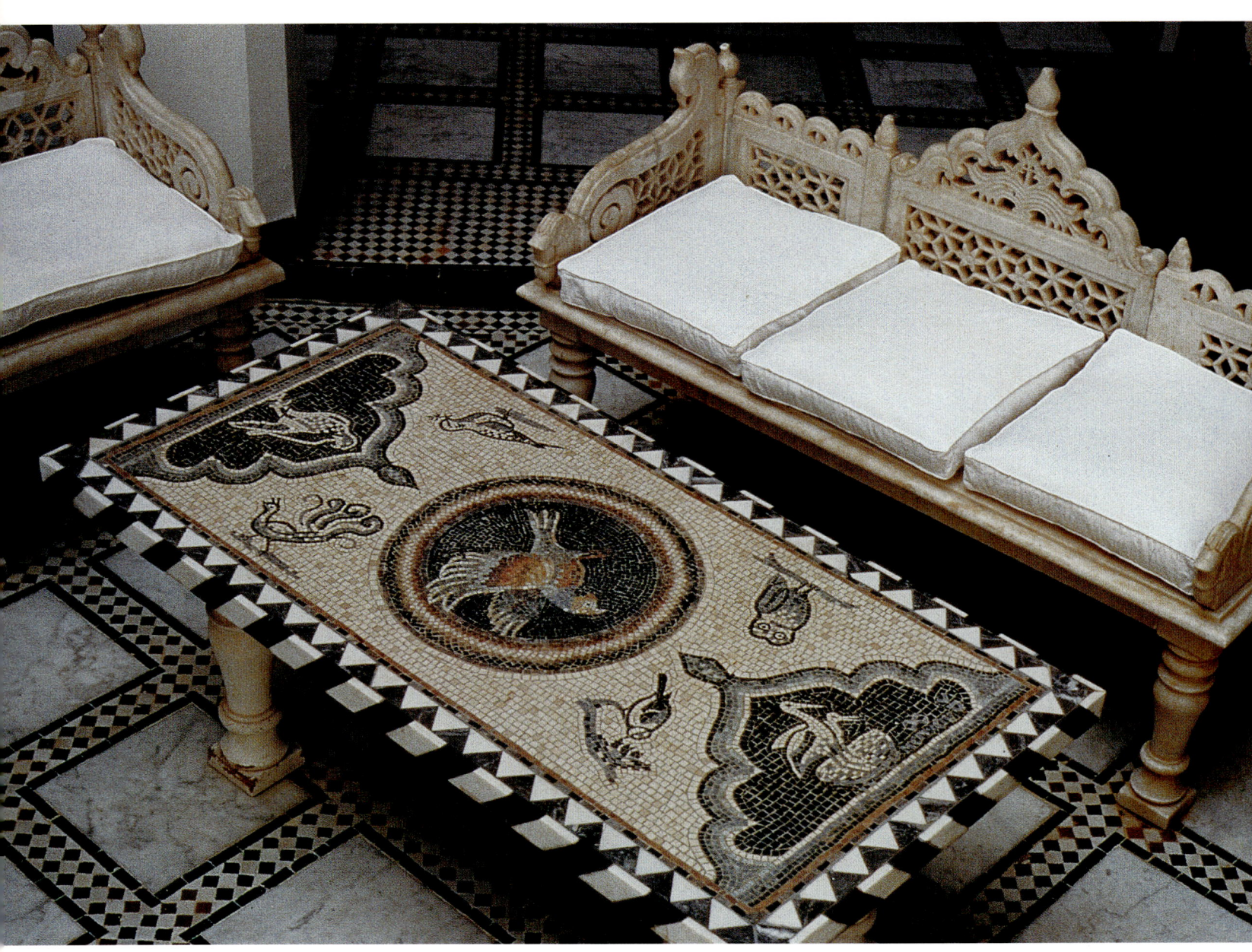

7 Virtues, 1995. Glass and marble mosaic, h. 27 x 47 inches.

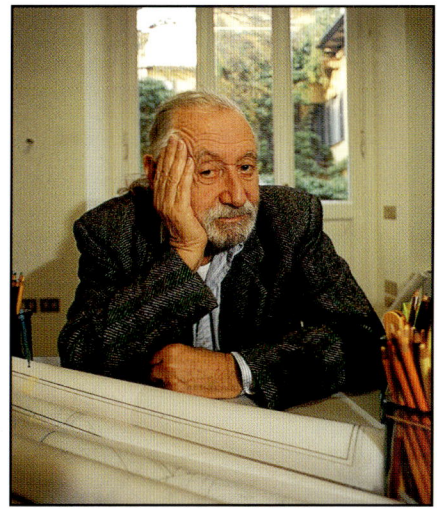

MILAN, ITALY

Ettore Sottsass
(b. 1917)

Photo: Fancesco Barasciutti

Yemen, 1994. Blown glass, h. 10 x 12 inches.
Courtesy Venini, Murano, Italy.

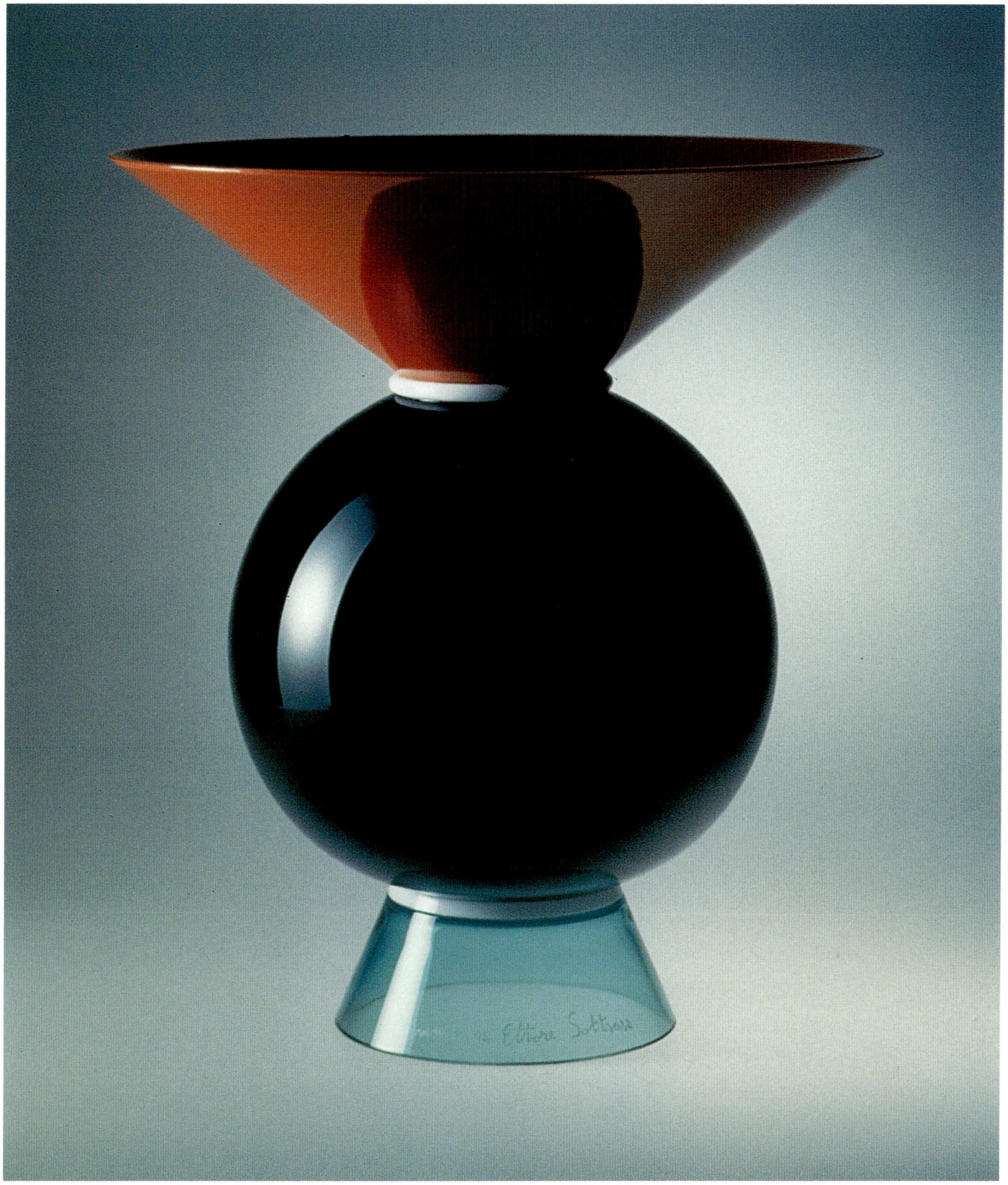

ETTORE SOTTSASS

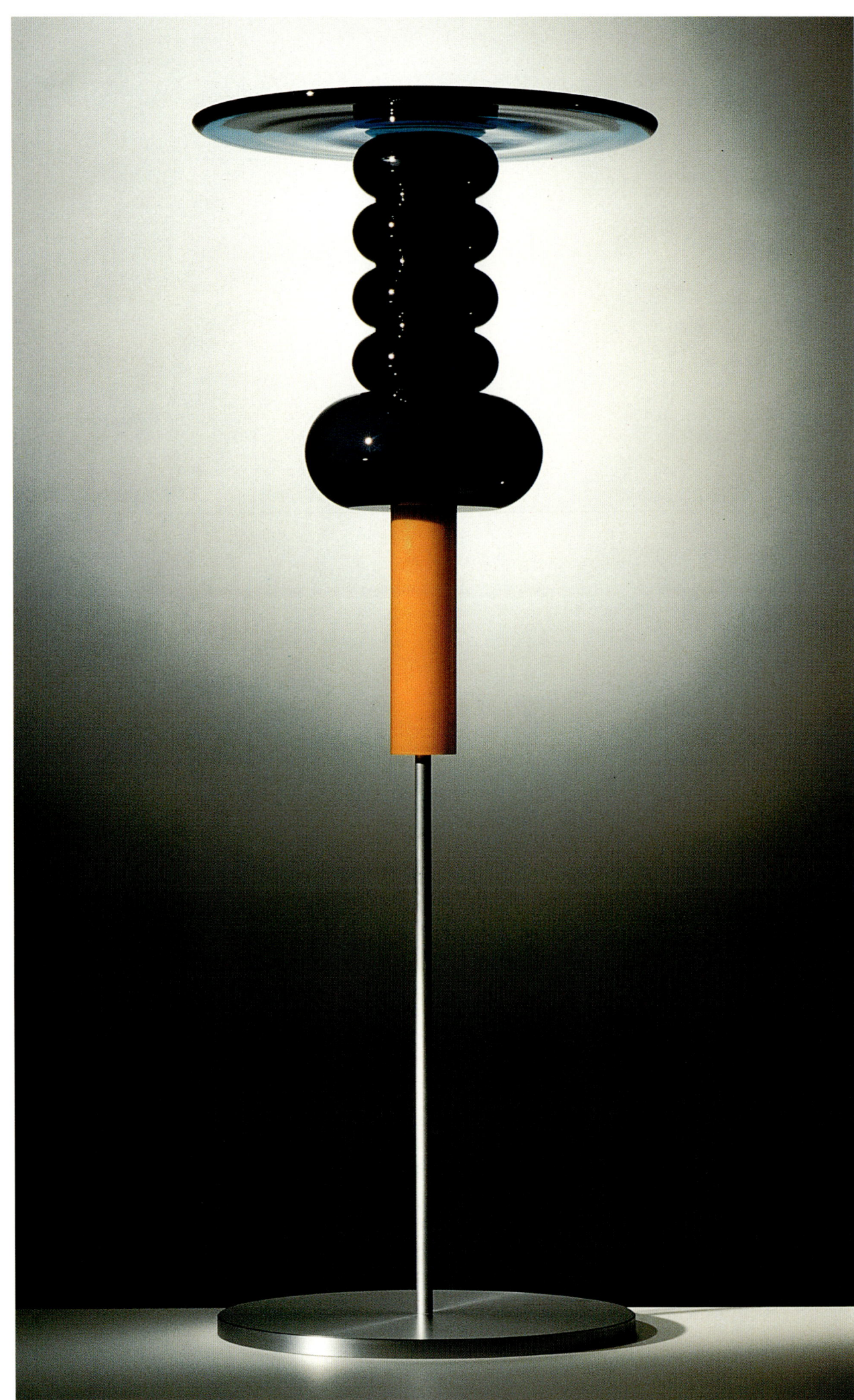

Ko Thod; Capricci Series, 1998. Glass sculpture on metal base, h. 34 inches. Courtesy Galleria Marina Barovier, Venice, Italy.

Marianne Spottswood
(b. 1938)
PORTSMOUTH, RHODE ISLAND

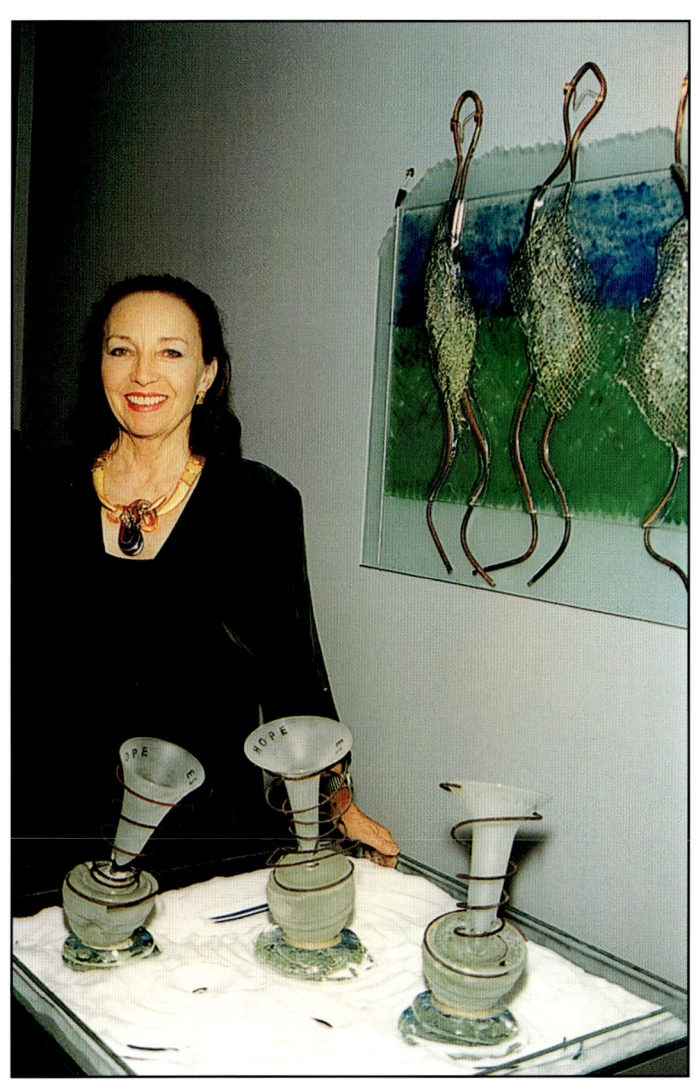

Left:
Necklace; Galathea, (top to bottom) Rhinemaidens, and Hope Springs Eternal.

Below:
Progression, 1999. Sand-cast glass, copper mesh, and nails, h. 7 x 20 x 8 inches. Courtesy LuniVerre, Paris, France.

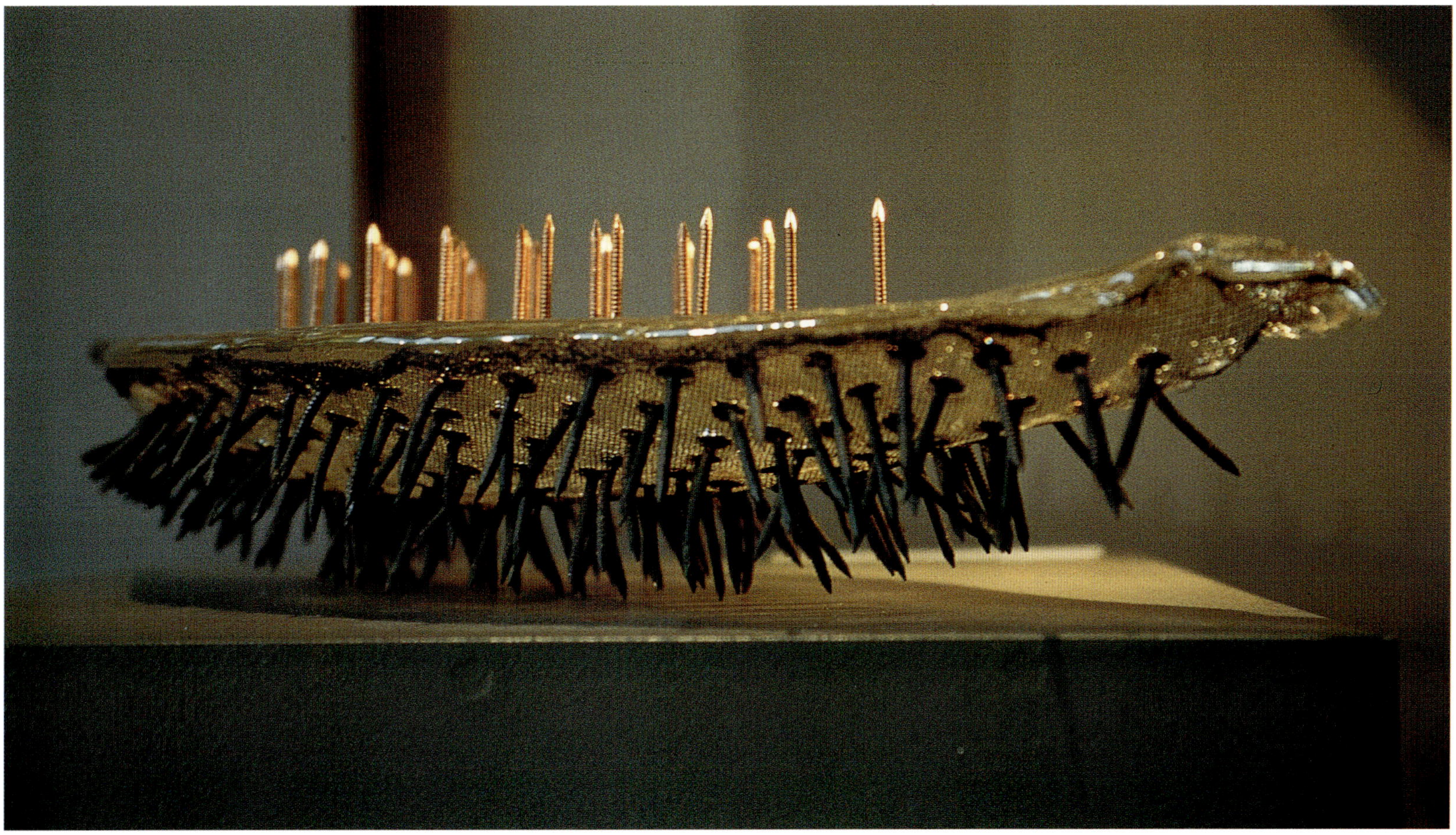

Sam Stang
(b. 1959)

AUGUSTA, MISSOURI

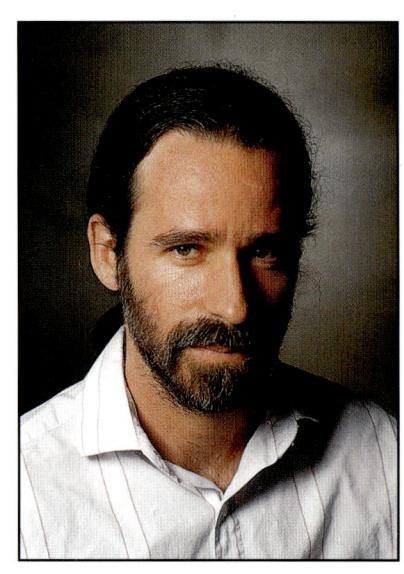

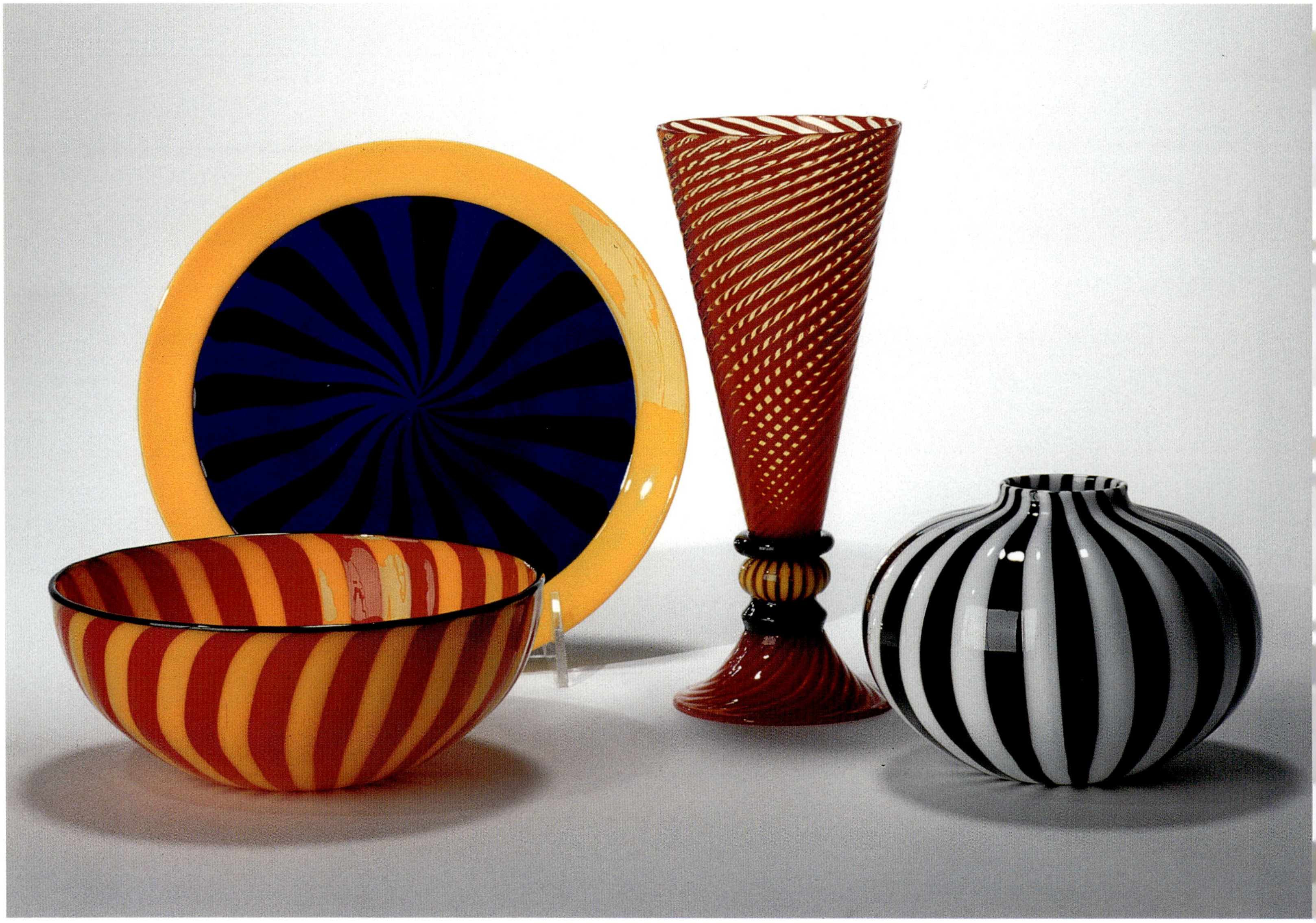

Moretti; Cane Bowl, Plate, Chalice, and Vase, 1995. Blown glass; tallest, h. 8.5 inches. Photo: David Kingsbury.

MANTUA, NEW JERSEY

Paul Stankard
(b. 1943)

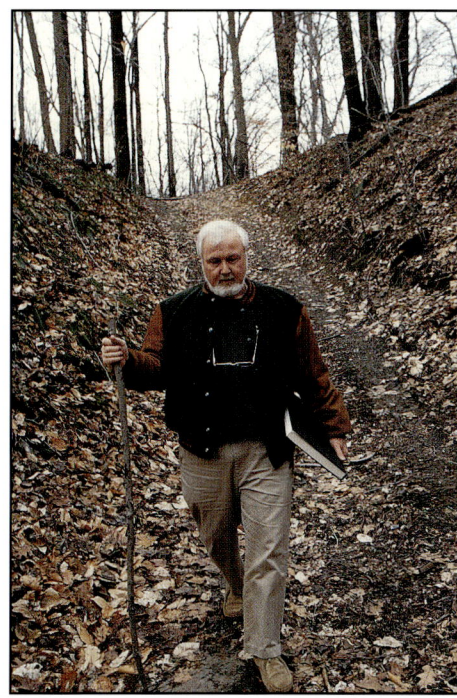

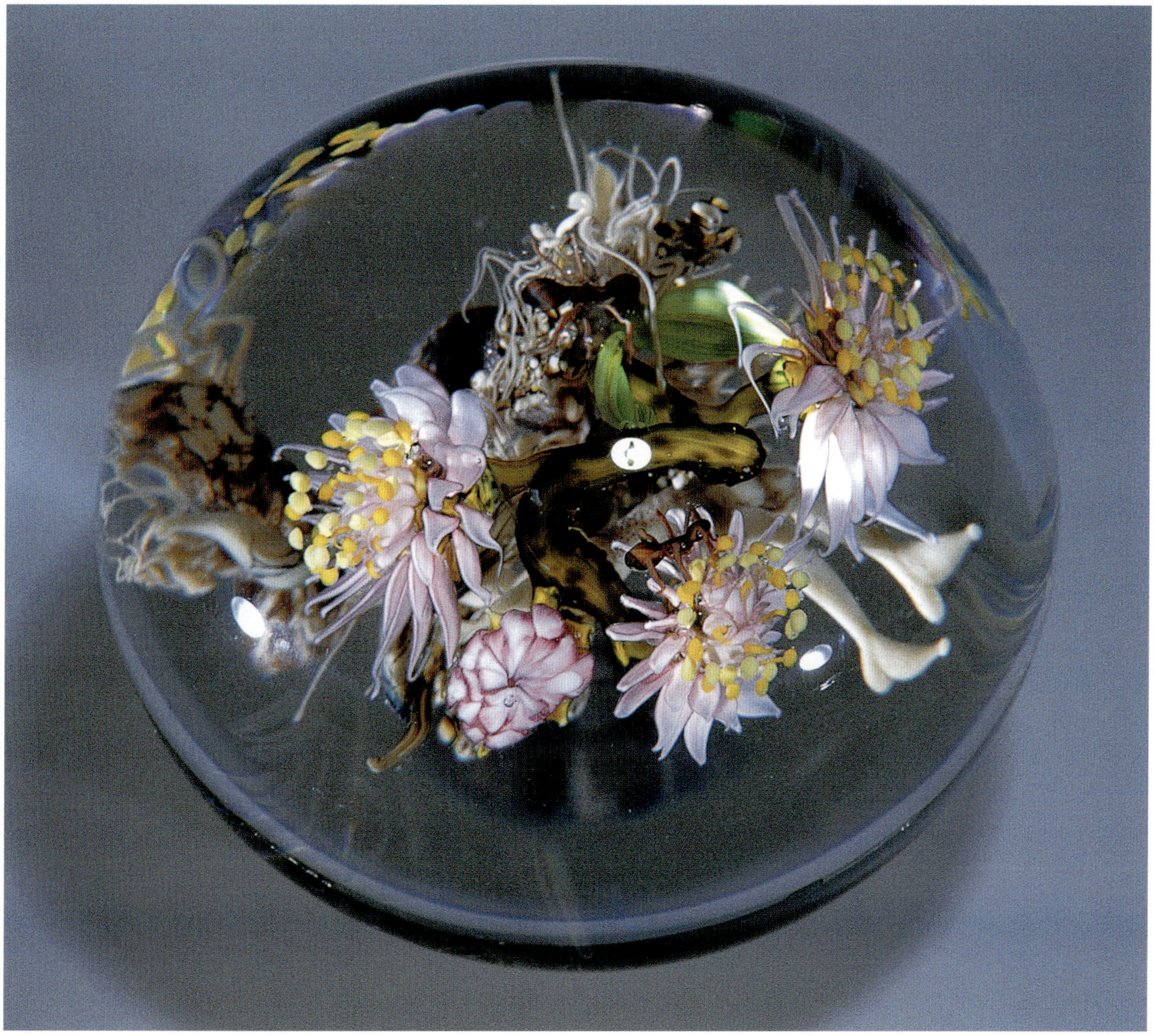

Pineland Pickerel Weed, 1998.
Flameworked glass, h. 3.25 inches.

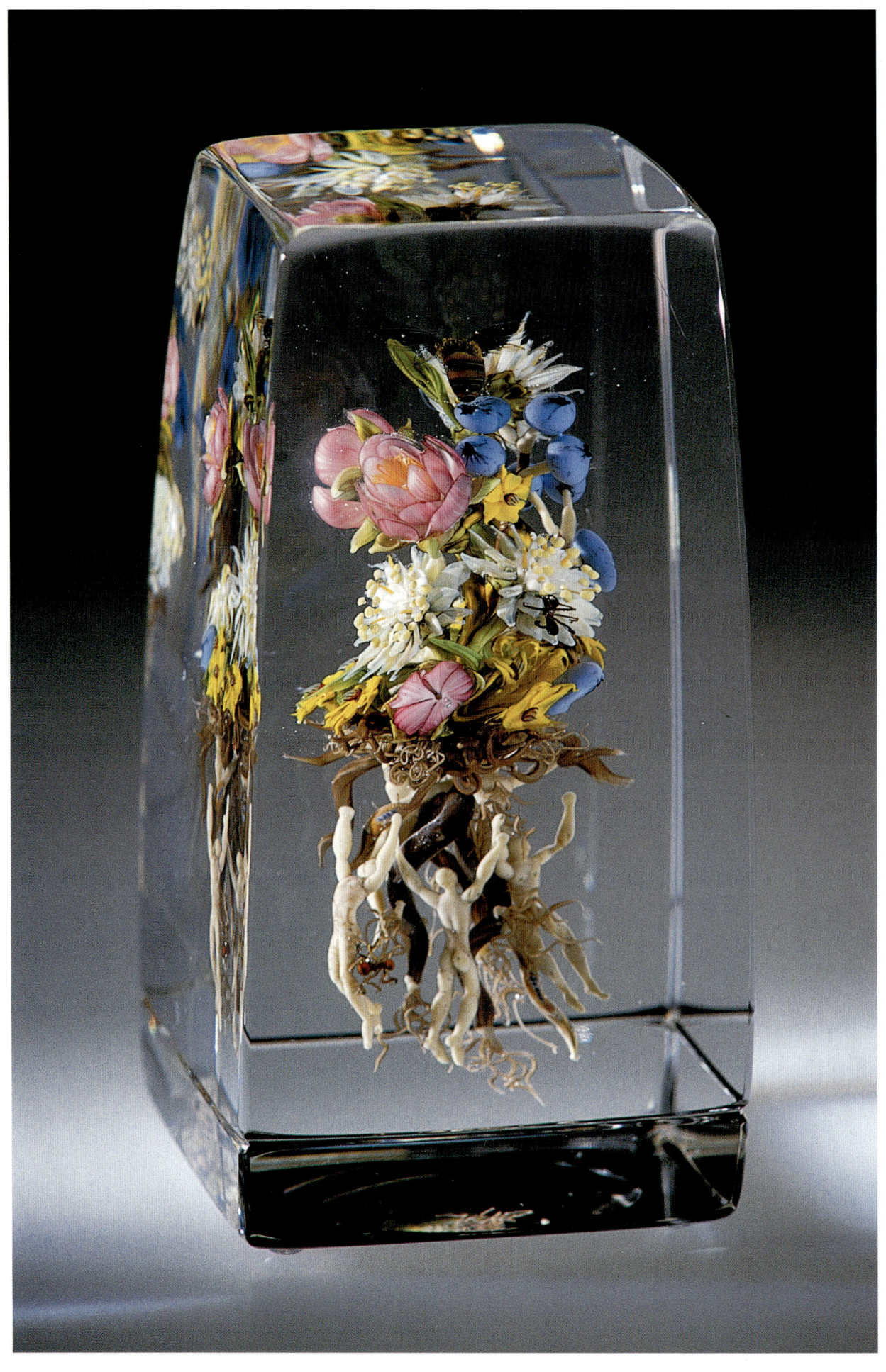

Tea Roses Bouquet With Ants; Botanical, *1998.*
Flameworked glass, h. 5 x 3 inches.

ESCONDIDO, CALIFORNIA

Therman Statom
(b.1953)

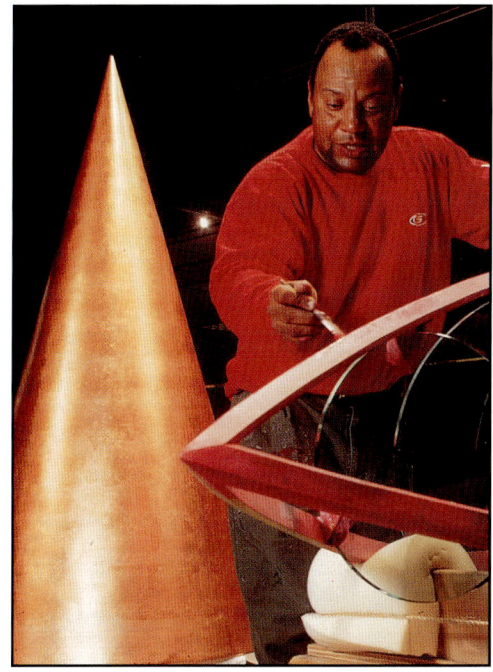

Left:
Corning Installation, New York, 1999.

Below left:
Botanica; Color Study, 1999. Glass and mixed media, h. 69 x 46 x 7 inches. Courtesy Leo Kaplan Modern.

Below right:
Two Histories; Sky, 1999. Glass and mixed media, h. 80 x 37 x 11 inches.

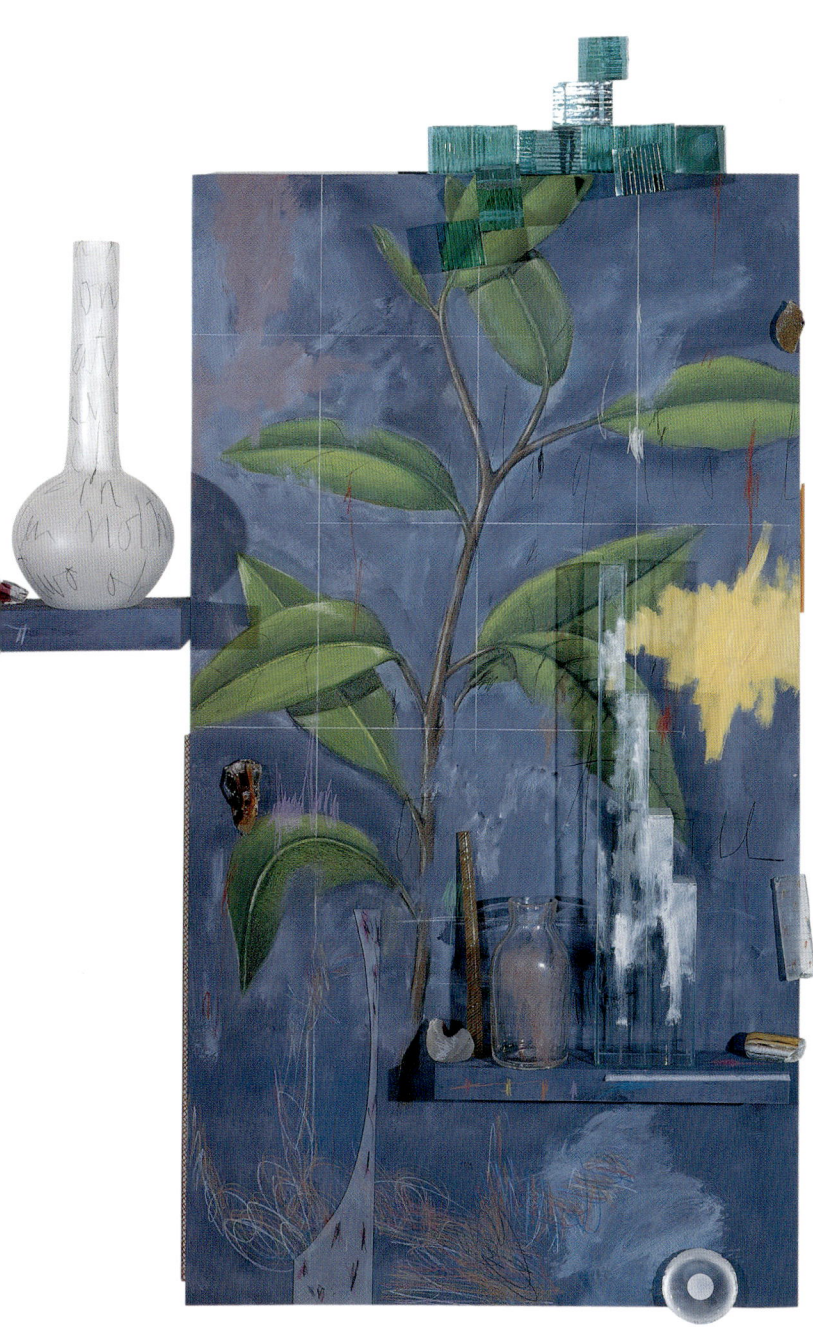

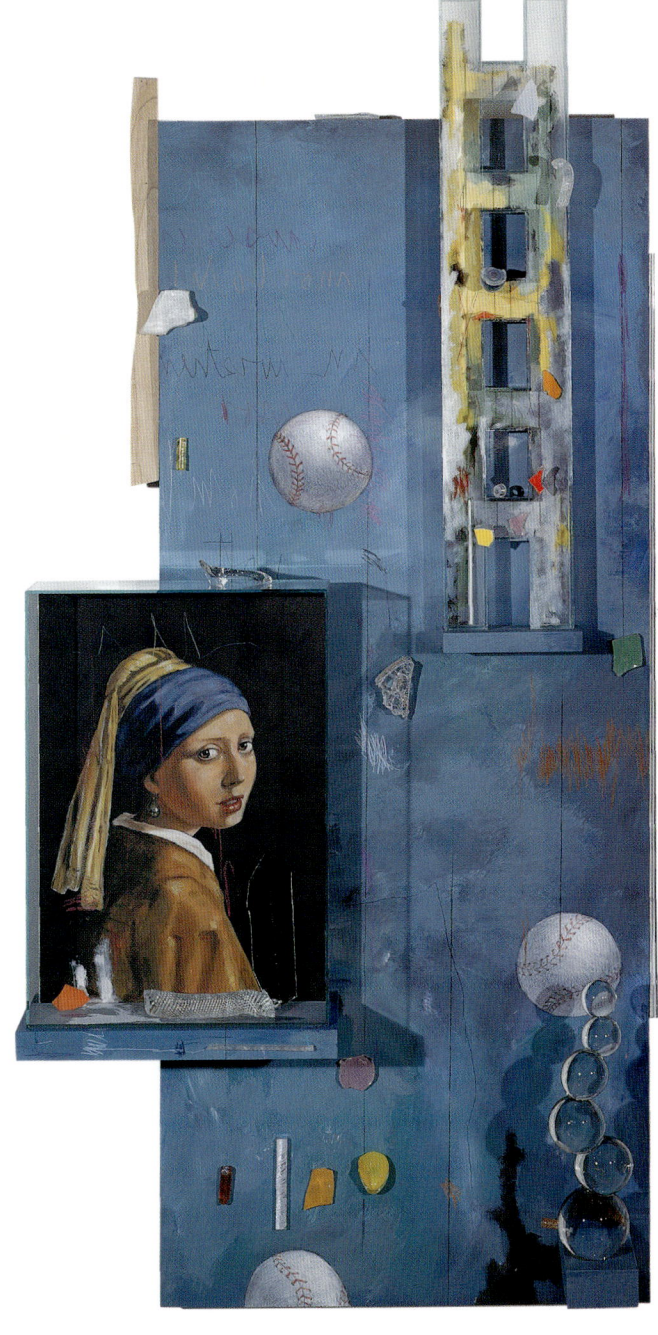

257

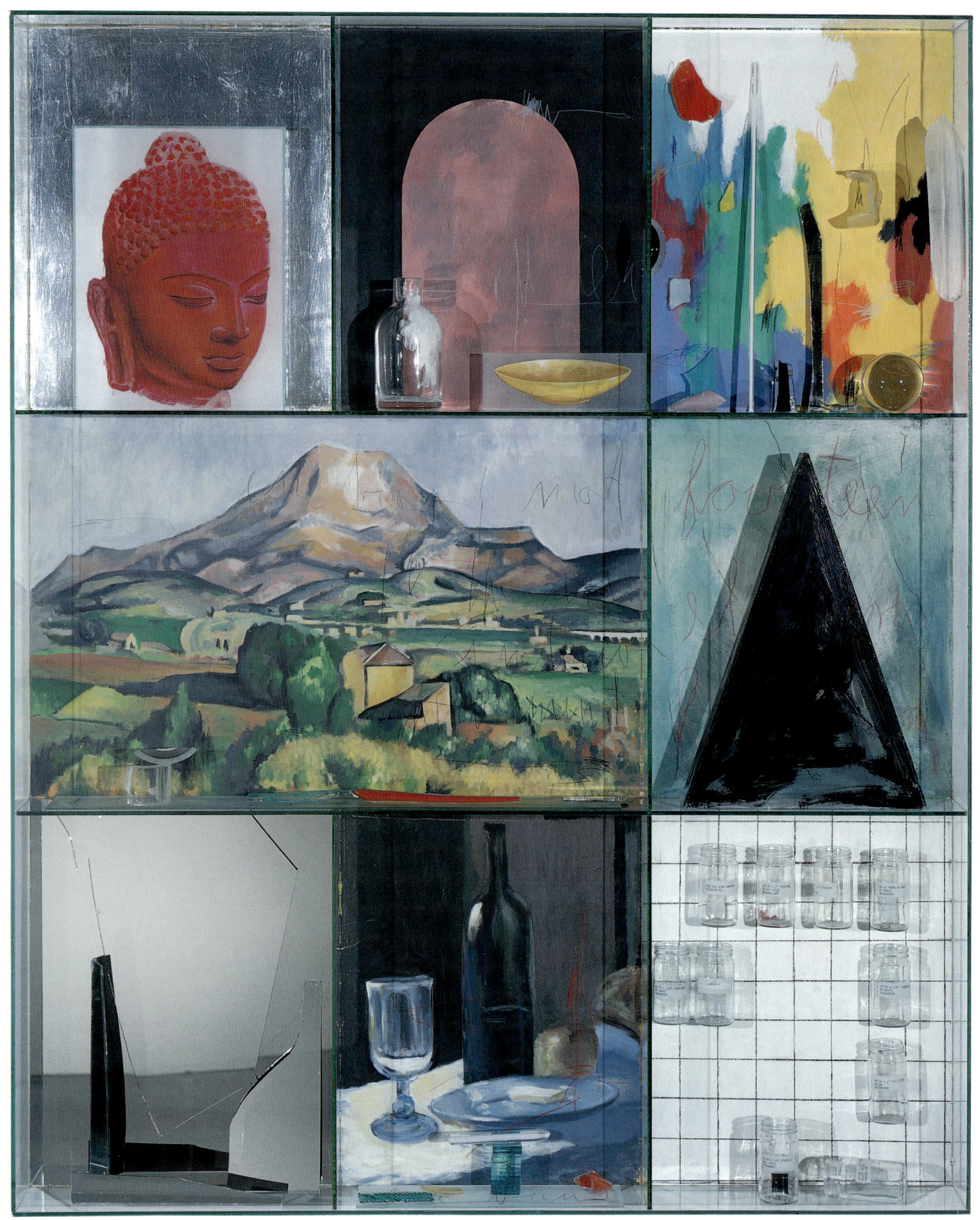

Mythological Landscape; France, 1999. Glass and mixed media, h. 60 x 48 x 5.5 inches.

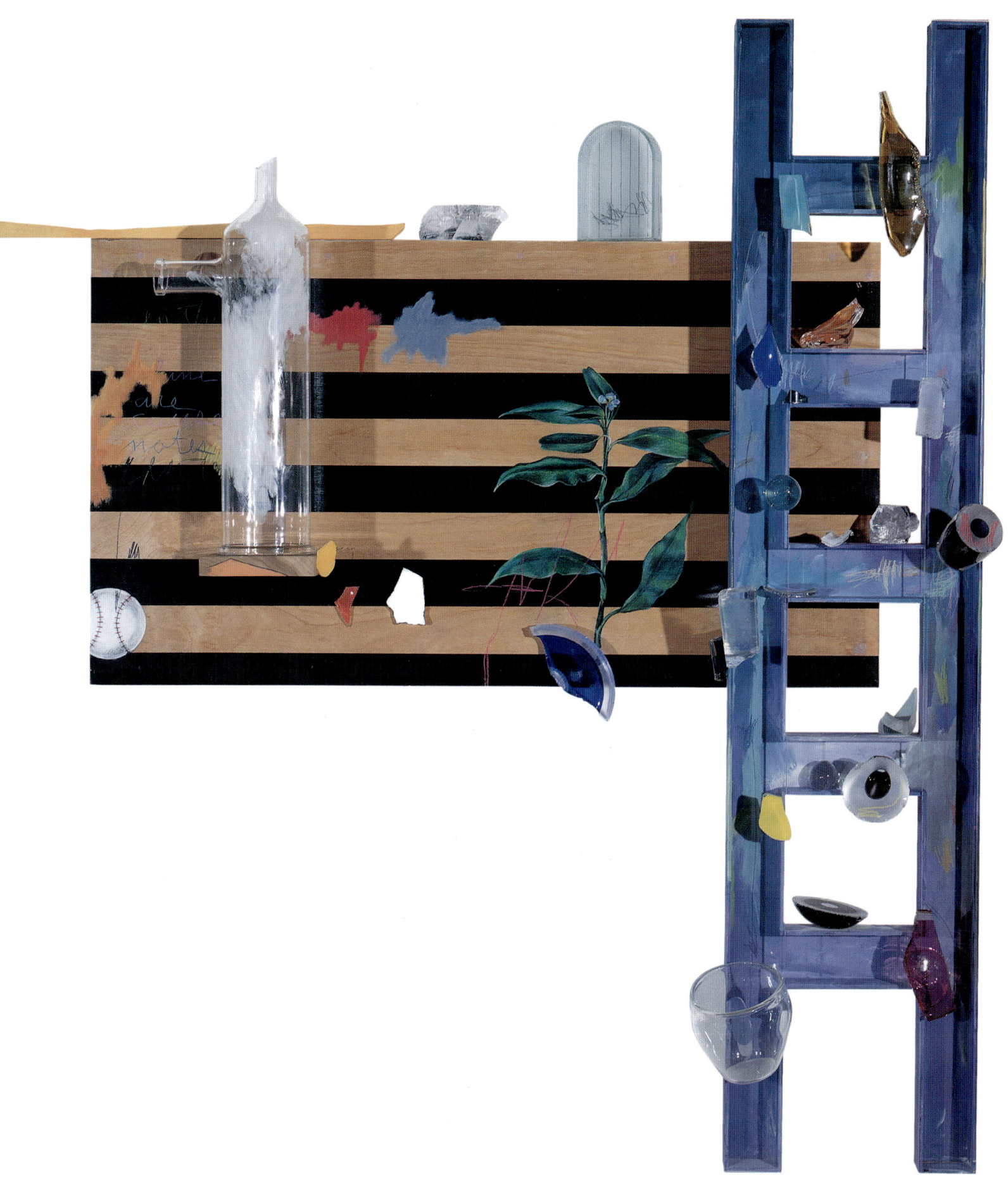

Blue Silence; Science, 1999. Glass and mixed media, h. 60 x 48 x 9 inches.

Susan Stinsmuehlen-Amend
(b.1948)

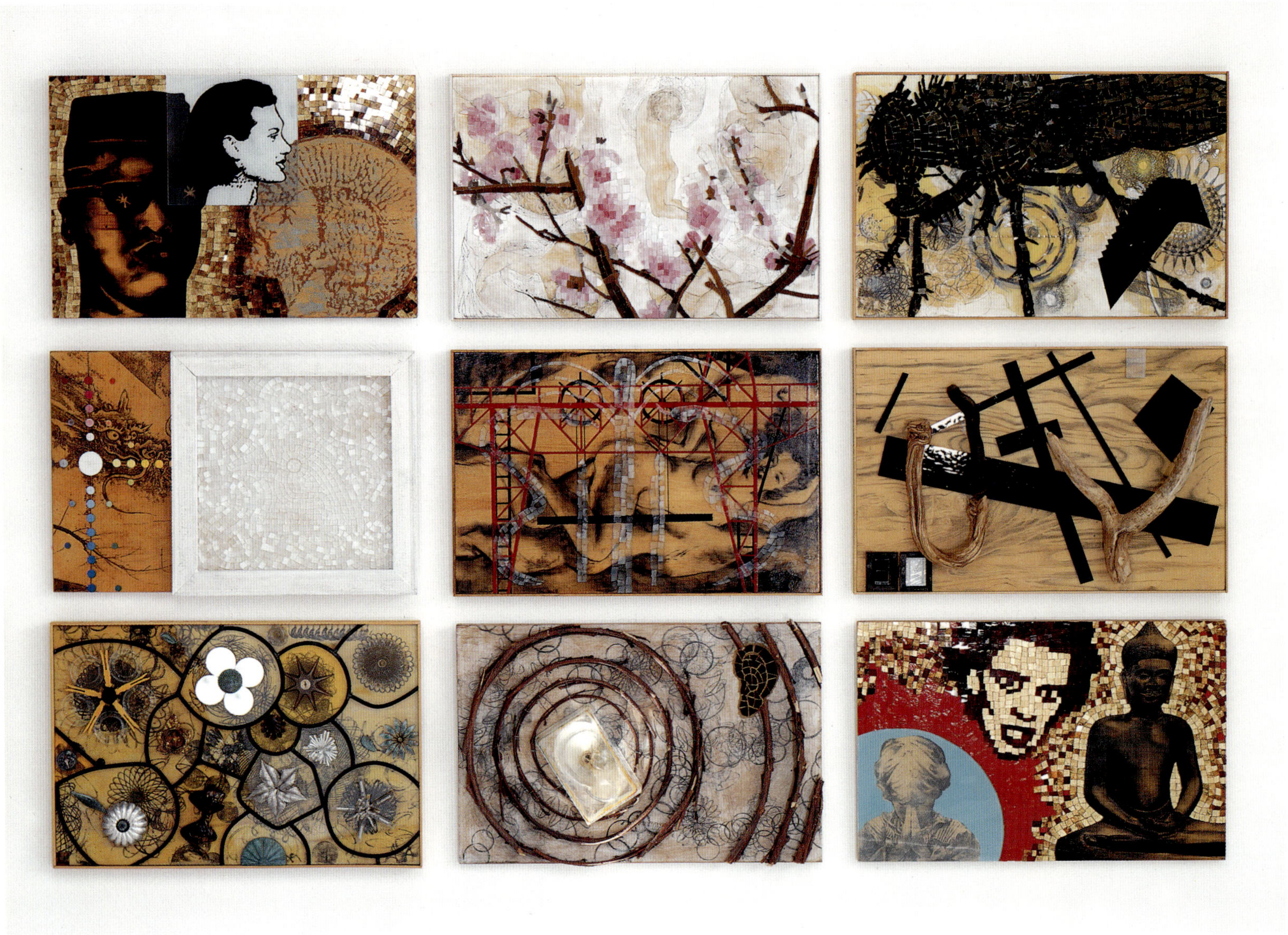

OJAI, CALIFORNIA

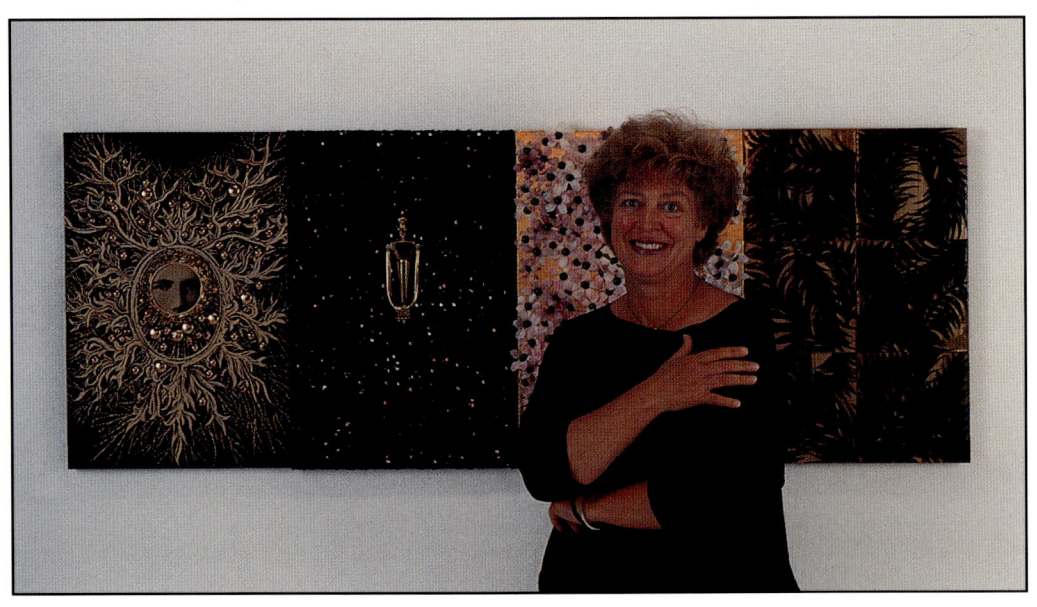

Top:
Ode to Geraldine (Mom), 1999. Painted fired glass and mixed media, h. 24 x 64 inches. Photo: Tom Kelly.

Bottom:
Remnants, 1995-96. Glass, wood, and mixed media, h. 52 x 76 inches. Photo: Tom Kelly.

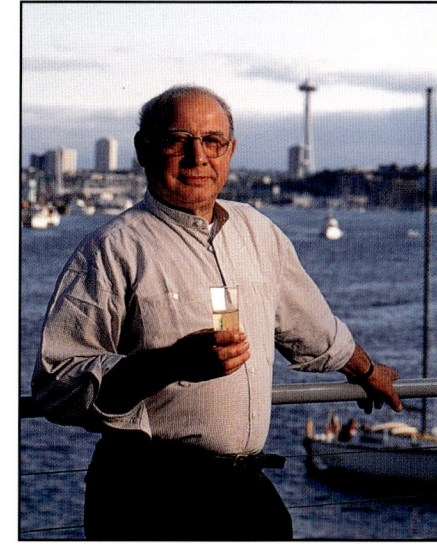

Photo: Russell Johnson

SEATTLE, WASHINGTON

Lino Tagliapietra
(b.1934)

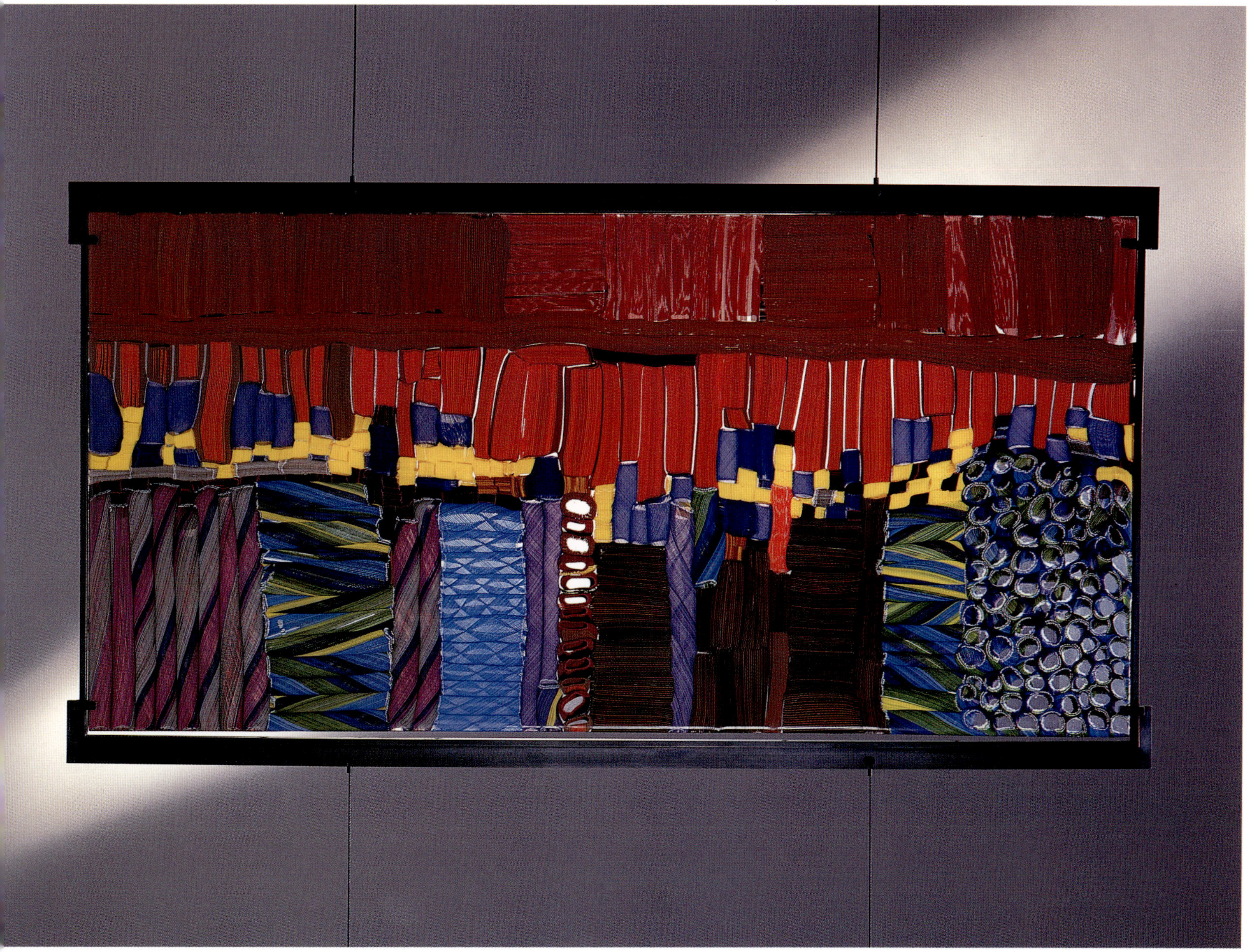

First Avenue, 1999. Fused glass, h. 30 x 60.25 inches.
Courtesy Lino Tagliapietra, Inc. Photo: Russell Johnson.

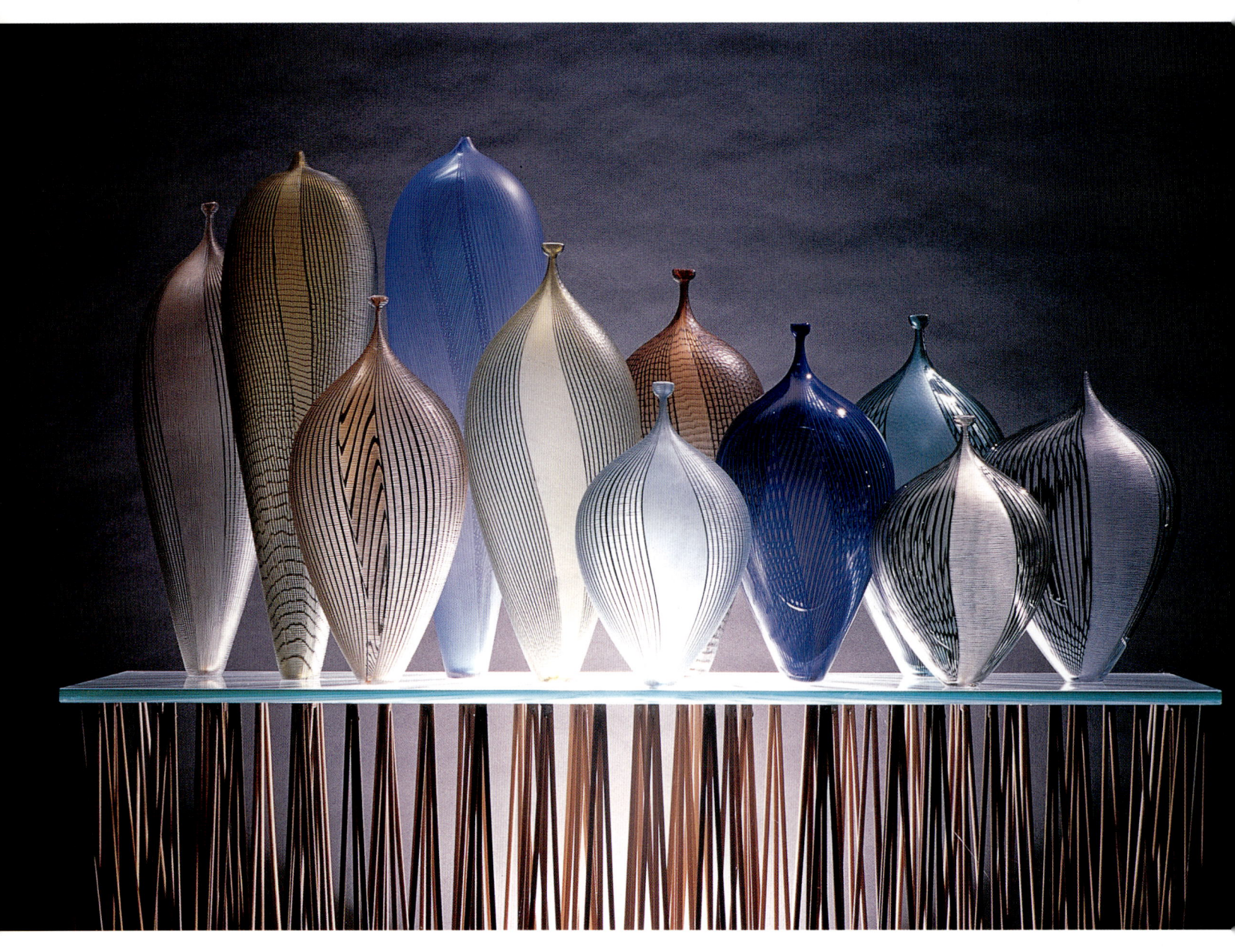

Above:
Manhattan Sunset, 1999. Blown glass, h. 67 x 60 x 20 inches. First piece of the International Glass Museum's permanent collection. Gift of Frank Russell Company.

Opposite:
Dinosaur, 1998. Blown glass, h. 34.75 x 9.5 x 4.75 inches. Photo: Russell Johnson

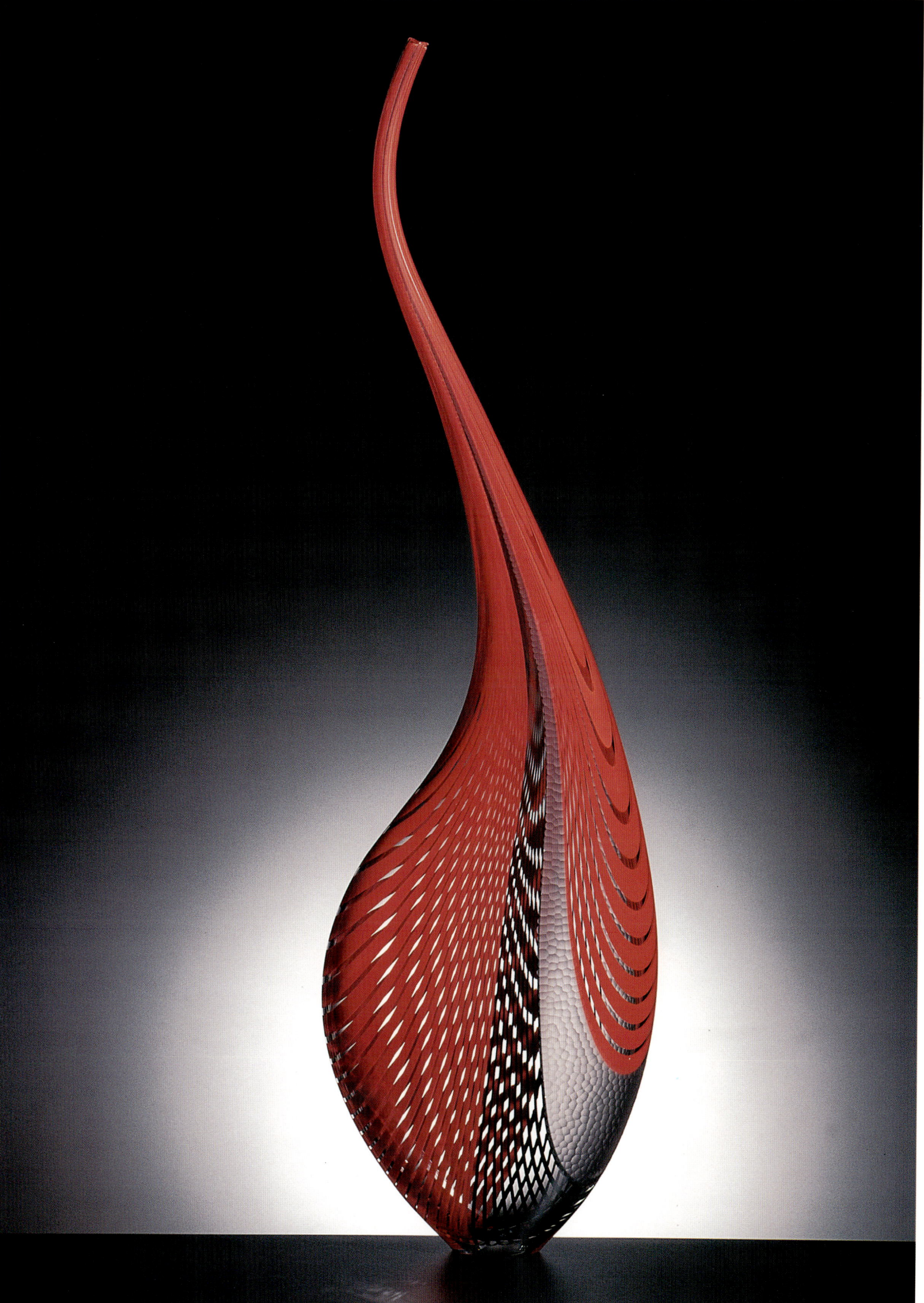

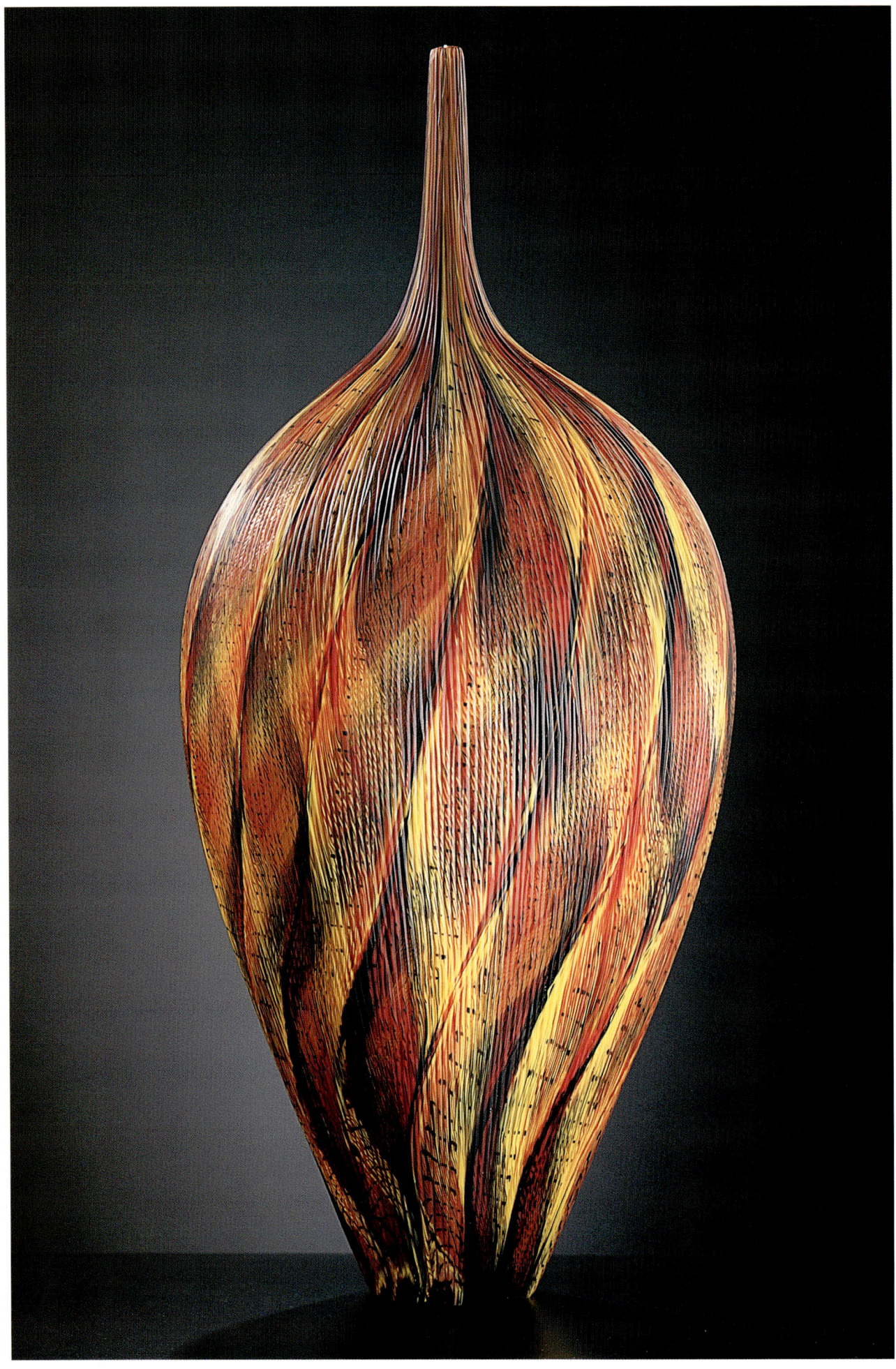

Tucson, 1997. Blown glass, h. 21.5 x 9.25 x 6.5 inches.
Photo: Russell Johnson.

ROCHESTER, NEW YORK # Michael Taylor
(b.1944)

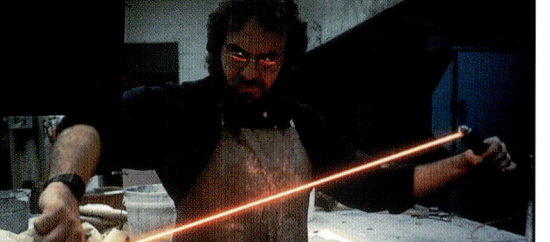

Radio Red Reprise II, 1999. Optical, dichroic, doll, vitrolite, drawn, and float glass, laminated, constructed, and cast, h. 28 x 16. Photo: Earl Kage.

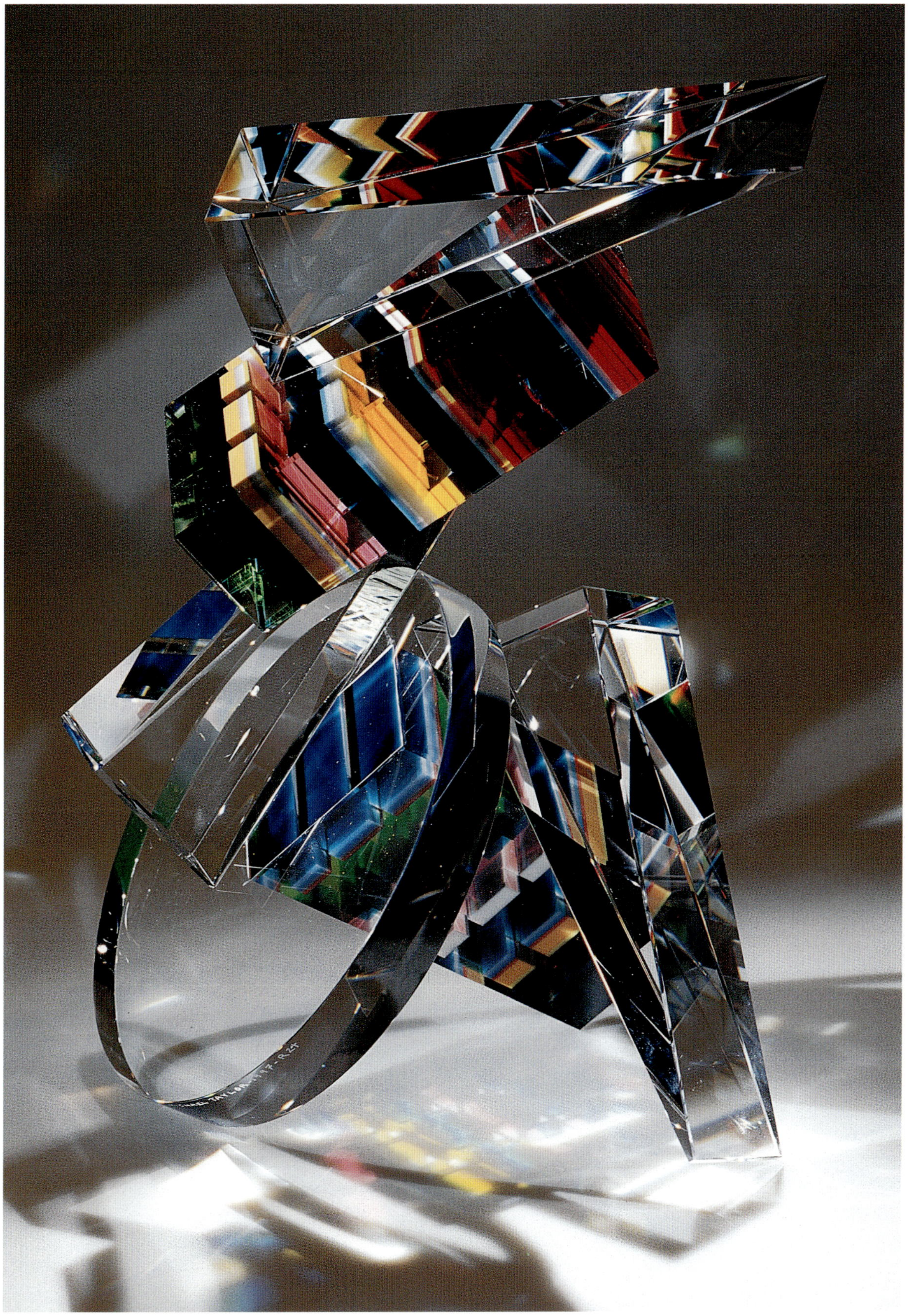

Cappy Thompson
(b.1952)

SEATTLE, WASHINGTON

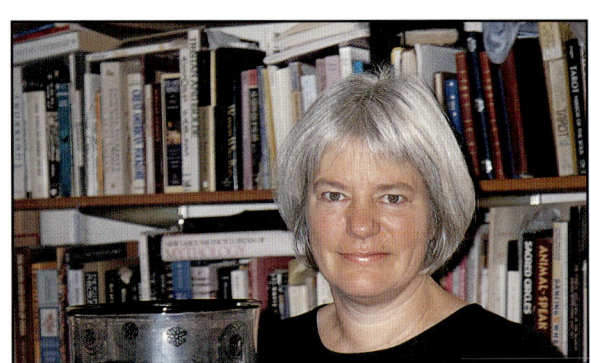

Below:
I Receive a Great Blessing from the Sun and the Moon: I Will Be an Artist and Walk the Path of Beauty, 1995. Vitreous enamels reverse-painted on blown glass, h. 16 x 16 x 16 inches.

Opposite:
Dancing with Ganesha, 1993. Vitreous enamels reverse-painted on blown glass, h. 19 x 12 x 12 inches.

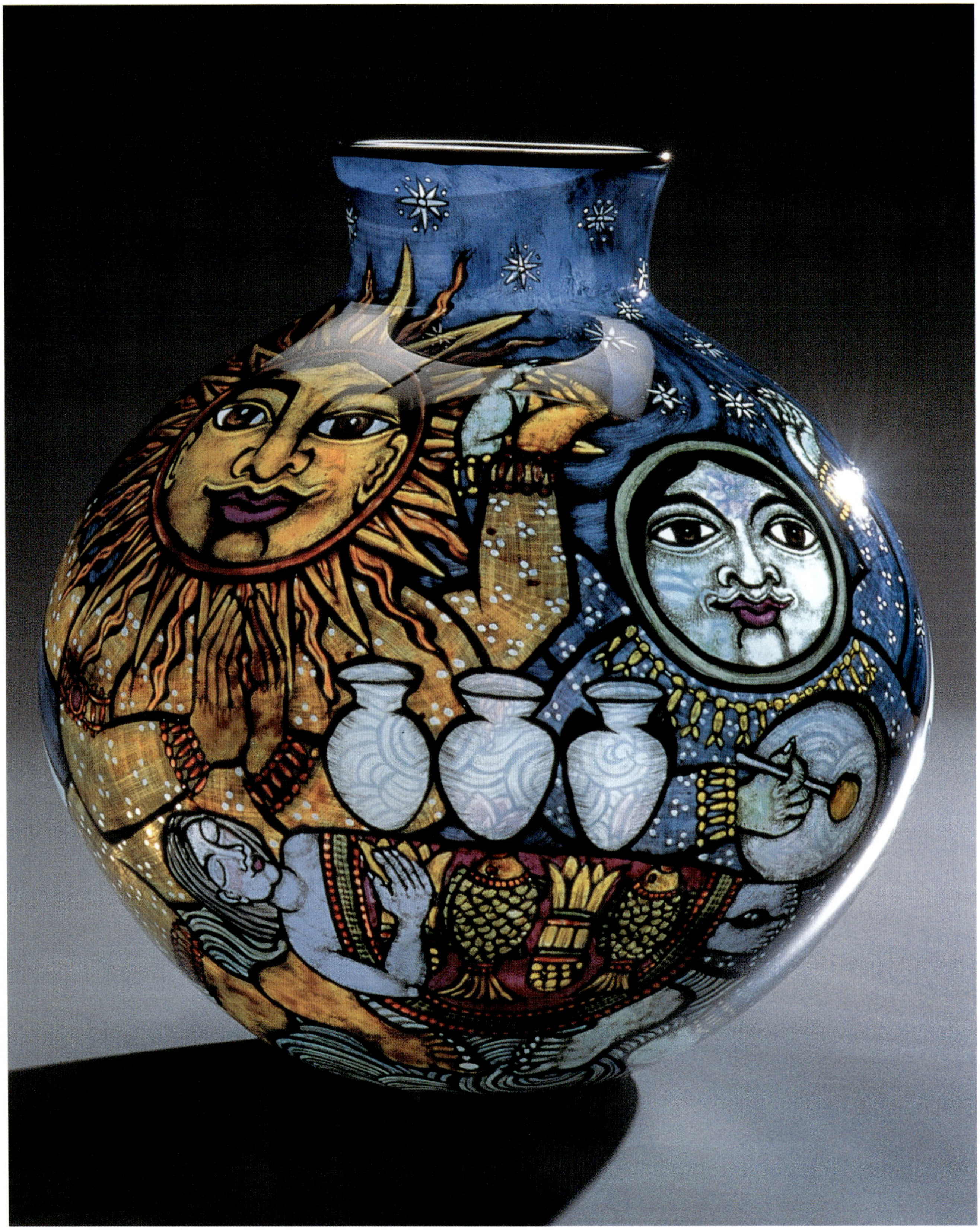

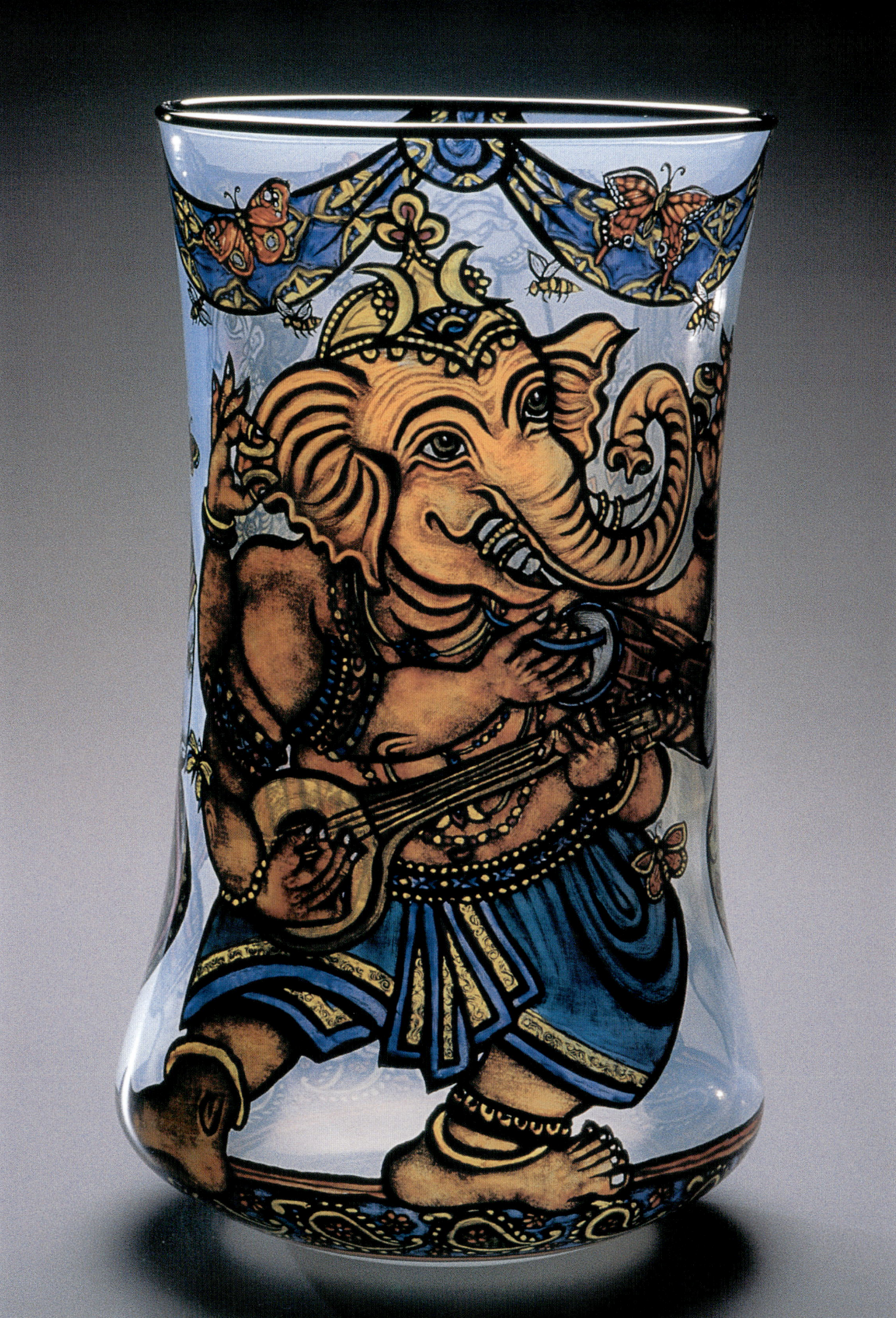

Steve Tobin
(b.1957)

COOPERSBURG, PENNSYLVANIA

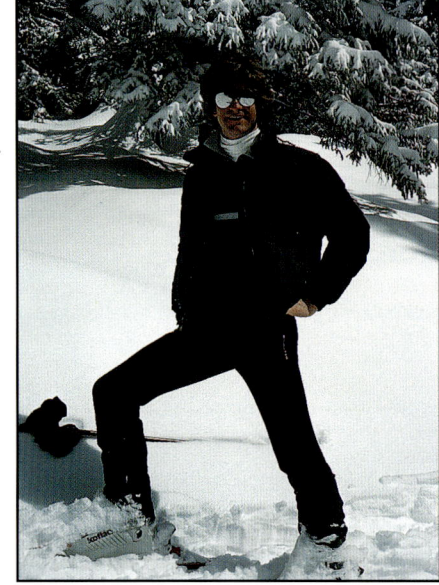

Below:
Cocoons; Artist's Studio, 1998. Cast glass, h. 6 to 15 feet. Photo: George Erml.

Opposite:
Adobe; Interior Detail View at Artist's Studio, 1998. Glass M-60 tank windows, and mixed media, h. 6 x 6 feet. Photo: George Erml.

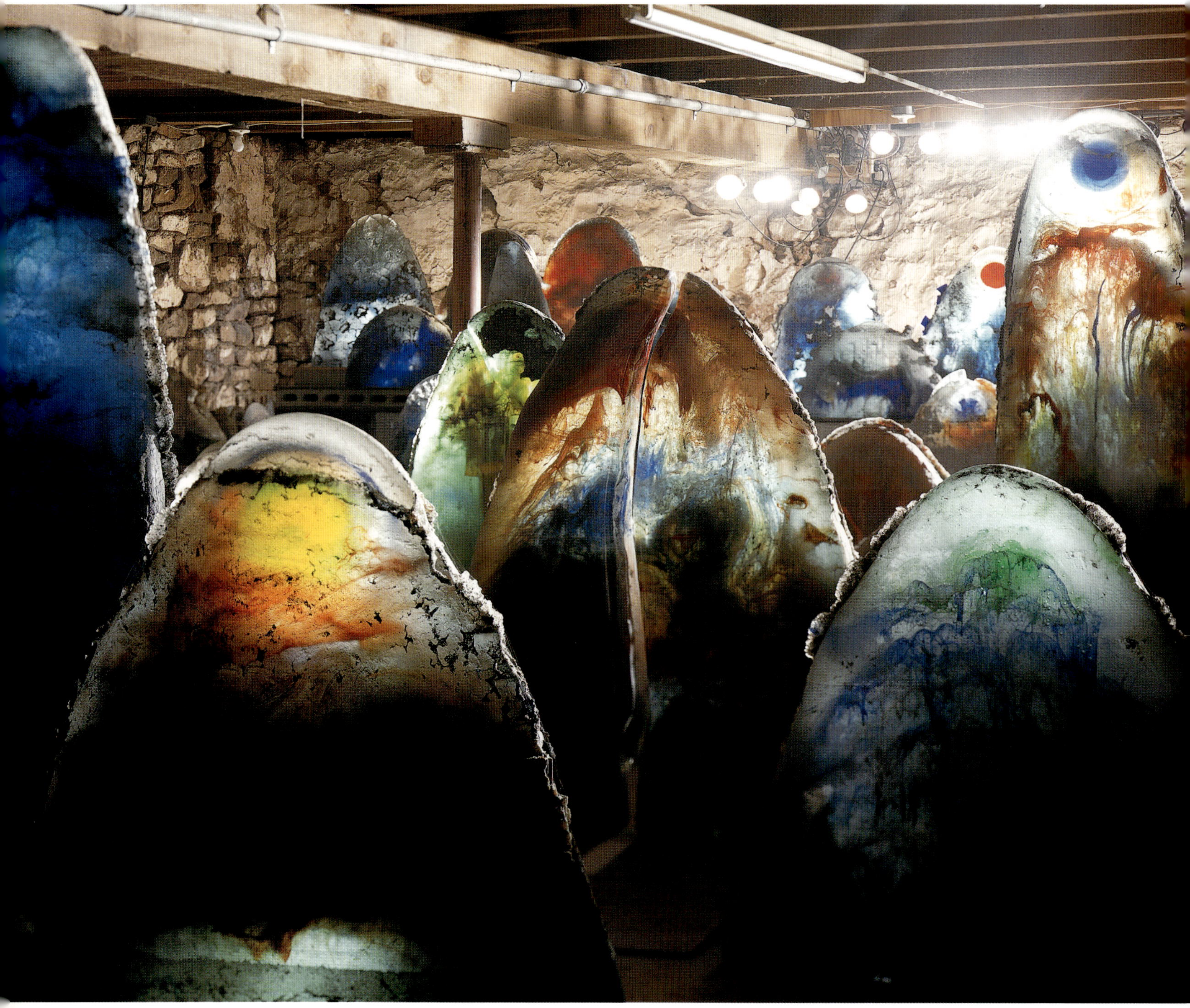

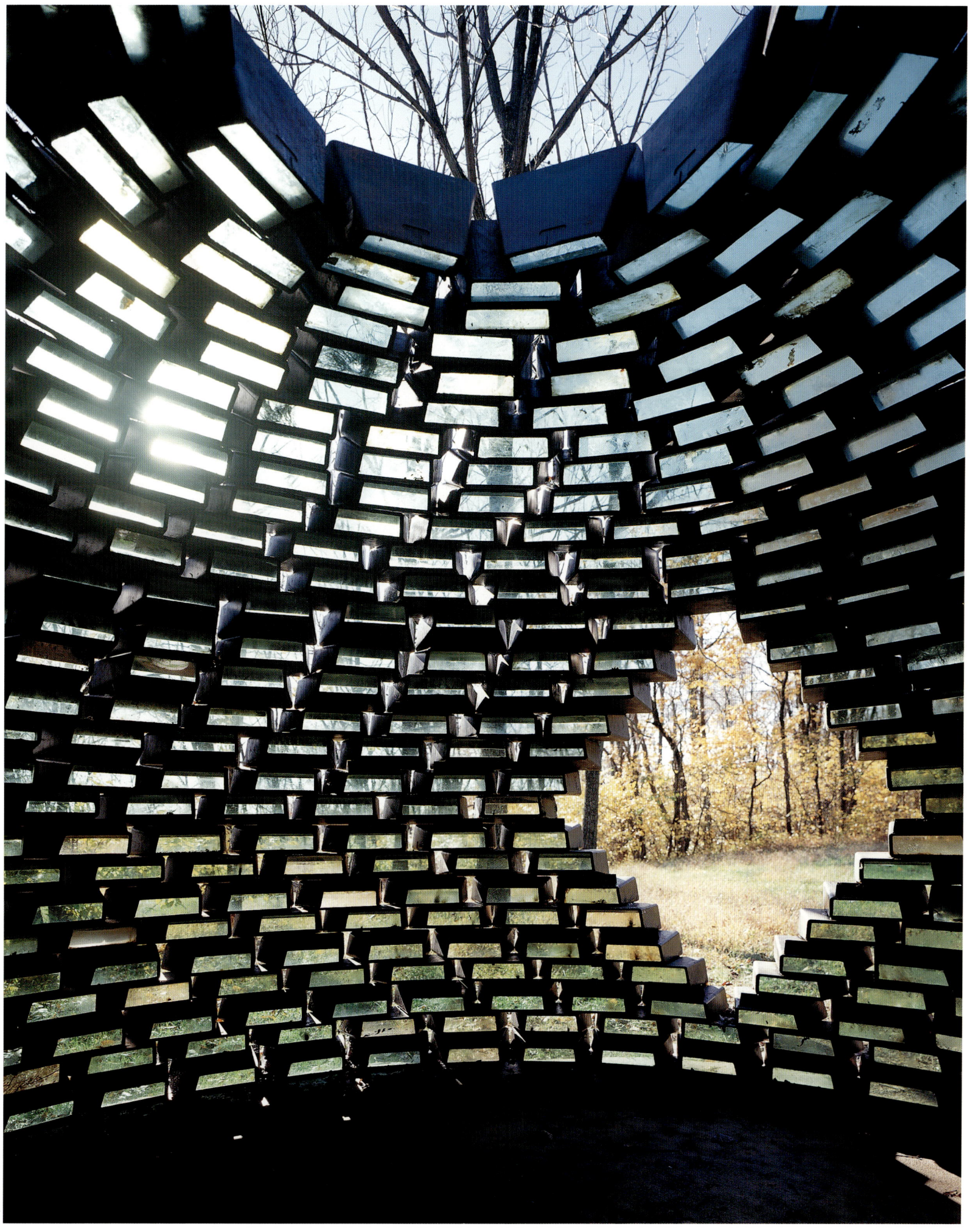

Karla Trinkley
(b. 1956)

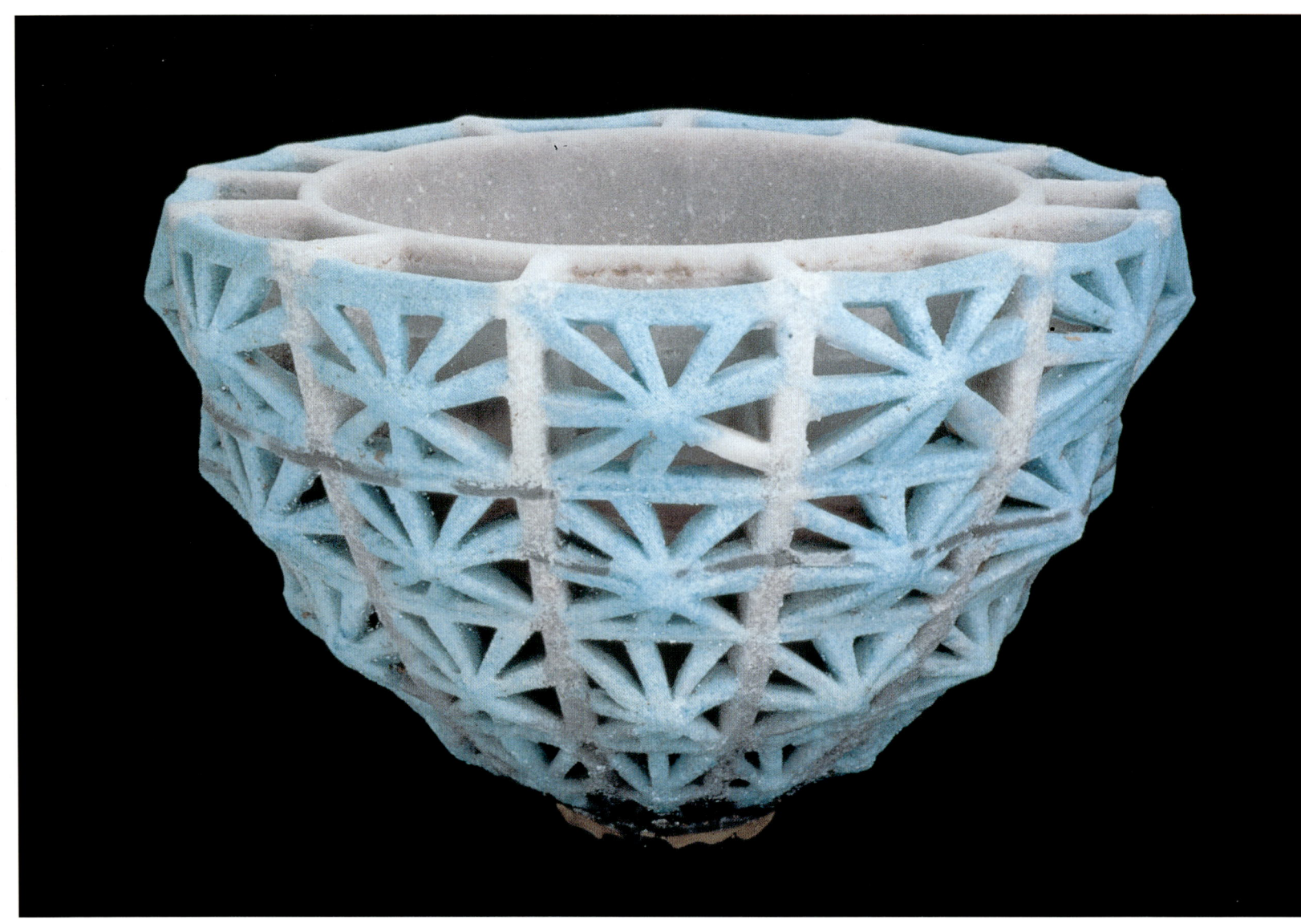

Terrapene, 1994. Cast glass (pâte de verre),
h. 13 x 21 inches. Collection of Ian Friedman.

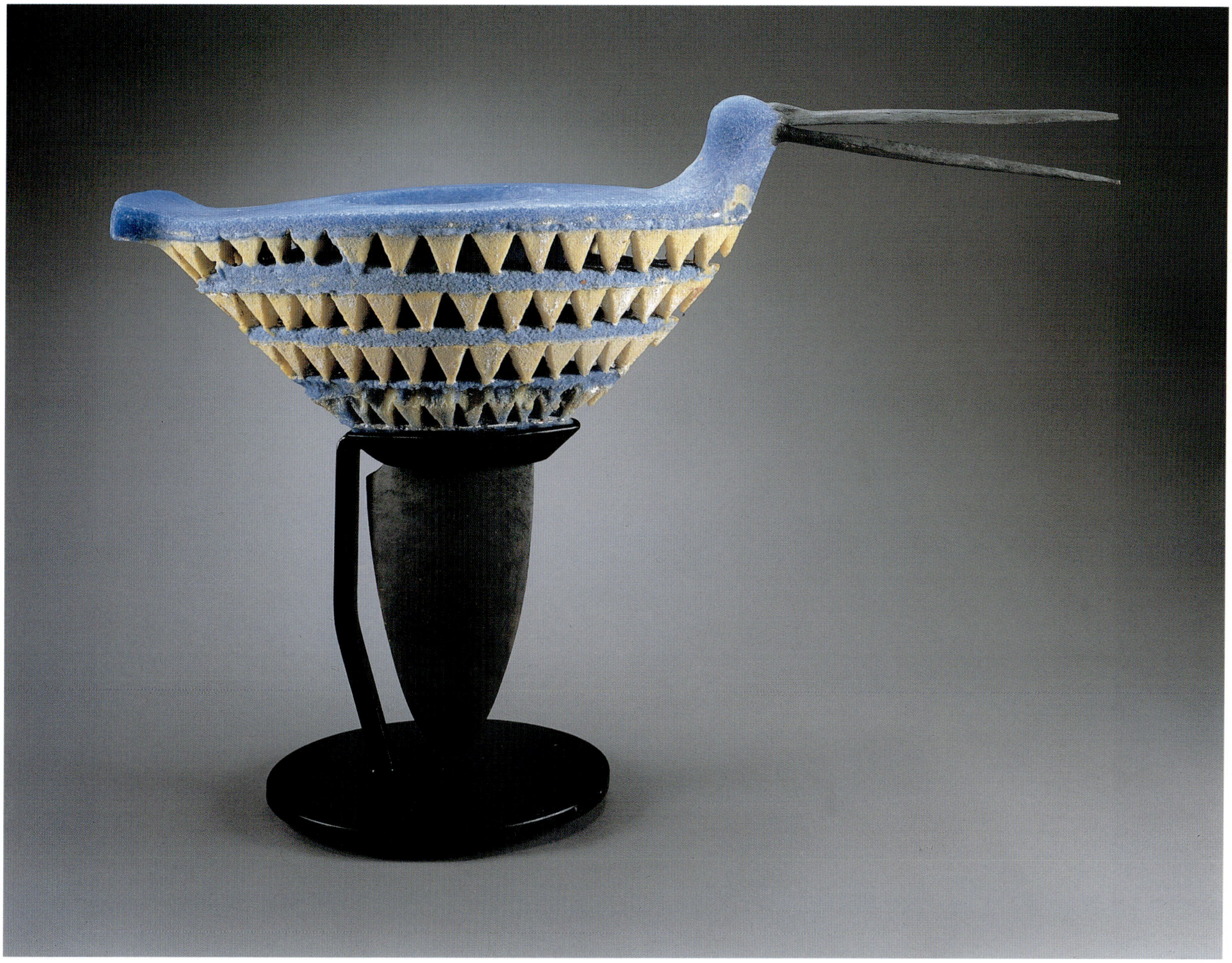

BOYERTOWN, PENNSYLVANIA

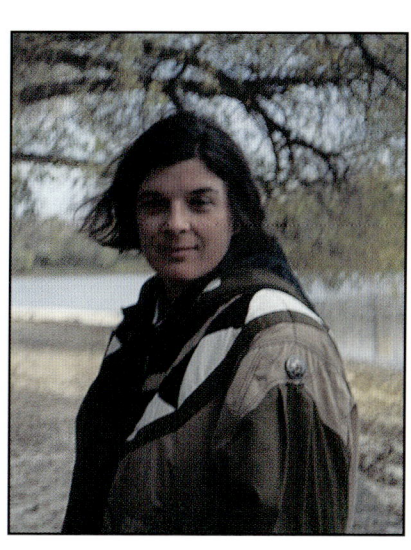

Peela Peela Boatbird, 1994. Glass, poplar, cedar, graphite, and metal, h. 25 x 36 x 12 inches. Los Angeles County Museum of Art. Gift of Daniel Greenberg and Susan Steinhauser.

Bertil Vallien
(b.1938)

ERIKSMALA, SWEDEN

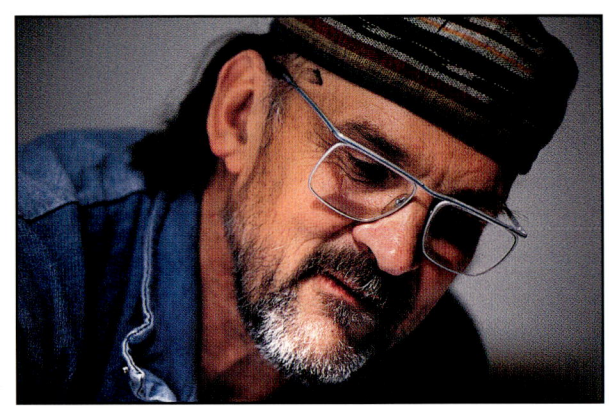

Photo: Göran Örtegren

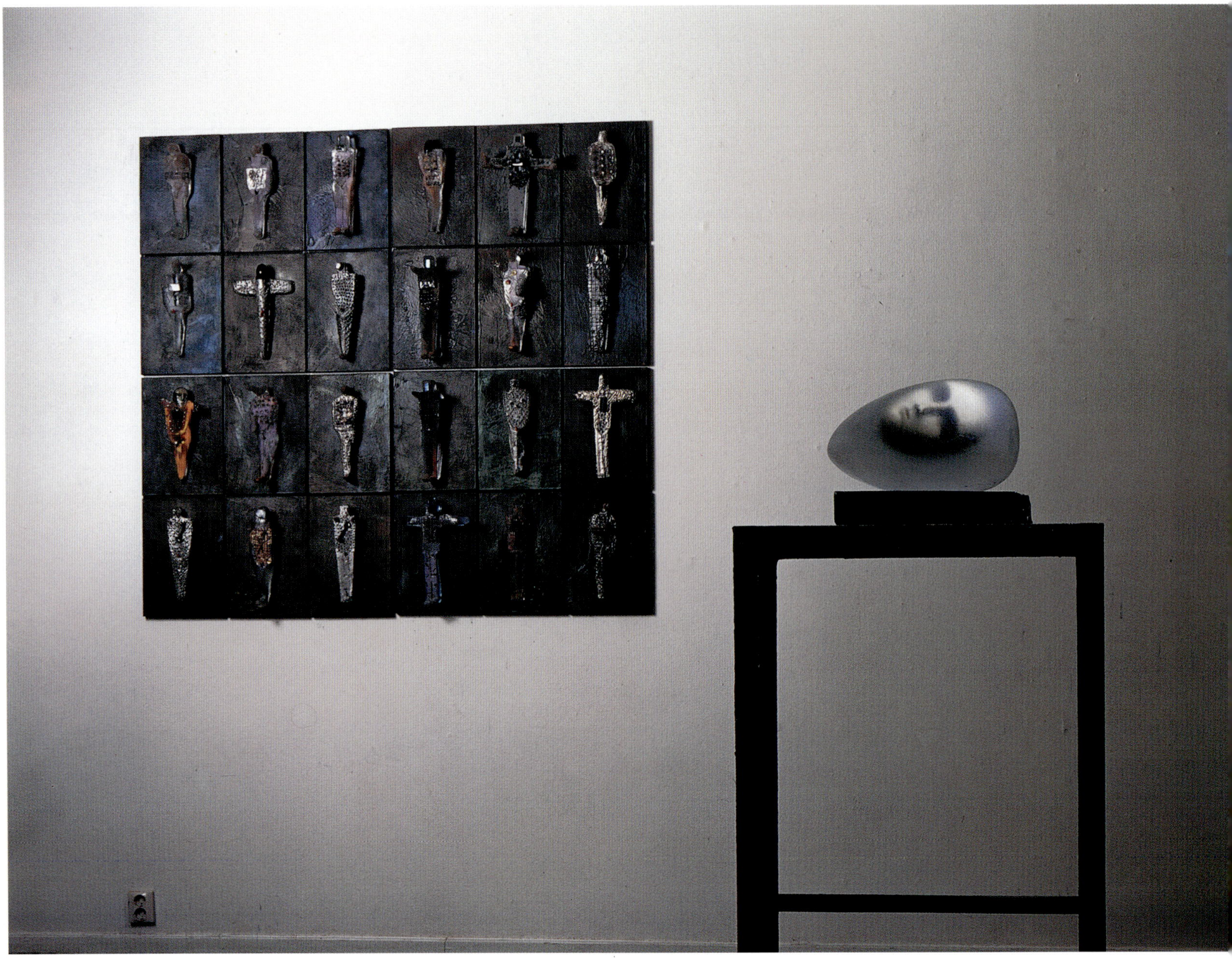

Above:
***Journey**,* 1998. Glass, mixed media, and steel, h. 9 x 14 feet. Photo: Eva Eje.

Opposite:
***Heads; Kosta Boda Unique**,* 1998. Glass and metal, h. 6 feet. Collection of Cynthia and Jeffrey Manocherian. Photo: Eva Heyd.

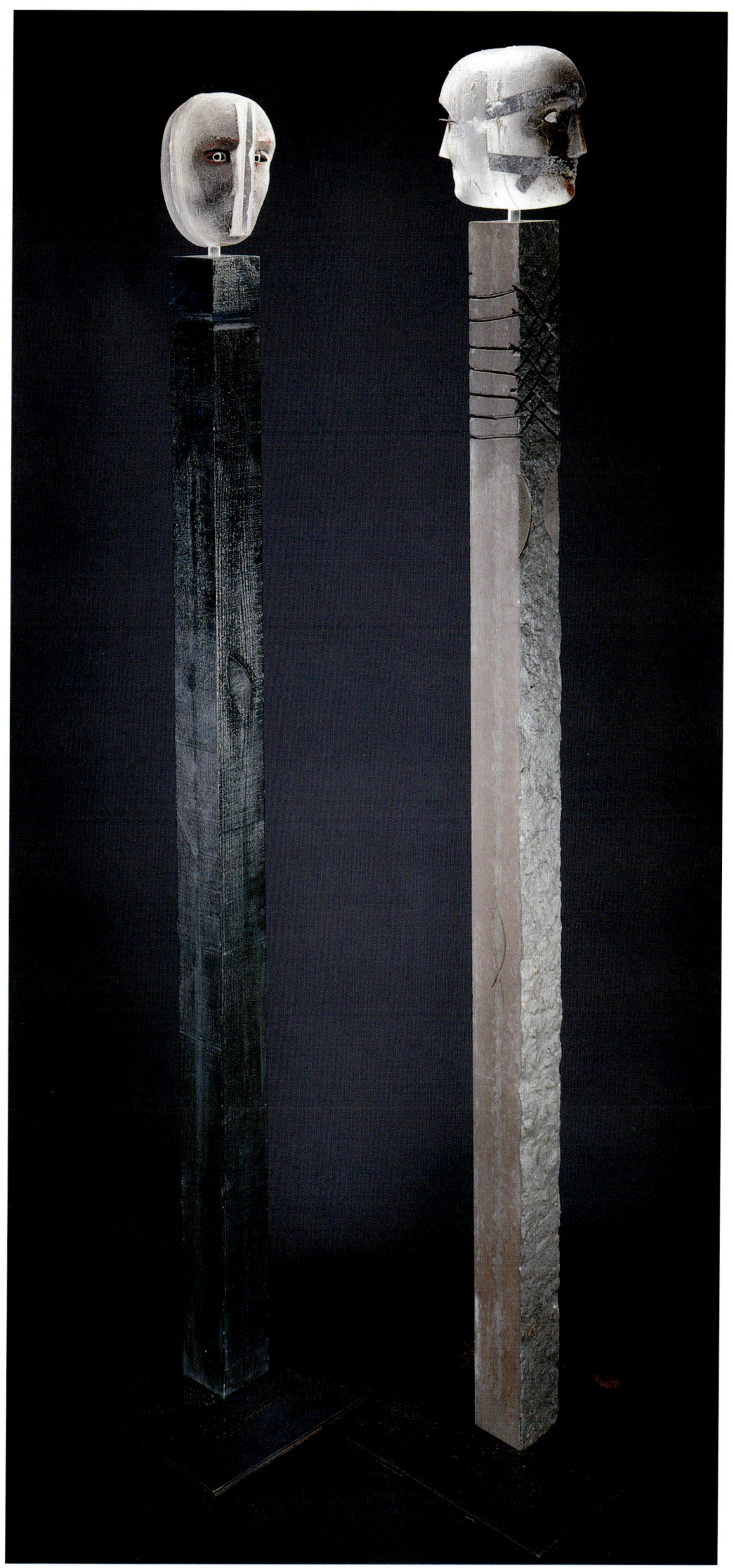

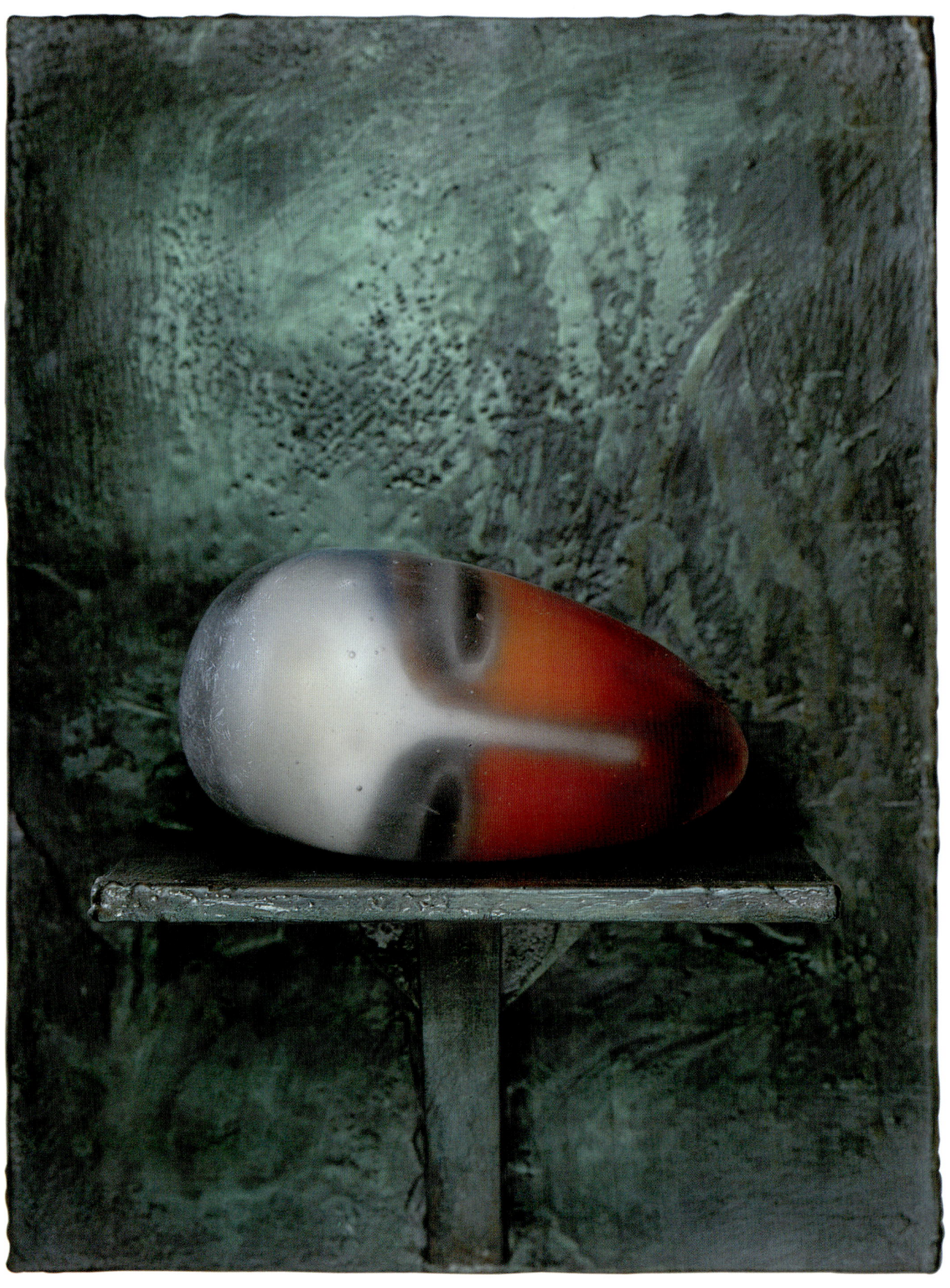

Resting Head, 1998. Glass and mixed media, h. 24 x 20 inches. Photo: G. Örtegren.

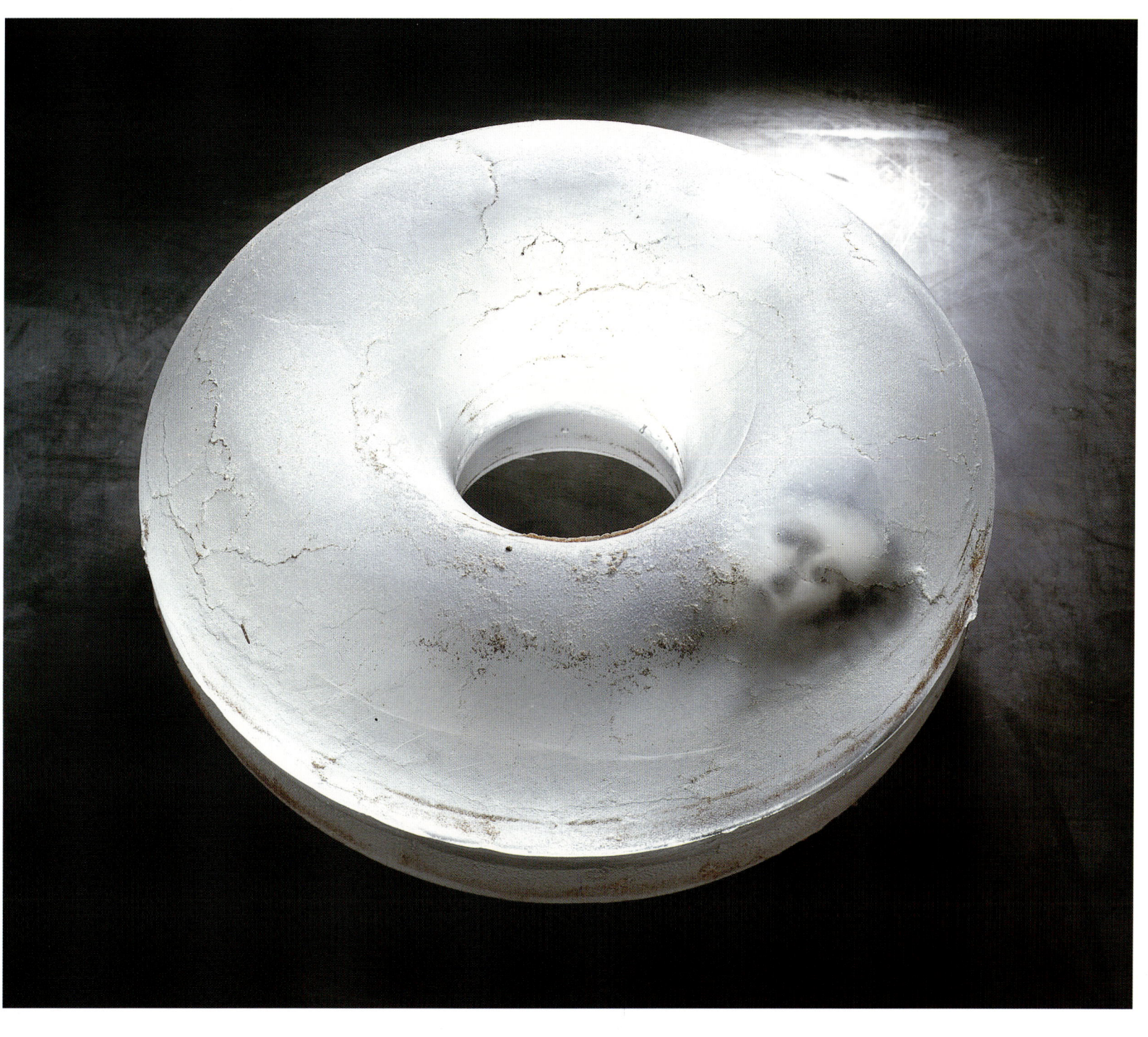

Circle, 1998, Glass, h. 20 inches. Courtesy Heller Gallery. Photo: G. Örtegren.

Mary Van Cline
(b.1954)

SEATTLE, WASHINGTON

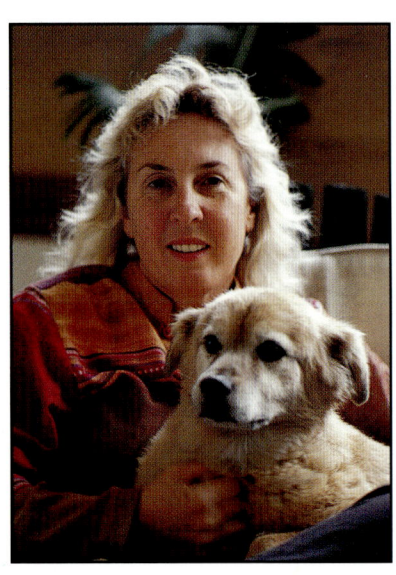

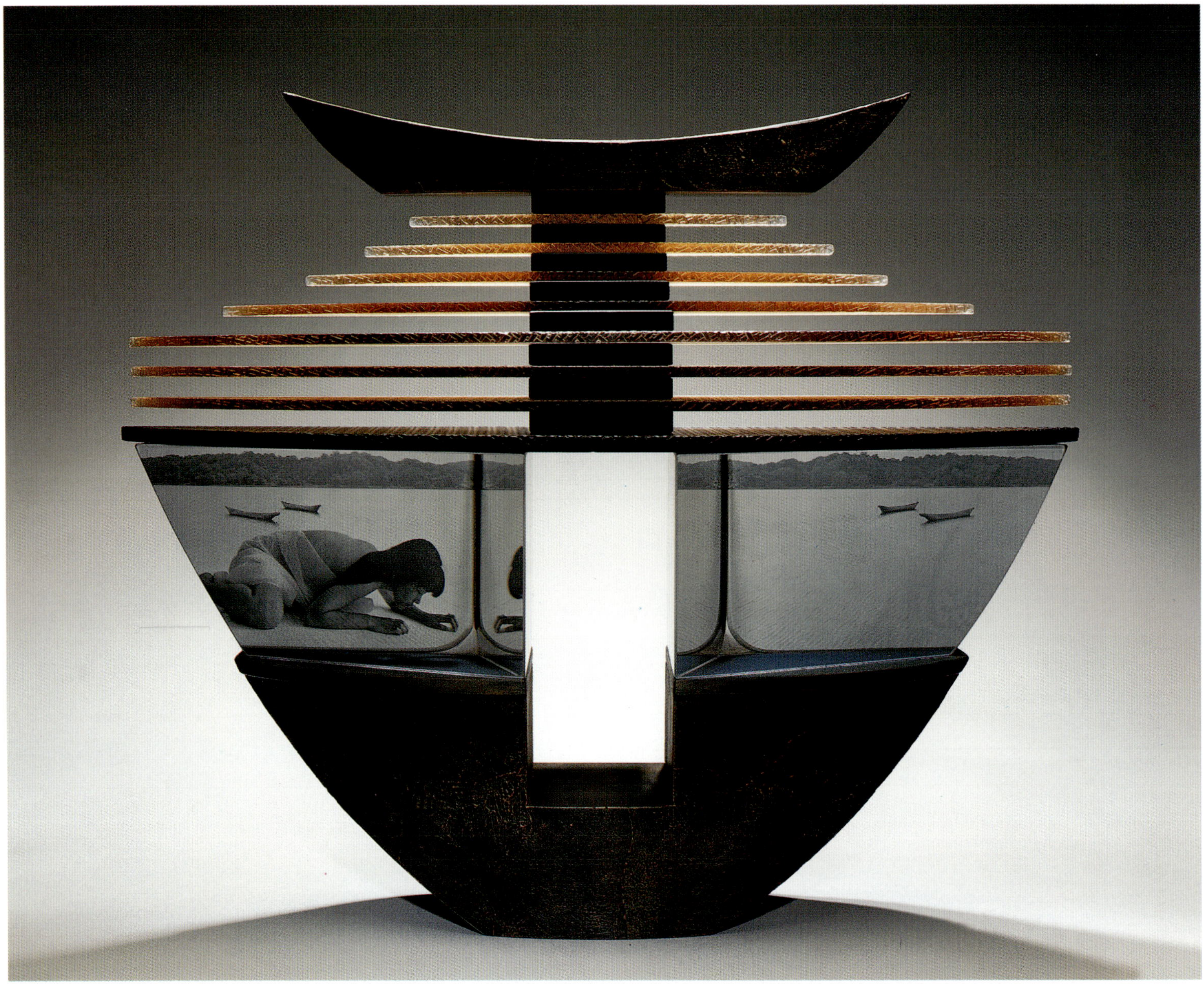

The Voyage Along the Curve of Time, 1997. Photosensitive glass, cast glass, and copper patina, h. 24 x 20 x 6 inches. Collection of Amye and Paul S. Gumbinner.

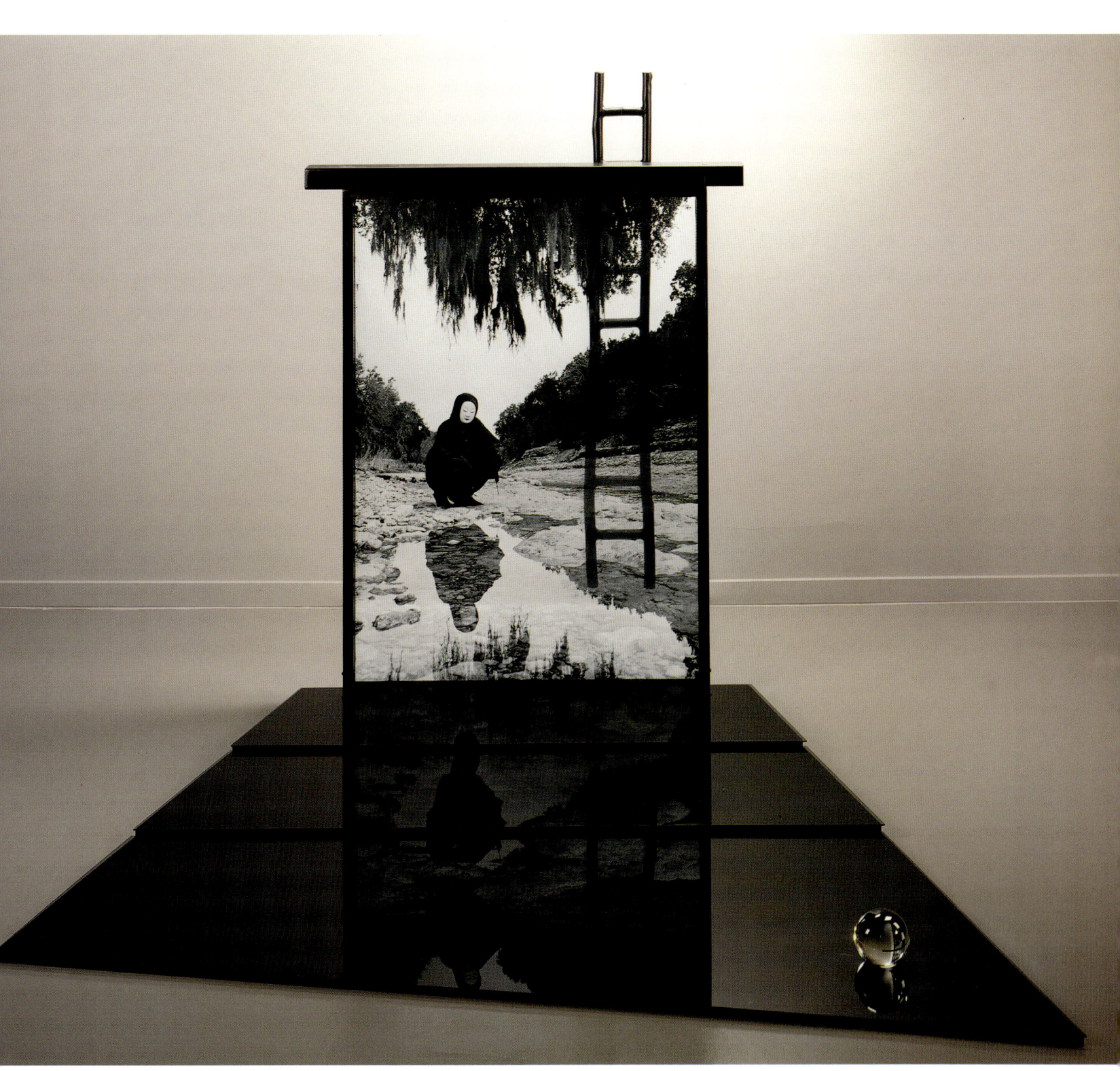

The Listening Point, 1993. Photosensitive glass, plateglass, and metal, h. 6 x 10 x 8 feet.

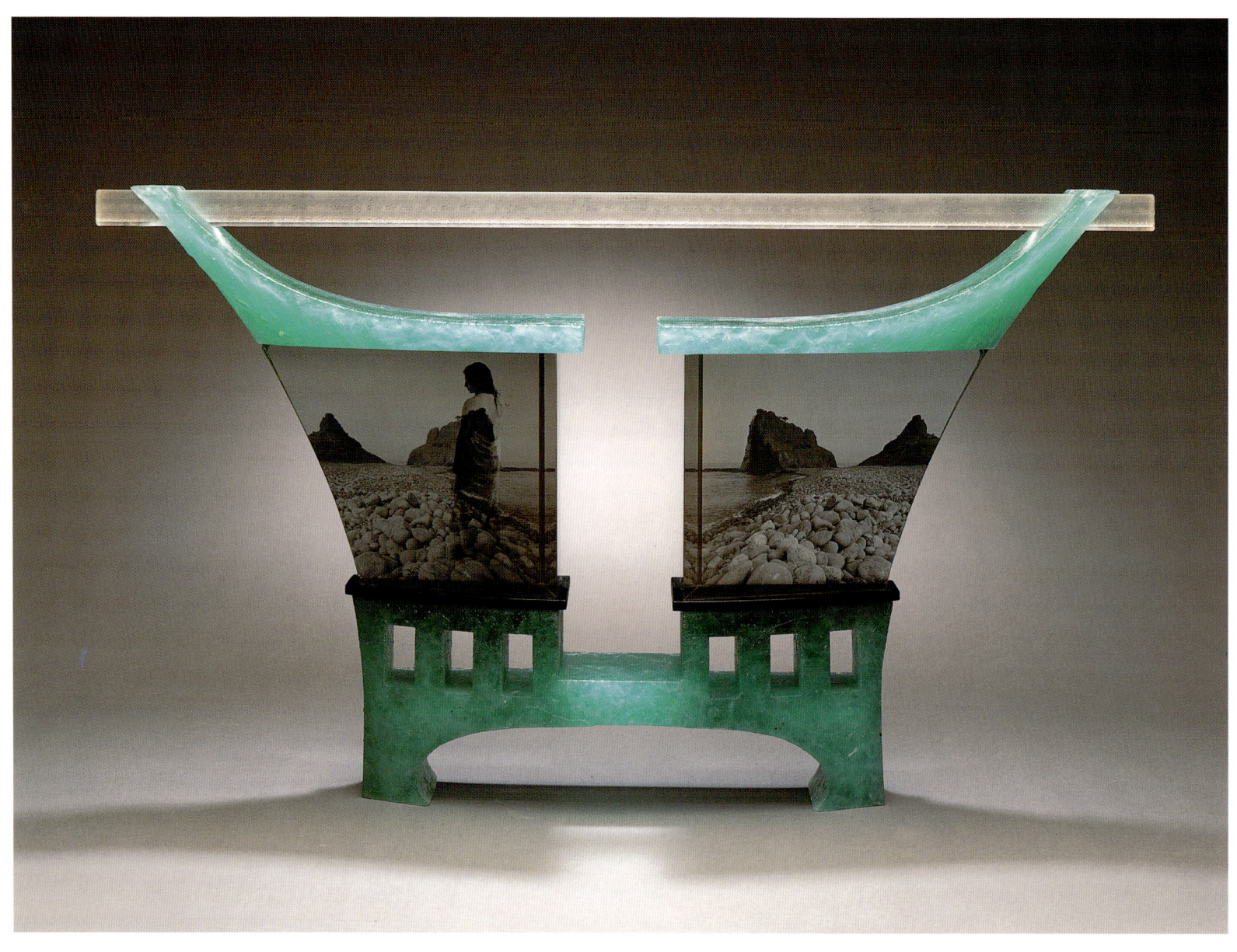

The Ocean of Memory, 1999. Photosensitive glass, and pâte de verre, h. 22 x 35 x 6 inches. Courtesy Leo Kaplan Modern.

CZECH REPUBLIC

Frantisek Vízner
(b.1936)

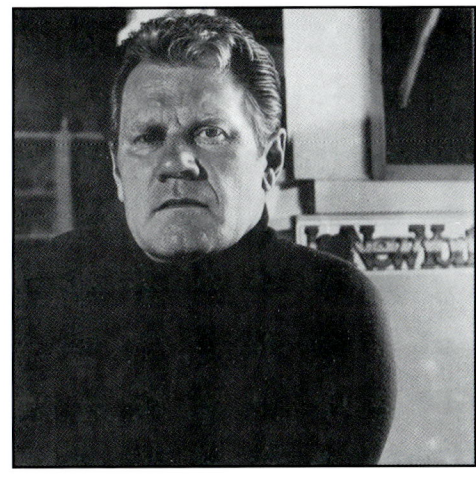

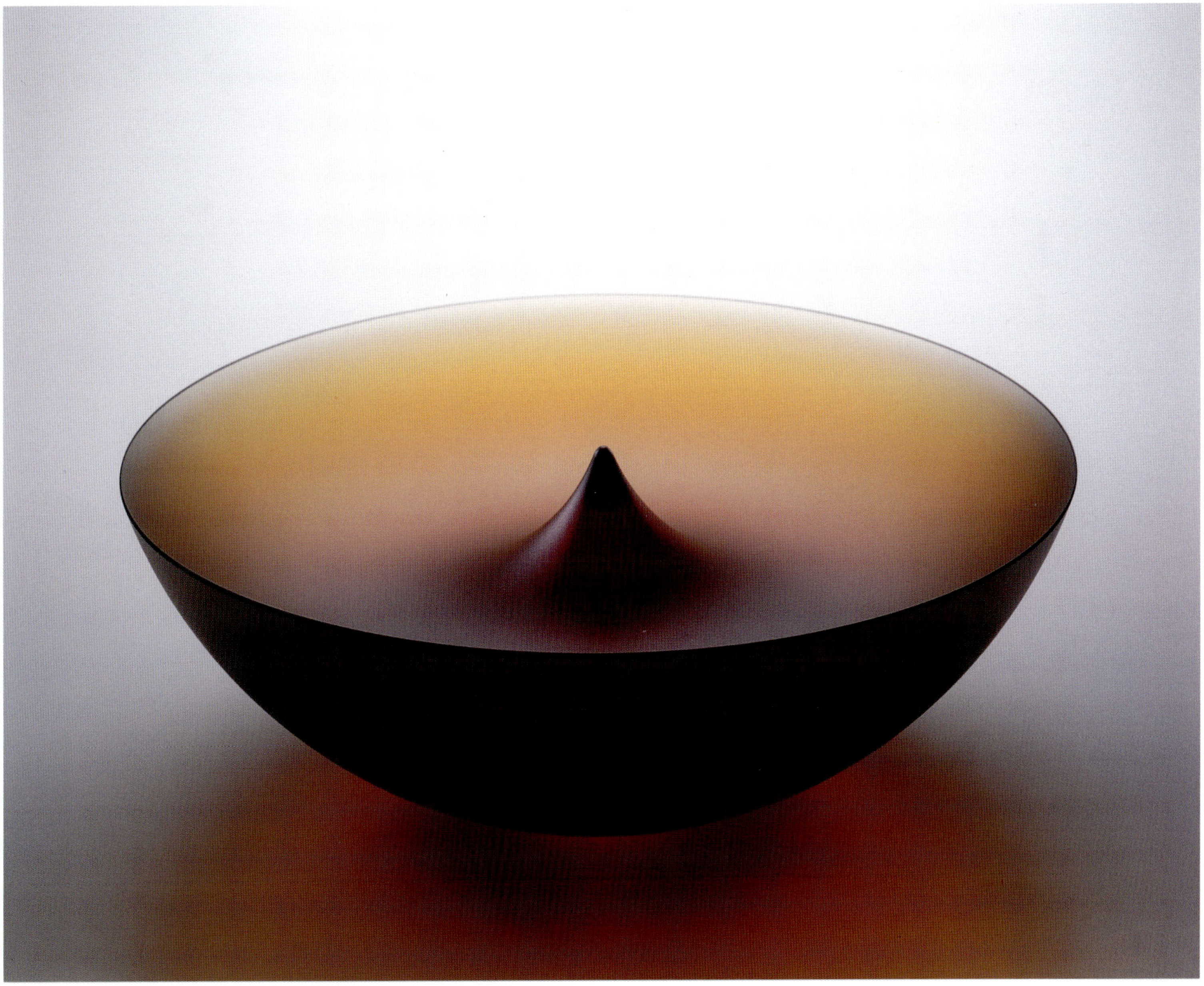

Amber Bowl with Point, 1978. Cast glass, cut, sandblasted, ground, and polished, h. 4 x 11.6 inches. Courtesy Barry Friedman Ltd., New York.

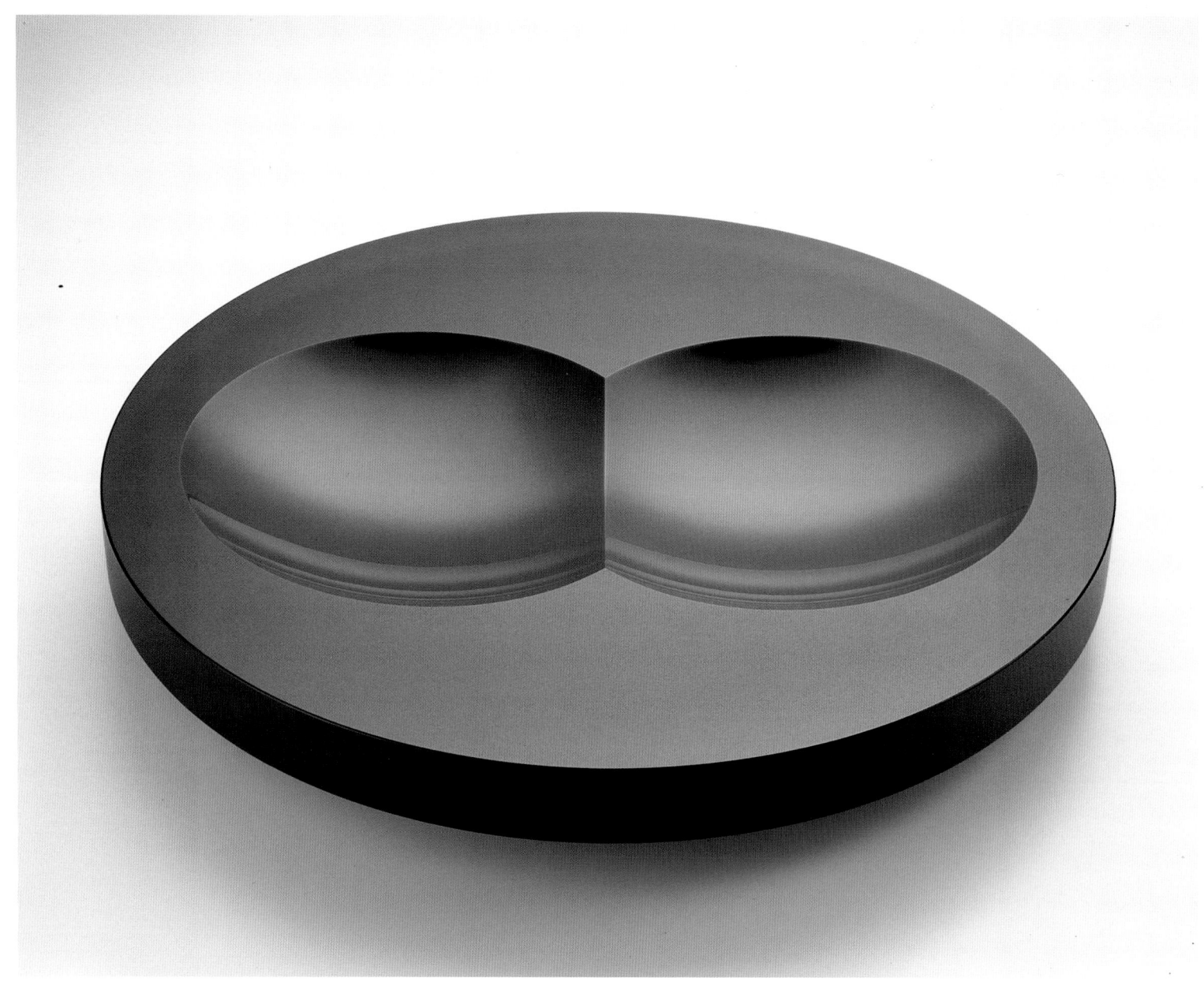

Blue Plate with Two Indentions, 1987. Cast glass, cut, sandblasted, ground, and polished, h. 2 x 14 inches. Collection of Cynthia and Jeffrey Manocherian.

BAKERSVILLE, NORTH CAROLINA

Kate Vogel & John Littleton
(b.1956) (b.1957)

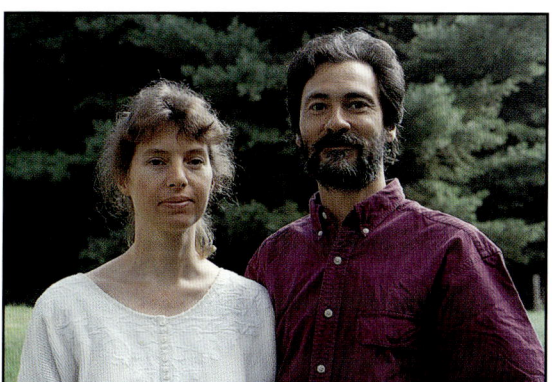

Imago Bag, 1999. Blown glass, acid etched, h. 19.5 x 14.25 x 12.5 inches.

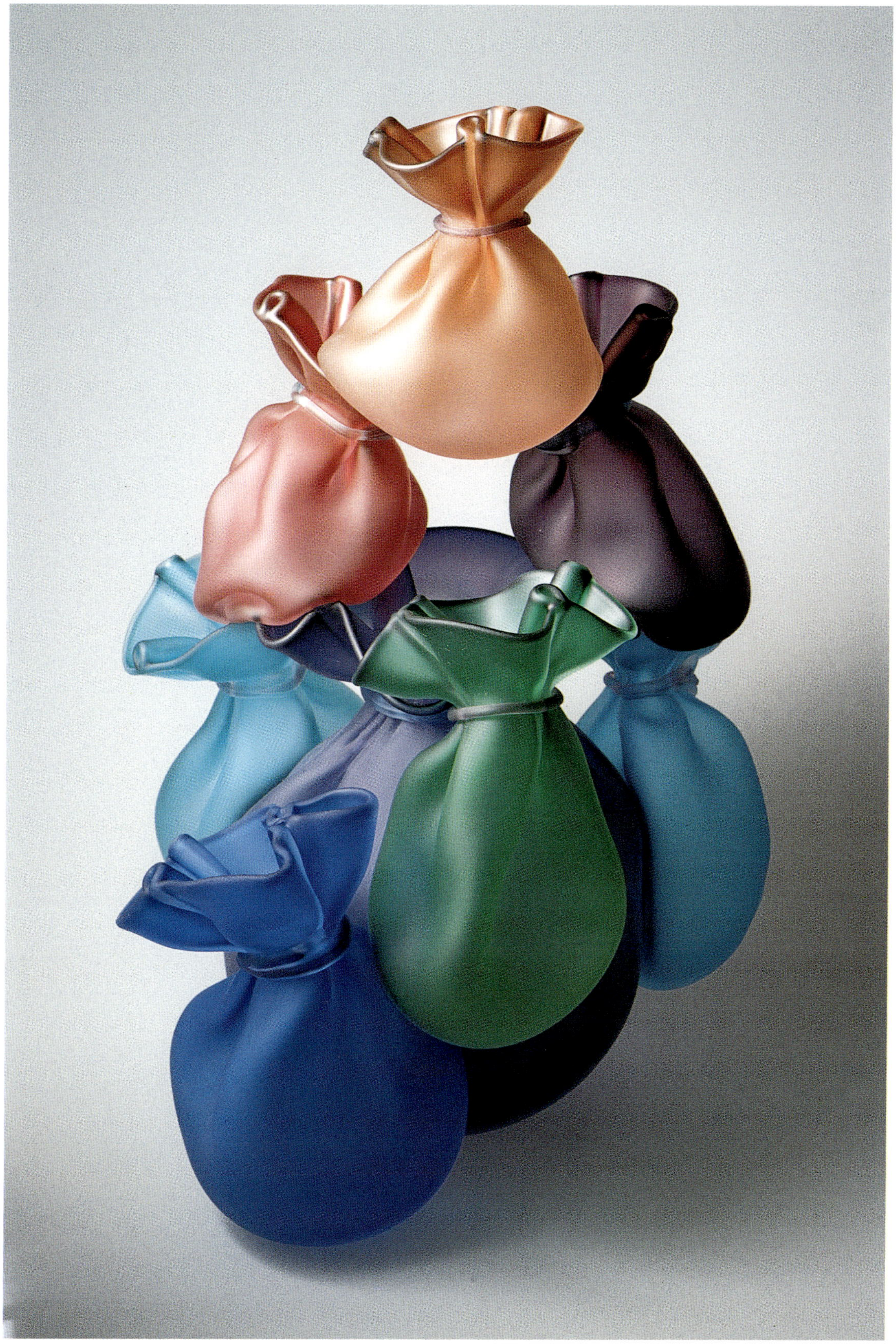

Ann Wåhlström
(b. 1957)

KOSTA, SWEDEN

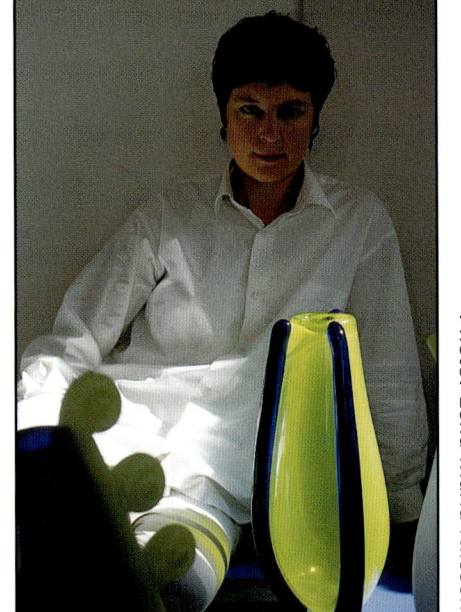

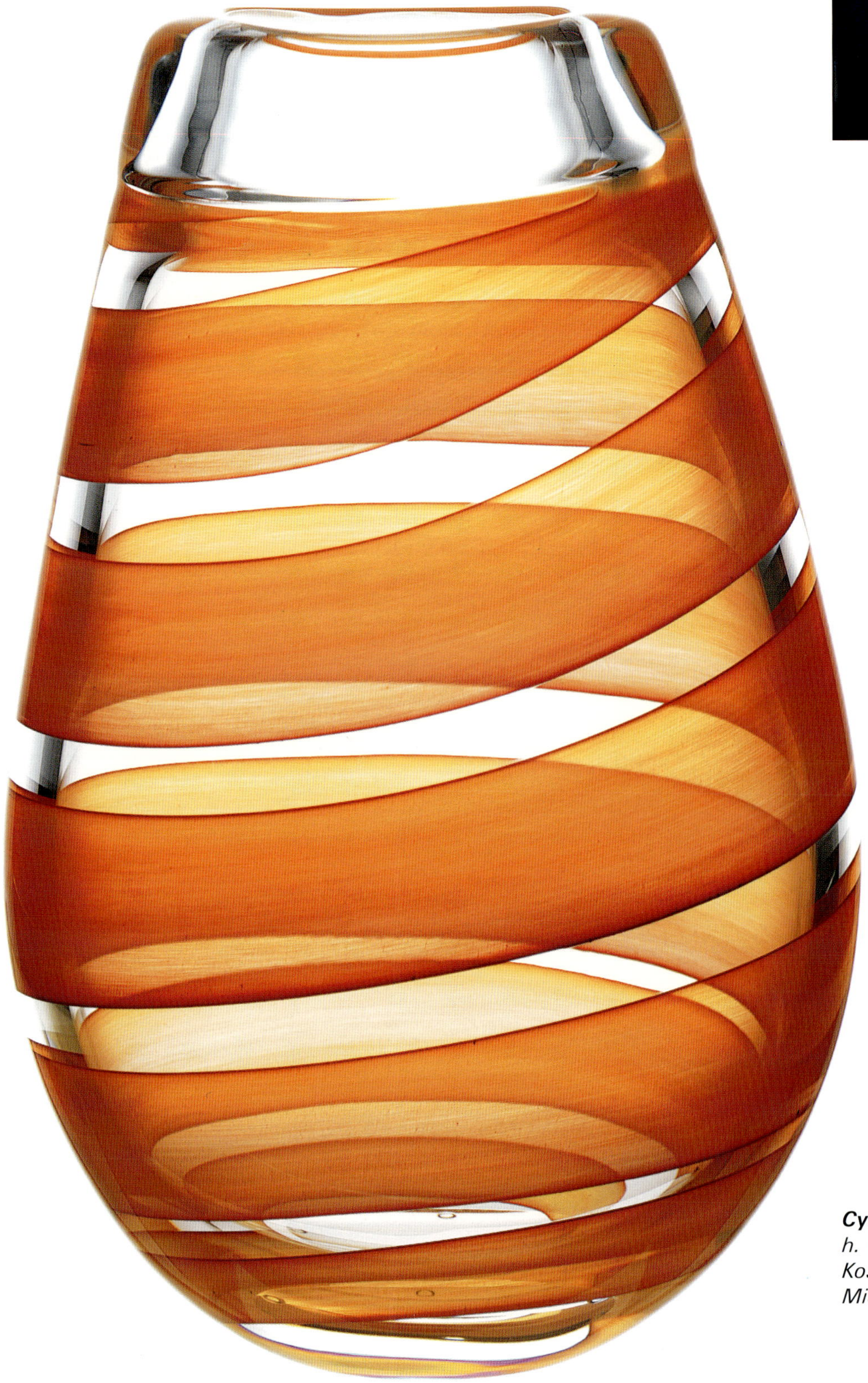

Cyklon, 1998. Blown glass, h. 17 inches. Limited edition, Kosta Boda, Sweden. Photo: Michael Förster.

BROOKLYN, NEW YORK

Peter Waldman
(b. 1963)

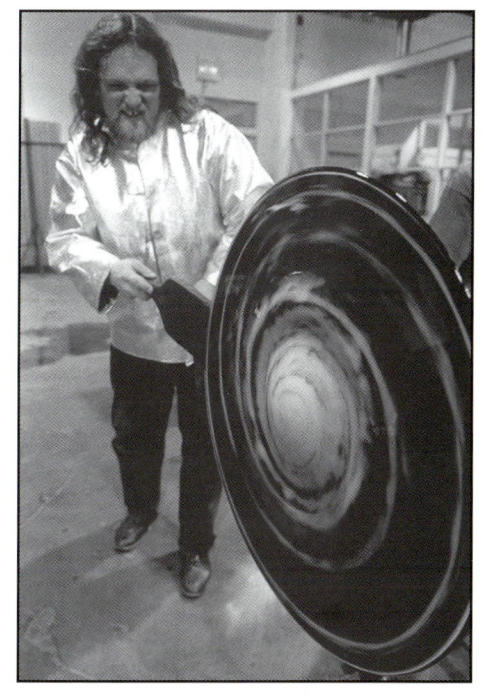
Photo: George Erml

8728; Galaxy Series, 1999. Blown glass, h. 30 inches. Photo: George Erml.

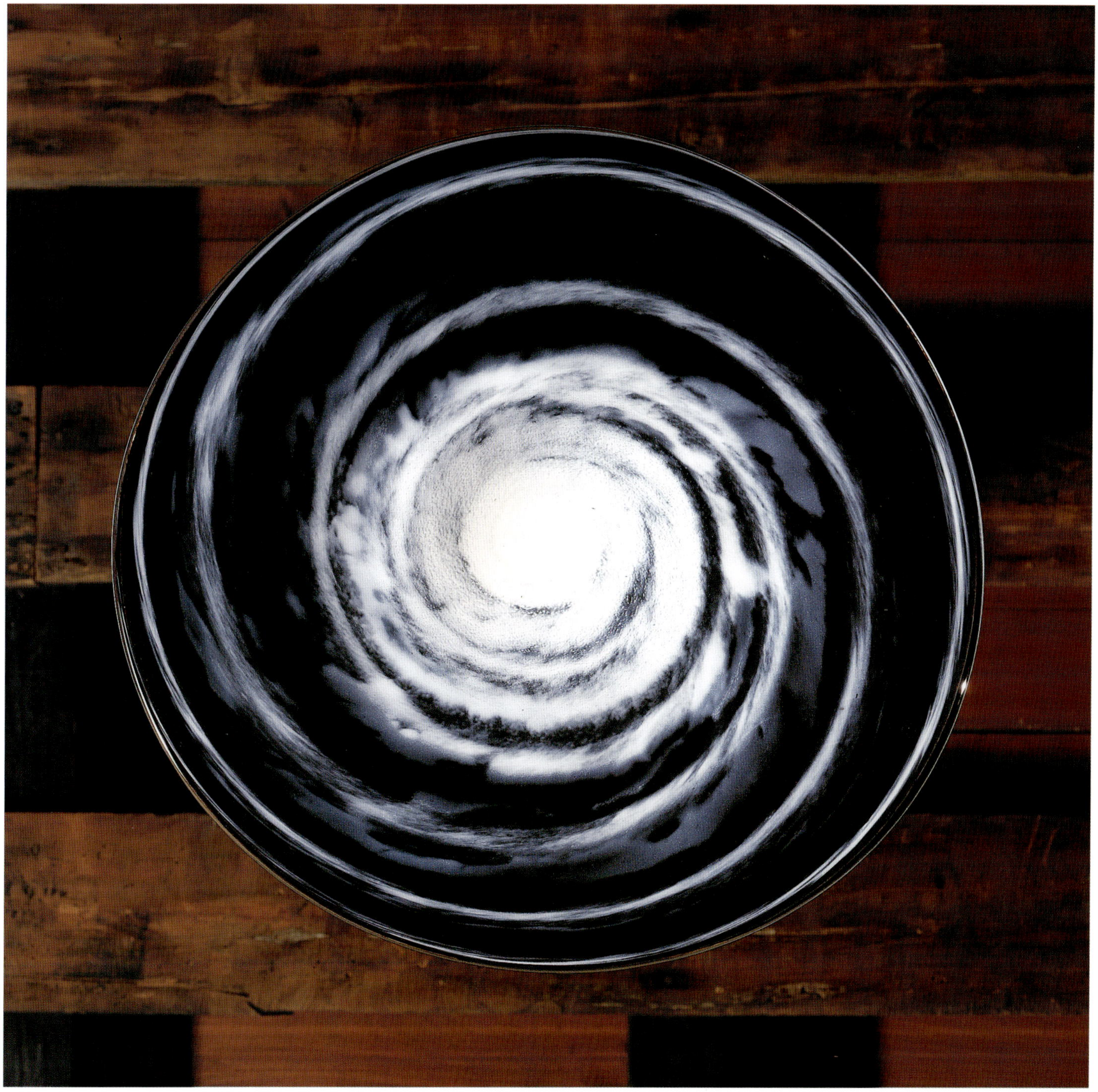

Rosita Walsh
(b. 1950)

BROOKLYN, NEW YORK

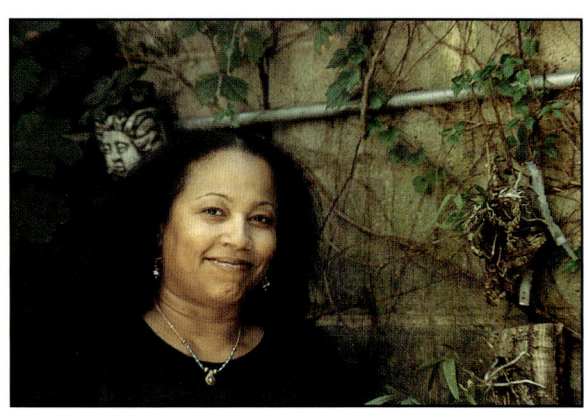

Top:
*A Collection of "**Eye Beads**"
inspired and made in Italy*

Bottom:
*Four "**Standing Core Vessel Beads**" inspired and made in Italy*

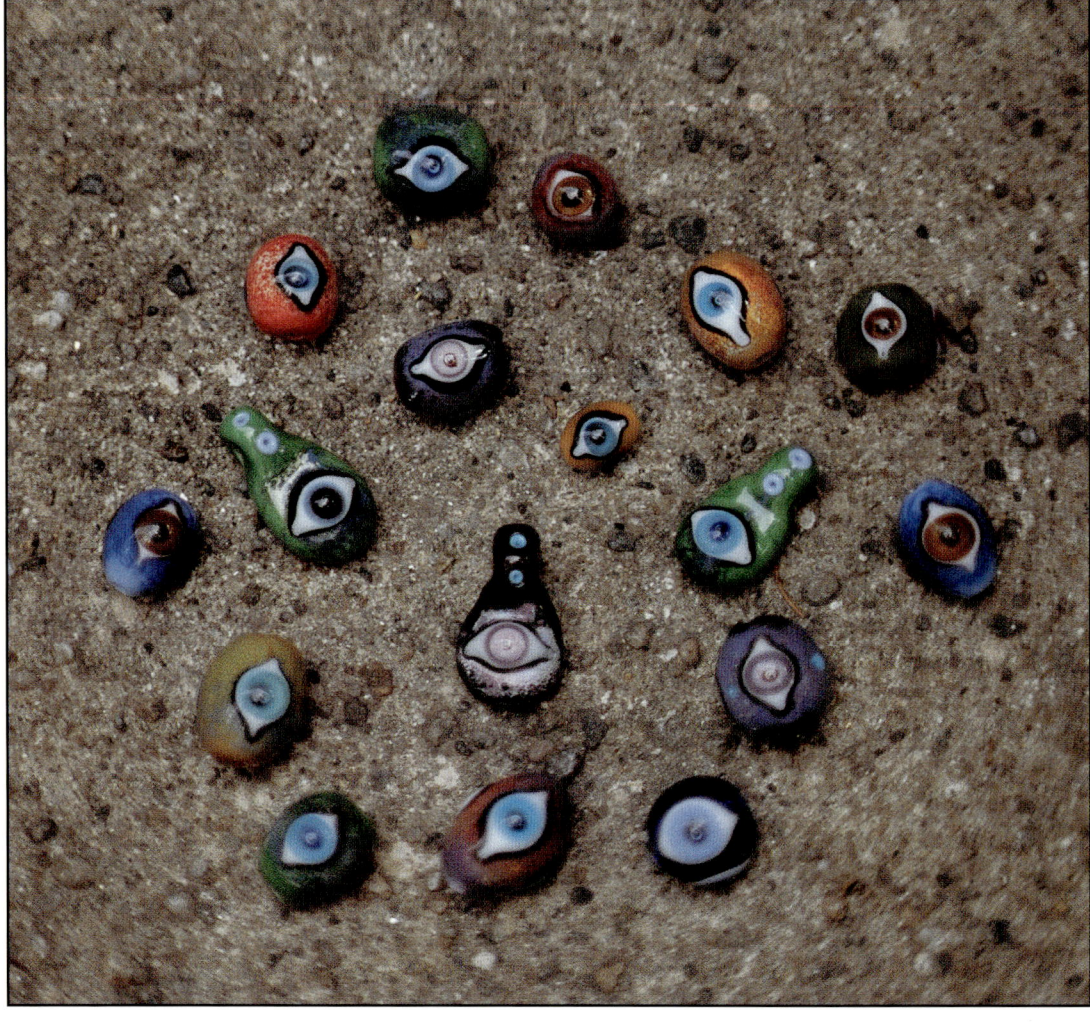

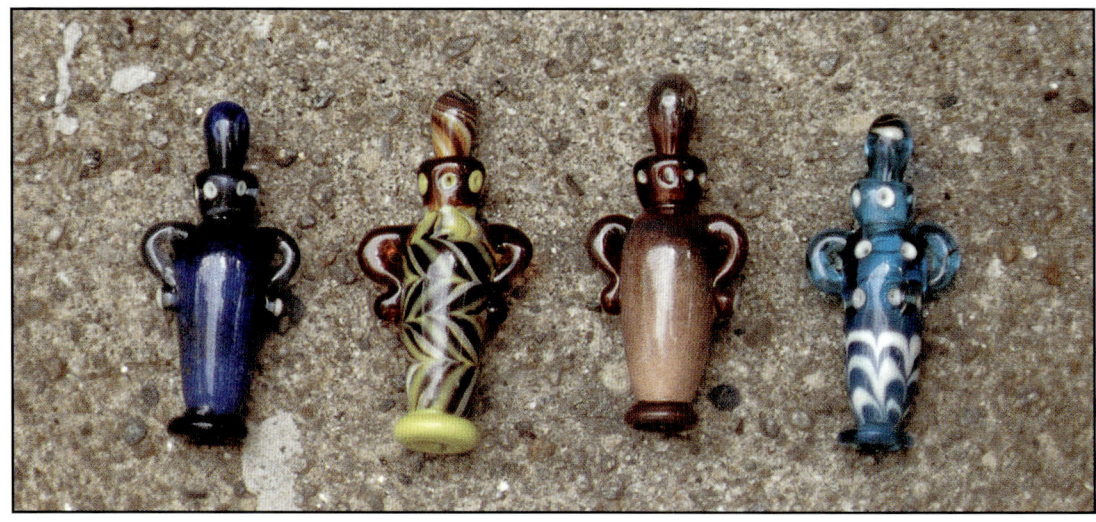

PAWTUCKET, RHODE ISLAND

James Watkins
(b. 1955)

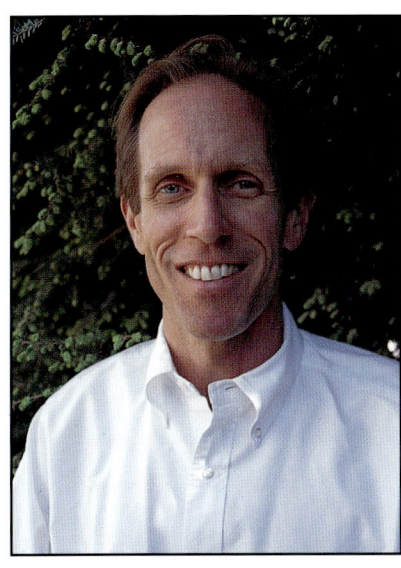

***Windows**, 1991. Pâte de cristal, h. 21 x 11 x 5 inches. Photo: James Beards.*

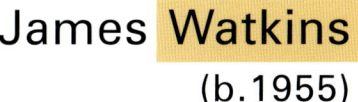

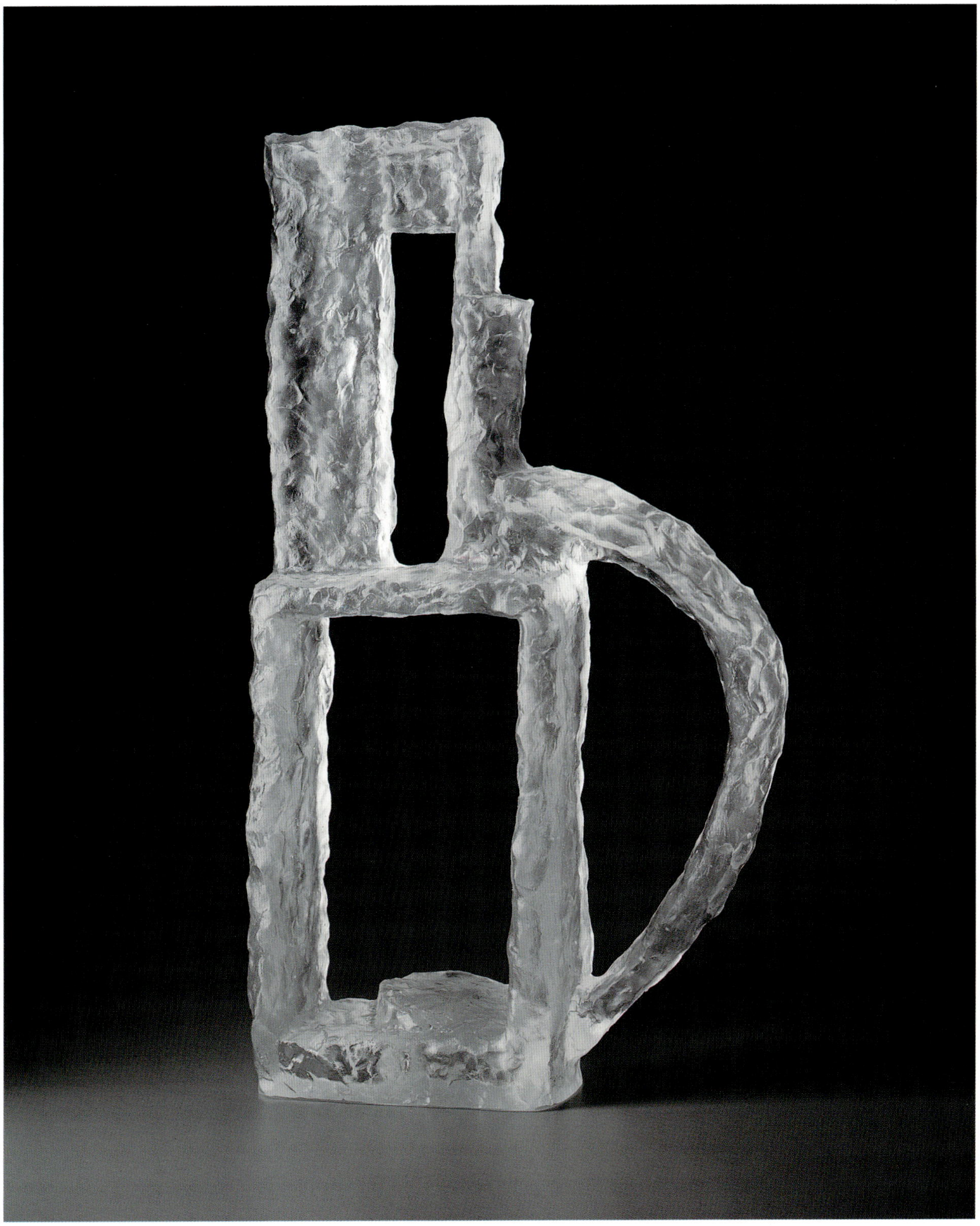

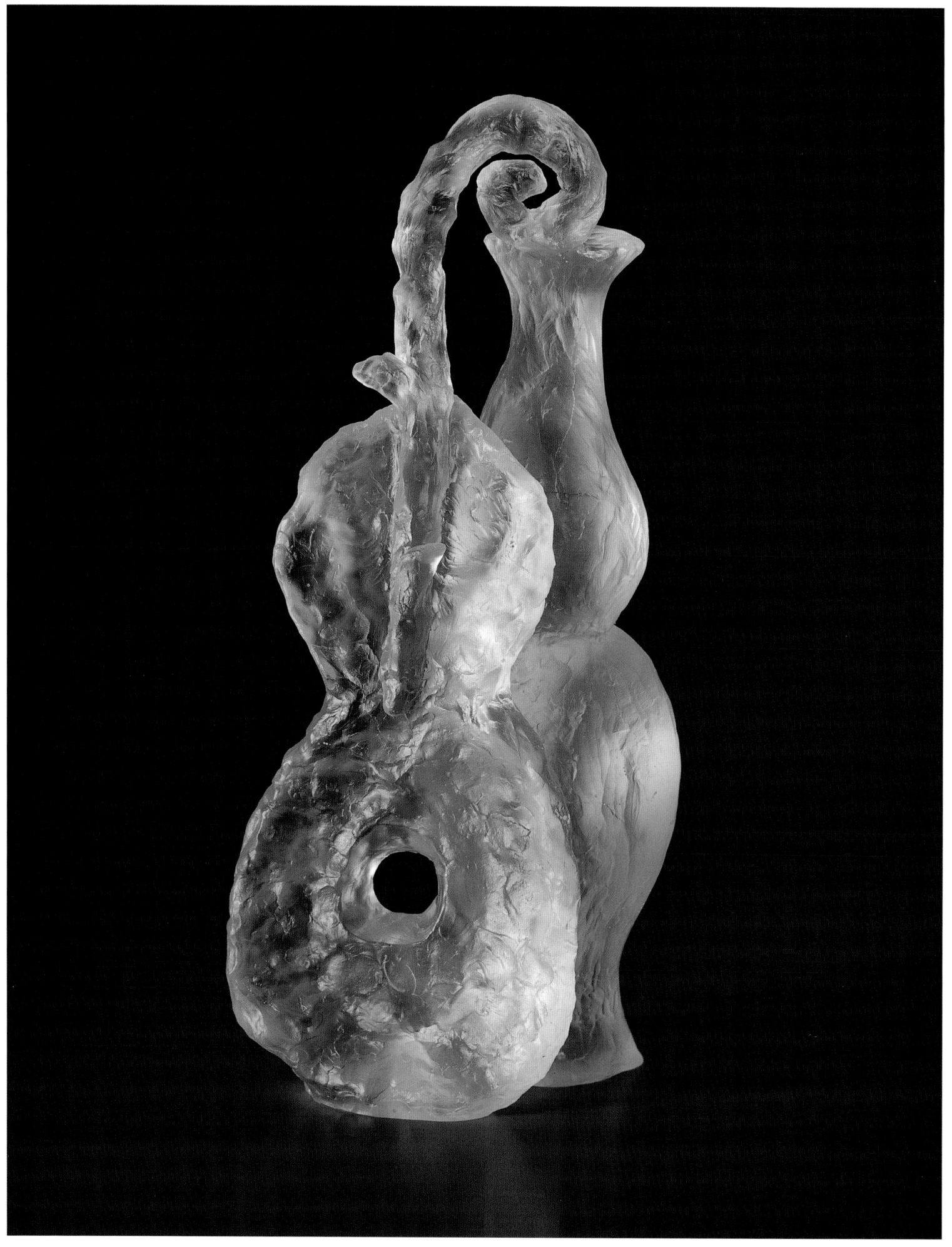

Fiddlehead With Crystal, 1994. Pâte de verre, h. 20 x 9 x 6 inches. Photo: James Beards.

PAWTUCKET, RHODE ISLAND

Steven I. Weinberg
(b.1954)

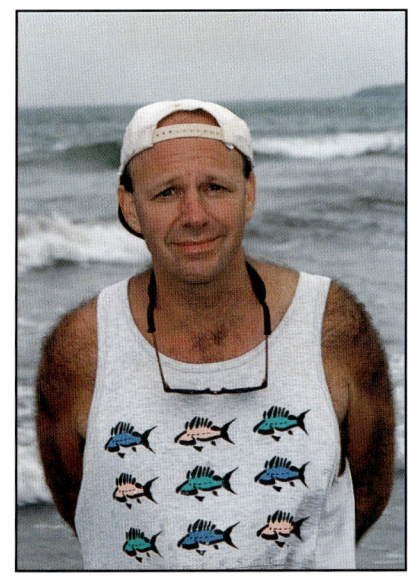

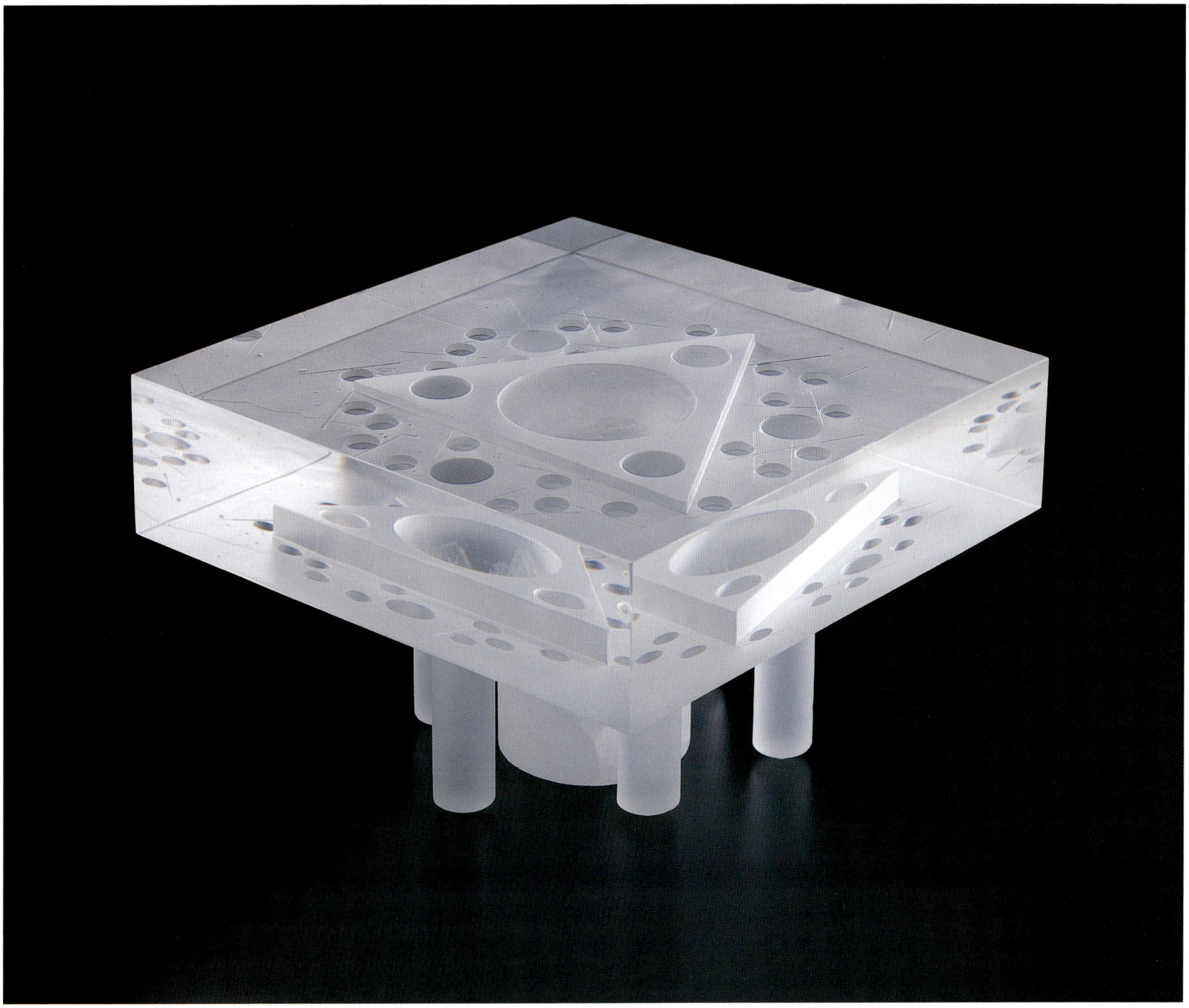

Untitled, 1984. Lead crystal glass, cast, cut, sandblasted, and polished, h. 6 x 9.5 x 9.5 inches. American Craft Museum. Gift of Mike Belkin. Photo: Eva Heyd.

STEVEN I. WEINBERG

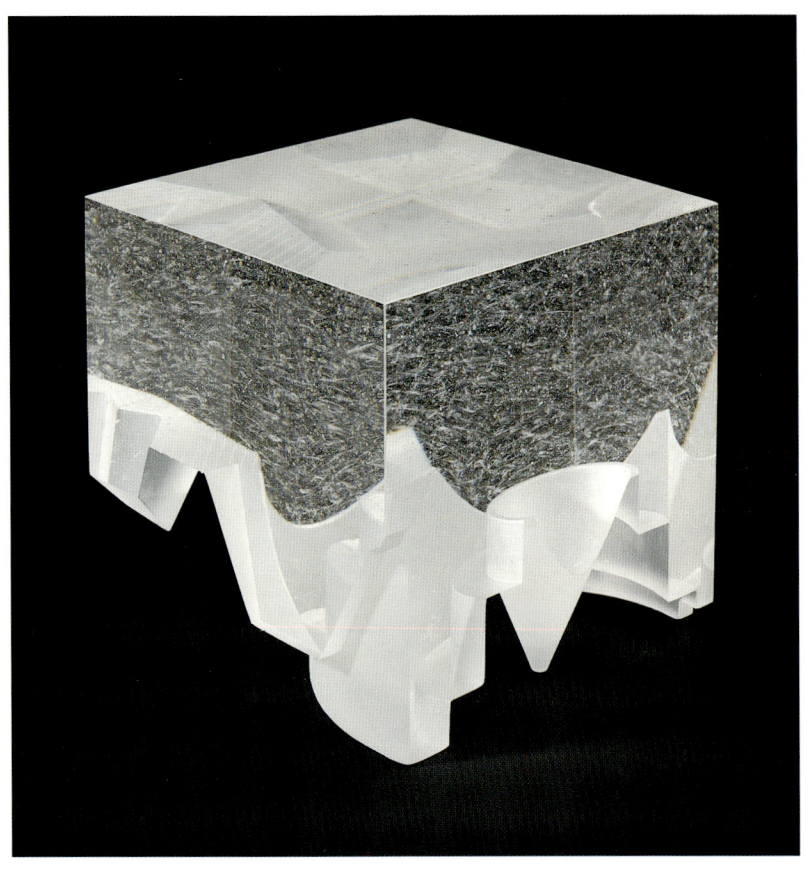

Right:
Untitled (Series cubes), 1987. Lead crystal glass, cast, cut, sandblasted, and polished, h. 7.5 x 7.5 x 7.5 inches. American Craft Museum. Gift of Simona and Jerome Chazen. Photo: Eva Heyd.

Below:
Boat Form: Block Island Blue, 1999. Cast lead crystal, cut, ground, polished, glue chip and ground lens. h. 6.5 x 14 x 4 inches. Courtesy Habatat Galleries. Photo: Douglas Schaible.

Opposite:
Brenton Reef Buoy, 1999. Cast cobalt glass, acid polished, and ground lens, h. 13 x 8 inches. Courtesy Habatat Galleries. Photo: Douglas Schaible.

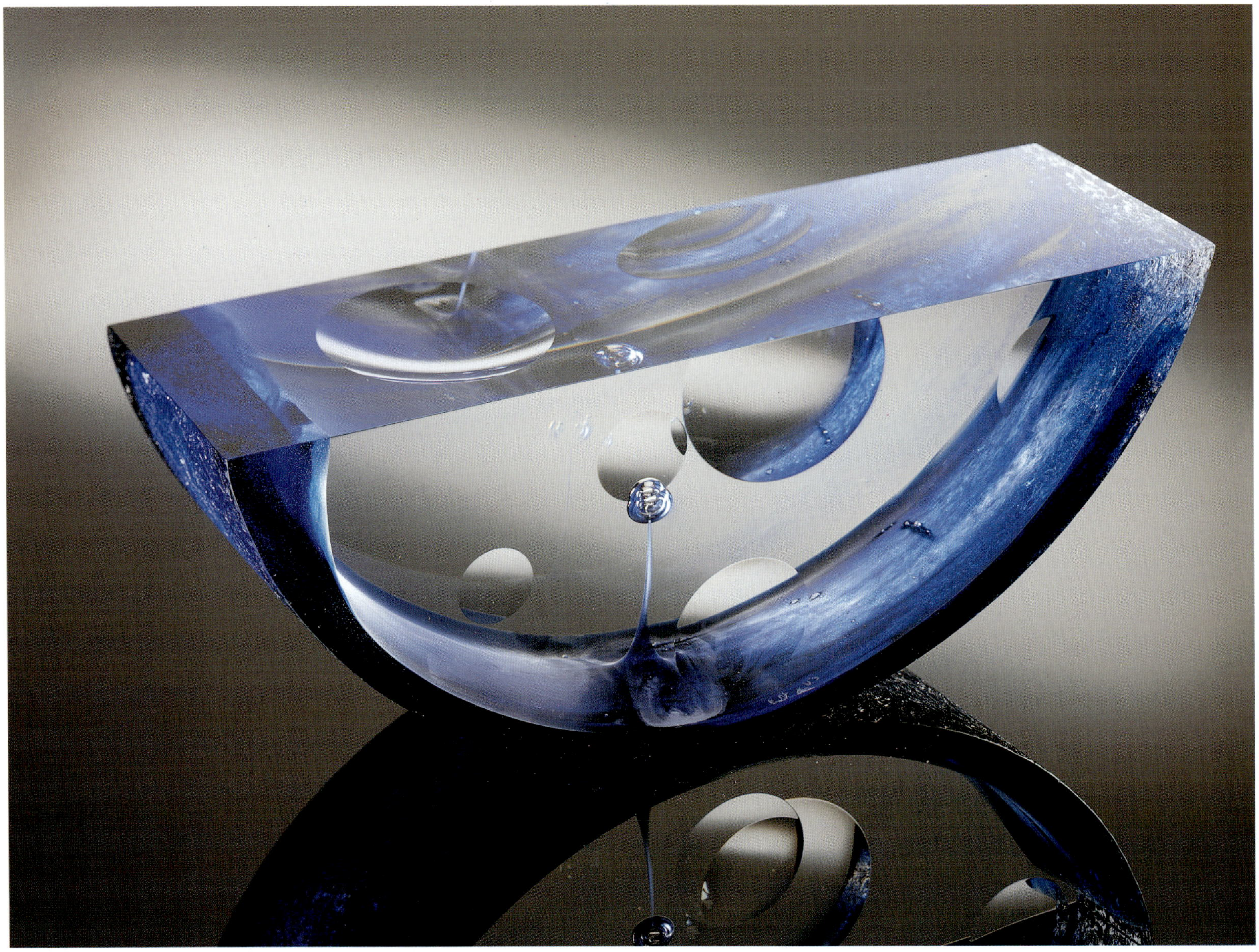

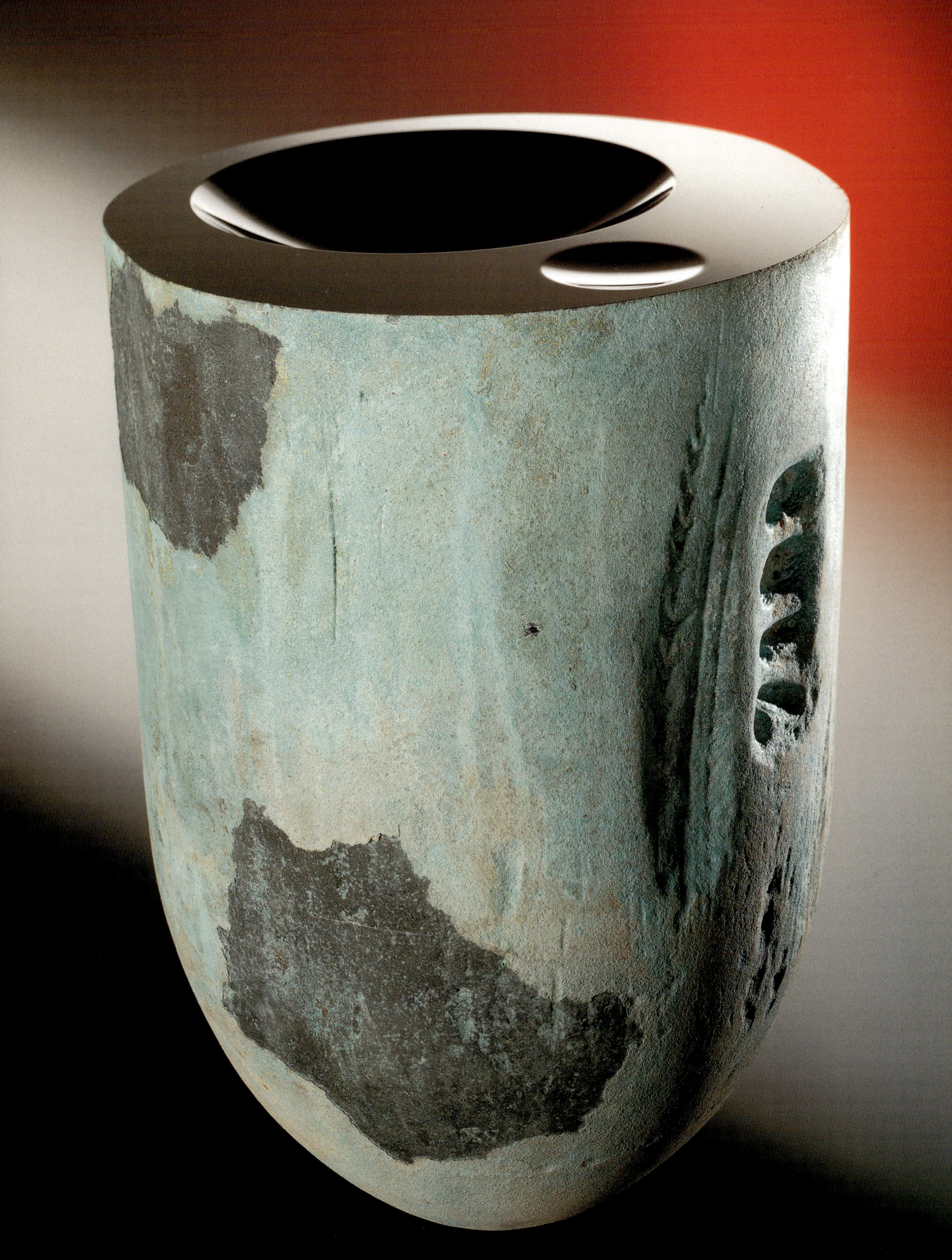

Dick Weiss
(b.1946)

SEATTLE, WASHINGTON

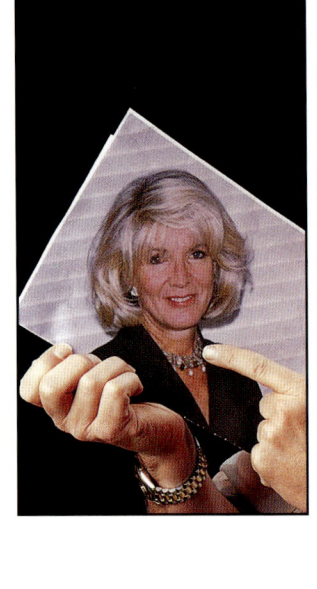

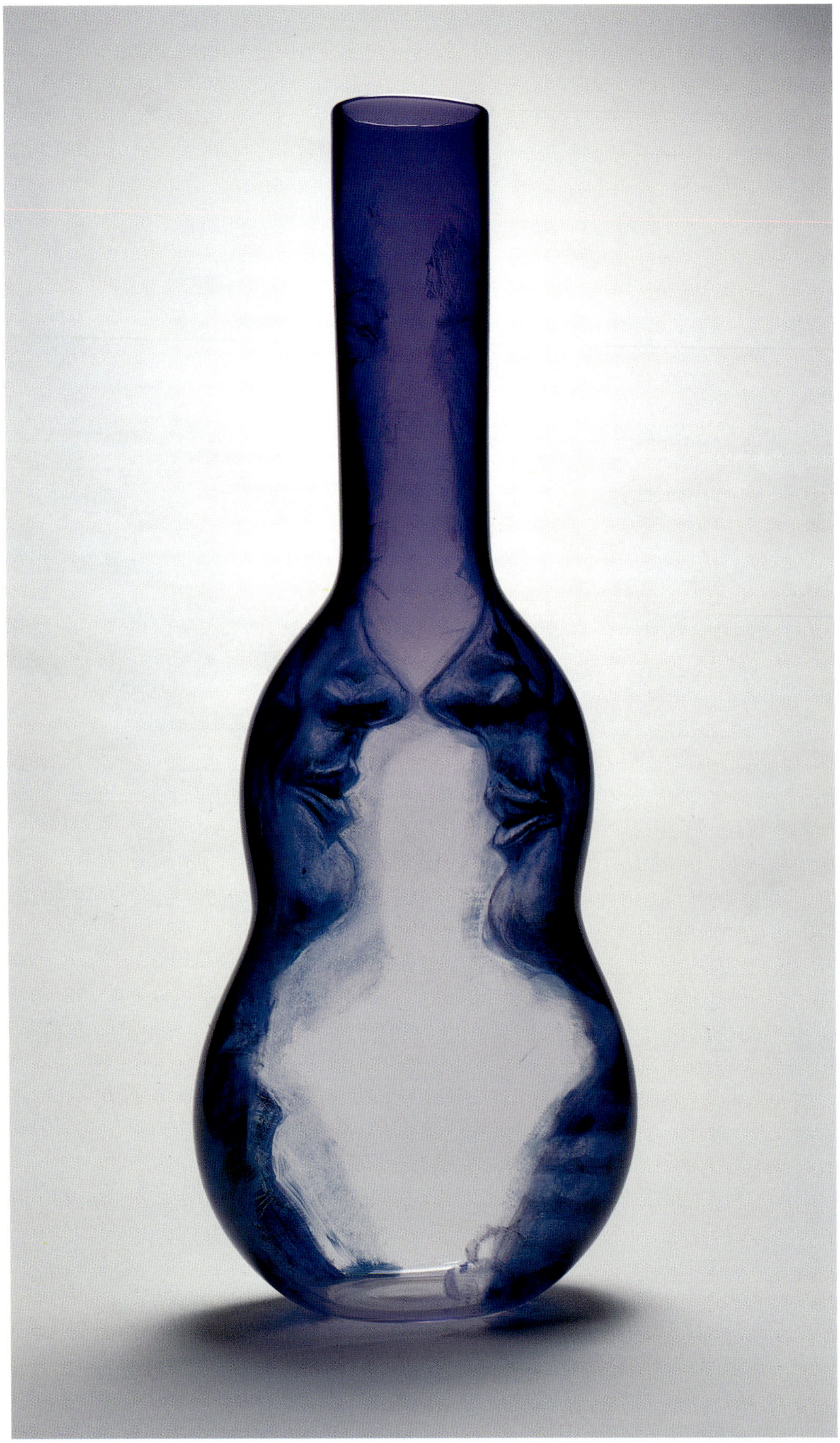

Left:
2 Profiles: Blue, 1997. Enamel fired onto blown glass, h. 26 x 12 x 4 inches. Vessel blown by Ben Moore and Dante Marioni. Photo: Roger Schreiber.

Opposite:
Black Hand Series; No.3, 1997. Enamels on blown glass, h. 26 x 13 x 5 inches. Vessel blown by Ben Moore and Dante Marioni.

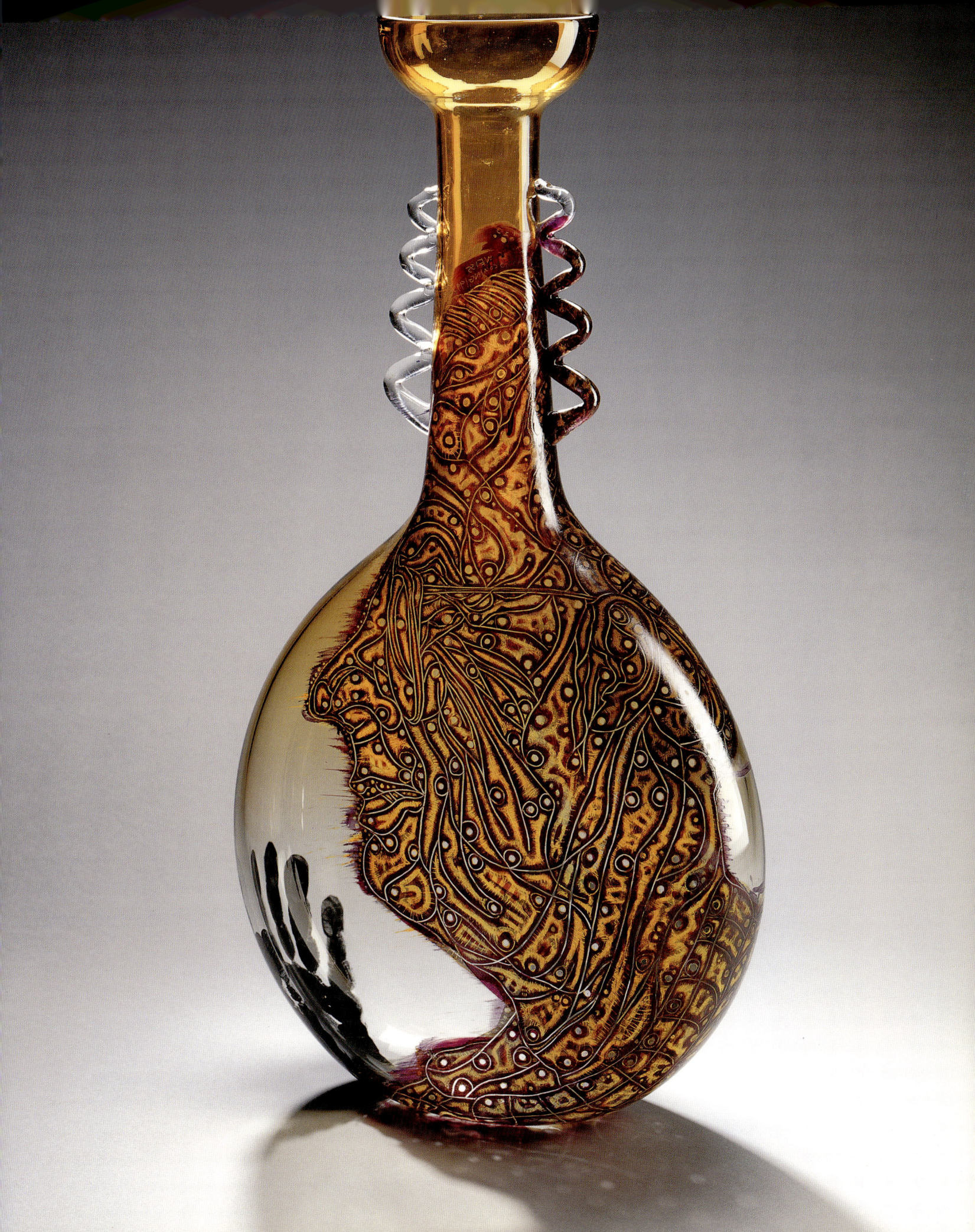

Christopher Wilmarth
(1943-1987)

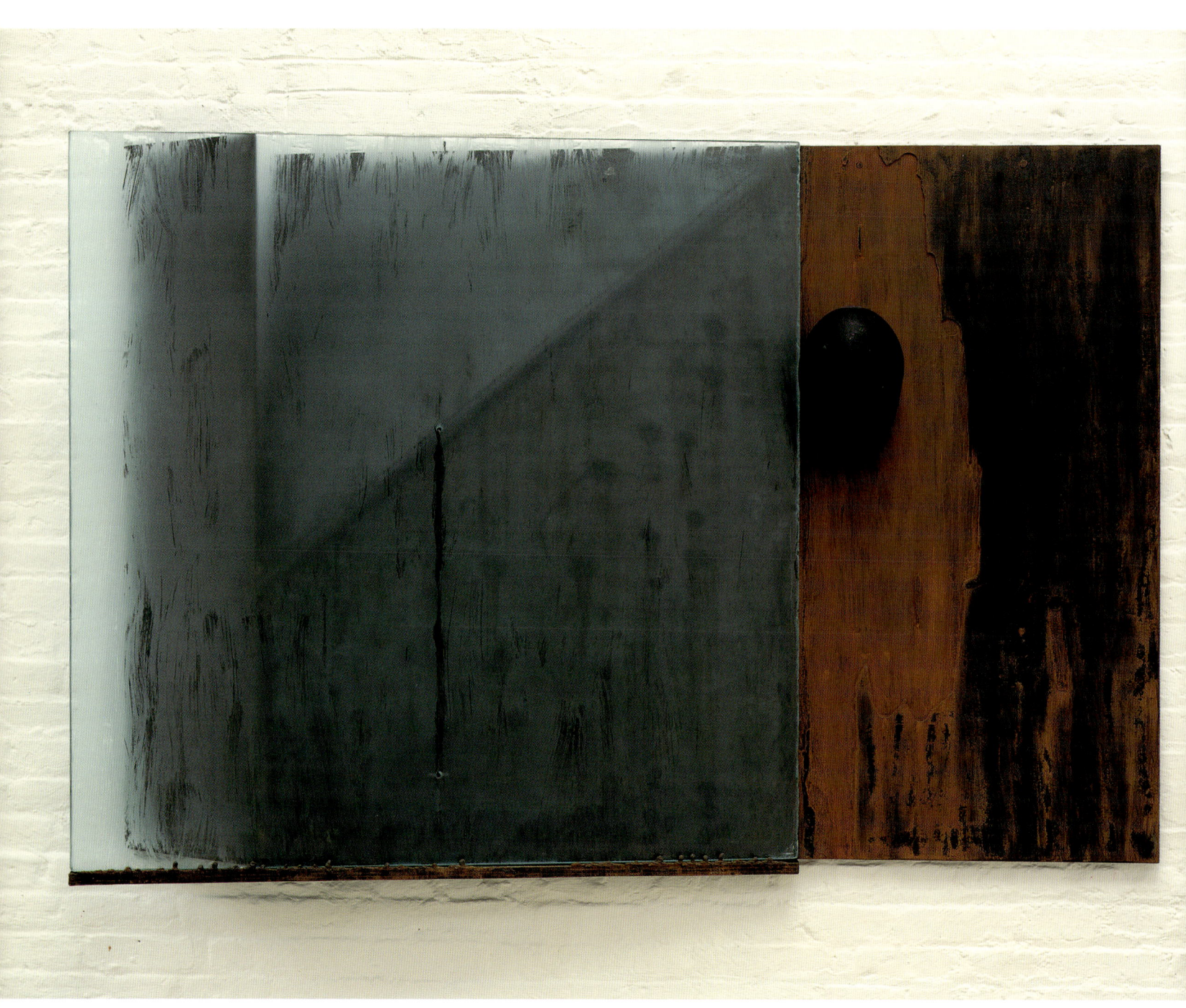

Street Leaf; Mayaquez, *1978-86. Etched flat glass, etched brown glass, bronze, and steel, h. 48 x 72 x 9 inches. Courtesy Susan Wilmarth-Rabineau.*

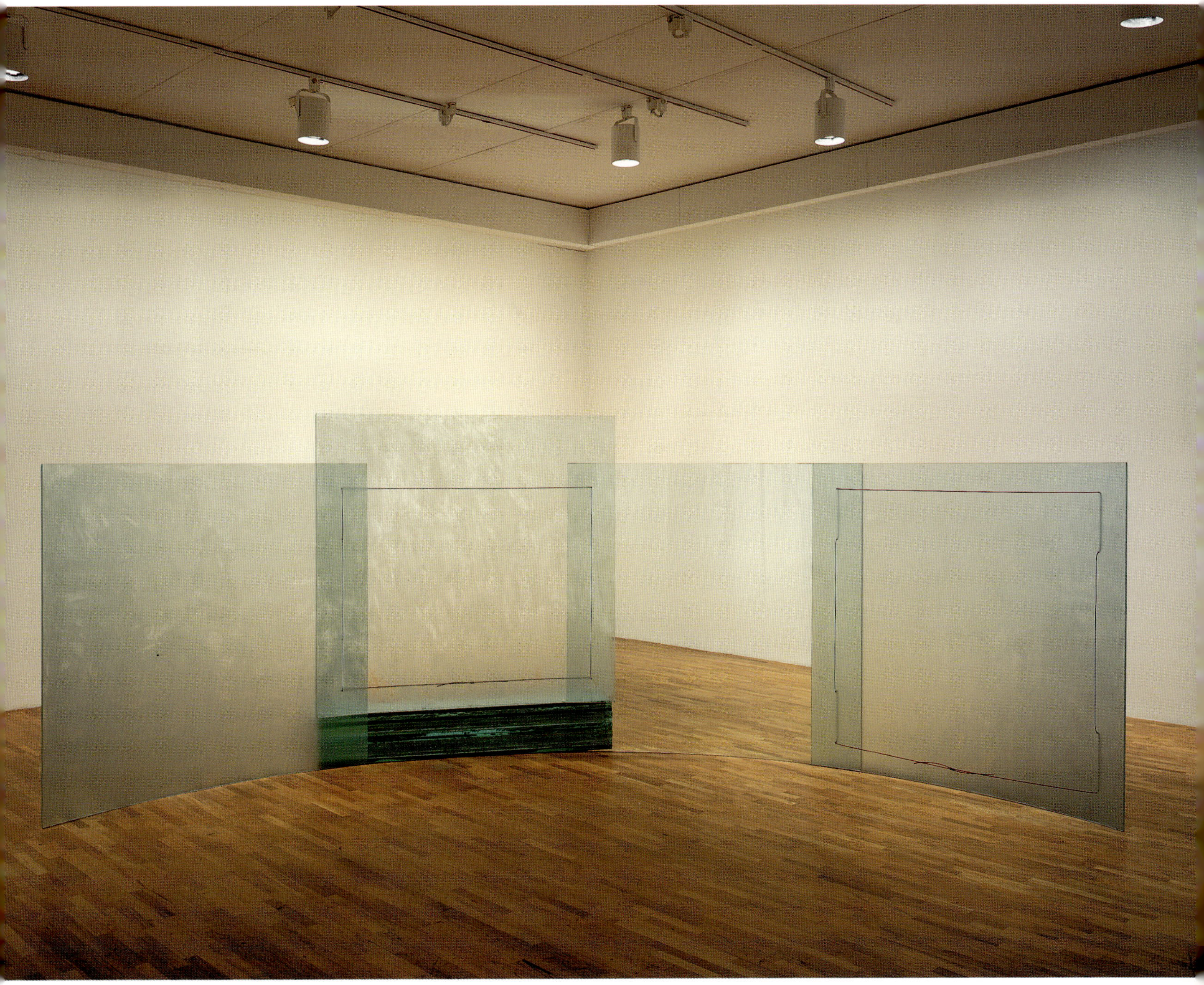

BROOKLYN, NEW YORK

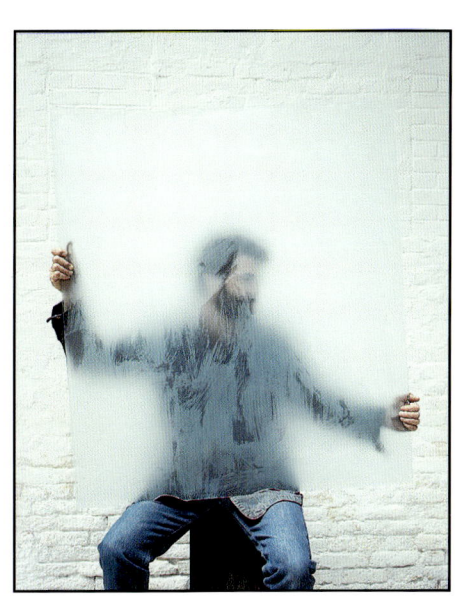

Tina Turner, 1971. Bent glass (clear and etched), glass planks, and steel cable, h. 69.75 x 177 x 58 inches. Courtesy Susan Wilmarth-Rabineau.

CHRISTOPHER WILMARTH

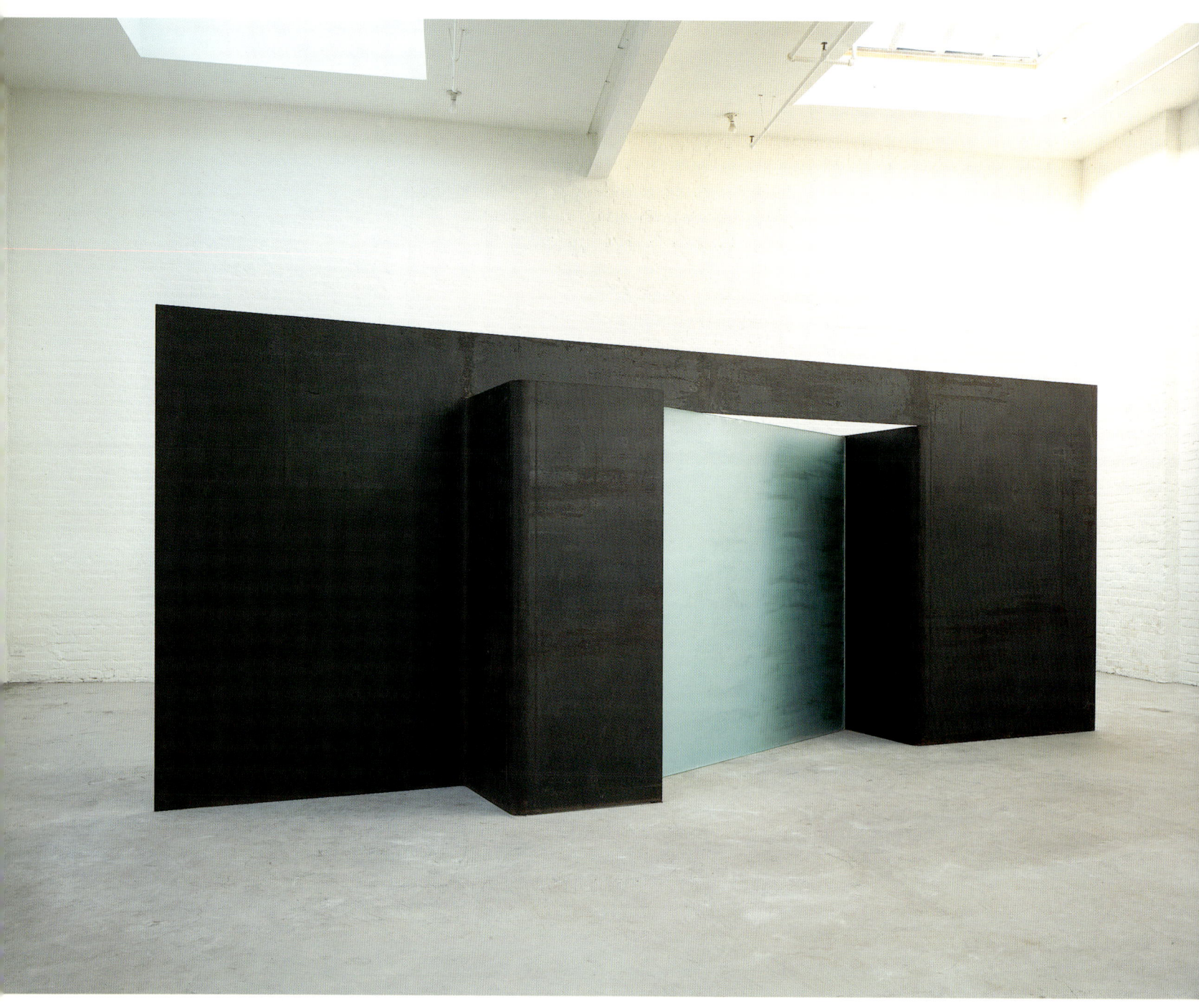

Days on Blue, 1974-77. Etched glass, and steel, h. 84 x 210 x 60 inches.
Courtesy Susan Wilmarth-Rabineau.

NEW YORK, NEW YORK

J. Raven Wilson
(b.1971)

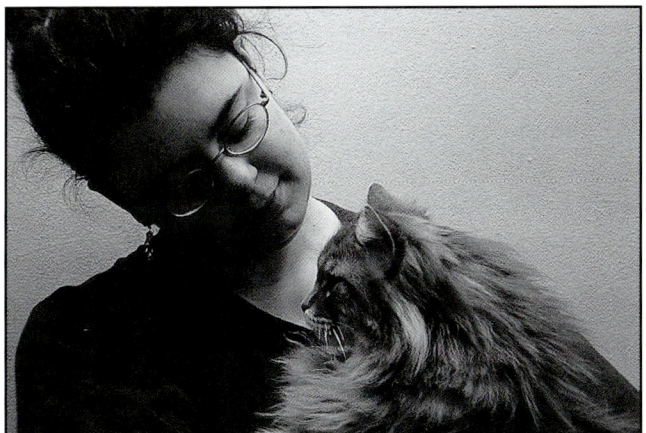

Photo: R.S. Carter

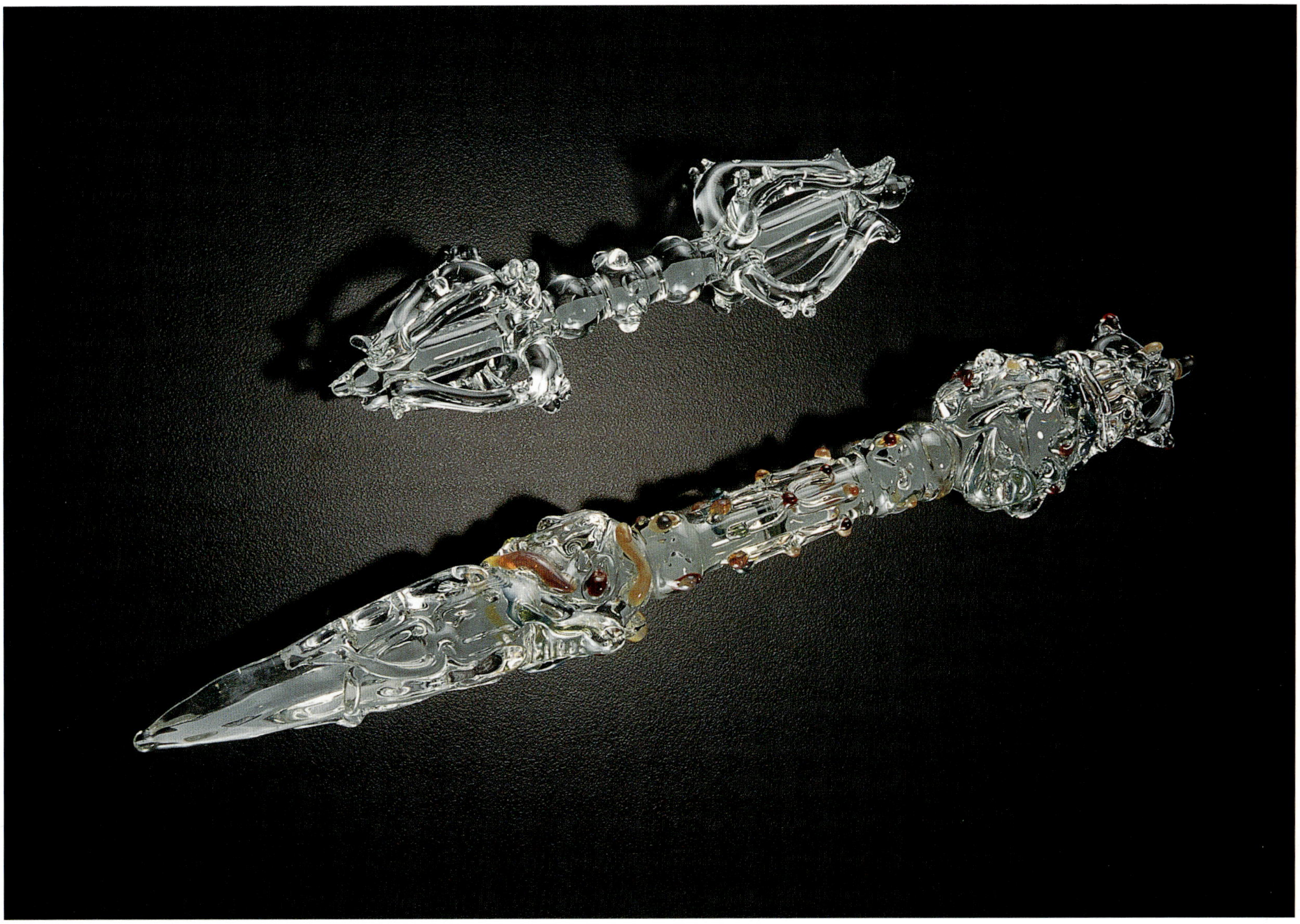

Dorje and Pudubu, 1998-99. Lampworked glass, (top to bottom) h. 5.37 x 1.25 and h. 9.8 x 1.5 inches. Photo: Tommy O. Elder.

Julian Wolff
(b.1925)

WANTAGH, NEW YORK

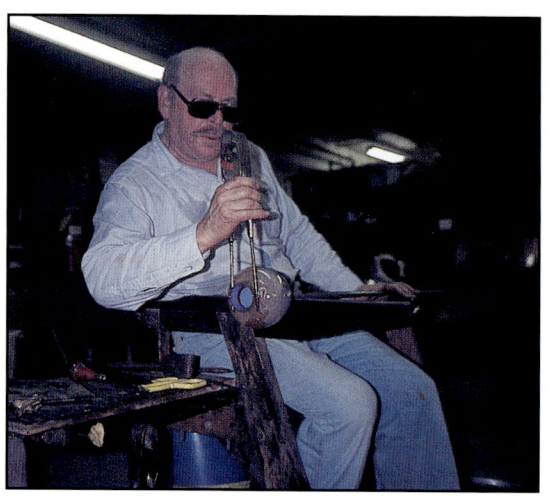

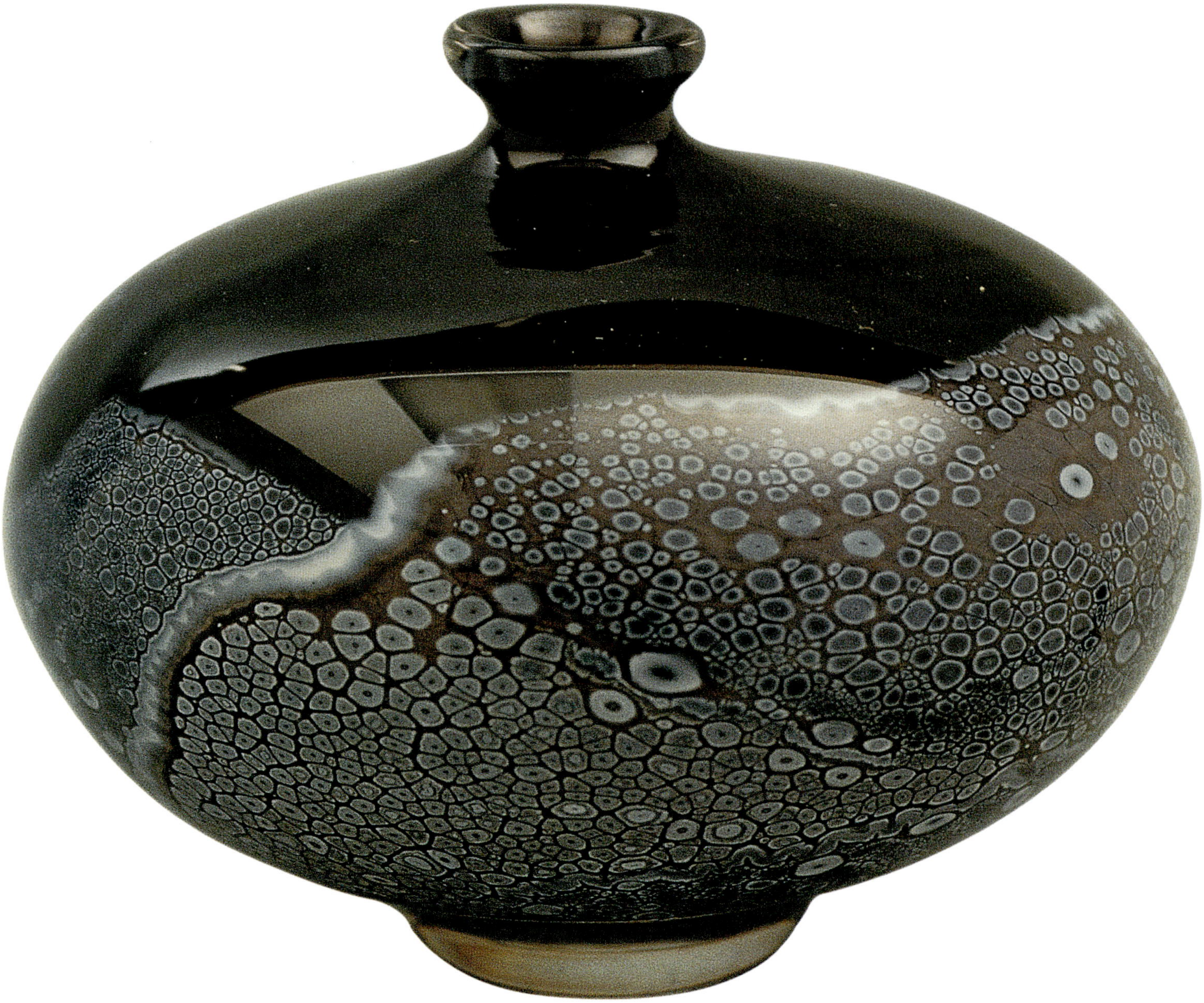

Untitled, 1999. Blown glass, h. 6 x 8 inches.

NEW YORK, NEW YORK

Ronnie Wolf
(b.1954)

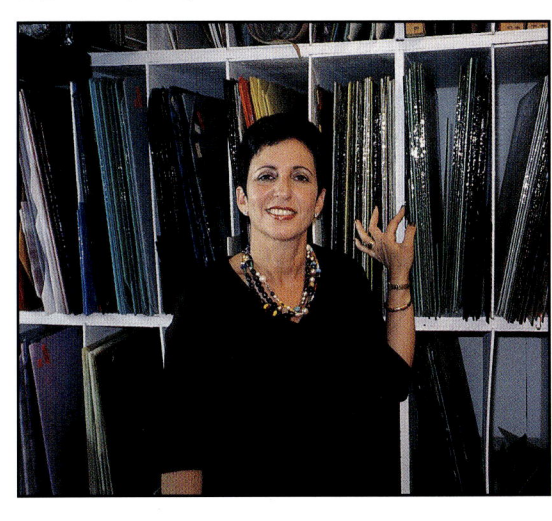

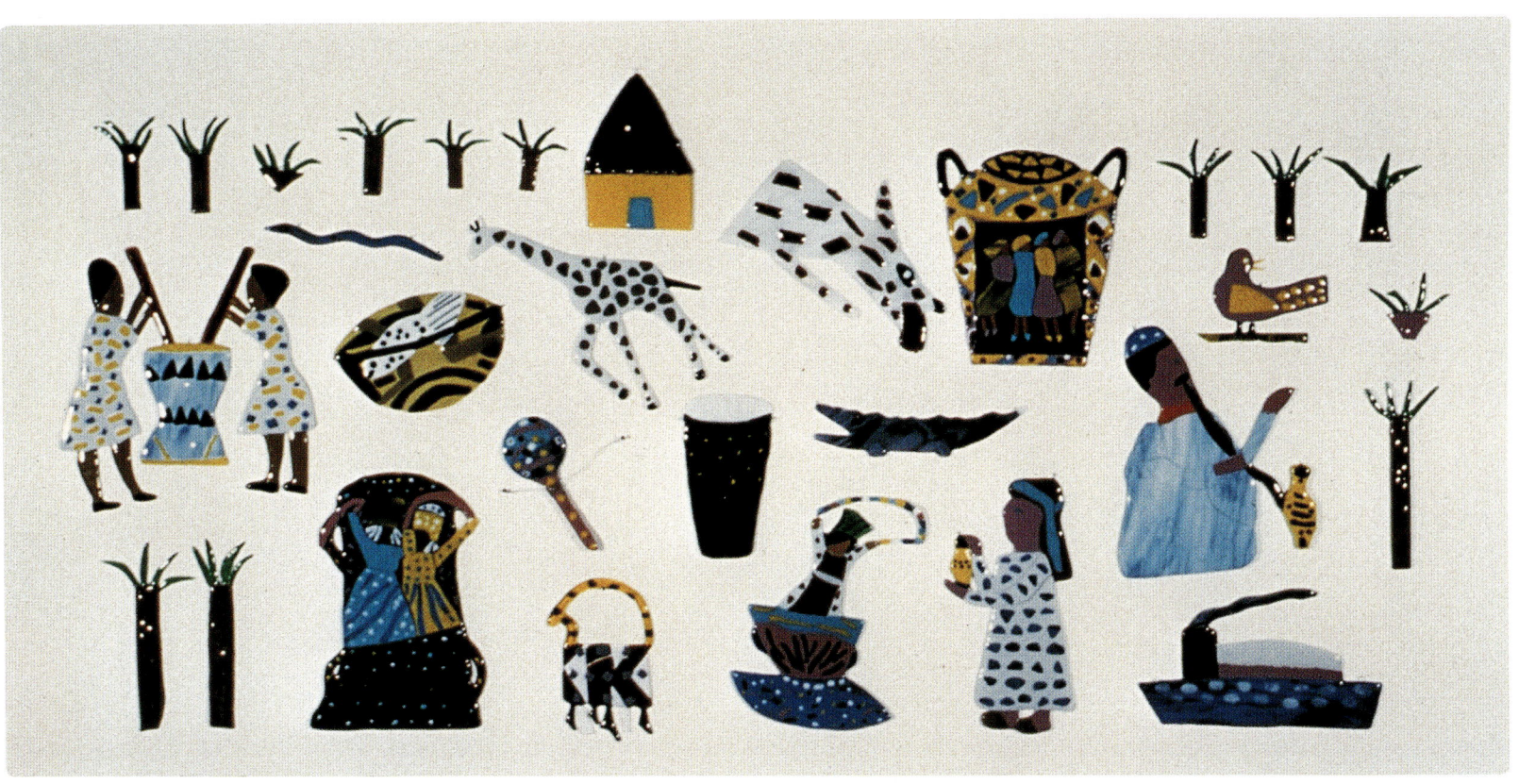

Travel Reflections, 1999. Fused glass wall mural, h. 4 x 6 feet.

Betty Woodman
(b.1930)

NEW YORK, NEW YORK

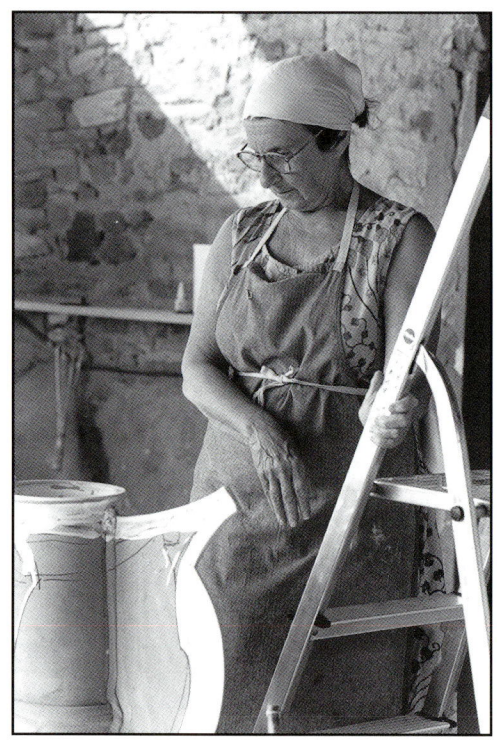

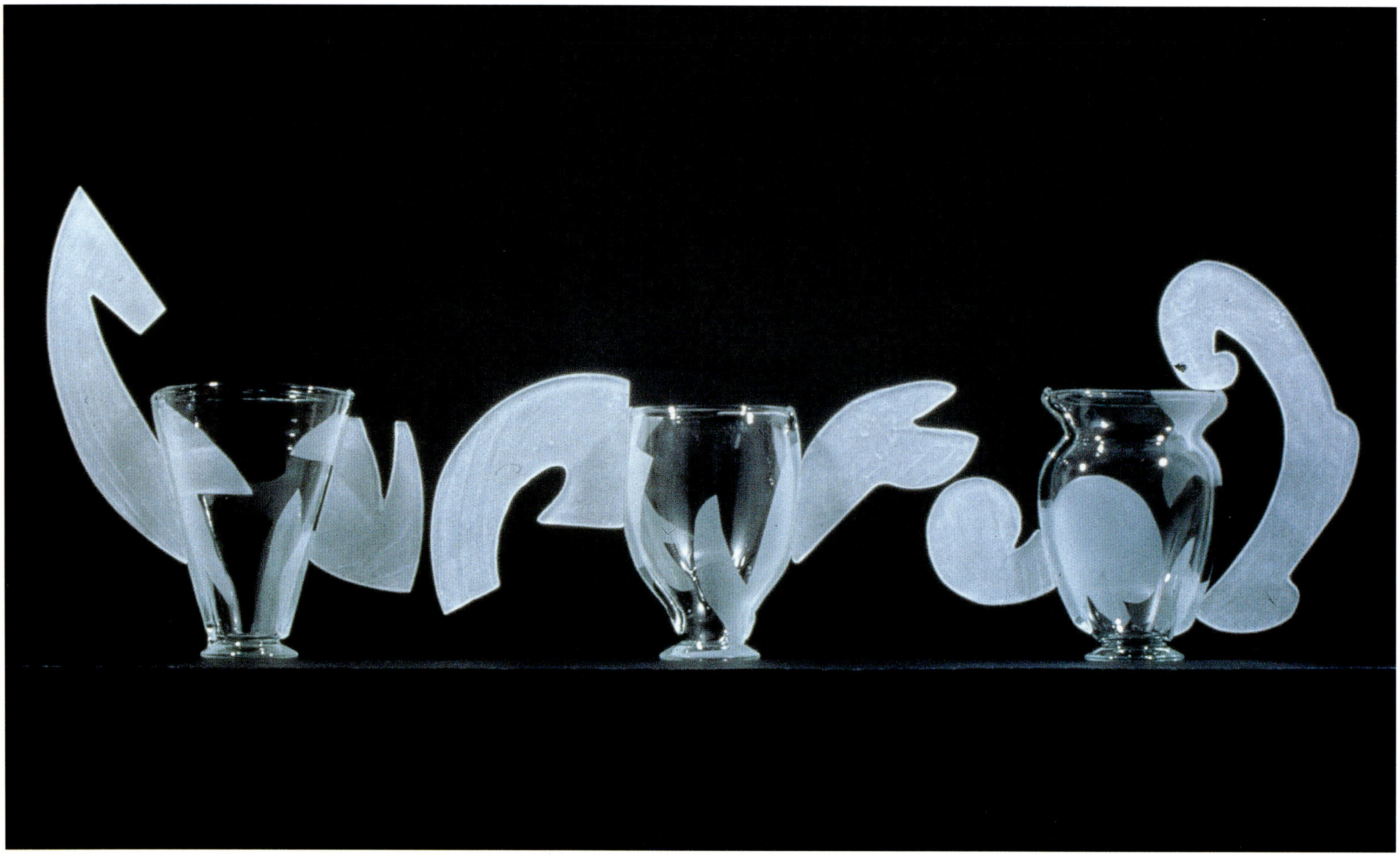

Above:
Triptych D, 1993-96. Blown glass, h. 66.1 x 7.7 x 23.4 inches. Courtesy Max Protetch Gallery.

Opposite:
Solo Vase 2, 1993-96. Blown glass, h. 19.1 x 5.7 x 21.3 inches. Courtesy Max Protetch Gallery.

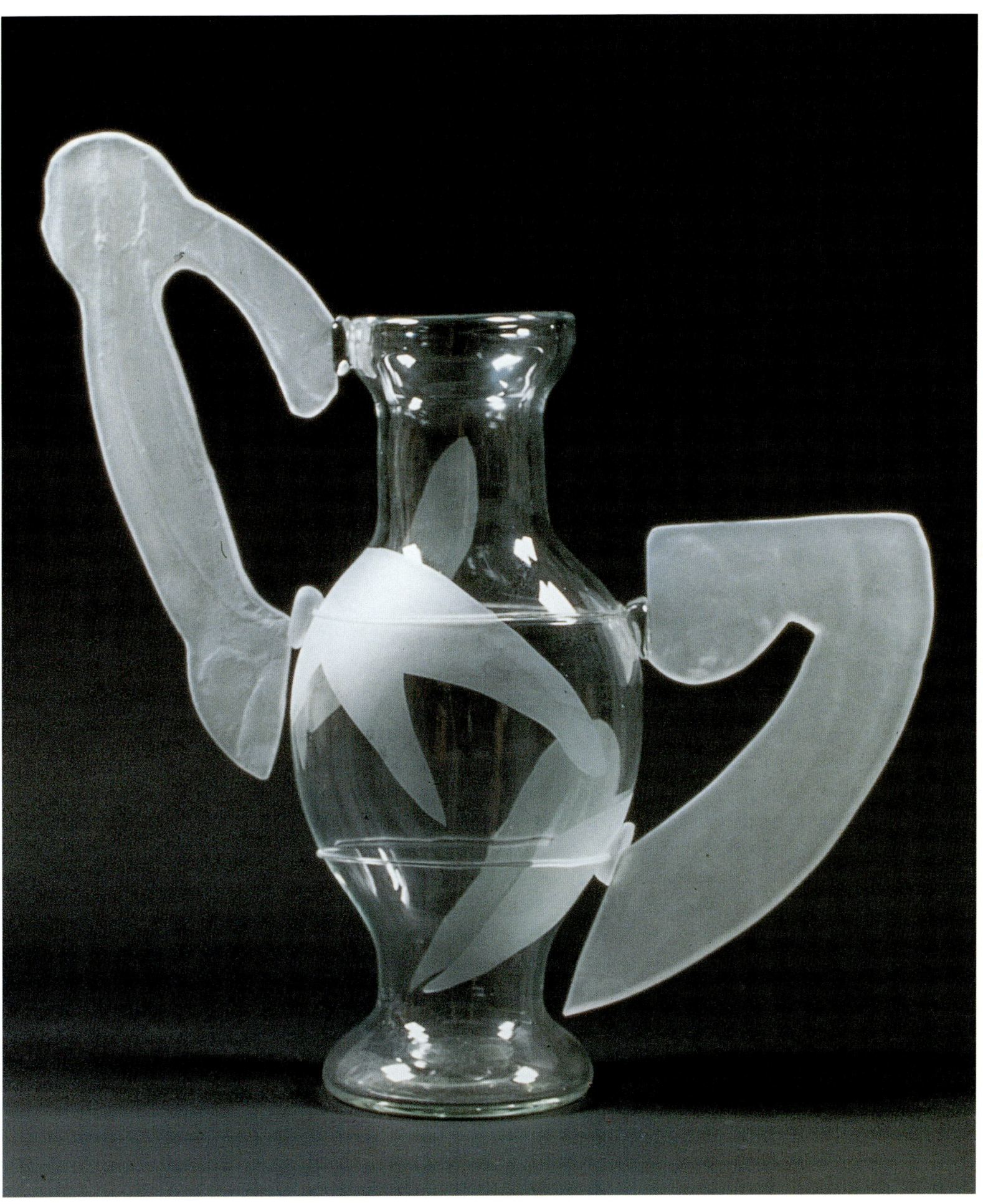

299

Richard Wilfred Yelle
(b.1951)

NORTH SALEM, NEW YORK

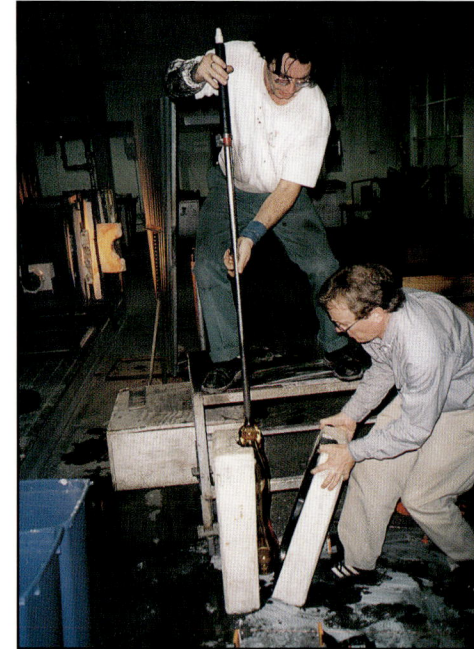

Artist in Residence, Richard Yelle (right) with gaffer Jeff Zimmerman removing blown glass form (from the new series ChipHeads!) from a plaster mold, UrbanGlass hot shop, November 1999.

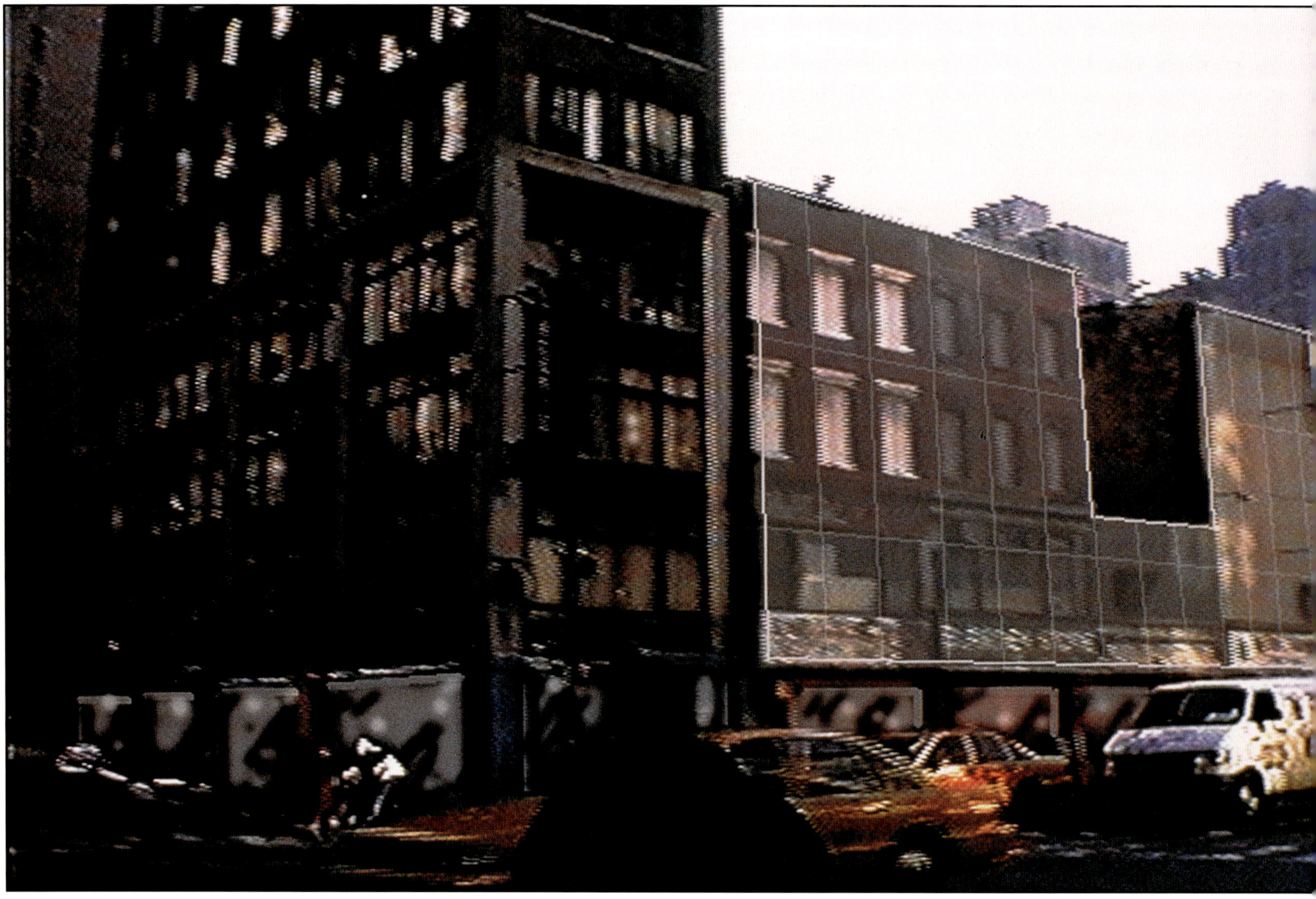

Virtual Tenants; 42nd Street, Interaction/Intersection, *(Day view) 1996. Projec[tions] Collaborative, Parsons School of Design. Tishman Construction Company proposal for glass filter screen on vacant buildings at Forty-Second and Seventh Avenue, New York City. Projec[tions] team: Dean Charles O. Olton, Christopher Grant Kirwan, Michael Lucero, and Richard Wilfred Yelle, Producer.*

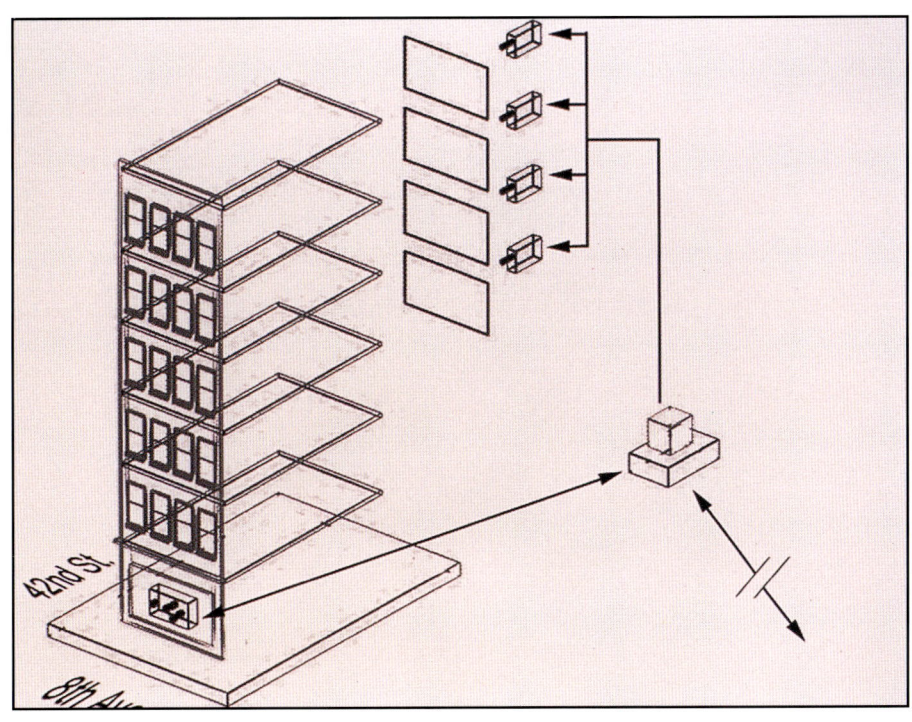

Virtual Tenants, (Digital Projection Plan) 1996.

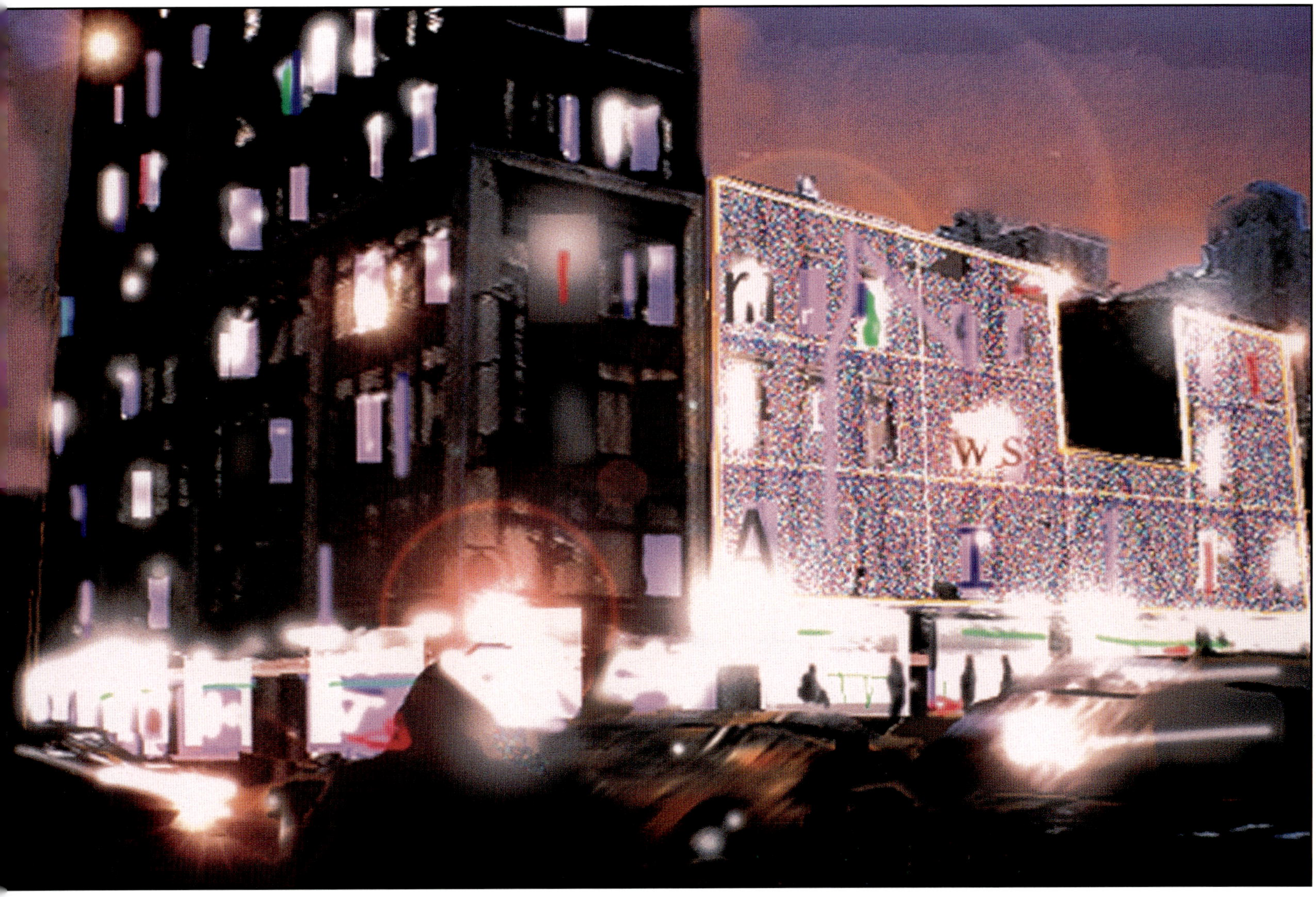

Virtual Tenants, (Night View) 1996.

301

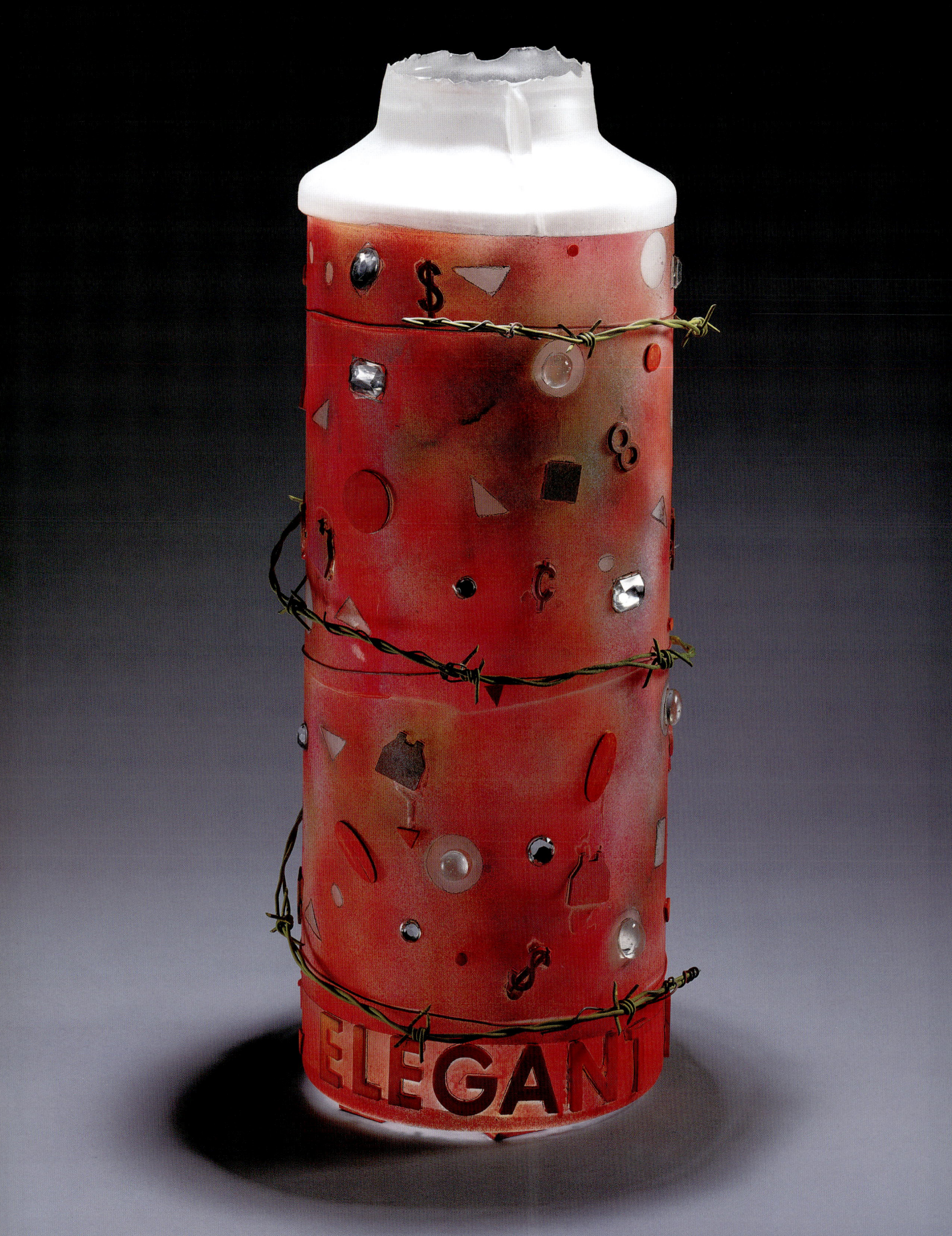

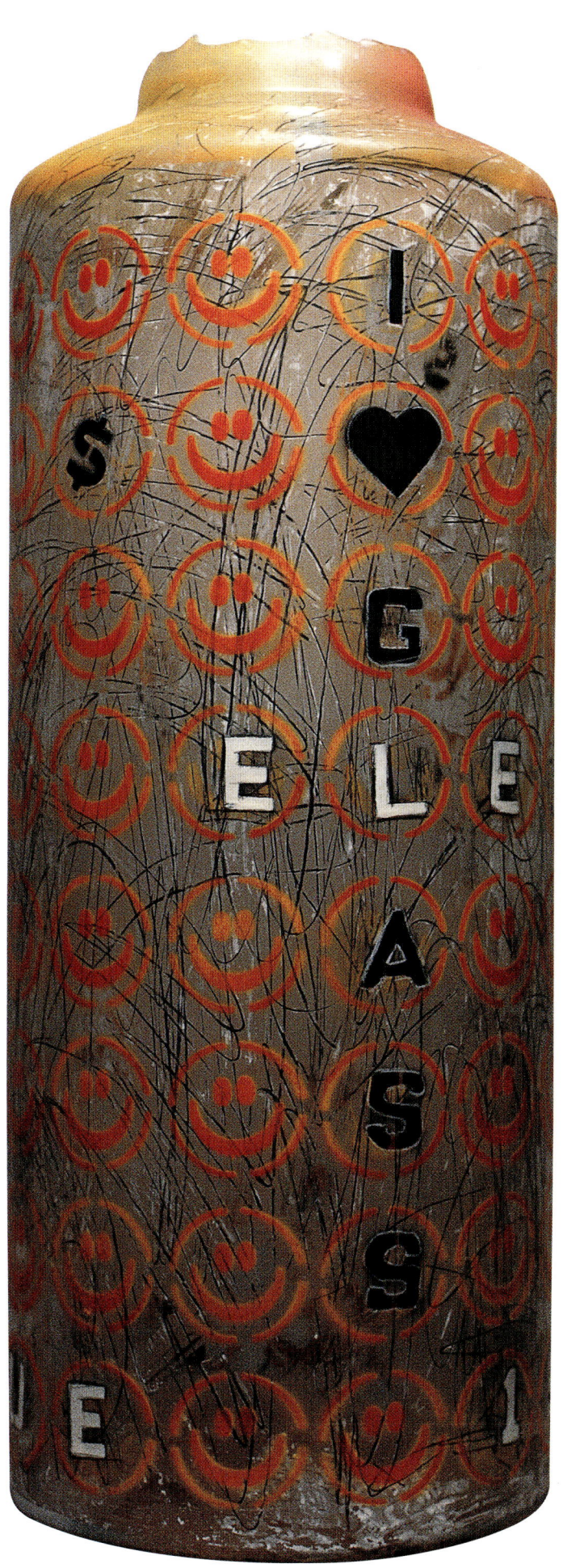

Opposite:
***Elegant Vase; No. 38**,* 1991. Blown glass, acid etched, oil, wax, pencil, barbed wire, and mixed media, h. 22.75 x 9.74 inches. The Metropolitan Museum of Art. Gift of Gary and Mary Pforzheimer.

Left:
***I Love Glass**;* Elegant Vase Series, 1993. Blown glass, acid etched, oil, and pencil, h. 23 x 8.5 inches.

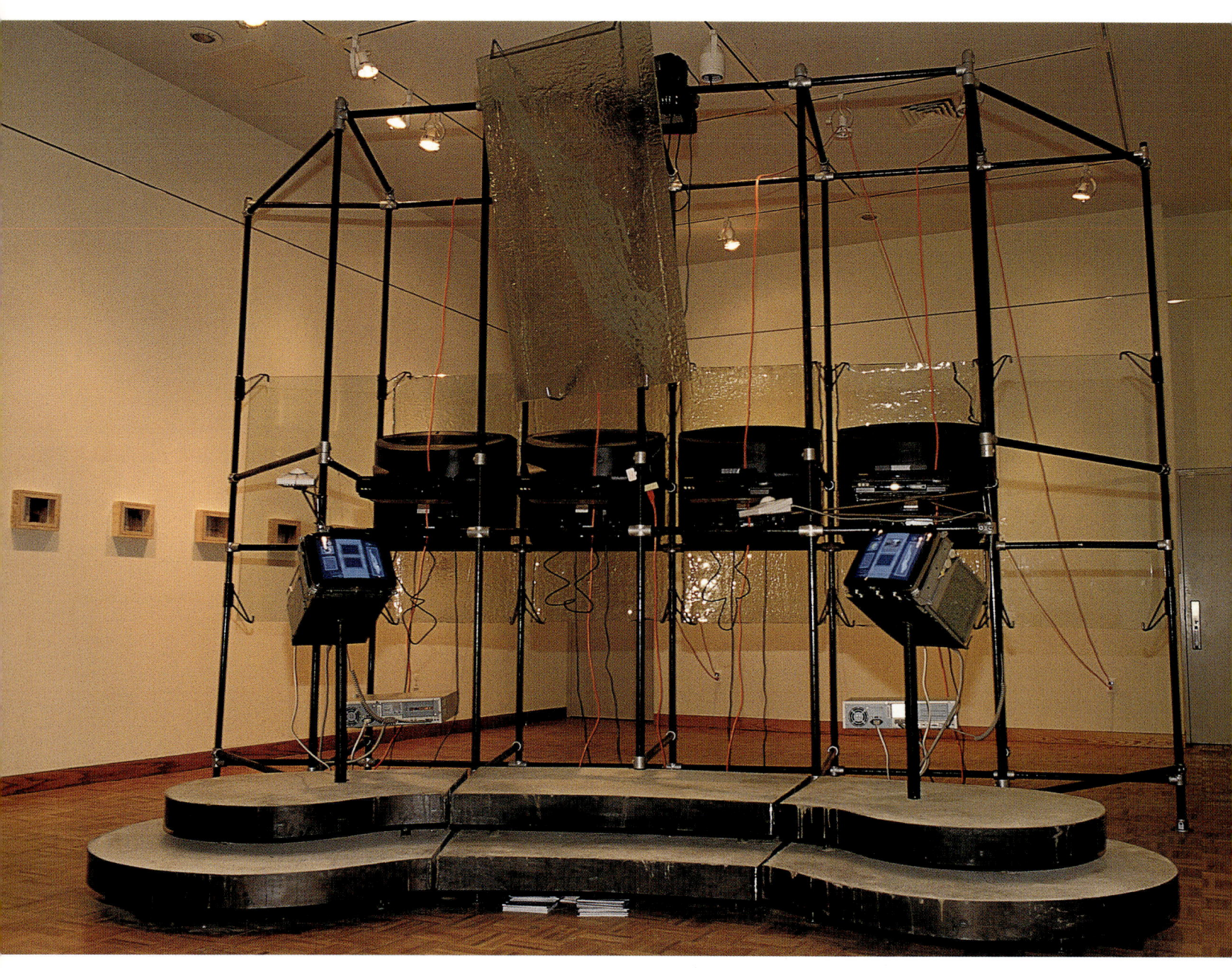

Multiple Identities, A Digital Map of New York City with Urban Kiosk, 1998. Projec[tions] Collaborative Installation; Aronson Galleries, Parsons School of Design. Digital avatars, slumped glass filters and map, cement, and steel, h. 16x14 feet. Projec[tions] Collaborative Team: Lura Albee, Suk Jae Chang, Richard Day, Cameron Jack, Christopher Grant Kirwan, Michael Lucero, Kenzo Minami, Trinh Huu Nguyen, Darren Roberts, Sven Travis, and Richard Wilfred Yelle, Producer. Photo: Matthew Septimus.

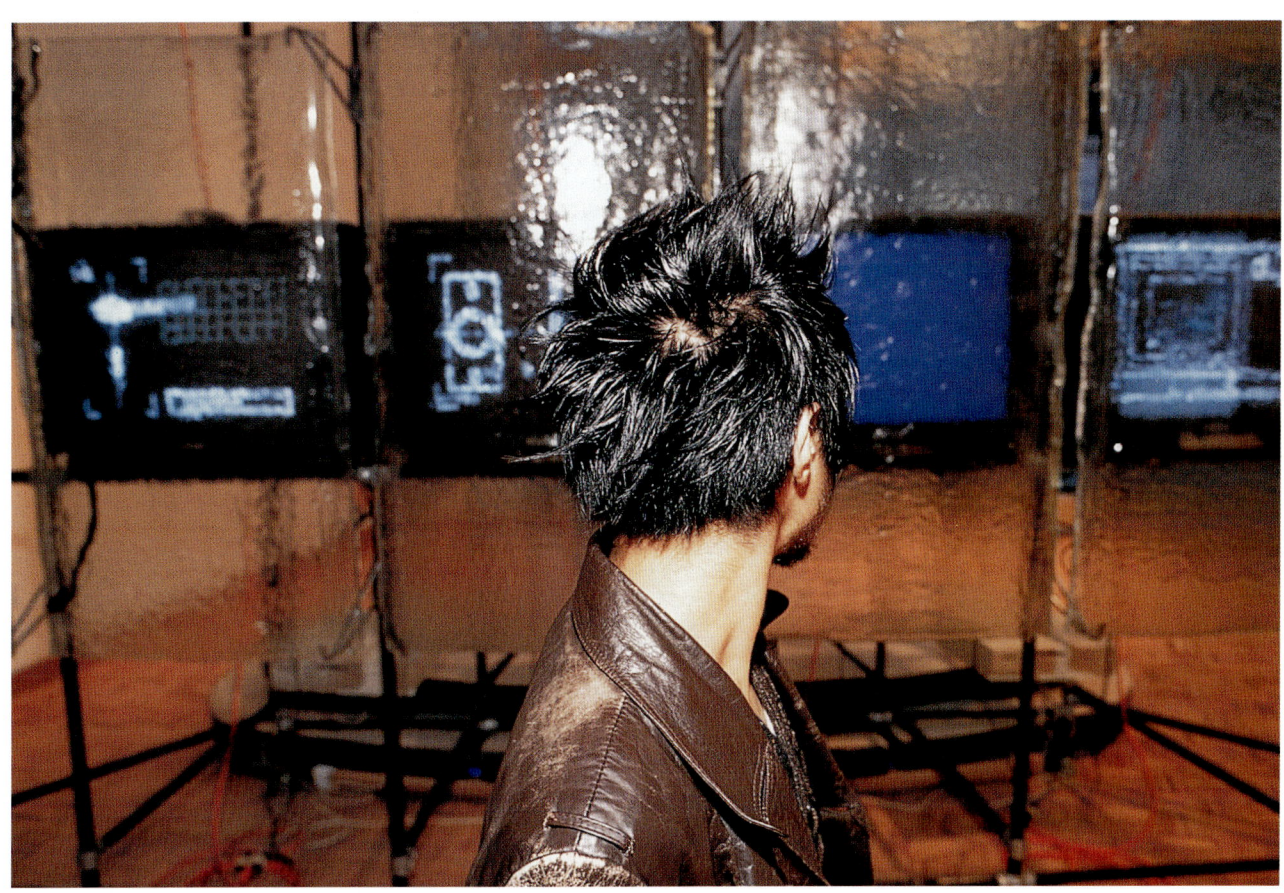

Multiple Identities; Detail of slumped glass filters (a metaphor for the digital age), with graphic design team member Kenzo Minami, 1998. Photo: Matthew Septimus.

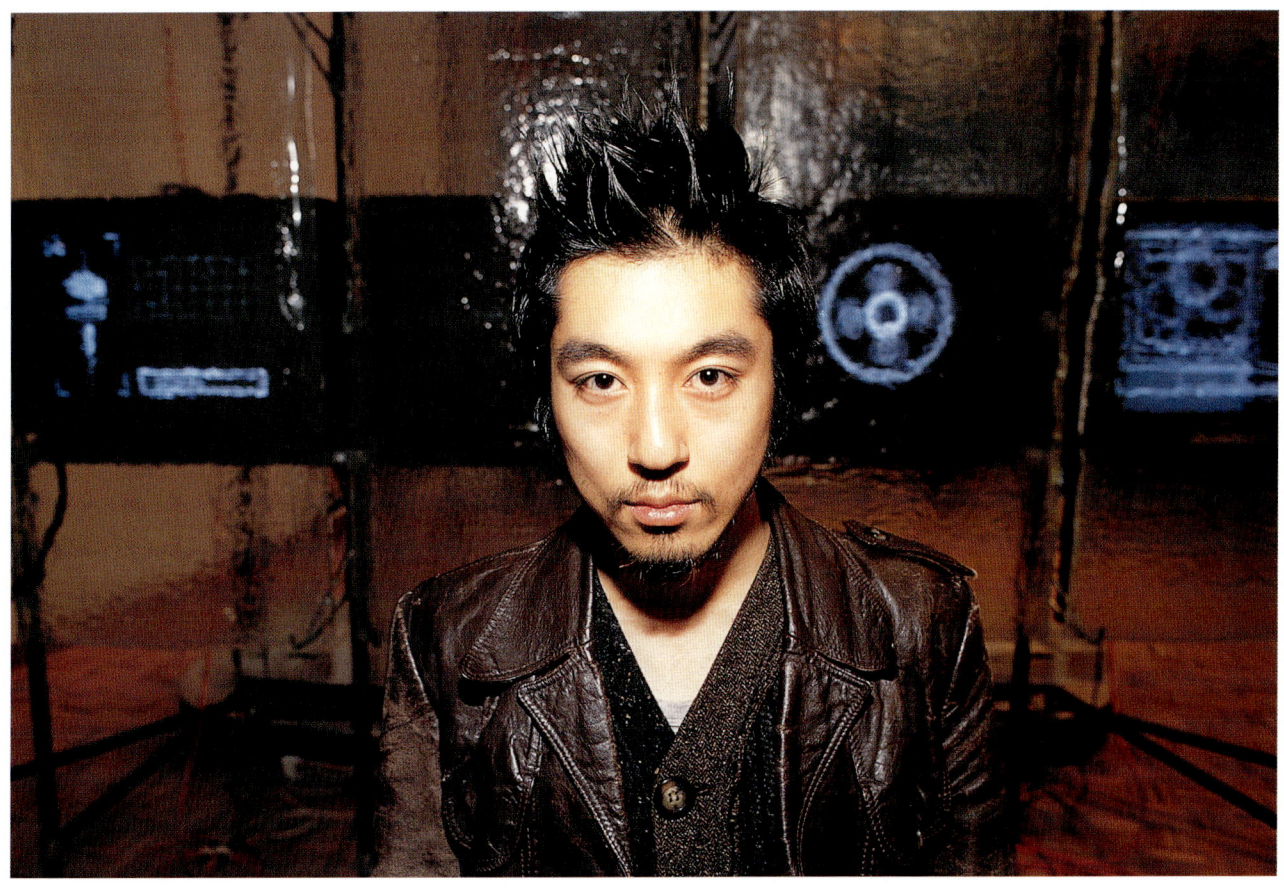

Multiple Identities; Detail of slumped glass filters, 1998.

Dana Zámecníková
(b.1945)

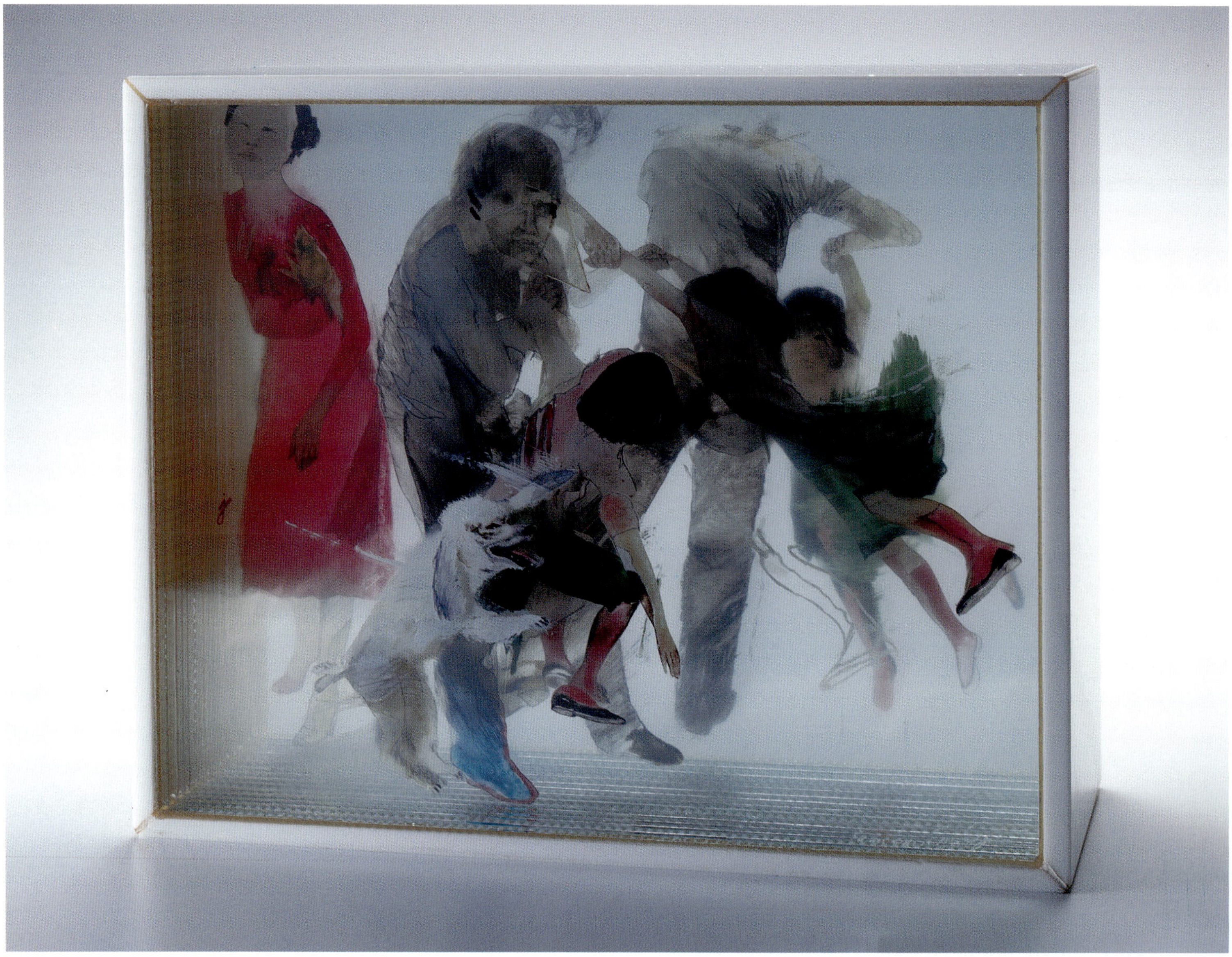

CZECH REPUBLIC

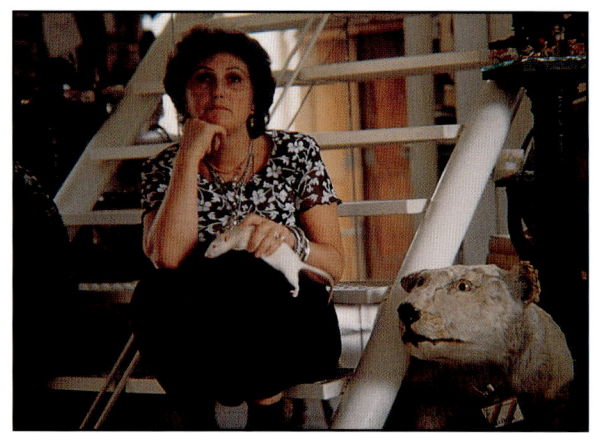

Above:
Marian Karel With Next Door Neighbors, 1986. Layered sheet glass and paint, h. 7.25 x 8.75 x 4 inches. Collection of Cynthia and Jeffrey Manocherian. Photo: Eva Heyd.

Opposite:
Women; Sink Deep and Deep, 1999. Painted glass and metal, h. 128.8 x 59.2 x 36 inches. Museum Rouen, France.

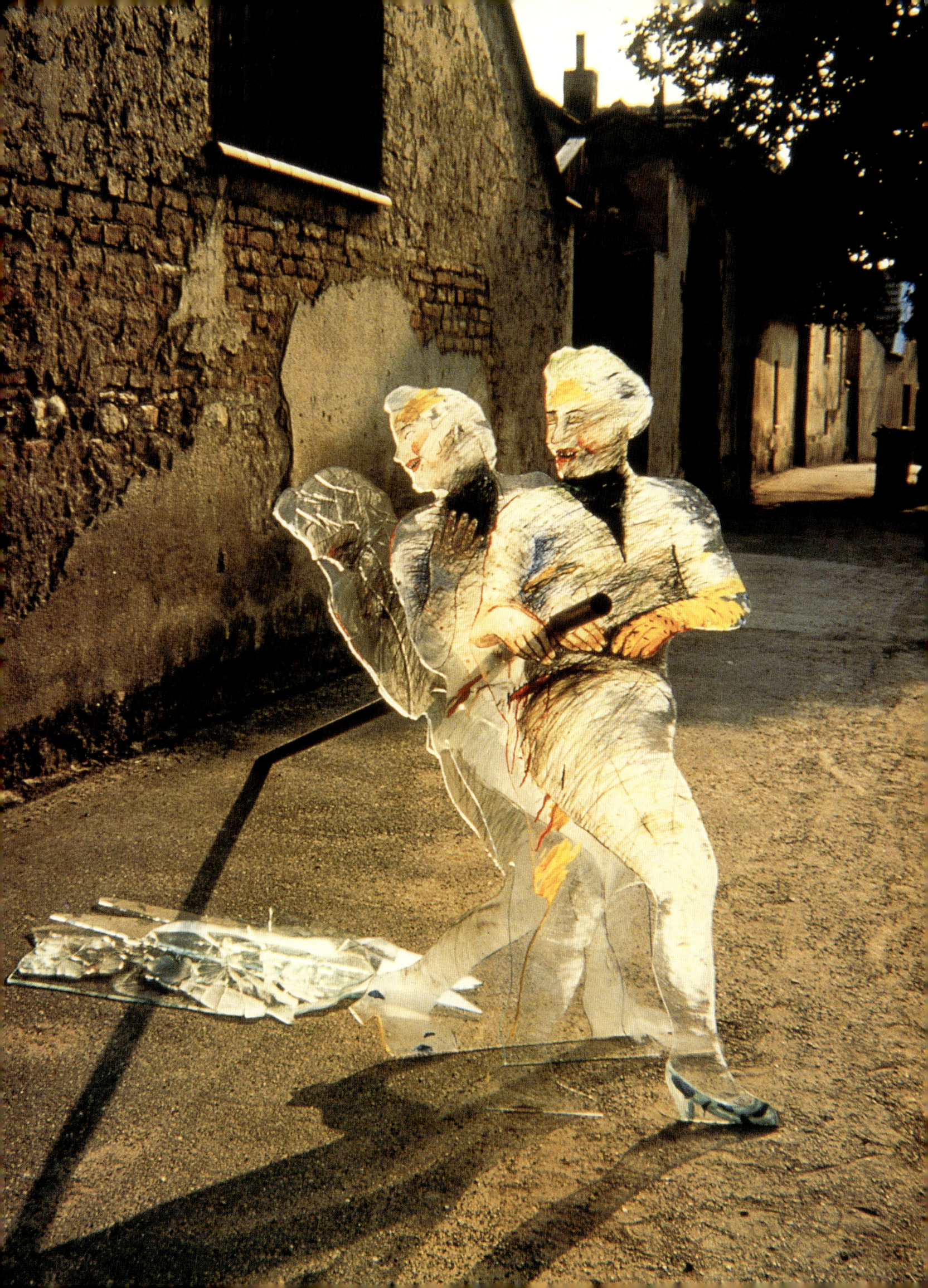

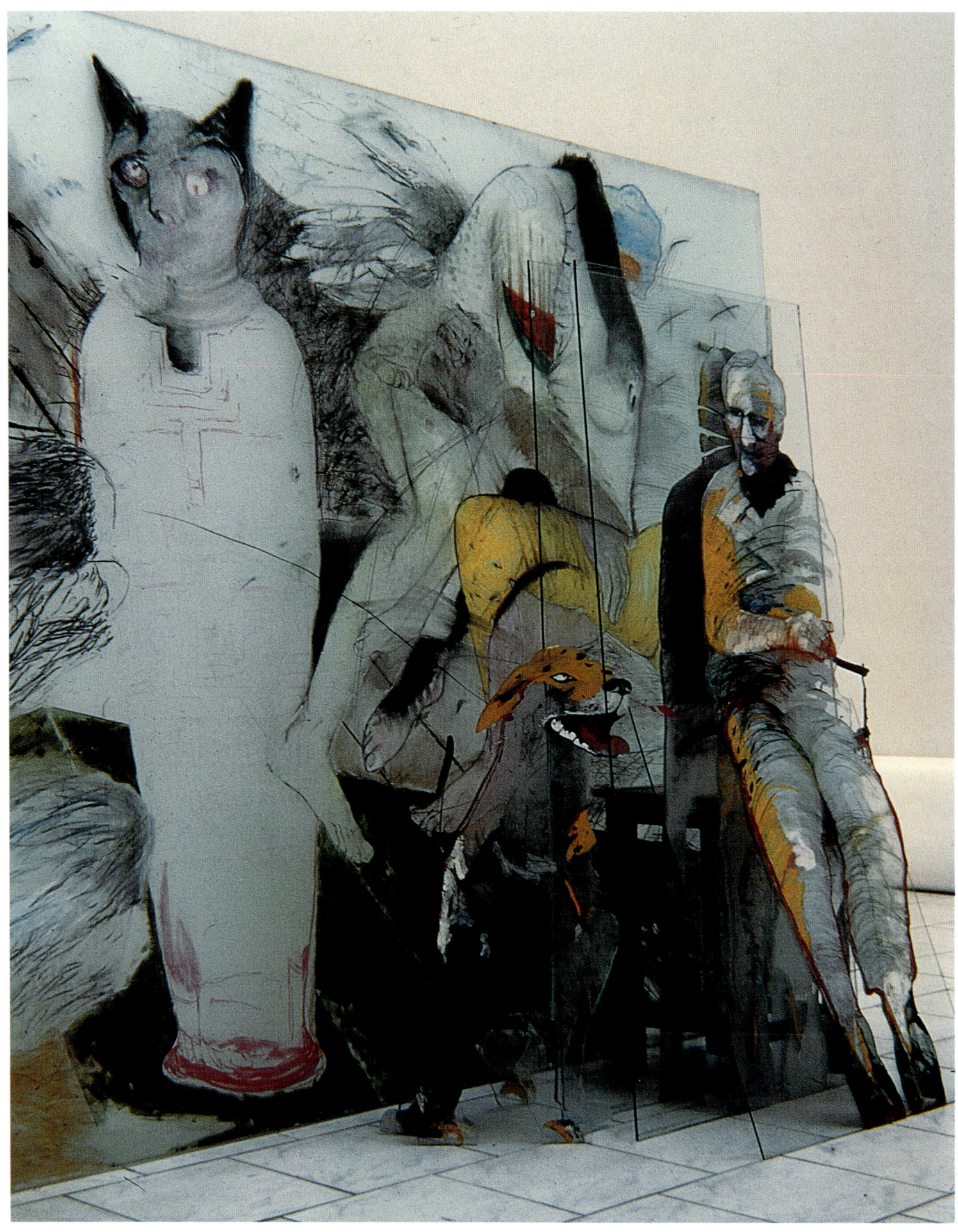

Behind Looking-Glass; Installation, Prague, 1994.
Painted flat glass, h. 81.2 x 121.2 x 72 inches.

BROOKLYN, NEW YORK

Jeff Zimmerman
(b.1968)

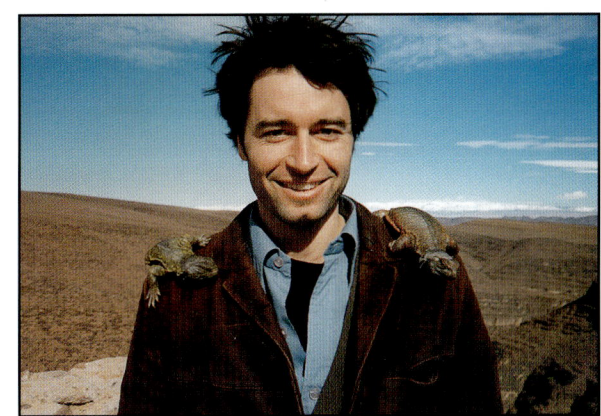

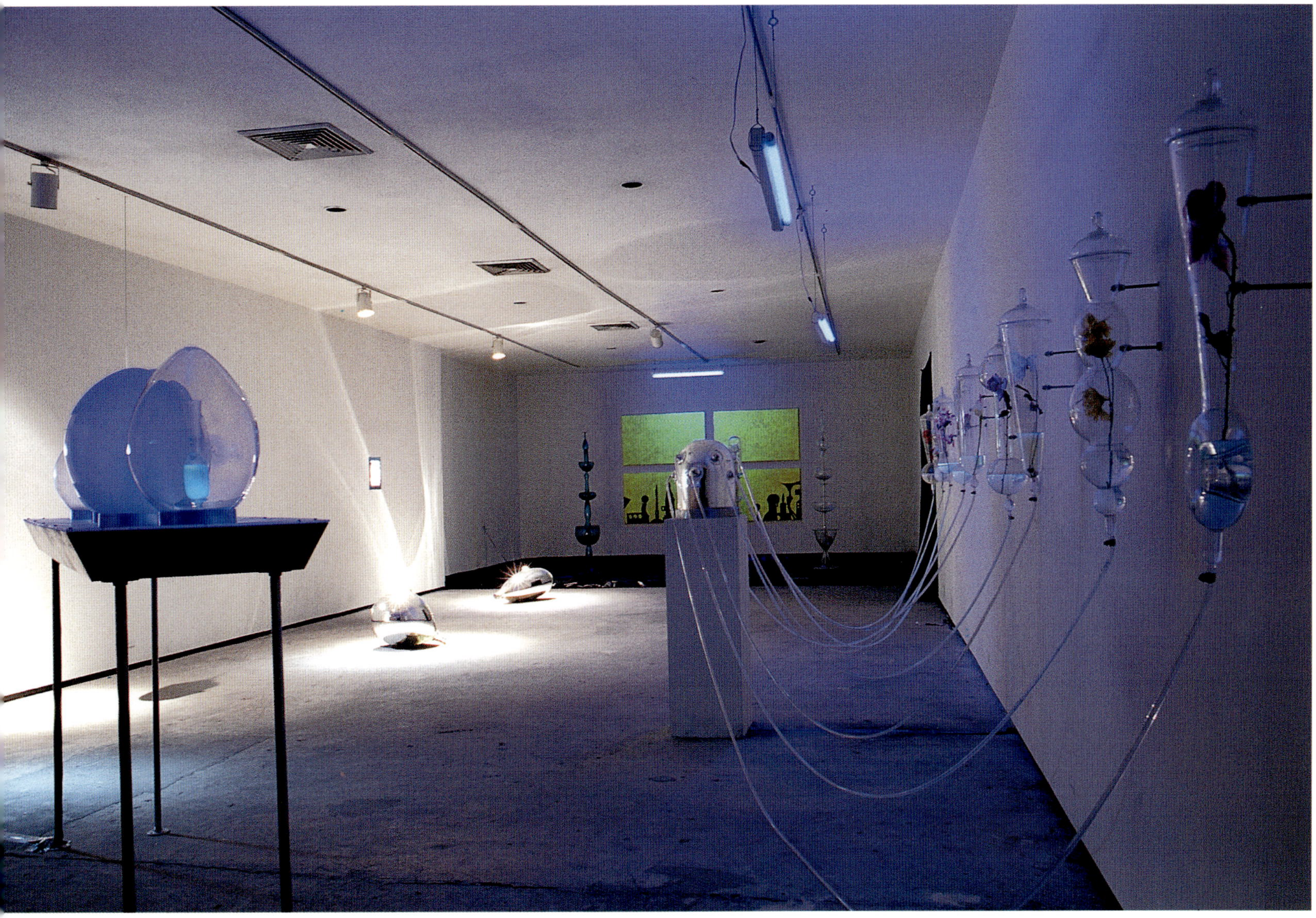

Future Fetish; Installation, Robert Lehman Gallery, UrbanGlass, 1999. Blown glass, flowers, pump system, and black lights, h. 8 x 30 feet. Photo: Eva Heyd.

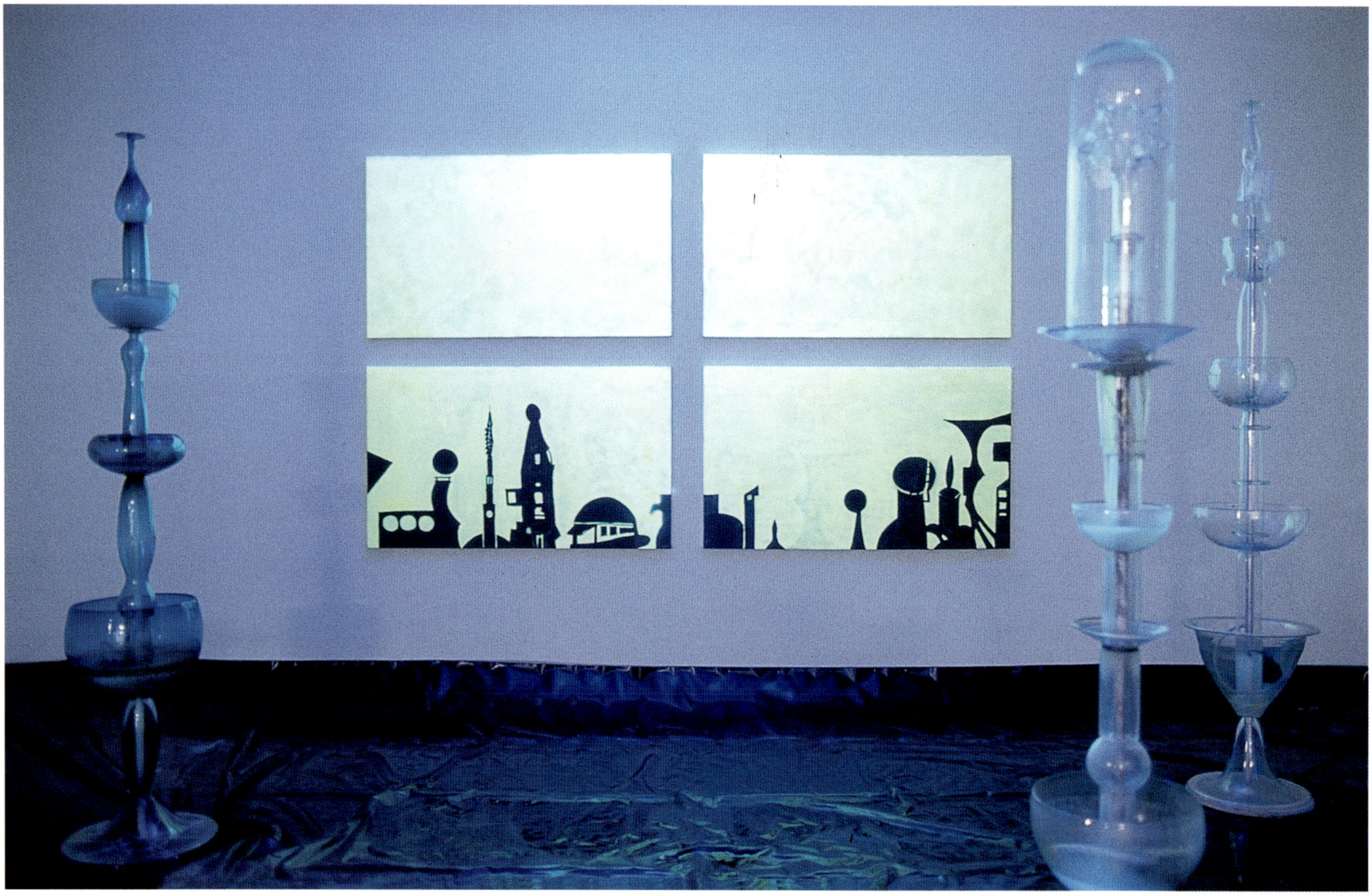

JEFF ZIMMERMAN

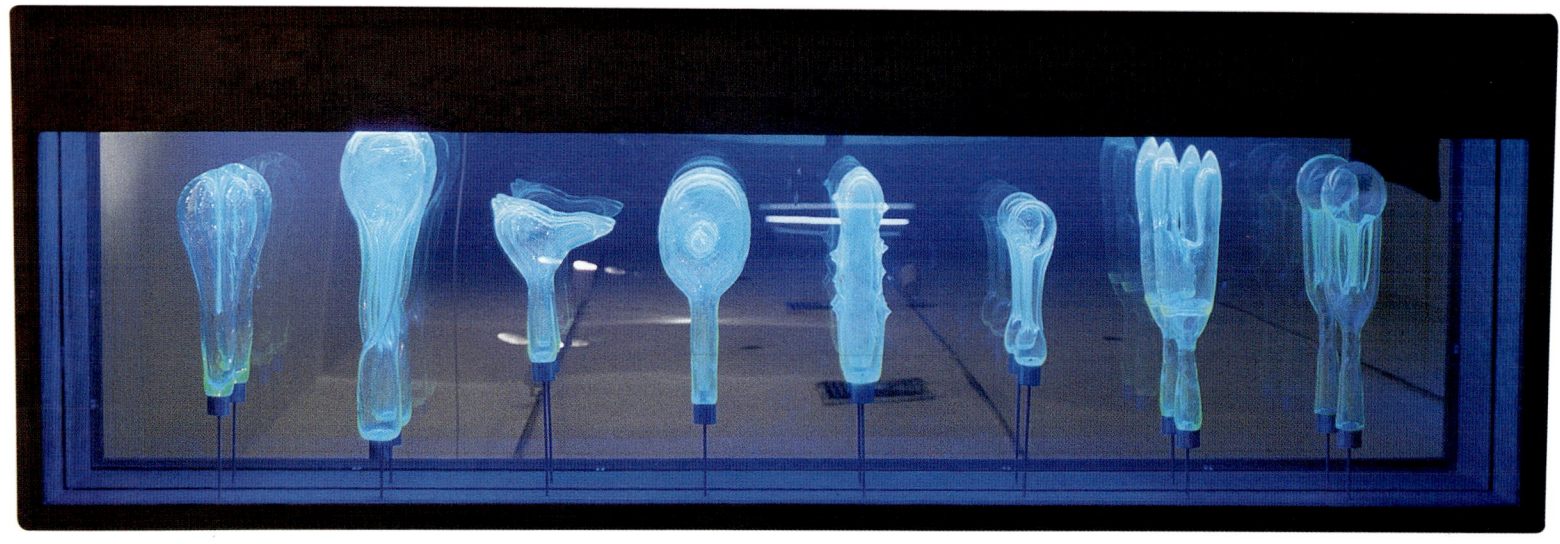

Top:
Future Fetish; Installation Detail, 1999. Blown glass and black light, h. 4 x 8 feet. Photo: Eva Heyd.

Bottom:
Future Fetish; Installation Detail, 1999. Blown glass and black light, h. 2 x 4 feet. Photo: Eva Heyd.

JERSEY CITY, NEW JERSEY

Walter Zimmerman
(b. 1946)

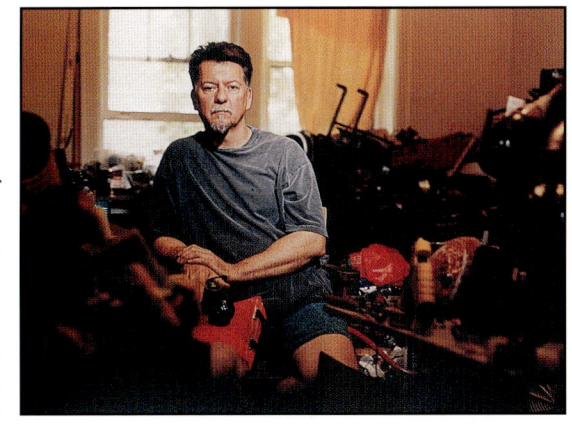
Photo: Brian Kennedy

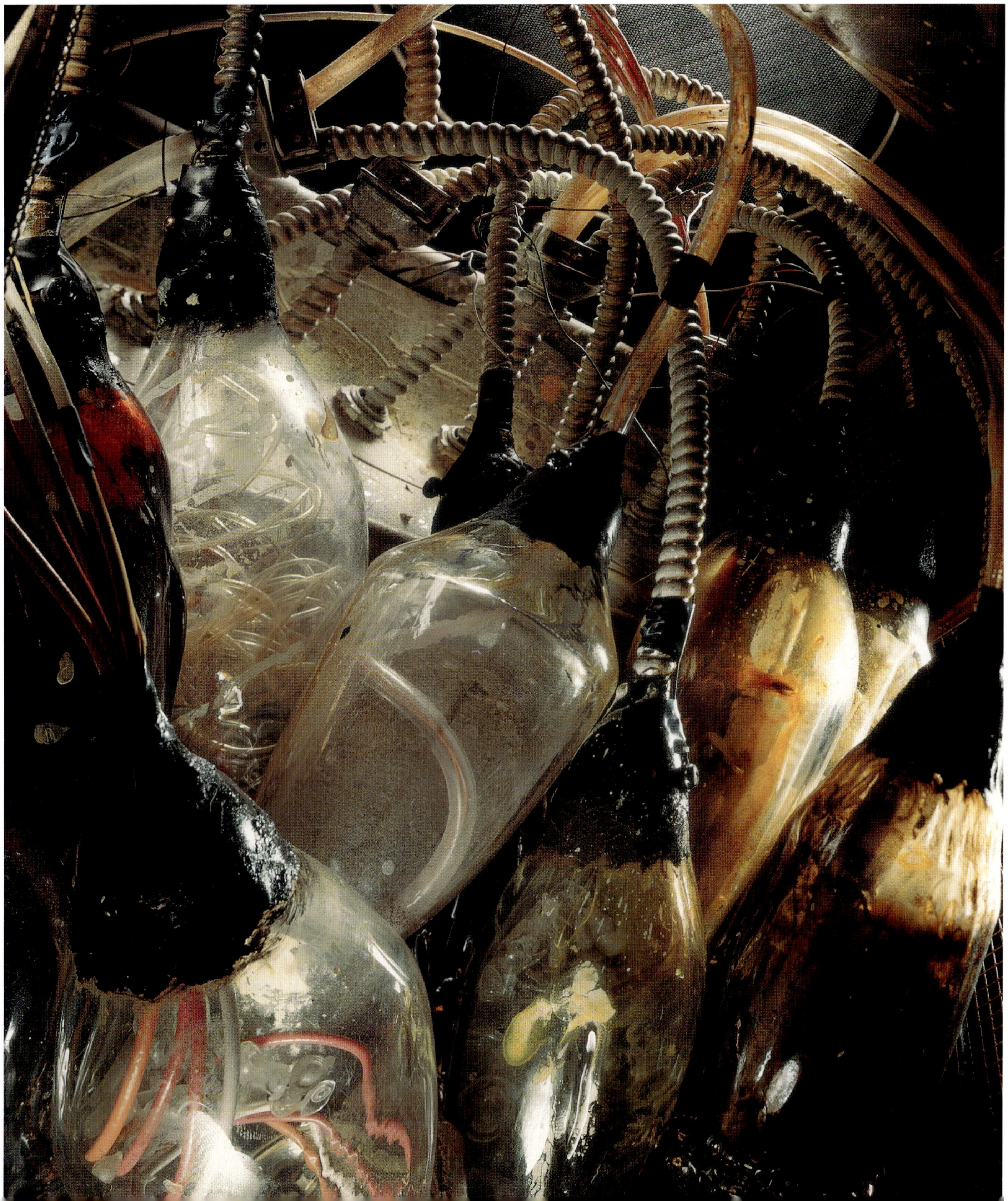

Safety Yellow; Detail, 1996. Blown glass and mixed media, h. 52 x 40 x 24 inches.

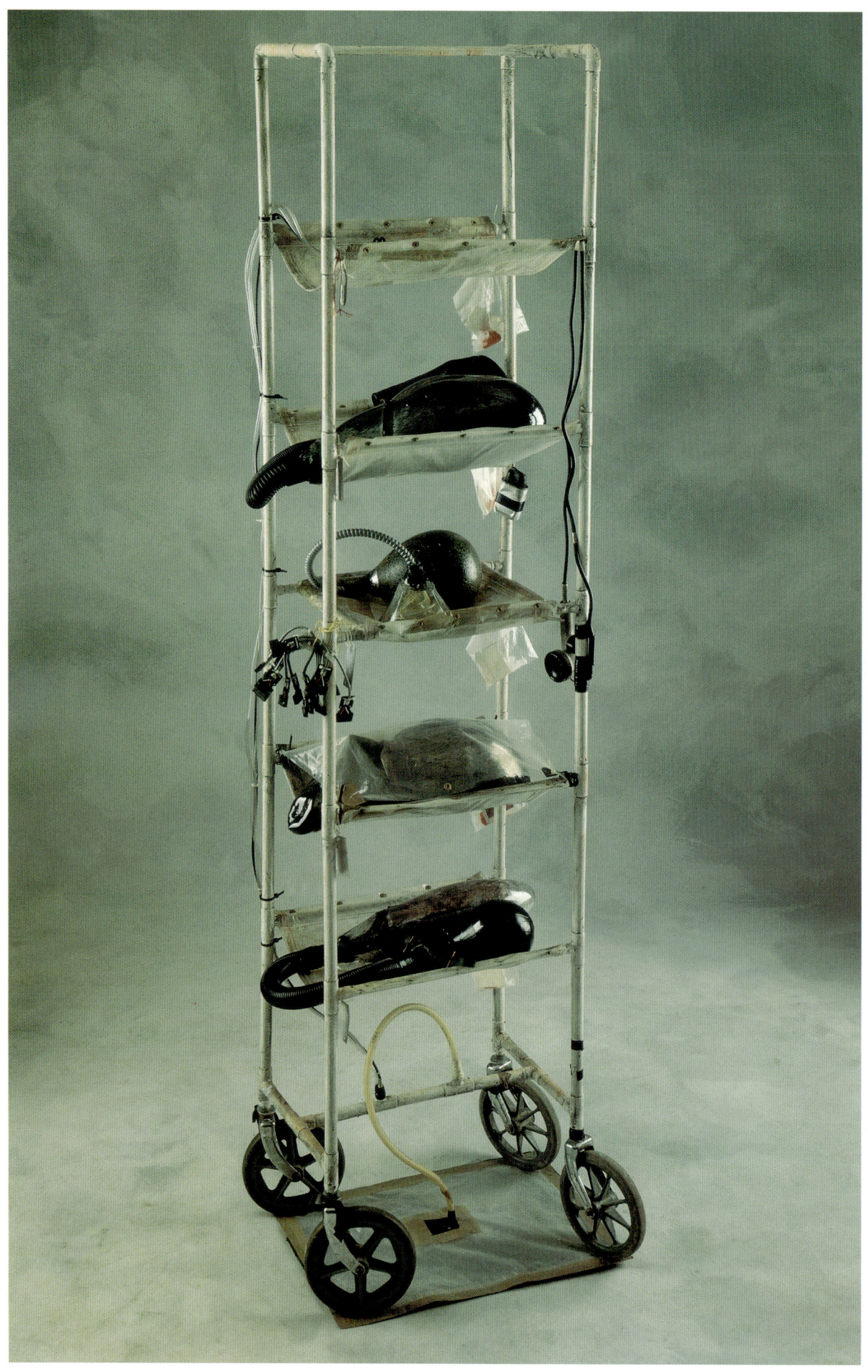

RSVD/4U, *1995. Blown glass and mixed media, h. 74 x 19 x 13 inches.*

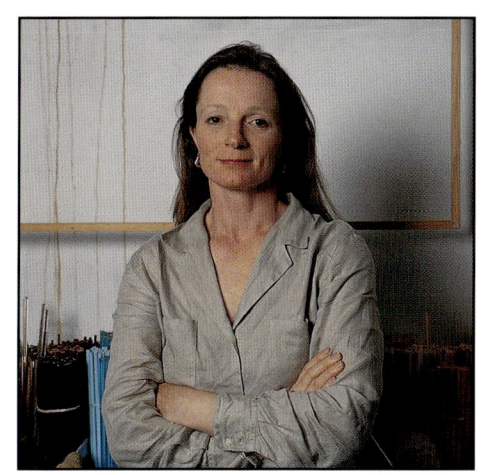

PROVIDENCE, RHODE ISLAND

Toots Zynsky
(b.1951)

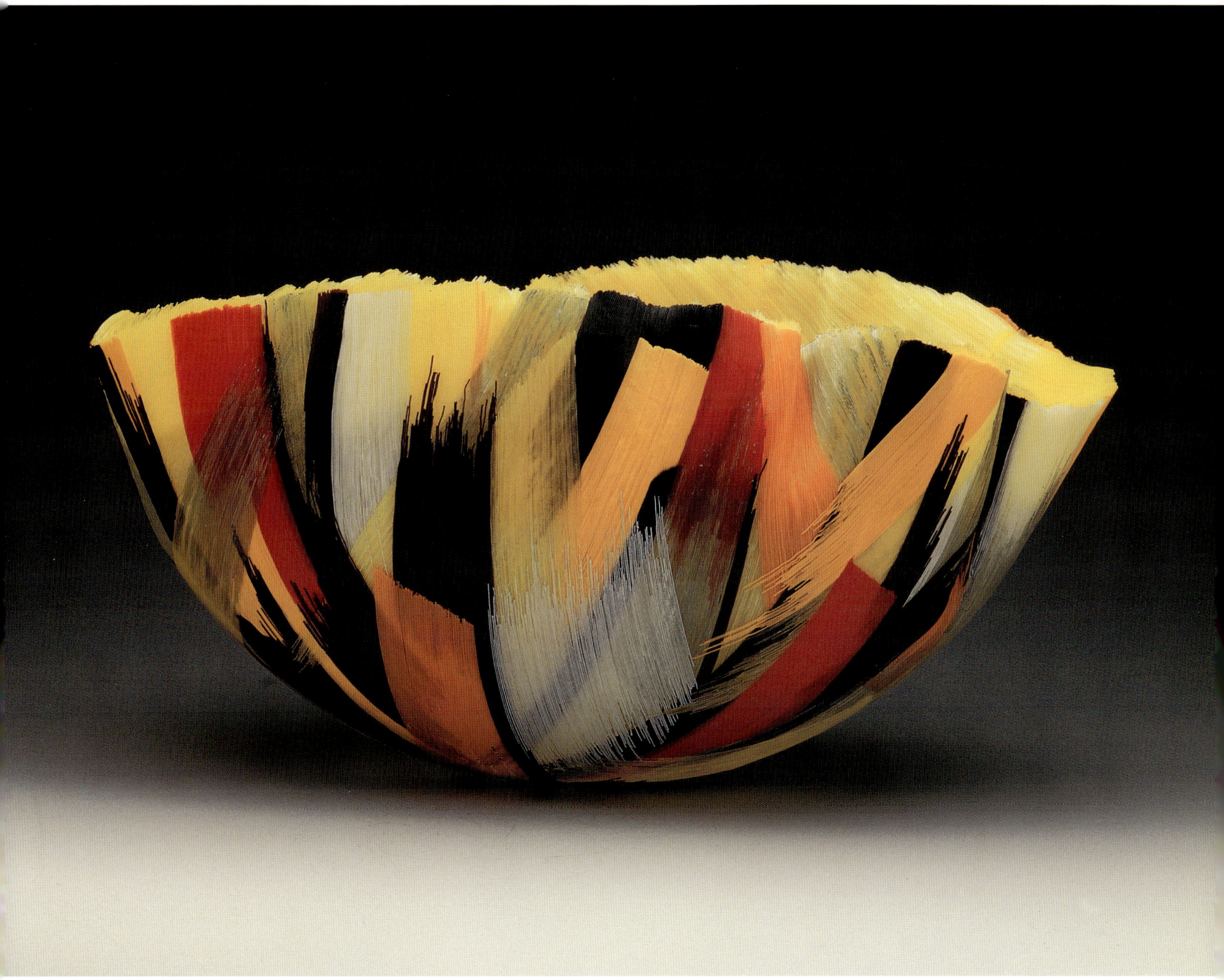

City Lights, 1993. Fused and thermo-formed glass threads, h. 6.8 x 13.2 x 8.8 inches. Courtesy Elliott Brown Gallery, Seattle.

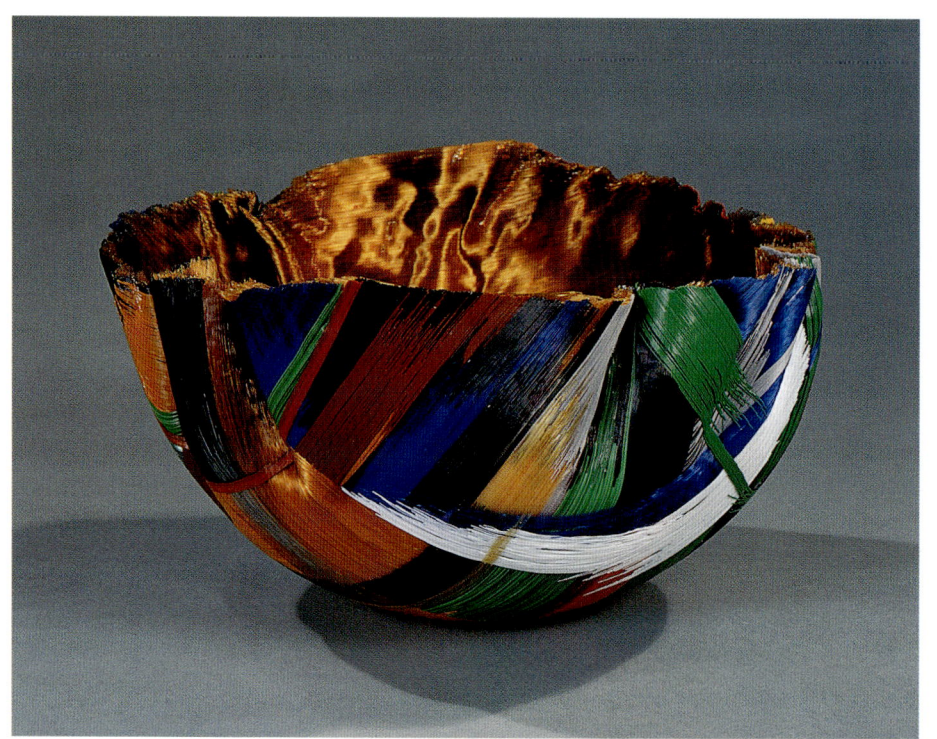

Right:
Untitled, 1992. Fused and thermo-formed glass threads, h. 6.75 x 10 x 9 inches. Norton Museum of Art, West Palm Beach, Florida. Gift of Dale and Doug Anderson.

Below:
Patagonian Serena, 1999. Fused and thermo-formed glass threads, 11.6 x 24 x 12 inches. Collection of Dorothy and George Saxe.

Opposite:
Night Street Chaos, 1998. Fused and thermo-form glass threads, h. 7.15 x 13 x 7 inches. Tampa Museum of Art, Florida. Gift of Dale and Doug Anderson.

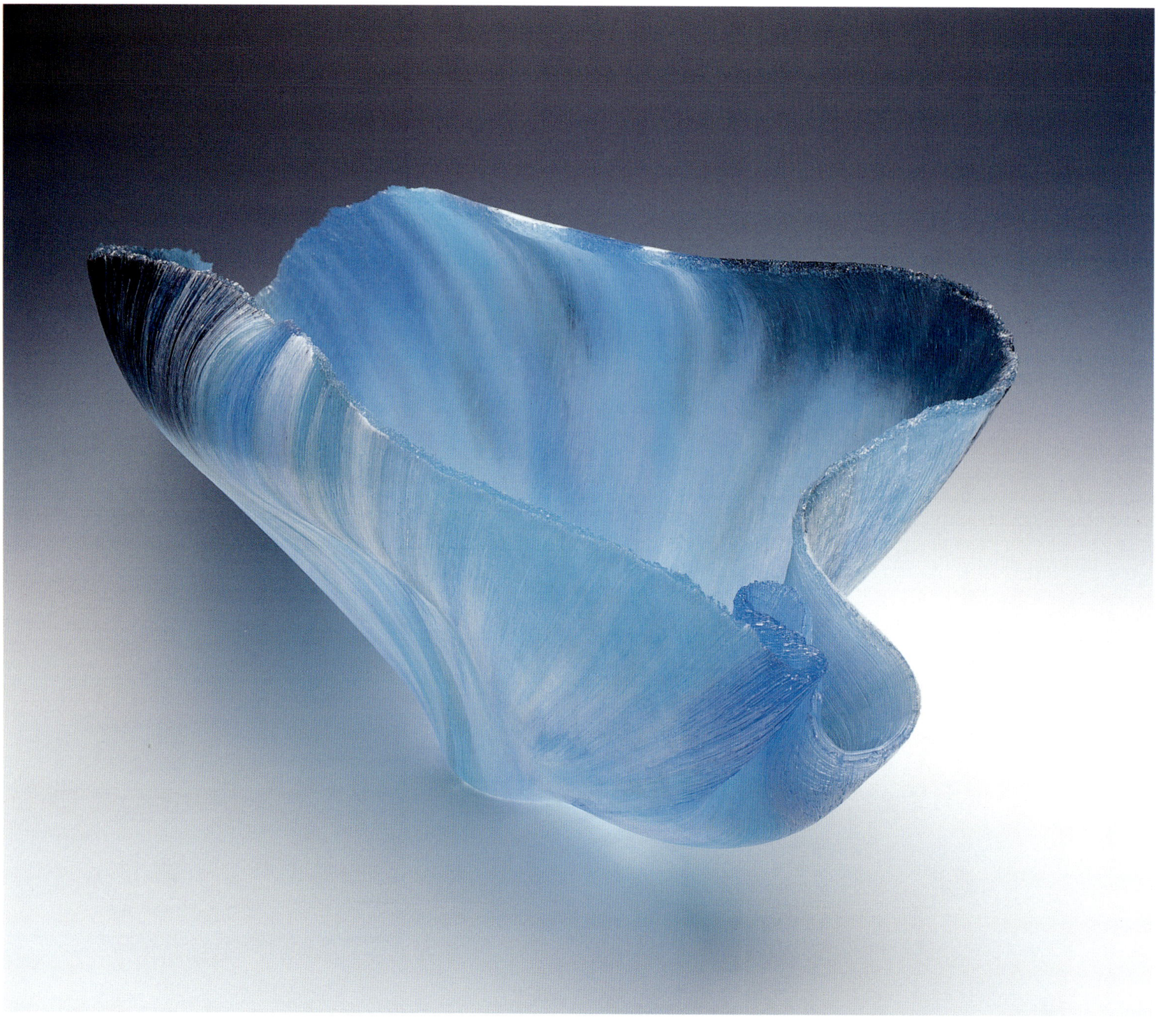

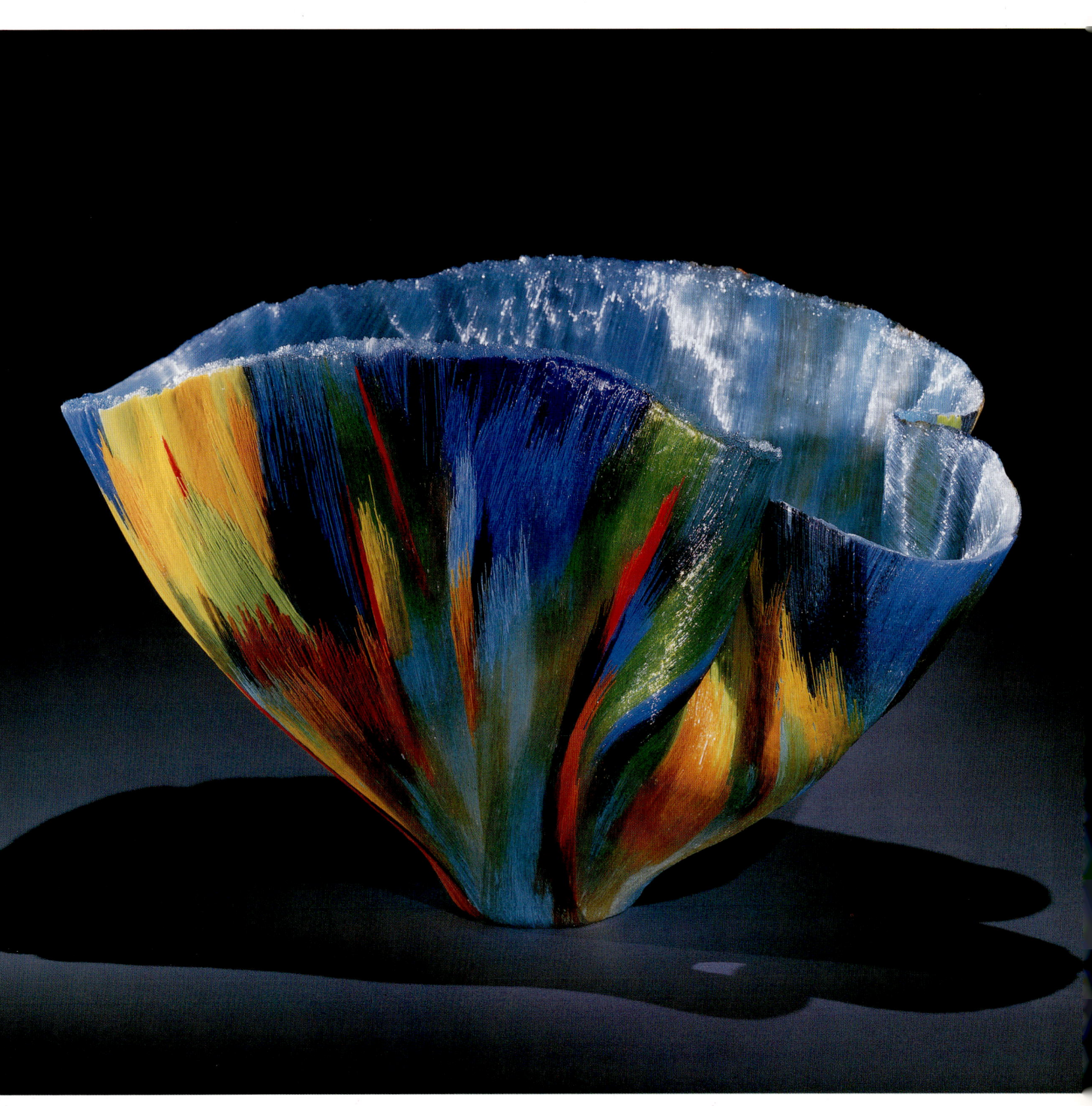

THE GLASS WORLD:
ESSAYS BY PROMINENT CURATORS, CRITICS, AND WRITERS

Questioning Glass

Why glass? That's a question I have asked frequently in the nearly 20 years that I have been writing about studio glass. I have asked artists, collectors, and even myself—why glass? What is it about the medium that is so powerful that artists dedicate years to mastering the skills necessary to bend it to their will or sometimes spend thousands of dollars for others' expertise? What is it about the medium that collectors become obsessed with acquiring just one more piece, sometimes even carefully budgeting to buy just one more seductive object? Why do I, who also write about subjects as diverse as abstract painting, photography, and graphic design, always find myself returning to glass, writing about it and curating exhibitions focused on it?

I think the reason is that glass is a versatile, even paradoxical medium. Nothing else can be blown to create a form, but glass can also be cast by pouring the molten metal or fusing powdered glass together in a mold. It can be worked cold, assembled into forms by the most mechanical of means or gluing. Glass can be transparent, translucent, opaque. It can convey color more purely than any other medium. Its surface can be the support for a pictorial representation by being painted on, abraded with acid, scratched by a diamond point, or bombarded with grains of sand.

With all of those qualities, it becomes an ideal medium for artists to use to convey their ideas. If you flip through the many catalogues of glass exhibitions that may be called surveys of the state of the art, it is clear that glass can be used to create the most pristine formal abstractions as well as the most expressionistic. It can appear archaic or futuristic, delicious or dangerous, dumbly beautiful or intellectually challenging. It can record a virtuoso performance or physically manifest a conceptual artwork.

Just as artists use the material for vastly different effects, glass appeals to collectors for various reasons. Some collections consist of pretty baubles sitting politely on shelves while others commandeer vast spaces, physically as well as conceptually. And some collectors of glass, like collectors of other media, are drawn by the personalities of the makers.

And for me, what sustains my interest in glass is all of these things. I like that glass can satisfy my desire for beauty and engage my mind. I like working in a field where I have the opportunity to know the artists, to question them about their intentions, and sometimes provide some insight into the work for those who are interested.

Of course, sometimes I feel that artists have yet to use glass to its fullest aesthetic potential to create masterpieces that will become icons for the age. Often I find that some collectors' passionate defense of glass as a museum-worthy medium (some of it is, even if it doesn't reach masterwork levels) is naïve boosterism. Still, glass arouses my interest as an art historian. I look forward to the next developments, whether studio glass continues as an identifiable field or glass leaves the ghetto and those who use it are simply called artists.

Karen S. Chambers
Freelance Curator and
Critic-at-Large, New York, New York

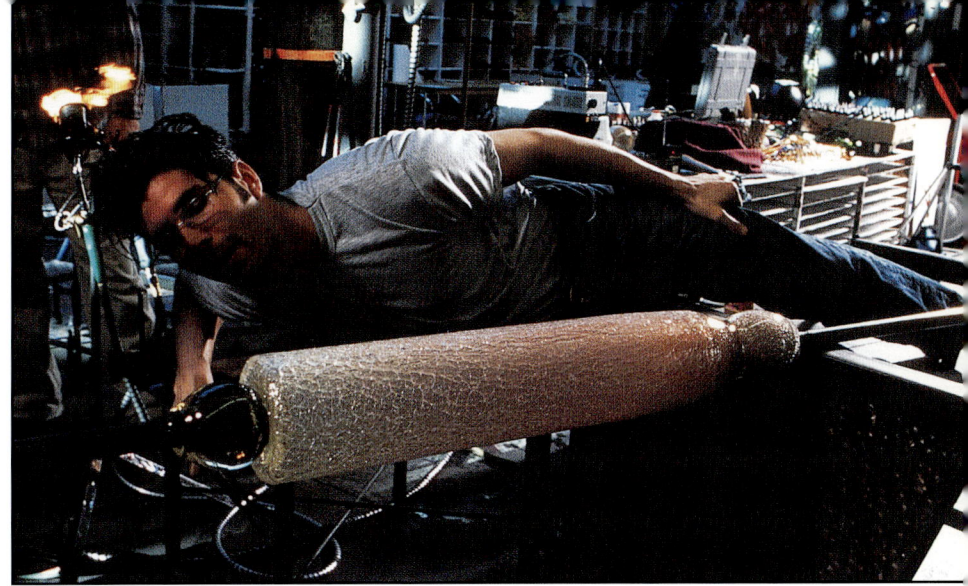

James Mongrain making Jerusalem cylinders for Dale Chihuly, 1999. Photo: T. Batty

The Current State of Contemporary Studio Glass

A prevailing perception exists that contemporary studio glass is a success with the public because it is a truly American form of expression. Although this notion may be comforting, even romantic, I believe it is false. Rather, glass' universal popularity proves that it represents an international rather than a national voice, one which engages and challenges its audience, addresses artistic rather than merely decorative concerns, and makes significant contributions to the history of art. Glass, therefore, should not be relegated simply to the craft sphere, but should be considered within the broader context of post World War II international art.

It is because glass is emerging as a major force in the arts that museums are organizing significant exhibitions and building important collections of it today. The Tampa Museum of Art's 1999 exhibition, *Clearly Inspired: Contemporary Glass and Its Origins*, guest-curated by Karen S. Chambers, demonstrated that the museum-going public finds glass not only accessible, but also widely appealing and engaging. That is perhaps due in part to glass' unique and myriad qualities (its translucency and opaqueness, its vibrant color and sensuous material, its intimate relationship between technique and content) as well as the skills of its makers, whose imaginative designs, fine craftsmanship, and innovative ideas know no bounds. The manual and technical skills involved in making glass—the very ones which in the past have perhaps limited glass to the sphere of craft—are often as astounding to glass neophytes such as myself as the final product.

Today studio glass deals as much with artistic invention as other contemporary media, i.e. painting and sculpture. However, unlike those media, most glass pieces are still moderately priced and thus affordable to a larger audience, especially to emerging collectors and museums with limited acquisition funds. For collectors, glass is a good way to "get one's feet wet," both in terms of understanding contemporary art and the fine art market. Museums are generally able to acquire pieces that further their missions—and are of tremendous appeal to their audiences—without consuming their acquisition funds. Yet, as the field develops and as more and more artists who have had commercial success in other media adopt or incorporate glass into their repertoire, lending further cachet to the medium, prices will undoubtedly rise to more appropriately reflect the mainstream art market.

For those who wish to become more involved with collecting glass, I recommend getting involved with a collectors group at an art museum. This type of organization not only provides opportunities to meet other collectors with similar interests, but also enhances one's understanding and appreciation of art through guest speakers (artists, curators, critics, and collectors) and by offering special events such as studio, collection or gallery visits. In addition, by working directly with an art museum's staff, collectors can become better knowledgeable of the museum's acquisition goals and future directions and thus be able to have a more significant impact on its growth.

Glass today is indeed one of the most exciting art mediums being explored. The work of the 175 artists included in this book illustrates glass at its full expressive range and intimates future possibilities and challenges. Many thanks and hearty congratulations to UrbanGlass for supporting and promoting the field for over twenty years.

Elaine D. Gustafson
Curator of Contemporary Art
Tampa Museum of Art
Tampa, Florida

Glass: A New Role in a New Century

The contemporary glass movement has experienced a level of public reception that exceeds expectations for a medium that is only thirty-five years old. Important glass exhibitions held at major museums are evidence of a new receptivity on the part of institutions and their audiences. Often visitors to glass exhibitions display a distinct sense of familiarity that places them at ease with this seductive material.

Functional glass is not often found exhibited in art museums; nevertheless, exposure to it in everyday life creates a basic familiarity with this medium. This understanding tends to encourage greater public acceptance of ideas communicated through most craft media than those found in painting and sculpture, because the public has an affection for the material. The basic ingredients used in painting can be as prosaic as those used in the hot shop. However, the public's shared perception of the technical acumen utilized in working glass appears to break down the apprehension of seeing unconventional forms or subject matter. This medium encourages viewers to engage with the work and the concept behind it.

The versatility of glass is one of its attractions for artists. Hot and cold working techniques provide surface and structural opportunities that guarantee that both the artist and viewer will always be challenged and surprised. Few people may have a clear impression of what takes place inside a painting studio, but many have a basic idea of or a desire to learn about the process of creating a work of glass.

Glass has the ability to transmit color and light. As light passes through it, the intensity and purity of hue is heightened, similar to the white of paper illuminating layers of transparent watercolor paint. This quality of transmitting color combines with the sparkling, reflective surfaces to create works that are often conventionally beautiful. Contemporary art critics are not always comfortable with glass and its connection with beauty. For the better part of this century, modern art has viewed beauty with the suspicion reserved for representational imagery, as if both have little relevance to present-day concerns. However, it is this same quality of attraction that draws many viewers and collectors to this medium.

Many institutions have collected historic ceramics and textiles for decades and this has ultimately led to the inclusion of contemporary works in their collections and exhibitions. The brief history of studio glass has not provided the same longstanding relationships between artists and institutions. Museums are now presenting glass because, after thirty years, it has evolved into a more mature medium deserving serious study. Glass can serve as a portal, through which a broader public can be introduced to other contemporary art forms.

Programs, such as those at UrbanGlass and the Pilchuck Glass School, that introduce painters and sculptors to working in the glass medium, can be of particular benefit by encouraging fresh viewpoints and applications. When these varied artists approach the medium, they employ glass because it creates a desired effect. The technical achievements of the past three decades were necessary steps to investigate and demonstrate the capabilities for expression in this new medium. Now that these artists have created a vernacular in which to speak, we have entered an era in which they are more involved in communicating concepts and content. By considering meaning in their work to be more important than the method of presenting the message, glass artists match the efforts of their counterparts in contemporary painting and sculpture.

Creating cerebral works in a medium that attracts a broad audience could expand the role of glass as a gateway for the public into contemporary art. The universal appeal of glass will lead to appreciation of the content found in these works. This understanding will transfer to contemporary paintings and sculptures as well. As we enter a new century, glass is poised to assume the role as the means through which museums and galleries can introduce consistently wider audiences to many different art forms, and more importantly, to foster better understanding and appreciation of contemporary art and artists.

Bruce W. Pepich, Director
Charles A. Wustum Museum
of Fine Arts, Racine, Wisconsin

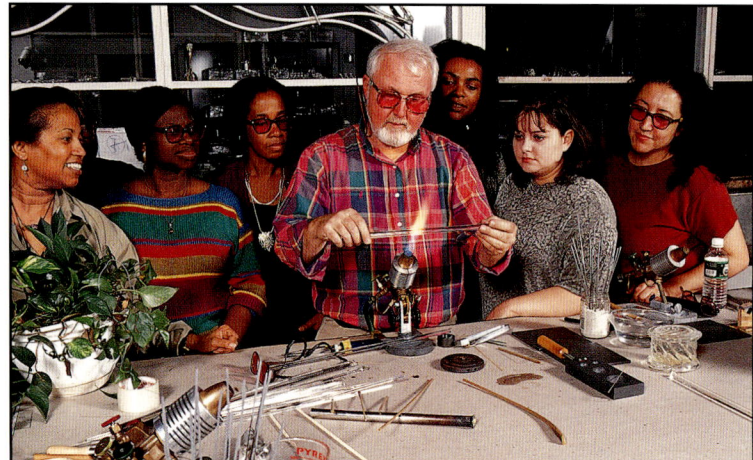

"The Bead Project" class at UrbanGlass with teacher Paul Stankard.

Valuing Glass

I see three ways of valuing glass as an art form, and they all derive from the essential American love-hate relationship between beauty and the marketing of beauty, between art and industry. We saw it in 1942 when Harvey Littleton set out on a long course to reclaim glass as a medium for art by removing it from the industrial context. We see it in 1999 as we anticipate the future of the medium: will financial success lead to a return to industrial marketing techniques and an abandonment of the pioneering spirit that forced studio glass onward in the 1960s and 1970s? I would look, in the decades ahead, for how the balance shifts in the following value relationships.

THE AESTHETIC FRONT: BEAUTY AND KITSCH

Glass is all about beauty, a term I define much as Elaine Scarry does in her book *On Beauty and Being Just.* Beauty is sacred, unprecedented, lifesaving; in Augustine's words, "a plank amid the waves of the sea." But beauty is intimately linked to kitsch, the faking of beauty. Kitsch is formulated beauty. A great deal of studio glass is kitsch, but there is just enough beautiful studio glass out there to make the search for it fulfilling. Five beautiful studio glass artworks: A Chihuly chandelier, a Tagliapietra vase, a Gudenrath goblet, a Vizner bowl, a Patti sculpture.

THE ETHICAL FRONT: IDEALISM AND PROFESSIONALISM

The idealism and raw energy that characterized studio glass until around the middle of the 1980s has been increasingly replaced by a professionalism that has secured for the most successful artists a steady livelihood and produced technically assured work. Increasingly, collectors can follow a formula for building collections by acquiring work by two dozen or so blue chip artists. Without a doubt, many of these artists are at present producing artworks of extraordinary beauty. The danger is if the balance shifts too far toward formulaic works. As Clement Greenberg wrote in his 1939 essay Avant-Garde and Kitsch: "The precondition for kitsch...is the availability close at hand of a fully matured cultural tradition, whose discoveries, acquisitions, and perfected self-consciousness kitsch can take advantage of for its own ends. It borrows from it devices, tricks, stratagems, rules of thumb, themes, converts them into a system and discards the rest." Greenberg wrote that three years before Harvey Littleton made the first studio glass object, at a time when there was no mature tradition of studio glass. Now there is, and the question of how to maintain the originality of the movement will be central to its vitality in the decades ahead. I see this as an ethical question, for I think it may be unethical for artists to copy others and make forgeries of the beautiful: we expect nothing less from them than truly original artworks.

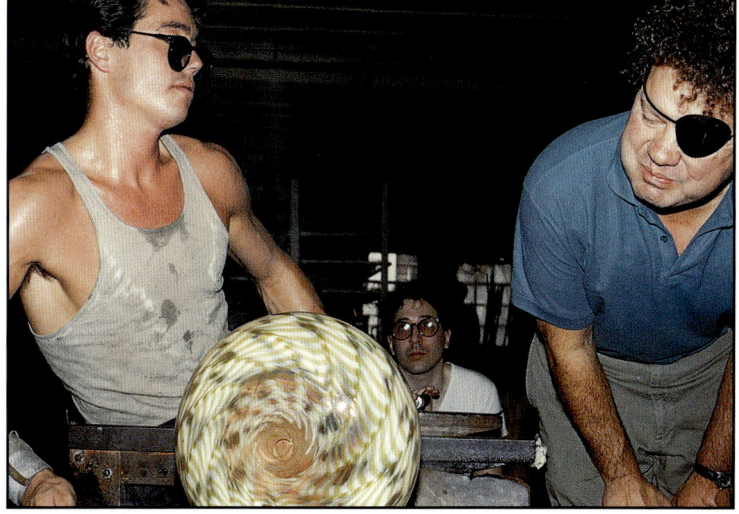

Billy Morris and Dale Chihuly at UrbanGlass, 1983. Photo: G. Rose

THE ECONOMIC FRONT: WORTH AND INVESTMENT

The first generation of collectors of studio glass is fading away. Will their values be passed along to the next generation? A central element in the success of studio glass was the willingness of the collectors to follow the artists into the wilderness of an unexplored medium. And these same collectors built collections without much interest in investment value but with a lot of interest in the inherent worth of the artworks. And they enjoyed each other's company as a kind of friendly competition for the most beautiful artworks developed. This made studio glass a community, and led to a relatively stable market. When there is a scramble for the most precious artworks on the secondary market, led by outsiders, what will happen to the values that have developed within the community over the last six decades?

William Warmus, Writer, Lansing, New York

What Will Last: The Challenge of Glass

Is it meaningful to continue to debate the distinction between art and craft? Doesn't it seem fruitless, if not a little absurd, to debate craft's inclusion in the contemporary art canon when artists are suspending sharks in tanks or drawing on the floor with hair saturated in Loving Care? It's a free-for-all out there. Forms expand. Barriers fall. Divisions blur. And it all happens at the accelerated point-and-click pace of contemporary culture. The contemporary curator who has time to make judgments about whether the medium of glass is craft or art is wasting time.

But curators are in the business of judgment, after all. Back in the early 1970s, when I was studying painting and printmaking at the Rhode Island School of Design, I wasn't thinking about judgments. I was gobbling up instruction as fast as I could. Studio glass was in its infancy, and Dale Chihuly was head of the glass department. He was also one of the coolest teachers around. I was fortunate enough to have the opportunity to take his flat glass course. I can't say that I was among his stellar students, but I was struck with Dale's vision of where glass was heading, and the fact that he saw no divisions, no barriers between what he did and what other artists did. For the first time, I connected glass to sculpture, glass to drawing, glass to paint.

Since that experience, I had always wanted to visit the Pilchuck Glass School in Washington State. Twenty-five years later, I got my wish. Last May I was invited to participate in their curator's workshop, and it was everything I had hoped. To stand in the hot shop and encounter close up the jump-back blistering heat of the furnaces and see the glassblowers perform their seemingly choreographed dance is to glimpse the remarkable progress of the studio glass movement as well as where it's headed.

Studio glass is a collaborative effort. The material requirements are demanding and costly, the help and assistance of others a necessity. That fact doesn't limit glass; it expands it. It charges and challenges artists. You can feel it all at Pilchuck, permeating Washington State's thick fog-laden air: passion, challenge, generosity, rivalry, vision. Even now, studio glass is still young. During the early 1960s when artists were experimenting with glass, their ambition was often hindered by the size of the work that could be created. With the advancements of furnaces and their capabilities and techniques, as well as a large dose of ingenuity, the artists were able to create larger scaled work. Trailblazers such as Harvey Littleton and Dale Chihuly were instrumental in bringing studio glass to the forefront and effectively giving it a popular appeal. At the same time, artists such as Toots Zynsky, Judith Schaechter, Christopher Wilmarth, and longtime collaborators Joey Kirkpatrick and Flora C. Mace have pushed the boundaries of the medium to a point where the glass has become an integral component of a larger idea. Today's artists are not constrained by medium; in their search for meaning, they slip back and forth across the borders of craft and art and, in the process, push us all in a new direction.

Much like photography, glass, when in the hands of gifted artists, becomes something altogether different from its traditional and more narrowly focused beginnings. Glass can be many things: smooth or coarse, opaque or clear, intimate or heroic, subtle or eye-popping. It can also be seductive—some critics say too seductive. In the world of contemporary art these days, beauty often annoys. It can be a problem. Beauty can't be taken seriously, after all. The impulse to beauty, some think, is an easy road, especially if the artist is technically proficient.

This is one of the challenges facing today's contemporary glass artists. Their technical virtuosity is unquestionable. But the artist who relies too heavily on technique will always be anchored to craft. In the end it will be the artists working with glass who look to art history as well as the work of their contemporaries who are non-glass artists who will have the greatest chance of being judged on their own terms as artists.

It is the job of the museum curator to try to make sense of it all. Finally, what all of these issues distill down to is what is good, what will last. All the heated discussions regarding the validity of glass as art will eventually disappear, and what will be left is the work, whether a classic vessel or a sculpture formed from thousands of carefully extruded colored glass threads. Talk fades. Vision endures.

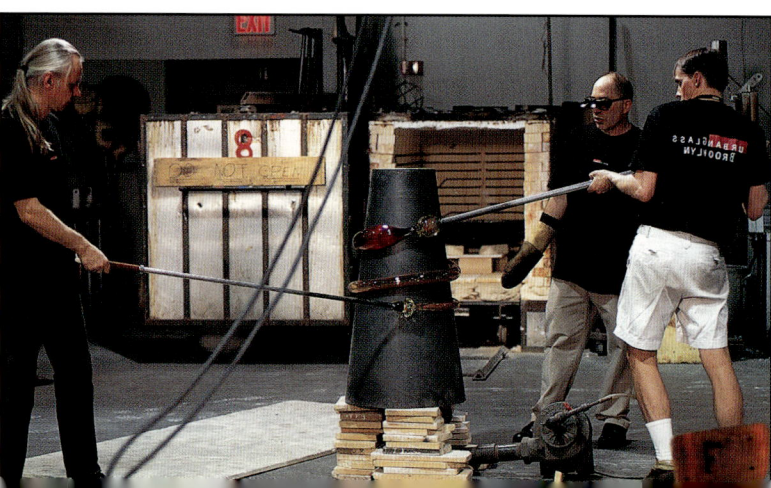

Paul Seide (center) pulling neon tubes, assisted by Reino Björk (left) and John Brekke (right).

Neil Watson
Curator of Exhibitions and Contemporary Art
Norton Museum of Art
West Palm Beach, Florida

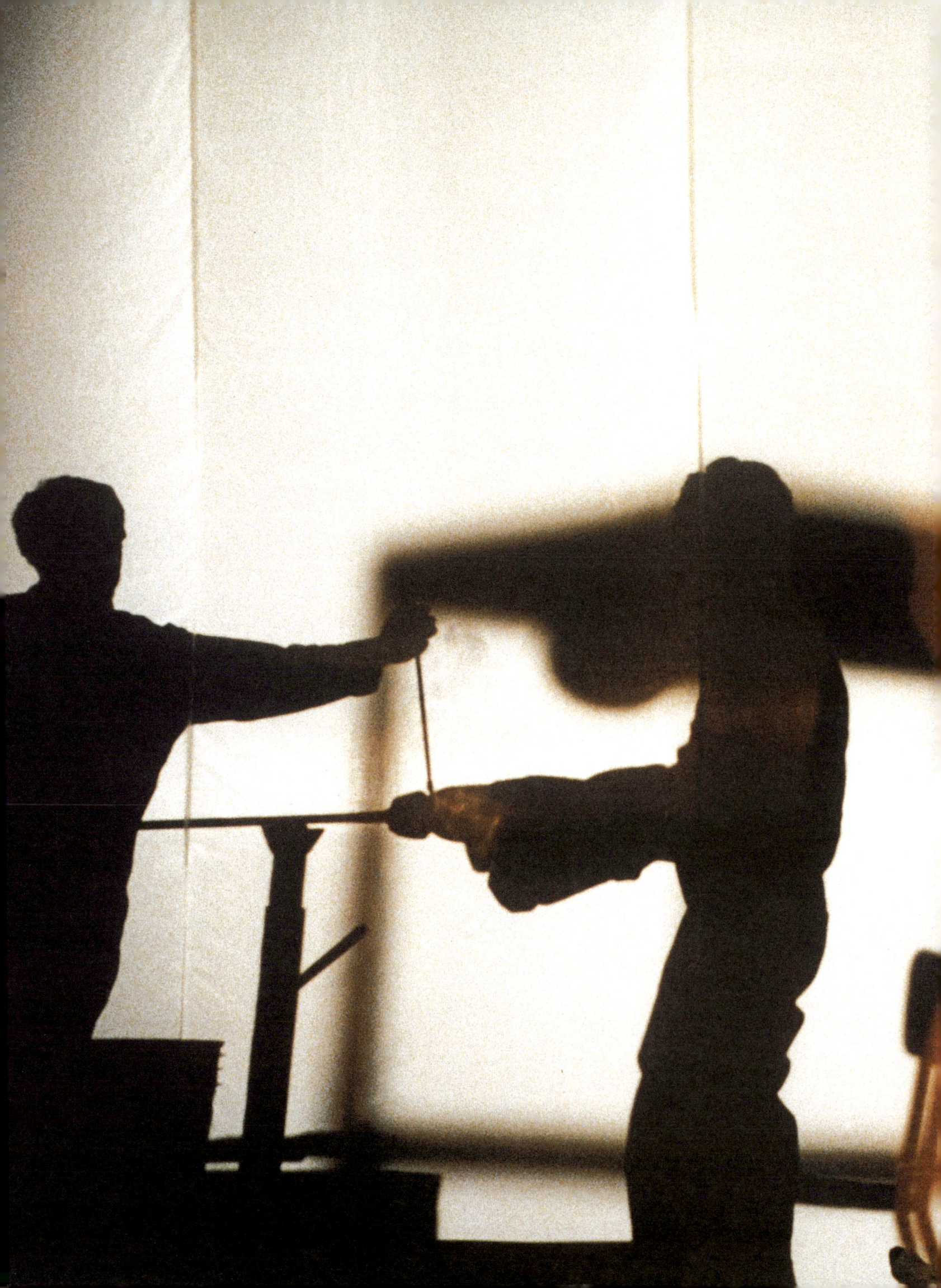